CD-ROM INCLUDED

SAMS

Teach Yourself

Game

Programming

with Visual Basic®

in 21 Days

SAMS

201 West 103rd St., Indianapolis, Indiana, 46290 USA

Sams Teach Yourself Game Programming with Visual Basic in 21 Days

Copyright © 2001 by Sams Publishing

International Standard Book Number: 0-672-31987-X

Library of Congress Catalog Card Number: 00-103210

Printed in the United States of America

First Printing: December 2000

03 02 01 00   4 3 2 1

Trademarks

Warning and Disclaimer

ACQUISITIONS EDITOR
Sharon Cox

DEVELOPMENT EDITOR
Kevin Howard

MANAGING EDITOR
Charlotte Clapp

PROJECT EDITOR
Elizabeth Finney

COPY EDITOR
Sean Medlock

INDEXER
Sandra Henselmeier

PROOFREADER
Tony Reitz

TECHNICAL EDITOR
Andy Indovina

TEAM COORDINATOR
Meggo Barthlow

MEDIA DEVELOPER
Matt Bates

INTERIOR DESIGNER
Gary Adair

COVER DESIGNER
Aren Howell

Contents at a Glance

Contents

About the Author

Award-winning author **CLAYTON WALNUM** has a degree in computer science and has written or co-authored more than 40 books (translated into many languages), covering everything from computer gaming to 3D graphics programming. He's also written hundreds of magazine articles and software reviews, as well as countless programs. His books include *Creating Turbo C++ Games*, *Creating Windows 95 Applications with Visual Basic*, *The Windows 95 Game SDK Strategy Guide*, and *The Complete Idiot's Guide to Visual Basic 6*. Feel free to visit Clay online at www.claytonwalnum.com.

Dedication

To Lynn

Acknowledgments

The author would like to thank all of the many people who contributed, either knowingly or unknowingly, to this book. Of special note are Sharon Cox for keeping things rolling and for her patience when things got bogged down, Kevin Howard for helping to shape the book, Kimberly Campanello, Sean Medlock, and Katie Robinson for their editing skills, and Andy Indovina for making sure everything worked the way it was supposed to.

Tell Us What You Think!

As the reader of this book, *you* are our most important critic and commentator. We value your opinion and want to know what we're doing right, what we could do better, what areas you'd like to see us publish in, and any other words of wisdom you're willing to pass our way.

As an Associate Publisher for Sams Publishing, I welcome your comments. You can fax, email, or write me directly to let me know what you did or didn't like about this book— as well as what we can do to make our books stronger.

Please note that I cannot help you with technical problems related to the topic of this book, and that due to the high volume of mail I receive, I might not be able to reply to every message.

When you write, please be sure to include this book's title and author as well as your name and phone or fax number. I will carefully review your comments and share them with the author and editors who worked on the book.

Fax: 317-581-4770
Email: samsfeedback@macmillanusa.com
Mail: Linda Engelman
         Associate Publisher
         Sams Publishing
         201 West 103rd Street
         Indianapolis, IN 46290 USA

Introduction

If you don't count the huge number of business packages bought by major corporations, more game software is sold than any other kind of software. This fact is not surprising when you consider that a good computer game is almost as effective as a good novel at drawing you into a fantasy world and making our mundane existence seem as far away as the next galaxy. Whether you're a fan of quick-reflex games like Tetris, brain-numbing puzzles like Lemmings, or spooky treks into magical realms like the Ultima line of role-playing adventures, you know that once you sit down to play a good game, nothing short of nuclear war is going to tear you away until you're good and ready to turn off the computer.

As you were playing your latest computer game late into the night, it may have crossed your mind that it might be even more fun to write computer games than to play them. After all, *you'd* be the one who determined how the computer game's world worked. *You'd* be the wizard who constructed that dungeon and populated it with all manner of creepy-crawly creatures. *You'd* be the one with all the answers, watching smugly as your friends struggled to defeat that final evil demon.

And believe it or not, it's a blast to sit down at a computer and play a few rounds of your own game. Along with the fun of playing a good game, you also get that glowing feeling that comes from producing a significant piece of work. No matter how many days, weeks, or months you spend honing your game program to perfection, it'll still be fun for you to play when you're done.

What Should You Already Know about Programming?

This book is *not* an introductory text for programmers who are interested in learning Visual Basic programming. To understand the lessons included here, you must have a working knowledge of Visual Basic and must be comfortable with the Visual Basic development system.

What Hardware and Software Do You Need?

To compile and run the programs that are included on this book's companion disk and to get the most out of the upcoming lessons, you must have the following:

- An IBM-compatible with a Pentium processor
- Windows 95 or later
- A CD-ROM drive and hard drive
- A Microsoft-compatible mouse
- Super VGA graphics
- Visual Basic 6.0 Professional Edition

As always, the faster your processor the better. Fast processors mean fast compiles and zippy programs. This is especially true for many game programs, which tend to push your hardware to the limit.

Conventions Used in This Book

This book uses different typefaces to differentiate between code and regular English, and also to help you identify important concepts.

Text that you type and text that should appear on your screen is presented in monospace type.

```
It will look like this to mimic the way text looks on your screen.
```

Placeholders for variables and expressions appear in *monospace italic* font. You should replace the placeholder with the specific value it represents.

This arrow (➥) at the beginning of a line of code means that a single line of code is too long to fit on the printed page. Continue typing all characters after the ➥ as though they were part of the preceding line.

Note

A Note presents interesting pieces of information related to the surrounding discussion.

Tip

A Tip offers advice or teaches an easier way to do something.

> **Caution**   A Caution advises you about potential problems and helps you steer clear of disaster.

 New Term icons provide clear definitions of new, essential terms. The term appears in italic.

INPUT The Input icon identifies code that you can type in yourself. It usually appears next to a listing.

ANALYSIS The Analysis icon alerts you to the author's line-by-line analysis of a program.

Let the Games Begin!

Now it's time to start programming games with Visual Basic. You'll soon discover that not only is game programming fun, but it's also a great way to get the most out of both your computer and Visual Basic.

Clayton Walnum

August, 2000

www.claytonwalnum.com

WEEK 1

At a Glance

This week you'll be introduced to some introductory game-programming concepts, and you'll get started on programming several simple (and not-so-simple) games of your own. On Day 1, your introduction to game programming starts with an overview of the elements of game design, including graphics design, sound effects, user interfaces, animation, and more. On Day 2, you move into programming by exploring how to draw graphics with Visual Basic commands and objects. This discussion continues on Day 3, where you'll learn how to draw game screens with Visual Basic graphics and fonts.

Day 4 gets into a bit of computer science as you develop algorithms that make your games run faster and better. Day 5, on the other hand, explores using images in Visual Basic game programs. Here you'll learn about the Image and PictureBox controls, as well as how to use Visual Basic's `PaintPicture` method. Day 6 covers the important topic of calling Windows API functions from Visual Basic. Finally, on Day 7, you'll study real-time games.

At the end of Week 1, you will have programmed the following games:

- *Face Catch*—A simple game in which you try to tag a smiley face that bounces around the game's window.
- *Nightshade*—An old-fashioned text adventure in which you try to save the dream world of Nightshade from the horrible Troll King.
- *The Game of Life*—A classic simulation in which single-celled creatures live and die based on the results of simple mathematical calculations.

- *Letter Tiles*—A popular puzzle game in which you try to place the letters of the alphabet in the correct order.
- *Battle Bricks*—An arcade game in which you control a bouncing ball in order to destroy a wall of bricks.

DAY 1

The Art of Game Programming

On your first day of studying game programming, you'll examine why you might want to program games and why you might want to use Visual Basic to do it. In addition, you'll take a brief look at the general process of creating a game. You'll learn about the many areas of expertise you need to design and create a computer game. In short, today you'll learn the following:

- How game programming can make you a better programmer.
- Why Visual Basic is a good language for game programming.
- The many skills needed to create a quality game.

Complex, But Not *Too* Complex

In my wild-and-wooly youth, I was a guitarist in a semiprofessional rock group. I'll never forget the first time I walked into a recording studio to record a demo song with my band. In the control room was a huge mixing board with more buttons and switches than there are teeth in a great white shark. To the right was a patch bay from which snaked dozens of patch cords, each one connecting some vital piece of equipment to another. Lights blinked. Reels spun. Sound processing equipment with fancy names like phase shifter, digital delay, and multiband equalizer clicked on and off.

When I looked at all that complex machinery and considered that I was paying $60 an hour (the equivalent of about $150 an hour today) for the privilege of being there, I almost turned around and walked out the door. It seemed to me that just learning my way around this complicated studio would cost me my life savings. I could see myself being ejected from the premises, penniless, without having recorded even a note.

Luckily, I'd had some studio training, so I at least knew in a general way how a studio worked. Like everything else in life (well, almost everything), a recording studio isn't really as complicated as it looks.

The same thing can be said about computer games. When you sit down at your computer and play the latest arcade hit or plunge into the newest state-of-the-art adventure game, you may be in awe of the talent and hard work that went into the glowing pixels that you see before your eyes. (And you *should* be.) But just like recording a song in a studio, writing games isn't as difficult as you may think.

If you've had some programming experience, you already have much of the knowledge and skills that you need to program a computer game. You need only refine those skills with an eye toward games. Today you'll get a quick look at some of the skills required to develop and write computer games.

The Hidden Benefits of Programming Games

You probably bought this book because you wanted to have a little fun with your computer. There you were in the bookstore, digging through all those very serious programming manuals, when this volume leaped out at you from the stack. But when you were walking to the cash register with this book in hand, you might have felt a little guilty. After all, games aren't serious computing, are they? You should be learning to write spreadsheet programs, databases, and word processors, right?

Let me tell you a quick story.

Way back in the dark ages of home computing (1981, to be exact), I got my first computer. It was an Atari 400, and like everything Atari made at that time, this powerful little computer was best known for its game-playing capabilities. After all, 1981 was the beginning of the golden age of video games, and Atari was the reigning king.

Unfortunately, after a few phenomenally successful years, video games spiraled into rapid decline and took many companies in the industry down with them. Computers became serious again. Although Atari managed to survive (barely), it would never be regarded as the designer and manufacturer of serious computers, thanks to its status as a game-computer maker. This is a shame, because the Atari 400/800's successor, the Atari ST—along with the Macintosh and the Amiga—were way ahead of their time. Certainly, these products were light years more advanced than the "serious" IBM clones that were popular at that time.

The problem was that darn gaming image with which Atari had been saddled. Who wanted to use a game computer to manage a spreadsheet, balance a bank account, or track an investment portfolio? That would be kind of dumb, wouldn't it?

Not really. The irony is that a computer that's capable of playing sophisticated games is a computer that's capable of just about anything. A good computer game taxes your computer to the maximum, including its capability to process data quickly, to generate graphics and animation, and to create realistic sound effects. Only a state-of-the-art computer can keep up with today's high-powered games, such as flight simulators and 3D action games. In fact, there are few business applications in existence that require more computing power than a sophisticated computer game.

Similarly, a programmer who can write commercial-quality computer games can write just about any other type of software as well, especially considering today's focus on graphics and sound in applications. You may have purchased this book to have a little fun with your computer, but before you're done, you'll learn valuable lessons in software design and programming—lessons that you can apply to many different kinds of software.

So, why program computer games? Mostly because it's fun! But remember that your game-programming experience will help you with every other program that you ever write.

Why Use Visual Basic?

I could probably come up with dozens of reasons why you'd want to use Visual Basic to learn about game programming. I could also easily come up with reasons why you wouldn't. The truth is that there are a lot of factors to consider when you're choosing a language for game programming, not the least of which is the types of games you want to write. You may want to use Visual Basic to learn game programming for the following reasons:

- It's one of the easiest languages to learn.
- It features a set of controls that make creating user interfaces quick and easy.

- Visual Basic and its programming environment enable much faster application development than is possible with a language like C++.
- It's a powerful language that can handle all but the most complex applications.
- Its drawing commands and tools enable you to create applications with professional-looking graphical displays.
- It features controls and commands that manage bitmapped images with very little effort on your part.
- Its extended implementation of the BASIC language allows not only user-definable data types, but also classes. This enables you to use some features of an object-oriented language.
- It can call Windows API functions, which puts a huge library of advanced commands at your fingertips.

Types of Games Best Suited to Visual Basic

Let's get something out of the way right now. If you want to write the next *Quake* or *Might and Magic*, forget Visual Basic. Such top-shelf games require programming power that's very difficult, if not outright impossible, to get out of a language like Visual Basic (not to mention requiring many man-years of intensive labor). Most games in this class are written in C or C++ along with a healthy dose of assembly language—and even then, the programmers employ dozens of tricks to get the most out of the computer's hardware. The intensive calculations and complex image handling needed in a real-time 3D game not only require a programmer with a degree in mathematics, but also a much faster language. What types of games, then, can you write with Visual Basic?

Games Using Straight Visual Basic

Although 3D games like *Quake* get a lot of attention, they represent only one genre in a marketplace packed with all types of games. Many other games, particularly those of the shareware variety, require much less programmer labor and processing power to create and run. By using straight Visual Basic without making calls to the Windows API or third-party libraries, you can write puzzle games, strategy games, card games, simple arcade games, and virtually any other type of game that doesn't require intensive processing or fast frame rates. Many programmers also use VB to write prototypes for games. If those games turn out to be worthwhile ventures, the programmers will then develop the final games using C++ or some other language.

NEW TERM   A game's *frame rate* is the number of times the display is redrawn every second. Animation at frame rates much less than 30 FPS (frames per second) appears jerky and disorienting.

Visual Basic Games that Call the Windows API

As I mentioned previously, Visual Basic can call Windows API functions. Compared to Visual Basic's intrinsic commands, in many cases Windows API functions exert extra power over a computer and allow your program to do things that cannot be duplicated with straight Visual Basic. For this reason, calls from Visual Basic to the Windows API may be just the trick to get a game running at its best. Although calls to the Windows API do not greatly extend the types of games you can write with Visual Basic, they can add pizzazz to what otherwise might be a lackluster game.

NEW TERM   An *application programming interface (API)* is one or more libraries of functions that give a programmer access to a programming technology. For example, the Windows API is a set of libraries for programming Windows applications, whereas the Direct3D API is a set of libraries for writing graphically intensive applications.

The Elements of Game Programming

As you've already discovered, a good computer game pushes your computer to its limits. In fact, a game must excel in many areas. To write computer games that people will want to play, then, you must gain some expertise in the related areas of game programming:

- Game design
- Graphic design
- Sound generation
- Controls and interfaces
- Image handling
- Animation
- Algorithms
- Artificial intelligence
- Game testing

These elements overlap to an extent. For example, to learn graphic design for computer games, you need to know how a computer handles graphic images. Moreover, game design draws on all the other elements in the list. After all, you can't design a game unless you know how the graphics, sound, controls, and computer algorithms fit together to form the final product.

Game Design

Whether your game is a standard shoot-'em-up, in which the player's only goal is to blast everything on the screen, or a sophisticated war game, requiring sharp wits and clever moves, first and foremost your game must be fun. If a game isn't fun, it doesn't matter how great the graphics are, how realistic the sound effects are, or how well you designed the computer player's algorithms. A boring game will almost certainly get filed away in a closet to gather dust.

Many things determine what makes a game fun. The most important thing, of course, is the game's concept. Often, a game's concept is based on some real-world event or circumstance. For example, chess—one of the most popular board games of all time—is really a war game. Monopoly, on the other hand, is a financial simulation in which players try to bankrupt their competition.

Computer games are no different from their real-world cousins. They too must have some logical goal for the player, and—with rare exceptions—they must be set in some sort of believable world. This world can be as simple as an onscreen maze or as complex as an entire planet with continents, countries, and cities. In the insanely addictive computer game *Tetris*, the world is simply a narrow onscreen channel in which the player must stack variously shaped objects. On the other hand, in the fabulous *Ultima* series of graphic adventures, the player's world is filled with forests, swamps, cities, monsters, and the other elements that make up a complete fantasy scenario.

No matter what type of world you envision for your game, it must have consistent rules that the player can master. For a game to be fun, the player must be able to figure out how to surmount the various obstacles that you place in his path. When a player loses a computer game, it should be because he hasn't mastered the subtleties of the rules yet, not because some random bolt out of the blue blasted him into digital bits and pieces.

Of course, to build a logical, fair, and effective gaming world, you must draw on all your skills as a programmer. All the other areas of programming listed earlier come into play here. Graphics, sound, interface design, computer algorithms, and more can make the difference between a fun game and just another dime-a-dozen hack job whose disk will be used as a Frisbee at the next family picnic.

Not only do you need consistent rules for your game, but you also need a consistent game world. Every element of your game—fonts, graphics, sound, story—contributes to this goal. For example, if you're writing a game in which the player must battle zombies and werewolves, you probably won't need those cute little bunny characters you drew. (That is, unless the bunnies suddenly grow fangs and horns and develop an unquenchable desire to consume human flesh!) Similarly, your zombie game will need suitably eerie sound effects and spooky music. The "Sugarplum Fairies" theme just ain't gonna cut it.

Graphic Design

There's a good reason why so many computer game packages are covered with exciting illustrations and awe-inspiring screen shots. In spite of how hard people try to make intelligent buying decisions, everyone is swayed by clever packaging. Although your smart side may tell you to ignore that fabulous wizard on the box cover, your impulsive side sees that wizard as just a hint of the excitement that you'll find in the box. Of course, reality usually falls far short of packaging. Buyer beware.

The lesson here is not that you should make your games look better than they play, but rather that how a game looks is often as important as how well it performs. You want your gaming screens to be neat and uncluttered, logically laid out, and above all exciting to look at. Your screens should scream "Play me!" to anyone who comes into viewing distance.

Like anything else, graphic design is a professional skill that takes many years of study and practice to master. Luckily, though, you don't have to be a graphic-design whiz to create attractive game screens. You can look at other games to get design ideas, and you can experiment with different screen designs to see which are the most attractive and work best with your game world. Use your favorite paint program to draw different layouts and compare them. Trial and error is not only a powerful technique for devising improved designs, but it's also a great learning tool. The more you experiment, the more you'll learn about what looks good on a computer screen and what doesn't.

Sound Generation

The word we live in is a noisy place indeed. There's hardly a moment in our lives when we're not assaulted by hundreds of sounds simultaneously. If your game world is to seem realistic to the player, it too must provide sound. That's not to say you have to recreate the full spectrum of sounds that a player hears in the real world, though. With today's computers, that task would be impossible.

Although you shouldn't fill your player's ears with unnecessary noise, you should provide as many sound cues as appropriate. When the player selects an onscreen button, she should hear the button click. When she slams a home run, she should hear the crack of the bat and the roar of the crowd.

There's not a computer game on the planet (or, I'd venture to say, in the universe) that couldn't be improved by better sound effects. Luckily, thanks to powerful sound cards, many of today's games include fabulous digitized sound effects.

Although music isn't as important as sound effects, it can also add a lot to a computer game. The most obvious place for music is at the beginning of the game, usually accompanying a title screen. You might also want to use music when the player advances to the next level or accomplishes some other important goal in the game.

To add music to a computer game, however, you must have some knowledge of music composition. Bad music in a game is worse than none at all. If you have no musical training, chances are that you have a friend who does. You can work together to compose the music for your computer game magnum opus. If you're lucky, she won't even ask for a share of the royalties!

Controls and Interfaces

The game programmer must provide some sort of interface to enable the player to play the game. In a computer game, menus and onscreen buttons enable the user to select options and commands. In addition, the player uses the keyboard or mouse to move and otherwise manipulate objects on the screen.

A good game interface makes playing the game as easy as possible. The game commands should be logical and readily available. The more your game works like a real-world game, the easier it will be for the player to learn its controls. For example, in a computer chess game, you might enable the player to move a game piece with her mouse pointer instead of typing in the position of the square where she wants to move the piece.

Image Handling

Every computer game must deal with various types of images. These images may be full-screen background graphics, icons that represent game commands or game pieces, or tiles that you use to create a map or some other complex game screen. When you design your game, you must decide which types of images you need. Should you draw your game's background screen at runtime? Or should you create the screen with a paint program and just load it in your game? If you need to conserve memory, maybe you should create your game screens from small tiles?

NEW TERM   In game-programming lingo, a *tile* is a small graphical object that can be used with other similar objects to assemble a complex game screen. For example, several tiles depicting trees can be used to create an entire forest. Various types of tiles—trees, grass, water, mountains, and so on—can be used to assemble an entire world map.

You must consider questions like these as you design your computer game's graphics. You want your game to look as professional as possible (which means that you may need to find an artist), but you also must consider the amount of memory the graphics will consume and how long it takes to move graphic images from the disk to the computer's memory. Most gamers hate to wait for files to load from the disk. On the other hand, keeping too much data in memory may make your game clunky on computers that have smaller amounts of free memory.

Another important issue is the amount of time it takes to create your game's graphics. You can't spend the next 10 years drawing detailed graphics for every aspect of your game. You need to use shortcuts (such as tiling) to speed up the graphic design process. In other words, although every tree in the real world looks different, many trees in a computer game look identical.

Animation

Once you've learned to design and manipulate computer graphic images, you're ready to take the next step: animation. This is the process of making objects appear to come to life and move around the computer screen. By using a series of images, you can make a chicken waddle across a road, a rock tumble from a cliff side, or a spaceship blast off from a launch pad.

NEW TERM *Animation* is the process of moving or changing a graphical game object in some way. For example, a ball that bounces around the screen is an animation, as is a game creature that falls to the ground when shot.

For example, when a player moves a game piece, instead of simply having the piece disappear from its current location and reappear at its new one, you might make the piece dissolve and then reform itself. Or, if the playing piece represents a human being or an animal, you could make the piece saunter over to its new location.

Such animation effects can make your game much more interesting and even more fun to play. Although animation requires a lot of work on the programmer's part, it's well worth the effort.

Algorithms

Although the term *algorithm* sounds like the most horrid technobabble, it's really a simple word. An algorithm is nothing more than a series of steps that solves a problem. You use algorithms every day of your life. When you make pancakes for breakfast, you must follow an algorithm. When you drive to work, you must follow another algorithm. Algorithms enable you to solve all of life's simple (and sometimes not-so-simple) tasks.

Computer algorithms enable you to solve computing problems. In other words, to write computer games, you need to figure out how to get your computer to do things that you may not have tried to do on a computer before. For example, how can you determine who has the best hand in a poker game? Or how do you create a smart computer player? You must write an algorithm. Once you know how to solve a problem with your computer, you can write the specific code in whatever programming language you're using. Throughout this book, you'll see many algorithms for solving game problems.

NEW TERM A *computer algorithm* is a set of program steps that solves a programming problem. For example, a function that determines whether a player has a full house in
a computer card game uses an algorithm to analyze the cards in the player's hand.

Artificial Intelligence

Artificial intelligence routines are algorithms that make computers seem smart. By
"smart," I don't mean the ability to calculate the player's score or process his input. I
mean the computer's ability to act as an opponent. If you want to write a computer game
that features computer-generated players, you must create algorithms that enable the
computer to compete with human players. How involved this algorithm turns out to be
depends on how complex the game is and how well you want the computer to play.

For example, it can be difficult to write good algorithms for creating a computer chess
player because winning a game of chess requires a great deal of strategy. You could simply have the computer choose a random move each turn, but such a computer player
would be easy to beat. The algorithm that you write can determine the difficulty of your
game.

Game Testing

After you've read this book and learned how to design and program your computer
game, you'll get to work on your own masterpiece (I hope). However, after you write
your game, you then must test it extensively to ensure that it works properly.

The best way to test a game is to give it to a few trusted friends and watch as they play,
taking notes about things that don't work quite the way you expected. Remember to
watch for not only program bugs that make the program do unexpected things and may
even crash the computer, but also interface bugs that may make your program confusing
to use.

After your friends have played the game for a while, ask them what they liked or didn't
like. Find out how they think the game could be improved. You don't have to agree with
everything they say, but always be polite, taking their suggestions seriously and writing
them down so that you can review them later. Don't be defensive. Your friends aren't
criticizing your work so much as helping you to make it better. Remember: There's no
such thing as a perfect computer program. There's always room for improvement. After
the testing is complete, implement those suggestions that you think are valuable.

The only way to test a game is to have several people play it repeatedly. Of course,
before you pass the game on to a few close friends, you should have already played the
game so much that you would rather read a phone book from cover to cover than see
your opening screen again!

Summary

Writing a computer game requires you to bring the best of your programming skills into play. To create a successful game, you must first design it. You must think about the game's graphic design and interface, experiment with it, and finally implement it. As you design your game, you need to consider the types of images and sounds that will bring the game to life. Animation and smart algorithms can also make your game the next best-seller.

On Day 2, "Drawing Graphics with Visual Basic," you'll learn more about these topics. Specifically, you'll learn how to design and create effective computer graphics. With a few basic techniques and tools at your disposal, you may be surprised at how easy it is to create competent computer graphics for games—or for any other computer application.

Q&A

Q Visual Basic programs tend to run slower than programs written in a lower-level language like C++. Does this mean that I can't use animation and sprites in my games?

A No, animation and sprites are still available. However, they're more limited than they might be in a language like C++ because Visual Basic doesn't give you access to the hardware at a near-assembly-language level.

Q Is it hard to call Windows API functions from Visual Basic?

A No, although it can be tricky. You need to code such calls very carefully, and you must be sure you understand the differences between the data types used in Visual Basic and those used in a language like C++.

Q How good do I need to be at Visual Basic programming to write game programs?

A Programming a game isn't all that different from programming any other type of application. The biggest difference is that game programs tend to be more graphically oriented than other types of programs, such as utilities or productivity applications. This means that you need to know all the ways to deal with graphics in Visual Basic. This book will teach you those skills.

Workshop

The workshop includes quiz questions to help gauge your grasp of the material. You'll find the answers to this quiz in Appendix A. Even if you feel that you totally understand the concepts presented here, you should work through the quiz anyway. The last section has an exercise to help reinforce your learning.

Quiz

1. Why does programming games make you a better all-around programmer?

2. Give at least four reasons why Visual Basic is a good language to use for game programming.

3. Why isn't Visual Basic a good language for programming real-time 3D games such as *Quake*?

4. What's a computer algorithm?

5. How are artificial intelligence and computer algorithms related in game programming?

Exercises

1. Imagine that you're going to write a computer version of checkers. How would you create the main game screen? What type of user interface would you use? What images would you need to design?

DAY 2

Drawing Graphics with Visual Basic

If there's one thing you can say about most games, it's that they display a lot of graphics. The bottom line is that if you can't draw and manipulate lines, shapes, and images, you can't program a modern game, no matter how clever you are with the Basic language. That's why, on only your second day of lessons, you're going to study Visual Basic's graphics abilities. Specifically, today you'll learn how to do the following:

- Manage colors
- Draw lines and shapes
- Use line styles and fill styles
- Use drawing modes
- Use Visual Basic's Line and Shape controls
- Use the Image and PictureBox controls

Using Colors in Visual Basic

One of the most important aspects of drawing graphics is, of course, color. Luckily, Visual Basic is very versatile, providing five ways to specify colors programmatically:

- Using Visual Basic's predefined color constants
- Using the RGB function
- Using Windows' system colors
- Using the QBColor function
- Using hexadecimal values

Today you'll examine these different methods of specifying colors. (Note that you can also specify colors for some object properties within the Visual Basic IDE.)

The Color Constants

If you're not too fussy about the colors you have to choose from, you can call upon Visual Basic's predefined color constants, which represent the typical colors used in computer programs. Using these predefined colors is more efficient than using custom colors, helping Visual Basic to give you exactly the color you request. Moreover, the color constants yield an easy-to-understand program code because a specific color is represented by a human-readable symbol, not a hard-to-interpret number. Table 2.1 lists and describes Visual Basic's standard color constants.

TABLE 2.1   The Visual Basic Color Constants

Constant	Hexadecimal Value
vbBlack	&H000000
vbBlue	&HFF0000
vbCyan	&HFFFF00
vbGreen	&H00FF00
vbMagenta	&HFF00FF
vbRed	&H0000FF
vbWhite	&HFFFFFF
vbYellow	&H00FFFF

Using the color constants is easy. For example, to set the background color of a form, you'd write something like this:

```
Form1.BackColor = vbWhite
```

Notice how much easier this line is to read than the equivalent that uses a hexadecimal color value instead:

```
Form1.BackColor = &HFFFFFF
```

The System Colors

You've undoubtedly noticed that Windows enables the user to set custom colors for the graphical elements that make up the user interface. For example, a user can specify the color of button faces, window title bars, menu bars, message boxes, and so on. The user does this through the Appearance tab on the Display Properties property sheet, as shown in Figure 2.1.

FIGURE 2.1

The user can change the Windows system colors.

If your Visual Basic game needs to incorporate system colors into its displays, you can use the Visual Basic system-color constants to specify the colors. For example, you might want a window's background color to be the same as the menu bar color. If the user changes his Windows color settings, you want your window's background color to change accordingly. Table 2.2 lists and describes the handy color constants that enable you to handle colors in this way.

TABLE 2.2   The Visual Basic System Color Constants

Constant	Description
vb3DDKShadow	Darkest 3D shadow color
vb3DFace	Text face color
vb3DHighlight	3D highlight color
vb3DLight	Second-lightest 3D color

TABLE 2.2　continued

Constant	Description
vb3Dshadow	Text shadow color
vbActiveBorder	Active window's border color
vbActiveTitleBar	Active window's title bar color
vbApplicationWorkspace	Multiple-document interface background color
vbButtonFace	Command button face-shading color
vbButtonShadow	Command button edge-shading color
vbButtonText	Buttons text color
vbDesktop	Desktop color
vbGrayText	Disabled text color
vbHighlight	Background color of selected items
vbHighlightText	Text color of selected items
vbInactiveBorder	Inactive window border color
vbInactiveCaptionText	Inactive caption text color
vbInactiveTitleBar	Inactive window title bar color
vbInfoBackground	ToolTip background color
vbInfoText	ToolTip text color
vbMenuBar	Menu background color
vbMenuText	Menu text color
vbScrollBars	Scroll bar color
vbTitleBarText	Caption, size box, and scroll arrow text color
vbWindowBackground	Window background color
vbWindowFrame	Window frame color
vbWindowText	Window text color

The *RGB* Function

If you can't get the color you want using one of the predefined constants, you can still avoid hard-to-interpret hexadecimal numbers by using the RGB function, which takes as arguments values for the red, green, and blue elements of the color. A value of 0 for a color element eliminates that element from the resulting color, whereas a value of 255 adds as much of the color element as possible. The three color elements combine to form the final color, much like mixing paint in a bucket. For example, the following code lines set a form's background color to black, bright red, bright green, bright blue, medium purple, and white, one after the other:

```
Form1.BackColor = RGB(0, 0, 0)        ' Black
Form1.BackColor = RGB(255, 0, 0)      ' Red
Form1.BackColor = RGB(0, 255, 0)      ' Green
Form1.BackColor = RGB(0, 0, 255)      ' Blue
Form1.BackColor = RGB(128, 0, 128)    ' Purple
Form1.BackColor = RGB(255, 255, 255)  ' White
```

The *QBColor* Function

If you've used computers long enough, you remember the old VGA displays that could show only 16 colors at a time. Those 16 colors were stored in a palette. To specify a color, you'd supply the index of the palette entry you wanted to use. These days, programmers have little use for such color-limited displays. However, if you have a hankering to do things the old-fashioned way, Visual Basic provides the QBColor function, which takes as its single argument the index of the palette color you want. To specify a white form background with the QBColor function, you might write the following:

```
Form1.BackColor = QBColor(15)
```

Table 2.3 lists the standard VGA colors and the palette indexes you use with the QBColor function.

TABLE 2.3   Color Values for the QBColor Function

Value	Color
0	Black
1	Blue
2	Green
3	Cyan
4	Red
5	Magenta
6	Yellow
7	Light Gray
8	Gray
9	Light Blue
10	Light Green
11	Light Cyan
12	Light Red
13	Light Magenta
14	Light Yellow
15	White

2

Hexadecimal Numbers

You can also use plain hexadecimal values to specify colors, although I don't suggest this method because you'll end up with code that's hard to read. For example, the following line sets a form's background color to green:

```
Form1.BackColor = &HFF00
```

As well as being hard to read, hexadecimal numbers are tricky to calculate.

Drawing Shapes

If you were programming your games using assembly language, you'd have to draw shapes one pixel at a time. This is a laborious process that requires you to create your own library of graphics routines, or maybe you could purchase such a library from a third-party vendor. Visual Basic, however, features powerful drawing methods that can create everything from simple lines to rectangles, circles, and more. This section introduces you to these methods, which are important to game programmers.

The *Line* Method

Visual Basic's Line method serves double duty, drawing both lines and "boxes," which most programmers call *rectangles*. Why VB doesn't have a Rectangle method is beyond me (in fact, when I was a new VB programmer, I spent quite a long time looking for a Rectangle method). Unconventional or not, in the following sections, you will master the Line method.

Drawing Lines

To draw a simple line, you need only a starting point and an ending point. Visual Basic requires that you provide these points as X,Y coordinates enclosed in parentheses, with the coordinate sets separated by a hyphen. For example, to draw a line from the point 20,20 to the point 200,350 (see Figure 2.2), call the Line method like this:

```
Line (20, 20)-(100, 150)
```

FIGURE 2.2

Drawing a simple line.

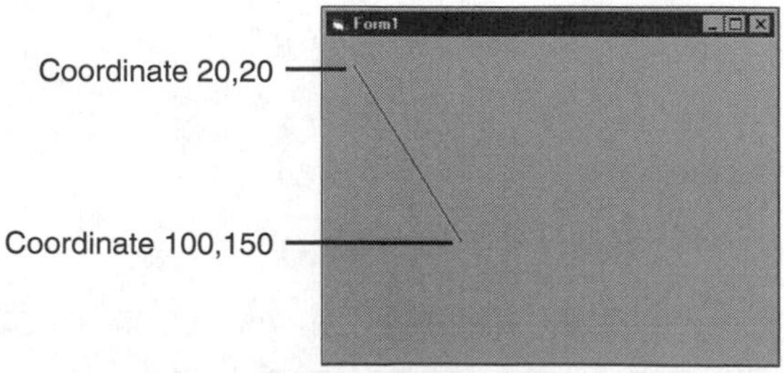

Note

> If you try out the code sample here, you should set your form's ScaleMode property to pixels. Otherwise, the results will be hard to see.

2

You can complicate matters a bit by using the Step keyword, which specifies that the line's starting and ending coordinates are relative to the value of the CurrentX and CurrentY properties of the object that you're drawing. VB always sets the CurrentX and CurrentY properties to the final coordinates of the last drawing command. For example, suppose you want to draw a line from 20,20 to 200,350 and then draw a line that starts 10 units to the right and 10 units down from the end of the original line, with the new line ending at the point 100,50 (see Figure 2.3). You'd write something like this:

```
Line (20, 20)-(100, 150)
Line Step(10, 10)-(150, 50)
```

FIGURE 2.3

Drawing lines using relative coordinates.

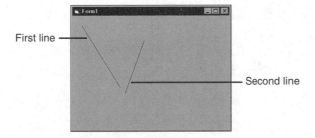

First line

Second line

If you want the line's ending point to be relative to the previous line's starting point, put the Step keyword in front of the second set of coordinates, like this:

```
Line (10, 10)-Step(150, 50)
```

Of course, you can make both points relative by including the Step keyword twice:

```
Line Step(10, 10)-Step(150, 50)
```

Note

> The coordinates used with the Line method and other drawing methods, depend upon the ScaleMode property of the object that you're drawing. For example, if you have a form's ScaleMode set to Twip (the default), the units used for the Line method's coordinates are twips. Similarly, if ScaleMode is set to Pixel, the units used are pixels. Most game programmers like to work with pixels.

NEW TERM   A *pixel* is the smallest dot that a program can display on a computer screen. When your computer's screen is set to 800×600 resolution, for example, it can display 800 pixels horizontally and 600 pixels vertically.

Finally, you can specify a line's color by adding it as a third argument. For example, to draw a green line, you might write this:

```
Line (20, 20)-(100, 150), vbGreen
```

Drawing Boxes

As mentioned previously, the Line method also draws rectangles, both hollow and filled. When you use the Line method this way, the first coordinate represents the rectangle's upper-left corner and the second coordinate represents the lower-right corner. You must also include the B flag, which tells VB to use the coordinates to draw a box. For example, to draw a hollow red rectangle with its upper-left corner at 20,20 and its lower-right corner at 100,150 (see Figure 2.4), you'd write the following:

```
Line (20, 20)-(100, 150), vbRed, B
```

FIGURE 2.4

Drawing a hollow rectangle.

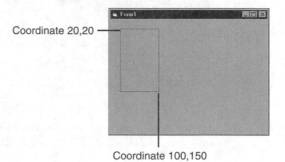

Finally, to draw a filled rectangle (see Figure 2.5), just add the F flag to the B flag, like this:

```
Line (20, 20)-(100, 150), vbRed, BF
```

FIGURE 2.5

Drawing a filled rectangle.

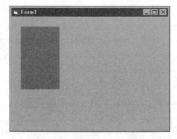

The *Circle* Method

Drawing lines and rectangles is all well and good, but occasionally you'll want to draw circles, ellipses, and arcs as well. Not to worry. Visual Basic features the `Circle` method, which you'll examine next.

Drawing Circles

To draw a circle, Visual Basic requires two values: the circle's center point and its radius. As with the `Line` method, the `Circle` method requires a coordinate's X,Y pair of values to be enclosed in parentheses. To draw a circle centered at point 100,75 with a radius of 50 (see Figure 2.6), type this:

```
Circle (100, 75), 50
```

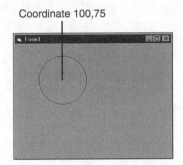

FIGURE 2.6

Drawing a circle.

Easy enough, but the process can get more complicated, of course. For example, you can use the `Step` keyword to specify that the circle's center coordinate is relative to the `CurrentX` and `CurrentY` properties, like this:

```
Circle Step(100, 75), 50
```

You can also set the circle's drawing color:

```
Circle Step(100, 75), 50, vbBlue
```

Drawing Ellipses

Drawing an ellipse (an oval) is almost as easy as drawing a circle. You need only add one argument (the ellipse's aspect ratio) to the `Circle` method call. For example, to draw an oval that's twice as wide as it is high (see Figure 2.7), you might write the following:

```
Circle (100, 75), 50, vbRed, , , 0.5
```

The two extra commas in this line represent two optional arguments that, in this case, the programmer has not supplied. You'll learn about these arguments in the following section on arcs.

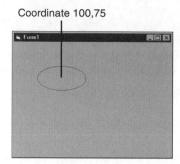

FIGURE 2.7

Drawing an ellipse.

NEW TERM   *Aspect ratio* is the proportion between a shape's height and width. For example, a
rectangle that's twice as high as it is wide has an aspect ratio of 2:1, meaning that
for every two units of height there's only one unit of width. You can express an aspect
ratio by changing the colon to a division symbol and doing the math. That is, an aspect
ratio of 2:1 can be expressed as 2/1 or simply 2, whereas an aspect ratio of 1:4 can be
expressed as 1/4 or 0.25.

Drawing Arcs

Drawing arcs can be tricky because you need to specify starting and ending angles. Even
worse, the angles must be specified in radians, rather than in degrees. For example, to
draw an arc that's 1/4 of a circle (see Figure 2.8), you might write this:

```
Circle (150, 125), 100, vbBlack, 0, 1.5708
```

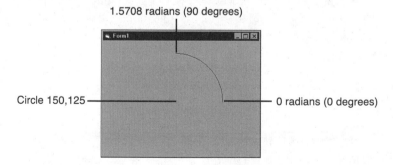

FIGURE 2.8

Drawing an arc.

If you're more comfortable working with degrees, a couple of simple formulas will get
you on track. Here are two functions that will help, one that converts radians to degrees
and one that converts degrees to radians:

```
Function RadiansToDegrees(Radians As Single) As Integer
  RadiansToDegrees = Radians * 180 / 3.14159265
```

```
End Function

Function DegreesToRadians(Degrees As Integer) As Single
  DegreesToRadians = Degrees / 180 * 3.14159265
End Function
```

Using these helper functions, you might write the following to create the arc shown in Figure 2.8:

```
Dim Start As Single
Dim Finish As Single
Start = DegreesToRadians(0)
Finish = DegreesToRadians(90)
Circle (150, 125), 100, vbBlack, Start, Finish
```

Besides supplying the starting and ending angles for your arc, you can also supply the aspect ratio:

```
Circle (150, 125), 100, vbBlack, 0, 1.5708
```

This call to the `Circle` method produces the arc shown in Figure 2.9.

FIGURE 2.9

Drawing a flattened arc.

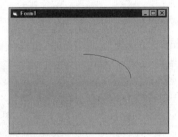

Line and Fill Properties

Visual Basic objects that can display graphics have a set of properties that control how Visual Basic draws lines and shapes. These properties are as follows:

- `DrawWidth`—The width of lines
- `DrawStyle`—The style used when drawing lines
- `DrawMode`—The drawing mode used to display graphics
- `FillColor`—The color used to fill shapes
- `FillStyle`—The style used to fill shapes

The *DrawWidth* Property

The DrawWidth property determines how thick lines will be. For example, the following code lines create the image shown in Figure 2.10:

```
Dim x As Integer
For x = 1 To 10
  Form1.DrawWidth = x
  Line (20, 20 * x)-(200, 20 * x)
Next x
```

FIGURE 2.10

*Drawing lines of vary-
ing thickness.*

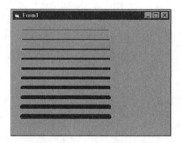

The *DrawMode* Property

The DrawMode property specifies the drawing mode to use, determining the way that Visual Basic combines the source and destination colors. There are actually 16 modes, represented by these predefined VB constants: vbBlackness, vbNotMergePen, vbMaskNotPen, vbNotCopyPen, vbMaskPenNot, vbInvert, vbXorPen, vbNotMaskPen, vbMaskPen, vbNotXorPen, vbNop, vbMergeNotPen, vbCopyPen, vbMergePenNot, vbMergePen, and vbWhiteness. However, only two of these modes—vbCopyPen and vbInvert—are especially useful to game programmers.

The vbCopyPen mode is the default drawing mode, in which you get what you ask for. That is, if you draw a red line, you get a red line. The vbInvert mode, on the other hand, combines the source and destination colors in such a way that performing the same draw-ing operation a second time returns the display to its original condition, as demonstrated by the following code lines:

```
Form1.DrawMode = vbInvert
Line (20, 20)-(200, 20) ' Draw the line
Line (20, 20)-(200, 20) ' Erase the line
```

If you try out this example, you will see no lines on the screen. As soon as the first line of source code draws its line, the line is immediately erased by the second line of source code.

The DrawStyle Property

You can create lines of various styles by setting the DrawStyle property to one of these values: vbSolid, vbDash, vbDot, vbDashDot, vbDashDotDot, vbInvisible, or vbInsideSolid. For example, to draw a dashed line (see Figure 2.11), you might write this:

```
Form1.DrawStyle = vbDash
Line (20, 50)-(250, 50)
```

FIGURE 2.11

Drawing a dashed line.

The DrawStyle property only affects lines with a DrawWidth value of 1.

The *FillColor* and *FillStyle* Properties

As you can probably guess by its name, the FillColor property determines the color used to fill shapes. It works hand-in-hand with the FillStyle property, which determines the style of the fill. For example, to draw a circle with a black outline and a solid-red fill, you might write this:

```
Form1.FillColor = vbRed
Form1.FillStyle = vbFSSolid
Circle (100, 100), 50
```

The FillStyle property can be set to one of eight values, each of which is represented in VB by a predefined constant. These constants are vbFSSolid, vbFSTransparent, vbHorizontalLine, vbVerticalLine, vbUpwardDiagonal, vbDownwardDiagonal, vbCross, and vbDiagonalCross. The vbFSTransparent style, which results in a hollow shape, is the default. The other styles specify a pattern that VB uses to fill the object. For example, the following lines create the circle shown in Figure 2.12:

```
Form1.FillColor = vbRed
Form1.FillStyle = vbUpwardDiagonal
Circle (100, 100), 50
```

FIGURE 2.12

Using fill colors and styles.

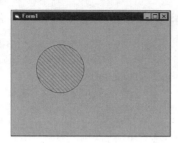

 Tip

Throughout this chapter, you've seen a lot of predefined VB constants used to represent things like colors, line styles, and fill styles. Remember that a constant is just a symbol that represents a number. That is, you don't need to use the constants. You can use their equivalent numbers instead—which can be very handy when you want to do something like change a property repeatedly within a loop. You can find the equivalent values for constants in your Visual Basic documentation.

The Graphics Controls

Visual Basic features several controls that represent graphical objects, anything from a simple line to a photograph. Like the Form object, one of these controls can provide drawing surfaces for VB's graphics methods, such as Line and Circle. In this section, you'll get a brief introduction to these handy controls.

The Line and Shape Controls

Previously in this chapter, you learned how to use Visual Basic's graphics methods to draw various types of lines and shapes. Another way to add lines and shapes to a display is to call upon the Line and Shape controls. The Line control features a set of properties that enable you to set a line's color, thickness, style, drawing mode, and more.

The Shape control, on the other hand, enables you to easily display six different shapes: rectangle, square, oval, circle, rounded rectangle, and rounded square. You change the shape simply by setting the control's Shape property. Other properties enable you to set the shape's color, style, fill color, fill style, height, width, and so on.

 Tip

If you need a line or shape that you can easily move around your application's display, use the Line or Shape control. This is because the Line and Shape controls support the Move method. Using the Move method is infinitely easier than trying to draw, erase, and redraw a shape using graphics methods such as Line and Circle.

The Image and PictureBox Controls

If you need to display bitmaps or other types of images from files on your disk, the Image and PictureBox controls fit the bill nicely. The Image control is a kind of stripped-down version of the PictureBox control with fewer capabilities and properties. Still, displaying a photographic-quality image on your application's display is as easy as setting an Image control's `Picture` property to the file containing the image.

The PictureBox control can also display image files, but it also acts as a drawing surface, just as a Form object does, and it can be a container for other controls. In many ways, a PictureBox control is much like a Form object, except it doesn't look like a standard window (that is, it doesn't have a title bar, menu bar, and so on). When you have complex graphics or collections of controls that you want to manipulate easily, a PictureBox control is the perfect choice.

You'll learn more about the Image and PictureBox controls as you use them throughout the rest of this book.

The Face Catch Game

You've learned quite a lot about Visual Basic's drawing commands and objects in this chapter, but you haven't yet seen how this information can help you write a game. In this section, you'll write your first Visual Basic game program, a simple little contest affectionately known as Face Catch. In the following sections, you'll discover how to play and program this example game.

Playing Face Catch

You can find the Face Catch game in the Chap02\FaceCatch directory on this book's CD-ROM. If you've installed the CD-ROM onto your hard disk drive, you can find the game in the same directory there. To run the game, double-click the FaceCatch.exe file. You'll see the window shown in Figure 2.13.

As you can see, the game has two menus, Game and Difficulty. The Game menu contains only two commands, Start Game and Exit. The Difficulty menu enables you to set the game to one of four difficulty levels.

To start playing, select the Start Game command or just press Ctrl+S. The face on the screen starts jumping from one place to another, leaving a color "footprint" each place it stops. Your task is to click the face with your mouse as many times as possible before the game ends. After the face jumps 30 times, the game ends and a message box displays your score, as shown in Figure 2.14.

FIGURE 2.13

The Face Catch game when it's first run.

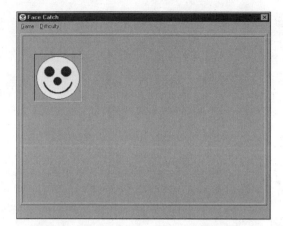

FIGURE 2.14

Face Catch at the end of a game.

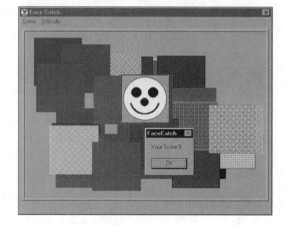

Although Face Catch will never win any awards, it's a cute diversion that you can play when you get tired of loading numbers into that spreadsheet or while you're waiting for Web pages to download. In the next section, you'll learn how to build the program from scratch.

Building Face Catch

This section is a fairly simple programming exercise that will show you how to use Visual Basic's drawing commands and graphics objects to create a game. In the following sections, you'll build the Face Catch program piece by piece, starting with the user interface.

Building the Face Catch User Interface

To build the game's user interface, perform the following steps:

1. Start a new Visual Basic Standard EXE project. Save the form as FaceCatch.frm, and save the project as FaceCatch.vbp.

2. In the VB Properties window, set the following form properties to the values shown:

```
AutoRedraw    =    True
BorderStyle   =    Fixed Single
Caption       =    "Face Catch"
Height        =    6285
Width         =    7995
ScaleMode     =    Pixel
```

Setting AutoRedraw to True ensures that the form will repaint its display automatically as needed, whereas the BorderStyle of Fixed Single prevents the user from changing the size of the window. The ScaleMode setting of Pixel causes positioning statements and drawing commands to use a measurement of pixels, which is the smallest dot on the screen.

3. Set the form's Icon property to the FaceCatch.ico file, which you can find in the Images\FaceCatch directory on this book's CD-ROM (or on your hard disk, if you installed the CD-ROM there).

The icon will appear in the upper-left corner of the window, as well as in Windows Explorer displays and on the taskbar.

4. Using the menu editor, create menus for the form, as shown in Figure 2.15. (Don't forget the Ctrl+S shortcut, also shown in Figure 2.15, for the Start Game command.) Use the following captions and menu names:

&Game	mnuGame
&Start Game	mnuStartGame
–	mnuSep
E&xit	mnuExit
&Difficulty	mnuDifficulty
&Easy	mnuEasy
&Moderate	mnuModerate
&Hard	mnuHard
&Impossible	mnuImpossible

FIGURE 2.15

*Creating the Face
Catch menu bar.*

5. Add a PictureBox control to the form, as shown in Figure 2.16.
    This PictureBox will hold the face image.

FIGURE 2.16

*Adding the PictureBox
control.*

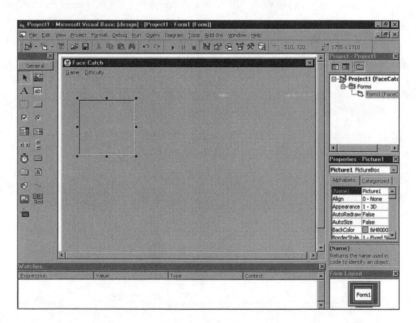

6. In the VB Properties window, set the following PictureBox properties to the values
    shown:

```
AutoRedraw     =    True
Height         =    100
ScaleMode      =    Pixel
Width          =    100
```

7. Add a Timer control to the form, as shown in Figure 2.17.

The Timer control determines how fast the face image jumps around the window.

FIGURE 2.17

Adding the Timer control.

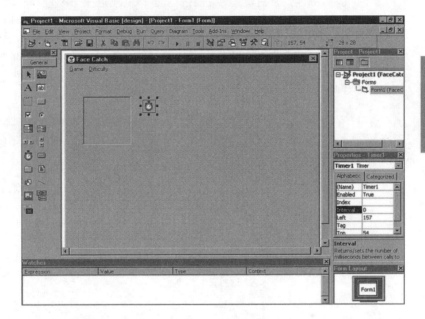

You've now completed the game's user interface. In the next section, you'll add the program code that gets the game working.

Adding the Program code

To add the game's program code to the Face Catch project, perform the following steps:

1. Add the following lines to the project's code window, as shown in Figure 2.18:

LISTING 2.1   Program Options and Variables

```
 1: '==================================================
 2: ' Face Catch for Visual Basic 6
 3: '    by Clayton Walnum
 4: ' Copyright 2000 by Macmillan Computer Publishing
 5: '==================================================
 6: Option Explicit
 7:
 8: '==================================================
 9: ' Global Variables.
10: '==================================================
11: Dim Score As Integer
12: Dim MoveCount As Integer
13: Dim Difficulty As Integer
14: Dim OldCheckedMenu As Menu
```

ANALYSIS This code sets the program's options and declares a set of global variables. As you'll see later in this chapter, these global variables hold important game values. The `Option Explicit` statement in Line 6 specifies that Visual Basic should warn you whenever it comes across a variable that hasn't been declared previously. This option helps avoid program bugs by enabling you to find misspelled variables easily. The variables declared in Lines 11 through 14 are global, so they can be shared between subroutines in the program without having to be passed explicitly to a called subroutine or function.

FIGURE 2.18

Adding global variable declarations.

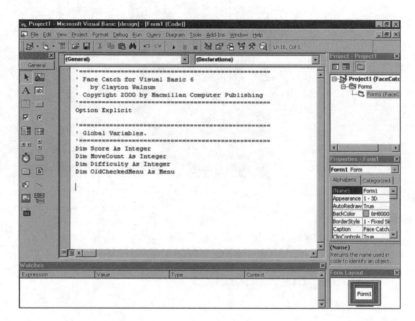

2. Add the following form subroutine to the project's code window, right after the code you added in Step 1:

LISTING 2.2   The Form_Load Event Handler

```
1: '=================================================
2: ' Form subroutines.
3: '=================================================
4: Private Sub Form_Load()
5:    InitGame
6: End Sub
```

ANALYSIS Visual Basic calls this subroutine when it first loads the game's main form. This gives your program a chance to perform any initialization it needs to do before the form becomes visible. In this case, Line 5 calls the `InitGame` subroutine, which sets the starting values for the game's variables.

3. Add the following `Picture1` handler subroutine to the project's code window, right after the code you added in Step 2:

LISTING 2.3   The Picture1_Click Event Handler

```
1: '==================================================
2: ' Picture1 subroutines.
3: '==================================================
4: Private Sub Picture1_Click()
5:   If Timer1.Interval > 100 Then
6:     Beep
7:     Score = Score + 1
8:   End If
9: End Sub
```

ANALYSIS Visual Basic calls this subroutine whenever the user clicks the `Picture1` object. This event handler increases the player's score (Line 7) whenever the player manages to click the face. The `If` statement in Line 5 ensures that the Timer control is running, which means that the face image is moving. You don't want the player to get points before the game starts!

4. Add the following `Timer1` handler subroutine to the project's code window, right after the code you added in Step 3:

LISTING 2.4   The Timer Handler

```
1:  '==================================================
2:  ' Timer1 Handler.
3:  '==================================================
4:  Private Sub Timer1_Timer()
5:    Dim x As Integer, y As Integer
6:    Dim BoxX As Integer, BoxY As Integer
7:
8:    x = Int(391 * Rnd + 20)
9:    y = Int(231 * Rnd + 20)
10:   BoxX = Picture1.Left
11:   BoxY = Picture1.Top
12:   Form1.ForeColor = RGB(Rnd * 256, Rnd * 256, Rnd * 256)
13:   Form1.Line (BoxX, BoxY)-(BoxX + 100, BoxY + 100), , BF
14:   Picture1.Move x, y
15:
```

LISTING 2.4 continued

```
16:    MoveCount = MoveCount + 1
17:    If MoveCount = 30 Then
18:       Timer1.Interval = 0
19:       MsgBox "Your Score:" & Score
20:    End If
21: End Sub
```

ANALYSIS Visual Basic calls this subroutine whenever the Timer1 object reaches its interval value, which is determined by the control's Interval property. When the timer is activated, it moves the face to a new random location. Lines 8 and 9 calculate the new location, and Lines 10 through 13 draw a rectangle at the face's current position before Line 14 moves the face. Lines 16 through 20 count each move and end the game when the face has moved 30 times.

5. Add the following menu-handler subroutines to the project's code window, right after the code you added in Step 4:

LISTING 2.5 The Menu Handlers

```
1:  '=====================================================
2:  ' Menu Handlers.
3:  '=====================================================
4:  Private Sub mnuEasy_Click()
5:     Difficulty = 1000
6:     OldCheckedMenu.Checked = False
7:     Set OldCheckedMenu = mnuEasy
8:     mnuEasy.Checked = True
9:  End Sub
10:
11: Private Sub mnuHard_Click()
12:    Difficulty = 500
13:    OldCheckedMenu.Checked = False
14:    Set OldCheckedMenu = mnuHard
15:    mnuHard.Checked = True
16: End Sub
17:
18: Private Sub mnuImpossible_Click()
19:    Difficulty = 250
20:    OldCheckedMenu.Checked = False
21:    Set OldCheckedMenu = mnuImpossible
22:    mnuImpossible.Checked = True
23: End Sub
24:
25: Private Sub mnuModerate_Click()
26:    Difficulty = 700
```

```
27:    OldCheckedMenu.Checked = False
28:    Set OldCheckedMenu = mnuModerate
29:    mnuModerate.Checked = True
30: End Sub
31:
32: Private Sub mnuStartGame_Click()
33:    Form1.Cls
34:    DrawScreen
35:    Score = 0
36:    MoveCount = 0
37:    Timer1.Interval = Difficulty
38: End Sub
39:
40: Private Sub mnuExit_Click()
41:    Unload Form1
42: End Sub
```

ANALYSIS   Visual Basic calls one of these subroutines whenever the user selects a command from the game's menu bar. Each of these event procedures performs the tasks required by its associated menu command. For example, Lines 4 through 8 set the game to its easy skill level when the player clicks the Difficulty menu's Easy command. Lines 33 through 37 prepare the program for a new game when the player clicks the Game menu's Start Game command.

6. Add the following general game subroutines to the project's code window, right after the code you added in Step 5:

LISTING 2.6   The General Subroutines

```
1:  '=================================================
2:  ' Game subroutines.
3:  '=================================================
4:  Sub InitGame()
5:     Difficulty = 500
6:     mnuModerate.Checked = True
7:     Set OldCheckedMenu = mnuModerate
8:     Randomize
9:     DrawScreen
10:    DrawFace
11: End Sub
12:
13: Sub DrawScreen()
14:    Form1.ForeColor = vbBlack
15:    Form1.Line (10, 10)-(517, 10)
16:    Form1.Line (10, 10)-(10, 358)
17:    Form1.Line (522, 5)-(522, 362)
18:    Form1.Line (522, 362)-(5, 362)
19:    Form1.ForeColor = vbWhite
```

LISTING 2.6 continued

```
20:   Form1.Line (5, 5)-(522, 5)
21:   Form1.Line (5, 5)-(5, 363)
22:   Form1.Line (517, 10)-(517, 358)
23:   Form1.Line (517, 358)-(10, 358)
24: End Sub
25:
26: Sub DrawFace()
27:   Picture1.FillStyle = vbSolid
28:   Picture1.FillColor = vbYellow
29:   Picture1.Circle (48, 48), 45
30:   Picture1.FillColor = vbBlack
31:   Picture1.Circle (30, 35), 10
32:   Picture1.Circle (65, 35), 10
33:   Picture1.Circle (47, 55), 8
34:   Picture1.DrawWidth = 2
35:   Picture1.Circle (48, 50), 30,  , 3.4, 6, 1#
36: End Sub
```

ANALYSIS These subroutines initialize the game variables and draw the graphics. The subroutine in Lines 4 through 11 gets the game ready to play for the first time. Lines 13 through 24 draw the screen display on the main form, whereas Lines 26 through 36 draw the face image in the PictureBox control.

You've now completed the Face Catch game project. You can run the program from within Visual Basic, or you can compile it into an executable file.

Understanding Face Catch

The Face Catch game relies on four global variables, which the program declares near the top of the program. Table 2.4 lists the variables and their descriptions.

TABLE 2.4 The Face Catch Game Variables

Variable	Type	Description
Score	Integer	The player's current score. The program increments this value each time the player manages to click on the jumping face.
MoveCount	Integer	The number of times the face has jumped. When this value reaches 30, the game is over.
Difficulty	Integer	The setting for the Timer1 control's Interval property. This value starts with an initial value of 500, but the user can change it by selecting a command on the game's Difficulty menu.
OldCheckedMenu	Menu	The Menu object associated with the command (on the Difficulty menu) that must be unchecked before a new command can be checked.

When the game starts, Visual Basic calls the `Form1` object's `Form_Load` subroutine, which does nothing more than call the game subroutine `InitGame`. `InitGame` first initializes several variables:

```
Difficulty = 500
mnuModerate.Checked = True
Set OldCheckedMenu = mnuModerate
```

This initialization sets the game difficulty to 500, which the program uses as the starting interval for the `Timer1` object. That is, when the player first runs the game, the face image is set to jump every 500 milliseconds. The remaining initialization lines coordinate the Difficulty menu with the initial difficulty setting when you checkmark the Moderate command in the menu.

The `InitGame` subroutine next calls the VB command `Randomize`, which ensures that the program can generate a different set of random numbers each time it's played:

```
Randomize
```

 Caution
> Most computer games rely heavily on random numbers. If you forget to call the `Randomize` command before acquiring random numbers, the game will generate the same set of random numbers each time it's played. This results in a game that's entirely predictable.

Finally, `InitGame` calls two other general game subroutines, as shown here:

```
DrawScreen
DrawFace
```

As you can tell by these subroutine's names, they draw the main game screen and the face image, all using the VB drawing commands you learned in this chapter. The `DrawScreen` subroutine draws a 3D border around the edge of the form's display area, like this:

LISTING 2.7   Drawing the Display's Border

```
 1:  Form1.ForeColor = vbBlack
 2:  Form1.Line (10, 10)-(517, 10)
 3:  Form1.Line (10, 10)-(10, 358)
 4:  Form1.Line (522, 5)-(522, 362)
 5:  Form1.Line (522, 362)-(5, 362)
 6:  Form1.ForeColor = vbWhite
 7:  Form1.Line (5, 5)-(522, 5)
 8:  Form1.Line (5, 5)-(5, 363)
 9:  Form1.Line (517, 10)-(517, 358)
10:  Form1.Line (517, 358)-(10,  358)
```

The DrawFace subroutine, on the other hand, draws the face image in the Picture1 control, like this:

LISTING 2.8   Drawing the Face

```
1:  Picture1.FillStyle = vbSolid
2:  Picture1.FillColor = vbYellow
3:  Picture1.Circle (48, 48), 45
4:  Picture1.FillColor = vbBlack
5:  Picture1.Circle (30, 35), 10
6:  Picture1.Circle (65, 35), 10
7:  Picture1.Circle (47, 55), 8
8:  Picture1.DrawWidth = 2
9:  Picture1.Circle (48, 50), 30,  , 3.4, 6, 1#
```

After reading this chapter, you should understand how these two subroutines draw their images. If a drawing command or object property doesn't ring a bell, review the appropriate sections of this chapter.

There's not a lot to be said about the Difficulty menu handlers, except that they set the Difficulty variable and checkmark the associated menu command. For example, when the user clicks the Easy menu command, the mnuEasy_Click subroutine handles the request like this:

```
Difficulty = 1000
OldCheckedMenu.Checked = False
Set OldCheckedMenu = mnuEasy
mnuEasy.Checked = True
```

For all intents and purposes, the Timer1_Timer handler manages all the game action. Every time the Timer1 object counts up to the value contained in its Interval property, VB calls the Timer1_Timer subroutine. This subroutine first declares a set of local variables:

```
Dim x As Integer, y As Integer
Dim BoxX As Integer, BoxY As Integer
```

The x and y variables represent the coordinates where the face will jump next. The program sets these variables' values by calling the VB Rnd command, which returns a value between 0 and 1. A little simple math converts these values to integers between 20 and 410 for the x coordinate and between 20 and 230 for the y coordinate:

```
x = Int(391 * Rnd + 20)
y = Int(231 * Rnd + 20)
```

> **Tip**
>
> Calculating a range of random numbers can sometimes be tricky. To make this task easier, remember the following formula: `Int((upper - lower + 1) * Rnd + lower)`. The formulas for the x and y coordinates in the Face Catch game are actually the same formula after they've been simplified. For example, `x = Int((410 - 20 + 1) * Rnd + 20)` simplifies to `x = Int (391 * Rnd + 20)`.

After setting the location for the next face jump, the program draws a rectangle on the form at the face's current location. Then the program moves the face to its new random location:

```
BoxX = Picture1.Left
BoxY = Picture1.Top
Form1.ForeColor = RGB(Rnd * 256, Rnd * 256, Rnd * 256)
Form1.Line (BoxX, BoxY)-(BoxX + 100, BoxY + 100), , BF
Picture1.Move x, y
```

The last task for the timer handler is to increment the jump count and check whether the game is over. If the game is over, the timer shuts itself off (by setting its `Interval` property to 0) and displays a message box containing the player's score:

```
MoveCount = MoveCount + 1
If MoveCount = 30 Then
  Timer1.Interval = 0
  MsgBox "Your Score:" & Score
End If
```

Summary

Writing computer games requires good graphics programming skills. In this, your second day of study, you learned how to use Visual Basic's drawing methods `Line` and `Circle` to draw lines, rectangles, circles, ovals, and arcs. You then discovered many properties that determine how Visual Basic draws its graphics. Finally, you got a quick look at the special graphics controls Line and Shape, as well as the very important Form object, Image control, and PictureBox control.

In Day 3, "Creating Game Screens with Fonts and VB Graphics," you'll learn how to manipulate graphical text to create attractive displays. Because every game combines graphics and text, these skills will take you a long way toward being the game programmer you want to be.

Q&A

Q **Is there any compelling reason to use one type of color constant rather than another, or can I specify colors any way I find comfortable?**

A In most cases, you should choose a method that suits your way of working. It's always better to use constants (even if you have to define your own) so that your code is easier to read. However, the predefined system-color constants can be very important if you want your game program to respond to changes that the user might make in his current Windows colors. For example, if you draw your own buttons rather than using Visual Basic's CommandButton controls, you might want the buttons to change colors appropriately when the system's button colors change. In that case, use the system-color constants to specify colors for your custom buttons.

Q **If I choose to use a `ScaleMode` setting of Twip, which is the VB default, is there a way I can convert twip coordinates to pixel coordinates and vice versa?**

A Sure is. Visual Basic provides the `TwipsPerPixelX` (for horizontal screen measurements) and `TwipsPerPixelY` (for vertical screen measurements) properties, which return the number of twips per screen pixel. You can use the return values from these properties to perform conversions between twips and pixels.

Q **You said that the DrawStyle property only affects lines with a DrawWidth setting of 1. What if I want to draw a stylized line that's two or more pixels wide?**

A Although you can't draw a single stylized line with a width greater than 1, there's nothing to stop you from drawing several of such lines, one after the other, to create a stylized line of the required width. For example, to create a dashed line two pixels wide, just draw two dashed lines, one on top of the other.

Workshop

The workshop includes quiz questions to help gauge your grasp of the material. You'll find the answers to this quiz in Appendix A, "Quiz and Exercise Answers." Even if you feel that you totally understand the concepts presented here, you should work through the quiz anyway. The last section has some exercises that you might work through to reinforce your learning.

Quiz

1. What are the five ways you can specify a color in a Visual Basic programs?

2. Why might you want to use system colors in your programs?

3. What are the three color elements of an RGB color value, and what are their minimum and maximum values?

4. What shapes can you draw with the `Line` method?

5. What shapes can you draw with the `Circle` method?

6. How does the `Step` keyword affect the coordinates given to the `Line` and `Circle` methods?

7. If you want to draw a shape filled with a predefined pattern, what property will you set for the object on whose surface you want to draw?

8. What is the purpose of a drawing mode?

9. Why are the `vbCopyPen` and `vbInvert` drawing modes especially useful?

10. Which two Visual Basic controls can display shapes without your program having to draw them by using drawing methods?

11. What Visual Basic object and control can act as drawing surfaces for the drawing methods?

12. Which two Visual Basic controls can display complex images such as bitmaps stored in a file?

Exercises

1. Start a new Visual Basic project and draw a blue, two-pixel-wide line on the form from point 30,50 (measured in pixels) to point 100,75. (Hint: You can perform your drawing in the form's `Form_Load` method, but you must first set the form's `AutoRedraw` property to `True`.)

2. In the same form, draw a yellow-filled rectangle with corners located at 20,30 and 75,60.

3. Add a PictureBox control to the form, and use the drawing methods to draw a scene in the PictureBox that includes a simple house on a green lawn and a sun in a blue sky. (Don't forget to set the PictureBox's `AutoRedraw` property to `True`.)

2

DAY **3**

Creating Game Screens with Fonts and VB Graphics

Whether it's something as simple as the player's score or as large as the status of a dozen or more characters, most games need to display text. And often, you won't want to stick to the default font and its attributes. In the following sections, you'll learn all you need to know to use text in your Visual Basic games. Today you'll learn the following:

- How to set text colors
- How to display transparent and nontransparent text
- How to set a font's typeface and size
- How to display italic, bold, underlined, or strikethrough text
- How to combine text and graphics to create a game screen

Setting Text Colors

The most obvious text attribute that affects your game displays is color. You want the text color to fit in well with the game's graphics. Color is also a good way to make certain text stand out more than other text. There are two object properties that determine the colors used for displaying text: ForeColor and FontTransparent.

The *ForeColor* Property

An object's ForeColor property determines the drawing color used by the object when it displays graphics (in this case, you can consider text to be graphics). For example, if you set a form's ForeColor property to the color red, graphics, such as lines, and text will be drawn in red. To put it simply, to change the text color, set the object's ForeColor property. The following lines display the message "This is red text" in red:

```
Form1.ForeColor = vbRed
Print "This is red text"
```

The *FontTransparent* Property

Another property that affects text color is FontTransparent. This property also determines whether or not background graphics will be blocked out by the text line. By default, Visual Basic sets the FontTransparent property to True, meaning that background graphics show through the displayed text. For example, Listing 3.1 draws a black rectangle in a form and then displays transparent white text over the rectangle. Figure 3.1 shows the result.

LISTING 3.1   Displaying Transparent Text

```
1: Form1.ScaleMode = vbPixels
2: Form1.Line (40, 40)-(270, 170), vbBlack, BF
3: Form1.FontTransparent = True
4: Form1.ForeColor = vbWhite
5: Form1.CurrentX = 80
6: Form1.CurrentY = 80
7: Form1.Print "This is transparent text"
```

ANALYSIS   Line 1 sets measurements in the form to pixels, and Line 2 draws a black, filled box. Lines 3 and 4 set the text attributes, Lines 5 and 6 set the position for text output, and Line 7 prints the transparent text.

Listing 3.2 is similar, except that the FontTransparent property is set to False and the text color is now black. Thus, the area around the text blocks out any graphics beneath. Figure 3.2 shows the result.

FIGURE 3.1

Transparent text displayed in a form.

LISTING 3.2 Displaying Opaque Text

```
1: Form1.ScaleMode = vbPixels
2: Form1.Line (40, 40)-(270, 170), vbBlack, BF
3: Form1.FontTransparent = False
4: Form1.ForeColor = vbWhite
5: Form1.CurrentX = 80
6: Form1.CurrentY = 80
7: Form1.Print "This is non-transparent text"
```

ANALYSIS Line 1 sets measurements in the form to pixels, and Line 2 draws a black, filled box. Lines 3 and 4 set the text attributes, Lines 5 and 6 set the position for text output, and Line 7 prints the text, this time opaque.

FIGURE 3.2

Non-transparent text displayed in a form.

Note
The background color of non-transparent text is the same as the object's background color. For example, whether a form's background color is white or not, non-transparent text drawn on the form will also have a white background. This means that any text not drawn on top of previously drawn graphics will always look transparent, regardless of the FontTransparent property's setting.

3

Working with Fonts

Besides color, the type of font and the font's attributes also play a big role in how text appears on your game's screen. Each object that can display text has a Font property that determines the font settings. In the following sections, you'll discover how to handle Font objects in your programs.

 A *font* is a set of attributes that determine how text looks on the screen.

The *Font* Property

As already mentioned, any object that can display text has a Font property that determines the type of font and its attributes. That is, the Font property determines the typeface that will be used to display text, as well as the size of the text and whether it will be italic, bold, underlined, and so on. To access a Font object's properties, just use the object name Font followed by a period and the name of the property you want to access. For example, here's how you set a form's font to bold:

```
Form1.Font.Bold = True
```

Properties of Fonts

The Font object features eight properties that determine the appearance of the text. Table 3.1 lists the properties and their descriptions.

TABLE 3.1   Properties of the Font Object

Property	Description
Bold	A Boolean value that determines whether text will be bold
Charset	An integer value that determines the font's character set
Italic	A Boolean value that determines whether text will be italic
Name	A string valuethat determines the typeface to use
Size	An integer value that determines the size (in points) of the font
Strikethrough	A Boolean value that determines whether text will be strikethrough
Underline	A Boolean value that determines whether text will be underlined
Weight	An integer value that represents the weight (boldness) of the font

Listing 3.3 sets a font to a 24-point, bold, italic, Courier typeface.

LISTING 3.3   Setting Up a Font

```
1: Form1.ScaleMode = vbPixels
2: Form1.Font.Name = "Courier"
3: Form1.Font.Size = 24
4: Form1.Font.Italic = True
5: Form1.Font.Bold = True
6: Form1.CurrentX = 80
7: Form1.CurrentY = 40
8: Form1.Print "This is Courier text"
```

ANALYSIS   Line 2 sets the font object to the Courier type face, and line 3 sets the font's size to 24 points. Lines 4 and 5 turn on the italic and bold attributes, Lines 6 and 7 set the output position, and Line 8 displays a line of text.

Figure 3.3 shows what this font looks like when a program prints text in a form.

FIGURE 3.3

Courier text displayed in a form.

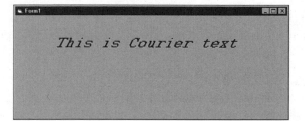

The Nightshade Text Adventure Game

Now that you know how to handle fonts in your Visual Basic games, it's time to put your font knowledge to the test. I can't think of a better example of using text in a game than a good old-fashioned text adventure.

Playing Nightshade

You can find the Nightshade game in the Chap03\Nightshade directory on this book's CD-ROM. If you've installed the CD-ROM onto your hard drive, you can find the game in the same directory there. To run the game, double-click the Nightshade.exe file. Figure 3.4 shows a game of Nightshade in progress.

Most adventure games start off with some sort of background story. In order to understand your quest in Nightshade, please read the following fairy tale.

3

The Story

*There's a land that exists in the unconscious flickers passing through a mind embraced
by sleep. It hides in the shadows of dreams and shuns the bright light of reality. It is a
land called Nightshade.*

*Ten-year-old Denny Wayne first finds Nightshade not in the dark realm of sleep, but in a
book he discovers tucked into a dusty library shelf. Each night, Denny perches on his bed
and reads, turning the pages with trembling fingers, eyes as round as full October moons.*

*In the story, the Troll King has decided that all of Nightshade should be under his rule.
His armies are even now preparing to march on the Elf capital of Gandolese. The city
will remain under siege until the Elves pledge fealty to the Troll King.*

*Denny closes the book reluctantly, crawls beneath his blankets and settles back. Soon,
he's asleep. In his mind's eye, he relives each moment of the story as if he were there. It
is he who must overthrow the Troll King. In his dreams, Nightshade comes into being,
acting out the script that has been laid down so carefully in the book by some long-for-
gotten author.*

*The book rests on the bed. Each of Denny's movements nudge it closer to the edge. What
secrets lay hidden in its final passages? According to the book, the Troll King's plans are
doomed to failure. On the very last page, the Elf armies banish him from Nightshade for-
ever.*

*Denny sleeps. Denny dreams. The book falls from the bed to the floor. The pages flutter,
opening to the final paragraphs before coming to rest. Suddenly, a face looms from
Denny's dream, the face of the Troll King. The King sees the book, reads the words that
spell his downfall, and bellows in fury. He will not be defeated! An idea begins to form...*

Yes! the Troll King thinks. That should work! He will send one of his henchmen from Nightshade into Denny's world and steal the last page. If Denny can't read that page, his dreams will take another path and he, the Troll King, will be victorious instead of defeated.

Denny wakes with a start. He scrambles up, looks wildly about. Nothing there. Only a dream.

His breath whispers past his lips in a quiet sigh as he eases back. His eyelids creep shut. He remembers seeing the book lying on the floor. Wasn't there something different? Something missing, perhaps? Sleep enfolds Denny in its dark arms, and, in his last moment of wakefulness, his mind focuses on the book. The last page was torn out! It's up to him to recover the missing page and place it back in the book. Only then will the Troll King's defeat be assured.

Denny sleeps. Nightshade wakes.

Getting Into the Game

Nightshade is a nonviolent fantasy text adventure suitable for the entire family. There's no fighting or dying. If you make a "fatal" mistake during play, Denny simply wakes from his dream. Your job is to guide Denny through the realm of Nightshade, recover the missing page, and replace it in the book.

Nightshade is open to your communication via two-word commands. These commands are in a verb/noun format (such as GET BOOK, GO DOOR). There are a few exceptions. All directions are abbreviated to a single letter (N, S, E, W, U, D).

If you've never played a text adventure before, you might find Nightshade a bit (byte?) confusing at first. You'll see messages like "Denny can't do that!" at times when it seems completely illogical. For instance, why can't Denny MOVE BOOK? It's right there in plain sight! Is he just stupid? Well, yes and no. It's important to realize that the game will respond only to those commands it's been programmed to accept. There's no computer in the galaxy that's big enough to hold all the possible replies to all the possible commands. Sometimes, rewording your command will yield a result. How about GET BOOK instead?

Draw a map! That's the only way you can keep track of your location. The most common mapping technique for adventure games is to represent each room (every location is a "room," even if it's outside) by a small box. You then write the room's name, as well as any items found there, inside the box. Each possible exit is indicated by a small line leading toward the next room. When you enter a new room, be sure to take note of all exits. It's imperative that you try each one, or else you're likely to miss something important.

To start your adventure, try eachavailable exit and note any items found. When you can go no farther, stop and think about everything you've discovered. What should Denny do with the bed? Is the closet significant in some way? How about the clothes? Are they important? When you solve a puzzle, repeat the process, moving from room to room, gathering items and information until you get stuck again. Eventually, you'll find your way to the game's solution.

Note

> For you computer history buffs, I should mention that a guy named Scott Adams was pretty much responsible for bringing text adventures to the masses. At one point, his series of adventures were on every computer-game player's shelf. After Adams, a company named Infocom took over the market for text adventures with the famous Zork series, and they continued with a long line of comedy, mystery, and science fiction adventures that are still available today.
>
> Back when I was working for an Atari computer magazine, I had the honor of traveling to the Infocom offices and writing an up-close article on the whole game-development process. If you're interested, that article and interviews with the Infocom staff are available online at `http://www.claytonwalnum.com/infocom.html`.

Nightshade Hints

To use the following hints, load up the Translate application in the same directory as the game. This application translates between Nightshadish and English, and vice versa. Figure 3.5 shows Translate in action. To use a hint, find the question that relates to your problem, and then type in the first encrypted hint beneath it. (Click Translate's Nightshadish to English button first.) Each line is a separate hint, and some questions have several hints. After you decode the first one, try to solve the puzzle on your own. If you're still stuck, decode the next hint.

FIGURE 3.5

The Translate applica-tion.

How can Denny get out of his room?

MPPL!JO!UIF!DMPTFU/

NPWF!UIF!DMPUIFT/

What are the trees for?

FYBNJOF!UIFN/

POF!DBO!CF!DMJNCFE/

POF!IBT!B!EPPS/

How can Denny cross the swamp?

WJTJU!UIF!FMWFT/

UBML!UP!UIF!FMWFT/

How can Denny cross the pond?

EJE!IF!HFU!JO!UIF!CPBU@

MPPL!BU!UIF!NVTJD/

EFOOZ!JT!B!HPPE!TJOHFS/

Where's the page from the book?

JO!B!TUPOF!SPPN/

VTF!UIF!NJSSPS/

FYBNJOF!GBJOUFE!USPMM/

What about the dwarf?

UBML!UP!IJN/

Troll won't let Denny leave?

SFGMFDU!PO!UIBU/

IF(T!BXGVMMZ!VHMZ/

HJWF!IJN!UIF!NJSSPS/

How can Denny "survive" the silver door?

IF!DBO(U/!JHOPSF!JU/

How can Denny open the fancy box?

IBWF!UIF!CMVF!TDSPMM@

TFF!XIBU!UIF!CMVF!TDSPMM!TBZT/

TBZ!QSFTUP/

What about the giant?

UBML!UP!IJN/

How can Denny get the hammer?

IF!NVTU!CF!TUSPOHFS/

EPFT!IF!IBWF!UIF!QPUJPO@

FYBNJOF!JU/

ESJOL!UIF!QPUJPO/

What about the stream?

FYBNJOF!JU/

HFU!UIF!BMHBF/

What about the old hag?

UBML!UP!IFS/

CBE!JEFB-!IVI@

TIF!IBT!OPUIJOH!PG!VTF/

What about the boulders?

EFOOZ!OFFET!DSZTUBMT/

CSFBL!UIFN!PQFO/

XJUI!UIF!IBNNFS/

Nightshade's Help Menu

On Nightshade's help menu, you can call up the game's background story and view the commands that Denny understands. Of course, you can also view the program's About dialog box.

Building Nightshade

Nightshade is a much larger program than the Face Catch game you built in Day 2. Still, the game uses conventional programming techniques that you should already know. Keep in mind that although the entire program listing is lengthy, much of the code performs similar tasks with different data. That is, the program isn't as complex as you might first think. In any case, this program's main purpose is to demonstrate how to create a simple game screen using Visual Basic's drawing commands and fonts. Let's start with the user interface.

Building Nightshade's User Interface

To build the game's user interface, perform the following steps:

1. Start a new Visual Basic Standard EXE project. Save the form as Nightshade.frm, and save the project as Nightshade.vbp.

2. In the VB Properties window, set the following form properties to the values shown:

    AutoRedraw = True

    BorderStyle = Fixed Single

    Caption = "Nightshade"

    Height = 6650

    ScaleMode = Pixel

    Width = 4755

3. Set the form's Icon property to the Nightshade.ico file, which you can find in the Images\Nightshade directory on this book's CD-ROM (or on your hard disk, if you installed the CD-ROM there).

4. Using the menu editor, create menus for the form, as shown in Figure 3.6&File
    mnuFile

&New	mnuNew
&Load	mnuLoad
&Save	mnuSave
—	mnuSep
E&xit	mnuExit
&Help	mnuHelp
The &Story	mnuStory
The &Commands	mnuCommands
&About Nightshade	mnuAbout

FIGURE 3.6

*Creating the
Nightshade menu bar.*

5. Add a TextBox control to the form, as shown in Figure 3.7

FIGURE 3.7

*Adding the TextBox
control.*

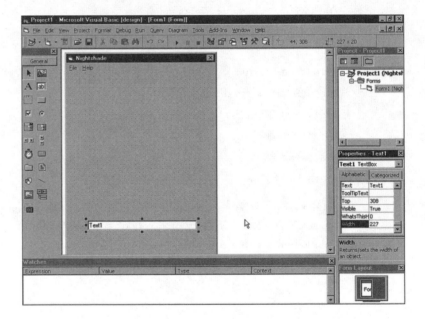

6. In the VB Properties window, set the following TextBox properties to the values
shown:

Name = "txtInput"

Height = 20

Left = 27

Text = ""

Top = 300

Width = 260

7. Add two Label controls to the form, as shown in Figure 3.8

FIGURE 3.8

Adding the Label controls.

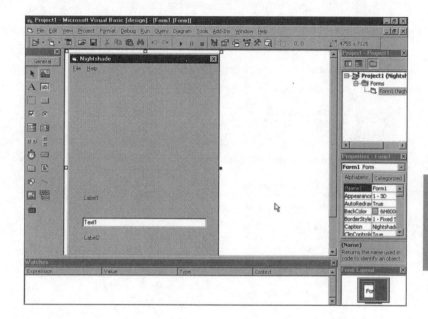

8. In the VB Properties window, set the labels' properties to the values shown here:

First Label Control:

Caption = "COMMAND:"

Height = 13

Left = 29

Top = 284

Width = 70

Second Label Control:

Name = "lblResult"

BorderStyle = Fixed Single

Caption = """

Height = 20

Left = 27

Top = 337

Width = 260

9. Add a new form to the project (select the Project menu's Add Form command) and
    set its properties to the following values:

    AutoRedraw = True

    BorderStyle = Fixed Dialog

    Caption = "The Story"

    Height = 6630

    Width = 5715

10. Add a TextBox control and a CommandButton control to the form, giving them the
    following property settings:

    ### TextBox Control:

    Font = MS Sans Serif, Regular, 10-point

    Height = 5145

    Left = 255

    MultiLine = True

    ScrollBars = Vertical

    Text = ""

    Top = 390

    Width = 5055

    ### CommandButton Control:

    Caption = "OK"

    Height = 345

    Left = 1200

    Top = 5715

    Width = 3120

You've now completed the game's user interface, which should look like Figure 3.9. In
the next section, you'll add the program code that makes the game work.

Adding the Program code

Because Nightshade consists of nearly 1,000 lines of source code, it doesn't make any
sense for you to type it in. Instead, you can find the program code under the name
Nightshade.txt in the Chap03/Code folder of this book's CD-ROM. To complete the program, double-click the Form1 form and copy the contents of the Nightshade.txt file to the

form's code window. Then, double-click the Form2 form and copy the contents of the Nightshade2.txt file into its code window. Now you can compile the program. Before trying to run your compiled program, however, make sure you copy the Nightshade.dat and Nightshade2.dat files into the game's directory. You can find these files in the CD-ROM's Chap03/Nightshade folder. The following sections will examine the parts of the source code that require explaining.

Figure 3.9

The complete Nightshade user interface.

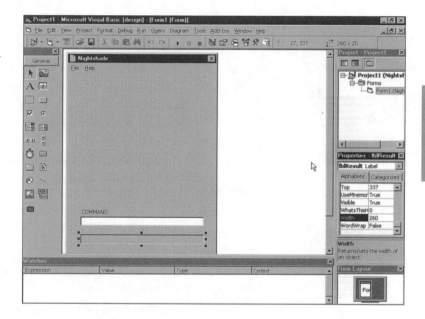

Understanding Nightshade

Nightshade contains a lot of source code, although many of the subroutines are so similar that once you understand one, you're on your way to understanding them all.

Nightshade's Variables

Nightshade relies on two sets of global variables, which the program declares near the top of the program. There's nothing special about the first set of global variables. However, the second set comprises those variables that must be saved to disk by the game-save routine. Table 3.1 lists the general global variables and their descriptions, and Table 3.2 lists the second set, the game-save variables.

TABLE 3.1 Nightshade's General Game Variables

Variable	Type	Description
CompleteNoun	String	The complete noun (that is, not abbreviated to three letters)
Directions	String	The single-letter direction characters: N, S, E, W, U, D
Exits()	Integer	An array containing the destination room numbers for each of the six directions in which the player can travel from the current room
ItemNames()	String	An array containing the full-length item (noun) names for display on the screen
Noun	String	The current noun, abbreviated to three letters
NounIndexes()	Integer	A companion array to NounNames(); this array contains the noun numbers that match the noun names
NounNames()	String	An array containing the abbreviated, three-letter names for the game's nouns
RoomDesc	String	The description of the current room
Verb	String	The current verb, abbreviated to three letters

TABLE 3.2 Nightshade's Game-Save Variables

Variable	Type	Description
ItemLocations()	Integer	An array containing the location (room number) of every item in the game
NumGlueIngredients	Integer	The number of ingredients the player has placed in the glue jug
NumItemsInInventory	Integer	The number of items currently in the player's inventory
PrevBoatRoom	Integer	The room number where the boat last appeared
Room	Integer	The number of the current room
TrollFainted	Boolean	A flag indicating whether the troll has fainted yet

Nightshade's Constants and Enumerations

When you're writing large programs like games, I can't stress enough the importance of *creating easily readable code*! Someday, you'll look at your code and try to remember what the heck it does. Using lots of constants, as well as self-explanatory variable and subroutine names, changes your program from indecipherable gobbledygook to something that's almost as readable as a newspaper.

That's why most of the programs in this book, including Nightshade, use constants instead of literal values. You'll also see some lengthy variable and subroutine names as well. Do you want to see how well this technique works? How much sense can you make of the following code fragment?

```
If NumGI = 3 Then
  ItLoc(7) = -1
  ItLoc(8) = -4
  ItLoc(15) = -19
End If
```

Now look at how this code appears in Nightshade:

```
If NumGlueIngredients = 3 Then
  ItemLocations(JUGWITHGLUE) = IN_INVENTORY
  ItemLocations(JUG) = NOT_IN_GAME
  ItemLocations(TROLL) = -19
End If
```

Even though you haven't looked at any of Nightshade's source code yet, you can almost figure out what's going on in this code fragment.

This brings us to enumerations, which come in handy when you need to create a set of related constants. For example, notice the constants JUGWITHGLUE, JUG, and TROLL used in the previous code example. Those constants are part of Nightshade's ItemsEnum enumeration, which looks like Listing 3.4.

LISTING 3.4   The ItemsEnum Enumeration

```
 1:  Enum ItemsEnum
 2:     BOOK
 3:     BED
 4:     CLOTHES
 5:     GLOWINGDOOR
 6:     REDSCROLL
 7:     TREES
 8:     WOODENDOOR
 9:     BLUESCROLL
10:     ELFFAMILY
11:     WATERSHOES
12:     HUT
13:     SIGN
14:     JUGWITHGLUE
15:     FAINTEDTROLL
16:     MIRROR
17:     JUG
18:     BOAT
19:     DWARF
20:     TUNNEL
21:     GOLDDOOR
22:     SILVERDOOR
23:     BRASSDOOR
```

3

LISTING 3.4 continued

```
24:    GLASSDOOR
25:    PAGE
26:    TROLL
27:    STREAM
28:    CRYSTALS
29:    MUD
30:    GIANT
31:    HUGEHAMMER
32:    BOULDERS
33:    FANCYBOX
34:    POTION
35:    RECIPECARD
36:    ALGAE
37:    SWAMP
38:    SHEETMUSIC
39:    BITSOFROCK
40:    OLDHAG
41: End Enum
```

The ItemsEnum enumeration creates a set of constants with values that run consecutively from 0 to 38. It's exactly as if the constants were defined in the normal way.

LISTING 3.5 An Alternative Definition for the Constants

```
1:  Const BOOK = 0
2:  Const BED = 1
3:  Const CLOTHES = 2
4:  Const GLOWINGDOOR = 3
5:  Const REDSCROLL = 5
6:  Const TREES = 6
7:  '
8:  ' Some constants not shown for brevity
9:  '
10: Const OLDHAG = 38
```

Nightshade defines one other enumeration, ExitEnum. This defines values for the six directions in which the player can move.

LISTING 3.6 The ExitEnum Enumeration

```
1: Enum ExitEnum
2:    NORTH
3:    SOUTH
4:    EAST
5:    WEST
```

```
6:    UP
7:    DOWN
8: End Enum
```

Nightshade also defines a set of nonenumerated constants (that is, not defined in enumerations), as shown in Table 3.3.

TABLE 3.3   Nightshade's Constants

Constant	Description
ENTER	The ASCII value of the Enter key
IN_INVENTORY	The value indicating that an item is in the player's inventory
ITEM_USED	The value indicating that an item has been used and is no longer in the game world
MAX_ITEMS_IN_INVENTORY	The maximum number of items that can fit in the player's inventory
MAX_ITEMS_IN_ROOM	The maximum number of items that can fit in a room
NOT_IN_GAME	The value indicating that an item isn't currently in the game world
NOT_VALID	The value indicating that the direction selected by the player isn't valid for the current room
NUM_NOUN_NAMES	The number of three-letter noun names (including aliases for some items) that the game understands
NUM_NOUNS	The number of items in the game
NUM_VERBS	The number of verbs the game understands

Starting the Game

Now that you have a handle on what all those variables and constants mean, it's time to dig deeper into the program's source code. As always, when the game starts, Visual Basic calls the Form1 object's Form_Load subroutine, which does nothing more than call the subroutine StartNewGame. StartNewGame, in turn, calls two other subroutines, InitGame and UpdateGameScreen.

LISTING 3.7   The Form_Load and StartNewGame Subroutines

```
1: Private Sub Form_Load()
2:    StartNewGame
3: End Sub
4:
5: Sub StartNewGame()
6:    InitGame
7:    UpdateGameScreen
8: End Sub
```

The `InitGame` subroutine sets the initial values for all the game's variables, as shown in Listing 3.8.

LISTING 3.8   The InitGame Subroutine

```
 1:  Sub InitGame()
 2:    Dim i As Integer
 3:    Directions = "NSEWUD"
 4:    Open "Nightshade.dat" For Input As #1
 5:    For i = 0 To NUM_NOUNS - 1
 6:      Input #1, ItemNames(i), ItemLocations(i)
 7:    Next i
 8:    Close #1
 9:    Open "Nightshade2.dat" For Input As #1
10:    For i = 0 To NUM_NOUN_NAMES - 1
11:      Input #1, NounNames(i), NounIndexes(i)
12:    Next i
13:    Close #1
14:    Room = 5
15:    PrevBoatRoom = 12
16:    NumItemsInInventory = 0
17:    NumGlueIngredients = 0
18:    TrollFainted = False
19:    txtInput.Text = ""
20:    lblResult.Caption = ""
21: End Sub
```

Notice how the game loads values from two files, Nightshade.dat (Lines 4 through 8) and Nightshade2.dat (Lines 9 through 13). These files must be in the same folder as the game's executable file.

The `UpdateGameScreen` subroutine calls all the other subroutines needed to draw the game's display. This task includes drawing the graphics, drawing text labels, and displaying the data that represents the player's current location and status. `UpdateGameScreen` looks like Listing 3.9.

LISTING 3.9   The UpdateGameScreen Subroutine

```
 1:  Sub UpdateGameScreen()
 2:    DrawGraphics
 3:    DrawText
 4:    ResetExits
 5:    SetRoomData
 6:    ShowRoomDescription
 7:    ShowExits
 8:    ShowVisibleItems
 9:    ShowInventory
10: End Sub
```

The DrawGraphics subroutine does nothing more than draw a bunch of black and white lines on the display, creating the display's 3D borders. There's no need to show that subroutine here. It's on the CD if you need a refresher.

However, the DrawText subroutine is where some of the stuff you learned about fonts gets put to use. In DrawText, the program changes font colors and attributes to create the display, like Listing 3.10.

LISTING 3.10 The DrawText Subroutine

```
1:  Sub DrawText()
2:    Form1.Font.Bold = True
3:    Form1.Font.Underline = True
4:    Form1.ForeColor = vbBlue
5:    Form1.CurrentX = 20
6:    Form1.CurrentY = 20
7:    Form1.Print "PLACE:"
8:    Form1.CurrentX = 20
9:    Form1.CurrentY = 70
10:   Form1.Print "EXITS:"
11:   Form1.CurrentX = 20
12:   Form1.CurrentY = 120
13:   Form1.Print "DENNY SEES:"
14:   Form1.CurrentX = 180
15:   Form1.CurrentY = 120
16:   Form1.Print "DENNY HAS:"
17:   Form1.ForeColor = vbBlack
18:   Form1.Font.Underline = False
19: End Sub
```

ANALYSIS Lines 2 through 4 set font attributes, and Lines 5 and 6 set the position for the text output printed in Line 7. The rest of the listing works similarly.

The ResetExits subroutine (see Listing 3.11) initializes the Exits array, which removes the room numbers for the old room in preparation for filling the array with the room numbers for the new room.

LISTING 3.11 The ResetExits Subroutine

```
1:  Sub ResetExits()
2:    Dim i As Integer
3:    For i = 0 To 5
4:      Exits(i) = 0
5:    Next i
6:  End Sub
```

The `SetRoomData` subroutine (see Listing 3.12) is where the `Exits` array gets its new values. The `Exits` array has six elements, which are the room numbers for north, south, east, west, up, and down, respectively. That is, if the player requests to move north, the array element `Exits(NORTH)` (notice the use of that handy constant from the `ExitEnum` enumeration) contains the room number where the player will move. For example, look at this abbreviated form of the `SetRoomData` subroutine.

LISTING 3.12   The SetRoomData Subroutine

```
 1:  Sub SetRoomData()
 2:    Select Case Room
 3:    Case 5
 4:      RoomDesc = "In Denny's bedroom."
 5:      Exits(NORTH) = 6
 6:    Case 6
 7:      RoomDesc = "In Denny's stuffy closet."
 8:      Exits(SOUTH) = 5
 9:    '
10:    ' Some statements not shown for brevity
11:    '
12:    Case 30
13:      RoomDesc = "On a dusty, well-used trail."
14:      Exits(NORTH) = 25
15:    End Select
16: End Sub
```

ANALYSIS   The `Room` variable contains the number of the current room. The program uses this number in a `Select Case` statement (Line 2) to jump to the `Case` clause that sets the room's description string, `RoomDesc`, and the valid exits (Lines 3 through 15). For example, if `Room` is 5, the `Case 5` clause of the `Select Case` statement (Line 3) is executed. There, the program sets the room's description to "In Denny's bedroom" (Line 4) and sets a valid exit to the north (Line 5), leading to room 6. If you look at `Case 6` (Lines 6 through 8), you can see that room 6 has an exit to the south, leading to room 5. That makes perfect sense because if you go north and then south, you'll end up back where you started.

If an element of the `Exits` array is 0, there's no exit in the corresponding direction. For example, room 22 has four exits—north, south, west, and down—as you can see here:

```
Case 22
  RoomDesc = "By a rocky mountainside."
  Exits(NORTH) = 24
  Exits(SOUTH) = 25
  Exits(WEST) = 19
  Exits(DOWN) = 23
```

The elements `Exits(EAST)` and `Exits(UP)` retain their 0 value, to which the `ResetExits` subroutine initialized the `Exits` array.

The `ShowRoomDescription` subroutine (see Listing 3.13) simply displays the room-description string, `RoomDesc`, at the appropriate location in the Nightshade window.

LISTING 3.13   The ShowRoomDescription Subroutine

```
1: Sub ShowRoomDescription()
2:    Dim Txt As String
3:    Form1.CurrentX = 20
4:    Form1.CurrentY = 40
5:    Form1.Print RoomDesc
6: End Sub
```

The `ShowExits()` subroutine (see Listing 3.14) displays the directions that the player can move from the current room. It does this by checking which elements of the `Exits` array are non-zero and printing the equivalent character in the `Directions` string (which contains the characters "NSEWUD") that coincides with the direction, as shown in Listing 3.14.

LISTING 3.14   The ShowExits Subroutine

```
 1:  Sub ShowExits()
 2:     Dim i As Integer
 3:     Form1.CurrentX = 20
 4:     Form1.CurrentY = 90
 5:     For i = 0 To 5
 6:       If Exits(i) Then
 7:          Form1.Print Mid$(Directions, i + 1, 1) & " ";
 8:       Else
 9:          i = i
10:       End If
11:    Next i
12:  End Sub
```

The next step is to show any items that are visible in the current room. The `ShowVisibleItems` subroutine handles this task. This subroutine first declares a set of local variables:

```
Dim i As Integer
Dim Txt As String
Dim NothingVisible As Boolean
Dim y As Integer
```

The subroutine then initializes two of the local variables to their starting values:

```
NothingVisible = True
y = 0
```

Next, the subroutine starts a `For` loop that iterates through the `ItemLocations` array, which contains the locations of every item in the game, to find items that are in the current room:

```
For i = 0 To NUM_NOUNS - 1
```

Inside the loop, the subroutine first sets the display location for the next item to print:

```
Form1.CurrentX = 20
Form1.CurrentY = 140 + y * 20
```

The loop then checks the current value in the `ItemLocations` array (indexed by the loop variable `i`):

```
If Abs(ItemLocations(i)) = Room Then
```

Notice that before the program compares the `ItemLocations` element to the current room number, it gets the absolute value of the array element. This is because items in a room can have two values: the room number or the negative room number. Items that have a positive value can be picked up by the player and thus added to her inventory. Items with a negative value cannot be picked up by the player and are permanent fixtures of the room.

If the value of the array element matches the room number, that item appears in the current room. Therefore, the program sets the `NothingVisible` flag to `False`, translates the item name stored in the `ItemNames` array, displays the item name on the screen, and increments the y variable, which keeps track of the current display row:

```
NothingVisible = False
Txt = TranslateText(ItemNames(i))
Form1.Print Txt
y = y + 1
```

What's this bit about translating the item name, you ask? The Nightshade.dat file holds the complete item names and their associated room numbers. However, because this is just a plain text file, you don't want the user to look at the file and see all the item names. That would ruin the game! For this reason, the item names are encoded. For example, here are the first two item entries in the Nightshade.dat file:

```
CPPL
5
CFE
-5
```

The first line is the encoded item name BOOK, which is associated with the room number 5. (Because 5 is positive, the player can pick up the book, thus adding it to her inventory.) The second item is BED, which is associated with the room number -5. This means that although the bed is located in room 5, the player cannot add the bed to her inventory. You might have noticed that all you have to do is move the encoded letter back one position in the alphabet to get the decoded letter. That is, C is B, P is O, L is K, and so on. The TranslateText subroutine accepts these encoded values and returns the actual item name for display.

Let's get back to the ShowVisibleItems subroutine. After the For loop, if the NothingVisible flag retains its False value, there are no visible items in the room. In this case, the program prints the word "Nothing" where the item names would have appeared:

```
If NothingVisible Then
  Form1.CurrentX = 20
  Form1.CurrentY = 140
  Form1.Print "Nothing"
End If
```

The ShowInventory subroutine, shown in Listing 3.15, works similarly to ShowVisibleItems, except that it checks for the value -1 (represented by the IN_INVENTORY constant), indicating that the item is in the player's inventory.

LISTING 3.15 The ShowInventory Subroutine

```
1:  Sub ShowInventory()
2:    Dim i As Integer
3:    Dim y As Integer
4:    Dim Txt As String
5:    Dim HasNothing As Boolean
6:    HasNothing = True
7:    y = 0
8:    For i = 0 To NUM_NOUNS - 1
9:      Form1.CurrentX = 180
10:     Form1.CurrentY = 140 + y * 20
11:     If ItemLocations(i) = IN_INVENTORY Then
12:       HasNothing = False
13:       Txt = TranslateText(ItemNames(i))
14:       Form1.Print Txt
15:       y = y + 1
16:     End If
17:    Next i
18:    If HasNothing Then
19:      Form1.CurrentX = 180
20:      Form1.CurrentY = 140
21:      Form1.Print "Nothing"
22:    End If
23:  End Sub
```

Processing Commands

To enter a command into the game, the player types the command in the TextBox.
Thanks to the txtInput_KeyPress event handler, typing in the TextBox also clears the
previous command's result from the lblResult Label control:

```
Private Sub txtInput_Change()
  lblResult.Caption = ""
End Sub
```

When the user presses Enter, the txtInput_KeyPress event handler calls the
ProcessInput subroutine to process the player's command:

```
Private Sub txtInput_KeyPress(KeyAscii As Integer)
  If KeyAscii = ENTER Then ProcessInput
End Sub
```

The ProcessInput subroutine first gets the verb and the noun that make up the current
command:

```
Verb = GetCommandVerb
Noun = GetCommandNoun
```

The GetCommandVerb and GetCommandNoun functions look like Listing 3.16.

LISTING 3.16   The GetCommandVerb and GetCommandNoun Subroutines

```
 1: Function GetCommandVerb() As String
 2:   Dim Position As Integer
 3:   Dim str As String
 4:   Position = InStr(1, txtInput.Text, " ")
 5:   If Position <> 0 Then
 6:     str = Left$(txtInput.Text, Position - 1)
 7:   Else
 8:     str = txtInput.Text
 9:   End If
10:   GetCommandVerb = UCase(str)
11: End Function
12:
13: Function GetCommandNoun() As String
14:   Dim Position As Integer
15:   Dim str As String
16:   Position = InStr(1, txtInput.Text, " ")
17:   If Position <> 0 Then
18:     str = Right$(txtInput.Text, _
19:       Len(txtInput.Text) - Position)
20:   Else
21:     str = ""
22:   End If
23:   GetCommandNoun = UCase(str)
24: End Function
```

ANALYSIS These functions work by finding the space that separates the verb from the noun in the input string (Lines 4 and 16), separating the verb and the noun (Lines 5 through 9 and Lines 17 through 22), and setting them to uppercase (Lines 10 and 23).

ProcessInput then removes all text from the input TextBox:

```
txtInput.Text = ""
```

Next, if the length of the verb is only one character, the player must be entering a direction to move. In this case, the program calls the MovePlayer subroutine:

```
If Len(Verb) = 1 Then
  MovePlayer
```

If the player has entered a one-word command (that is, the noun is missing), the program like this:

```
ElseIf Noun = "" Then
   lblResult.Caption = _
      "Denny doesn't understand what you're saying."
```

Next, the program changes the verb and noun into three letters each (after saving the full-length noun for possible future use) and then calls the ProcessVerb subroutine, which routes the program to the correct subroutine (ProcessInput) for the verb the player entered, as shown in Listing 3.17.

LISTING 3.17   Manipulating the Noun and Verb

```
1:    Else
2:       CompleteNoun = Noun
3:       Noun = Left$(Noun, 3)
4:       If Verb = "GO" Then Verb = "GO "
5:       Verb = Left$(Verb, 3)
6:       ProcessVerb
7:    End If
8: End Sub
```

The ProcessVerb subroutine examines the current three-letter verb and determines which subroutine to call. ProcessVerb is little more than a big Select Case statement, as you can see in Listing 3.18.

LISTING 3.18   The ProcessVerb Subroutine

```
1: Sub ProcessVerb()
2:    Select Case Verb
3:    Case "EXA"
4:       DoExamine
5:    Case "LOO"
```

LISTING 3.18 continued

```
 6:      DoExamine
 7:    Case "TAK"
 8:      DoGet
 9:    Case "GET"
10:      DoGet
11:    Case "DRO"
12:      DoDrop
13:    Case "GIV"
14:      DoDrop
15:    Case "PUT"
16:      DoDrop
17:    Case "TAL"
18:      DoTalk
19:    Case "DRI"
20:      DoDrink
21:    Case "MOV"
22:      DoMove
23:    Case "CLI"
24:      DoClimb
25:    Case "SIN"
26:      DoSing
27:    Case "GO "
28:      DoGo
29:    Case "ENT"
30:      DoGo
31:    Case "SAY"
32:      DoSay
33:    Case "HIT"
34:      DoHit
35:    Case "SMA"
36:      DoHit
37:    Case "GLU"
38:      DoGlue
39:    Case Else
40:      lblResult.Caption = _
41:      "Denny doesn't know how to do that."
42:    End Select
43: End  Sub
```

ANALYSIS Notice how some verbs get directed to the same subroutine. For example, `ProcessVerb` routes both EXA (examine, Line 3) and LOO (look, Line 5) to the subroutine `DoExamine` (Lines 5 and 6). This method enables the program to accept different versions of the same command. Notice also that if the `Select Case` statement has no match for the current verb, the program displays "Denny doesn't know how to do that" (Lines 39 through 41).

Moving the Player

If the player enters N, S, E, W, U, or D, she's trying to move from one room to another. The MovePlayer subroutine handles this task. First, MovePlayer calls the GetDirection function to change the command letter to a direction number:

```
Dim Direction As Integer
Direction = GetDirection(Verb)
```

If GetDirection returns -1 (represented by the constant NOT_VALID), the player entered a one-letter command other than a direction. Otherwise, GetDirection returns the direction as an integer (with 0 meaning north, 1 meaning south, and so on, as you can see in the ExitEnum enumeration). The program then calls the IsMoveOK function to determine whether the requested exit exists in the current room:

```
If Direction <> NOT_VALID Then
  If IsMoveOK(Direction) Then
```

If the direction is invalid or doesn't exist, the program prints an appropriate response, as shown in Listing 3.19.

LISTING 3.19 Displaying a Response for an Invalid Direction

```
1:    Else
2:       lblResult.Caption = "Denny can't move that way."
3:    End If
4: Else
5:    lblResult.Caption = "Denny doesn't understand."
6: EndIf
```

If all the checks go okay, it's time to move the player in the requested direction. First, the program prints a response and sets the current room to the destination room:

```
lblResult.Caption = "Okay"
Room = Exits(Direction)
```

At this point, the player has moved to the new room but the screen display doesn't show it. In order for the new room data to appear, the program must update and display all data for the new room:

```
ResetExits
SetRoomData
UpdateGameScreen
```

The GetDirection and IsMoveOK functions (see Listing 3.20) aren't all that interesting, so I won't go into any details other than to list them here. You should be able to figure them out for yourself.

3

LISTING 3.20   The GetDirection and IsMoveOK Subroutines

```
 1:  Function GetDirection(Command As String) As Integer
 2:     Dim i As Integer
 3:     Dim Direction As Integer
 4:     Direction = -1
 5:     For i = 1 To 6
 6:        If Mid$(Directions, i, 1) = Command Then _
 7:           Direction = i - 1
 8:     Next i
 9:     GetDirection = Direction
10: End Function
11:
12: Function IsMoveOK(Direction As Integer) As Boolean
13:     If Exits(Direction) = 0 Then
14:        IsMoveOK = False
15:     Else
16:        IsMoveOK = True
17:     End If
18: EndFunction
```

Getting and Dropping Items

Nightshade can handle many different commands, but the get and drop commands are special cases. If the player drops an item, the item must vanish from the player's inventory and appear in the current room. If the player gets an item, the item must vanish from the current room and appear in the player's inventory.

The DoGet subroutine handles the get command. Its first task is to call GetItemNumber to get the item number that matches the noun that the player entered as the second word in the command:

```
Dim ItemNum As Integer
ItemNum = GetItemNumber()
```

If GetItemNumber returns -1, the program doesn't recognize the noun the player typed:

```
If ItemNum = -1 Then
  lblResult.Caption = "No such item."
```

If the item exists, it must also be in the player's current room:

```
ElseIf Room <> Abs(ItemLocations(ItemNum)) Then
  lblResult.Caption = "That item isn't here."
```

Next, if the item has a negative room number, it can't be picked up:

```
ElseIf ItemLocations(ItemNum) = -Room Then
  lblResult.Caption = "Denny can't pick that up!"
```

Also, if the player's inventory is full, a new item can't be picked up:

```
ElseIf NumItemsInInventory = MAX_ITEMS_IN_INVENTORY Then
    lblResult.Caption = "Denny can't carry anymore."
```

Whew! If the requested item makes it past all the checks, it's okay to add it to the player's inventory:

```
Else
    ItemLocations(ItemNum) = IN_INVENTORY
    NumItemsInInventory = NumItemsInInventory + 1
    lblResult.Caption = "Denny got it."
    UpdateGameScreen
End If
```

Notice that after a new item is added to the player's inventory, the screen display must be updated. Otherwise, the new item won't appear on the screen even though it's in the player's inventory.

There's one special case of the get command in the game—when the player tries to pick up the giant's hammer. To pick up the hammer, the player must have used the strength potion:

```
ElseIf Room = 26 And (Noun = "HAM" Or Noun = "HUG") And _
    ItemLocations(POTION) <> ITEM_USED Then
    lblResult.Caption = "The hammer's too heavy."
```

The DoDrop subroutine works similarly to the DoGet subroutine, except that it removes items from the player's inventory and places them in the current room. Because the DoDrop subroutine has many special cases and therefore is large, I won't show it here. A couple of special cases are worth examining in detail, however. The first (see Listing 3.21) is when the player drops a glue ingredient into the jug.

LISTING 3.21 Getting Glue into the Jug

```
1: ElseIf ItemLocations(JUG) = IN_INVENTORY And _
2:     (Noun = "CRY" Or Noun = "MUD" Or Noun = "ALG") Then
3:     lblResult.Caption = "In the jug..."
4:     ItemLocations(ItemNum) = ITEM_USED
5:     NumGlueIngredients = NumGlueIngredients + 1
6:     NumItemsInInventory = NumItemsInInventory - 1
7:     If NumGlueIngredients = 3 Then
8:       ItemLocations(JUGWITHGLUE) = IN_INVENTORY
9:       ItemLocations(JUG) = NOT_IN_GAME
10:       ItemLocations(TROLL) = -19
11:       lblResult.Caption = "Denny made the magical glue!"
12:     End If
```

ANALYSIS Here, the program checks whether the jug is in the player's inventory (Line 1). If the player has the jug and the current command's noun is CRY (crystals), MUD (mud), or ALG (algae) (Line 2), the item goes into the jug instead of into the current room (Lines 3 and 4). Then the program increments the NumGlueIngredients variable,(Line 5) which keeps track of how many items are in the jug and decrements the player's inventory count (Line 6). If there are three items in the jug (Line 7), the program removes the jug from the player's inventory (Line 9) and replaces it with the jug with glue (Line 8). (Also, at this point in the game, the troll appears in room 19, as you can see in Line 10.)

Another special case (see Listing 3.22) is when the player drops the mirror in the same room with the troll, who then sees his own ugly face and faints dead away.

LISTING 3.22   Giving the Mirror to the Troll

```
1:    ElseIf Room = 19 And TrollFainted = False And _
2:        Noun = "MIR" And _
3:        ItemLocations(MIRROR) = IN_INVENTORY Then
4:    lblResult.Caption = _
5:      "The troll saw himself in the mirror and fainted!"
6:    TrollFainted = True
7:    ItemLocations(MIRROR) = Room
8:    ItemLocations(FAINTEDTROLL) = -Room
9:    ItemLocations(TROLL) = NOT_IN_GAME
10:   NumItemsInInventory = NumItemsInInventory - 1
```

ANALYSIS Line 1 checks that the player is in room 19 and the troll hasn't fainted yet, and Line 2 makes sure that the noun the player specified is the mirror. Line 3 checks that the mirror is in the player's inventory. If all these checks are true, Lines 4 through 9 make the troll faint. Line 10 decrements the player's inventory count since he no longer has the mirror.

The last two parts of the get and drop puzzle are the GetItemNumber and GetNumItemsInRoom subroutines, shown in Listing 3.23.

LISTING 3.23   The GetItemNumber and GetNumItemsInRoom Subroutines

```
1:  Function GetItemNumber()
2:    Dim i As Integer
3:    Noun = Left$(Noun, 3)
4:    GetItemNumber = -1
5:    For i = 0 To NUM_NOUN_NAMES - 1
6:      If Noun = NounNames(i) Then _
7:        GetItemNumber = NounIndexes(i)
8:    Next i
```

```
 9:  End Function
10:
11: Function GetNumItemsInRoom() As Integer
12:   Dim i As Integer
13:   For i = 0 To NUM_NOUNS - 1
14:     If ItemLocations(i) = Room Then _
15:       GetNumItemsInRoom = GetNumItemsInRoom + 1
16:   Next i
17: End Function
```

Executing the Player's Commands

A large part of the Nightshade program is made up of the source code needed to execute the player's commands. The code for each command works similarly, so there's no need to examine the whole lot. The program must carefully evaluate each command, ensuring that the game's state is correct for the command to be executed. Often, this means checking the room number, the current noun, the contents of the room, the contents of the player's inventory, and other variables that might need to be in a certain state. Some commands are simple. For example, the code that enables the player to examine the book (in the DoExamine subroutine) depends upon whether the book is in the current room or in the player's inventory:

```
If Noun = "BOO" And ItemLocations(BOOK) = Room Then
  lblResult.Caption = "It looks interesting."
ElseIf Noun = "BOO" And _
    ItemLocations(BOOK) = IN_INVENTORY Then
  lblResult.Caption = "The last page is missing."
```

Other commands require a little more work. For example, if the player looks at a certain tree, he'll notice a wooden door in it. Here's the code that handles that eventuality:

```
ElseIf Noun = "TRE" And Room = 10 And _
    ItemLocations(WOODENDOOR) = NOT_IN_GAME Then
  lblResult.Caption = "There's a door in it."
  ItemLocations(WOODENDOOR) = -Room
```

There's no blueprint you can use for the code that responds to a player's command. You need to think about all the requirements for the command's execution and make sure all those requirements have been met. It's in this part of the program that the likelihood of bugs is very high. For example, if the player drinks a potion, you have to make sure that he can't drink it again.

Saving and Loading the Game

Because it takes a long time to complete a text adventure, and because the player isn't likely to want to start from the beginning every time, Nightshade requires a game-save mechanism. The player can save a game by selecting the Save command on the game's

File menu. This causes Visual Basic to call the `mnuSave_Click` subroutine. In that sub-routine, the program first asks if the player really wants to save the game and overwrite an existing game-save file:

```
Dim Answer As Integer
Answer = MsgBox("Are you sure you want" & _
    vbCrLf & "to save your game?" & vbCrLf & _
    "You may overwrite an existing game.", _
    vbQuestion Or vbYesNo, "Save Game")
```

If the player answers yes, the program opens the game-save file and writes all pertinent variable values to the file, as shown in Listing 3.24.

LISTING 3.24   Saving the Game

```
 1:  If Answer = vbYes Then
 2:    On Error GoTo FileError
 3:    Open "Nightshade.sav" For Output As #1
 4:    For i = 0 To NUM_NOUNS - 1
 5:      Write #1, ItemNames(i), ItemLocations(i)
 6:    Next i
 7:    Write #1, Room
 8:    Write #1, NumItemsInInventory
 9:    Write #1, NumGlueIngredients
10:    Write #1, TrollFainted
11:    Write #1, PrevBoatRoom
12:    Close #1
13:    MsgBox "Game saved."
14: End If
```

ANALYSIS Line 3 opens the save game file, and Lines 4 through 6 save the contents of the `ItemNames()` and `ItemLocations()` arrays. Lines 7 through 11 save the values of the remaining game variables.

In order for the game save to be successful (meaning that reloading the data will restore the game to where the player left off), it's important that you know which variables in the game contain data that must be restored. That's why I created a special section for declaring variables that need to be saved, as shown in Listing 3.25.

LISTING 3.25   Variables That Need Saving

```
 1:  '=====================================================
 2:  ' Global variables that must be saved in a
 3:  ' game-save file.
 4:  '=====================================================
 5:  Dim Room As Integer
 6:  Dim ItemLocations(NUM_NOUNS - 1) As Integer
```

```
 7:  Dim NumItemsInInventory As Integer
 8:  Dim NumGlueIngredients As Integer
 9:  Dim TrollFainted As Boolean
10: Dim PrevBoatRoom As Integer
```

Every time I added a variable to the game, I determined whether that variable would need to be saved. If not, I declared it in with the general variables. If the variable did need to be saved, I declared it in the variable declaration section shown previously. If you don't handle your variables this way and later you try to find all the variables you need to save, you're almost certain to miss some. This will cripple the player's ability to save a game. Missing important variables will cause minor side effects at the least, and at worst it can make the game impossible to complete.

The `mnuLoad_Click` subroutine is essentially the reverse of `mnuSave_Click`, reading values from the file instead of writing them. The important difference is that after reading in the variables from the file, the program must update the game screen. The `mnuLoadGame_Click` subroutine looks like Listing 3.26.

LISTING 3.26   Loading a Game

```
 1:  Private Sub mnuLoad_Click()
 2:     Dim i As Integer
 3:     Dim Answer As Integer
 4:     Answer = MsgBox("Are you sure you want" & _
 5:          vbCrLf & "to load your previous game?", _
 6:          vbQuestion Or vbYesNo, "Save Game")
 7:     If Answer = vbYes Then
 8:        On Error GoTo FileError
 9:        Open "Nightshade.sav" For Input As #1
10:        For i = 0 To NUM_NOUNS - 1
11:          Input #1, ItemNames(i), ItemLocations(i)
12:        Next i
13:        Input #1, Room
14:        Input #1, NumItemsInInventory
15:        Input #1, NumGlueIngredients
16:        Input #1, TrollFainted
17:        Input #1, PrevBoatRoom
18:        Close #1
19:        UpdateGameScreen
20:        txtInput.Text = ""
21:        lblResult.Caption = ""
22:        MsgBox "Game loaded."
23:     End If
24:     Exit Sub
25: FileError:
26:    MsgBox "File error."
27:    Close #1
28: End Sub
```

ANALYSIS Lines 4 through 6 ask the player if he wants to load a game. If he answers yes
          (Line 7), Lines 8 through 18 load the game's saved data. The program must then
update the game's display with the new data, which it does in Lines 19 through 22.

Summary

Most games don't incorporate as much text as an old-fashioned text adventure does
(although some do), but you still need to know how to display text in various colors and
fonts. There will always be data to display for the player, including game scores and
game status values.

Day 4 will examine how to solve computing problems and write effective algorithms.
Often, a good algorithm can make the difference between a game that people want to
play and one that collects dust on a shelf.

Q&A

Q What happens if I set a font to a typeface that doesn't exist on the computer?

A No matter what typeface you set a Font object's Name property to, you'll always get
a font. However, if the typeface you request doesn't exist on the computer running
the program, you can't know in advance what typeface Visual Basic will pick. For
this reason, it's a good idea to use only typefaces that are commonly installed on
all computers. You could also install the correct font along with your program, or
you could tell the player where to get the font.

**Q Can I assign the Font object of one control to the Font object of another
control?**

A Absolutely. In fact, this is an easy way to set not only a font, but also all the font
properties at the same time. Keep in mind that you must use the Set keyword, as
you do when making any type of object assignment, to assign the font to the
object. For example, to assign a TextBox control's font to a Label control, you
might write something like Set Label1.Font = Text1.Font.

Q If I assign a size to a font, is that the actual size I'll get?

A Not necessarily. Not every font can be shown in any size. If you want to know the
exact size font you'll end up with, check the value of the Font.Size property after
assigning the size. You might very well end up with something slightly different
than you requested.

Workshop

The workshop includes quiz questions to help gauge your grasp of the material. You'll find the answers to this quiz in Appendix A. Even if you feel that you totally understand the concepts presented here, you should work through the quiz anyway. The last section contains some exercises to help reinforce your learning.

Quiz

1. Which object property determines text color?
2. Which object property determines whether a line of text enables background graphics to show through?
3. Which object property holds the attributes of the object's font?
4. Name four font properties.
5. How does the `Weight` property affect the appearance of text?
6. Which property enables a program to change the typeface of text?
7. Can you set a single font to display several different attributes, such as bold, italic, and underline?

Exercises

1. Change the Nightshade text adventure so that all text appears as 10-point Arial.
2. In the `DoExamine` subroutine, add the code needed to handle the command LOOK BED. The response to the command will be, "The bed has a blue comforter."

3

DAY 4

Developing Program Code

Writing a game program requires a wide range of skills, not the least of which is the ability to get the computer to do what you need it to do. Moreover, it should do what you want efficiently so that the game runs at a peppy speed, rather than crawling along like a slow-motion movie. Designing algorithms is the skill in question here, a skill that requires you to have thorough knowledge of the tools at your disposal (the programming language) and the ability to solve problems with those tools. Today, you'll study a simulation-type game called Life and see how algorithms solve some tricky problems. Specifically, today you will learn the following:

- The mathematical rules of the game of Life
- How to create algorithms that solve complex problems
- How to use advanced data structures when implementing an algorithm
- How to implement linked lists in Visual Basic
- How to use object-oriented programming techniques to improve the Visual Basic linked-list implementation
- How to write a game loop that shares processor time with other applications

The Story of Life

About 30 years ago, a fine English fellow by the name of John Conway created a system that simulated the lives of special one-celled animals. Although the rules of the simulation were simple, the results were fascinating. Before long, every computer scientist worth his or her diploma had written a version of Life and had spent hours trying different combinations of cells to see which patterns might emerge.

Today, people are still fascinated by Conway's computer simulation. Many computer science books at least mention Life, and each year thousands of computer science students write versions of Life as part of their programming curriculum. The simplest of these programs accurately portray the simulation, but they run too slowly to be practical. Other implementations blaze across the screen in wonderfully vivid colors and kaleidoscopic patterns, hypnotizing any viewer that happens to glance in their direction.

This chapter will show you how to think about and create effective algorithms for your computer games, and you'll implement the Life simulation. Warning: After you start dabbling with Life, you might find it hard to tear away. The author and publisher cannot be held responsible for lost productivity!

 An *algorithm* is a set of steps that solves a problem.

The Rules of Life

The Life simulation is played on a grid of any size. Under the original rules the grid is unbounded, but you can limit it to the screen. Think of the screen display as a petri dish holding a culture of microscopic cells. Cells are placed randomly on the grid and the simulation is started. The cells then run through their life cycles for a given number of generations, living and dying according to the rules set forth by Mr. Conway.

Those rules are simple and elegant: Any live cell with less than two neighbors dies of loneliness. Any live cell with more than three neighbors dies of crowding. Any dead cell with exactly three neighbors comes to life. And finally, any live cell with two or three neighbors lives on, unchanged, to the next generation.

Life Implementation

As you might imagine, a large grid can contain hundreds if not thousands of cells living and dying every generation. The computer must work furiously, calculating the number of neighbors for each cell in the grid and then creating or killing cells based on these counts. Keep in mind that counting the neighbors for a single cell requires checking each adjacent cell—as many as eight.

Suppose that you implement the grid as a two-dimensional array of integers, like this:

```
Const MAXCOL = 50
Const MAXROW = 28
Dim World(MAXCOL - 1, MAXROW - 1) As Integer
```

Each element of the world map can be one of two values: 0 if the cell is dead, and 1 if the cell is alive. The logical way to process this grid is to check each element of the array, counting its neighbors and marking it as alive or dead.

In the example 50-by-28 array, 1,400 cells must be processed every generation. Each cell processed must check the status of as many as eight adjacent cells. That's about 11,000 operations for the entire grid. Worse, this processing must be performed for every generation of the simulation. A single run of the simulation might have as many as 10,000 generations!

All this calculating wouldn't be a problem if you planned to let the simulation run all night. However, to make the simulation interesting, you must update the screen as quickly as possible, ideally several times a second. Obviously, the amount of processing required creates a problem in the speed department. You can solve this problem with an efficient algorithm.

But speed isn't the only problem. You also must consider the effects of prematurely creating or killing cells. It's not enough for your algorithm to scan though the grid, creating and killing cells as it goes, because the cells that are created or killed might affect cells not yet processed. Suppose that cell X in a grid has only two neighbors, and that one of those cells dies as you process the grid. Although this cell has died, cell X should still remain alive for this generation because it has two neighbors; it won't be lonely until the next generation. When you finally process cell X, however, the counting function recognizes cell X as having only one neighbor. As a result, cell X dies prematurely.

Confused? Look at Figure 4.1. There are three cells in the first-generation grid on the left. In this generation, the uppermost cell must die because it has only one neighbor. The middle cell must remain alive until the next generation, because it has two neighbors. The bottom cell must die because, like the top cell, it has only one neighbor. The empty cells to the left and right of the center cell must be brought to life because both have exactly three neighbors. After processing the grid, you should have the second-generation grid, which is on the right.

FIGURE **4.1**

Applying the rules of
Life to three cells.

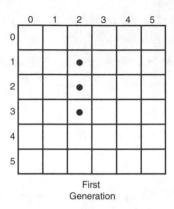

First
Generation

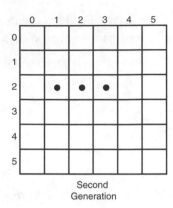

Second
Generation

However, if you start at the top and process the grid by creating and killing cells as you go, you get incorrect results. First, you kill the top cell, because it has only one neighbor. Then, when you get to empty cell 1,2, even though it should have come to life, you determine that it has only two neighbors and leave it alone. When you get to cell 2,2, you think it has only one neighbor and kill it, even though this cell should have survived to the next generation. After processing the entire grid, you don't have the correct second-generation result. Instead, you have an empty grid!

In short, in each generation, you must determine which cells will live or die without changing the grid. When you finish, you must simultaneously create and kill the appropriate cells. This requires tricky algorithms, especially when you consider that all these calculations must be performed at a speed that allows fast screen updates. Sound like fun?

 Note

> When you're designing algorithms, there's usually a tradeoff between code complexity and speed. That is, the more speed you manage to squeeze out of an algorithm, the more complex the algorithm tends to become.

The Speed Problem

What can you do to speed things up? First, add another array to keep a running count of each cell's neighbors. When the simulation starts, the program does a full update of the neighbor count. From then on, instead of recalculating the entire grid in each generation, the program changes neighbor counts for only those cells adjacent to cells that have just been created or killed. This method cuts processing time significantly: In a given generation, the program must change the neighbor counts of only a small number of cells rather than the entire grid.

Then, even though the original map grid records the status of each cell, you add two lists of cells: one for cells about to be created, and another for cells about to die. These are the only cells that affect the map, so why check the entire grid every generation?

This brings us to using the tools at your disposal to create an efficient algorithm. Dealing with algorithms means dealing with data structures. Which type of data structure enables you to build lists of items—lists that can grow or shrink dynamically? The answer is a linked list.

NEW TERM   A *linked list* is a data structure composed of data nodes, each of which has a pointer to the next node in the list.

Linked Lists

To create a linked list, first you must decide which information makes up the items, or nodes, that will be stored in the list. In the simulation program, you must store enough data to identify a cell. The only information that you need to identify a cell are its X and Y coordinates in the grid, so a node could be a Visual Basic class, named Node, that holds the following data:

```
Public X As Integer
Public Y As Integer
```

NEW TERM   A *node* is a data set that's part of a linked list.

When a cell is born, you can create a node for the cell like this:

```
Dim n As Node
Set n = New Node
n.X = x
n.Y = y
```

This code creates a new Node object and sets its X and Y properties to the coordinates of a cell.

But what good is it to have a bunch of these nodes sitting around in memory? You must link them into a list. To do this, you must add to your class a reference to a Node. You can then use this reference to point to the next node in the list. The new Node class, then, looks like this:

```
Public X As Integer
Public Y As Integer
Public NextNode As Node
```

In addition to the data structure for a node, you also need a reference to the first node of the list (a *head pointer*) and a reference to the end of the list (a *tail pointer*). Having a reference to the head of the list is the most important. Without it, you cannot find the list in memory. A tail pointer is just a convenience. You can use it to add new nodes to the end of the list quickly, without having to scan the list from the first node. The head and tail pointers look like this:

```
Public ListHead As Node
Public ListTail As Node
```

Figure 4.2 illustrates how a linked list looks in memory. The `ListHead` pointer points to the first node in the list. Each node has a pointer that leads to the next node in the list. The next pointer in the last node is left set to `Nothing`, which indicates the end of the list. Finally, the `ListTail` pointer points to the last node in the list.

FIGURE 4.2

A linked list in memory.

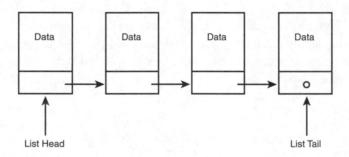

To get a little practice with linked lists, you'll now construct a program that manipulates lists using a Visual Basic `Node` class, which you'll also create. The first step is to create the `Node` class, which you can do by following these steps:

1. Create a new Visual Basic Standard EXE project.

2. From the Project menu, select the Add Class Module command. The Add Class Module property sheet appears.

   A Visual Basic class enables you to encapsulate the data and the functions that operate on that data in much the same way a C++ class does.

3. Double-click the Class Module icon on the New page of the property sheet. Visual Basic adds the class module to your project.

4. In the class module's Properties window, set the `Name` property to Node.

   The class's name identifies the data type represented by the class. A class is nothing more than a fancy, user-defined data type.

5. Paste the following lines into the class module's code window:

```
Public X As Integer
Public Y As Integer
Public NextNode As Node
```

These lines define the class's properties, which are the variables controlled by the class.

6. Save the project files, saving the class file as Node.cls, the form file as Lists.frm, and the project file as Lists.vbp.

You now have a Visual Basic project that includes a class you can use to represent node objects in a program. Next, open the form's code window and add the following source code lines (see Listing 4.1) to complete the program. If you don't want to type the source code (although I suggest that you do because you'll learn better that way), you can just paste the contents of the Lists.txt file into the form's code window. That file is located in the Chap04\Code folder of this book's CD-ROM.

LISTING 4.1 Testing the Node Class

```
 1: Option Explicit
 2:
 3: Private Sub Form_Load()
 4:    Dim i As Integer
 5:    Dim n As Node
 6:    Dim ListHead As Node
 7:    Dim ListTail As Node
 8:
 9:    For i = 1 To 10
10:       Set n = New Node
11:       n.X = i
12:       n.Y = i * 10
13:       If ListHead Is Nothing Then
14:          Set ListHead = n
15:       Else
16:          Set ListTail.NextNode = n
17:       End If
18:       Set ListTail = n
19:       Set ListTail.NextNode = Nothing
20:    Next i
21:
22:    While Not ListHead Is Nothing
23:       Set n = ListHead
24:       Set ListHead = ListHead.NextNode
25:       Form1.Print n.X & "," & n.Y
26:       Set n = Nothing
27:    Wend
28: End Sub
```

Study this short program carefully to make sure you understand how to create and manage a linked list. In this program, the Node class is the type of item stored in the list. This class contains two data members, as well as a pointer to a Node object. This Node reference, NextNode, points to the next node in the list.

The program begins with a For loop that creates and links 10 nodes. In the loop, the New keyword creates a new node, after which the program sets the node's X and Y properties to the values of i and i*10. (These values hold no particular significance.) After creating the node, the program checks whether ListHead is equal to Nothing. If it is, the program has a new list, so it sets ListHead to point to the node. Then the program sets ListTail to point to the same Node object (if the list has only one node, the head and tail of the list are the same), and sets ListTail's NextNode pointer to Nothing, indicating that there are no other items in the list.

Getting back to the If statement, if ListHead isn't Nothing, there's already at least one node in the list. In this case, the program shouldn't change ListHead. Rather, the program must add the new node to the end of the list. This is where ListTail comes in handy. Instead of having to scan through the whole list, looking for Nothing in a NextNode pointer, the program can use ListTail to tack the new node onto the end of the list. It does this by setting ListTail's NextNode pointer so that it points to the new node and then changing ListTail so that it points to the new last node. Figures 4.3 through 4.6 illustrate this process.

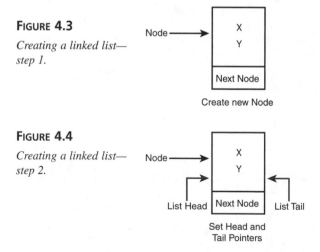

FIGURE 4.3

Creating a linked list—step 1.

FIGURE 4.4

Creating a linked list—step 2.

FIGURE 4.5

Creating a linked list—step 3.

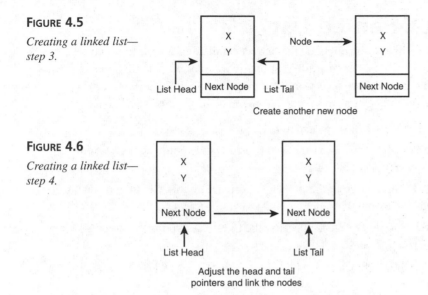

Create another new node

FIGURE 4.6

Creating a linked list—step 4.

Adjust the head and tail
pointers and link the nodes

After the program creates the linked list, a `While` loop scans the list, printing each node's contents before deleting the node. Notice how the temporary node pointer keeps track of the current node. By setting n to `ListHead` and then setting `ListHead` to point to the next node in the list, you effectively "pop off" the first node. Unless you save the pointer in n, you cannot access this node. The program's output looks like this:

```
1,10
2,20
3,30
4,40
5,50
6,60
7,70
8,80
9,90
10,100
```

 Note

A linked list is just one of many data structures that can help you design effective and efficient algorithms. Other data structures you should explore are stacks, queues, and tables, just to mention a few.

An Object-Oriented List

If you think that a linked list might be the perfect candidate for a class, you'd be correct, especially if you need to use many different lists in a program. For example, let's convert the Lists program into a more object-oriented program by adding a List class. Perform the following steps to create a new version of the Lists project, named Lists2:

1. Create a new Visual Basic Standard EXE project.
2. From the Project menu, select the Add Class Module command. The Add Class Module property sheet appears.
3. Select the Existing page of the property sheet and double-click the Node.cls file. Visual Basic adds the Node class module to your project.

    You need to add this reference because the List class you're developing will use the Node class to represent its nodes.
4. Again, select the Add Class Module command. The Add Class Module property sheet appears.
5. Double-click the Class Module icon on the New page of the property sheet. Visual Basic adds the new class module to your project.
6. In the class module's Properties window, set the Name property to List.
7. Type the following lines (see Listing 4.2) into the class module's code window (or paste the code from the ListClass.txt file located in the Chap04\Code folder of this book's CD-ROM).

LISTING 4.2 Source Code for the List Class

```
1:  Option Explicit
2:
3:  Public ListHead As Node
4:  Public ListTail As Node
5:
6:  Private Sub Class_Initialize()
7:    Set ListHead = Nothing
8:    Set ListTail = Nothing
9:  End Sub
10:
11: Private Sub Class_Terminate()
12:    ClearList
13: End Sub
14:
15: Sub MakeNewNode(n1 As Integer, n2 As Integer)
16:    Dim n As Node
17:    Set n = New Node
18:    n.X = n1
```

```
19:    n.Y = n2
20:    If ListHead Is Nothing Then
21:      Set ListHead = n
22:    Else
23:      Set ListTail.NextNode = n
24:    End If
25:    Set ListTail = n
26:    Set ListTail.NextNode = Nothing
27: End Sub
28:
29: Sub TransferList(list2 As List)
30:    Set list2 = New List
31:    Set list2.ListHead = ListHead
32:    Set list2.ListTail = ListTail
33:    Set ListHead = Nothing
34:    Set ListTail = Nothing
35: End Sub
36:
37: Sub GetNode(column As Integer, row As Integer)
38:    Dim n As Node
39:    If Not ListHead Is Nothing Then
40:      Set n = ListHead
41:      column = n.X
42:      row = n.Y
43:      Set ListHead = ListHead.NextNode
44:      If ListHead Is Nothing Then Set ListTail = Nothing
45:      Set n = Nothing
46:    End If
47: End Sub
48:
49: Function HasNodes() As Boolean
50:    HasNodes = Not ListHead Is Nothing
51: End Function
52:
53: Sub ClearList()
54:    Dim n As Node
55:    While Not ListHead Is Nothing
56:      Set n = ListHead
57:      Set ListHead = ListHead.NextNode
58:      Set n = Nothing
59:    Wend
60: End Sub
61:
62: Sub DisplayList()
63:    Dim n As Node
64:    Set n = ListHead
65:    While Not n Is Nothing
66:      Debug.Print "X:" & n.X & " Y:" & n.Y
67:      Set n = n.NextNode
68:    Wend
69: End Sub
```

4

ANALYSIS   This complete class listing includes the definitions for the class's properties, as
            well as its methods, which are the functions that operate on the properties and
give the class its functionality. Notice how the List class creates objects from the Node
class in Lines 3, 4, 16, 38, 54, and 63.

   8. Type the following lines (see Listing 4.3) into the form's code window (or paste
      the code from the Lists2.txt file located in the Chap04\Code folder of this book's
      CD-ROM).

LISTING 4.3   Testing the List Class

```
 1:  Option Explicit
 2:
 3:  Private Sub Form_Load()
 4:     Dim TestList As List
 5:     Dim i As Integer
 6:
 7:     Form1.ScaleMode = vbPixels
 8:     Form1.AutoRedraw = True
 9:     Set TestList = New List
10:     For i = 1 To 10
11:        TestList.MakeNewNode i, i * 10
12:     Next i
13:     TestList.DisplayList
14: End Sub
```

ANALYSIS   This short program shows how using classes can make your main program much
            simpler and easier to understand. Only three lines—9, 11, and 13—deal directly
with the List class.

   9. Save the project files, saving the List class as List.cls, the form as Lists2.frm, and
      the project as Lists2.vbp.

You now have a Visual Basic project that includes classes for both nodes and lists. When
you run the Lists2 program, you'll see the same output you saw with the Lists program,
except that the output is now routed to Visual Basic's Immediate window. This is a good
place to display debugging information. However, notice how simple the main program
is when most of the details of handling the list are delegated to the List class.

Exploring the List Class

As you can see, all the list-handling operations have been taken out of Lists2's main program and placed into the List class. The data that defines the list—the node pointers and
declarations—are placed inside the class also. The main program no longer has to know
how a linked list works. It only has to draw on the capabilities of the class.

Look at the class's `Initialize` method first:

```
Private Sub Class_Initialize()
  Set ListHead = Nothing
  Set ListTail = Nothing
End Sub
```

This method initializes a new list by setting its head and tail pointers to `Nothing`. This creates an empty list. Of course, an empty list isn't particularly useful. Now the class needs a way to add nodes to the list, as shown in Listing 4.4.

LISTING 4.4   The MakeNewNode Subroutine

```
1:  Sub MakeNewNode(n1 As Integer, n2 As Integer)
2:    Dim n As Node
3:    Set n = New Node
4:    n.X = n1
5:    n.Y = n2
6:    If ListHead Is Nothing Then
7:      Set ListHead = n
8:    Else
9:      Set ListTail.NextNode = n
10:   End If
11:   Set ListTail = n
12:   Set ListTail.NextNode = Nothing
13: End Sub
```

ANALYSIS   This method takes as parameters (Line 1) the values for the new node's X and Y members. First, Lines 2 and 3 allocate a new node, after which Lines 4 and 5 set the X and Y members to their appropriate values. Then, Lines 6 through 12 add the new node to the list.

To display the contents of the list, you can call the class's `DisplayList` method, shown in Listing 4.5.

LISTING 4.5   The DisplayList Subroutine

```
1:  Sub DisplayList()
2:    Dim n As Node
3:    Dim LineCount As Integer
4:    Set n = ListHead
5:    LineCount = 0
6:    While Not n Is Nothing
7:      Debug.Print "X:" & n.X & " Y:" & n.Y
8:      Set n = n.NextNode
9:    Wend
10: End Sub
```

ANALYSIS This method simply scans the list (using the temporary n pointer so that it doesn't destroy `ListHead`), printing the contents of X and Y. Unlike the Lists program, this program doesn't delete each node after printing its contents.

Deleting nodes is left for the class's `Terminate` and `ClearList` methods, shown in Listing 4.6.

LISTING 4.6   The Class_Terminate and ClearList Subroutines

```
1:  Private Sub Class_Terminate()
2:    ClearList
3:  End Sub
4:
5:  Sub ClearList()
6:    Dim n As Node
7:    While Not ListHead Is Nothing
8:      Set n = ListHead
9:      Set ListHead = ListHead.NextNode
10:     Set n = Nothing
11:   Wend
12: End Sub
```

ANALYSIS Visual Basic calls the `List` class's `Terminate` method when a `List` object goes out of scope or when it's set to `Nothing`, which deletes the object from memory. Line 2 in the `Terminate` method then deletes every node in the list by calling the `ClearList` subroutine. In Line 6, `ClearList` defines a `Node` object that the subroutine will use as temporary storage. Lines 7 through 11 remove the head node from the list until there are no nodes left.

A Cell List

There's a lot more to `List`, the linked-list class, than the Lists2 program takes advantage of. The methods you've yet to study will help you build lists of cells for the Life program. Let's start by examining the `TransferList` method (see Listing 4.7).

LISTING 4.7   The TransferList Subroutines

```
1: Sub TransferList(list2 As List)
2:    Set list2 = New List
3:    Set list2.ListHead = ListHead
4:    Set list2.ListTail = ListTail
5:    Set ListHead = Nothing
6:    Set ListTail = Nothing
7: End Sub
```

ANALYSIS This method enables you to transfer the contents of one list to another. TransferList doesn't actually move or copy any data. Instead, it transfers the contents simply by setting the destination-list pointers to the same values as the source-list pointers (Lines 3 and 4). The danger here is that after copying the pointers, you'll have two sets of pointers to the same data. When one of the lists is deleted, its destructor deletes all the nodes in the list. That leaves pointers to nodes that have been deleted, which is a dangerous situation. However, Lines 5 and 6 avoid this problem by setting the source-list pointers to Nothing after copying them. This way, only one set of pointers to the nodes is in the list.

You'll use TransferList often in the Life program to shift the contents of lists. Another method you'll use often is GetNode (see Listing 4.8).

LISTING 4.8   The GetNode Subroutines

```
 1:  Sub GetNode(column As Integer, row As Integer)
 2:    Dim n As Node
 3:    If Not ListHead Is Nothing Then
 4:      Set n = ListHead
 5:      column = n.X
 6:      row = n.Y
 7:      Set ListHead = ListHead.NextNode
 8:      If ListHead Is Nothing Then Set ListTail = Nothing
 9:      Set n = Nothing
10:    End If
11: End Sub
```

ANALYSIS Line 4 retrieves the first cell node in a list, Lines 5 and 6 return its contents in the variables column and row, and then Lines 7 through 9 move the list head forward one node and delete the old head node from the list. Calling GetNode for every node in a list results in an empty list.

One handy function is HasNodes, which returns a Boolean value that indicates whether the list is empty or includes nodes:

```
Function HasNodes() As Boolean
  HasNodes = Not ListHead Is Nothing
End Function
```

This function is particularly useful with a function such as GetNode. By using HasNodes as the conditional for a While statement, you can scan an entire list, ending the looping when the list is empty—that is, when HasNodes returns False.

The last new method in the List class is ClearList, shown in Listing 4.9.

LISTING 4.9   The ClearList Subroutines

```
1: Sub ClearList()
2:   Dim n As Node
3:   While Not ListHead Is Nothing
4:      Set n = ListHead
5:      Set ListHead = ListHead.NextNode
6:      Set n = Nothing
7:   Wend
8: End Sub
```

ANALYSIS   This method enables you to empty a list at any time. It simply reads through the list, deleting nodes as it goes. List's destructor calls this function, but you can also use it in your programs (and you'll use it in the Life program).

The Life Program

Now you know how to handle linked lists. You've even created a handy cell-list class that you can use in your program to track cells as they're created and killed. It's time to put your knowledge of linked lists to work by examining the full Life program. But first, how about playing the completed game?

Playing Life

When you run Life, the main screen appears. Most of the screen consists of the grid in which your cells will live and die. (Figure 4.7 shows the simulation in progress.) Above the grid are the command buttons with which the user controls the program. At the top-right corner of the screen is the generation count. While the simulation is running, the readout shows the number of the current generation.

FIGURE 4.7

The main screen of Life.

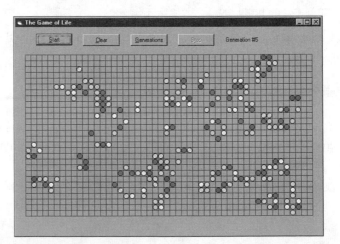

To get started, you must first seed the grid with cells. Place your mouse pointer where you want to place a cell and click the left mouse button. A green cell appears there. If you want to place cells quickly, you can paint them onto the grid by holding down the left mouse button as you drag the pointer across the screen.

When you've placed your cells, activate the simulation by either clicking the Start button or pressing Alt+S. The simulation springs into action, with cells living and dying as they speed through their life cycles. To stop the simulation before the generations run out, click the Stop button or press Alt+T.

Next to the Start button is the Clear button, which removes all cells from the grid. The Generations button sets the generation count. When you choose this button, the Generations dialog box appears, as shown in Figure 4.8. To change the generation setting, type a number from 1 to 10,000. Invalid entries yield the default value of 10000.

FIGURE 4.8

The Generations dialog box.

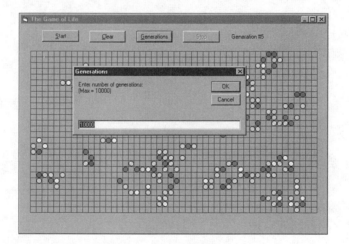

Building Life

Now that you've seen Life in action, it's time to learn to build the program yourself. In the following sections you'll build the program, starting with the user interface.

Building Life's User Interface

To build the game's user interface, perform the following steps:

1. Start a new Visual Basic Standard EXE project.

2. Set the following form properties in the form's Properties window:

   AutoRedraw = True

   Caption = "The Game of Life"

   Height = 6900

   ScaleMode = Pixels

   Width = 9705

3. Add four CommandButton controls to the form, giving them the following property settings:

   ### CommandButton #1

   Name = cmdStart

   Caption = "&Start"

   Height = 360

   Left = 660

   TabIndex = 0

   Top = 195

   Width = 1140

   ### CommandButton #2

   Name = cmdClear

   Caption = "&Clear"

   Height = 360

   Left = 2130

   TabIndex = 1

   Top = 210

   Width = 1140

CommandButton #3

```
Name = cmdGenerations

Caption = "&Generations"

Height = 360

Left = 3615

TabIndex = 2

Top = 210

Width = 1140
```

CommandButton #4

```
Name = cmdStop

Caption = "S&top"

Height = 360

Left = 5085

TabIndex = 3

Top = 210

Width = 1140
```

4

These four buttons will be the objects that make up the game's control panel. You can tell what each button does by looking at its name and caption.

4. Add a Label control to the form, giving it the following property settings:

```
Name = lblGenerations

Caption = "Generation #10000"

Height = 270

Left = 6585

Top = 285

Width = 1500
```

When you've added all the controls, your form should look like Figure 4.9.

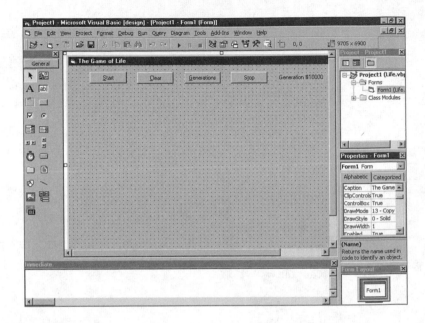

Adding the Program Code

Now that you've completed the program's user interface, you need to add the source code that implements the game and the user interface's actions. The following is the source code for the Life program. Type it into the form's code window, or, if you'd rather not type, paste it from the Life.txt file (found in the Chap04\Code folder of this book's CD-ROM) into the form's code window.

```
'===================================================
' The Game of Life for Visual Basic 6
'    by Clayton Walnum
' Copyright 2000 by Macmillan Computer Publishing
'===================================================
Option Explicit


'===================================================
' Constants
'===================================================
Const DEAD = 0
Const ALIVE = 1
Const CELLWIDTH = 12
Const CELLHEIGHT = 12
Const MAXCOL = 50
Const MAXROW = 28
Const XOFFSET = 20
Const YOFFSET = 56
Const MAXX = MAXCOL * CELLWIDTH + XOFFSET
```

```
Const MAXY = MAXROW * CELLHEIGHT + YOFFSET
Const CIRCLERADIUS = 5
Const MAXGENERATIONS = 10000


'==================================================
' Global Variables
'==================================================
Dim Generations As Integer
Dim Drawing As Boolean
Dim World(MAXCOL - 1, MAXROW - 1) As Integer
Dim Neighbors(MAXCOL - 1, MAXROW - 1)
Dim StopLife As Boolean
Dim LiveList As New List
Dim DieList As New List
Dim NextDieList As New List
Dim NextLiveList As New List


'==================================================
' Form Handler
'==================================================
Private Sub Form_Load()
  InitGame
  DrawScreen
End Sub


'==================================================
' CommandButton Handlers
'==================================================
Private Sub cmdClear_Click()
  Dim column As Integer
  Dim row As Integer
  For column = 0 To MAXCOL - 1
    For row = 0 To MAXROW - 1
      If World(column, row) = ALIVE Then
        World(column, row) = DEAD
        Form1.ForeColor = vbButtonFace
        Form1.FillStyle = vbSolid
        Form1.FillColor = vbButtonFace
        Form1.Circle (column * CELLWIDTH + XOFFSET + _
            CELLWIDTH / 2, row * CELLHEIGHT + _
            YOFFSET + CELLHEIGHT / 2), CIRCLERADIUS
      End If
    Next row
  Next column
  ReleaseNodes
End Sub

Private Sub cmdGenerations_Click()
  On Error GoTo Inputerror
  Generations = InputBox("Enter number of generations:" & _
    vbCrLf & "(Max = " & MAXGENERATIONS & ")", _
```

4

```
            "Generations", MAXGENERATIONS)
        If Generations < 1 Or Generations > MAXGENERATIONS Then _
            Generations = MAXGENERATIONS
Inputerror:
End Sub

Private Sub cmdStop_Click()
    StopLife = True
End Sub

Private Sub cmdStart_Click()
    cmdStart.Enabled = False
    cmdGenerations.Enabled = False
    cmdStop.Enabled = True
    cmdClear.Enabled = False
    RunLife
End Sub

'=====================================================
' Mouse Handlers
'=====================================================
Private Sub Form_MouseDown(Button As Integer, _
        Shift As Integer, x As Single,  Y As Single)
    Drawing = True
    AddCell x, Y
End Sub

Private Sub Form_MouseMove(Button As Integer, _
        Shift As Integer, x As Single, Y As Single)
    If Drawing Then AddCell x, Y
End Sub

Private Sub Form_MouseUp(Button As Integer, _
        Shift As Integer, x As Single, Y As Single)
    Drawing = False
End Sub

'=====================================================
' Initialization Subroutines
'=====================================================
Sub InitGame()
    Dim row As Integer
    Dim column As Integer
    For row = 0 To MAXROW - 1
        For column = 0 To MAXCOL - 1
            World(column, row) = DEAD
        Next column
    Next row
    Generations = 10000
    StopLife = False
End Sub
```

```
Sub DrawScreen()
  Dim x As Integer
  Dim Y As Integer
  Form1.ForeColor = vbBlue
  For Y = YOFFSET To MAXY Step CELLHEIGHT
    Form1.Line (XOFFSET, Y)-(MAXX + 1, Y)
  Next Y
  For x = XOFFSET To MAXX Step CELLWIDTH
    Form1.Line (x, YOFFSET)-(x, MAXY + 1)
  Next x
  lblGenerations.Caption = "Generation #10000"
End Sub


'==================================================
' General Subroutines
'==================================================
Sub RunLife()
  Dim gen As Integer
  For gen = 1 To Generations
    CreateLists
    If StopLife Then Exit For
    lblGenerations.Caption = "Generation #" & gen
    SetCellColor gen
    Live
    Die
    AddNeighbors
    SubtractNeighbors
    NextLiveList.TransferList LiveList
    NextDieList.TransferList DieList
    DoEvents
  Next gen
  StopLife = False
  cmdStart.Enabled = True
  cmdGenerations.Enabled = True
  cmdStop.Enabled = False
  cmdClear.Enabled = True
End Sub

Sub DisplayNeighbors()
  Dim x As Integer
  Dim Y As Integer
  Debug.Print "NEIGHBORS"
  For x = 0 To MAXCOL - 1
    For Y = 0 To MAXROW - 1
      Debug.Print x & ":" & Y & " -> " & Neighbors(x, Y)
    Next Y
  Next x
End Sub

Sub SetCellColor(Generation As Integer)
  Dim ColorNum
```

4

```
      ColorNum = Generation Mod 6
      Select Case ColorNum
      Case 0
        Form1.FillColor = vbBlue
      Case 1
        Form1.FillColor = vbRed
      Case 2
        Form1.FillColor = vbGreen
      Case 3
        Form1.FillColor = vbYellow
      Case 4
        Form1.FillColor = vbMagenta
      Case 5
        Form1.FillColor = vbCyan
      End Select
End Sub

Sub CreateLists()
   Dim column As Integer
   Dim row As Integer
   ReleaseNodes
   For column = 0 To MAXCOL - 1
     For row = 0 To MAXROW - 1
       Neighbors(column, row) = 0
       If World(column, row) = ALIVE Then _
         LiveList.MakeNewNode column, row
     Next row
   Next column
   AddNeighbors
   For column = 0 To MAXCOL - 1
     For row = 0 To MAXROW - 1
       If ((((Neighbors(column, row) < 2) Or _
           (Neighbors(column, row) > 3)) And _
           (World(column, row) = ALIVE)) Then _
         NextDieList.MakeNewNode column, row
     Next row
   Next column
   NextLiveList.TransferList LiveList
   NextDieList.TransferList DieList
End Sub

Sub Live()
   Dim row As Integer
   Dim column As Integer
   Dim TempList As List
   LiveList.TransferList TempList
   While (TempList.HasNodes)
     TempList.GetNode column, row
     If ((World(column, row) = DEAD) And _
         (Neighbors(column, row) = 3)) Then
       World(column, row) = ALIVE
```

```
            Form1.ForeColor = vbBlack
            Form1.FillStyle = vbSolid
            Form1.Circle (column * CELLWIDTH + XOFFSET + _
                CELLWIDTH / 2, row * CELLHEIGHT + _
                YOFFSET + CELLHEIGHT / 2), CIRCLERADIUS
            LiveList.MakeNewNode column, row
        End If
    Wend
End Sub

Sub Die()
    Dim temp As List
    Dim column As Integer
    Dim row As Integer
    Dim TempList As List
    DieList.TransferList TempList
    While (TempList.HasNodes)
        TempList.GetNode column, row
        If World(column, row) = ALIVE And _
            Neighbors(column, row) <> 2 And _
            Neighbors(column, row) <> 3 Then
          World(column, row) = DEAD
          Form1.ForeColor = vbButtonFace
          Form1.FillStyle = vbSolid
          Form1.FillColor = vbButtonFace
          Form1.Circle (column * CELLWIDTH + XOFFSET + _
              CELLWIDTH / 2, row * CELLHEIGHT + _
              YOFFSET + CELLHEIGHT / 2), CIRCLERADIUS
          DieList.MakeNewNode column, row
        End If
    Wend
End Sub

Sub AddNeighbors()
    Dim xLow As Integer, xHigh As Integer
    Dim yLow As Integer, yHigh As Integer
    Dim column As Integer
    Dim row As Integer
    Dim x As Integer, Y As Integer
    While LiveList.HasNodes
        LiveList.GetNode column, row
        CalcLimits column, row, xLow, xHigh, yLow, yHigh
        For x = xLow To xHigh
          For Y = yLow To yHigh
            If (x <> column) Or (Y <> row) Then
               Neighbors(x, Y) = Neighbors(x, Y) + 1
               Select Case Neighbors(x, Y)
                 Case 3:
                   If World(x, Y) = DEAD Then _
                     NextLiveList.MakeNewNode x, Y
                 Case 4:
```

4

```
                    If World(x, Y) = ALIVE Then _
                        NextDieList.MakeNewNode x, Y
                End Select
            End If
        Next Y
      Next x
  Wend
End Sub

Sub SubtractNeighbors()
  Dim xLow As Integer, xHigh As Integer
  Dim yLow As Integer, yHigh As Integer
  Dim column As Integer
  Dim row As Integer
  Dim x As Integer, Y As Integer
  While (DieList.HasNodes)
    DieList.GetNode column, row
    CalcLimits column, row, xLow, xHigh, yLow, yHigh
    For x = xLow To xHigh
      For Y = yLow To yHigh
        If (x <> column) Or (Y <> row) Then
          Neighbors(x, Y) = Neighbors(x, Y) + 1
          Select Case Neighbors(x, Y)
            Case 1:
              If World(x, Y) = ALIVE Then _
                NextDieList.MakeNewNode x, Y
            Case 3:
              If World(x, Y) = DEAD Then _
                NextLiveList.MakeNewNode x, Y
          End Select
        End If
      Next Y
    Next x
  Wend
End Sub

Sub CalcLimits(c As Integer, r As Integer, _
    xLow As Integer, xHigh As Integer, _
    yLow As Integer, yHigh As Integer)
  If c = 0 Then
    xLow = 0
  Else
    xLow = c - 1
  End If
  If c = MAXCOL - 1 Then
    xHigh = MAXCOL - 1
  Else
    xHigh = c + 1
  End If
  If r = 0 Then
    yLow = 0
```

```
      Else
        yLow = r - 1
      End If
      If r = MAXROW - 1 Then
        yHigh = MAXROW - 1
      Else
        yHigh = r + 1
      End If
  End Sub

  Sub ReleaseNodes()
    LiveList.ClearList
    DieList.ClearList
    NextLiveList.ClearList
    NextDieList.ClearList
  End Sub

  Sub AddCell(x As Single, Y As Single)
    Dim column As Integer
    Dim row As Integer
    If Drawing Then
      If x > XOFFSET And x < MAXX And _
          Y > YOFFSET And Y < MAXY Then
        column = (x - XOFFSET) \ CELLWIDTH
        row = (Y - YOFFSET) \ CELLHEIGHT
        If Not World(column, row) Then
          Form1.ForeColor = vbBlack
          Form1.FillStyle = vbSolid
          Form1.FillColor = vbGreen
          Form1.Circle (column * CELLWIDTH + XOFFSET + _
              CELLWIDTH / 2, row * CELLHEIGHT + _
              YOFFSET + CELLHEIGHT / 2), CIRCLERADIUS
          World(column, row) = ALIVE
        End If
      End If
    End If
  End Sub
```

Finally, use the Add Class Module on the Project menu to add the Node.cls and List.cls modules to the project. When you're finished, save the entire project, naming the form file Life.frm and the project file Life.vbp.

Understanding Life

Now that you know how the program operates, take a look at the code, starting with the game's constants and variables.

Life's Variables and Constants

Life relies on a set of global variables and constants that are declared near the top of the program. Table 4.1 lists the general global variables and their descriptions, and Table 4.2 lists the constants.

TABLE 4.1   Life's General Game Variables

Variable	Type	Description
DieList	List	A linked list that contains the cells that will die in the current generation
Drawing	Boolean	A flag that indicates whether the user is using the mouse to draw cells on the screen
Generations	Integer	The number of generations the simulation should run
LiveList	List	A linked list that contains the cells that will live in the current generation
Neighbors()	Integer	An array containing the number of living neighbors for each cell
NextDieList	List	A linked list that acts as temporary storage for cells that might die in the next generation
NextLiveList	List	A linked list that acts as temporary storage for cells that might live in the next generation
StopLife	Boolean	A flag that indicates the player has clicked the Stop button
World()	Integer	An array containing the contents of the entire grid; a value of 0 means the cell is dead, and 1 means the cell is alive

TABLE 4.2   Life's Constants

Constant	Description
ALIVE	The value for a living cell
CELLHEIGHT	The height of each cell in the display grid
CELLWIDTH	The width of each cell in the display grid
CIRCLERADIUS	The radius of the circle that represents a living cell
DEAD	The value for a dead cell
MAXCOL	The maximum number of columns in the cell-world display grid
MAXGENERATIONS	The maximum number of generations the simulation should run
MAXROW	The maximum number of rows in the cell-world display grid
MAXX	The maximum X value the mouse can have when clicking in the grid

Constant	Description
MAXY	The maximum Y value the mouse can have when clicking in the grid
XOFFSET	The position, from the left of the window, in which to start drawing the world grid
YOFFSET	The position, from the top of the window, in which to start drawing the world grid

Starting the Game

Now that you know what all those variables and constants mean, it's time to dig deeper into the program's source code. As always, when the game starts, Visual Basic calls the Form1 object's Form_Load subroutine, which does nothing more than call the subroutines InitGame and DrawScreen:

```
Private Sub Form_Load()
  InitGame
  DrawScreen
End Sub
```

The InitGame subroutine sets the initial values for all the game's variables. First, the subroutine sets all the cells in the world to DEAD, as shown in 4.10.

LISTING 4.10   Initializing the Cells

```
1: Dim row As Integer
2: Dim column As Integer
3: For row = 0 To MAXROW - 1
4:   For column = 0 To MAXCOL - 1
5:     World(column, row) = DEAD
6:   Next column
7: Next row
```

Then, InitGame sets the Generations and StopLife variables to their initial values:

```
Generations = 10000
StopLife = False
```

The DrawScreen subroutine draws the game's display, starting with the horizontal lines:

```
Form1.ForeColor = vbBlue
For Y = YOFFSET To MAXY Step CELLHEIGHT
  Form1.Line (XOFFSET, Y)-(MAXX + 1, Y)
Next Y
```

Notice how the program uses constants to calculate loop values and drawing locations.
Because of this technique, you can change the size of the game's world just by changing
the values of the MAXCOL and MAXROW constants. The entire game will then run just fine
with a smaller or larger grid.

After drawing the horizontal lines, DrawScreen draws the vertical lines:

```
For x = XOFFSET To MAXX Step CELLWIDTH
  Form1.Line (x, YOFFSET)-(x, MAXY + 1)
Next x
```

Finally, DrawScreen draws the caption for the generation count:

```
lblGenerations.Caption = "Generation #10000"
```

Processing Commands

Now that the initialization is complete, the program waits for the player to either draw
cells on the screen or click one of the buttons. The player can click in the grid to draw a
single cell or paint cells into the grid by holding down the left mouse button and drag-
ging the mouse. In either case, the Form_MouseDown, Form_MouseMove, and
Form_MouseUp event handlers (see Listing 4.11) perform the task of adding cells by calling the AddCell subroutine with the current location of the mouse pointer.

LISTING 4.11   Handling Mouse Events

```
 1: Private Sub Form_MouseDown(Button As Integer, _
 2:     Shift As Integer, x As Single, y As Single)
 3:   Drawing = True
 4:   AddCell x, y
 5: End Sub
 6:
 7: Private Sub Form_MouseMove(Button As Integer, _
 8:     Shift As Integer, x As Single, y As Single)
 9:   If Drawing Then AddCell x, y
10: End Sub
11:
12: Private Sub Form_MouseUp(Button As Integer, _
13:     Shift As Integer, x As Single, y As Single)
14:   Drawing = False
15: End Sub
```

The AddCell subroutine checks the mouse position to ensure that the mouse pointer is
over the grid and not over some other part of the window:

```
If x > XOFFSET And x < MAXX And _
    Y > YOFFSET And Y < MAXY Then
```

If the mouse is over the grid, the program calculates the column and row of the cell over which the mouse pointer is positioned:

```
column = (x - XOFFSET) \ CELLWIDTH
row = (Y - YOFFSET) \ CELLHEIGHT
```

Then, if the cell over which the mouse is positioned isn't already alive, the program draws the cell and adds it to the World array, as shown in Listing 4.12.

LISTING 4.12 Adding a Cell to the Game

```
1:    If Not World(column, row) Then
2:       Form1.ForeColor = vbBlack
3:       Form1.FillStyle = vbSolid
4:       Form1.FillColor = vbGreen
5:       Form1.Circle (column * CELLWIDTH + XOFFSET + _
6:          CELLWIDTH / 2, row * CELLHEIGHT + _
7:          YOFFSET + CELLHEIGHT / 2), CIRCLERADIUS
8:       World(column, row) = ALIVE
9:    End If
```

ANALYSIS Again, notice the use of constants to calculate cell positions (Lines 5 through 7). Not only does this make the code more readable, but it also ensures that it will work with any size grid.

The remaining command handlers are attached to the CommandButton controls. For example, when the player clicks the Start button, Visual Basic calls the cmdStart_Click event handler, which looks like Listing 4.13.

LISTING 4.13 The cmdStart_Click Event Handler

```
1: Private Sub cmdStart_Click()
2:    cmdStart.Enabled = False
3:    cmdGenerations.Enabled = False
4:    cmdStop.Enabled = True
5:    cmdClear.Enabled = False
6:    RunLife
7: End Sub
```

ANALYSIS The cmdStart_Click event handler disables all buttons except the Stop button, and then it calls the RunLife subroutine, which starts the simulation.

When the player clicks the Clear button, Visual Basic calls the cmdClear_Click event handler, which looks like Listing 4.14.

LISTING 4.14   The cmdClear_Click Event Handler

```
 1:  Private Sub cmdClear_Click()
 2:    Dim column As Integer
 3:    Dim row As Integer
 4:    For column = 0 To MAXCOL - 1
 5:      For row = 0 To MAXROW - 1
 6:        If World(column, row) = ALIVE Then
 7:          World(column, row) = DEAD
 8:          Form1.ForeColor = vbButtonFace
 9:          Form1.FillStyle = vbSolid
10:          Form1.FillColor = vbButtonFace
11:          Form1.Circle (column * CELLWIDTH + XOFFSET + _
12:              CELLWIDTH / 2, row * CELLHEIGHT + _
13:              YOFFSET + CELLHEIGHT / 2), CIRCLERADIUS
14:        End If
15:      Next row
16:    Next column
17:    ReleaseNodes
18: End Sub
```

ANALYSIS   As you can see, this event handler does nothing more than scan the World array, killing every living cell (Line 7) and erasing them from the screen (Lines 8 through 11), providing the simulation with a fresh start.

When the player clicks the Generations button, Visual Basic calls the cmdGenerations_Click event handler (see Listing 4.15). This displays an input box in order to obtain the new generations setting from the user.

LISTING 4.15   The cmdGenerations_Click Event Handler

```
 1:  Private Sub cmdGenerations_Click()
 2:    On Error GoTo Inputerror
 3:    Generations = InputBox("Enter number of generations:" & _
 4:      vbCrLf & "(Max = " & MAXGENERATIONS & ")", _
 5:      "Generations", MAXGENERATIONS)
 6:    If Generations < 1 Or Generations > MAXGENERATIONS Then _
 7:      Generations = MAXGENERATIONS
 8:  Inputerror:
 9:  End Sub
```

Finally, clicking the Stop button causes the program to set the StopLife flag to true, which ends the currently running simulation (as you'll see in the next section):

```
Private Sub cmdStop_Click()
  StopLife = True
End Sub
```

Processing the Simulation

When the user clicks the Start button, the RunLife subroutine, which is the main simulation loop, takes over. This subroutine performs the simulation by calling the subroutines that count cell neighbors, create cells, and kill cells. To get started, it calls CreateLists, which creates the starting lists and neighbor count for the simulation:

```
CreateLists
```

When CreateLists (which you'll examine a little later in this section) finishes initializing the starting lists, program execution returns to RunLife and enters the main simulation loop. This loop is controlled by a For statement that compares its loop variable to Generations, which is the number of generations that the simulation will run:

```
For gen = 1 To Generations
```

First, the loop checks whether the player has clicked the Stop button. If so, the program terminates the For loop, which also terminates the current simulation:

```
If StopLife Then Exit For
```

If the simulation should continue, the program sets the current onscreen generation count and the cell color:

```
lblGenerations.Caption = "Generation #" & gen
SetCellColor gen
```

Then, it's time to process the LiveList and DieList lists by calling the Live and Die subroutines:

```
Live
Die
```

The Live subroutine brings to life those cells in LiveList that meet the requirements for life, whereas Die kills off those cells in DieList that meet the requirements for death.

After processing the lists, the program must update the Neighbors array for all cells whose neighbor count has changed. The AddNeighbors and SubtractNeighbors subroutines handle this task:

```
AddNeighbors
SubtractNeighbors
```

The program then transfers the new lists into LiveList and DieList, where they'll be for the next iteration of the loop:

```
NextLiveList.TransferList LiveList
NextDieList.TransferList DieList
```

4

Because the For loop runs for quite a while, the RunLife subroutine must relinquish the processor now and then so that Windows can handle messages. The program does this by calling the DoEvents method at the end of each loop:

```
DoEvents
```

After the For loop completes its processing or the player forces the loop to exit by clicking the Stop button, RunLife resets the StopLife flag and the command buttons to their normal states:

```
StopLife = False
cmdStart.Enabled = True
cmdGenerations.Enabled = True
cmdStop.Enabled = False
cmdClear.Enabled = True
```

The CreateLists subroutine is responsible for initializing LiveList and DieList, the two linked lists that the simulation needs to get started. Also, it initializes the starting neighbor counts. The subroutine first calls ReleaseNodes, which simply makes sure that all lists are empty:

```
ReleaseNodes
```

(When the program first starts, the lists are empty. But in subsequent calls to RunLife, your linked lists probably won't be empty because it's rare that every cell onscreen is dead after the generations run out.)

After clearing the lists, CreateLists scans the newly created World array, creating a new node for each living cell in the array. As CreateLists scans the World array, it also takes advantage of the loop to initialize all the neighbor counts in the Neighbors array to 0, as shown in Listing 4.16.

LISTING 4.16   Initializing Neighbor Counts

```
1:    For column = 0 To MAXCOL - 1
2:      For row = 0 To MAXROW - 1
3:        Neighbors(column, row) = 0
4:        If World(column, row) = ALIVE Then _
5:          LiveList.MakeNewNode column, row
6:      Next row
7:    Next column
```

After creating the LiveList linked list, the subroutine calls the AddNeighbors subroutine, which updates the neighbor counts and creates a NextLiveList and NextDieList list for cells that might (or might not) live or die in the next generation:

```
AddNeighbors
```

After the call to AddNeighbors, the CreateLists subroutine must scan the neighbor counts, looking for cells with less than two neighbors or more than three neighbors. The subroutine adds these cells to the NextDieList list that AddNeighbors started, as shown in Listing 4.17.

LISTING 4.17   Initializing Neighbor Counts

```
1:   For column = 0 To MAXCOL - 1
2:     For row = 0 To MAXROW - 1
3:       If (((Neighbors(column, row) < 2) Or _
4:           (Neighbors(column, row) > 3)) And _
5:           (World(column, row) = ALIVE)) Then _
6:         NextDieList.MakeNewNode column, row
7:     Next row
8:   Next column
```

After building the NextLiveList and NextDieList lists, CreateLists finally transfers these lists to the LiveList and DieList lists, where RunLife expects to find them:

```
NextLiveList.TransferList LiveList
NextDieList.TransferList DieList
```

Calculating Cell Neighbors

Now let's look at the AddNeighbors subroutine. AddNeighbors scans the LiveList list, which contains all the cells that have just come to life. The While loop iterates until this list is empty:

```
While LiveList.HasNodes
```

The subroutine first gets the cell's coordinates by calling the list's GetNode method:

```
LiveList.GetNode column, row
```

(Remember: GetNode also deletes the node.)

It then calls the CalcLimits subroutine, which determines the minimum and maximum coordinates for cells adjacent to the live cell:

```
CalcLimits column, row, xLow, xHigh, yLow, yHigh
```

The program requires this calculation because cells on any edge of the grid do not have eight adjacent cells.

After calculating the coordinates, nested For loops increment the neighbor count for every adjacent cell:

```
For x = xLow To xHigh
  For y = yLow To yHigh
    If (x <> column) Or (y <> row) Then
      Neighbors(x, y) = Neighbors(x, y) + 1
```

After the loops increment a cell's neighbor count, the Select Case statement checks the count, adding new nodes to the NextLiveList or NextDieList list as appropriate, as shown in Listing 4.18.

LISTING 4.18   Checking Cell Counts

```
1:              Select Case Neighbors(x, y)
2:                Case 3:
3:                  If World(x, y) = DEAD Then _
4:                    NextLiveList.MakeNewNode x, y
5:                Case 4:
6:                  If World(x, y) = ALIVE Then _
7:                    NextDieList.MakeNewNode x, y
8:              End Select
```

Keep in mind that the nodes on the list are only "maybes." That is, when you add nodes to these two lists, you're telling the program that when it finishes counting all the neighbors, it should check those cells again to see whether they'll actually live or die. Not every cell on the NextLiveList list will come to life, and not every cell on the NextDieList list will die. Some cells might appear in both lists at the same time. With these temporary lists, you can keep track of cells that might change without changing the grid—which, as you've learned, can really mess up the simulation.

The SubtractNeighbors routine works similarly to its counterpart, AddNeighbors. The difference is that it processes the DieList list, adding to the NextLiveList list any cells that have three neighbors (even though the cells might not keep all three neighbors) and adding to the NextDieList list any cells with less than two neighbors (even though the cell's final neighbor count might not qualify it to die).

Creating and Killing Cells

Next up is the Live subroutine, which checks all the nodes on the LiveList list, bringing to life only the nodes that meet the requirements for life. The first step in this process is to transfer the LiveList list to the TempList list:

```
Dim TempList As List
LiveList.TransferList TempList
```

The subroutine then starts a While loop that iterates through the entire list:

```
While (TempList.HasNodes)
```

The first thing the loop does is remove a node from the list:

```
TempList.GetNode column, row
```

The loop then checks whether the cell should come to life:

```
If ((World(column, row) = DEAD) And _
    (Neighbors(column, row) = 3)) Then
```

If so, the subroutine adds the cell to the World array and draws the cell on the screen:

```
World(column, row) = ALIVE
Form1.ForeColor = vbBlack
Form1.FillStyle = vbSolid
Form1.Circle (column * CELLWIDTH + XOFFSET + _
    CELLWIDTH / 2, row * CELLHEIGHT + _
    YOFFSET + CELLHEIGHT / 2), CIRCLERADIUS
```

Finally, the subroutine adds any newly alive cells to the NextLiveList list so that they can be counted in the next generation:

```
        LiveList.MakeNewNode column, row
    End If
  Wend
End Sub
```

The Die subroutine (see Listing 4.19) is Live's counterpart.

LISTING 4.19   The Die Subroutine

```
 1:  Sub Die()
 2:    Dim temp As List
 3:    Dim column As Integer
 4:    Dim row As Integer
 5:    Dim TempList As List
 6:    DieList.TransferList TempList
 7:    While (TempList.HasNodes)
 8:      TempList.GetNode column, row
 9:      If World(column, row) = ALIVE And _
10:          Neighbors(column, row) <> 2 And _
11:          Neighbors(column, row) <> 3 Then
12:        World(column, row) = DEAD
13:        Form1.ForeColor = vbButtonFace
14:        Form1.FillStyle = vbSolid
15:        Form1.FillColor = vbButtonFace
16:        Form1.Circle (column * CELLWIDTH + XOFFSET + _
17:            CELLWIDTH / 2, row * CELLHEIGHT + _
18:            YOFFSET + CELLHEIGHT / 2), CIRCLERADIUS
19:        DieList.MakeNewNode column, row
20:      End If
21:    Wend
22: End Sub
```

ANALYSIS `Die` checks the `DieList` list, killing the cells that meet the requirements for death and deleting from the list the cells that don't. (Remember that `GetNode` deletes a cell after getting it.) Any cells that die are placed back onto the `DieList` list so they can be accounted for in the next generation.

Summary

The Life program is an excellent example of an interactive, event-driven application with a game loop that continuously updates the game screen while still allowing other Windows messages to get through to the system. The program also introduces the linked list, which is a data structure that enables you to build lists of items. But aside from demonstrating all these features, the program is fun—and addictive. I've spent far too many hours watching little creatures live and die onscreen. Time to get back to work.

Q&A

Q How important are efficient algorithms in a world where computer speeds double nearly every two years?

A Good question. It's true that programmers today can get away with a lot more inefficiency than they could back when computers ran at 16MHz or slower. Still, game programmers like to push computers to their limits. For this reason, efficient algorithms will never go out of style.

Q Is there a way to make a linked list that can be easily traversed both forward and backward?

A Yep. You'll need to create something called a *doubly-linked list*, in which each node has a pointer to both the previous and next nodes. The two pointers enable a program to search through the nodes from front to back or back to front.

Q Does the use of so many constants in a program slow it down?

A Not much. When you compile your program, Visual Basic replaces all constants with the values they represent. The only processing time you might lose is the time it takes to perform mathematical operations such as addition or subtraction. In most cases, this is insignificant.

Q I know that the `DoEvents` method enables my game program to process Windows messages within a game loop, but does `DoEvents` also allow other currently running Windows applications to receive their messages?

A Yes. When you call `DoEvents`, you're telling the operating system to process all pending messages. This ensures that your game program will share processor time fairly with all other processes that are running.

Q **What happens if I forget to call** `DoEvents` **from within a game loop?**

A The game loop will completely take over the system, leaving you with what appears to be a lockup. No Windows applications will be able to function, including your game.

Workshop

The workshop includes quiz questions to help gauge your grasp of the material. You'll find the answers to this quiz in Appendix A. Even if you feel that you totally understand the concepts presented here, you should work through the quiz anyway. The last section has an exercise or two that will help reinforce your learning.

Quiz

1. What's an algorithm?
2. Why do algorithms need to be efficient?
3. How does the complexity of an algorithm relate to its efficiency?
4. How does a program store the location of a linked list in memory?
5. What does the Life program use the `LiveList` and `DieList` linked lists for?
6. In the Life program, what's the `World` array used for?
7. How does the `Neighbors` array in the Life program help to speed the simulation's algorithm?
8. Why must a program call the `DoEvents` method within a game loop?

Exercises

1. Come up with an algorithm that completely shuffles an array of 20 values, from 0 to 19. Write a short program that implements your algorithm and displays the shuffled values in the application's form.
2. Add constants to the program you wrote in Exercise 1 so that you can easily change the size of the array and the location where the program prints the array values.
3. Modify the Life program so that it runs in a 30¥18 grid, with cells that are 20 pixels high and 20 pixels wide. Change the size of the cell circles to a radius of 8. (Hint: Study the program's constants.)

4

WEEK 1

DAY 5

Displaying and Manipulating Images

Most computer games are heavily graphical. Luckily, Visual Basic includes two
controls—the Image control and the PictureBox control—that make performing
many graphical operations a snap. These controls enable you to do things with
graphics that only a highly trained programmer can do in another language
such as C++. Previously in this book, you gained a little experience with these
controls. In today's lesson, you'll learn everything you need to know to take
full advantage of these graphical powerhouses:

- The main differences between the Image and PictureBox controls
- The properties and methods of Image and PictureBox controls
- How to load picture files into controls
- How to resize a picture in an Image control
- How to combine PictureBox and Image controls
- How to draw images with the `PaintPicture` method

The Image Control in Detail

The Image control is the simpler of the two graphical controls and is useful when you don't need as much control over a picture as you can get with the more powerful PictureBox. The most significant difference between the Image control and the PictureBox control is that the PictureBox control can act as a container in the same way a form can. That is, a PictureBox control can contain other controls (and can act as a drawing surface), but an Image control cannot. This section will examine the Image control's properties and methods, as well as ways to use the control in your programs.

Important Image Control Properties, Methods, and Events

Table 5.1 lists the most commonly used of the Image control's 20 properties. These are the properties that are the most useful to game programmers, and most of them should already be familiar to you as a Visual Basic programmer.

TABLE 5.1   Most Useful Image Control Properties

Property	Description
BorderStyle	Determines the type of border that's drawn around the control
Height	Specifies the control's height
Left	Specifies the location of the control's left edge
Name	Specifies the control's name
Picture	Specifies the picture to display in the control
Stretch	Determines whether the control changes size to fit the picture or the picture changes size to fit the control
Top	Specifies the location of the control's top edge
Visible	Determines whether the control is visible
Width	Specifies the control's width

The Image control supports the usual set of Visual Basic control methods. However, the only one of these that's particularly useful to you as a game programmer is the Move method, which repositions and resizes the control. Of course, you can also resize or reposition an Image control by setting its Left, Top, Width, and Height properties.

 Note

> You can resize an Image control only when its Stretch property is set to True. If the Stretch property is set to False, the control always takes the size of the picture it contains, and trying to change its size will have no effect.

The Image control also responds to many events, most of which should be familiar to you. Table 5.2 lists the most commonly used of these events.

TABLE 5.2 The Most Commonly Used Image Control Events

Event	Description
Click	Occurs when the control is clicked
DblClick	Occurs when the control is double-clicked
MouseDown	Occurs when a mouse button is pressed and the mouse pointer is over the control
MouseUp	Occurs when a mouse button is released and the mouse pointer is over the control
MouseMove	Occurs when the mouse pointer moves over the control

Loading Pictures into an Image Control

There are two ways to get a picture into an Image control. First, at design time you can assign a picture to the Picture property in the control's Properties window. Visual Basic then loads the picture into the control at design time, and the picture becomes part of the program's executable. The second way is to assign a picture to the control's Picture property at runtime by calling the LoadPicture method:

```
Image1.Picture = LoadPicture("picture.jpg")
```

Note

The type of file you use for your pictures depends on a number of things. JPEG files (with the .jpg file extension) are best used with photos because you can control the amount of compression used, which enables you to create a small file that still looks good. GIF picture files are good for line drawings and less complex graphics. Bitmap files (with the .bmp file extension) are perfect reproductions of images because no compression is used. However, they can take up a lot of disk space.

5

There are advantages and disadvantages to each of these picture-loading methods. If you assign a picture to the control at design time, the picture becomes part of the control and you don't need to package a separate image file with the program. However, if you do this, editing the picture becomes a matter of editing the original image, loading the Visual Basic project, setting the Image control's Picture property to the new image, and then recompiling the program. If you load the picture at runtime, you must package the separate image file with the program, but editing the image doesn't require recompiling.

Sizing Pictures with an Image Control

The Image control has a Stretch property, which determines whether the control stretches to fit the picture or the picture stretches to fit the control. The Stretch property is one of the advantages of using an Image control rather than a PictureBox control, which doesn't have the Stretch property. If you set the Stretch property to True, whenever you change the size of the Image control, the picture resizes as well. Scaling pictures has never been easier!

The Stretch Example program, which you can find on this book's CD-ROM, demonstrates this advantage of the Image control. When you first run the program, you see the window shown in Figure 5.1. Click the Image control (the picture on the left), and the control and picture get scaled by three. Click the PictureBox control (the picture on the right), and the control gets scaled by three but the picture stays the same size. Figure 5.2 shows both the controls after they've been enlarged.

FIGURE **5.1**

Stretch Example when it's first run.

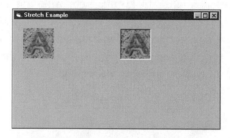

FIGURE **5.2**

Both controls after being scaled by three.

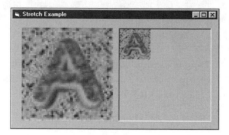

The source code that implements the Stretch Example program is fairly simple, as you can see in Listing 5.1.

LISTING **5.1**   The Stretch Example Program

```
1:  Option Explicit
2:
3:  Dim ImageWidth As Integer
4:  Dim ImageHeight As Integer
5:
```

```
 6:  Private Sub Form_Load()
 7:     ImageWidth = Image1.Width
 8:     ImageHeight = Image1.Height
 9:     Picture1.Width = ImageWidth
10:     Picture1.Height = ImageHeight
11:  End Sub
12:
13:  Private Sub Image1_Click()
14:     If Image1.Width = ImageWidth Then
15:        Image1.Width = ImageWidth * 3
16:        Image1.Height = ImageHeight * 3
17:     Else
18:        Image1.Width = ImageWidth
19:        Image1.Height = ImageHeight
20:     End If
21:  End Sub
22:
23:  Private Sub Picture1_Click()
24:     If Picture1.Width = ImageWidth Then
25:        Picture1.Width = ImageWidth * 3
26:        Picture1.Height = ImageHeight * 3
27:     Else
28:        Picture1.Width = ImageWidth
29:        Picture1.Height = ImageHeight
30:     End If
31:  End Sub
```

ANALYSIS The Form_Load procedure (Lines 6 through 11), which Visual Basic calls when it loads the form, sets the size of the PictureBox to control to the size of the image. The Image1_Click event procedure (Lines 13 through 21) stretches the Image control or returns the control to its normal size when the user clicks it. The Picture1_Click event procedure (Lines 23 through 31) does the same thing for the PictureBox control that Image1_Click does for the Image control.

5

The PictureBox Control in Detail

When discussing the Image control, it's almost impossible not to cover some aspects of the PictureBox control as well. Still, there's a lot more to this versatile control than what you might have picked up in the previous section. In this section, you'll get a closer look at the PictureBox control, one of the most versatile objects in your Visual Basic toolbox.

Important PictureBox Control Properties

The PictureBox control is a full-fledged container, like a form, so it boasts nearly twice as many properties as the Image control. These properties give you extra power over your graphics. Moreover, because the PictureBox is a full-fledged container, you can use it to organize output or sets of controls within the main window represented by a form. However, all this power comes with a price, because a PictureBox control is more of a resource hog than an Image control is.

Table 5.3 lists the most commonly used PictureBox properties, most of which should already be familiar to you as a Visual Basic programmer.

TABLE 5.3   The Most Commonly Used PictureBox Control Properties

Property	Description
Appearance	Determines whether the control is drawn flat or 3D
AutoRedraw	Determines whether Visual Basic keeps a persistent graphic in memory to refresh the control's display
AutoSize	Determines whether the control automatically sizes itself to the size of the picture it contains
BorderStyle	Specifies the type of border to draw around the control
CurrentX	The ending horizontal location of the last drawing operation
CurrentY	The ending vertical location of the last drawing operation
DrawMode	Specifies the mode to use when combining pixels during drawing operations
DrawStyle	Specifies the style of drawing for lines in the control
DrawWidth	Specifies the width of lines drawn in the control
FillColor	Specifies the color to use for fill operations
FillStyle	Specifies the pattern to use for fill operations
Font	Specifies the font to use when displaying text in the control
Height	Specifies the height of the control
Left	Specifies the location of the control's left edge
Picture	Specifies the picture to display in the control
ScaleMode	Specifies the type of measurement to use for coordinates within the control
Top	Specifies the location of the control's top edge
Visible	Determines whether the control is visible
Width	Specifies the width of the control

The PictureBox control supports the usual set of Visual Basic control methods. However, because a PictureBox control supports drawing, it also implements the complete set of graphical methods. Table 5.4 lists and describes these methods.

TABLE 5.4 The PictureBox Control's Graphical Methods

Method	Description
Circle	Draws a circle, oval, or ellipse
Cls	Clears the control's display area
Line	Draws a line or a box
PaintPicture	Draws all or part of a picture in the control
Point	Gets the RGB value of a point in the control
PSet	Draws a point in the control
Scale	Sets the control's scaling to user-defined values

The PictureBox control also responds to many events, most of which should be familiar to you as a Visual Basic programmer. Table 5.5 lists the most commonly used of these events.

TABLE 5.5 The Most Useful PictureBox Control Events

Event	Description
Change	Occurs when the control's contents change
Click	Occurs when the control is clicked
DblClick	Occurs when the control is double-clicked
MouseDown	Occurs when a mouse button is pressed and the mouse pointer is over the control
MouseUp	Occurs when a mouse button is released and the mouse pointer is over the control
MouseMove	Occurs when the mouse pointer moves over the control
Paint	Occurs when the contents of the control must be repainted
Resize	Occurs when the control is resized

5

Loading Pictures into a PictureBox Control

Loading pictures into a PictureBox control works the same as with an Image control. You can set the control's Picture property in the control's Properties window at design time, or you can call the LoadPicture method to load a picture into the control at runtime.

Sizing Pictures with a PictureBox Control

You might think that because the PictureBox control doesn't have a Stretch property, scaling pictures in the control would require some fancy finagling—but that isn't really true. There are actually two fairly easy ways to handle scaling. The first is to combine the advantages of an Image control with a PictureBox control.

Remember that a PictureBox control is a container, which means that can hold other controls, including an Image control. By placing an Image control inside a PictureBox control, you can easily scale an image. When you change the size of the PictureBox control, you also change the size of the Image control. (Just don't forget to set the Image control's Stretch property to True.)

The Stretch2 program, found on this book's CD-ROM, demonstrates how this technique works. When you run the program, you see the window shown in Figure 5.3. Click the picture and it expands to three times its normal size, shown in Figure 5.4. Listing 5.2 contains the source code that accomplishes this bit of trickery.

LISTING 5.2   The Stretch2 Example Program

```
1:  Option Explicit
2:
3:  Dim ImageWidth As Integer
4:  Dim ImageHeight As Integer
5:
6:  Private Sub Form_Load()
7:    Image1.Move 0, 0
8:    ImageWidth = Image1.Width
9:    ImageHeight = Image1.Height
10:   Picture1.Width = ImageWidth
11:   Picture1.Height = ImageHeight
12: End Sub
13:
14: Private Sub Image1_Click()
15:   If Image1.Width = ImageWidth Then
16:     Picture1.Width = ImageWidth * 3
17:     Picture1.Height = ImageHeight * 3
18:     Image1.Width = ImageWidth * 3
19:     Image1.Height = ImageHeight * 3
20:   Else
21:     Picture1.Width = ImageWidth
22:     Picture1.Height = ImageHeight
23:     Image1.Width = ImageWidth
24:     Image1.Height = ImageHeight
25:   End If
26: End Sub
```

ANALYSIS   The Form_Load procedure (Lines 6 through 12), which Visual Basic calls when it loads the form, sets the Image control's position inside the PictureBox control and sets the size of the PictureBox to control to the size of the image. The Image1_Click event procedure (Lines 14 through 26) stretches the Image and PictureBox controls or returns them to their normal sizes when the user clicks the image.

FIGURE 5.3

Stretch2 when it's first run.

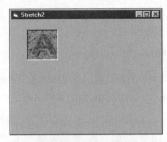

FIGURE 5.4

The control after being scaled by three.

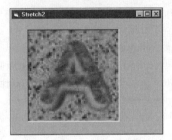

The second way to scale a picture in a PictureBox control is called the `PaintPicture` method, which you'll examine in the next section.

The `PaintPicture` Method

The `PaintPicture` method of the PictureBox control gives you almost total control over how a picture is displayed. Using this method, you can draw a picture at any size or draw only parts of a picture. Moreover, you can specify the drawing mode so you can combine the source and destination pixels. A call to `PaintPicture` looks like this:

```
Picture1.PaintPicture picture, x1, y1, _
  width1, height1, x2, y2, width2, height2, opcode
```

The `PaintPicture` method's arguments are the following:

- `picture`—The source picture, which must be an object's `Picture` property
- `x1`—The X coordinate where the picture will be drawn
- `y1`—The Y coordinate where the picture will be drawn
- `width1`—The width of the picture
- `height1`—The height of the picture
- `x2`—The X coordinate within the source picture from which the destination picture will be taken
- `y2`—The Y coordinate within the source picture from which the source picture will be taken

5

- width2—The width of the area of the source picture that will be drawn
- height2—The height of the area of the source picture that will be drawn
- opcode—The drawing mode that will be used

All these arguments are optional except picture, x1, and y1. That is, you can draw the picture simply by supplying a reference to the picture and the coordinate position at which to draw the picture, like this:

```
Picture1.PaintPicture Image1.Picture, 10, 10
```

To scale the picture, use the width1 and height1 arguments. The Stretch3 program, which you can find on this book's CD-ROM, demonstrates using the PaintPicture method to scale a picture. The program's form contains two controls, an Image control and a PictureBox control. The Image control holds the picture to be displayed. However, this control is invisible, so the image can't be seen until it's drawn in the PictureBox control. When you click the PictureBox control, the picture toggles between normal and enlarged size, as shown in Figures 5.5 and 5.6. The program's source code looks like Listing 5.3.

LISTING 5.3   The Stretch3 Example Program

```
1:  Option Explicit
2:
3:  Dim ImageWidth As Integer
4:  Dim ImageHeight As Integer
5:  Dim Scaled As Boolean
6:
7:  Private Sub Form_Load()
8:    Image1.Visible = False
9:    ImageWidth = Image1.Width
10:   ImageHeight = Image1.Height
11:   Picture1.Width = ImageWidth * 3
12:   Picture1.Height = ImageHeight * 3
13:   Scaled = False
14:   Picture1.PaintPicture Image1.Picture, 10, 10
15: End Sub
16:
17: Private Sub Picture1_Click()
18:   Picture1.Cls
19:   If Scaled Then
20:     Picture1.PaintPicture Image1.Picture, 10, 10
21:   Else
22:     Picture1.PaintPicture Image1.Picture, 10, 10, _
23:         ImageWidth * 3, ImageHeight * 3
24:   End If
25:   Scaled = Not Scaled
26: End Sub
```

ANALYSIS The Form_Load procedure (Lines 7 through 15), which Visual Basic calls when it loads the form, makes the Image control invisible (Line 8). Then it sets the PictureBox control to three times the size of the image (Lines 9 through 12), initializes the Scaled flag to False (Line 13), and paints the contents of the Image control in the PictureBox control (Line 14). The Picture1_Click event procedure (Lines 17 through 26) stretches the image (Lines 22 and 23), or returns it to its normal size (Line 20), when the user clicks the PictureBox control.

FIGURE 5.5

The picture at normal size.

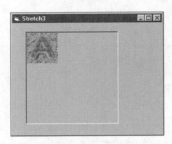

FIGURE 5.6

The picture enlarged.

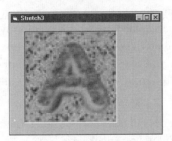

The Letter Tiles Puzzle Game

The Letter Tiles game is a version of a classic puzzle and is a good example of how easy Visual Basic makes it to manipulate images. The game incorporates 25 different images, all created with Microsoft PhotoDraw 2000.

Playing Letter Tiles

To play the game, run the LetterTiles.exe file. You'll see the window shown in Figure 5.7. The object of the game is to put the letters in order. To make this task tricky, there's only one blank tile in the game. You can swap the blank tile with any adjacent letter tile (no diagonal moves) by clicking the letter tile you want to move. When you click an adjacent tile, the blank tile and the letter tile switch places. (When you move a letter into its correct position, it blinks.) With some skill (not to mention a good helping of luck and a lot of swearing), eventually you can shuffle the letter tiles into their correct order.

FIGURE 5.7

*Letter Tiles when it's
first run.*

Letter Tiles is easy at first. But as you put more and more tiles in their correct positions, you have less room to maneuver the remaining tiles. By the time you get to the last row, you'll find out just how hard this puzzle can be. If you're easily frustrated, Letter Tiles has a secret cheat mode. To activate it, place the mouse pointer over the blank tile, hold down the Shift and Ctrl keys, and then right-click. A message box appears, telling you that the cheat mode is active. Now you can swap any letter tile on the board with the blank tile, not just adjacent tiles. To turn off cheat mode, perform the same actions you used to turn it on.

When you manage to get the letter tiles in their correct order, the tiles go a little crazy, shuffling themselves around the grid at breakneck speed.

Building Letter Tiles

Now that you've seen Letter Tiles in action, it's time to build the program yourself. Let's start with the user interface.

Building Letter Tiles' User Interface

To build the game's user interface, perform the following steps:

1. Start a new Visual Basic Standard EXE project.
2. Set the following form properties in the form's Properties window:

   AutoRedraw = True

   BorderStyle = Fixed Single

   Caption = "Letter Tiles"

```
Height = 6765
```

```
ScaleMode = Pixel
```

```
Width = 6045
```

As you may remember, the `AutoRedraw` property enables the form to automatically update its contents as necessary (such as when the form is uncovered by another window), whereas the Fixed Single `BorderStyle` creates a window that cannot be resized by the player. Setting the `ScaleMode` to Pixel causes all coordinates in the form to be measured in pixels, which gives program measurements a one-to-one relationship to screen coordinates.

3. Add an Image control (not a Picture control) to the form, giving it the following property settings:

```
Name = imgLetters
```

```
BorderStyle = Fixed Single
```

```
Height = 68
```

```
Left = 17
```

```
Top = 23
```

```
Width = 68
```

This Image control, and all the other Image controls you create in the next few steps, will hold the game's letter images. Because each letter is contained in its own Image control, it's easy for the program to move the letters around the form.

4. With the Image control selected in the form, press Ctrl+C to copy it and then Ctrl+V to paste the copy into the form. When Visual Basic asks whether you want to create a control array, answer Yes.

5. Give the second Image control the following property settings:

```
Left = 91
```

```
Top = 23
```

6. Paste 23 more copies of the Image control into the form, giving them the following property settings:

Image #3

```
Left = 165
```

```
Top = 23
```

5

Image #4

Left = 239

Top = 23

Image #5

Left = 313

Top = 23

Image #6

Left = 17

Top = 97

Image #7

Left = 91

Top = 97

Image #8

Left = 165

Top = 97

Image #9

Left = 239

Top = 97

Image #10

Left = 313

Top = 97

Image #11

Left = 17

Top = 171

Image #12

Left = 91

Top = 171

Image #13

Left = 165

Top = 171

Image #14

Left = 239

Top = 171

Image #15

Left = 313

Top = 171

Image #16

Left = 17

Top = 245

Image #17

Left = 91

Top = 245

Image #18

Left = 165

Top = 245

Image #19

Left = 239

Top = 245

Image #20

Left = 313

Top = 245

Image #21

Left = 17

Top = 319

5

Image #22

Left = 91

Top = 319

Image #23

Left = 165

Top = 319

Image #24

Left = 239

Top = 319

Image #25

Left = 313

Top = 319

7. Create menus for the form using the menu editor, as shown in Figure 5.8. (Don't forget the Ctrl+N shortcut, also shown in Figure 5.8, for the New Game command.) Use the following captions and menu names:

&File	mnuFile
&New Game	mnuNewGame
–	mnuSep
E&xit	mnuExit
&Help	mnuHelp
&About Letter Tiles...	mnuAbout

FIGURE 5.8

Creating Letter Tiles' menu bar.

8. Set the `Picture` properties of the Image controls to the letter graphics files in the Images\LetterTiles folder of this book's CD-ROM. Set the first Image control to the A.jpg file, the second to the B.jpg file, and so on. Set the last Image control to the Blank.jpg file.

These files contain the actual letter images, which I created using Microsoft PhotoDraw 2000.

9. Place a Timer control anywhere on the form.

The Timer will control the speed of the blinking letters.

10. Save the project's form file as LetterTiles.frm and the project file as LetterTiles.vbp.

You've now completed Letter Tiles' user interface. At this point, your project's form will look like Figure 5.9. If you run the program now, the game's window looks exactly as it will when you've completed the program. The only problem is that nothing works! In the following sections, you'll remedy that little oversight.

FIGURE 5.9

Letter Tiles' completed form.

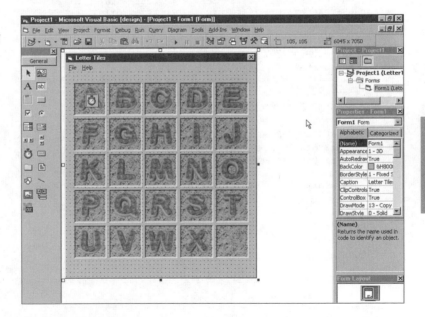

Adding the Program code

Type the following source code for the Letter Tiles program into the form's code window. If you'd rather not type, paste the source code from the LetterTiles.txt file (found in the Chap05\Code folder of this book's CD-ROM. Remember to save the form file often, if you're typing it in.

```
'===================================================
' Letter Tiles for Visual Basic 6
'    by Clayton Walnum
' Copyright 2000 by Macmillan Computer Publishing
'===================================================
Option Explicit


'===================================================
' Constants.
'===================================================
Const MAXCOL = 5
Const MAXROW = 5
Const NUMOFTILES = MAXCOL * MAXROW
Const BLANKTILE = 24
Const SPACEBETWEENTILES = 10
Const TILEWIDTH = 64
Const TILEHEIGHT = 64
Const CELLHEIGHT = TILEHEIGHT + SPACEBETWEENTILES
Const CELLWIDTH = TILEWIDTH + SPACEBETWEENTILES
Const XOFFSET = 17
Const YOFFSET = 23
Const RIGHTBUTTON = 2
Const SHIFTANDCTRL = 3


'===================================================
' General Game Variables.
'===================================================
Dim Cheating As Boolean
Dim BlinkingTile As Integer
Dim GameOver As Boolean


'===================================================
' Form Handlers.
'===================================================
Private Sub Form_Load()
  InitGame
End Sub


'===================================================
' Initialization Routine.
'===================================================
Sub InitGame()
  ShuffleTiles
  Cheating = False
  GameOver = False
End Sub
```

```
'====================================================
' Image Control Handlers.
'====================================================
Private Sub imgLetters_Click(Index As Integer)
  If Not GameOver Then
    If CanSwapTiles(Index) Then
      Swap imgLetters(Index), imgLetters(BLANKTILE)
      If IsInRightPlace(Index) Then
        BlinkTile (Index)
        WaitForTimer
      End If
    End If
    CheckForEndOfGame
  End If
End Sub

Private Sub imgLetters_MouseDown(Index As Integer, _
    Button As Integer, Shift As Integer, _
    X As Single, Y As Single)
  If Index = BLANKTILE And Button = RIGHTBUTTON _
      And Shift = SHIFTANDCTRL Then
    Cheating = Not Cheating
    If Cheating Then
      MsgBox "Cheating mode on."
    Else
      MsgBox "Cheating mode off."
    End If
  End If
End Sub

'====================================================
' Timer Control Handler.
'====================================================
Private Sub Timer1_Timer()
  Static pic As Picture
  Static BlinkCount As Integer
  If BlinkCount Mod 2 = 0 Then
    Set pic = imgLetters(BlinkingTile).Picture
    Set imgLetters(BlinkingTile).Picture = _
        imgLetters(BLANKTILE).Picture
  Else
    Set imgLetters(BlinkingTile).Picture = pic
  End If
  BlinkCount = BlinkCount + 1
  If BlinkCount = 6 Then
    BlinkCount = 0
    Timer1.Interval = 0
  End If
End Sub
```

5

```
'===================================================
' Menu Handlers.
'===================================================
Private Sub mnuNewGame_Click()
  InitGame
End Sub

Private Sub mnuExit_Click()
  Unload Form1
End Sub

Private Sub mnuAbout_Click()
  MsgBox "Letter Tiles" & vbCrLf & "by Clayton Walnum" & _
      vbCrLf & vbCrLf & "Copyright 2000" & vbCrLf & _
      "by Macmillan Computer Publishing", vbInformation, _
      "About Letter Tiles"
End Sub


'===================================================
' General Game Subroutines.
'===================================================
Sub Swap(img1 As Image, img2 As Image)
  Dim Left As Integer, Top As Integer
  Left = img1.Left
  Top = img1.Top
  img1.Move img2.Left, img2.Top
  img2.Left = Left
  img2.Top = Top
End Sub

Sub CheckForEndOfGame()
  Dim i As Integer
  GameOver = True
  For i = 0 To NUMOFTILES - 1
    If Not IsInRightPlace(i) Then GameOver = False
  Next i
  If GameOver Then
    DoWinningAnimation
    MsgBox "You win!"
  End If
End Sub

Sub DoWinningAnimation()
  Dim i As Integer
  For i = 0 To 10
    ShuffleTiles
    DisplayInOrder
  Next i
End Sub
```

```
Sub ShuffleTiles()
  Dim i As Integer
  Dim Index As Integer
  Randomize
  For i = 0 To NUMOFTILES - 1
    Index = Int(Rnd * (NUMOFTILES - 1))
    Swap imgLetters(i), imgLetters(Index)
  Next i
End Sub

Sub DisplayInOrder()
  Dim i As Integer
  Dim Top As Integer, Left As Integer
  Dim Column As Integer, Row As Integer
  For i = 0 To NUMOFTILES - 1
    Column = i Mod MAXCOL
    Row = i \ MAXCOL
    Left = Column * CELLWIDTH + XOFFSET
    Top = Row * CELLHEIGHT + YOFFSET
    imgLetters(i).Left = Left
    imgLetters(i).Top = Top
  Next i
End Sub

Sub BlinkTile(Index As Integer)
  BlinkingTile = Index
  Timer1.Interval = 100
End Sub

Sub WaitForTimer()
  While Timer1.Interval <> 0
    DoEvents
  Wend
End Sub

'===================================================
' Game Functions.
'===================================================
Function CanSwapTiles(Index As Integer) As Boolean
  If BlankIsAbove(Index) Or BlankIsBelow(Index) Or _
     BlankIsLeft(Index) Or BlankIsRight(Index) Then
    CanSwapTiles = True
  Else
    CanSwapTiles = False
  End If
  If Cheating Then CanSwapTiles = True
End Function

Function BlankIsAbove(Index As Integer) As Boolean
  If imgLetters(Index).Top = _
     imgLetters(BLANKTILE).Top + CELLHEIGHT And _
```

5

```
      imgLetters(Index).Left = imgLetters(BLANKTILE).Left Then
    BlankIsAbove = True
  Else
    BlankIsAbove = False
  End If
End Function

Function BlankIsBelow(Index As Integer) As Boolean
  If imgLetters(Index).Top = _
     imgLetters(BLANKTILE).Top - CELLHEIGHT And _
     imgLetters(Index).Left = imgLetters(BLANKTILE).Left Then
    BlankIsBelow = True
  Else
    BlankIsBelow = False
  End If
End Function

Function BlankIsLeft(Index As Integer) As Boolean
  If imgLetters(Index).Left = _
     imgLetters(BLANKTILE).Left + CELLWIDTH And _
     imgLetters(Index).Top = imgLetters(BLANKTILE).Top Then
    BlankIsLeft = True
  Else
    BlankIsLeft = False
  End If
End Function

Function BlankIsRight(Index As Integer) As Boolean
  If imgLetters(Index).Left = _
     imgLetters(BLANKTILE).Left - CELLWIDTH And _
     imgLetters(Index).Top = imgLetters(BLANKTILE).Top Then
    BlankIsRight = True
  Else
    BlankIsRight = False
  End If
End Function

Function IsInRightPlace(Index As Integer) As Boolean
  Dim Column As Integer, Row As Integer
  Dim Left As Integer, Top As Integer
  IsInRightPlace = False
  Column = Index Mod MAXCOL
  Row = Index \ MAXCOL
  Left = Column * CELLWIDTH + XOFFSET
  Top = Row * CELLHEIGHT + YOFFSET
  If imgLetters(Index).Left = Left And _
     imgLetters(Index).Top = Top Then _
    IsInRightPlace = True
End Function
```

Understanding Letter Tiles

Now that you know how to the program operates, take a look at the code, starting with the game's constants and variables.

Letter Tiles' Variables and Constants

Letter Tiles relies on a set of global variables and constants that the program declares near the top of the program. Table 5.6 lists the general global variables and their descriptions, and Table 5.7 lists the constants.

TABLE 5.6 Letter Tiles' General Game Variables

Variable	Type	Description
BlinkingTile	Integer	The index of the image control that is to blink
Cheating	Boolean	A flag that indicates whether the game is currently in the cheat mode
GameOver	Boolean	A flag that indicates whether the current game has ended

TABLE 5.7 Letter Tiles' Constants

Constant	Description
BLANKTILE	The index of the image control that displays the blank tile
CELLHEIGHT	The height in pixels of each cell in the display grid
CELLWIDTH	The width in pixels of each cell in the display grid
MAXCOL	The maximum number of columns in the letter-tile grid
MAXROW	The maximum number of rows in the letter-tile grid
NUMOFTILES	The number of tiles in the grid
RIGHTBUTTON	The integer value that represents a right button click
SHIFTANDCTRL	The integer value that represents that both the Shift and Ctrl keys are being held down
SPACEBETWEENTILES	The amount of space between tiles in the grid
TILEHEIGHT	The height in pixels of a tile
TILEWIDTH	The width in pixels of a tile
XOFFSET	The position, from the left of the window, of the first tile
YOFFSET	The position, from the top of the window, of the first tile

5

Starting the Game

Now let's see how all that game source code works. As always, when the game starts, Visual Basic calls the Form object's Form_Load subroutine, which does nothing more than call the subroutine InitGame:

```
Private Sub Form_Load()
  InitGame
End Sub
```

Listing 5.4 shows the InitGame subroutine.

LISTING 5.4   The InitGame Subroutine

```
1: Sub InitGame()
2:    ShuffleTiles
3:    Cheating = False
4:    GameOver = False
5: End Sub
```

ANALYSIS The InitGame subroutine simply calls ShuffleTiles (Line 2) to mix the letter tiles up, and then it sets the Cheating and GameOver flags to false (Lines 3 and 4).

Thanks to the Image controls in which the program displays the letter images, scrambling the tiles is just a matter of moving the Image controls themselves around, as shown in Listing 5.5. You don't even want to know how tough this little operation would be in a language like C++!

LISTING 5.5   The ShuffleTiles Subroutine

```
1: Sub ShuffleTiles()
2:    Dim i As Integer
3:    Dim Index As Integer
4:    Randomize
5:    For i = 0 To NUMOFTILES - 1
6:       Index = Int(Rnd * (NUMOFTILES - 1))
7:       Swap imgLetters(i), imgLetters(Index)
8:    Next i
9: End Sub
```

ANALYSIS Line 4 randomizes the random-number generator. Line 5 starts a For loop that iterates through the Image controls. Line 6 gets a random tile number, and Line 7 swaps the currently indexed control with the randomly indexed control.

Note that it's actually the Swap subroutine that moves the Image controls. That subroutine looks like Listing 5.6.

LISTING 5.6 The Swap Subroutine

```
1: Sub Swap(img1 As Image, img2 As Image)
2:   Dim Left As Integer, Top As Integer
3:   Left = img1.Left
4:   Top = img1.Top
5:   img1.Move img2.Left, img2.Top
6:   img2.Left = Left
7:   img2.Top = Top
8: End Sub
```

ANALYSIS As you can see here, moving an Image control is as easy as calling its Move method (Line 5) or setting its Left and Top properties (Lines 6 and 7). Either method works fine.

Enabling the Player to Move Tiles

Now the game is ready to go. The user can start clicking on tiles in order to swap them with the blank tile. When the user clicks a tile, Visual Basic calls the imgLetters_Click event handler, shown in Listing 5.7.

LISTING 5.7 The imgLetters_Click Event Procedure

```
 1:  Private Sub imgLetters_Click(Index As Integer)
 2:    If Not GameOver Then
 3:      If CanSwapTiles(Index) Then
 4:        Swap imgLetters(Index), imgLetters(BLANKTILE)
 5:        If IsInRightPlace(Index) Then
 6:          BlinkTile (Index)
 7:          WaitForTimer
 8:        End If
 9:      End If
10:      CheckForEndOfGame
11:    End If
12: End Sub
```

ANALYSIS This subroutine first checks the GameOver flag (Line 2). If GameOver is True, the game is over and the player isn't allowed to move tiles until he starts a new game. If GameOver is False, it's okay for the player to move a tile but the program must check whether the clicked tile is able to move (Line 3). Remember that only a tile adjacent to the blank tile (not counting diagonals) can move. The CanSwapTiles function returns True if the move is legal. If CanSwapTiles returns True, the move is legal and a call to Swap (Line 4) does the deed. Next, the function IsInRightPlace checks whether the player has moved the tile into its correct position (Line 5). If this function returns

5

True, the `BlinkTile` subroutine blinks the tile and the `WaitForTimer` subroutine ensures that the blinking finishes before the program moves on (Lines 6 and 7). Finally, the subroutine ends by calling `CheckForEndOfGame` (Line 10), which ends the game if the player has positioned all the tiles correctly.

 Note   Because `imgLetters` is not a single Image control but rather an array of 25 controls, the `imgLetters_Click` event handler receives as a parameter a value that specifies the index of the clicked control.

Let's look at the other functions that are called from within `imgLetters_Click`. First is `CanSwapTiles` (see Listing 5.8), which determines whether the clicked tile is able to move.

LISTING 5.8   The `CanSwapTiles` Function

```
1: Function CanSwapTiles(Index As Integer) As Boolean
2:   If BlankIsAbove(Index) Or BlankIsBelow(Index) Or _
3:      BlankIsLeft(Index) Or BlankIsRight(Index) Then
4:     CanSwapTiles = True
5:   Else
6:     CanSwapTiles = False
7:   End If
8:   If Cheating Then CanSwapTiles = True
9: End Function
```

ANALYSIS   The `CanSwapTiles` function must figure out whether the clicked tile is above, below, to the left, or to the right of the blank tile. Although this process isn't particularly hard, it does require a messy set of checks. To simplify what would be a ridiculously complex and completely unreadable `If` statement, `CanSwapTiles` calls the functions `BlankIsAbove`, `BlankIsBelow`, `BlankIsLeft`, and `BlankIsRight` (Lines 2 and 3). These functions do all the location checking so that `CanSwapTiles` has a nice, clean, and understandable `If` statement. (For now, ignore the `If` statement with the `Cheating` flag.)

The `BlankIsAbove`, `BlankIsBelow`, `BlankIsLeft`, and `BlankIsRight` functions all work similarly, so we'll examine only one, `BlankIsAbove`, shown in Listing 5.9.

LISTING 5.9   The `BlankIsAbove` Function

```
1: Function BlankIsAbove(Index As Integer) As Boolean
2:   If imgLetters(Index).Top = _
3:      imgLetters(BLANKTILE).Top + CELLHEIGHT And _
4:      imgLetters(Index).Left = imgLetters(BLANKTILE).Left Then
```

```
5:      BlankIsAbove = True
6:   Else
7:      BlankIsAbove = False
8:   End If
9: End Function
```

ANALYSIS In order to determine whether the blank tile is above the clicked tile, `BlankIsAbove` must compare the positions of the two tiles. First, the `Left` properties of the blank tile and the clicked tile must be the same (Line 4). Second, the clicked tile's `Top` property must be one grid cell higher than the blank tile's `Top` property (Lines 2 and 3). If both of these conditions are true, the blank tile is above the clicked tile.

As you now know, the `IsInRightPlace` function determines whether the player has moved a tile into its correct location in the grid. `IsInRightPlace` looks like Listing 5.10.

LISTING 5.10   The `IsInRightPlace` Function

```
1:  Function IsInRightPlace(Index As Integer) As Boolean
2:     Dim Column As Integer, Row As Integer
3:     Dim Left As Integer, Top As Integer
4:     IsInRightPlace = False
5:     Column = Index Mod MAXCOL
6:     Row = Index \ MAXCOL
7:     Left = Column * CELLWIDTH + XOFFSET
8:     Top = Row * CELLHEIGHT + YOFFSET
9:     If imgLetters(Index).Left = Left And _
10:        imgLetters(Index).Top = Top Then _
11:      IsInRightPlace = True
12: End Function
```

5

ANALYSIS Because the Image controls in the control array are in alphabetical order, the program can use the Image control indexes to calculate where the tiles belong in the grid. The `IsInRightPlace` function first calculates the column and row where the tile belongs (Lines 5 and 6). It then converts the column and row values to pixel coordinates (Lines 7 and 8). If these pixel coordinates match the Image control's `Left` and `Top` properties, the image is in its correct position (Lines 9 through 11).

To blink a tile, the `BlinkTile` subroutine sets the `BlinkingTile` variable to the tile's index and then starts the Timer control ticking:

```
Sub BlinkTile(Index As Integer)
  BlinkingTile = Index
  Timer1.Interval = 100
End Sub
```

It's the Timer control's `Timer` event handler that blinks the tile as shown in Listing 5.11.

LISTING 5.11 The Timer1_Timer Event Procedure

```
1:  Private Sub Timer1_Timer()
2:    Static pic As Picture
3:    Static BlinkCount As Integer
4:    If BlinkCount Mod 2 = 0 Then
5:      Set pic = imgLetters(BlinkingTile).Picture
6:      Set imgLetters(BlinkingTile).Picture = _
7:          imgLetters(BLANKTILE).Picture
8:    Else
9:      Set imgLetters(BlinkingTile).Picture = pic
10:   End If
11:   BlinkCount = BlinkCount + 1
12:   If BlinkCount = 6 Then
13:     BlinkCount = 0
14:     Timer1.Interval = 0
15:   End If
16: End Sub
```

ANALYSIS   The program declares the pic and BlinkCount variables as Static (Lines 2 and 3) so that they will retain their values even after the Timer1_Timer event handler exits. Timer1_Timer gets called once every 100 milliseconds, as specified by its Interval property, which was set by the BlinkTile subroutine. Every time it's called, Timer1_Timer checks whether BlinkCount is odd or even (Line 4). If it's even, the program stores the Image control's picture in the pic variable and sets the Image control's picture to the picture contained in the blank tile (Lines 5 through 7). If BlinkCount is odd, the program restores the Image control's picture (Line 9). This switching between the blank picture and the letter picture makes the tile blink. After switching pictures, Line 11 increments BlinkCount. When BlinkCount reaches 6 (Line 12), the program resets it to 0 and turns off the timer by setting the Timer control's Interval property to 0 (Lines 13 and 14).

The WaitForTimer subroutine (see Listing 5.12) puts the program to sleep until the Timer control has finished blinking the tile.

LISTING 5.12 The WaitForTimer Subroutine

```
1: Sub WaitForTimer()
2:   While Timer1.Interval <> 0
3:     DoEvents
4:   Wend
5: End Sub
```

ANALYSIS `WaitForTimer` is nothing more than a loop that continually checks the value of the Timer control's `Interval` property. When `Interval` is 0, the Timer control has finished its task and the loop ends, enabling the program to continue. Notice the call to `DoEvents` in Line 3. Without this call, not only won't the program be able to receive timer events, but the entire Windows system will come to a screeching halt.

Ending the Game

Every time the player moves a tile, the program must check whether the game is over. The game is over when all the tiles are in their correct positions in the grid, of course. And in case you can't tell by its name, the `CheckForEndOfGame` subroutine (see Listing 5.13) determines when the game is over.

LISTING 5.13 The `CheckForEndOfGame` Subroutine

```
 1: Sub CheckForEndOfGame()
 2:   Dim i As Integer
 3:   GameOver = True
 4:   For i = 0 To NUMOFTILES - 1
 5:     If Not IsInRightPlace(i) Then GameOver = False
 6:   Next i
 7:   If GameOver Then
 8:     DoWinningAnimation
 9:     MsgBox "You win!"
10:   End If
11: End Sub
```

ANALYSIS `CheckForEndOfGame` calls the `IsInRightPlace` function on behalf of every tile in the grid (Lines 4 through 6). If all the tiles are in the right place, the `GameOver` flag ends up being `True`. In that case, the `DoWinningAnimation` subroutine (Line 8) performs a little soft-shoe shuffle with the tiles.

Listing 5.14 shows the `DoWinningAnimation` and `DisplayInOrder` subroutines.

LISTING 5.14 The `DoWinningAnimation` and `DisplayInOrder` Subroutines

```
 1: Sub DoWinningAnimation()
 2:   Dim i As Integer
 3:   For i = 0 To 10
 4:     ShuffleTiles
 5:     DisplayInOrder
 6:   Next i
 7: End Sub
 8:
 9: Sub DisplayInOrder()
```

5

LISTING 5.14   continued

```
10:   Dim i As Integer
11:   Dim Top As Integer, Left As Integer
12:   Dim Column As Integer, Row As Integer
13:   For i = 0 To NUMOFTILES - 1
14:     Column = i Mod MAXCOL
15:     Row = i \ MAXCOL
16:     Left = Column * CELLWIDTH + XOFFSET
17:     Top = Row * CELLHEIGHT + YOFFSET
18:     imgLetters(i).Left = Left
19:     imgLetters(i).Top = Top
20:   Next i
21: End Sub
```

ANALYSIS   In DoWinningAnimation, Lines 3 through 6 shuffle and unshuffle the letters 11 times, which is all it takes to create the winning animation. The DisplayInOrder subroutine uses a For loop (Line 13) to iterate through each of the letter images. Inside the loop, Lines 14 and 15 determine the column and row in which the current letter belongs, and Lines 16 and 17 convert the column and row to pixel coordinates. Finally, Lines 18 and 19 move the letter to its correct position.

Creating a Game Cheat

Computer game cheat codes are the latest big thing. You might think that creating game cheats is just another way for programmers to stir up interest in their products, but that's a major oversimplification. The truth is that programmers create game cheats to help them when they're programming and testing a game. A programmer doesn't want to start a game from the beginning every time just to get to a part that needs testing. He wants to jump directly to that part, complete with whatever game statistics must be set to enable him to test a situation.

In case you didn't notice, Letter Tiles can be a difficult puzzle to solve. Getting that last row in order is especially tough. For this reason, Letter Tiles includes its very own cheat code. You can turn the cheat mode on and off by holding down the Shift and Ctrl keys while right-clicking the blank tile. When the cheat mode is on, any tile in the grid can be swapped with the blank tile, not just adjacent tiles. The imgLetters_MouseDown event procedure implements the cheat, as shown in Listing 5.15.

LISTING 5.15   The imgLetters_MouseDown Event Procedure

```
1:   Private Sub imgLetters_MouseDown(Index As Integer, _
2:       Button As Integer, Shift As Integer, _
3:       X As Single, Y As Single)
```

```
4:    If Index = BLANKTILE And Button = RIGHTBUTTON _
5:        And Shift = SHIFTANDCTRL Then
6:      Cheating = Not Cheating
7:      If Cheating Then
8:        MsgBox "Cheating mode on."
9:      Else
10:       MsgBox "Cheating mode off."
11:     End If
12:   End If
13: End Sub
```

ANALYSIS   This subroutine simply checks that the blank tile is being clicked by the right mouse button and that the Shift and Ctrl keys are held down (Lines 4 and 5). If the proper conditions have been met, Line 6 toggles the value of the Cheating flag. The Not operator reverses the value of a Boolean expression. So, if Cheating is False, Not Cheating is True, and vice versa (see Listing 5.16). The single line Cheating = Not Cheating replaces this longer If statement.

LISTING 5.16   Toggling a Flag the Long Way

```
1: If Cheating Then
2:    Cheating = False
3: Else
4:    Cheating = True
5: End If
```

If the Cheating flag is True, the CanSwapTiles function always returns True, meaning that any tile can be swapped with the blank tile. Ain't cheating fun?

Summary

Visual Basic's Image and PictureBox controls make manipulating images almost child's play. Using these controls, you can easily perform image manipulations that would require the knowledge of an expert graphics programmer in other languages.

Q&A

Q **What if I need to do some kind of image manipulation that can't be handled well in Visual Basic with an Image or PictureBox control?**

A There's good news, bad news, and more good news. The good news is that you can always call upon the Windows API when you want to sidestep Visual Basic for a complex task. The bad news is that such a sidestep can be difficult if you're not familiar with Windows programming in C or C++. The other good news is that the next chapter gives you some hands-on experience with the Windows API's graphical functions.

Q If I set a control's `Picture` property at runtime by calling `LoadPicture`, I understand that I will have to include the picture file to load. Does this mean that anyone can change the appearance of the program by editing the image files that the program loads?

A Yep. Giving your game's players such power might or might not be a good thing. Players love to customize games, but you have to make sure that they can't change graphics that might affect how the game runs or that mess up the basic game display.

Q What's with these drawing modes that I can use with the `PaintPicture` method?

A There are really only a few drawing modes that are useful to a games programmer. You'll learn about them later in this book when you discover how to animate sprites.

Q Is it possible to use the `PaintPicture` method to flip a picture upside down or sideways?

A Sure is. All you have to do is use negative coordinates for the height or width.

Workshop

The workshop includes quiz questions to help gauge your grasp of the material. You'll find the answers to this quiz in Appendix A. Even if you feel that you totally understand the concepts presented here, you should work through the quiz anyway. The last section is an exercise to help reinforce your learning.

Quiz

1. What is a significant difference between the Image and PictureBox controls?
2. Which Image control property enables the control to scale pictures?
3. What are two ways to move and resize an Image or PictureBox control?
4. When is it impossible to resize an Image control?
5. What are two techniques for loading a picture into a control?
6. Which of the two graphical controls can act as a drawing surface?
7. Is it possible to scale a picture in a PictureBox control?

Exercise

1. Modify the Stretch3 program so that the PictureBox control displays the A.jpg picture file cut into two equal pieces when the user clicks the control. (Hint: You'll need the `PaintPicture` method.)

DAY 6

Graphics Programming with the Windows API

Although Visual Basic features powerful and flexible graphical objects, such as the Image and PictureBox controls, there might be times when you want even more flexibility. For example, Visual Basic provides the `PSet` and `Point` commands for manipulating individual pixels in an image, but these methods are slow compared with handling images through the Windows API. In this chapter, you'll learn to use the Windows API's graphical functions:

- The steps required to call a Windows API function
- Windows API functions that draw lines
- Windows API functions that draw shapes
- How to modify a Visual Basic object's bitmap through the Windows API
- How to handle the different bitmap pixel formats

Calling the Windows API

To take advantage of Windows' graphical functions, you first need to know how to call Windows API (Application Programming Interface) functions from Visual Basic. This might seem like a tricky task at first, but thanks to the tools supplied with Visual Basic, it's an easy three-step process:

1. Provide a declaration for the Windows API function you want to call.
2. Provide declarations for any data types required by the Windows API function.
3. Call the Windows API function.

In the following sections, you'll take a closer look at each of these steps.

Provide the Windows API Function Declaration

Visual Basic knows nothing about the Windows API functions—it can process its own methods, such as `PaintPicture` and `PSet`, but it doesn't know what to do with Windows functions like `GetObject()` or `GetBitmapBits()`. That's not to say that Visual Basic can't call these Windows functions (if that were the case, we wouldn't be having this discussion). However, you must give Visual Basic the information it needs to call these functions by adding their declarations to your program's source code.

Providing such a declaration can be difficult or easy, depending on your method. The difficult way requires looking up the function you want in a Windows programming reference, figuring out how to translate the C argument types into Visual Basic types, and then coding the function declaration. This process requires a lot of knowledge about both C and Visual Basic, and it's prone to errors. The first time you try to run a program with such a function declaration and call, I'm willing to bet that you'll see the system come to a crashing halt.

More than likely, you'll prefer the easy method, which involves using the handy tools that Microsoft so graciously supplies. (Okay, maybe not graciously; you did pay for them, after all.) There are two files you need to locate in your Visual Basic installation: Win32api.txt and Apiload.exe. The default location for these files is Program Files\Microsoft Visual Studio\Common\Tools\Winapi.

The Win32api.txt file contains ready-to-use Visual Basic declarations for Windows API functions, data types, and constants. Apiload.exe is the executable file for a handy (that's an understatement) program called API Viewer, which enables you to quickly locate and copy the information you need from the Win32api.txt file. If you're going to call a lot of Windows API functions in your programs, you'll want to create a shortcut to Apiload.exe on your desktop or taskbar so you have quick access to this invaluable program.

When you run Apiload.exe, you'll see the window shown in Figure 6.1. To begin, you must first load the Win32api.txt file into the program by selecting the File menu's Load

Text File command and then selecting the Win32api.txt file. The available selections in the file will appear in API Viewer's Available Items box. The setting you choose (Declares, Constants, or Types) from the API Type box will determine what actually appears in the VAI box.

FIGURE 6.1

The API Viewer application when it's first run.

Suppose that you want to find the Visual Basic declaration of the Windows API function CreateBitmap(). First, set the API Type box to Declares, and then type the first few letters of the function in the next box down. (This causes the available items list to scroll down to the location of the desired function.) Highlight the appropriate function and click the Add button (or just double-click the function's name). The function's Visual Basic declaration appears in the Selected Items box, as shown in Figure 6.2. You can paste the function into your Visual Basic source code from the Clipboard after clicking the Copy button to copy the declaration.

FIGURE 6.2

The API Viewer application showing a function declaration.

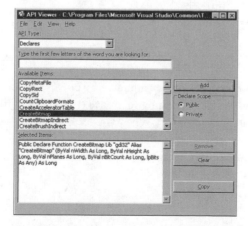

6

Provide the Windows API Type Declarations

If you examine the Visual Basic declaration for a Windows API function, you might discover curious data types such as the GetObject() declaration:

```
Public Declare Function GetObject Lib "gdi32" Alias "GetObjectA" _
  (ByVal hObject As Long, ByVal nCount As Long, lpObject As Any) As Long
```

The first two arguments are long values. Nothing to be concerned with there. But the third argument has the data type Any. As a Visual Basic programmer, you know that the Any keyword means that the function will accept any type of argument without checking the value passed for it. (This is similar to the C and C++ void pointer type of argument.) The Windows API function, however, needs a specific data type for this argument, depending on how the function is being used. For example, to get information about a bitmap, the GetObject() function's third argument must be a pointer to a BITMAP structure, which you can locate using API Viewer. That structure, in Visual Basic form, looks like Listing 6.1.

LISTING 6.1   The BITMAP Structure

```
1: Public Type BITMAP '14 bytes
2:          bmType As Long
3:          bmWidth As Long
4:          bmHeight As Long
5:          bmWidthBytes As Long
6:          bmPlanes As Integer
7:          bmBitsPixel As Integer
8:          bmBits As Long
9: End Type
```

How do you know the data type for this argument? You have to look up the Windows API function in a Windows programming reference (a Windows programming book or the help that comes with Visual Basic). When you look up GetObject(), you'll then see that the function requires a pointer to different types of values depending upon the type of object for which you need information. To get information about a bitmap, you must supply a pointer to a BITMAP structure.

Call the Windows API Function

Now that you have all the pieces of the puzzle, you can call the Windows API function. For example, here's a short program you can find on this book's CD-ROM, under the name GetBitmap. It acquires and displays the width and height of a PictureBox control's picture, as shown in Listing 6.2.

LISTING 6.2   Displaying the Width and Height of a Picture

```
 1:  Option Explicit
 2:
 3:  Private Type BITMAP '14 bytes
 4:     bmType As Long
 5:     bmWidth As Long
 6:     bmHeight As Long
 7:     bmWidthBytes As Long
 8:     bmPlanes As Integer
 9:     bmBitsPixel As Integer
10:     bmBits As Long
11:  End Type
12:
13:  Private Declare Function GetObject Lib "gdi32" _
14:      Alias "GetObjectA" (ByVal hObject As Long, _
15:      ByVal nCount As Long, lpObject As Any) As Long
16:
17:  Private Sub Form_Load()
18:     Dim bmp As BITMAP
19:
20:     GetObject Picture1.Image, Len(bmp), bmp
21:     MsgBox "Width: " & bmp.bmWidth & vbCrLf & _
22:         "Height: " & bmp.bmHeight
23:  End Sub
```

ANALYSIS   Lines 3 through 11 declare the BITMAP structure needed by the Windows API GetObject() function. Lines 13 through 15 declare the GetObject() function, Line 20 calls the function, and Lines 21 and 22 display values from the BITMAP structure, which was filled in by the call to GetObject().

You'll learn more about the GetObject() function and other wonders of the Windows API throughout the rest of this chapter.

6

Note   You must be comfortable with Windows programming techniques before you can take advantage of the Windows API. Otherwise, you can use the examples in this chapter as a starting point, but you still need to pick up a good Windows programming book for reference.

Drawing with the Windows API

In earlier chapters, you learned how to use Visual Basic's drawing commands to create displays for your games. Although these commands are powerful enough for most of the things you'll want to do, there may come a time when you wish you had some of the graphical power of the Windows API. Not to worry! Now that you know how to call Windows API functions, you can certainly call upon the many graphical ones.

The Windows API is worth bothering with to draw game displays because it offers more drawing functions than Visual Basic. For example, the Polyline() Windows API function can draw a whole series of lines with a single function call. Also, many of the API functions are faster than their Visual Basic counterparts. You might find that the Windows API is the only way to do more complex drawing. The following sections are a quick primer on Windows API drawing functions.

Drawing Lines with the Windows API

The most common way to draw straight lines with Windows API is to use the MoveToEx() and LineTo() functions. Like setting a Visual Basic object's CurrentX and CurrentY properties, MoveToEx() determines the starting point of a drawing operation. It looks like this:

```
Public Declare Function MoveToEx Lib "gdi32" Alias _
   "MoveToEx" (ByVal hdc As Long, ByVal x As Long, _
   ByVal y As Long, lpPoint As POINTAPI) As Long
```

This function requires four arguments. The hdc argument is a handle to the device context for the object. Visual Basic objects that support device contexts have a hDC property, which is the handle you need for this function. The x and y arguments are the coordinates of the location where the objects move. Finally, the lpPoint argument is a POINTAPI structure, which is where the function call will store the previous X and Y points. The structure's definition looks like this:

```
Private Type POINTAPI
   x As Long
   y As Long
End Type
```

 A *device context* is a collection of attributes that describe a graphical device, including color depth, image size, pen color, brush type, and so on.

The LineTo() API function actually draws the line. Its Visual Basic declaration looks like this:

```
Public Declare Function LineTo Lib "gdi32" Alias _
   "LineTo" (ByVal hdc As Long, ByVal x As Long, _
   ByVal y As Long) As Long
```

The function's three arguments are the device context handle and the X and Y coordinates of the line's ending point. The line's starting point is the previous line's ending point or the location set by a call to MoveToEx().

 Note

> If you don't need to receive the previous point from the MoveToEx() function, declare the fourth argument as Any, rather than as POINTAPI, and pass vbNullString as the argument's value.

This book's CD-ROM contains the WinLines application, which uses the Windows API MoveToEx() and LineTo() functions to draw lines in a PictureBox control. When you run the application, you'll see the window shown in Figure 6.3. The source code looks like Listing 6.3.

LISTING 6.3 The WinLines Application

```
 1: Option Explicit
 2:
 3: Private Type POINTAPI
 4:    x As Long
 5:    y As Long
 6: End Type
 7:
 8: Private Declare Function MoveToEx Lib "gdi32" _
 9:    (ByVal hdc As Long, ByVal x As Long, _
10:    ByVal y As Long, lpPoint As POINTAPI) As Long
11:
12: Private Declare Function LineTo Lib "gdi32" _
13:    (ByVal hdc As Long, ByVal x As Long, _
14:    ByVal y As Long) As Long
15:
16: Private Sub Form_Load()
17:    Dim PrevPoint As POINTAPI
18:    Dim i As Integer
19:    Picture1.AutoRedraw = True
20:    Picture1.ScaleMode = vbPixels
21:    For i = 1 To 90
22:       MoveToEx Picture1.hdc, 20, i * 3 + 5, PrevPoint
23:       LineTo Picture1.hdc, 400, i * 3 + 5
24:    Next i
25: End Sub
```

6

ANALYSIS Lines 3 through 6 declare the POINTAPI structure needed by the Windows API MoveToEx() function. Lines 8 through 14 declare the MoveToEx() and LineTo() Windows API functions, and Lines 22 and 23 call the functions to draw lines on the screen.

FIGURE 6.3

The WinLines *application.*

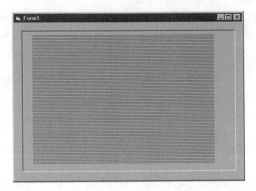

Another way to draw lines is with the Polyline() function, whose Visual Basic declaration looks like this:

```
Public Declare Function Polyline Lib "gdi32" Alias _
   "Polyline" (ByVal hdc As Long, lpPoint As POINTAPI, _
   ByVal nCount As Long) As Long
```

This function's arguments are the device context handle, an array of POINTAPI structures, and the number of points in the array. Each point in the array describes one point in the set of lines that Polyline() will draw. The drawing starts at the first point in the array, with a line being drawn between each of the remaining points.

This book's CD-ROM contains the Polyline application, which uses the Windows API Polyline() function to draw a design in a PictureBox control. When you run the application, you'll see the window shown in Figure 6.4. The program's source code looks like Listing 6.4.

LISTING 6.4   The Polyline Application

```
1:  Option Explicit
2:
3:  Const MAXPOINTS = 100
4:
5:  Private Type POINTAPI
6:     x As Long
7:     y As Long
8:  End Type
9:
10: Private Declare Function Polyline Lib "gdi32" _
11:    (ByVal hdc As Long, lpPoint As POINTAPI, _
12:    ByVal nCount As Long) As Long
13:
14: Private Sub Form_Load()
15:    Dim Points(1 To MAXPOINTS) As POINTAPI
```

```
16:    Dim i As Integer
17:    Picture1.AutoRedraw = True
18:    Picture1.ScaleMode = vbPixels
19:    For i = 1 To MAXPOINTS Step 2
20:       Points(i).x = i * 4 + 10
21:       Points(i).y = 10
22:       Points(i + 1).x = i * 2 + 10
23:       Points(i + 1).y = 200
24:    Next i
25:    Polyline Picture1.hdc, Points(1),  MAXPOINTS
26: End Sub
```

ANALYSIS Lines 5 through 9 declare the POINTAPI structure needed by the Windows API Polyline() function. Lines 10 through 12 declare the Polyline() function, Lines 19 through 24 initialize the Points() array with line coordinates, and Line 25 calls Polyline() to draw the lines.

FIGURE 6.4

The Polyline application.

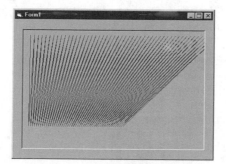

Drawing Shapes with the Windows API

The Windows API also features functions for drawing various types of shapes, including rectangles, ellipses (ovals and circles), and even polygons. The function that draws rectangles is called Rectangle(), and its Visual Basic declaration looks like this:

```
Private Declare Function Rectangle Lib "gdi32" _
  (ByVal hdc As Long, ByVal X1 As Long, ByVal Y1 As Long, _
  ByVal X2 As Long, ByVal Y2 As Long) As Long
```

This function requires as arguments the device context handle, the X and Y coordinates of the rectangle's upper-left corner, and the X and Y coordinates of the rectangle's lower-right corner.

This book's CD-ROM contains the Rectangles application, which uses the Windows API Rectangle() function to draw a design in a PictureBox control. When you run the application, you'll see the window shown in Figure 6.5. The program's source code looks like Listing 6.5.

6

LISTING 6.5   The Rectangles Application

```
1:  Option Explicit
2:
3:  Private Declare Function Rectangle Lib "gdi32" _
4:    (ByVal hdc As Long, ByVal X1 As Long, ByVal Y1 As Long, _
5:    ByVal X2 As Long, ByVal Y2 As Long) As Long
6:
7:  Private Sub Form_Load()
8:    Dim i As Integer
9:    Picture1.ScaleMode = vbPixels
10:   Picture1.AutoRedraw = True
11:   For i = 1 To 10
12:     Rectangle Picture1.hdc, i * 10 + 5, i * 10 + 5, _
13:         i * 5 + 100, i * 5 + 100
14:   Next i
15: End Sub
```

ANALYSIS Lines 3 through 5 declare Rectangle() function, and Lines 11 through 14 use the Rectangle() function to draw 10 rectangles.

FIGURE 6.5

The Rectangles appli-cation.

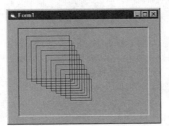

To draw a circle or oval, you can use the Windows API Ellipse() function with the following Visual Basic declaration:

```
Private Declare Function Ellipse Lib "gdi32" _
  (ByVal hdc As Long, ByVal X1 As Long, ByVal Y1 As Long, _
  ByVal X2 As Long, ByVal Y2 As Long) As Long
```

This function requires the same arguments as the Rectangle() function: the device context handle, the X and Y coordinates of the rectangle's upper-left corner, and the X and Y coordinates of the rectangle's lower-right corner. The function draws an ellipse that fits inside the specified rectangle.

This book's CD-ROM contains the Ellipse application, which uses the Windows API Ellipse()function to draw a design in a PictureBox control. When you run the application, you'll see the window shown in Figure 6.6. The program's source code looks like Listing 6.6.

LISTING 6.6 The Ellipse Application

```
1:  Option Explicit
2:
3:  Private Declare Function Ellipse Lib "gdi32" _
4:    (ByVal hdc As Long, ByVal X1 As Long, ByVal Y1 As Long, _
5:    ByVal X2 As Long, ByVal Y2 As Long) As Long
6:
7:  Private Sub Form_Load()
8:    Dim i As Integer
9:    Picture1.ScaleMode = vbPixels
10:   Picture1.AutoRedraw = True
11:   For i = 1 To 10
12:     Ellipse Picture1.hdc, i * 10 + 5, i * 10 + 5, _
13:         i * 5 + 100, i * 5 + 100
14:   Next i
15: End Sub
```

ANALYSIS Lines 3 through 5 declare Ellipse() function, and Lines 11 through 14 use the Ellipse() function to draw 10 ellipses.

FIGURE 6.6

The Ellipse application.

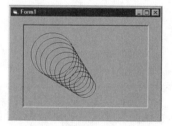

Another way to draw shapes is with the Polygon() function, whose Visual Basic declaration looks like this:

```
Public Declare Function Polygon Lib "gdi32" Alias "Polygon" _
  (ByVal hdc As Long, lpPoint As POINTAPI, _
  ByVal nCount As Long) As Long
```

This function's arguments are the same as those in the Polyline() function: the device context handle, an array of POINTAPI structures, and the number of points in the array. Each point in the array describes one point in the set of lines that Polygon() will draw. The drawing starts at the first point in the array, with a line being drawn between each of the remaining points. The function closes the polygon by drawing a line between the first and last points.

This book's CD-ROM contains the Polygon application, which uses the Windows API Polygon() function to draw a shape in a PictureBox control. When you run the application, you'll see the window shown in Figure 6.7. The source code looks like Listing 6.7.

6

LISTING 6.7 The Polygon Application

```
1:  Option Explicit
2:
3:  Private Type POINTAPI
4:     x As Long
5:     y As Long
6:  End Type
7:
8:  Private Declare Function Polygon Lib "gdi32" _
9:     (ByVal hdc As Long, lpPoint As POINTAPI, _
10:    ByVal nCount As Long) As Long
11:
12: Private Sub Form_Load()
13:    Dim Points(1 To 5) As POINTAPI
14:    Picture1.AutoRedraw = True
15:    Picture1.ScaleMode = vbPixels
16:    Points(1).x = 20
17:    Points(1).y = 20
18:    Points(2).x = 300
19:    Points(2).y = 30
20:    Points(3).x = 280
21:    Points(3).y = 200
22:    Points(4).x = 200
23:    Points(4).y = 150
24:    Points(5).x = 40
25:    Points(5).y = 100
26:    Polygon Picture1.hdc, Points(1), 5
27: End Sub
```

ANALYSIS Lines 3 through 6 declare the POINTAPI data type needed by the Polygon() function. Lines 8 through 10 declare the Polygon() Windows API function, Lines 16 through 25 initialize the coordinates for the polygon, and Line 26 calls Polygon() to draw the polygon.

FIGURE 6.7

The Polygon application.

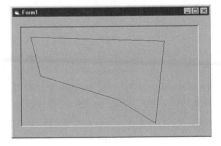

For a list of other useful Windows API functions, look at Appendix C, "Resources."

Manipulating a Control's Picture with the Windows API

When you set a form object or PictureBox control's `AutoRedraw` property to `True`, Windows will create a bitmap in memory. Whenever the form or PictureBox's display needs to be redrawn, Visual Basic will simply copy the bitmap from memory. This process is usually much faster than having to redraw the display command by command.

When Visual Basic creates such a bitmap in memory, it's called a *device-dependent bitmap (DDB)*. This bitmap is device-dependent because it can be displayed correctly only on the device for which it was created. In the case of Visual Basic forms and controls, the bitmap's display device is the screen. DDBs are usually found only in a computer's memory, rather than in the form as a disk file, because it usually doesn't make sense to load such an image from a file.

Visual Basic provides access to an object's bitmap through the object's `Image` property. The `Image` property is actually a *handle* to the bitmap. In Windows programming, you run into many handles, which are really little more than IDs for an object. Identifying an object with a handle rather than a pointer (a memory address) enables Windows to move things around in memory.

Once your program has access to an object's DDB, it can draw directly on the bitmap using Windows API functions, which are much faster than the Visual Basic equivalents. (This last statement assumes that Visual Basic even *has* an equivalent function. One advantage of using the Windows API is that you have many more graphical functions at your beck and call. Most of these functions do not have Visual Basic equivalents.)

There are four steps to drawing directly on a bitmap:

1. Obtain information about the bitmap.
2. Retrieve the bitmap data.
3. Modify the bitmap data.
4. Copy the data back to the bitmap.

Note You have to copy data to and from a bitmap because, as you already learned, Windows reserves the right to move data objects, including bitmaps, around in memory without your knowledge. Thus the need for handles.

6

Obtaining Bitmap Information

To obtain bitmap information, you must first get information about the bitmap you want to manipulate by calling the Windows API function GetObject(). (You've already had some experience with this function, but now you'll explore it in detail.) Here's the Visual Basic declaration for GetObject(), as copied from the API Viewer application:

```
Private Declare Function GetObject Lib "gdi32" _
    Alias "GetObjectA" (ByVal hObject As Long, _
    ByVal nCount As Long, lpObject As Any) As Long
```

Looking up GetObject() in your trusty Windows API reference, you discover that this function's arguments are described as follows:

- hObject—A handle to the graphical object.
- nCount—The number of bytes that will be written to the buffer given in the lpObject argument.
- lpObject—A pointer to the structure that will receive information about the object.

In the case of a bitmap, the hObject argument is equivalent to the Visual Basic object's Image property. The nCount argument is the size of a BITMAP structure, and lpObject is a pointer to the BITMAP structure. The BITMAP structure, as obtained from the API Viewer application, looks like Listing 6.8.

LISTING 6.8   The BITMAP Structure

```
1: Private Type BITMAP '14 bytes
2:    bmType As Long
3:    bmWidth As Long
4:    bmHeight As Long
5:    bmWidthBytes As Long
6:    bmPlanes As Integer
7:    bmBitsPixel As Integer
8:    bmBits As Long
9: End Type
```

Each of the BITMAP structure's fields (except bmType) contains useful information that you'll need to manipulate the bitmap. Here's a description of each of these fields:

- bmType — Always 0
- bmWidth — The bitmap's width in pixels
- bmHeight — The bitmap's height in pixels
- bmWidthBytes — The bitmap's width in bytes

- bmPlanes — The number of color planes in the bitmap
- bmBitsPixel — The number of bits required for each pixel of the image
- bmBits — A pointer to the bitmap's image data

Okay, now that you're thoroughly confused, let's examine this information in detail. First, you might wonder why the BITMAP structure describes the bitmap's width in two different ways, using the bmWidth and bmWidthBytes fields. The bmWidth field is the width of the bitmap in pixels. A pixel, of course, is a single dot of color in an image. If the bitmap is 35 dots wide, its bmWidth field will be set to 35 after calling GetObject().

Unfortunately, knowing the bitmap's pixel width isn't enough information to manipulate the bitmap. One complication is the graphics mode of the computer. Your system might be displaying its images in any one of the following common modes:

- 4-bit, 16-color
- 8-bit, 256-color
- 16-bit, High Color
- 24-bit, True Color
- 32-bit, True Color

If your computer is set to 16-bit color mode, each pixel in the image requires 16 bits, or two bytes. This means that if bmWidth is 35, bmWidthBytes will be 70. And if your computer is set to 24-bit color, each pixel requires 24 bits, or three bytes. So if bmWidth is 35, bmWidthBytes is 105, right?

Wrong. The last detail is that DDBs must have an even byte width. Therefore, in the case of the 35-pixel-wide image, the bitmap actually has a bmWidthBytes of 106—an extra byte is tacked onto each row of pixels in the image.

To demonstrate this little anomaly, set your system's color mode and run the Modes program you can find on this book's CD-ROM. A window will appear, showing the size of the application's PictureBox control and the size of its associated bitmap. For example, if you set your system to 256 colors and run the Modes program, you'll see the window shown in Figure 6.8. If you set your system to 24-bit color mode, you'll see the window shown in Figure 6.9.

FIGURE 6.8

The Modes application in 256-color mode.

6

Figure 6.9

The Modes application in 24-bit color mode.

The source code for the Modes program looks like Listing 6.9.

Listing 6.9   The Modes Program

```
1:  Option Explicit
2:
3:  Private Type BITMAP '14 bytes
4:    bmType As Long
5:    bmWidth As Long
6:    bmHeight As Long
7:    bmWidthBytes As Long
8:    bmPlanes As Integer
9:    bmBitsPixel As Integer
10:   bmBits As Long
11: End Type
12:
13: Private Declare Function GetObject Lib "gdi32" _
14:     Alias "GetObjectA" (ByVal hObject As Long, _
15:     ByVal nCount As Long, lpObject As Any) As Long
16:
17: Private Sub Form_Load()
18:   Dim BitmapWidth As Long
19:   Dim BitmapHeight As Long
20:   Dim bmp As BITMAP
21:
22:   Form1.AutoRedraw = True
23:   Form1.ScaleMode = vbPixels
24:   Form1.Width = 200 * Screen.TwipsPerPixelX()
25:   Form1.Height = 200 * Screen.TwipsPerPixelY()
26:   Picture1.AutoRedraw = True
27:   Picture1.BorderStyle = vbBSNone
28:   Picture1.Width = 35
29:   Picture1.Height = 50
30:   Picture1.Left = 20
31:   Picture1.Top = 100
32:   GetObject Picture1.Image, Len(bmp), bmp
33:   BitmapWidth = bmp.bmWidthBytes
34:   BitmapHeight = bmp.bmHeight
35:   Form1.Font.Size = 12
36:   Form1.FontTransparent = False
37:   Form1.Print "  PictureBox: " & Picture1.Width & _
```

```
38:     " x " & Picture1.Height & "   "
39:    Form1.Print "  Bitmap: " & BitmapWidth & " x " & _
40:        BitmapHeight & "   "
41: End Sub
```

ANALYSIS Lines 3 through 11 declare the `BITMAP` data type needed by the `GetObject()` function. Lines 13 through 15 declare the `GetObject()` Windows API function, and Line 32 calls `GetObject()` to obtain information about the Picture control's bitmap. Lines 33 through 40 display information about the bitmap.

Manipulating the Bitmap

Now that you have information about the bitmap, you can start doing some cool stuff. This book's CD-ROM contains the ImageBits application, which uses the Windows API to set each pixel of a PictureBox control's display area to a random color. When you run the program, click the Modify Pixels button and you'll see something like Figure 6.10. Click the button as many times as you like to fill the PictureBox with different sets of random colors.

FIGURE 6.10

The ImageBits application.

Listing 6.10 is the source code for the ImageBits application.

LISTING 6.10   The ImageBits Program

6

```
1:  Option Explicit
2:
3:  Private Type BITMAP '14 bytes
4:     bmType As Long
5:     bmWidth As Long
6:     bmHeight As Long
7:     bmWidthBytes As Long
8:     bmPlanes As Integer
9:     bmBitsPixel As Integer
10:    bmBits As Long
```

LISTING 6.10   continued

```
11: End Type
12:
13: Private Declare Function GetObject Lib "gdi32" _
14:     Alias "GetObjectA" (ByVal hObject As Long, _
15:     ByVal nCount As Long, lpObject As Any) As Long
16: Private Declare Function GetBitmapBits Lib "gdi32" _
17:     (ByVal hBitmap As Long, ByVal dwCount As Long, _
18:     lpBits As Any) As Long
19: Private Declare Function SetBitmapBits Lib "gdi32" _
20:     (ByVal hBitmap As Long, ByVal dwCount As Long, _
21:     lpBits As Any) As Long
22:
23: Private Sub Form_Load()
24:    Picture1.AutoRedraw = True
25: End Sub
26:
27: Private Sub Command1_Click()
28:    Dim BitmapSize As Long
29:    Dim BitmapBits() As Byte
30:    Dim x As Long
31:    Dim y As Integer
32:    Dim bmp As BITMAP
33:
34:    GetObject Picture1.Image, Len(bmp), bmp
35:    BitmapSize = bmp.bmWidthBytes * bmp.bmHeight
36:    ReDim BitmapBits(1 To BitmapSize)
37:    GetBitmapBits Picture1.Image, BitmapSize,  BitmapBits(1)
38:    For x = 1 To BitmapSize
39:      BitmapBits(x) = Int(Rnd * 256)
40:    Next x
41:    SetBitmapBits Picture1.Image, BitmapSize, BitmapBits(1)
42: End Sub
```

ANALYSIS   Lines 3 through 11 declare the BITMAP data type needed by the GetObject()
function. Lines 13 through 21 declare the GetObject(), GetBitmapBits(), and
SetBitmapBits() Windows API functions, and Line 34 calls GetObject() to obtain
information about the Picture control's bitmap. Line 37 gets the image's bitmap data, and
Lines 38 through 41 modify the bitmap data.

As you can see, the ImageBits application calls upon three Windows API functions:
GetObject(), GetBitmapBits(), and SetBitmapBits(). We'll look first at
GetBitmapBits(). This function's Visual Basic declaration looks like this:

```
Private Declare Function GetBitmapBits Lib "gdi32" _
    (ByVal hBitmap As Long, ByVal dwCount As Long, _
    lpBits As Any) As Long
```

The declaration shows that `GetBitmapBits()` requires three arguments. If you look up the function in your Windows programming reference, you'll see that the arguments are as follows:

- `hBitmap` — A handle to the bitmap
- `dwCount` — The number of bytes to copy
- `lpBits` — A pointer to the buffer that will receive the copied bytes

As you already know, the bitmap handle is just a reference to the Visual Basic object's `Image` property. The `dwCount` argument is just a `Long` variable, and `lpBits` is just a two-dimensional array of bytes. However, before you can supply values for these last two arguments, you need to know the size of the bitmap. You get that information with the `GetObject()` call:

```
GetObject Picture1.Image, Len(bmp), bmp
```

Next, you must get the data from the bitmap and store it in your array. First, calculate the amount of data the array needs to hold:

```
BitmapSize = bmp.bmWidthBytes * bmp.bmHeight
```

Then you can change the byte array to the correct size:

```
ReDim BitmapBits(1 To BitmapSize)
```

Finally, call `GetBitmapBits()` to retrieve the data:

```
GetBitmapBits Picture1.Image, BitmapSize, BitmapBits(1)
```

Now that you have the bitmap's image data in your array, you can modify it any way you like. As a simple example, the ImageBits application simply sets each byte to a random value. After manipulating the bitmap's data, you copy it back to the bitmap by calling the `SetBitmapBits()` Windows API function:

```
SetBitmapBits Picture1.Image, BitmapSize, BitmapBits(1)
```

The Visual Basic declaration for `SetBitmapBits()` is as follows. Notice that the arguments are exactly the same as those for `GetBitmapBits()`:

```
Private Declare Function SetBitmapBits Lib "gdi32" _
    (ByVal hBitmap As Long, ByVal dwCount As Long, _
    lpBits As Any) As Long
```

Understanding Pixel Formats

Setting each byte of a bitmap to a random value, as you did in the ImageBits applications, is a bit of a cheat because it oversimplifies an important aspect of working with bitmaps: pixel formats. Each graphics mode displays its pixels in a different way. In this section, you'll see how important pixel formats can be to your applications.

6

The 8-Bit Pixel Format

An 8-bit value can range from 0 to 255, which is why this pixel format is often referred to as 256-color mode. In the 8-bit pixel format, each byte in the bitmap specifies an index to a color palette, which is essentially an array of colors. For example, if a pixel in the bitmap has a value of 100, Windows sets the pixel to the color found in the 100th entry in the color palette.

Listing 6.11 handles 8-bit bitmaps, setting the bitmap to either white or black. This code comes from the 8Bits application that you can find on this book's CD-ROM.

LISTING 6.11   Handling an 8-Bit Bitmap

```
1:    GetObject Picture1.Image, Len(bmp), bmp
2:    If bmp.bmBitsPixel = 8 Then
3:      BitmapSize = bmp.bmWidthBytes * bmp.bmHeight
4:      ReDim BitmapBits(BitmapSize)
5:      GetBitmapBits Picture1.Image, BitmapSize, BitmapBits(1)
6:      PaletteIndex = 255
7:      If BitmapBits(1) = 255 Then PaletteIndex = 0
8:      For x = 1 To BitmapSize
9:        BitmapBits(x) = PaletteIndex
10:     Next x
11:     SetBitmapBits Picture1.Image, BitmapSize, BitmapBits(1)
12:   Else
13:     MsgBox "Please run this program in 256-color mode."
14:   End If
```

ANALYSIS   Line 1 calls `GetObject()` to obtain information about the Picture control's bitmap. Then Line 2 checks that the image is 8-bit. Lines 4 and 5 get the image data into the `BitmapBits()` array, and Lines 7 through 11 modify the bitmap data.

The 16-Bit Pixel Format

The 16-bit (or High Color) pixel format can display more than 65,000 different colors. In this format, each pixel is represented by two bytes of data that contain the color's RGB (red, green, and blue) color values. The red and blue color elements get five bits each, with the green color element getting six bits. There are a couple of variations of this format. Things get so sticky with the 16-bit pixel format that it's not often used.

The 24-Bit Pixel Format

Things get a lot simpler with the 24-bit pixel format, which can display millions of colors. Each pixel of the bitmap gets three bytes of data, one byte each for the red, green, and blue color elements. Thanks to its logical byte layout, handling 24-bit images is a heck of a lot easier than managing the 16-bit or 8-bit formats.

There *is* a complication, though. (Isn't there always?) Because each pixel is represented by an odd number of bytes, at times you must pad each line of the bitmap with an extra byte to ensure that the bitmap's width is always an even number.

Listing 6.12 sets a PictureBox's image to red when run on a 24-bit display.

LISTING **6.12**   Handling a 24-Bit Bitmap

```
1:    GetObject Picture1.Image, Len(bmp), bmp
2:    If bmp.bmBitsPixel = 24 Then
3:      BitmapSize = bmp.bmWidthBytes * bmp.bmHeight
4:      ReDim BitmapBits(BitmapSize)
5:      GetBitmapBits Picture1.Image, BitmapSize, BitmapBits(1)
6:      For x = 1 To BitmapSize Step 3
7:        BitmapBits(x) = 0 ' Blue color element
8:        BitmapBits(x + 1) = 0 ' Green color element
9:        BitmapBits(x + 2) = 255 ' Red color element
10:     Next x
11:     SetBitmapBits Picture1.Image, BitmapSize, BitmapBits(1)
12:   Else
13:     MsgBox "Please run this program in 24-bit color mode."
14:   End If
```

ANALYSIS   Line 1 calls `GetObject()` to obtain information about the Picture control's bitmap. Then Line 2 checks to be sure that the image is 24-bit. Lines 4 and 5 get the image data into the `BitmapBits()` array, and Lines 6 through 11 modify the bitmap data.

The 32-Bit Pixel Format

The 32-bit pixel format works virtually identically to the 24-bit format, except each pixel in the image gets four bytes. Generally, the fourth byte is ignored, but its presence ensures that every bitmap has an even width. Some advanced graphics applications might use the fourth byte for alpha information, which specifies a transparency value for a pixel.

Listing 6.13 sets a PictureBox's image to blue when run on a 32-bit display.

LISTING **6.13**   Handling a 32-Bit Bitmap

```
1:    GetObject Picture1.Image, Len(bmp), bmp
2:    If bmp.bmBitsPixel = 32 Then
3:      BitmapSize = bmp.bmWidthBytes * bmp.bmHeight
4:      ReDim BitmapBits(BitmapSize)
5:      GetBitmapBits Picture1.Image, BitmapSize, BitmapBits(1)
6:      For x = 1 To BitmapSize Step 4
7:        BitmapBits(x) = 255 ' Blue color element
8:        BitmapBits(x + 1) = 0 ' Green color element
```

6

LISTING 6.13   continued

```
 9:        BitmapBits(x + 2) = 0 ' Red color element
10:        BitmapBits(x + 3) = 0 ' Alpha color element
11:      Next x
12:      SetBitmapBits Picture1.Image, BitmapSize, BitmapBits(1)
13:    Else
14:      MsgBox "Please run this program in 32-bit color mode."
15:    End If
```

ANALYSIS   Line 1 calls GetObject() to obtain information about the Picture control's
bitmap. Then Line 2 checks that the image is 32-bit. Lines 4 and 5 get the image
data into the BitmapBits() array, and Lines 6 through 12 modify the bitmap data.

Summary

Depending upon the kinds of games you write, you might never need the information
covered in this day. Still, it's good to have some Windows API experience under your
belt because sooner or later you're likely to need it. However, this chapter has been only
an introduction to some of the things you can do with the Windows API graphical functions. If you're interested in this stuff, you'll need to study the Windows API and keep a
good API reference at your side while you're programming.

Q&A

Q How dangerous is it to call the Windows API from a Visual Basic program?

A It's no more dangerous than calling such a function from a program in any other
language. However, Windows API functions tend to be more complex than the
Visual Basic methods you're used to using. If you call an API function with the
wrong types of arguments, you can easily crash the system. Make sure you save
your work before you test API function calls!

**Q The Windows API is so overwhelmingly immense—do I need to know all those
functions?**

A I doubt that there's a single programmer on the planet who's fluent with every single function in the Windows API. They all use Windows reference books when
programming to check the types of arguments that functions need and to find just
the right functions. As a Visual Basic programmer, you'll use the API only to
enhance your VB programs. You'll need to know only a fraction of the API functions, if you bother with them at all.

Q If a Visual Basic object uses a device-independent bitmap, what are those bitmaps I see all the time in disk files with the BMP filename extension?

A Those are device-independent bitmaps (DIBs), which carry much more information than you'll find in a device-dependent bitmap's BITMAP structure. DIBs can be extremely complex, and they require advanced programming skills to manage. Just be glad that Visual Basic knows how to load them for you!

Workshop

The workshop includes quiz questions to help gauge your grasp of the material. You'll find the answers to this quiz in Appendix A. Even if you feel that you totally understand the concepts presented here, you should work through the quiz anyway. The last section contains some exercises to help reinforce your learning.

Quiz

1. What are the three steps needed to call a Windows API function from a Visual Basic program?
2. What's an easy way to get Windows API function, type, and constant declarations for your Visual Basic programs?
3. Name three bitmap attributes that you can find in a BITMAP structure.
4. Which two Windows API functions enable you to draw single lines?
5. Which Windows API function enables you to draw a set of lines?
6. Name three Windows API functions that draw shapes.
7. How can you get the handle of a bitmap associated with a Visual Basic object?
8. What does DDB stand for?
9. What Windows API function retrieves information about a bitmap?
10. What are the five most common pixel formats?
11. Why must some bitmaps be padded with extra bytes?

Exercises

1. Modify the 24-bit program so that it displays the color purple rather than red. (Hint: Purple is a combination of red and blue.)
2. Write a short program that uses the Windows API to draw a circle that fits exactly inside a rectangle.
3. Write a program that uses the Windows API to set the pixels of a PictureBox control's bitmap to display alternating lines of black and white. (Hint: Load the bitmap's data into a two-dimensional array.)

6

DAY 7

Programming Real-Time Games

One of the biggest challenges that you can take on as a game programmer is to write an action or arcade game. Action games require every ounce of power that you can extract from your computer. Keeping track of many moving objects while performing other game-program tasks is enough to bog down all but the most carefully written programs.

Although Visual Basic is an excellent programming language, it's not well suited for writing action games. Its graphics-handling functions are too limited, and a compiled Visual Basic program is often too slow to handle multiple *sprites* (moving objects) on the screen. To write sophisticated action games on your PC, in many cases you should use a third-party graphics library like DirectDraw, which is part of DirectX. The good news is that although sophisticated action games are often too much for Visual Basic, you can use the language to write simple action games—if you minimize the number of moving objects.

In this chapter, you'll design and write a Breakout-type arcade game called Battle Bricks. This game features only two moving objects, a ball and a paddle, so even a fairly slow language like Visual Basic is fast enough to handle it. Along the way, you'll learn the basics of programming arcade games. Specifically, today you will learn the following:

- How to play Battle Bricks
- How to build Battle Bricks
- How to program a game loop for a real-time game
- How to use the keyboard as a game controller
- How to add simple animation sequences to a game

Playing Battle Bricks

Before examining the programming for Battle Bricks, you should play the game a few times so that you know how it works from the player's point of view. Figure 7.1 shows the game's main screen.

FIGURE 7.1

The Battle Bricks main screen.

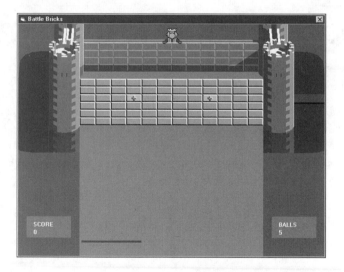

To start the game, press F2. A message box asks whether you're ready. Click OK, and a ball starts bouncing around the screen. Your task is to keep the ball going by using your paddle to bounce the ball back at the brick wall. When the ball hits a brick in the wall, the brick is destroyed. The objective is to destroy the entire wall and make the king surrender his castle. To move the paddle, use your keyboard's left and right arrow keys.

You get 10 points for every brick that you destroy. However, each time you hit a bonus brick (one of the green bricks that have plus signs on them), the score values double. The doubling stays in effect until you lose the current ball.

The king near the top of the castle doesn't affect the game in any way, but he does perform a few amusing antics. For example, when the ball manages to get past the last row in the wall, the king ducks. Also, when you lose a ball, the king (who is not exactly a good sport) taunts you by sticking out his tongue. Finally, when you manage to destroy the entire front wall, the king ducks down behind the rear wall and surrenders by waving a white flag.

You get five balls. After you lose them all, you can play another game or quit.

Note that the game operates at three speeds, which are controlled by the F3, F4, and F5 keys. Select the speed that works best for your computer.

Building Battle Bricks

Now that you've had a chance to play Battle Bricks, you'll learn to build the program yourself. In the following sections, you'll build the program one piece at a time.

Creating the Battle Bricks User Interface

The first step is to create the game's user interface:

1. Start a new Standard EXE Visual Basic project.

2. Set the form's properties to the values listed here:

   AutoRedraw = True

   BorderStyle = Fixed Single

   Caption = "Battle Bricks"

   Height = 7575

   ScaleMode = Pixel

   Width = 9675

3. Set the form's Picture property to the Battlebr.gif image that you can find in the Images\BattleBricks directory of this book's CD-ROM.

7

4. Add seven Image (not PictureBox) controls to the form, giving them the property values listed here:

Image #1

Name = imgBrick

Picture = Images\BattleBricks\Brick.bmp

Image #2

Name = imgBonus2

Picture = Images\BattleBricks\BonusBrick2.bmp

Image #3

Name = imgKing1

Picture = Images\BattleBricks\King1.bmp

Image #4

Name = imgKing2

Picture = Images\BattleBricks\King2.bmp

Image #5

Name = imgKing3

Picture = Images\BattleBricks\King3.bmp

Image #6

Name = imgKing4

Picture = Images\BattleBricks\King4.bmp

Image #7

Name = imgKing5

Picture = Images\BattleBricks\King5.bmp

5. Save your work, giving the main form the filename BattleBricks.frm and the project the filename BattleBricks.vbp.

You've now completed the Battle Bricks user interface. Figure 7.2 shows what your main form should look like at this point. In the next section, you'll add handlers for the main form.

Adding the Form Handlers

To complete the form's handlers, add the source code from Listing 7.1 to the project's code window. You can either type the code or copy it from the file BattleBricks1.txt, located in the Chap07\BattleBricks\Code directory of this book's CD-ROM.

FIGURE 7.2

The completed Battle Bricks user interface.

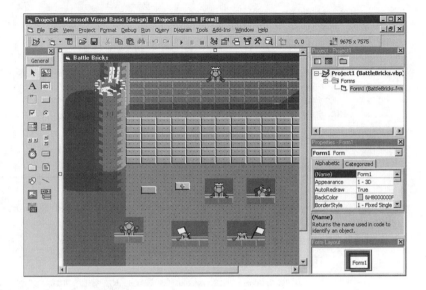

LISTING 7.1 The Form Handlers

```
1:  '====================================================
2:  ' Form Handlers.
3:  '====================================================
4:  Private Sub Form_Load()
5:    InitObjects
6:    InitGame
7:   DrawScoreBoxes
8:  End Sub
9:
10: Private Sub Form_KeyDown(KeyCode As Integer, _
11:    Shift As Integer)
12:   If KeyCode = vbKeyF2 Then
13:     GameLoop
14:   ElseIf KeyCode = vbKeyF3 Then
15:     Speed = SLOW
16:     BallVecX = -1
17:     BallVecY = -1
18:     MsgBox "Set to slow speed."
19:   ElseIf KeyCode = vbKeyF4 Then
20:     Speed = MEDIUM
21:     BallVecX = -1
22:     BallVecY = -1
23:     MsgBox "Set to medium speed."
24:   ElseIf KeyCode = vbKeyF5 Then
25:     Speed = FAST
26:     BallVecX = -2
```

7

LISTING 7.1   continued

```
27:      BallVecY = -2
28:      MsgBox "Set to fast speed."
29:   Else
30:      MovePaddle KeyCode
31:   End If
32: End Sub
33:
34: Private Sub Form_Unload(Cancel As Integer)
35:    Done = True
36: End Sub
```

ANALYSIS   The Form_Load subroutine (Lines 4 to 8) initializes the game, and the
Form_KeyDown subroutine captures and interprets keystrokes for the game.

Adding the Initialization Routines

To complete the game's initialization routines, add the source code from Listing 7.2 to
the project's code window, below the form routines you added in the previous section.
You can either type the code or copy it from the file BattleBricks2.txt, located in the
Chap07\BattleBricks\Code directory of this book's CD-ROM.

LISTING 7.2   The Initialization Routines

```
 1:  '================================================
 2:  ' Initialization Routines.
 3:  '================================================
 4:  Sub InitObjects()
 5:     Form1.Height = 7575
 6:     Form1.Width = 9675
 7:     Form1.FillColor = vbRed
 8:     Form1.FillStyle = vbSolid
 9:     Form1.Font.Bold = True
10:     imgBrick.Visible = False
11:     imgBonus2.Visible = False
12:     imgKing1.Visible = False
13:     imgKing2.Visible = False
14:     imgKing3.Visible = False
15:     imgKing4.Visible = False
16:     imgKing5.Visible = False
17:  End Sub
18:
19:  Sub InitGame()
20:     BallX = 300
21:     BallY = 300
22:     Speed = MEDIUM
```

LISTING 7.2 continued

```
23:     BallVecX = 1
24:     BallVecY = -1
25:     PaddleX = 134
26:     BallCount = NUMBALLSPERGAME
27:     Score = 0
28:     Done = False
29:     Ducking = False
30:     ScoreMultiplier = 1
31:     GrassColor = RGB(0, 162, 0)
32:     ShadowGrassColor = RGB(0, 112, 0)
33:     ScoreBoxColor = RGB(128, 128, 128)
34:     DrawPaddle
35:     InitBricks
36: End Sub
37:
38: Sub InitBricks()
39:     Dim Col As Integer
40:     Dim Row As Integer
41:     Dim BrickPixelX As Integer
42:     Dim BrickPixelY As Integer
43:     BrickCount = 72
44:     For Col = 0 To COLCOUNT - 1
45:       For Row = 0 To ROWCOUNT - 1
46:         Bricks(Col, Row) = BRICK
47:         BrickPixelX = Col * BRICKWIDTH + OFFSETX
48:         BrickPixelY = Row * BRICKHEIGHT + OFFSETY
49:         Form1.PaintPicture imgBrick.Picture, _
50:             BrickPixelX, BrickPixelY
51:       Next Row
52:     Next Col
53:     Form1.PaintPicture imgBonus2.Picture, 224, 146
54:     Form1.PaintPicture imgBonus2.Picture,  384, 146
55: End Sub
```

ANALYSIS The InitObjects subroutine in Lines 4 to 17 initializes properties for the form and some of the game's images, and the InitGame subroutine (Lines 19 to 36) initializes the game's many variables. Finally, the InitBricks subroutine in Lines 38 to 55 initializes and paints the brick wall.

Adding the General Game Subroutines

Next come the game's general subroutines. To take care of them, add the source code from Listing 7.3 to the project's code window, below the initialization routines you added in the previous section. You can either type the code or copy it from the file BattleBricks3.txt, located in the Chap07\BattleBricks\Code directory of this book's CD-ROM.

7

LISTING 7.3   The General Game Subroutines

```
'=====================================================
' General Game Subroutines.
'=====================================================
Sub GameLoop()
  WaitForReady
  Do
    MoveBall
    If Speed = SLOW Then SlowBall
    DoEvents
  Loop While Not Done
End Sub

Sub SlowBall()
  Dim x As Integer
  Dim y As Integer
  For x = 1 To 32000
    For y = 1 To 10
    Next y
  Next x
End Sub

Sub MoveBall()
  Dim BrickGridX As Integer
  Dim BrickGridY As Integer
  Dim BrickPixelX As Integer
  Dim BrickPixelY As Integer
  Dim HitBrick As Boolean
  Form1.DrawWidth = 1
  Form1.ForeColor = GrassColor
  Form1.FillColor = GrassColor
  Form1.FillStyle = vbSolid
  Form1.Circle (BallX + BALLWIDTH / 2, _
      BallY + BALLHEIGHT / 2), BALLHEIGHT / 2
  BallX = BallX + BallVecX
  BallY = BallY + BallVecY
  HandleBallActions
  If Not Done Then
    If BallY < MAXBRICKY And BallY > MINBRICKY Then
      HitBrick = FindBrick(BrickGridX, BrickGridY, _
          BrickPixelX, BrickPixelY)
      If HitBrick Then DestroyBrick BrickGridX, _
          BrickGridY, BrickPixelX, BrickPixelY
    End If
    Form1.FillColor = vbRed
    Form1.ForeColor = vbBlack
    Form1.DrawWidth = 1
    Form1.Circle (BallX + BALLWIDTH / 2, _
        BallY + BALLHEIGHT / 2), BALLHEIGHT / 2
```

LISTING 7.3   continued

```
      If BrickCount = 0 Then
        KingSurrenders
      End If
    End If
  End If
End Sub

Sub HandleBallActions()
  If BallY > PADDLEY Then
    StartNewBall
  End If
  If Not Done Then
    CheckWalls
    CheckPaddle
    CheckKing
  End If
End Sub

Sub CheckKing()
  If BallY < OFFSETY - 1 And Not Ducking Then
    Form1.PaintPicture imgKing2.Picture, 290, 0
    Ducking = True
  ElseIf BallY > 250 And Ducking Then
    Form1.PaintPicture imgKing1.Picture, 290, 0
    Ducking = False
  End If
End Sub

Sub CheckWalls()
  If ((BallX < MINBALLX) Or (BallX > MAXBALLX)) Then
    BallVecX = -BallVecX
    If BallX < MINBALLX Then
        BallX = MINBALLX
    Else
        BallX = MAXBALLX
    End If
  End If
  If BallY < MINBALLY Then
    BallVecY = -BallVecY
  End If
End Sub

Sub StartNewBall()
  BallCount = BallCount - 1
  Form1.Line (5, 375)-(125, 385), ShadowGrassColor, BF
  Form1.Line (517, 375)-(635, 385), ShadowGrassColor, BF
  Form1.Line (540, 424)-(620, 434), ScoreBoxColor, BF
  Form1.ForeColor = vbWhite
  Form1.CurrentX = 544
```

7

LISTING 7.3   continued

```
      Form1.CurrentY = 424
      Form1.Print BallCount
      ErasePaddle
      If BallCount = 0 Then
        GameOver
      Else
        Form1.PaintPicture imgKing3.Picture, 290, 0
        Form1.FillColor = GrassColor
        Form1.ForeColor = GrassColor
        Form1.Circle (BallX + BALLWIDTH / 2, _
            BallY + BALLHEIGHT / 2), BALLHEIGHT / 2
        BallY = 300
        If Speed = FAST Then
          BallVecX = -2
          BallVecY = -2
        Else
          BallVecX = -1
          BallVecY = -1
        End If
        ScoreMultiplier = 1
        DrawPaddle
        WaitForReady
        Form1.PaintPicture imgKing1.Picture, 290, 0
      End If
End Sub

Sub DrawPaddle()
  Form1.ForeColor = vbBlue
  Form1.DrawWidth = 4
  Form1.Line (PaddleX, PADDLEY)- _
      (PaddleX + PADDLEWIDTH, PADDLEY)
End Sub

Sub ErasePaddle()
  Form1.ForeColor = GrassColor
  Form1.DrawWidth = 4
  Form1.Line (PaddleX, PADDLEY)- _
      (PaddleX + PADDLEWIDTH, PADDLEY)
End Sub

Sub MovePaddle(KeyCode As Integer)
  If KeyCode = vbKeyLeft Then
    If PaddleX > MINPADDLEX Then
      ErasePaddle
      PaddleX = PaddleX - 12
      DrawPaddle
    End If
  ElseIf KeyCode = vbKeyRight Then
```

LISTING 7.3   continued

```
      If PaddleX < MAXPADDLEX Then
        ErasePaddle
        PaddleX = PaddleX + 12
        DrawPaddle
      End If
    End If
End Sub

Sub DrawScoreBoxes()
  Form1.Line (20, 400)-(108, 440), ScoreBoxColor, BF
  Form1.ForeColor = vbWhite
  Form1.CurrentX = 32
  Form1.CurrentY = 408
  Form1.Print "SCORE"
  Form1.CurrentX = 32
  Form1.CurrentY = 424
  Form1.Print "0"
  Form1.Line (532, 400)-(620, 440), ScoreBoxColor, BF
  Form1.CurrentX = 544
  Form1.CurrentY = 408
  Form1.Print "BALLS"
  Form1.CurrentX = 544
  Form1.CurrentY = 424
  Form1.Print "5"
End Sub

Sub CheckPaddle()
  If ((BallY + BALLHEIGHT > PADDLEY - 3) And _
      (BallX + BALLWIDTH >= PaddleX) And _
      (BallX <= PaddleX + PADDLEWIDTH)) Then
    If (BallX + BALLWIDTH < PaddleX + PADDLEWIDTH / 6) Then
      If Speed = FAST Then
        BallVecX = -4
      Else
        BallVecX = -2
      End If
    ElseIf (BallX > PaddleX + PADDLEWIDTH - _
        PADDLEWIDTH / 6) Then
      If Speed = FAST Then
        BallVecX = 4
      Else
        BallVecX = 2
      End If
    ElseIf (BallX + BALLWIDTH < PaddleX + _
        PADDLEWIDTH / 3) Then
      If Speed = FAST Then
        BallVecX = -2
      Else
```

7

LISTING 7.3   continued

```
            BallVecX = -1
          End If
        ElseIf (BallX > PaddleX + PADDLEWIDTH - _
            PADDLEWIDTH / 3) Then
          If Speed = FAST Then
            BallVecX = 2
          Else
            BallVecX = 1
          End If
        End If
        BallVecY = -BallVecY
      End If
    End Sub

    Sub DestroyBrick(BrickGridX As Integer, _
        BrickGridY As Integer, BrickPixelX As Integer, _
        BrickPixelY As Integer)
      BallX = BallX - BallVecX
      BallY = BallY - BallVecY
      Bricks(BrickGridX, BrickGridY) = NOBRICK
      BallVecY = -BallVecY
      Form1.Line (BrickPixelX, BrickPixelY)- _
          (BrickPixelX + BRICKWIDTH - 1, _
          BrickPixelY + BRICKHEIGHT - 1), GrassColor, BF
      BrickCount = BrickCount - 1
      Score = Score + 10 * ScoreMultiplier
      Form1.Line (25, 424)-(90, 434), ScoreBoxColor, BF
      Form1.ForeColor = vbWhite
      Form1.CurrentX = 32
      Form1.CurrentY = 424
      Form1.Print Score
      If ((BrickGridY * COLCOUNT + BrickGridX) = BONUSBRICK1 Or _
          (BrickGridY * COLCOUNT + BrickGridX) = BONUSBRICK2) Then
        ScoreMultiplier = ScoreMultiplier * 2
        Form1.Line (5, 375)-(125, 385), ShadowGrassColor, BF
        Form1.Line (517, 375)-(635, 385),  ShadowGrassColor, BF
        Form1.ForeColor = vbRed
        Form1.CurrentX = 30
        Form1.CurrentY = 375
        Form1.Print "SCORE x " & ScoreMultiplier
        Form1.CurrentX = 542
        Form1.CurrentY = 375
        Form1.Print "SCORE x " & ScoreMultiplier
      End If
    End Sub

    Sub KingSurrenders()
      Form1.Line (BallX, BallY)-(BallX + BALLWIDTH, _
```

LISTING 7.3   continued

```
      BallY + BALLHEIGHT), GrassColor, BF
  Dim x As Integer
  For x = 0 To 5
    Form1.PaintPicture imgKing4.Picture, 290, 0
    Delay (0.25)
    Form1.PaintPicture imgKing5.Picture, 290, 0
    Delay (0.25)
  Next x
  Form1.Line (290, 0)-(400, 30), ShadowGrassColor, BF
  Form1.PaintPicture imgKing1.Picture, 290, 0
  WaitForReady
  StartNewWall
End Sub

Sub Delay(Amount As Single)
  Dim StartTime As Single
  Dim CurrentTime As Single
  StartTime = Timer
  Do
    CurrentTime = Timer
    DoEvents
  Loop While CurrentTime < StartTime + Amount
End Sub

Sub StartNewWall()
  BallY = 300
  If Speed = FAST Then
    BallVecY = -2
  Else
    BallVecY = -1
  End If
  InitBricks
End Sub

Sub WaitForReady()
  MsgBox "Are you ready?"
End Sub

Sub GameOver()
  Dim Response As Integer
  ErasePaddle
  Response = MsgBox("Game Over.  Do you want to play again?", _
      vbYesNo Or vbQuestion, "Game Over")
  If Response = vbYes Then
    InitGame
    DrawScoreBoxes
    WaitForReady
    StartNewWall
```

7

LISTING 7.3   continued

```
    Else
      Done = True
      Unload Form1
    End If
End Sub
```

Adding the `FindBrick` Function

You're getting near the end. To complete the game's functions, of which there is only
one, add the source code from Listing 7.4 to the project's code window, below the general subroutines you added in the previous section. You can either type the code or copy it
from the file BattleBricks4.txt, located in the Chap07\BattleBricks\Code directory of this
book's CD-ROM.

LISTING 7.4   The General Game Functions

```
'==================================================
' Game Functions.
'==================================================
Function FindBrick(GridCol As Integer, GridRow As Integer, _
    PixelX As Integer, PixelY As Integer) As Boolean
  Dim BrickX(4) As Integer
  Dim BrickY(4) As Integer
  Dim LeftOrRightSide As Integer
  Dim OverlapY1 As Integer
  Dim OverlapY2 As Integer
  Dim OverlapX1 As Integer
  Dim OverlapX2 As Integer
  Dim x As Integer
  Dim GridX As Integer
  Dim GridY As Integer

  FindBrick = False
  BrickX(0) = ((BallX - OFFSETX) \ BRICKWIDTH) * _
      BRICKWIDTH + OFFSETX
  BrickY(0) = ((BallY - OFFSETY) \ BRICKHEIGHT) * _
      BRICKHEIGHT + OFFSETY
  BrickX(1) = ((BallX + BALLWIDTH - OFFSETX) \ _
      BRICKWIDTH) * BRICKWIDTH + OFFSETX
  BrickY(1) = ((BallY - OFFSETY) \ BRICKHEIGHT) * _
      BRICKHEIGHT + OFFSETY
  BrickX(2) = ((BallX + BALLWIDTH - OFFSETX) \ _
      BRICKWIDTH) * BRICKWIDTH + OFFSETX
  BrickY(2) = ((BallY + BALLHEIGHT - OFFSETY) \ _
      BRICKHEIGHT) * BRICKHEIGHT + OFFSETY
```

LISTING 7.4   continued

```
    BrickX(3) = ((BallX - OFFSETX) \ BRICKWIDTH) * _
        BRICKWIDTH + OFFSETX
    BrickY(3) = ((BallY + BALLHEIGHT - OFFSETY) \ _
        BRICKHEIGHT) * BRICKHEIGHT + OFFSETY

    If BallVecY < 0 Then
      LeftOrRightSide = (BallY - OFFSETY - 1) Mod BRICKHEIGHT
    Else
      LeftOrRightSide = (BallY + BALLHEIGHT - OFFSETY + 1) _
        Mod BRICKHEIGHT
    End If

    For x = 0 To 3
      GridX = (BrickX(x) - OFFSETX) \ BRICKWIDTH
      GridY = (BrickY(x) - OFFSETY) \ BRICKHEIGHT
      If ((GridX > -1) And (GridX < COLCOUNT) And _
          (GridY > -1) And (GridY < ROWCOUNT) And _
          (Bricks(GridX, GridY) = BRICK)) Then
        If LeftOrRightSide Then
          OverlapY1 = BrickY(1) - BallY
          OverlapY2 = BALLHEIGHT - OverlapY1
          If (((GridY = 5) Or _
              (Bricks(GridX, GridY + 1) = NOBRICK)) Or _
              ((x < 2) And (OverlapY1 > BALLHEIGHT / 2)) Or _
              ((x > 1) And (OverlapY2 > BALLHEIGHT / 2))) Then
            PixelX = BrickX(x)
            PixelY = BrickY(x)
            GridCol = GridX
            GridRow = GridY
            FindBrick = True
          End If
        Else
          OverlapX1 = BrickX(1) - BallX
          OverlapX2 = BALLWIDTH - OverlapX1
          If (GridX = 11 Or Bricks(GridX + 1, GridY) = NOBRICK) Or _
              ((x = 0 Or x = 3) And OverlapX1 > BALLWIDTH / 2) Or _
              ((x = 1 Or x = 2) And OverlapX2 > BALLWIDTH / 2) Then
            PixelX = BrickX(x)
            PixelY = BrickY(x)
            GridCol = GridX
            GridRow = GridY
            FindBrick = True
          End If
        End If
      End If
    Next x
End Function
```

7

Completing the Game

Finally, you must add the constant and variable declarations to the program. To do this, add the source code from Listing 7.5 at the top of the project's code window. You can either type the code or copy it from the file BattleBricks5.txt, located in the Chap07\BattleBricks\Code directory of this book's CD-ROM.

LISTING 7.5   The Declarations

```
 1:  '=====================================================
 2:  ' Battle Bricks for Visual Basic 6
 3:  '    by Clayton Walnum
 4:  ' Copyright 2000 by Macmillan Computer Publishing
 5:  '=====================================================
 6:  Option Explicit
 7:
 8:  '=====================================================
 9:  ' Constants.
10:  '=====================================================
11:  Const COLCOUNT = 12
12:  Const ROWCOUNT = 6
13:  Const BALLWIDTH = 10
14:  Const BALLHEIGHT = 10
15:  Const BRICKWIDTH = 32
16:  Const BRICKHEIGHT = 16
17:  Const PADDLEWIDTH = 120
18:  Const PADDLEY = 450
19:  Const NUMBALLSPERGAME = 5
20:  Const MINBALLX = 130
21:  Const MAXBALLX = 509 - BALLWIDTH
22:  Const MINBALLY = 100
23:  Const MINPADDLEX = 136
24:  Const MAXPADDLEX = 380
25:  Const MINBRICKY = 113 - BALLHEIGHT
26:  Const MAXBRICKY = 210
27:  Const OFFSETX = 128
28:  Const OFFSETY = 114
29:  Const BONUSBRICK1 = 27
30:  Const BONUSBRICK2 = 32
31:
32:  Enum BrickEnum
33:     NOBRICK
34:     BRICK
35:  End Enum
36:
37:  Enum SpeedEnum
38:     SLOW
39:     MEDIUM
```

LISTING 7.5   continued

```
40:    FAST
41: End Enum
42:
43: '==================================================
44: ' General Game Variables.
45: '==================================================
46: Dim BallX As Integer
47: Dim BallY As Integer
48: Dim BallVecX As Integer
49: Dim BallVecY As Integer
50: Dim Ducking As Boolean
51: Dim PaddleX As Integer
52: Dim BrickCount As Integer
53: Dim Done As Boolean
54: Dim Score As Long
55: Dim BallCount As Integer
56: Dim ScoreMultiplier As Integer
57: Dim Bricks(12, 6)
58: Dim GrassColor As Long
59: Dim ShadowGrassColor As Long
60: Dim ScoreBoxColor As Long
61: Dim Speed As Integer
```

ANALYSIS   Lines 11 to 30 define the many constants used in the game, and Lines 32 to 41 define the game's enumerations. Lines 46 to 61 declare the game's global variables.

Understanding Battle Bricks

Now that you've built your own version of Battle Bricks, it's time to examine the source code, starting with the game's constants and variables.

The Battle Bricks Variables and Constants

Battle Bricks relies on a set of global variables and constants that it declares near the top of the program. Table 7.1 lists the general global variables and their descriptions, and Table 7.2 lists the constants.

TABLE 7.1   The Battle Bricks General Game Variables

Variable	Type	Description
BallCount	Integer	The number of balls remaining in the current game
BallVecX	Integer	The direction (left or right) and number of pixels the ball should move horizontally

7

TABLE 7.1   continued

Variable	Type	Description
BallVecY	Integer	The direction (up or down) and number of pixels the ball should move vertically
BallX	Integer	The ball's current horizontal location
BallY	Integer	The ball's current vertical location
BrickCount	Integer	The total number of bricks in a newly built wall
Bricks()	Integer	An array that indicates the remaining bricks in the wall
Done	Boolean	Specifies whether the game is over
Ducking	Boolean	Indicates whether the king is currently ducking
GrassColor	Long	The color used to draw grass
PaddleX	Integer	The paddle's horizontal position
Score	Long	The current score
ScoreBoxColor	Long	The color used to draw the score boxes
ScoreMultiplier	Integer	The value by which the score value of a brick should be multiplied
ShadowGrassColor	Long	The color used to draw the darker grass
Speed	Integer	The game's current speed setting

TABLE 7.2   The Battle Bricks Constants

Constant	Description
BALLHEIGHT	The height of the ball
BALLWIDTH	The width of the ball
BONUSBRICK1	The number of the first bonus brick
BONUSBRICK2	The number of the second bonus brick
BRICKHEIGHT	The height of a single brick
BRICKWIDTH	The width of a single brick
COLCOUNT	The number of columns in the wall
MAXBALLX	The maximum allowable X coordinate for the ball
MAXBRICKY	The Y coordinate of the row of bricks farthest from the king
MAXPADDLEX	The maximum allowable X coordinate for the paddle
MINBALLX	The minimum allowable X coordinate for the ball
MINBALLY	The minimum allowable Y value for the ball

Constant	Description
MINBRICKY	The Y coordinate of the row of bricks closest to the king
MINPADDLEX	The minimum allowable X coordinate for the paddle
NUMBALLSPERGAME	The number of balls the player has for each game
OFFSETX	The horizontal offset of the left-hand wall
OFFSETY	The vertical offset of the brick wall
PADDLEWIDTH	The width of the paddle
PADDLEY	The vertical position of the paddle
ROWCOUNT	The number of rows in the wall

The Battle Bricks program also defines two enumerations. The BrickEnum enumeration defines the NOBRICK and BRICK constants, and the SpeedEnum enumeration defines the SLOW, MEDIUM, and FAST constants.

The Game Loop

As you already know, the toughest task in a game like Battle Bricks is to keep everything moving at a reasonable speed. If the ball moves too slowly, the game will be too easy. Conversely, if the paddle moves too slowly, the player will be unable to keep the ball in action.

To keep the game's actions running smoothly, you must program a loop that continually updates the ball's position. The Battle Bricks main game loop looks like Listing 7.6.

LISTING 7.6   The Game Loop

```
1: Sub GameLoop()
2:    WaitForReady
3:    Do
4:       MoveBall
5:       If Speed = SLOW Then SlowBall
6:       DoEvents
7:    Loop While Not Done
8: End Sub
```

ANALYSIS   Here, the call to the function WaitForReady (Line 2) displays the "Are you ready?" message box, which keeps the game from starting until the player clicks the OK button or presses Enter on the keyboard. Then the Do loop (Lines 3 to 7) iterates constantly throughout the entire game, moving the ball and enabling other Windows messages to get through. The flag Done, which controls the Do loop (Line 7), becomes True

7

only when the player quits the game. The SlowBall routine is a simple set of loops that helps slow the ball on fast computer systems (Line 5).

Moving the Ball

Another programming challenge in Battle Bricks is to keep the ball moving while at the same time checking the ball's position and performing any corresponding actions. Each time through the game loop, the ball moves horizontally and vertically, after which its position is compared to the positions that trigger some sort of action, like hitting a wall or a brick.

The subroutine MoveBall (see Listing 7.7) updates the ball's position according to its current X,Y vectors (which are stored in BallVecX and BallVecY) and calls the required functions to handle any actions initiated by the ball's position.

LISTING 7.7   The MoveBall Subroutine

```
 1:  Sub MoveBall()
 2:     Dim BrickGridX As Integer
 3:     Dim BrickGridY As Integer
 4:     Dim BrickPixelX As Integer
 5:     Dim BrickPixelY As Integer
 6:     Dim HitBrick As Boolean
 7:     Form1.DrawWidth = 1
 8:     Form1.ForeColor = GrassColor
 9:     Form1.FillColor = GrassColor
10:     Form1.FillStyle = vbSolid
11:     Form1.Circle (BallX + BALLWIDTH / 2, _
12:         BallY + BALLHEIGHT / 2), BALLHEIGHT / 2
13:     BallX = BallX + BallVecX
14:     BallY = BallY + BallVecY
15:     HandleBallActions
16:     If Not Done Then
17:        If BallY < MAXBRICKY And BallY > MINBRICKY Then
18:           HitBrick = FindBrick(BrickGridX, BrickGridY, _
19:              BrickPixelX, BrickPixelY)
20:           If HitBrick Then DestroyBrick BrickGridX, _
21:              BrickGridY, BrickPixelX, BrickPixelY
22:        End If
23:        Form1.FillColor = vbRed
24:        Form1.ForeColor = vbBlack
25:        Form1.DrawWidth = 1
26:        Form1.Circle (BallX + BALLWIDTH / 2, _
27:           BallY + BALLHEIGHT / 2), BALLHEIGHT / 2
28:        If BrickCount = 0 Then
29:           KingSurrenders
30:        End If
31:     EndIf
32:  End Sub
```

NEW TERM   A *vector* is nothing more than a line that points in a specific direction. In the case of Battle Bricks, a vector indicates the direction in which the ball should move.

ANALYSIS   The function first erases the ball from the screen (Lines 7 to 12). It then calculates the ball's new coordinates by adding the values of BallVecX and BallVecY to BallX and BallY, respectively (Lines 13 and 14). The variables BallX and BallY are the ball's current screen coordinates. The variables BallVecX and BallVecY contain values that change the ball's position by the number of pixels stored in the variables. For example, when BallVecX and BallVecY are each -1, the ball moves left and up. This is because adding BallVecX and BallVecY to BallX and BallY decrements the ball's X,Y coordinates. Similarly, if BallVecX is 1 and BallVecY is -1, the ball moves right and up. Figure 7.3 summarizes the effect of BallVecX and BallVecY on the ball's movement.

FIGURE 7.3

Vectors and the ball's movement.

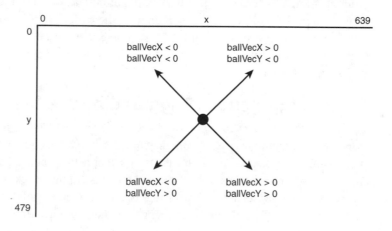

Note

One way to make an object move faster on the screen is to move it more than one pixel at a time. However, if you try to move the object too far at once, the object's motion will be jerky rather than fluid. Such a jerky motion can be disorienting to the player and make the game hard to play. To ensure smooth motion, move your objects in small steps rather than large ones.

After updating the ball's position, MoveBall calls HandleBallActions (Line 15), which compares the ball's position to certain predetermined locations on the screen and performs any actions that are initiated when the ball is in one of those positions. You'll examine HandleBallActions soon. For now, just be aware that this function handles

7

such actions as bouncing the ball off the walls or the paddle and making the king duck when the ball gets past the wall of bricks.

Next, MoveBall checks whether the ball is in the brick grid area (Line 17). If it is, the program must determine whether the ball has hit a brick (Line 18). The function FindBrick handles this task. If the ball hits a brick, FindBrick returns True, with the brick's coordinates in the given integer variables. If the ball doesn't hit a brick, FindBrick returns False.

If the ball has hit a brick, not only does a call to DestroyBrick remove the brick from the screen, but it also updates the player's score, calculates the ball's new direction, and checks whether the brick that the ball hit is a score-doubling brick (one of the two green bricks with plus signs).

After handling all the actions that the ball might initiate, MoveBall draws the ball in its new location (Lines 23 to 27). After redrawing the ball, MoveBall checks the brick count to determine whether there are still bricks on the screen (Line 28). If BrickCount equals 0, the player has destroyed the entire wall and the function KingSurrenders shows the king waving a white flag.

Performing Actions Triggered by the Ball

Everything that happens in Battle Bricks is governed by the ball's position. For example, if the ball is about to overlap a wall, the ball must reverse its horizontal or vertical direction so that it appears to bounce off the wall. Other actions in the game are equally important. After all, you can't have the ball passing through bricks or the player's paddle any more than you can have it burrowing its way through a wall. Every time the ball strikes an object, the ball must bounce away so that the object looks solid.

Checking for Actions

As stated previously, the subroutine HandleBallActions (see Listing 7.8) checks the ball's location and then initiates any actions that the location specifies.

LISTING 7.8   The HandleBallActions Subroutine

```
1: Sub HandleBallActions()
2:    If BallY > PADDLEY Then StartNewBall
3:    If Not Done Then
4:       CheckWalls
5:       CheckPaddle
6:       CheckKing
7:    End If
8: End Sub
```

ANALYSIS HandleBallActions first checks that the ball hasn't moved beyond the paddle at the bottom of the screen (Line 2). If it has, HandleBallActions calls StartNewBall to put a new ball into play (assuming, of course, that the player hasn't already used all five balls). HandleBallActions then calls CheckWalls, CheckPaddle, and CheckKing (Lines 4 to 6) to determine whether the ball has struck a wall, struck the paddle, or is in a location that makes the king duck.

Bouncing the Ball off the Walls

The subroutine CheckWalls (see Listing 7.9) bounces the ball off a wall.

LISTING 7.9 The CheckWalls Subroutine

```
 1: Sub CheckWalls()
 2:   If ((BallX < MINBALLX) Or (BallX > MAXBALLX)) Then
 3:     BallVecX = -BallVecX
 4:     If BallX < MINBALLX Then
 5:         BallX = MINBALLX
 6:     Else
 7:         BallX = MAXBALLX
 8:     End If
 9:   End If
10:   If BallY < MINBALLY Then
11:     BallVecY = -BallVecY
12:   End If
13: End Sub
```

ANALYSIS If the ball's X coordinate indicates that it's hitting a side wall (Line 2), CheckWalls reverses the ball's X vector (Line 3). For example, if BallVecX is -1 when the ball hits the left wall (and it would have to be -1 because the ball is moving to the left), CheckWalls changes BallVecX to 1, which starts the ball moving to the right, away from the wall. After reversing the ball's horizontal direction, CheckWalls checks the ball's X coordinate to ensure that the ball doesn't get stuck in the left or right wall (Lines 4 to 8). The function must check this because sometimes the ball moves horizontally more than one pixel at a time.

If the ball reaches the castle's top wall—that is, if the ball moves as high up as it can go—CheckWalls reverses the ball's Y vector (Lines 10 to 12).

7

Note To keep things simple, the background over which the ball in Battle Bricks must pass is a solid color. This makes it easy to erase the ball because then the program needs only a block of background color to replace the ball's image. In some games, you may have seen objects that pass over detailed graphics without disturbing them, in much the same way that your mouse pointer can move around the screen without changing its display. These objects are called *sprites*. To move a sprite over a background image, you must first save the background image before you draw the sprite, and then restore the background image after the sprite moves. To keep your program running fast, you'll probably need to use a library like DirectX to save and transfer these images.

Bouncing the Ball off the Paddle

The program must enable the player to bounce the ball off his paddle so that he can keep the ball in play. The subroutine CheckPaddle (Listing 7.10) handles this action.

LISTING 7.10   The CheckPaddle Subroutine

```
 1:  Sub CheckPaddle()
 2:    If ((BallY + BALLHEIGHT > PADDLEY - 3) And _
 3:        (BallX + BALLWIDTH >= PaddleX) And _
 4:        (BallX <= PaddleX + PADDLEWIDTH)) Then
 5:      If (BallX + BALLWIDTH < PaddleX + PADDLEWIDTH / 6) Then
 6:        If Speed = FAST Then
 7:          BallVecX = -4
 8:        Else
 9:          BallVecX = -2
10:        End If
11:      ElseIf (BallX > PaddleX + PADDLEWIDTH - _
12:          PADDLEWIDTH / 6) Then
13:        If Speed = FAST Then
14:          BallVecX = 4
15:        Else
16:          BallVecX = 2
17:        End If
18:      ElseIf (BallX + BALLWIDTH < PaddleX + _
19:          PADDLEWIDTH / 3) Then
20:        If Speed = FAST Then
21:          BallVecX = -2
22:        Else
23:          BallVecX = -1
24:        End If
25:      ElseIf (BallX > PaddleX + PADDLEWIDTH - _
26:          PADDLEWIDTH / 3) Then
```

LISTING 7.10   continued

```
27:        If Speed = FAST Then
28:           BallVecX = 2
29:        Else
30:           BallVecX = 1
31:        End If
32:     End If
33:     BallVecY = -BallVecY
34:   End If
35: End Sub
```

ANALYSIS   This subroutine first checks that the ball is just above the paddle (Lines 2 to 4). If it is, the function must determine exactly which area of the paddle the ball is about to hit. This determines the ball's angle and direction. Changing the ball's angle with the paddle gives the player more control over where the ball goes, and it also keeps the ball from getting stuck in boring patterns.

It's in CheckPaddle that BallVecX may double its current value (Lines 5 to 10). This happens when the ball strikes the paddle on the left or right end. Figure 7.4 summarizes the paddle's effects on the ball.

FIGURE 7.4

How the paddle affects the ball.

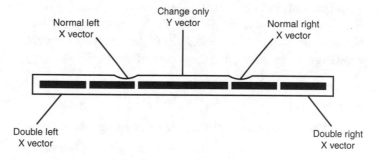

Finally, no matter where the ball strikes the paddle, CheckPaddle reverses the ball's Y vector so that the ball reverses direction and moves away from the paddle.

Making the King Duck

The subroutine CheckKing (see Listing 7.11) makes the king duck.

7

LISTING 7.11   The CheckKing Subroutine

```
1: Sub CheckKing()
2:   If BallY < OFFSETY - 1 And Not Ducking Then
3:     Form1.PaintPicture imgKing2.Picture, 290, 0
4:     Ducking = True
5:   ElseIf BallY > 250 And Ducking Then
6:     Form1.PaintPicture imgKing1.Picture, 290, 0
7:     Ducking = False
8:   End If
9: End Sub
```

ANALYSIS   Here, if the ball gets past the castle's front wall (Line 2), the subroutine displays an image of the king ducking (Line 3). When the ball returns to the middle of the screen (Line 5), CheckKing redisplays the normal king graphic (Line 6). Simple, no?

Hitting a Brick

The most complex function in the program is FindBrick, which determines whether the ball has hit a brick. To make this task a little easier, the program treats the ball as a square rather than a round object. Trying to calculate whether a round object is overlapping another object is way too difficult to be worth the effort. This is because computers work best with rectangular areas. Determining whether two rectangles overlap is relatively easy because you need only consider horizontal and vertical coordinates, without having to do a lot of fancy calculations involving geometry. Such calculations require knowledge of geometry, and they also perform slowly on computers.

To determine whether the ball has struck a brick, the program first must answer several questions:

- Which candidate bricks are the ball's corners overlapping?
- Is the ball striking the side, top, or bottom of a brick?
- Which candidate brick is the ball overlapping the most?
- Is the candidate brick with the most overlap still onscreen?

To understand the preceding questions, you must first know the difference between an actual brick and a candidate brick. An *actual brick* is a brick that is currently displayed onscreen because the ball has not yet struck it. A *candidate brick* is a location where a brick may or may not be. In other words, candidate bricks make up the entire brick grid, as shown in Figure 7.5. However, a candidate brick may or may not contain an actual brick.

FIGURE 7.5

Candidate bricks and actual bricks.

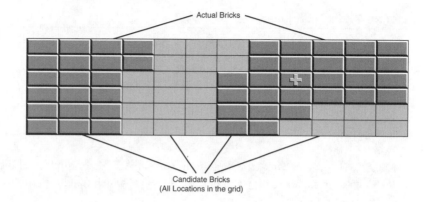

FIGURE 7.6

The ball overlapping four candidate bricks, but only one actual brick.

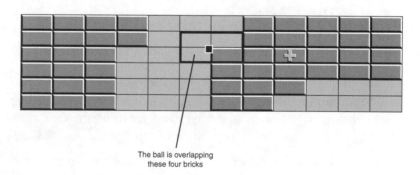

The first step in determining whether the ball has struck a brick is to determine which candidate bricks the ball's corners are overlapping. For example, in Figure 7.6 the ball overlaps four candidate bricks, only one of which is an actual brick.

The ball always overlaps four candidate bricks, except when the ball is in the first or last rows of the grid. Therefore, FindBrick() always calculates the X,Y screen coordinates for four candidate bricks first and handles any exceptions later (see Listing 7.12).

LISTING 7.12 Determining Candidate Bricks

```
1:  BrickX(0) = ((BallX - OFFSETX) \ BRICKWIDTH) * _
2:      BRICKWIDTH + OFFSETX
3:  BrickY(0) = ((BallY - OFFSETY) \ BRICKHEIGHT) * _
4:      BRICKHEIGHT + OFFSETY
5:  BrickX(1) = ((BallX + BALLWIDTH - OFFSETX) \ _
6:      BRICKWIDTH) * BRICKWIDTH + OFFSETX
7:  BrickY(1) = ((BallY - OFFSETY) \ BRICKHEIGHT) * _
8:      BRICKHEIGHT + OFFSETY
9:  BrickX(2) = ((BallX + BALLWIDTH - OFFSETX) \ _
```

7

LISTING 7.12   continued

```
10:     BRICKWIDTH) * BRICKWIDTH + OFFSETX
11: BrickY(2) = ((BallY + BALLHEIGHT - OFFSETY) \ _
12:     BRICKHEIGHT) * BRICKHEIGHT + OFFSETY
13: BrickX(3) = ((BallX - OFFSETX) \ BRICKWIDTH) * _
14:     BRICKWIDTH + OFFSETX
15: BrickY(3) = ((BallY + BALLHEIGHT - OFFSETY) \ _
16: BRICKHEIGHT) * BRICKHEIGHT + OFFSETY
```

ANALYSIS   As you can see, the program stores the X,Y coordinates of the candidate bricks in the `BrickX()` and `BrickY()` arrays, which makes it easy to access the coordinates in a loop.

After calculating these coordinates, `FindBrick` determines whether the ball's position indicates that the ball is hitting a candidate brick's side or a candidate brick's top or bottom:

```
If BallVecY < 0 Then
  LeftOrRightSide = (BallY - OFFSETY - 1) Mod BRICKHEIGHT
Else
  LeftOrRightSide = (BallY + BALLHEIGHT - OFFSETY + 1) _
      Mod BRICKHEIGHT
End If
```

If the ball's upper-left corner is located somewhere between the top and bottom of a candidate brick, the modulus division stores a remainder in the flag `LeftOrRightSide`, making it `True`. Otherwise, `LeftOrRightSide` ends up set to 0, making it `False`.

A `For` loop then iterates through the four sets of coordinates in the `BrickX()` and `BrickY()` arrays, checking whether the candidate bricks in question actually exist and which candidate brick the ball is overlapping the most. In the loop, the program first calculates the current candidate brick's grid locations, which are its row and column positions in the brick grid:

```
GridX = (BrickX(x) - OFFSETX) \ BRICKWIDTH
GridY = (BrickY(x) - OFFSETY) \ BRICKHEIGHT
```

You can also use the grid coordinates `GridX` and `GridY` as indexes into the global `Bricks()` array, which contains values that indicate which bricks are still displayed onscreen. Two constants, `NOBRICK` and `BRICK`, indicate the presence or absence of a brick in the grid. For example, if `Bricks(0,1)` is equal to `NOBRICK`, the first brick in the second row is no longer displayed onscreen. On the other hand, if `Bricks(3,5)` is equal to `BRICK`, the fourth brick in the sixth row is still displayed onscreen.

The program uses `GridX` and `GridY` to determine whether the current candidate brick's grid coordinates are valid and whether a brick is actually in that location:

```
If ((GridX > -1) And (GridX < COLCOUNT) And _
    (GridY > -1) And (GridY < ROWCOUNT) And _
    (Bricks(GridX, GridY) = BRICK)) Then
```

If everything checks out okay, the program checks whether the ball is hitting the brick on one of its sides:

```
If LeftOrRightSide Then
```

If it is, the program calculates the amount of overlap for the upper and lower pairs of candidate bricks:

```
OverlapY1 = BrickY(1) - BallY
OverlapY2 = BALLHEIGHT - OverlapY1
```

If one of three sets of conditions is met, `FindBrick` determines that the ball is hitting an actual brick. Those conditions are as follows:

- The brick below the current brick does not exist:
  ```
  If (((GridY = 5) Or _
      (Bricks(GridX, GridY + 1) = NOBRICK)) Or _
  ```
- The current candidate brick is the upper brick of the pair, and the upper overlap is larger:
  ```
  ((x < 2) And (OverlapY1 > BALLHEIGHT / 2)) Or _
  ```
- The current candidate brick is the lower of the pair, and the lower overlap is the larger:
  ```
  ((x > 1) And (OverlapY2 > BALLHEIGHT / 2))) Then
  ```

If any of the preceding sets of conditions is met, `FindBrick` sets its return values:

```
PixelX = BrickX(x)
PixelY = BrickY(x)
GridCol = GridX
GridRow = GridY
FindBrick = True
```

`FindBrick` checks horizontal pairs of candidate bricks in almost exactly the same way.

Destroying Bricks

The whole point of Battle Bricks is to destroy the castle's front wall, so just bouncing the ball off a brick isn't good enough. Instead, the ball must both destroy the brick and bounce away. This extra complication is taken care of in the subroutine `DestroyBrick` (see Listing 7.13).

7

LISTING 7.13 The DestroyBrick Subroutine

```
 1: Sub DestroyBrick(BrickGridX As Integer, _
 2:     BrickGridY As Integer, BrickPixelX As Integer, _
 3:     BrickPixelY As Integer)
 4:   BallX = BallX - BallVecX
 5:   BallY = BallY - BallVecY
 6:   Bricks(BrickGridX, BrickGridY) = NOBRICK
 7:   BallVecY = -BallVecY
 8:   Form1.Line (BrickPixelX, BrickPixelY)- _
 9:      (BrickPixelX + BRICKWIDTH - 1, _
10:       BrickPixelY + BRICKHEIGHT - 1), GrassColor, BF
11:   BrickCount = BrickCount - 1
12:   Score = Score + 10 * ScoreMultiplier
13:   Form1.Line (25, 424)-(90, 434), ScoreBoxColor, BF
14:   Form1.ForeColor = vbWhite
15:   Form1.CurrentX = 32
16:   Form1.CurrentY = 424
17:   Form1.Print Score
18:   If ((BrickGridY * COLCOUNT + BrickGridX) = BONUSBRICK1 Or _
19:       (BrickGridY * COLCOUNT + BrickGridX) = BONUSBRICK2) Then
20:     ScoreMultiplier = ScoreMultiplier * 2
21:     Form1.Line (5, 375)-(125, 385), ShadowGrassColor, BF
22:     Form1.Line (517, 375)-(635, 385), ShadowGrassColor, BF
23:     Form1.ForeColor = vbRed
24:     Form1.CurrentX = 30
25:     Form1.CurrentY = 375
26:     Form1.Print "SCORE x " & ScoreMultiplier
27:     Form1.CurrentX = 542
28:     Form1.CurrentY = 375
29:     Form1.Print "SCORE x " & ScoreMultiplier
30:   End If
31: End Sub
```

ANALYSIS Because the ball's coordinates currently overlap those of the brick (which is how the program knows that the ball is hitting the brick), DestroyBrick first adjusts the ball's position to move it off the brick (Lines 4 and 5). The subroutine then sets the brick's entry in the Bricks() array to NOBRICK (Line 6) and changes the ball's direction (Line 7). Then DestroyBrick erases the brick from the screen, decrements the brick count, and increments the player's score (Lines 8 to 12).

The subroutine calculates the score for the brick by multiplying the base score of 10 by the variable ScoreMultiplier, which is 1 when the score doubler is off and can be any multiple of 2, depending on how many times the player has hit a bonus brick since he last lost a ball. After calculating the new score, DestroyBrick displays the score in the

SCORE box (Lines 13 to 17). Finally, DestroyBrick checks whether the brick that the ball hit was one of the score doublers (Line 18). If it was, the program multiplies ScoreMultiplier by 2 (Line 20).

Getting Keyboard Input and Moving the Paddle

The player uses the arrow keys to move the paddle, so the program's form implements the KeyDown event handler, shown in Listing 7.14.

Note

In Listing 7.14, you'll see keyboard key names such as vbKeyF3. Visual Basic defines these key constants, and you can find them in your Visual Basic help files. Just look for "Key Code Constants."

LISTING 7.14   The KeyDown Subroutine

```
1:  Private Sub Form_KeyDown(KeyCode As Integer, _
2:      Shift As Integer)
3:    If KeyCode = vbKeyF2 Then
4:      GameLoop
5:    ElseIf KeyCode = vbKeyF3 Then
6:      Speed = SLOW
7:      BallVecX = -1
8:      BallVecY = -1
9:      MsgBox "Set to slow speed."
10:   ElseIf KeyCode = vbKeyF4 Then
11:      Speed = MEDIUM
12:      BallVecX = -1
13:      BallVecY = -1
14:      MsgBox "Set to medium speed."
15:   ElseIf KeyCode = vbKeyF5 Then
16:      Speed = FAST
17:      BallVecX = -2
18:      BallVecY = -2
19:      MsgBox "Set to fast speed."
20:   Else
21:      MovePaddle KeyCode
22:   End If
23: End Sub
```

ANALYSIS KeyDown handles all keyboard input, including the F keys, which the program uses to start the game and set the ball speed. For example, when the user presses the F2 key, Lines 3 and 4 start the game, and if the player presses the F3 key, Lines 5 to 9 set the game to the slow speed. To move the paddle, KeyDown passes the key code of the pressed key to the MovePaddle subroutine (see Listing 7.15).

7

LISTING 7.15 The `MovePaddle` Subroutine

```
 1: Sub MovePaddle(KeyCode As Integer)
 2:    If KeyCode = vbKeyLeft Then
 3:       If PaddleX > MINPADDLEX Then
 4:          ErasePaddle
 5:          PaddleX = PaddleX - 12
 6:          DrawPaddle
 7:       End If
 8:    ElseIf KeyCode = vbKeyRight Then
 9:       If PaddleX < MAXPADDLEX Then
10:          ErasePaddle
11:          PaddleX = PaddleX + 12
12:          DrawPaddle
13:       End If
14:    End If
15: End Sub
```

ANALYSIS This subroutine checks whether the key code is for the left (Line 2) or right arrow key (Line 8) and moves the paddle in the appropriate direction, first checking the `MINPADDLEX` or `MAXPADDLEX` values to ensure that the paddle doesn't move out of its area.

The `ErasePaddle` subroutine then erases the paddle:

```
Sub ErasePaddle()
  Form1.ForeColor = GrassColor
  Form1.DrawWidth = 4
  Form1.Line (PaddleX, PADDLEY)- _
      (PaddleX + PADDLEWIDTH, PADDLEY)
End Sub
```

After updating the paddle's position, the `DrawPaddle` subroutine redraws the paddle. The paddle itself is nothing more than a wide line. Visual Basic can draw such a wide line, so you don't have to build the line from several smaller ones. To get the wide line, the program sets the form's `DrawWidth` property to 4. This happens in the `DrawPaddle` subroutine:

```
Sub DrawPaddle()
  Form1.ForeColor = vbBlue
  Form1.DrawWidth = 4
  Form1.Line (PaddleX, PADDLEY)- _
      (PaddleX + PADDLEWIDTH, PADDLEY)
End Sub
```

Note

Getting mouse input for your games is almost as easy as getting keyboard input. You need only implement your form's MouseMove and MouseDown event procedures. The MouseMove event procedure reports the position of the mouse as the mouse moves. MouseDown reports the coordinates of a mouse click, as well as providing the status of the Shift, Alt, and Ctrl keys at the time of the click.

Tearing Down the Walls

When the player manages to destroy all the bricks in the wall, the king surrenders his castle (at least until the next wall is built). The subroutine that handles this mini-animation is KingSurrenders (see Listing 7.16).

LISTING 7.16   The KingSurrenders Subroutine

```
 1:  Sub KingSurrenders()
 2:    Form1.Line (BallX, BallY)-(BallX + BALLWIDTH, _
 3:        BallY + BALLHEIGHT), GrassColor, BF
 4:    Dim x As Integer
 5:    For x = 0 To 5
 6:      Form1.PaintPicture imgKing4.Picture, 290, 0
 7:      Delay (0.25)
 8:      Form1.PaintPicture imgKing5.Picture, 290, 0
 9:      Delay (0.25)
10:    Next x
11:    Form1.Line (290, 0)-(400, 30), ShadowGrassColor, BF
12:    Form1.PaintPicture imgKing1.Picture, 290, 0
13:    WaitForReady
14:    StartNewWall
15: End Sub
```

ANALYSIS   This subroutine first erases the ball from the screen (Lines 2 and 3). It then iterates through a For loop six times (Line 5). In the loop, the program displays the first frame of the animation (Line 6) and then calls Delay (Line 7) to keep that frame on the screen for the appropriate amount of time. Then the program displays the second animation frame (Line 8), also delaying (Line 9) before going on to the next iteration of the loop. Figure 7.7 shows the two frames in the animation sequence.

After the loop finishes, the program draws a solid bar over the last frame of the animation and redraws the original king image. The program must first erase the animation frame because it's larger than the king image that normally sits in that location on the

7

wall. After restoring the regular king on the wall, KingSurrenders calls WaitForReady to give the player a chance to collect his wits and steel his nerves for the next round. When the player dismisses the message box that appears, KingSurrenders calls StartNewWall to build a new wall, after which the game is once again under way.

FIGURE 7.7

The frames of the surrender animation.

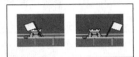

The surrender animation sequence consists of only two frames. However, the results are pretty effective: It really looks as though the king has ducked down behind his wall and is waving a white flag. This demonstrates how easily you can spice up a program with simple animation. One short subroutine is all it takes to create such an animation sequence. If you're feeling ambitious, you can produce more complex animation sequences by creating four or more frames.

Note

In some game programs, you may want to combine animation with movement so that a moving object —such as a spinning flying saucer—changes its form as it moves. You can achieve such an effect fairly easily by displaying the frames of the animation one after the other as the object moves. The only extra overhead in the program is a variable to keep track of which image is currently displayed. However, it's difficult to perform this type of animation in a Visual Basic program because in all but the simplest cases, it requires a lot of processing power.

Summary

Although Visual Basic is too slow and graphically limited for sophisticated, fast-action games, you just need a little ingenuity and elbow grease to use it to create simple arcade games. Of course, the better you optimize your code, the faster your program will run. There are probably several ways that you can make Battle Bricks run faster. Give it a try.

Q&A

Q So, it's not possible to create fast-action games with Visual Basic?

A You *can* use Visual Basic for such a game, but you'll need to call upon a special library such as Microsoft's DirectX to handle the graphically intensive parts of the game. See this book's Appendix D for an introduction to DirectX.

Q **How about the Windows API? Will that help me write action games in Visual Basic?**

A Although you can call Windows API functions from Visual Basic, the API itself isn't any better at handling action games than Visual Basic is. That's not to say that you won't come across a few handy and effective functions in the API, but you'll still need the graphics power of a library like DirectX.

Workshop

The workshop includes quiz questions to help gauge your grasp of the material. You'll find the answers to this quiz in Appendix A. Even if you feel that you totally understand the concepts presented here, you should work through the quiz anyway. The last section has an few exercises to help reinforce your learning.

Quiz

1. What's the purpose of a game loop in a real-time game?
2. Explain how the `BallX` and `BallY` variables are used in Battle Bricks.
3. What is a vector, and how is it used to control ball movement in Battle Bricks?
4. How does Battle Bricks finally manage to break out of its game loop?
5. What does the `Bricks()` array contain?
6. How does the Battle Bricks program determine when to bounce the ball off an object?
7. What is the difference between candidate bricks and actual bricks?
8. What does the program do to destroy a brick and remove it from the game?

Exercises

1. Modify Battle Bricks so that the paddle is 160 pixels wide.
2. Write a short program that bounces a ball around the display area of a form. Feel free to steal source code from the Battle Bricks game. Don't forget to use a game loop.

7

WEEK 1

In Review

There are several reasons to choose Visual Basic for learning game programming. First, it's one of the easiest languages to learn, and it features a set of controls that make creating user interfaces quick and easy. Also, Visual Basic and its programming environment enable fast application development. It's also a powerful language that's capable of handling all but the most complex applications, and its drawing commands and tools enable applications to create professional-looking graphical displays. Finally, Visual Basic's extended implementation of the BASIC language allows not only user-definable data types, but also classes, which enables you to take advantage of some features of an object-oriented language.

Using straight Visual Basic (that is, without making calls to the Windows API or third-party libraries), you can write puzzle games, strategy games, card games, simple arcade games, and virtually any other type of game that doesn't require intensive processing or fast framerates. However, because Visual Basic can call Windows API functions, you can imbue your program with capabilities that cannot be duplicated with straight Visual Basic.

To write computer games that people will want to play, you must gain some expertise in the related areas of programming: game design, graphic design, sound generation, controls and interfaces, image handling, animation, algorithms, artificial intelligence, and game testing.

One of the most important aspects of drawing graphics is color. Visual Basic is very versatile when it comes to color, providing five ways to specify colors. You can use Visual Basic's predefined color constants or the RGB function. You can also use Windows' system colors or the QBColor function, or specify a color's hexa-decimal value.

Visual Basic features powerful drawing methods that can create everything from simple lines to rectangles, circles, and more. Visual Basic's Line method draws lines and boxes, for example, and the Circle method draws circles, ellipses, and arcs.

Visual Basic objects that can display graphics have a set of properties that control how Visual Basic draws lines and shapes. These properties are DrawWidth, DrawStyle, DrawMode, FillColor, and FillStyle.

Visual Basic features several controls that represent graphical objects, from a simple line to a photograph. Like the Form object, the PictureBox control can provide a drawing surface for VB's graphics methods such as Line and Circle. The Line control features a set of properties that enable you to set a line's color, thickness, style, drawing mode, and more. The Shape control, on the other hand, enables you to easily display six different shapes: rectangle, square, oval, circle, rounded rectangle, and rounded square.

If you need to display bitmaps or other types of images from files on your disk, the Image and PictureBox controls fit the bill nicely. The Image control is a kind of stripped-down version of the PictureBox control, so it features fewer capabilities and properties. Still, displaying a photographic-quality image on your application's display is as easy as setting an Image control's Picture property to the file containing the image.

Most games need to display text, and often you won't want to stick to the default font and font attributes. The most obvious font attribute that affects your game displays is color. There are two object properties that determine the colors used for displaying text: ForeColor and FontTransparent.

Besides color, the type of font and its attributes also play a big role in how text appears on your game's screen. Each object that can display text has a Font property that determines the font settings. The Font object features seven properties: Bold, Charset, Italic, Name, Strikethrough, Underline, and Weight.

Writing a game program requires a wide range of skills, not the least of which is figuring out how to get the computer to do what you need it to do. Moreover, you need to get the game to run at a peppy speed, rather than crawling along like a slow-motion replay. Designing algorithms requires that you know the tools at your disposal (the program-ming language) and can apply those tools to solve problems.

When you're designing algorithms, there's usually a tradeoff between code complexity and speed. That is, the more speed you manage to squeeze out of an algorithm, the more complex the algorithm tends to become.

To design effective algorithms, you need to understand the different types of data structures you can use to store data in your program. A linked list is just one of these data structures. Other useful data structures include stacks, queues, and tables.

Although Visual Basic features powerful and flexible graphical objects, such as the Image and PictureBox controls, there may be times when you want even more flexibility. In these cases, you can call the Windows API from your Visual Basic program. There are three steps to calling a Windows API function from Visual Basic. First, you must provide a declaration for the Windows API function you want to call. Second, you must provide declarations for any datatypes required by the Windows API function. Finally, you need to call the Windows API function.

There are a couple of ways to draw straight lines using the Windows API. The most common way is to use the `MoveToEx()` and `LineTo()` functions. The Windows API also features functions for drawing various types of shapes, including not only rectangles and ellipses (ovals and circles), but also polygons. The function that draws rectangles is called (appropriately enough) `Rectangle()`. To draw a circle or oval, you can use the Windows API `Ellipse()` function. Other useful Windows API graphics functions include `Polygon()`, `Polyline()`, `Pie()`, `RoundRect()`, and `PolyPolygon()`.

Although Visual Basic is an excellent programming language, it isn't well suited to writing action games. Its graphics-handling functions are too limited, and a compiled Visual Basic program is often too slow to handle multiple sprites (moving objects) on the screen. Although sophisticated action games are too much for Visual Basic, you can use it to write simple action games if you minimize the number of moving objects.

To keep the game running smoothly, you must program a loop that continually updates each object's position. This is called the game loop. You can make an object move faster onscreen by moving it more than one pixel at a time. However, if you try to move the object too far at once, its motion will be jerky rather than fluid. To keep things simple, you might want to make the background a solid color. This makes it easy to erase and redraw objects.

WEEK 2

At a Glance

In Week 2, you'll study game-programming topics that are more advanced than those presented in Week 1. You'll start off on Day 8 by learning how to use Visual Basic classes to represent a real-world object, such as a deck of cards. You'll also begin to program your own card game. Day 9 continues with the card theme as you learn how to use Visual Basic code to analyze poker hands. Day 10 provides an introduction to the art of creating intelligent computer players. Here you'll get an introduction to artificial intelligence, and then you'll learn how to use a "brute force" method of creating a computer player for a strategy game.

On Day 11, you'll start adding the finishing touches to your games by learning how to play sound effects with the DirectSound component of DirectX. You'll learn how to create, record, and edit sound effects, and you'll discover the Visual Basic Multimedia control and the Windows API functions used to play sounds.

Day 12 begins a three-part section in which you design and program a simple RPG game. On Day 12, you'll learn some general information about RPGs, as well as how to play the Dragonlord RPG included with this book. On Day 13, you'll learn how to program Dragonlord from scratch. Finally, on Day 14, you'll create a level editor for Dragonlord so that you and other players can design their own dungeon adventures.

At the end of Week 2, you will have programmed the following games:

- *Blackjack*—A simple version of the classic card game in which you try to get as close to 21 as you can without going over.

- *Poker Squares*—This commercial-quality card game challenges you to create the best poker hands possible in a 5×5 grid of cards.

- *Crystals*—An ancient strategy game that pits you against the computer as you try to capture as many crystals as possible.

- *Battle Bricks #2*—This is the Battle Bricks game from Day 7, except now it's complete with sound effects.

- *Dragonlord*—A simple RPG in which you try to locate and tame a dragon hidden in a dungeon filled with treasures and deadly skeleton creatures.

DAY 8

Programming Card Games

Few types of games are more popular than card games. Most households have a deck of cards, and probably more fortunes are won and lost over a card table than on a roulette wheel or a slot machine. That popularity crosses over to computer card games as well. The bottom line is that if you're going to be a Visual Basic game programmer, you need to know how to use VB to handle a deck of virtual cards.

Fortunately, Lady Luck is smiling upon you. In this chapter, not only will you create a class for manipulating a deck of cards, but you'll also get a full set of graphical images for your cards. If there's one thing that discourages most programmers from creating card games, it's the daunting challenge of drawing images for 52 cards—especially the face cards, which are the most graphically complex cards in the deck.

Specifically, today you'll learn the following:

- How to write a class to represent a single card
- How to write a class to represent a deck of cards
- How to write card programs using classes
- How to write a simple blackjack game

Deck-Handling Functions

In the following sections, you'll create a class that you can use to program card games. Before creating a class, however, you have to consider carefully the different ways that you must manipulate the data encapsulated in the class. After you've analyzed your game's needs, you can then write the class's functions. Unfortunately for programmers, there are more card games than craters on the moon. This makes creating a complete card class a nearly impossible task. You can never predict all the different ways that you might need to manipulate cards in your programs.

Therefore, the best you can do is to write the functions that every card game needs—such as shuffling a deck and dealing hands—and then add more specific functions as you need them. That's the approach this chapter will take with the clsCard class, which will be used in the next few chapters. After you understand how the clsCard class works, you'll be able to add any other functions that you need to create specific card games.

The clsCard Class

The library of routines presented in this chapter actually consists of two classes: clsCard and clsDeck. The clsCard class includes the data members and methods required to manipulate a single card, and the clsDeck class draws on the clsCard class to create and manipulate a deck of 52 cards, each of which is an object of the clsCard class. The clsDeck class also enables you to group card objects into hands. Listing 8.1 shows the source code for the clsCard class.

LISTING 8.1   The clsCard Class

```
 1:  '//////////////////////////////////////////////////////////
 2:  '// The clsCard Class
 3:  '//////////////////////////////////////////////////////////
 4:
 5:  Option Explicit
 6:
 7:  Private m_xPosition As Integer
 8:  Private m_yPosition As Integer
 9:  Private m_value As Integer
10:
11:  '//////////////////////////////////////////////////////////
12:  '// Class_Initialize
13:  '//////////////////////////////////////////////////////////
14:  Private Sub Class_Initialize()
15:    m_xPosition = -1
16:    m_yPosition = -1
17:    m_value = 0
```

```
18: End Sub
19:
20: '//////////////////////////////////////////////////////////
21: '// Display
22: '//
23: '// This subroutine displays the card at the coordinates
24: '// x,y. The card is displayed face-up or face-down based
25: '// on the face parameter.
26: '//////////////////////////////////////////////////////////
27: Sub Display(x As Integer, y As Integer, face As Integer)
28:   xPosition = x
29:   yPosition = y
30:   If face = FaceUp Then
31:     ShowFace
32:   Else
33:     ShowBack
34:   End If
35: End Sub
36:
37: '//////////////////////////////////////////////////////////
38: '// ShowFace
39: '//
40: '// This subroutine displays the card's face. The card must
41: '// have been previously displayed with the Display()
42: '// subroutine, which sets the card's screen coordinates.
43: '//////////////////////////////////////////////////////////
44: Sub ShowFace()
45:   CardForm.PaintPicture frmCards.Picture1(m_value), _
46:       xPosition, yPosition
47: End Sub
48:
49: '//////////////////////////////////////////////////////////
50: '// ShowBack
51: '//
52: '// This subroutine displays the card's back. The card must
53: '// have been previously displayed with the Display()
54: '// subroutine function, which sets the card's screen
55: '// coordinates.
56: '//////////////////////////////////////////////////////////
57: Sub ShowBack()
58:   CardForm.PaintPicture frmCards.Picture1(52), _
59:       xPosition, yPosition
60: End Sub
61:
62: '//////////////////////////////////////////////////////////
63: '// EraseCard
64: '//
65: '// This subroutine erases the card from the CardForm
66: '// display.
67: '//////////////////////////////////////////////////////////
68: Sub EraseCard()
```

LISTING 8.1   continued

```
69:    CardForm.PaintPicture frmCards.Picture1(53), _
70:       xPosition, yPosition
71: End Sub
72:
73: '////////////////////////////////////////////////////////
74: '// Get and Let xPosition
75: '////////////////////////////////////////////////////////
76: Property Get xPosition() As Integer
77:    xPosition = m_xPosition
78: End Property
79:
80: Public Property Let xPosition(ByVal vNewValue As Integer)
81:    m_xPosition = vNewValue
82: End Property
83:
84: '////////////////////////////////////////////////////////
85: '// Get and Let yPosition
86: '////////////////////////////////////////////////////////
87: Property Get yPosition() As Integer
88:    yPosition = m_yPosition
89: End Property
90:
91: Public Property Let yPosition(ByVal vNewValue As Integer)
92:    m_yPosition = vNewValue
93: End Property
94:
95: '////////////////////////////////////////////////////////
96: '// Get and Let value
97: '////////////////////////////////////////////////////////
98: Public Property Get value() As Integer
99:    value = m_value
100: End Property
101:
102: Public Property Let value(ByVal vNewValue As Integer)
103:    m_value = vNewValue
104: End Property
```

ANALYSIS   The Display method (Lines 27 through 35) displays the card object at the pixel coordinates given as the method's x and y parameters. The face parameter determines whether the card is displayed face-up (by calling the ShowFace method) or face-down (by calling the ShowBack method). The Display method saves the card's screen location in the object's xPosition and yPosition properties.

ANALYSIS   The ShowFace method (Lines 44 through 47) displays the card object's face. The card must have been previously displayed with the Display method, which sets the card's screen coordinates and saves those coordinates in the xPosition and yPosition properties. ShowFace calls the PaintPicture method of the CardForm object (which should be your program's main form) to display the card image, which is one of the images in the Picture1 PictureBox control array.

ANALYSIS The ShowBack method (Lines 57 through 60) displays the card's back. As with the ShowFace method, the card must have been previously displayed with the Display method, which sets the card's screen coordinates and saves them in the xPosition and yPosition properties. ShowBack calls the PaintPicture method of the CardForm object (which should be your program's main form) to display the card-back image, which is the next-to-last image in the Picture1 PictureBox control array.

ANALYSIS The EraseCard method (Lines 68 through 71) erases a card from the screen. As with the ShowFace method, the card must have been previously displayed with the Display method, which sets the card's screen coordinates and saves them in the xPosition and yPosition properties. EraseCard calls PaintPicture method of the CardForm object (which should be your program's main form) to display the blank card image, which is the last image in the Picture1 PictureBox control array.

ANALYSIS The Get and Let methods for each of the properties (Lines 76 through 104) enable a program to obtain the values of the class object's properties. You should use the Let methods with caution because it's not a good idea to change the property values unless you're very sure of what you're doing. For example, if you change a card's xPosition and yPosition properties, a card will be drawn on the screen in one place while the class object thinks the card is in another place.

In this class, the properties xPosition and yPosition (stored in the m_xPosition and m_yPosition variables) are the card's x,y screen coordinates, and value (stored in m_value) is the card's value (which is really more an ID than a card value). The m_value property can be a number from 0 to 51, with the cards numbered as they appear in Figure 8.1.

You can use integer division to determine a card's suit. The formula is suit = value \ 13. This formula results in a value of 0, 1, 2, or 3, which indicates diamonds, clubs, spades, or hearts, respectively.

Use modulus division to determine a card's face value, as in the formula faceValue = value mod 13. This formula yields a result from 0 to 12, with 0 being an ace and 12 being a king. Of course, a specific card program must determine the actual point value of a card.

The clsCard class includes four methods, which are listed and described in Table 8.1.

FIGURE 8.1

*The order of the cards
from ID 0 to 51.*

TABLE 8.1   Methods of the clsCard Class

Method	Description
Display(x As Integer, y As Integer, face As Integer)	Sets the card's coordinates and displays the card at the x,y coordinates. The card is displayed face-up or face-down based on the face parameter, which will be the value FaceUp or FaceDown.
EraseCard	Erases the card from the CardForm display.
ShowFace	Displays the card's face. The card must have been previously displayed with the Display method, which sets the card's screen coordinates.
ShowBack	Displays the card's back. The card must have been previously displayed with the Display method, which sets the card's screen coordinates.

The clsDeck Class

Although Table 8.1 explains how the clsCard class works, you probably won't often need to access the clsCard class directly because it's handled mostly by the clsDeck class. The source code looks like Listing 8.2.

LISTING 8.2   The clsDeck Class

```
1:  '//////////////////////////////////////////////////////////
2:  '// The clsDeck class
3:  '//////////////////////////////////////////////////////////
```

8

```
4:
5:  Option Explicit
6:
7:  Private m_Hands(MAXHANDS) As hand
8:  Private m_Cards(51) As clsCard
9:  Private m_PositionInDeck As Integer
10: Private m_NumCardsInHand As Integer
11:
12: '//////////////////////////////////////////////////////////
13: '// Class_Initialize
14: '//////////////////////////////////////////////////////////
15: Private Sub Class_Initialize()
16:    Dim i As Integer
17:
18:    Randomize
19:    m_PositionInDeck = 0
20:    For i = 0 To 51
21:      Set m_Cards(i) = New clsCard
22:      m_Cards(i).value = i
23:    Next i
24:    Init_Hands
25: End Sub
26:
27: '//////////////////////////////////////////////////////////
28: '// Shuffle
29: '//
30: '// This subroutine shuffles the deck, resets the
31: '// m_PositionInDeck marker, and initializes the m_Hands.
32: '//////////////////////////////////////////////////////////
33: Sub Shuffle()
34:    Dim CardNum As Integer
35:    Dim temp As clsCard
36:    Dim i As Integer
37:
38:    m_PositionInDeck = 0
39:    For i = 0 To 51
40:      CardNum = Int(Rnd * 52)
41:      Set temp = m_Cards(i)
42:      Set m_Cards(i) = m_Cards(CardNum)
43:      Set m_Cards(CardNum) = temp
44:    Next i
45:    Init_Hands
46: End Sub
47:
48: '//////////////////////////////////////////////////////////
49: '// Deal
50: '//
51: '// This subroutine deals num cards into the given hand,
52: '// displaying the cards on screen starting at x,y and
53: '// spacing them each one card width over plus the spacing
54: '// parameter. The parameter face controls whether the cards
```

LISTING 8.2   continued

```
55: '// are dealt face-up or face-down.
56: '///////////////////////////////////////////////////////////
57: Sub Deal(num As Integer, hand As Integer, x As Integer, _
58:    y As Integer, spacing As Integer, face As Integer)
59:   Dim pos As Integer
60:   Dim i As Integer
61:
62:   For i = 0 To num - 1
63:     pos = m_Hands(hand).PositionInHand
64:     Set m_Hands(hand).cards(pos) = m_Cards(m_PositionInDeck)
65:     m_Cards(m_PositionInDeck).Display x, y, face
66:     m_PositionInDeck = m_PositionInDeck + 1
67:     If m_PositionInDeck > 51 Then m_PositionInDeck = 0
68:     m_Hands(hand).PositionInHand = _
69:         m_Hands(hand).PositionInHand + 1
70:     If m_Hands(hand).PositionInHand > 51 Then _
71:         m_Hands(hand).PositionInHand = 0
72:     x = x + 56 + spacing
73:   Next i
74: End Sub
75:
76: '///////////////////////////////////////////////////////////
77: '// ShowHand
78: '//
79: '// This subroutine shows all the cards in the given hand
80: '// starting at the screen coordinates x,y and spaced
81: '// apart according to the spacing parameter. The cards
82: '// are displayed face-up or face-down depending on the
83: '// face parameter.
84: '///////////////////////////////////////////////////////////
85: Sub ShowHand(hand As Integer, x As Integer, y As Integer, _
86:       spacing As Integer, face As Integer)
87:   Dim num As Integer
88:   Dim i As Integer
89:
90:   num = m_Hands(hand).PositionInHand
91:   For i = 0 To num - 1
92:     m_Hands(hand).cards(i).Display x, y, face
93:     x = x + 56 + spacing
94:   Next i
95: End Sub
96:
97: '///////////////////////////////////////////////////////////
98: '// DealReplace
99: '//
100:  '// This subroutine deals one card into the given hand,
101:  '// replacing the card at the position pos. The parameter
102:  '// face controls whether the card is displayed face-up
```

```
103:  '// or face-down.
104:  '//////////////////////////////////////////////////////
105:  Sub DealReplace(hand As Integer,  pos As Integer, _
106:      face As Integer)
107:    Dim x As Integer
108:    Dim y As Integer
109:
110:    x = m_Hands(hand).cards(pos).xPosition
111:    y = m_Hands(hand).cards(pos).yPosition
112:    Set m_Hands(hand).cards(pos) = m_Cards(m_PositionInDeck)
113:    m_Cards(m_PositionInDeck).Display x, y, face
114:    m_PositionInDeck = m_PositionInDeck + 1
115:    If m_PositionInDeck > 51 Then m_PositionInDeck = 0
116: End Sub
117:
118: '//////////////////////////////////////////////////////
119: '// Discard
120: '//
121: '// This subroutine removes the card at position pos from
122: '// the hand specified bt the hand parameter.
123: '//////////////////////////////////////////////////////
124: Sub Discard(hand As Integer, pos As Integer)
125:    Dim x As Integer
126:    Dim y As Integer
127:    Dim DiscardPos As Integer
128:    Dim i As Integer
129:
130:    DiscardPos = m_Hands(MAXHANDS - 1).PositionInHand
131:    m_Hands(MAXHANDS - 1).PositionInHand = _
132:        m_Hands(MAXHANDS - 1).PositionInHand + 1
133:    Set m_Hands(MAXHANDS - 1).cards(DiscardPos) = _
134:        m_Hands(hand).cards(pos)
135:    For i = pos To m_Hands(hand).PositionInHand - 1
136:      Set m_Hands(hand).cards(i) = m_Hands(hand).cards(i + 1)
137:    Next i
138:    m_Hands(hand).PositionInHand = m_Hands(hand).PositionInHand - 1
139: End Sub
140:
141: '//////////////////////////////////////////////////////
142: '// EraseCard
143: '//
144: '// This subroutine erases the card at position pos in
145: '// the hand specified by the hand parameter.
146: '//////////////////////////////////////////////////////
147: Sub EraseCard(HandNum As Integer, pos As Integer)
148:    m_Hands(HandNum).cards(pos).EraseCard
149: End Sub
150:
151: '//////////////////////////////////////////////////////
152: '// ShowHandCard
```

LISTING 8.2   continued

```
153: '//
154: '// This subroutine displays the card at position pos in
155: '// the given hand. The parameter face controls whether
156: '// the card is displayed face-up or face-down.
157: '//////////////////////////////////////////////////////////
158: Sub ShowHandCard(hand As Integer, pos As Integer, _
159:     face As Integer)
160:   If face = FaceUp Then
161:     m_Hands(hand).cards(pos).ShowFace
162:   Else
163:     m_Hands(hand).cards(pos).ShowBack
164:   End If
165: End Sub
166:
167: '//////////////////////////////////////////////////////////
168: '// MoveHandCard
169: '//
170: '// This subroutine moves the card at position pos in the
171: '// given hand to new screen coordinates. The parameter
172: '// face controls whether the card is displayed face-up or
173: '// face-down.
174: '//////////////////////////////////////////////////////////
175: Sub MoveHandCard(hand As Integer, pos As Integer, _
176:     x As Integer, y As Integer, face As Integer)
177:   m_Hands(hand).cards(pos).Display x, y, face
178: End Sub
179:
180: '//////////////////////////////////////////////////////////
181: '// GetCardValue
182: '//
183: '// This function returns the value of the card at pos in
184: '// the given hand. The value is a number from 0 to 51.
185: '//////////////////////////////////////////////////////////
186: Function GetCardValue(hand As Integer, _
187:     pos As Integer) As Integer
188:   GetCardValue = m_Hands(hand).cards(pos).value
189: End Function
190:
191: '//////////////////////////////////////////////////////////
192: '// Init_Hands
193: '//
194: '// This subroutine initializes the m_Hands property,
195: '// setting all cards in m_Hands to Nothing and setting
196: '// each hand's PositionInHand property to zero.
197: '//////////////////////////////////////////////////////////
198: Sub Init_Hands()
199:   Dim i As Integer
```

8

```
200:    Dim j As Integer
201:
202:    For i = 0 To MAXHANDS - 1
203:       m_Hands(i).PositionInHand = 0
204:       For j = 0 To 51
205:          Set m_Hands(i).cards(j) = Nothing
206:       Next j
207:    Next i
208: End Sub
209:
210: '///////////////////////////////////////////////////////////
211: '// Restore
212: '//
213: '// This subroutine sets the position in the deck back to
214: '// the beginning of the deck.
215: '///////////////////////////////////////////////////////////
216: Sub Restore()
217:    m_PositionInDeck = 0
218: End Sub
219:
220: '///////////////////////////////////////////////////////////
221: '// Get NumCardsInHand
222: '///////////////////////////////////////////////////////////
223: Property Get NumCardsInHand(hand As Integer) As Integer
224:    If hand < 0 Or hand > MAXHANDS - 1 Then Err.Raise 9
225:    NumCardsInHand = m_Hands(hand).PositionInHand
226: End Property
```

ANALYSIS In the class's Class_Initialize method, Line 18 ensures that the class is capable of producing a different shuffled deck every time it's used. Line 19 initializes the m_PositionInDeck property, and Lines 20 through 23 create 52 objects of the clsCard class. The Init_Hands call (Line 24) empties all the card hands.

ANALYSIS The Shuffle method shuffles the deck (Lines 39 to 44) by swapping each card with another randomly selected card. The method also resets the m_PositionInDeck marker (Line 38) to 0, which makes the first card in the deck the next card to be drawn. Finally, the method empties all hands (Line 45).

ANALYSIS The Deal method deals the requested number of cards (specified by the num parameter) into the hand specified by the hand parameter. The cards are displayed on the screen starting at x,y, with each card spaced one card width over plus the spacing parameter. The parameter face controls whether the cards are dealt face-up or face-down. Line 62 begins a For statement that iterates once for each card to display. Inside the For loop, Line 63 gets the position in the hand to which the current card should be dealt, and Line 64 sets the card in that hand position to the next card in the deck. Line 65 calls the card object's Display method to paint the card on the screen, and Lines 66 and 67 move the current position in the deck to the next card. Lines 68 to 71 move forward the location for the next card in the hand. Finally, Line 72 adds the spacing parameter to the horizontal position for the next card to display.

ANALYSIS
This ShowHand method shows all the cards in the given hand, starting at the screen coordinates x,y and spaced apart according to the spacing parameter. The cards are displayed face-up or face-down depending on the face parameter. Line 90 gets the number of cards in the hand, and Lines 91 to 94 call each card object's Display method to show the card on the screen. Notice how the Display method is a member of the currently indexed element of the cards() array, which is itself a member of the m_Hands() array.

ANALYSIS
The DealReplace method deals one card into the given hand, replacing the card at the position pos. The parameter face controls whether the card is displayed face-up or face-down. Lines 110 and 111 get the coordinates of the card to replace, and Line 112 places the next card in the deck into the given position in the hand. Line 113 then displays the new card on the screen. Finally, Lines 114 and 115 move the position in the deck to the next card.

ANALYSIS
The Discard method removes the card at position pos from the hand specified by the hand parameter. Line 130 gets the current position in the discard hand, and Lines 131 and 132 move the discard hand's current position forward one card. Line 133 removes the discarded card from the hand and places it into the discard hand, and then Lines 135 to 137 move the cards in the hand back one position in order to fill in the position where the discarded card used to be. Finally, Line 138 updates the position in the hand, setting it back one.

ANALYSIS
The EraseCard method erases the card at position pos in the hand specified by the hand parameter. Calling the card object's EraseCard method is all that's required to erase the card from the screen.

ANALYSIS
The ShowHandCard method displays the card at position pos in the given hand. The parameter face controls whether the card is displayed face-up or face-down. Lines 160 and 161 display the card's face if the face parameter is FaceUp, and Lines 162 and 163 display the card face-down if the face parameter is FaceDown.

ANALYSIS The MoveHandCard method moves the card at position pos in the given hand to new screen coordinates. The parameter face controls whether the card is displayed face-up or face-down. Line 177 calls the card object's Display method to display the card in its new position.

ANALYSIS The GetCardValue function returns the value of the card at pos in the given hand. The value is a number from 0 to 51 and is obtained from the card object's value property in Line 188.

ANALYSIS The Init_Hands method initializes the m_Hands property, setting all cards in m_Hands to Nothing (Lines 204 to 206) and setting each hand's PositionInHand property to zero (Line 203).

ANALYSIS The Restore method sets the position in the deck back to the beginning of the deck. It does this in Line 217 by setting m_PositionInDeck to 0. This method is handy when you want to reuse the same deck of cards.

In the clsDeck class, the variable m_Cards is a 52-element array of clsCard objects. These objects make up the deck of cards. The integer m_PositionInDeck keeps track of the next card to be dealt. That is, at the beginning of a program, m_PositionInDeck is 0, indicating that the first card in the deck will be dealt next. Each time a card is dealt, m_PositionInDeck increments. When m_PositionInDeck equals 51, there's only one card left to deal in the deck. To avoid array-indexing errors, if your program tries to deal more than 52 cards before reshuffling the deck, m_PositionInDeck starts back at 0 and goes through the deck again.

The variable m_Hands is an array of hand objects, which is a user-defined data type (defined in a module called Cards.bas). The hand data type is as follows:

```
Public Type hand
  PositionInHand As Integer
  cards(51) As clsCard
End Type
```

As you can see, the members of hand are similar to two members of the clsDeck class. The integer PositionInHand keeps track of the position in the hand where the next card will be dealt. The array cards holds the clsCard objects that make up the hand.

Although you cannot anticipate all the different ways that you might need to manipulate a deck of cards, the clsDeck class includes 10 methods that you can call in your programs. These methods, which are listed in Table 8.2, enable you to program many card games without adding anything to the class. Study this table now so that you understand how to use the clsDeck class.

TABLE 8.2   Methods of the `clsDeck` Class

Member Function	Description
`Shuffle`	Shuffles the deck and resets the `m_PositionInDeck` marker. It also calls the private member function `Init_Hands` to initialize all eight hands that the `clsDeck` class handles.
`Deal(num As Integer, hand As Integer, x As Integer, y As Integer, spacing As Integer, face As Integer)`	Deals `num` cards into the hand specified by the `hand` parameter and displays the cards onscreen, starting at the coordinates `x` and `y` and spacing the cards each one card-width over plus the `spacing` parameter. The parameter `face` must have the value `FaceUp` or `FaceDown`, which controls whether the cards are dealt face-up or face-down.
`ShowHand(hand As Integer, x As Integer, y As Integer, spacing As Integer, face As Integer)`	Shows all the cards in the hand specified by `hand`, starting at the screen coordinates `x` and `y` and spaced apart according to the `spacing` parameter. The cards are displayed face-up or face-down depending on the `face` parameter with a value that must be either `FaceUp` or `FaceDown`.
`DealReplace(hand As Integer, pos As Integer, face As Integer)`	Deals one card into the given hand, replacing the card at the position `pos`. The parameter `face`, which must be the value `FaceUp` or `FaceDown` controls whether the cards are displayed face-up or face-down.
`EraseCard(HandNum As Integer, pos As Integer)`	Erases the card at position `pos` in the hand specified by the `HandNum` parameter.
`Discard(hand As Integer, pos As Integer)`	Removes the card at position `pos` from `hands(hand)`, placing the card into `hands(7)`, which is the discard pile.
`Sub ShowHandCard(hand As Integer, pos As Integer, face As Integer)`	Displays the card at position `pos` in the given hand. The parameter `face`, which must have the value `FaceUp` or `FaceDown`, controls whether the cards are displayed face-up or face-down.
`MoveHandCard(hand As Integer, pos As Integer, x As Integer, y As Integer, face As Integer)`	Moves the card at position `pos` in the given hand to the new screen coordinates, `x` and `y`. The parameter `face`, which must have the value `FaceUp` or `FaceDown`, controls whether the card is displayed face-up or face-down.
`GetCardValue(hand As Integer, pos As Integer)`	Returns the value of the card at the position `pos` in the given hand. The value is a number from 0 to 51.
`Restore`	Sets the `m_PositionInDeck` data member back to 0, restoring the deck to the state it was in before the program dealt the first card.

Demonstrating the `clsCard` and `clsDeck` Classes

Now that you've looked over the classes, you might be a little unsure exactly how to use them in your own programs. In this section, you'll build a demo program that puts the classes to work.

Building the Program

Follow these steps to create the demo program:

1. Start a new Standard EXE Visual Basic project.

2. Set the following form properties to the values shown here. (Note that the form must be named CardForm because that's the name the `clsDeck` class expects it to have.)

   Name = CardForm

   AutoRedraw = True

   BackColor = Black

   Height = 7815

   ScaleMode = Pixel

   Width = 7995

3. Add a CommandButton control to the form, giving it the following properties:

   Caption = "Test Cards"

   Height = 40

   Left = 18

   Top = 439

   Width = 144

4. Use the Add Form command on the Project menu to add the frmCards.frm form file to the project. You can find this form in the Classes folder of this book's CD-ROM. The frmCards.frm contains the card images, as you can see in Figure 8.2.

   You need this form because it contains the card images.

5. Use the Add Class Module command on the Project menu to add the clsCard.cls and clsDeck.cls class module files to the project. You can find these class modules in the Classes folder of this book's CD-ROM.

   In order to use the `clsCard` and `clsDeck` classes in your program, you must add their files to your project, which you did in this step.

FIGURE 8.2

The frmCards.frm form.

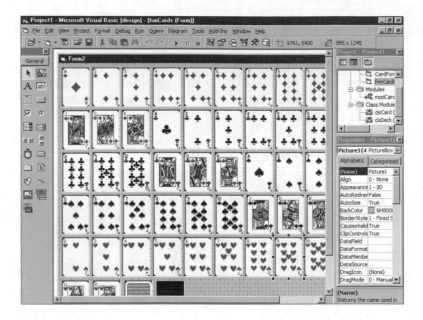

6. Use the Add Module command on the Project menu to add the Cards.bas module file to the project. You can find this module in the Classes folder of this book's CD-ROM.

   The Cards.bas module defines the constants, enumerations, and types needed by the program and the classes, as you can see in Listing 8.3.

LISTING 8.3   The Cards.bas Module

```
 1: Public Const MAXHANDS = 8
 2:
 3: Public Enum Orientation
 4:    FaceDown
 5:    FaceUp
 6: End Enum
 7:
 8: Public Type hand
 9:    PositionInHand As Integer
10:    cards(51) As clsCard
11: End Type
12:
13: Public Enum Suits
14:    Diamonds
15:    Clubs
16:    Spades
17:    Hearts
18: End Enum
```

8

```
19:
20: Public Enum CardNames
21:     Ace
22:     Two
23:     Three
24:     Four
25:     Five
26:     Six
27:     Seven
28:     Eight
29:     Nine
30:     Ten
31:     Jack
32:     Queen
33:     King
34: End Enum
```

7. Double-click the project's form in order to display the code window, and then type the following lines at the top of the program:

```
Option Explicit

Dim Deck As clsDeck
    Dim TestNumber As Integer
```

The Deck object will represent the deck of cards in the program.

8. Add to the code window the handlers in Listing 8.4 for the form object. You can either type them or copy them from the Cards1.txt file, which you can find in the Chap08\Code directory of this book's CD-ROM.

LISTING 8.4   The Form Handlers

```
1: Private Sub Form_Load()
2:     TestNumber = 0
3: End Sub
4:
5: Private Sub Form_Unload(Cancel As Integer)
6:     Unload frmCards
7: End Sub
```

ANALYSIS   The Unload command in the Form_Unload event handler ensures that the frmCards form will be removed from memory at the same time the main form is.

9. Add to the code window the command button handler for the form object, shown in Listing 8.5. You can either type the code or copy it from the Cards2.txt file, which you can find in the Chap08\Code directory of this book's CD-ROM.

LISTING 8.5   The Command1_Click Handler

```
 1:  Private Sub Command1_Click()
 2:    Select Case TestNumber
 3:    Case 0
 4:      ShowFullDeck
 5:    Case 1
 6:      ShowShuffledDeck
 7:    Case 2
 8:      ShowFaceDownDeck
 9:    Case 3
10:      Deal7CardHand
11:    Case 4
12:      ShowFaceDownHand
13:    Case 5
14:      ShowFaceUpHand
15:    Case 6
16:      ReplaceTwoCards
17:    Case 7
18:     DiscardEachCard
19:    Case 8
20:      MoveCards
21:    End Select
22:    TestNumber = TestNumber + 1
23:    If TestNumber > 8 Then
24:      TestNumber = 0
25:      Set Deck = Nothing
26:    End If
27: End Sub
```

ANALYSIS   The command button handler calls a different subroutine depending upon the value of the TestNumber variable. This causes the program to cycle through the various tests of the clsDeck and clsCard classes.

10. Add to the code window the general program subroutines shown in Listing 8.6, which are the subroutines that actually put the classes to the test. You can either type the code or copy it from the Cards3.txt file, which you can find in the Chap08\Code directory of this book's CD-ROM.

LISTING 8.6   The General Subroutines

```
 1:  Sub ShowFullDeck()
 2:    Set Deck = New clsDeck
 3:    Cls
 4:    CurrentX = 250
 5:    CurrentY = 430
 6:    Print "Full Unshuffled Deck"
 7:    Deck.Deal 13, 0, 20, 20, -20, FaceUp
```

```
 8:    Deck.Deal 13, 1, 20, 120, -20, FaceUp
 9:    Deck.Deal 13, 2, 20, 220, -20, FaceUp
10:    Deck.Deal 13, 3, 20, 320, -20, FaceUp
11: End Sub
12:
13: Sub ShowShuffledDeck()
14:    Cls
15:    CurrentX = 250
16:    CurrentY = 430
17:    Print "Full Shuffled Deck"
18:    Deck.Shuffle
19:    Deck.Deal 13, 0, 20, 20, -20, FaceUp
20:    Deck.Deal 13, 1, 20, 120, -20, FaceUp
21:    Deck.Deal 13, 2, 20, 220, -20, FaceUp
22:    Deck.Deal 13, 3, 20, 320, -20, FaceUp
23: End Sub
24:
25: Sub ShowFaceDownDeck()
26:    Cls
27:    CurrentX = 250
28:    CurrentY = 430
29:    Print "Full Face Down Deck"
30:    Deck.Deal 13, 0, 20, 20, -20, FaceDown
31:    Deck.Deal 13, 1, 20, 120, -20, FaceDown
32:    Deck.Deal 13, 2, 20, 220, -20, FaceDown
33:    Deck.Deal 13, 3, 20, 320, -20, FaceDown
34: End Sub
35:
36: Sub Deal7CardHand()
37:    Cls
38:    CurrentX = 250
39:    CurrentY = 430
40:    Print "7-Card Hand"
41:    Deck.Shuffle
42:    Deck.Deal 7, 0, 20, 20, 10, FaceUp
43: End Sub
44:
45: Sub ShowFaceDownHand()
46:    Dim i As Integer
47:
48:    Cls
49:    CurrentX = 250
50:    CurrentY = 430
51:    Print "Face Down Hand"
52:    For i = 0 To 6
53:      Deck.ShowHandCard 0, i, FaceDown
54:    Next i
55: End Sub
56:
57: Sub ShowFaceUpHand()
58:    Dim i As Integer
```

LISTING 8.6   continued

```
59:
60:    Cls
61:    CurrentX = 250
62:    CurrentY = 430
63:    Print "Face Up Hand"
64:    For i = 0 To 6
65:       Deck.ShowHandCard 0, i, FaceUp
66:    Next i
67: End Sub
68:
69: Sub ReplaceTwoCards()
70:    Dim i As Integer
71:
72:    PrepareScreen
73:    Print "Replace Two Cards"
74:    For i = 0 To 6
75:       Deck.ShowHandCard 0, i, FaceUp
76:    Next i
77:    Deck.DealReplace 0, 2, FaceDown
78:    Deck.DealReplace 0, 3, FaceDown
79: End Sub
80:
81: Sub DiscardEachCard()
82:    Dim i As Integer
83:
84:    PrepareScreen
85:    Print "Discard Cards"
86:    Deck.ShowHand 0, 20, 20, 10, FaceUp
87:    For i = 6 To 0 Step -1
88:       MsgBox "Click OK to discard a card"
89:       Deck.EraseCard 0, i
90:       Deck.Discard 0, 0
91:       Deck.ShowHand 0, 20, 20, 10, FaceUp
92:       Deck.ShowHand 7, 20, 110, -20, FaceUp
93:    Next i
94: End Sub
95:
96: Sub MoveCards()
97:    Dim i As Integer
98:
99:    PrepareScreen
100:    Print "Move Cards"
101:    For i = 0 To 6
102:       Deck.EraseCard 7, i
103:       Deck.MoveHandCard 7, i, i * 20 + 20, 200, FaceUp
104:    Next i
105: End Sub
106:
```

```
107: Sub PrepareScreen()
108:   Cls
109:   CurrentX = 250
110:   CurrentY = 430
111: End Sub
```

ANALYSIS These subroutines are the guts of the program. You'll look at this source code in detail a little later in this chapter.

11. Save the project's form file as CardForm.frm and the project file as Cards.vbp.

You've now completed the Cards demo program.

Running the Demo Program

When you run this program, you first see the screen shown in Figure 8.3. Here the program has dealt four hands of 13 cards each, all before shuffling the deck. As you can see, all the cards are in order. When you press Enter, the program shuffles the cards and redeals the four hands, as shown in Figure 8.4. You can see that the cards were indeed shuffled, so the program deals them randomly. Press Enter again and the program deals the same cards face-down.

FIGURE 8.3

The unshuffled deck.

After showing the entire deck, the program manipulates the hand. Each time that you press Enter or click the Test Cards button, the program performs a new function on the current hand. First, it deals a seven-card hand and displays it face-up. The program then shows the hand face-down and again face-up.

FIGURE 8.4

The deck after shuffling.

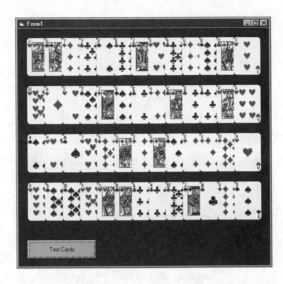

Next, the program deals two new face-down cards into the hand (see Figure 8.5) and then reveals them by turning them over. Then, each time you press Enter, the program discards a card from the hand and displays the new discard pile. Finally, the program moves the discard pile to a new location on the screen.

FIGURE 8.5

Dealing new cards into a hand.

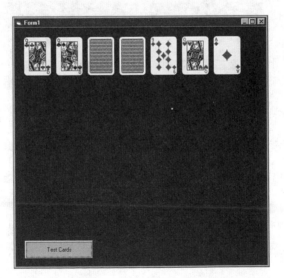

Using the `clsDeck` Class

The demonstration program shows most of what you need to know to use the `clsDeck` class. Before the program can access the `clsDeck` class, it must create a `Deck` object:

```
Dim Deck As clsDeck
```

8

Now, to deal four, 13-card hands from the deck, the program calls the `Deal` subroutine four times:

```
Deck.Deal 13, 0, 20, 20, -20, FaceUp
Deck.Deal 13, 1, 20, 120, -20, FaceUp
Deck.Deal 13, 2, 20, 220, -20, FaceUp
Deck.Deal 13, 3, 20, 320, -20, FaceUp
```

The `Deal` method's arguments are the number of cards to deal, the hand where the cards will be dealt, the x,y screen coordinates of the first card in the hand, the onscreen distance between each card in the hand, and the cards' orientation (either `FaceUp` or `FaceDown`). In the preceding code segment, notice that the distance between the cards is -20. A negative distance causes the cards to appear overlapped. Positive distances separate the right and left edges of adjacent cards by the given number of pixels.

Because the cards in the `Deck` object are all in order, the deck must be shuffled:

```
Deck.Shuffle
```

After the shuffle, the program redeals the 13-card hands in random order:

```
Deck.Deal 13, 0, 20, 20, -20, FaceUp
Deck.Deal 13, 1, 20, 120, -20, FaceUp
Deck.Deal 13, 2, 20, 220, -20, FaceUp
Deck.Deal 13, 3, 20, 320, -20, FaceUp
```

Next, the program deals a seven-card hand, which is displayed onscreen first face-up and then face-down. The program switches the cards' orientation by using the `ShowHandCard` method, which can display any card face-up or face-down:

```
For i = 0 To 6
  Deck.ShowHandCard 0, i, FaceUp
Next I
```

The arguments for `ShowHandCard` are the number of the hand where the card is located, the card's position in the hand (starting at 0 for the first card), and the card's new orientation (either `FaceUp` or `FaceDown`).

To replace cards in a hand, the program calls the `DealReplace` method:

```
Deck.DealReplace 0, 2, FaceDown
Deck.DealReplace 0, 3, FaceDown
```

This method's arguments are the number of the hand where the card to be replaced is located, the position in the hand of the card to be replaced, and the orientation of the new card's display. Note that `DealReplace` does not add replaced cards to the discard pile. To add cards to the discard pile, you must call the `Discard` method. The example program in Listing 8.7 does this.

LISTING 8.7   Discarding Cards

```
1:   For i = 6 To 0 Step -1
2:     MsgBox "Click OK to discard a card"
3:     Deck.EraseCard 0, i
4:     Deck.Discard 0, 0
5:     Deck.ShowHand 0, 20, 20, 10, FaceUp
6:     Deck.ShowHand 7, 20, 110, -20, FaceUp
7: Next I
```

ANALYSIS   In the For loop, the program discards each card from the hand one at a time (Lines 3 and 4), displaying the new discard pile after each discard (Lines 5 and 6). The Discard method's arguments are the number of the hand where cards must be discarded and the position within the hand of the card to discard. In the preceding code segment, Discard's arguments are always 0,0 because the first card in the hand is always the one being discarded. When a card is discarded, the other cards in the hand move back to fill in the empty space.

Finally, the example program moves the discard pile to a new screen location by calling the MoveHandCard method:

```
For i = 0 To 6
  Deck.EraseCard 7, i
  Deck.MoveHandCard 7, i, i * 20 + 20, 200, FaceUp
Next I
```

MoveHandCard moves a single card to a new screen location. Its arguments are the number of the hand that holds the card to move, the position of the card in the hand, the new x,y coordinates for the card, and the card's orientation.

Blackjack, Anyone?

The sample program shows how to call many of the clsDeck methods, but it doesn't show them in action in a real game. In the next chapter you'll design a complete card game called Poker Squares, but for now, something a little simpler is in order. It's time to create a bare-bones version of blackjack.

Creating Blackjack's User Interface

The first step is to create the game's user interface. Perform the following steps:

1. Start a new Standard EXE Visual Basic project.

2. Set the form's properties to the values listed here:

   Name = CardForm

   AutoRedraw = True

```
BackColor = Black
Caption = "Blackjack"
Height = 6015
ScaleMode = Pixel
```
Width = 8250

3. Add three CommandButton controls to the form, giving them the property values listed here:

CommandButton #1

```
Name = cmdStartGame
Caption = "&Start Game"
Height = 33
Left = 19
Top = 320
Width = 89
```

CommandButton #2

```
Name = cmdHit
Caption = "&Hit"
Height = 33
Left = 341
Top = 320
Width = 89
```

CommandButton #3

```
Name = cmdStay
Caption = "S&tay"
Height = 33
Left = 443
Top = 320
Width = 89
```

4. Add a Timer control to the form.

You've now completed blackjack's user interface. Figure 8.6 shows what your main form will look like at this point. In the next section, you'll add handlers for the program's various controls.

FIGURE 8.6

The completed user interface.

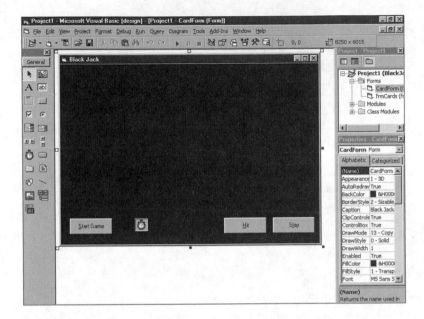

Adding the Object Handlers

Next, you need to associate code with the various objects—the form, buttons, and timer—that make up the user interface. To accomplish this task, perform the following steps:

1. Double-click the form to bring up the code window, and add the following form handlers to it. You can either type the code or copy it from the BlackJack1.txt file, which you can find in the Chap08\Code directory of this book's CD-ROM.

LISTING 8.8   The Form Handlers

```
1: Private Sub Form_Load()
2:   cmdHit.Enabled = False
3:   cmdStay.Enabled = False
4:   cmdStartGame_Click
5: End Sub
6:
7: Private Sub Form_Unload(Cancel As Integer)
8:   Unload frmCards
9: End Sub
```

ANALYSIS   The Form_Load subroutine, which Visual Basic calls when the user starts the program, disables the Hit and Stay buttons (Lines 2 and 4) and the starts a new game by simulating a click on the Start Game button (Line 4). Line 8 in the Form_Unload subroutine removes the frmCards form from memory at the same time the main form closes.

2. Add to the code window the CommandButton handlers in Listing 8.9. You can either type the code or copy it from the BlackJack2.txt file, which you can find in the Chap08\Code directory of this book's CD-ROM.

LISTING 8.9 The CommandButton Handlers

```
1:  Private Sub cmdHit_Click()
2:     PlayerCardCount = PlayerCardCount + 1
3:     Deck.Deal 1, Player, _
4:         PlayerCardCount * 80 + 20, 220, 0, FaceUp
5:     PlayerTotal = GetCardTotal(Player)
6:     If PlayerTotal > 21 Then
7:        MsgBox "You busted"
8:        DealerTotal = GetCardTotal(Dealer)
9:        EndGame
10:    End If
11: End Sub
12:
13: Private Sub cmdStartGame_Click()
14:    Cls
15:    cmdStartGame.Enabled = False
16:    cmdHit.Enabled = True
17:    cmdStay.Enabled = True
18:    Set Deck = New clsDeck
19:    Deck.Shuffle
20:    DealerCardCount = 1
21:    PlayerCardCount = 1
22:    CurrentX = 20
23:    CurrentY = 20
24:    Print "DEALER'S HAND"
25:    Deck.Deal 1, Dealer, 20, 60, 0, FaceDown
26:    Deck.Deal 1, Dealer, 100, 60, 0, FaceUp
27:    CurrentX = 20
28:    CurrentY = 180
29:    Print "PLAYER'S HAND"
30:    Deck.Deal 2, Player, 20, 220, 24, FaceUp
31: End Sub
32:
33: Private Sub cmdStay_Click()
34:    cmdHit.Enabled = False
35:    cmdStay.Enabled = False
36:    Timer1.Interval = 1000
37: End Sub
```

ANALYSIS The cmdHit_Click subroutine responds to the Hit button. Line 2 increases the player's card count, and Line 3 deals another card into the player's hand. A call to GetCardTotal (Line 5) gets the player's current score, and if the total is over 21 (Line 6), the game is over (Lines 7 to 9).

ANALYSIS The cmdStartGame_Click subroutine responds to the Start Game button. Line 14 clears the screen, and Lines 16 and 17 enable the Hit and Stay buttons. Then, Lines 18 and 19 create a new Deck object and shuffle it. Lines 20 and 21 initialize the card counts, and Lines 22 to 24 print the "DEALER'S HAND" label. Lines 25 and 26 deal two cards to the dealer, one of them face down, while Line 30 does the same thing for the player's hand, except this time both cards are dealt face-up.

ANALYSIS The cmdStay_Click subroutine responds to the Stay button. Lines 34 and 35 disable the Hit and Stay buttons in preparation for the dealer's turn. Line 36 turns on the timer, which gets the dealer's turn going.

3. Add to the code window the Timer handler shown in Listing 8.10. You can either type the code or copy it from the BlackJack3.txt file, which you can find in the Chap08\Code directory of this book's CD-ROM.

LISTING 8.10 The Timer Handler

```
 1:  Private Sub Timer1_Timer()
 2:    DealerTotal = GetCardTotal(Dealer)
 3:    If DealerTotal > 21 Then
 4:      MsgBox "Dealer busts"
 5:      Timer1.Interval = 0
 6:      EndGame
 7:    ElseIf DealerTotal > 16 Then
 8:      MsgBox "Dealer stays"
 9:      Timer1.Interval = 0
10:      EndGame
11:    Else
12:      DealerCardCount = DealerCardCount + 1
13:      Deck.Deal 1, Dealer, _
14:        DealerCardCount * 80 + 20, 60, 0, FaceUp
15:    End If
16:  End Sub
```

ANALYSIS The Timer1_Timer subroutine implements the computer player and gets called for each timer event. Line 2 gets the dealer's current card total. If the total is greater than 21, Line 4 notifies the player that the dealer has busted and Line 5 turns off the timer. If the dealer's total is greater than 16, the dealer stays (Lines 8 and 9) and the current game ends (Line 10). Finally, if the dealer's total is less than or equal to 16, Lines 12 to 14 add a card to the dealer's hand.

8

Completing the Game

Almost there! After you add the general game subroutines and the required modules, you'll be ready to play blackjack. Here are the final steps:

1. Add to the code window the general game subroutines shown in Listing 8.11. You can either type the code or copy it from the BlackJack4.txt file, which you can find in the Chap08\Code directory of this book's CD-ROM.

LISTING 8.11 The General Subroutines

```
 1: Function GetCardTotal(plyer As Integer) As Integer
 2:    Dim value As Integer
 3:    Dim total As Integer
 4:    Dim AceCount As Integer
 5:    Dim CardCount As Integer
 6:    Dim i As Integer
 7:
 8:    total = 0
 9:    AceCount = 0
10:    CardCount = Deck.NumCardsInHand(plyer)
11:    For i = 0 To CardCount - 1
12:      value = Deck.GetCardValue(plyer, i) Mod 13
13:      If value > Ten Then
14:          value = Ten
15:      ElseIf value = Ace Then
16:        AceCount = AceCount + 1
17:        value = 10
18:      End If
19:      total = total + value + 1
20:    Next i
21:
22:    If total > 21 And AceCount > 0 Then _
23:      total = total - AceCount * 10
24:    GetCardTotal = total
25: End Function
26:
27: Sub EndGame()
28:    Dim msg As String
29:
30:    Deck.ShowHandCard Dealer,  0, FaceUp
31:    DealerTotal = GetCardTotal(Dealer)
32:    PlayerTotal = GetCardTotal(Player)
33:    Set Deck = Nothing
34:    cmdStartGame.Enabled = True
35:    cmdHit.Enabled = False
36:    cmdStay.Enabled = False
37:    msg = "Dealer: " + CStr(DealerTotal) + _
38:        vbCrLf + "Player: " + CStr(PlayerTotal)
```

LISTING 8.11   continued

```
39:   If PlayerTotal > 21 Or _
40:       (PlayerTotal < DealerTotal And DealerTotal < 22) Then
41:     msg = msg + vbCrLf + vbCrLf + "You lose."
42:   Else
43:     msg = msg + vbCrLf + vbCrLf + "You win."
44:   End If
45:   MsgBox msg
46: End Sub
```

ANALYSIS The GetCardTotal function calculates the card total for the player or dealer, depending upon the value of the plyer parameter. You'll study this function in detail later in this chapter. The EndGame subroutine shows the dealer's hand (Line 30), gets the player's and dealer's card totals (Lines 31 and 32), deletes the deck (Line 33), sets the game's buttons (Lines 34 to 36), and displays a message telling the player who won (Lines 37 to 45).

2. Add to the top of the code window the variable declarations and enumerations in Listing 8.12. You can either type the code or copy it from the BlackJack5.txt file, which you can find in the Chap08\Code directory of this book's CD-ROM.

LISTING 8.12   The Declarations

```
1:  Option Explicit
2:
3:  Private Enum HandIDs
4:     Dealer
5:     Player
6:  End Enum
7:
8:  Dim DealerCardCount As Integer
9:  Dim PlayerCardCount As Integer
10: Dim Deck As clsDeck
11: Dim PlayerTotal As Integer
12: Dim DealerTotal As Integer
```

3. Add the Cards.frm form and the clsCard.cls, clsDeck.cls, and Cards.bas modules to the project, just as you did with the previous demo program.

4. Save the game's main form as CardForm.frm and the project file as BlackJack.vbp.

You've now completed the blackjack program.

Playing Blackjack

When you run the program, you see the screen shown in Figure 8.7. The dealer's hand is at the top of the screen, and the player's hand is at the bottom. The objective of the game is to get as close to 21 as you can without going over. (The cards 2 through 10 are worth 2–10 points. All face cards count as 10 points, and an ace can count as either 1 or 11 points.)

FIGURE 8.7

The main blackjack screen.

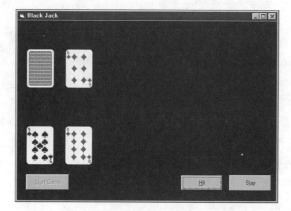

To draw a card, press Enter or click the Hit button. Continue to draw until you're ready to stop, and then click the Stay button. If you haven't gone over 21, the dealer then begins to draw cards. The dealer must continue to draw until it reaches 17 or better. The winning hand is the one that's closest to 21 without going over (see Figure 8.8).

FIGURE 8.8

Winning at blackjack.

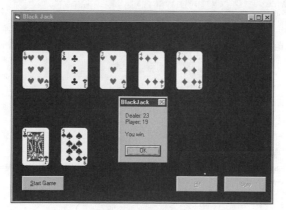

Programming Blackjack

Obviously, this program isn't a complete blackjack game. Many of the game's details are ignored (like doubling-down and insurance), there's no betting, and each game is only a single hand. However, the program does demonstrate how you can use the clsDeck and clsCard classes when programming an actual game. Much of the code in the program needs no explanation. However, one function, GetCardTotal, is the heart of the game and worthy of close examination.

GetCardTotal analyzes a blackjack hand and comes up with a total. This might seem like a trivial task until you recall that an ace can count as either 1 or 11 points. Moreover, a hand might have as many as four aces, further complicating the point-counting process.

To keep this task simple, GetCardTotal assumes that it will count all aces in a hand as the same value. The point value that the program chooses depends on the hand's point total. (Obviously, the program will never use 11 as an ace point value if the hand has more than one ace, because two 11-point aces will bring the hand to over 21.)

First, the program determines how many cards are in the hand by calling NumCardsInHand:

```
CardCount = Deck.NumCardsInHand(plyer)
```

This clsDeck method takes as its single parameter the number of the hand to check. The program uses the value returned from NumCardsInHand to set up a For loop that looks at each card in the hand. In the loop, the program first calculates the value of the current card:

```
value = Deck.GetCardValue(plyer, i) Mod 13
```

This calculation results in a value from 0 to 12 (ace to king). If the card's value is greater than 10, indicating a face card (jack, queen, or king), the program sets the card's value to Ten:

```
If value > Ten Then
    value = Ten
```

(The constants range from Ace, which equals 0, to King, which equals 12. Therefore, Ten is actually the integer value 9, not 10 as you might think.)

If the card turns out to be an ace, the program increments the number of aces in the hand and sets value to 10:

```
ElseIf value = Ace Then
    AceCount = AceCount + 1
    value = 10
End If
```

8

The program first assumes that it will treat the ace as a high card that is worth one point more than the face cards.

Next, the program adds the value of the current card to the total so far:

```
total = total + value + 1
```

Because the card values range from 0 to 12, the added point value is actually value+1.

After totaling the values of all cards in the hand, the program checks whether the hand is over 21. If it is, and it contains aces, the program subtracts 10 for each ace in the hand so that the values of the aces all change to 1:

```
If total > 21 And AceCount > 0 Then _
    total = total - AceCount * 10
```

The function then returns the total to the calling method:

```
GetCardTotal = total
```

That's all there is to analyzing a blackjack hand (although this is a simplified version of the game). Now you're ready to move on to more challenging card games.

Summary

There's a lot involved in programming card games, simply because there are so many of them. Each card game has its own set of rules and requires the deck of cards to be handled in a different way. This makes it difficult to create a comprehensive card class. Still, this day gave you a good start on a class that you can use in your own computer card games. Feel free to modify this class and add code as you discover different ways to manipulate cards in your programs.

In Day 9, you'll put the clsDeck and clsCard classes to a much greater test by creating a full-featured card game called Poker Squares. Not only will you learn more about using the clsDeck class, but you'll also learn to evaluate cards to determine the best poker hands.

Q&A

Q Do all my card games that use these card images have to be on a black background?

A Well, the card images look best on a black background because they're actually rectangular and use black to get the look of rounded corners. Still, you can use another color for the background if you don't mind this little detail. However, avoid white—it won't work because the white of the card faces blends right in.

Q What if I don't want to name my main form CardForm?

A As they stand now, the `clsCard` and `clsDeck` classes expect your form to be named
CardForm. However, there's nothing to stop you from customizing the classes to
expect any form name you want. You actually only need to change the `clsCard`
class in the `ShowFace`, `ShowBack`, and `EraseCard` methods.

Workshop

The workshop includes quiz questions to help gauge your grasp of the material. You'll
find the answers to this quiz in an Appendix A. Even if you feel that you completely
understand the concepts presented here, you should work through the quiz anyway. The
last section contains some exercises to help reinforce your learning.

Quiz

1. Which real-world objects do the `clsCard` and `clsDeck` classes represent?
2. How does the `clsDeck` class use the `clsCard` class?
3. How can you calculate the suit of a card represented by a `clsCard` object?
4. How can you calculate the card's suit?
5. Which modules do you need to add to your programs to use the card classes?
6. Which module defines the constants that are used with the card classes?
7. How do you get the cards represented by a `clsDeck` object into random order?
8. How can you ensure that the frmCards.frm is removed from memory when the
   player quits your card game?

Exercises

1. Write a short program that deals four six-card hands. Overlap the cards in each
   hand by 10 pixels.
2. Write a short program that shuffles the deck and then deals 10 cards, one each time
   the user clicks the form. After the 10th card, reset the deck so that the same 10
   cards are dealt again.

DAY 9

Poker Squares

Now that you're a master card-game programmer (all right, maybe a *novice* master card-game programmer), it's time to put your digital card-shark skills to the test. In the previous chapter, you wrote a simple version of a blackjack program. Although this program put the clsCard and clsDeck classes to good use, it wasn't exactly a challenging project. Evaluating a blackjack hand is almost as easy as counting your fingers when compared to evaluating a poker hand.

In this day, not only will you use the clsCard and clsDeck classes to design a commercial-quality card game, but you'll also learn how to evaluate poker hands—a fairly complicated task. Along the way, you'll also learn to handle a file that records the highest scores.

(A word of caution, though: Poker Squares, the game presented in this chapter, is highly addictive. Don't be surprised if you find yourself stuck in the "just one more" cycle.)

Specifically, today you'll learn the following:

- How to play Poker Squares
- How to build Poker Squares

- How to use the `clsCard` and `clsDeck` classes in a full-featured game
- How to analyze cards for scoring poker hands
- How to implement a high-score board

Playing Poker Squares

The objective of Poker Squares is to place cards in a five-by-five grid so that you create the best poker hands possible in both the horizontal and vertical directions. When you run the program, you'll see the Number of Players box shown in Figure 9.1. You can play Poker Squares with one or two players. Choose the number of players by clicking the Yes or No button.

FIGURE 9.1

The Number of Players box.

In a two-player game of Poker Squares, the program deals both players exactly the same cards in exactly the same order. This eliminates the element of chance in the dealing of the cards for both hands, giving both players an equal chance of scoring. Of course, when the first player is playing his hand, the second player shouldn't watch the screen because he'll see the cards the program deals to him during his turn.

After you close the Number of Players box, you see the screen shown in Figure 9.2. On the left side is the card grid in which you place the cards that the program deals to you. On the right is the card dispenser, which shows the current card to place in the grid. Next to the card dispenser are the final scores for up to two players, and below the card dispenser are the running totals for the current grid. Each time that you place a card in the grid, the program updates the grid scores. The program updates the final scores only after you've placed all 25 cards in the grid.

Below the grid scores are the game's control buttons. Select the Start button to begin a new hand or to start a game over from the beginning (with new cards). At the end of the first player's hand in a two-player game, the Start button resets the screen for the second player, leaving the first player's total score (not the grid scores) onscreen in the SCORES box.

FIGURE 9.2

The Poker Squares main screen.

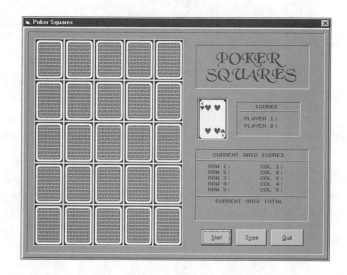

Choose the Score button to display the High Scores box (see Figure 9.3), which holds the highest 15 scores. After you play a hand of Poker Squares and your final score is higher than a score in the file that maintains a list of the 15 highest scores, the New High Score box appears (see Figure 9.4) and prompts you to enter your name. Your name and score are then added to the high-score file, and the High Scores box automatically appears with the new high score highlighted in blue. When you choose the Score button to display the High Score box, no score is highlighted.

FIGURE 9.3

The High Scores box.

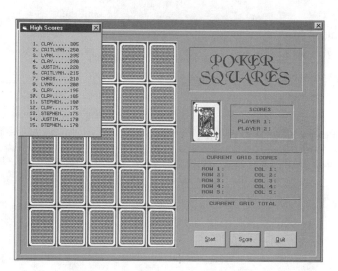

Figure 9.4

*Entering a name for
the high-score file.*

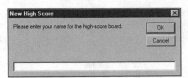

To exit from Poker Squares, click the Quit button. The program then asks you to confirm
that you want to exit. Choose Yes to exit Poker Squares or No to cancel the quit command.

As mentioned previously, your score is based on the best poker hands that you build in
both the horizontal and vertical directions. Table 9.1 describes how the program scores
the eight possible poker hands.

Table 9.1   Scoring for Poker Squares

Hand	Score	Description
One pair	5	Two cards of the same face value (such as two jacks or two deuces).
Two pair	15	Two sets of two cards of the same face value.
Three of a kind	20	Three cards of the same face value.
Straight	30	Any five cards whose face values can be placed in sequence, such as 8, 9, 10, jack, queen. The cards need not be displayed in any particular order in the grid.
Flush	35	Five cards of the same suit.
Full house	45	One pair and one three of a kind.
Four of a kind	60	Four cards of the same face value.
Straight flush	100	A straight that is also a flush.

Building Poker Squares

Now that you've had a chance to play some Poker Squares, you'll learn how to build the
program yourself. In the following sections, you'll build the program one piece at a time.

Creating Poker Square's User Interface

The first step is to create the game's user interface:

1. Start a new Standard EXE Visual Basic project.

2. Set the form's properties to the values listed here:

   Name = CardForm

   AutoRedraw = True

   BorderStyle = Fixed Single

   Caption = "Poker Squares"

   Height = 7590

   ScaleMode = Pixel

   Width = 9705

   This form is the game's main screen. It's important to name the form CardForm because that's the name that the card classes expect.

3. Set the form's Picture property to the screen.gif image that you can find in the Images\PokerSquares directory of this book's CD-ROM.

   Rather than draw the game's display using Visual Basic drawing commands, the program loads a completed screen image into the form.

4. Add three CommandButton controls to the form, giving them the property values listed here:

   CommandButton #1

   Name = cmdStart

   Caption = "&Start"

   Height = 34

   Left = 373

   Top = 418

   Width = 66

CommandButton #2

Name = cmdScore

Caption = "S&core"

Height = 34

Left = 448

Top = 418

Width = 66

CommandButton #3

Name = cmdQuit

Caption = "&Quit"

Height = 34

Left = 523

Top = 418

Width = 66

These are the buttons that enable the player to issue commands to the game. Specifically, these buttons start a new game, display the high-score board, and quit the program.

5. Add a form to the project by selecting the Add Form command from the Project menu. Give the new form the following property settings:

Name = ScoreForm

AutoRedraw = True

BorderStyle = Fixed Single

Caption = "High Scores"

Font = Terminal, Bold, 8-point

Height = 3570

ScaleMode = Pixel

Width = 2610

This form will display the high-score board at the end of a game or when the player clicks the Score button.

6. Save your work, giving the main form the filename CardForm.frm, the project the filename PokerSquares.vbp, and the second form the filename ScoreForm.frm.

You've now completed the Poker Squares user interface. Figure 9.5 shows what your main form should look like at this point. In the next section, you'll add handlers for the program's various controls.

9

FIGURE 9.5

The completed Poker Squares user interface.

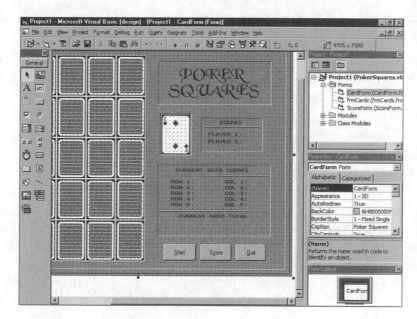

Adding the Object Handlers

Next, you need to associate code with the various objects—the forms and buttons—that make up the user interface:

1. Double-click the form to bring up the code window, and add the form handlers shown in Listing 9.1. You can either type the code or copy it from the PokerSquares1.txt file, which you can find in the Chap09\Code directory of this book's CD-ROM.

LISTING 9.1   The Form Handlers

```
1:  '====================================================
2:  ' Form Handlers.
3:  '====================================================
4:  Private Sub Form_Load()
5:    CardForm.Font.Bold = True
6:    CardForm.Height = 7590
7:    CardForm.Width = 9705
8:    Set Deck = New clsDeck
9:    Player = FirstPlayer
10:   NumPlayers = GetNumPlayers() - 1
11:   InitGame
12: End Sub
13:
14: Private Sub Form_MouseDown(Button As Integer, _
15:     Shift As Integer, X As Single, Y As Single)
16:   Dim CardNum As Integer
17:   Dim CardX As Integer, CardY As Integer
18:   Dim CardPosition As Integer
19:   If ((X > MINX) And (X < MAXX) And _
20:       (Y > MINY) And (Y < MAXY)) Then
21:     CardNum = CalcCardNumber(X, Y)
22:     If Grid(CardNum) = EMPTYCELL Then
23:       GetCardXY CardNum, CardX, CardY
24:       CardPosition = Deck.NumCardsInHand(0)
25:       Deck.MoveHandCard 0, CardPosition - 1, _
26:           CardX, CardY, FaceUp
27:       Grid(CardNum) = CardPosition - 1
28:       EvaluateHands
29:       Deck.Deal 1, 0, DISPENSERX, DISPENSERY, 0, FaceUp
30:       CardCount = CardCount + 1
31:       If CardCount = 26 Then ShowPlayerScore
32:     End If
33:   End If
34: End Sub
35:
36: Private Sub Form_Unload(Cancel As Integer)
37:   Unload frmCards
38:   Unload ScoreForm
39: End Sub
```

ANALYSIS   Visual Basic calls the Form_Load event handler in Lines 4 to 12 when the form is first loaded into memory. In that subroutine, the form sets a few of its own properties (Lines 5 to 7), creates a deck of cards (Line 8), and initializes game variables (Lines 9 to 11). Visual Basic calls the Form_MouseDown event procedure (Lines 14 to 34) when the player clicks the form. This procedure determines which cell in the grid that the player clicked, if any. In Lines 19 and 20, the program checks that the mouse click is within the boundaries of the grid. Then Line 21 calculates the cell on which the player clicked. If the clicked cell is empty, Lines 22 to 32 move the current card into the grid, checking for scoring poker hands and the end of the game. Finally, Visual Basic calls the Form_Unload event procedure in Lines 36 to 39 when the form is unloaded from memory. This subroutine ensures that the other forms are also unloaded.

2. Add the CommandButton handlers (see Listing 9.2) to the code window. You can either type the code or copy it from the PokerSqaures2.txt file, which you can find in the Chap09\Code directory of this book's CD-ROM.

LISTING 9.2   The Button Handlers

```
 1:  '====================================================
 2:  ' Button Handlers.
 3:  '====================================================
 4:  Private Sub cmdQuit_Click()
 5:    Dim Answer As Integer
 6:    Answer = MsgBox("Are you sure you want to quit?", _
 7:        vbYesNo Or vbQuestion, "Quit")
 8:    If Answer = vbYes Then Unload CardForm
 9:  End Sub
10:
11:  Private Sub cmdScore_Click()
12:    ShowScoreFile -1
13:  End Sub
14:
15:  Private Sub cmdStart_Click()
16:    Dim Answer As Integer
17:    Answer = MsgBox("Restart the game?", _
18:        vbYesNo Or vbQuestion, "Start Game")
19:    If Answer = vbYes Then
20:      If CardCount = 26 Then
21:        Player = Player + 1
22:        If Player > NumPlayers Then Player = FirstPlayer
23:      Else
24:          Player = FirstPlayer
25:      End If
26:      DrawNewCardsInGrid
27:      InitGame
28:    End If
29:  End Sub
```

ANALYSIS   These are the event procedures that respond when the player clicks one of the command buttons. The cmdQuit_Click event procedure in Lines 4 to 9 ends the game when the player clicks the Quit button, and the cmdScore_Click event procedure (Lines 11 to 13) displays the high-score board when the player clicks the Score button.

Finally, the `cmdStart_Click` event procedure in Lines 15 to 29 starts a new game when the player clicks the Start button, taking into account whether the game is a one- or two-player game.

Completing the Game

Now, add the general game subroutines, functions, constants, and variables:

1. Add the initialization subroutines (see Listing 9.3) to the code window. You can either type the code or copy it from the PokerSquares3.txt file, which you can find in the Chap09\Code directory of this book's CD-ROM.

LISTING 9.3   The Button Handlers

```
 1:  '=====================================================
 2:  ' Initialization Routines.
 3:  '=====================================================
 4:  Sub InitGame()
 5:    Dim j As Integer
 6:    If Player = FirstPlayer Or CardCount < 26 Then
 7:      Deck.Shuffle
 8:    Else
 9:      Deck.Restore
10:    End If
11:    Deck.Deal 1, 0, DISPENSERX, DISPENSERY, 0, FaceUp
12:    For j = 0 To CELLCOUNT - 1
13:      Grid(j) = EMPTYCELL
14:    Next j
15:    CardCount = 1
16:  End Sub
17:
18:  Function GetNumPlayers() As Integer
19:    Dim Answer As Integer
20:    Answer = MsgBox("Is this a two-player game?", _
21:        vbYesNo Or vbQuestion, "Poker Squares")
22:    GetNumPlayers = 1
23:    If Answer = vbYes Then GetNumPlayers = 2
24:  End Function
```

ANALYSIS   The `InitGame` subroutine (Lines 4 to 16) initialize the deck of cards (Lines 6 to 11) and the game grid (Lines 12 to 14). This subroutine also initializes the `CardCount` variable (Line 15). The `GetNumPlayers` function (Lines 18 to 24) retrieves the number of players from the user.

2. Add the general subroutines (see Listing 9.4) to the code window. You can either
   type the code or copy it from the PokerSquares4.txt file, which you can find in the
   Chap09\Code directory of this book's CD-ROM.

LISTING 9.4   The General Subroutines

```
 1:  '=================================================
 2:  ' General Game Subroutines.
 3:  '=================================================
 4:  Sub GetCardXY(Card As Integer, PixelX As Integer, _
 5:      PixelY As Integer)
 6:    PixelX = (Card Mod COLUMNCOUNT) * CELLWIDTH + MINX
 7:    PixelY = (Card \ COLUMNCOUNT) * CELLHEIGHT + MINY
 8:  End Sub
 9:
10:  Sub EvaluateHands()
11:    PlayerScores(Player) = 0
12:    EraseScores
13:    PlayerScores(Player) = _
14:        PlayerScores(Player) + GetRowScores
15:    PlayerScores(Player) = _
16:        PlayerScores(Player) + GetColumnScores
17:    ShowTotalScore
18:  End Sub
19:
20:  Sub EraseScores()
21:    CardForm.ForeColor = RGB(172, 172, 172)
22:    CardForm.Line (ROWSCORESX, SCOREOFFSETY)- _
23:        (ROWSCORESX + 40, SCOREOFFSETY + 60), , BF
24:    CardForm.ForeColor = RGB(160, 0, 0)
25:    CardForm.ForeColor = RGB(172, 172, 172)
26:    CardForm.Line (COLSCORESX, SCOREOFFSETY)- _
27:        (COLSCORESX + 40, SCOREOFFSETY + 60), , BF
28:    CardForm.ForeColor = RGB(160, 0, 0)
29:  End Sub
30:
31:  Sub ShowTotalScore()
32:    CardForm.ForeColor = RGB(172, 172, 172)
33:    CardForm.Line (TOTALSCOREX, TOTALSCOREY)- _
34:        (TOTALSCOREX + 100, TOTALSCOREY + 30), , BF
35:    CardForm.ForeColor = RGB(160, 0, 0)
36:    CardForm.CurrentX = TOTALSCOREX
37:    CardForm.CurrentY = TOTALSCOREY
38:    CardForm.Font.Size = 24
39:    CardForm.Print PlayerScores(Player)
40:    CardForm.Font.Size = 8
41:  End Sub
42:
43:  Sub ShowPlayerScore()
44:    Dim s As String
```

LISTING 9.4 continued

```
45:    CardForm.ForeColor = RGB(172, 172, 172)
46:    CardForm.Line (PLAYERSCOREX, Player * _
47:       LINESPACING + PLAYERSCOREY)- _
48:       (PLAYERSCOREX + 30, Player * (LINESPACING + 3) + _
49:       PLAYERSCOREY + 12), , BF
50:    CardForm.ForeColor = RGB(160, 0, 0)
51:    CardForm.CurrentX = PLAYERSCOREX
52:    CardForm.CurrentY = Player * (LINESPACING + 3) + PLAYERSCOREY
53:    CardForm.Print PlayerScores(Player)
54:    AddToScoreFile
55: End Sub
56:
57: Sub DrawNewCardsInGrid()
58:    Dim Col As Integer
59:    Dim Row As Integer
60:    For Col = 0 To COLUMNCOUNT - 1
61:      For Row = 0 To ROWCOUNT - 1
62:        CardForm.PaintPicture frmCards.Picture1(CARDBACK), _
63:           Col * CELLWIDTH + MINX, Row * CELLHEIGHT + MINY
64:      Next Row
65:    Next Col
66: End Sub
67:
68: Sub SortCards(cards() As Integer, hand() As Integer)
69:    Dim i As Integer
70:    For i = 0 To 13
71:      cards(i) = 0
72:    Next i
73:    cards(13) = 1
74:    For i = 0 To 4
75:      If hand(i) <> NOCARD Then
76:        Dim val As Integer
77:        val = hand(i) Mod 13
78:        cards(val) = cards(val) + 1
79:      End If
80:    Next i
81: End Sub
```

ANALYSIS The GetCardXY subroutine (Lines 4 to 8) gets the pixel X and Y coordinates of a given card in the grid, whereas EvaluateHands (Lines 10 to 18) calculates the scores for each column and row in the grid. The EraseScores subroutine (Lines 20 to 29) erases the old scores from the screen in preparation for displaying the new scores, which is handled by ShowTotalScore (Lines 31 to 41) and ShowPlayerScore (Lines 43 to 55). The DrawNewCardsInGrid subroutine (Lines 57 to 66) fills the grid with card backs, whereas the SortCards subroutine (Lines 68 to 81) sorts the cards in preparation for analyzing the hands.

3. Add the file-handling subroutines (see Listing 9.5) to the code window. You can
either type the code or copy it from the PokerSquares5.txt file, which you can find
in the Chap09\Code directory of this book's CD-ROM.

LISTING 9.5   The File-Handling Subroutines

```
 1:  '==================================================
 2:  ' File Handling Subroutines.
 3:  '==================================================
 4:  Sub WriteScoreFile(names() As String, scores() As Integer)
 5:    'ChDir "c:\TYVBGames\PokerSquares"
 6:    Open "highscr.dat" For Binary As #1
 7:    Put #1, , names
 8:    Put #1, , scores
 9:    Close #1
10:  End Sub
11:
12:  Sub ReadScoreFile(names() As String, scores() As Integer)
13:    'ChDir "c:\TYVBGames\PokerSquares"
14:    Open "highscr.dat" For Binary As #1
15:    Get #1, , names
16:    Get #1, , scores
17:    Close #1
18:  End Sub
19:
20:  Sub AddToScoreFile()
21:    Dim names(MAXHIGHSCORES - 1) As String
22:    Dim scores(MAXHIGHSCORES - 1) As Integer
23:    Dim name As String
24:    Dim i As Integer
25:    Dim X As Integer
26:    Dim NewHighScore As Boolean
27:    Dim HighScore As Integer
28:    Dim NameLen As Integer
29:    ReadScoreFile names, scores
30:    X = 0
31:    NewHighScore = False
32:    Do
33:      HighScore = scores(X)
34:      If PlayerScores(Player) > HighScore Then
35:        NewHighScore = True
36:        For i = MAXHIGHSCORES - 2 To X Step -1
37:          names(i + 1) = names(i)
38:          scores(i + 1) = scores(i)
39:        Next i
40:        name = InputBox _
41:            ("Please enter your name for the high-score board.",
42:  _
43:            "New High Score")
44:        NameLen = Len(name)
```

9

LISTING 9.5 continued

```
45:          If NameLen > 10 Then
46:            name = Left$(name, 10)
47:            NameLen = 10
48:          End If
49:          For i = NameLen To 9
50:            name = name & "."
51:          Next i
52:          name = UCase(name)
53:          names(X) = name
54:          scores(X) = PlayerScores(Player)
55:          WriteScoreFile names, scores
56:        End If
57:      X = X + 1
58:    Loop While ((Not NewHighScore) And (X < MAXHIGHSCORES))
59:    If NewHighScore Then ShowScoreFile (X - 1)
60: End Sub
61:
62: Sub ShowScoreFile(NameToHighlight As Integer)
63:   Dim names(MAXHIGHSCORES - 1) As String
64:   Dim scores(MAXHIGHSCORES - 1) As Integer
65:   Dim str As String
66:   Dim X As Integer
67:   ReadScoreFile names, scores
68:   ScoreForm.Left = CardForm.Left + 100
69:   ScoreForm.Top = CardForm.Top + 100
70:   ScoreForm.Show
71:   For X = 0 To MAXHIGHSCORES - 1
72:     If X < 9 Then
73:       str = " " & X + 1
74:     Else
75:       str = X + 1
76:     End If
77:     str = str & ". " & names(X) & scores(X)
78:     ScoreForm.CurrentX = 20
79:     ScoreForm.CurrentY = 20 + X * LINESPACING
80:     If X = NameToHighlight Then ScoreForm.ForeColor = vbBlue
81:     ScoreForm.Print str
82:     ScoreForm.ForeColor = vbBlack
83:   Next X
84: End Sub
```

ANALYSIS The WriteScoreFile subroutine (Lines 4 to 10) updates the high-score file with the latest set of player names and high scores. The ReadScoreFile subroutine reads the current player names and high scores from the high-score file, whereas AddToScoreFile (Lines 20 to 60) adds a new score to the high-score list, sorting the scores in descending order. Finally, ShowScoreFile displays the high-score file in the ScoreForm window.

4. Add the game functions (see Listing 9.6) to the code window. You can either type the code or copy it from the PokerSquares6.txt file, which you can find in the Chap09\Code directory of this book's CD-ROM.

LISTING 9.6   The Game Functions

```
 1: '=====================================================
 2: ' Game Functions.
 3: '=====================================================
 4: Function GetColumnScores()
 5:   Dim Col As Integer
 6:   Dim Start As Integer
 7:   Dim X As Integer
 8:   Dim i As Integer
 9:   Dim hand(4) As Integer
10:   Dim Score As Integer
11:   Dim BestHand As Integer
12:   For Col = 0 To COLUMNCOUNT - 1
13:     Start = Col
14:     For X = 0 To 4
15:       hand(X) = NOCARD
16:     Next X
17:     i = 0
18:     For X = 0 To 4
19:       If Grid(X * COLUMNCOUNT + Col) <> EMPTYCELL Then
20:           hand(i) = Deck.GetCardValue(0, _
21:             Grid(X * COLUMNCOUNT + Col))
22:         i = i + 1
23:       End If
24:     Next X
25:     BestHand = GetBestHand(hand)
26:     Score = GetScore(BestHand)
27:     CardForm.CurrentX = COLSCORESX
28:     CardForm.CurrentY = Col * LINESPACING + SCOREOFFSETY
29:     CardForm.Print Score
30:     GetColumnScores = GetColumnScores + Score
31:   Next Col
32: End Function
33:
34: Function GetRowScores() As Integer
35:   Dim Row As Integer
36:   Dim Start As Integer
37:   Dim X As Integer
38:   Dim i As Integer
39:   Dim hand(4) As Integer
40:   Dim BestHand As Integer
41:   Dim Score As Integer
42:   For Row = 0 To ROWCOUNT - 1
43:     Start = Row * COLUMNCOUNT
```

LISTING 9.6 continued

```
44:      For X = 0 To 4
45:        hand(X) = NOCARD
46:      Next X
47:      i = 0
48:      For X = Start To Start + 4
49:        If Grid(X) <> EMPTYCELL Then
50:          hand(i) = Deck.GetCardValue(0, Grid(X))
51:          i = i + 1
52:        End If
53:      Next X
54:      BestHand = GetBestHand(hand)
55:      Score = GetScore(BestHand)
56:      GetRowScores = GetRowScores + Score
57:      CardForm.CurrentX = ROWSCORESX
58:      CardForm.CurrentY = Row * LINESPACING + SCOREOFFSETY
59:      CardForm.Print Score
60:    Next Row
61: End Function
62:
63: Function CalcCardNumber(PixelX As Single, _
64:      PixelY As Single) As Integer
65:    Dim GridX As Integer
66:    Dim GridY As Integer
67:    GridX = (PixelX - MINX) \ CELLWIDTH
68:    GridY = (PixelY - MINY) \ CELLHEIGHT
69:    CalcCardNumber = GridY * COLUMNCOUNT + GridX
70: End Function
71:
72: Function GetScore(BestHand As Integer) As Integer
73:    Select Case BestHand
74:      Case NoHand
75:        GetScore = 0
76:      Case Pair
77:        GetScore = 5
78:      Case TwoPair
79:        GetScore = 15
80:      Case ThreeOfAKind
81:        GetScore = 20
82:      Case Straight
83:        GetScore = 30
84:      Case Flush
85:        GetScore = 35
86:      Case FullHouse
87:        GetScore = 45
88:      Case FourOfAKind
89:        GetScore = 60
90:      Case StraightFlush
91:        GetScore = 100
```

LISTING 9.6   continued

```
92:       End Select
93: End Function
94:
95: Function GetBestHand(hand() As Integer) As Integer
96:    Dim FlushFlag As Boolean
97:    Dim StraightFlag As Boolean
98:    Dim PairFlag As Boolean
99:    Dim TwoPairFlag As Boolean
100:    Dim ThreeOfAKindFlag As Boolean
101:    Dim FourOfAKindFlag As Boolean
102:    Dim cards(13) As Integer
103:
104:    FlushFlag = CheckForFlush(hand)
105:    SortCards cards, hand
106:    StraightFlag = CheckForStraight(cards, hand)
107:    PairFlag = CheckForPair(cards)
108:    TwoPairFlag = CheckForTwoPair(cards)
109:    ThreeOfAKindFlag = CheckForThreeOfAKind(cards)
110:    FourOfAKindFlag = CheckForFourOfAKind(cards)
111:
112:    If (StraightFlag) And (FlushFlag) Then
113:      GetBestHand = StraightFlush
114:    ElseIf FourOfAKindFlag Then
115:      GetBestHand = FourOfAKind
116:    ElseIf (PairFlag) And (ThreeOfAKindFlag) Then
117:      GetBestHand = FullHouse
118:    ElseIf FlushFlag Then
119:      GetBestHand = Flush
120:    ElseIf StraightFlag Then
121:      GetBestHand = Straight
122:    ElseIf ThreeOfAKindFlag Then
123:      GetBestHand = ThreeOfAKind
124:    ElseIf TwoPairFlag Then
125:      GetBestHand = TwoPair
126:    ElseIf PairFlag Then
127:      GetBestHand = Pair
128:    Else
129:      GetBestHand = NoHand
130:    End If
131: End Function
132:
133: Function CheckForTwoPair(cards() As Integer)
134:    Dim i As Integer
135:    Dim PairFlag As Boolean
136:    CheckForTwoPair = False
137:    PairFlag = False
138:    For i = Ace To King
139:      If cards(i) = 2 And PairFlag Then
```

9

LISTING 9.6 continued

```
140:      CheckForTwoPair = True
141:    ElseIf cards(i) = 2 Then
142:      PairFlag = True
143:    End If
144:  Next i
145: End Function
146:
147: Function CheckForThreeOfAKind(cards() As Integer) As Boolean
148:   Dim i As Integer
149:   CheckForThreeOfAKind = False
150:   For i = Ace To King
151:     If cards(i) = 3 Then CheckForThreeOfAKind = True
152:   Next i
153: End Function
154:
155: Function CheckForFourOfAKind(cards() As Integer) As Boolean
156:   Dim i As Integer
157:   CheckForFourOfAKind = False
158:   For i = Ace To King
159:     If cards(i) = 4 Then CheckForFourOfAKind = True
160:   Next i
161: End Function
162:
163: Function CheckForPair(cards() As Integer) As Boolean
164:   Dim i As Integer
165:   CheckForPair = False
166:   For i = Ace To King
167:     If cards(i) = 2 Then CheckForPair = True
168:   Next i
169: End Function
170:
171: Function CheckForFlush(hand() As Integer) As Boolean
172:   Dim i As Integer
173:   Dim Suit As Integer
174:   Suit = hand(0) \ 13
175:   CheckForFlush = True
176:   For i = 1 To 4
177:     If hand(i) \ 13 <> Suit Or hand(i) = NOCARD Then _
178:         CheckForFlush = False
179:   Next i
180: End Function
181:
182: Function CheckForStraight(cards() As Integer, _
183:     hand() As Integer) As Boolean
184:   Dim First As Integer
185:   Dim i As Integer
186:   First = -1
187:   i = Ace
```

LISTING 9.6   continued

```
188:   Do
189:     If ((cards(i)) And (i <> Ace Or cards(Two))) _
190:        Then First = i
191:     i = i + 1
192:   Loop While (First = -1)
193:   If (First > Ten) Then
194:     CheckForStraight = False
195:   Else
196:     CheckForStraight = True
197:     For i = First To First + 4
198:       If (cards(i) = 0) Then CheckForStraight = False
199:     Next i
200:   End If
201: End Function
```

ANALYSIS   These functions implement the scoring in the game and are discussed in detail later in this chapter.

5. Add the variable declarations and enumerations (see Listing 9.7) to the top of the code window. You can either type the code or copy it from the PokerSquares7.txt file, which you can find in the Chap09\Code directory of this book's CD-ROM.

LISTING 9.7   The Game's Declarations

```
 1: '==================================================
 2: ' Poker Squares for Visual Basic 6
 3: '    by Clayton Walnum
 4: ' Copyright 2000 by Macmillan Computer Publishing
 5: '==================================================
 6: Option Explicit
 7:
 8: '==================================================
 9: ' Constants.
10: '==================================================
11: Const EMPTYCELL = -1
12: Const NOCARD = -1
13: Const MINX = 28
14: Const MAXX = 332
15: Const MINY = 28
16: Const MAXY = 450
17: Const CELLWIDTH = 62
18: Const CELLHEIGHT = 86
19: Const COLUMNCOUNT = 5
20: Const ROWCOUNT = 5
21: Const DISPENSERX = 369
22: Const DISPENSERY = 151
```

LISTING 9.7 continued

```
23: Const LINESPACING = 12
24: Const ROWSCORESX = 441
25: Const PLAYERSCOREX = 535
26: Const PLAYERSCOREY = 182
27: Const CARDBACK = 52
28: Const MAXHIGHSCORES = 15
29: Const CELLCOUNT = 25
30: Const COLSCORESX = 553
31: Const SCOREOFFSETY = 281
32: Const TOTALSCOREX = 430
33: Const TOTALSCOREY = 365
34:
35: Public Enum PokerHandsEnum
36:    NoHand
37:    Pair
38:    TwoPair
39:    ThreeOfAKind
40:    Straight
41:    Flush
42:    FullHouse
43:    FourOfAKind
44:    StraightFlush
45: End Enum
46:
47: Public Enum PlayerEnum
48:    FirstPlayer
49:    SecondPlayer
50: End Enum
51:
52: '=================================================
53: ' General Game Variables.
54: '=================================================
55: Dim Player As Integer
56: Dim CardCount As Integer
57: Dim Grid(24) As Integer
58: Dim PlayerScores(2)
59: Dim Deck As clsDeck
60: Dim NumPlayers As Integer
```

ANALYSIS These lines declare all the global game variables and constants. Later in this chapter, you'll examine these symbols in detail.

6. Add the frmCards.frm form and the clsCard, clsDeck, and Cards.bas modules to the project, just as you did with the previous demo program.

7. Save your work.

You've now completed the Poker Squares program.

Understanding Poker Squares

Now that you've played the game and built your own version, it's time to examine the code, starting with the game's constants and variables.

The Poker Squares Variables and Constants

Poker Squares relies on a set of global variables and constants that it declares near the top of the program. Table 9.1 lists the general global variables and their descriptions, and Table 9.2 lists the constants.

TABLE 9.1 The Poker Squares General Game Variables

Variable	Type	Description
CardCount	Integer	The number of cards that have been dealt in the current game
Deck	clsDeck	The game's clsDeck object, which represents the deck of cards
Grid()	Integer	An array that holds the card numbers for each cell in the card grid
NumPlayers	Integer	The number of players in the current game
Player	Integer	The current player
PlayerScores()	Integer	An array that holds the scores for up to two players

TABLE 9.2 The Poker Squares Constants

Constant	Description
CARDBACK	The number of the card-back image
CELLCOUNT	The number of cells in the grid
CELLHEIGHT	The height of a cell in the card grid
CELLWIDTH	The width of a cell in the card grid
COLSCORESX	The X coordinate of the column scores
COLUMNCOUNT	The number of columns in the grid
DISPENSERX	The X coordinate of the card dispenser
DISPENSERY	The Y coordinate of the card dispenser
EMPTYCELL	The value that represents a grid cell that does not yet contain a card
LINESPACING	The amount of space between lines of text in the scoreboards
MAXHIGHSCORES	The maximum number of scores that will fit in the high score window
MAXX	The maximum X value that is a valid mouse click in the grid

TABLE 9.2 continued

Constant	Description
MAXY	The maximum Y value that is a valid mouse click in the grid
MINX	The minimum X value that is a valid mouse click in the grid
MINY	The minimum Y value that is a valid mouse click in the grid
NOCARD	The value that indicates an empty position in a hand
PLAYERSCOREX	The X coordinate of the player scores
PLAYERSCOREY	The Y coordinate of the player scores
ROWCOUNT	The number of rows in the grid
ROWSCORESX	The X coordinate of the row scores
SCOREOFFSETY	The Y coordinate of the row and column scores
TOTALSCOREX	The X coordinate of the total score for the current game
TOTALSCOREY	The Y coordinate of the total score for the current game

The Poker Squares program also defines two enumerations. The PokerHandsEnum enumeration defines constants for the nine different poker hands (including a non-scoring hand), and the PlayerEnum enumeration defines the FirstPlayer and SecondPlayer constants. (The SecondPlayer constant is not currently used in the program.)

Getting Row and Column Scores

Most of the source code in Poker Squares is easy to understand, especially now that you can handle the clsCard and clsDeck classes. However, the card-evaluation functions, which are the core of the game, require discussion.

The program calls the function EvaluateHands whenever the player places a new card in the card grid. This function calculates the current row and column scores by calling the GetRowScores and GetColumnScores functions. Also, EvaluateHands displays the player's new total score.

LISTING 9.8 The EvaluateHands Subroutine

```
1:  Sub EvaluateHands()
2:    PlayerScores(Player) = 0
3:    EraseScores
4:    PlayerScores(Player) = _
5:        PlayerScores(Player) + GetRowScores
6:    PlayerScores(Player) = _
7:        PlayerScores(Player) + GetColumnScores
8:    ShowTotalScore
9:  End Sub
```

ANALYSIS This subroutine calls the functions required to calculate the player's scores. Lines 4 and 5 get the row scores, and Lines 6 and 7 get the column scores.

The GetRowScores function starts a For loop that examines each of the five rows:

```
For Row = 0 To ROWCOUNT - 1
```

The function then calculates the cell number that starts the current row:

```
Start = Row * COLUMNCOUNT
```

Next, the function initializes the local hand array:

```
For X = 0 To 4
  hand(X) = NOCARD
Next X
```

Another For loop gets the cards from the current row and places them into the hand array.

LISTING 9.9 Initializing the Hand Array

```
1:    i = 0
2:    For X = Start To Start + 4
3:      If Grid(X) <> EMPTYCELL Then
4:        hand(i) = Deck.GetCardValue(0, Grid(X))
5:        i = i + 1
6:      End If
7:  Next X
```

ANALYSIS Line 1 initializes an index into the hand() array, and the loop in Lines 3 to 6 gets the value of each card and places that value into the hand() array.

With the cards assembled into the hand array, the function calls GetBestHand, which analyzes the cards in the hand array and returns the highest-scoring hand for those cards:

```
BestHand = GetBestHand(hand)
```

The GetScore function then returns the score for the hand returned by GetBestHand, and the function adds the score to the row scores total:

```
Score = GetScore(BestHand)
GetRowScores = GetRowScores + Score
```

Finally, GetRowScores displays the score for the current row, and the For loop continues to the next row:

```
CardForm.CurrentX = ROWSCORESX
CardForm.CurrentY = Row * LINESPACING + SCOREOFFSETY
CardForm.Print Score
Next Row
```

The function GetBestHand analyzes a hand of five cards and determines the highest-scoring combination. It declares a set of flags that represent the various combinations of cards:

```
Dim FlushFlag As Boolean
Dim StraightFlag As Boolean
Dim PairFlag As Boolean
Dim TwoPairFlag As Boolean
Dim ThreeOfAKindFlag As Boolean
Dim FourOfAKindFlag As Boolean
```

The GetBestHand function sets these flags by calling other functions that specialize in calculating each type of hand. Checking for a flush, for example, is the job of the CheckForFlush function:

```
FlushFlag = CheckForFlush(hand)
```

Checking for a flush is easy, as you'll see when you examine the CheckForFlush function. Other types of poker hands require some extra processing. To start this processing, GetBestHand defines an array that can hold 13 card values:

```
Dim cards(13) As Integer
```

Each element in the array represents a card of a specific face value. That is, cards(0) represents aces, cards(1) represents twos, cards(2) represents threes, and so on, up to cards(12), which represents kings. The element cards(13) represents aces when used as high cards.

The SortCards subroutine sorts the cards in the current hand into the cards array:

```
SortCards cards, hand
```

With the cards sorted, GetBestHand can call the other functions that check for poker hands:

```
StraightFlag = CheckForStraight(cards, hand)
PairFlag = CheckForPair(cards)
TwoPairFlag = CheckForTwoPair(cards)
ThreeOfAKindFlag = CheckForThreeOfAKind(cards)
FourOfAKindFlag = CheckForFourOfAKind(cards)
```

At this point, GetBestHand has set all the poker-hand flags. The final step is to check the flags in order to determine the best possible hand, as shown in Listing 9.10.

LISTING 9.10   Initializing the Hand Array

```
 1:    If (StraightFlag) And (FlushFlag) Then
 2:       GetBestHand = StraightFlush
 3:    ElseIf FourOfAKindFlag Then
 4:       GetBestHand = FourOfAKind
 5:    ElseIf (PairFlag) And (ThreeOfAKindFlag) Then
 6:       GetBestHand = FullHouse
 7:    ElseIf FlushFlag Then
 8:       GetBestHand = Flush
 9:    ElseIf StraightFlag Then
10:       GetBestHand = Straight
11:    ElseIf ThreeOfAKindFlag Then
12:       GetBestHand = ThreeOfAKind
13:    ElseIf TwoPairFlag Then
14:       GetBestHand = TwoPair
15:    ElseIf PairFlag Then
16:       GetBestHand = Pair
17:    Else
18:       GetBestHand = NoHand
19:    End If
```

ANALYSIS   This function must consider that some poker hands are actually combinations of two types of hands. For example, the best poker hand, a straight flush, is a straight that is also a flush (Line 1). Similarly, a full house has both a pair and three of a kind (Line 5).

Analyzing Poker Hands

As you've learned, the CheckForFlush, CheckForStraight, CheckForPair, CheckForTwoPair, CheckForThreeOfAKind, and CheckForFourOfAKind functions analyze the cards for the various poker card combinations.

The CheckForFlush function simply checks whether every card in the current hand is of the same suit. The function must also check that there are no empty elements (-1, represented by the NOCARD constant) in the hand array. This is because a flush must be five cards of the same suit.

LISTING 9.11   The CheckForFlush Function

```
1:    Function CheckForFlush(hand() As Integer) As Boolean
2:    Dim i As Integer
3:    Dim Suit As Integer
4:    Suit = hand(0) \ 13
5:    CheckForFlush = True
6:    For i = 1 To 4
```

LISTING 9.11 continued

```
 7:      If hand(i) \ 13 <> Suit Or hand(i) = NOCARD Then _
 8:          CheckForFlush = False
 9:    Next i
10: End Function
```

ANALYSIS In Line 4 of CheckForFlush, the program first calculates the suit of the first card in the hand array. It then compares this suit to the others in the hand (Lines 5 to 9). If the suit of any of the cards does not match or if the card position is empty, CheckForFlush returns False (Lines 7 and 8). Otherwise, CheckForFlush remains True throughout the entire loop.

To check for other card combinations, the program must first sort the cards in the current hand into the cards array, which it does with the SortCards subroutine, shown in Listing 9.12.

LISTING 9.12 The SortCards Function

```
 1: Sub SortCards(cards() As Integer, hand() As Integer)
 2:   Dim i As Integer
 3:   For i = 0 To 13
 4:     cards(i) = 0
 5:   Next i
 6:   cards(13) = 1
 7:   For i = 0 To 4
 8:     If hand(i) <> NOCARD Then
 9:       Dim val As Integer
10:       val = hand(i) Mod 13
11:       cards(val) = cards(val) + 1
12:     End If
13:   Next i
14: End Sub
```

ANALYSIS The array element cards(13) is always set to 1 (Line 6), which enables the program to treat an ace as the highest card in the deck. As you may recall, the hand array contains ID values of the cards in the hand. These values range from 0 (for the ace of diamonds) to 51 (for the king of hearts). The program performs modulus division to calculate the card's face value (Line 10). Then it uses the card's face value as an index into the cards array (Line 11), incrementing the count for that card type. The program stores the number of aces into cards(0), the number of twos into cards(1), the number of threes into cards(2), and so on.

Once the cards in the current hand have been sorted into the cards array, checking for a pair is easy, as seen in Listing 9.13.

LISTING 9.13   The CheckForPair Function

```
1: Function CheckForPair(cards() As Integer) As Boolean
2:    Dim i As Integer
3:    CheckForPair = False
4:    For i = Ace To King
5:       If cards(i) = 2 Then CheckForPair = True
6:    Next i
7: End Function
```

ANALYSIS   If there's any occurrence of 2 in the card array, meaning that there are two of that card in the hand, the player has a pair (Line 5). For example, a 2 in cards(2) means that the player has a pair of threes.

Checking for three of a kind is just as easy, except the function checks for a 3 in an element of the cards array, rather than for a 2, as shown in this snippet from the CheckForThreeOfAKind function:

```
For i = Ace To King
   If cards(i) = 3 Then CheckForThreeOfAKind = True
Next i
```

Checking for two pair is a little bit trickier because it has to check for a pair twice. Still, the process is straightforward and not unlike checking for a single pair.

LISTING 9.14   Checking for Two Pairs

```
1:    For i = Ace To King
2:       If cards(i) = 2 And PairFlag Then
3:          CheckForTwoPair = True
4:       ElseIf cards(i) = 2 Then
5:          PairFlag = True
6:       End If
7:    Next i
```

To check for a straight, the program calls the CheckForStraight function.

LISTING 9.15   The CheckForStraight Function

```
 1:  Function CheckForStraight(cards() As Integer, _
 2:       hand() As Integer) As Boolean
 3:    Dim First As Integer
 4:    Dim i As Integer
 5:    First = -1
 6:    i = Ace
 7:    Do
 8:      If ((cards(i)) And (i <> Ace Or cards(Two))) Then First = i
 9:      i = i + 1
10:    Loop While (First = -1)
11:    If (First > Ten) Then
12:      CheckForStraight = False
13:    Else
14:      CheckForStraight = True
15:      For i = First To First + 4
16:        If (cards(i) = 0) Then CheckForStraight = False
17:      Next i
18:    End If
19: End Function
```

ANALYSIS   CheckForStraight finds the first card in the cards array (Lines 7 to 10) and
then checks that five consecutive elements in cards contain a value other than 0
(Lines 14 to 17). Finding the first card is complicated by the fact that an ace, which is
stored in cards(0), can be counted as either the lowest or highest card in the deck. If an
ace is used as the high card in a straight, the cards array looks like Figure 9.6.

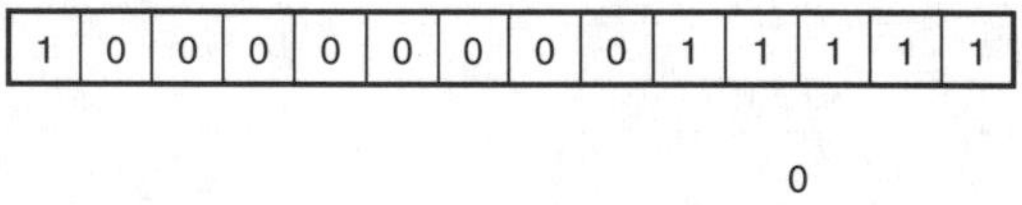

FIGURE 9.6

*An ace-high straight in
the* cards *array.*

| 1 | 0 | 0 | 0 | 0 | 0 | 0 | 0 | 0 | 1 | 1 | 1 | 1 | 1 |

                                              0

As you can see in Figure 9.6, the cards array contains a 1 in cards(0), which is the
hand's ace count, and a 1 in cards(13), which enables an ace to be counted as a high
card in a straight. The Do loop that finds the first card in the hand takes this ace complication into account.

In this loop, if cards contains no ace, the program simply finds the first element of
cards that contains a value. That element is considered to hold the first card in a possible
straight. If the cards array indicates an ace (cards(0) = 1), the ace is considered the
first card of a possible straight only if the cards array also indicates that the hand holds a
two (cards(1) = 1). Otherwise, the next element of cards after cards(0) that contains
a card is considered the first card in a possible straight.

After finding the first card in a possible straight, the program examines the rest of the cards to see whether a straight exists. If the first card is greater than TEN (that is, it's a jack, queen, or king), the hand cannot possibly hold a straight. Otherwise, the program sets CheckForStraight to True and then checks each consecutive element of cards for a value, starting with First. If any of the five elements of cards from First to First+4 contain a 0, there is no straight and the CheckForStraight returns False.

You could probably optimize the code in GetBestHand quite a bit, but at the cost of making it harder to understand. For example, the program can probably get by without a flag for each poker card combination, but the flags help you see exactly what the program is doing. If Poker Squares suffered in the speed department because of its lack of optimization, you would have to find a faster way to handle the cards. But Poker Squares runs fast enough, so the readability of the code is the most important factor in the design of an algorithm.

High-Score Files

Game players love to beat old scores, and little gives them more pleasure than seeing their name and score up in lights. Poker Squares uses a high-score file that holds 15 names and scores in descending order. That is, the highest score is the first in the file. There's no high-score file the first time that someone plays Poker Squares, so the program creates one. The default high-score file contains nothing but 15 sets of an empty string followed by a zero score.

When a player finishes a hand of Poker Squares, the program loads the high-score file and checks whether the player's score beats one already in the file. If it does, the program asks for a new name. Then the program inserts the new name and score into the file and writes the entire file back to disk.

The program handles the high-score file in the functions ShowScoreFile, AddToScoreFile, ReadScoreFile, and WriteScoreFile. You can easily modify these functions to create high-score files and displays for any of your games.

Summary

Poker Squares provides all the tools that you need to create many types of poker games. For example, you could write a version of a video poker machine, similar to those found in casinos. Instead of keeping track of scores, you could start each player with a specific amount of money. The player who lasts the longest before going broke gets his or her name on the high-score board. Use your imagination—maybe you can invent a whole new kind of poker game!

In Day 10, you'll learn a bit about writing an intelligent computer player by using the card classes to create a traditional poker game. Along the way, you'll use the tools that you developed in this chapter.

Q&A

Q Why does Poker Squares load a bitmap for its background image instead of drawing the game screen using Visual Basic drawing commands?

A When you have a complicated background, it's usually easier to draw it using a paint program like Microsoft Paint than it is to write all the code required to draw the same screen.

Q It seems to me that Poker Squares uses a lot of code to analyze poker hands. Isn't there an easier way?

A I don't know whether there's an *easier* way, but there are surely many *different* ways. When you're writing algorithms, you need to pick a method that you can easily understand but that doesn't bog down the program. There are surely faster, more efficient ways to analyze poker hands than the method used in Poker Squares, but the more efficient an algorithm becomes, the harder it tends to be to program and understand. The Poker Squares algorithms are plenty speedy enough for this game.

Q What if the player wants to get rid of all the high scores and start a new high-score file?

A All the player has to do is delete the highscr.dat file from the Poker Squares directory, and the program will automatically create a new file when it needs it.

Workshop

The workshop includes quiz questions to help gauge your grasp of the material. You'll find the answers to this quiz in Appendix A. Even if you feel that you totally understand the concepts presented here, you should work through the quiz anyway. The last section contains an exercise to help reinforce your learning.

Quiz

1. What method of the `clsDeck` class makes it possible for Poker Squares to deal the same cards to two players?

2. Explain how the `MINX`, `MAXX`, `MINY`, and `MAXY` constants are used in the Poker Squares program.

3. Why doesn't the Poker Squares program have `CheckForFullHouse` and `CheckForStraightFlush` functions?

4. In the `GetBestHand` function, what does the program store in the `cards` array?

5. What does the global `Grid` array contain?

6. Explain briefly how Poker Squares analyzes cards for scoring poker hands.

7. Why does the `cards` array have 14 elements instead of only 13?

Exercise

1. Modify Poker Squares so that a pair of aces is worth 25 points.

9

DAY **10**

Programming Computer Opponents

Most of the games in this book are single-player games that require computer "intelligence" only for the enforcing of the game's rules. Many other types of games require two or more players, however. What happens when you have a multiplayer computer game and there's nobody else to play? You, as the game's programmer, must supply a computer opponent.

Today you'll create a strategy game called Crystals, which pits a human player against the computer. Specifically, you'll learn the following:

- The different approaches to artificial intelligence
- How to build the strategy game Crystals
- How to use "brute force" algorithms to create a computer opponent
- How to analyze game moves for the best score

A Short Introduction to Artificial Intelligence

Artificial intelligence (AI) is one of the most controversial branches of computer science. Some scientists believe that eventually computers will be able to outthink people, whereas others believe such a claim is pure science fiction. AI research hasn't progressed as rapidly as its adherents would like, so the debate is still raging.

One thing's for sure: You can make a computer do some amazing things by implementing AI routines. For example, neural networks and fuzzy logic routines can help computers learn from experience, as well as make reasonable choices. Unless you're a computer scientist, though, or you're willing to spend years in school becoming one, these high-tech types of AI are out of the reach of the average game programmer.

So, how do you make a computer act as a game opponent? The solutions to this problem are as varied as the games to which you can apply them. The approach that you take can also vary. For example, do you want to program your computer to "understand" the strategy behind a game? Or do you just want the computer to fake its way through a game by calculating the results of moves before it makes them?

The first solution is the most difficult, not only because of the programming challenge, but also because the game opponent that you produce will be only as good as you are at playing the game. In fact, the game opponent will actually be significantly worse than you because it's unlikely that you can translate your creative-thinking process into equally effective computer code. Unless you're a chess champion, you shouldn't try to program your own strategies into a chess game because it will disappoint players who are more experienced than you.

The second method of creating a computer opponent is the easiest approach to take—letting the computer cheat a bit by using its calculating power. After you create a computer opponent in this "brute force" way, you can add strategy routines to plug some of the holes in the way that the computer plays. Once you've created a competent player, adding your own strategies can only make the player's routines better.

Introducing Crystals

Thousands of years ago, long before playing cards, dice, and video games, people entertained themselves using whatever items they could find lying around. Unfortunately, not all the world's locales offer as much of a variety of natural resources as others. For instance, the ancient Egyptians, being in the middle of the desert, had to be a little more creative in coming up with game materials than, say, the Native Americans in the lush forests of North America. Everywhere that those poor Egyptians looked, it was sand and stone, sand and stone.

Not to be put off by such petty matters, the Egyptians came up with a game called Oh-Wa-Ree (the spelling varies widely, depending on the source), which was played with nothing more than a bunch of pebbles and some pits dug in the sand. This game became so popular that it's still played even today. Crystals, this chapter's program, is a version of this ancient Egyptian game. As you begin to appreciate the hidden complexities of this basically simple game, you'll probably become as fascinated with it as millions of others have been throughout the ages.

Playing Crystals

When you first run the program, you see the screen shown in Figure 10.1. The message box requests the number of crystals that you want to place in each pit at the start of the game. The standard number is four, but you can try any number from three to nine.

FIGURE 10.1

Specifying the number of crystals per pit.

The playing board consists of two rows of eight pits each (see Figure 10.2). The top row belongs to you, and the bottom row belongs to the computer. Each pit starts with the number of crystals that you chose at the start. The object of the game is to maneuver the crystals so that you capture more than your opponent. A move consists of picking up the crystals from a pit in your row (just click the pit with your mouse) and then "sowing" them, one by one, in each succeeding pit until you've played all of them. The game performs the sowing action automatically when you select a pit.

FIGURE 10.2

The Crystals playing board.

In the original version of Oh-Wa-Ree, the pits are arranged in a circle and the pebbles are sown clockwise. However, in this version, you sow the crystals from left to right in each row. When you sow a crystal in the last pit of the bottom row, the play continues at the first pit of the top row. Likewise, when you sow the last pit of the top row, play continues at the first pit of the bottom row.

If the pit where you end is empty before you drop your last crystal into it, your turn is over. If the pit contains exactly three crystals (two plus the last one that you sowed), you capture the crystals in that pit. The crystals are removed from the board, placed in your storage pit, and added to your score. If the pit where you finish already contains other crystals (unless, of course, the total is three), you must pick up all of them and continue (the program does this automatically; you don't actually have to do anything). Then you must sow the crystals around the board until you run out again.

As play progresses, whenever the total number of crystals in any pit is three, the crystals in that pit are immediately captured by the player in whose row the pit resides (unless the play ends in the pit, as described in the previous paragraph). When you end in an empty pit, it's the computer's turn. The play continues in this manner until there are four or fewer crystals remaining, in which case the game ends. The player with the highest score wins.

Building Crystals

Now that you've had a chance to play Crystals, you'll learn how to build the program yourself, one piece at a time.

Creating Crystals' User Interface

The first step is to create the game's user interface:

1. Start a new Standard EXE Visual Basic project.

2. Set the form's properties to the values listed here:

   AutoRedraw = True

   Caption = "Crystals"

   Height = 7590

   ScaleMode = Pixel

   Width = 9705

3. Set the form's Picture property to the screen.gif image that you can find in the Images\Crystals directory of this book's CD-ROM.

4. Add three Image controls to the form, giving them the property values listed here:

   Image #1

   Name = imgCrystal

   Picture = Crystal.bmp

   Image #2

   Name = imgPit

   Picture = Pit.bmp

   Image #3

   Name = imgStoragePit

   Picture = Storage.bmp

5. Add a form to the project by selecting the Add Form command from the Project menu. Give the new form the following property settings:

   Name = frmMessage

   AutoRedraw = True

   BorderStyle = Fixed Single

   Caption = "Crystals"

   Font = MS Sans Serif, Regular, 14-point

   Height = 1470

   ScaleMode = Pixel

   Width = 3675

6. Save your work, naming the main form Crystals.frm, the project Crystals.vbp, and the second form frmMessage.frm.

10

You've now completed the Crystals user interface. Figure 10.3 shows what your main form should look like at this point. In the next section, you'll add handlers for the program's various controls.

FIGURE 10.3

The completed Crystals user interface.

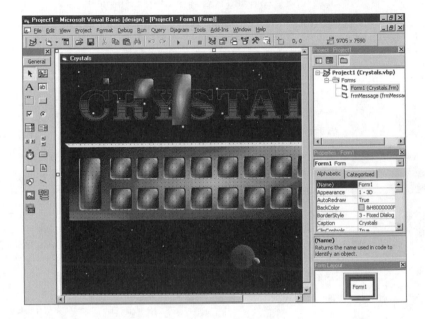

Adding the Object Handlers

Next, you need to associate code with the form that's the base object of the game's user interface. To accomplish this task, double-click the Form1 form to bring up the code window and add the following form handlers. You can either type the source code or copy it from the Crystals1.txt file, which you can find in the Chap10\Code directory of this book's CD-ROM.

LISTING 10.1   The Form Handlers

```
1:  '==================================================
2:  ' Form Handlers.
3:  '==================================================
4:  Private Sub Form_Load()
5:     InitObjects
6:     InitGame
7:  End Sub
8:
9:  Private Sub Form_MouseDown(Button As Integer, _
10:     Shift As Integer, x As Single, y As Single)
```

LISTING 10.1   continued

```
11:    Dim pitGridX As Integer
12:    Dim pitGridY As Integer
13:    If Player = HUMAN Then
14:      CalcPitGridCoords x, y, pitGridX, pitGridY
15:      If pitGridX <> -1 Then HumanPlay pitGridX, pitGridY
16:    End If
17: End Sub
18:
19: Private Sub Form_Unload(Cancel As Integer)
20:    Unload frmMessage
21: End Sub
```

Completing the Game

Now, add the general game subroutines, functions, constants, and variables by performing the following steps:

1. Add the following initialization subroutines to the code window. You can either type the code or copy it from the Crystals2.txt file, which you can find in the Chap10\Code directory of this book's CD-ROM.

LISTING 10.2   The Initialization Routines

```
 1:  '==================================================
 2:  ' Initialization Routines.
 3:  '==================================================
 4:  Sub InitObjects()
 5:    imgPit.Visible = False
 6:    imgCrystal.Visible = False
 7:    imgStoragePit.Visible = False
 8:    Form1.Left = 500
 9:    Form1.Top = 500
10:    Form1.Height = 7590
11:    Form1.Width = 9705
12:    Form1.Show
13: End Sub
14:
15: Sub InitGame()
16:    Randomize
17:    ReadData
18:    Scores(HUMAN) = 0
19:    Scores(COMPUTER) = 0
20:    Player = HUMAN
21:    SetNumCrystalsInPit
22:    CrystalCount = NumCrystalsInGame
23:    StartNewBoard
```

LISTING 10.2   continued

```
24:    DrawScoreBoxes
25: End Sub
26:
27: Sub ReadData()
28:    ChDir "d:\tyvbgames\crystals\"
29:    Open "crystals.dat" For Binary As #1
30:    Get #1, , CrystalXY
31:    Close #1
32: End Sub
33:
34: Sub SetNumCrystalsInPit()
35:    On Local Error Resume Next
36:    NumCrystalsInPit = _
37:        InputBox("How many crystals in each pit?" & _
38:        vbCrLf & "(3 - 9)", "Crystal Count", "4")
39:    If NumCrystalsInPit = 0 Then NumCrystalsInPit = 4
40:    NumCrystalsInGame = NumCrystalsInPit * 16
41:    Form1.PaintPicture Form1.Picture, 0, 0
42: End Sub
43:
44: Sub StartNewBoard()
45:    Dim x As Integer
46:    Dim y As Integer
47:    Form1.PaintPicture imgStoragePit, 41, 197
48:    Form1.PaintPicture imgStoragePit, 561, 197
49:    For x = 0 To NUMPITSPERPLAYER - 1
50:      Form1.PaintPicture imgPit, x * CELLWIDTH + OFFSETX, 196
51:      Form1.PaintPicture imgPit, x * CELLWIDTH + OFFSETX, 260
52:      For y = 0 To NumCrystalsInPit - 1
53:        Form1.PaintPicture imgCrystal, _
54:            OFFSETX + x * CELLWIDTH + CrystalXY(y * 2), _
55:            ROW1OFFSETY + CrystalXY(y * 2 + 1)
56:        Form1.PaintPicture imgCrystal, _
57:            OFFSETX + x * CELLWIDTH + CrystalXY(y * 2), _
58:            ROW2OFFSETY + CrystalXY(y * 2 + 1)
59:        If y < 2 Then Board(x, y) = NumCrystalsInPit
60:      Next y
61:    Next x
62: End Sub
```

2. Add the following general subroutines to the code window. You can either type the code or copy it from the Crystals3.txt file, which you can find in the Chap10\Code directory of this book's CD-ROM.

LISTING 10.3   The Game's Subroutines

```
 1: '=====================================================
 2: ' General Game Subroutines.
 3: '=====================================================
 4: Sub HumanPlay(pitGridX As Integer, pitGridY As Integer)
 5:   Dim numCrystals As Integer
 6:   If HaveMove(HUMAN) Then
 7:     numCrystals = PickUpCrystals(pitGridX, pitGridY)
 8:     DistributeCrystals numCrystals, pitGridX, pitGridY
 9:   Else
10:     PlayerMessage ("Human has no move.")
11:   End If
12:   Player = COMPUTER
13:   ComputerPlay
14: End Sub
15:
16: Sub ComputerPlay()
17:   Dim pitGridX As Integer
18:   Dim pitGridY As Integer
19:   Dim numCrystals As Integer
20:   If HaveMove(COMPUTER) Then
21:     PlayerMessage "Computer's turn."
22:     pitGridY = COMPUTER
23:     pitGridX = CalcMoves
24:     numCrystals = PickUpCrystals(pitGridX, pitGridY)
25:     DistributeCrystals numCrystals, pitGridX, pitGridY
26:   Else
27:     PlayerMessage ("Computer has no move.")
28:   End If
29:   Player = HUMAN
30:   PlayerMessage "Human's turn."
31: End Sub
32:
33: Sub PlayerMessage(msg As String)
34:   frmMessage.Left = Form1.Left + 1000
35:   frmMessage.Top = Form1.Top + 1000
36:   frmMessage.Cls
37:   frmMessage.CurrentX = 20
38:   frmMessage.CurrentY = 25
39:   frmMessage.Print msg
40:   frmMessage.Show
41:   Delay 2#
42:   frmMessage.Hide
43: End Sub
44:
45: Sub DistributeCrystals(numCrystals As Integer, _
46:     pitGridX As Integer, pitGridY As Integer)
47:   While numCrystals > 0
48:     GetNextGridXY pitGridX, pitGridY
```

10

LISTING **10.3**   continued

```
49:      PutCrystalInPit pitGridX, pitGridY, numCrystals
50:   Wend
51: End Sub
52:
53: Sub PutCrystalInPit(pitGridX As Integer, _
54:     pitGridY As Integer, numCrystals As Integer)
55:   Dim GameOver As Boolean
56:   numCrystals = numCrystals - 1
57:   Board(pitGridX, pitGridY) = Board(pitGridX, pitGridY) + 1
58:   ShowCrystal pitGridX, pitGridY
59:   GameOver = CalcScore(pitGridX, pitGridY, numCrystals)
60:   If Not GameOver And Board(pitGridX, pitGridY) > 1 _
61:       And numCrystals = 0 Then
62:     Delay 0.3
63:     numCrystals = PickUpCrystals(pitGridX, pitGridY)
64:   End If
65:   Delay 0.4
66: End Sub
67:
68: Sub ShowCrystal(pitGridX As Integer, pitGridY As Integer)
69:   Dim index As Integer
70:   Dim pitPixelX As Integer
71:   Dim pitPixelY As Integer
72:   If Board(pitGridX, pitGridY) < 25 Then
73:     index = Board(pitGridX, pitGridY) - 1
74:     pitPixelX = pitGridX * CELLWIDTH + OFFSETX
75:     pitPixelY = pitGridY * CELLHEIGHT + ROW1OFFSETY
76:     Form1.PaintPicture imgCrystal, _
77:         pitPixelX + CrystalXY(index * 2), _
78:         pitPixelY + CrystalXY(index * 2 + 1)
79:   End If
80: End Sub
81:
82: Sub StoreCrystals(Winner As Integer)
83:   Dim storagePitX As Integer
84:   Dim storagePitY As Integer
85:   Dim xPos As Integer
86:   Dim yPos As Integer
87:   Dim x As Integer
88:   storagePitY = 200
89:   If Winner = HUMAN Then
90:     storagePitX = 40
91:   Else
92:     storagePitX = 560
93:   End If
94:   For x = 0 To 2
95:     xPos = storagePitX + Int(Rnd * 25)
96:     yPos = storagePitY + Int(Rnd * 90)
```

LISTING 10.3   continued

```
97:      Form1.PaintPicture imgCrystal, xPos, yPos
98:   Next x
99: End Sub
100:
101:  Sub CalcPitGridCoords(mx As Single, my As Single, _
102:      pitGridX As Integer, pitGridY As Integer)
103:    pitGridX = (mx - OFFSETX) \ CELLWIDTH
104:    pitGridY = (my - ROW1OFFSETY) \ CELLHEIGHT
105:    If Not ClickIsOnValidPit(mx, my, _
106:       pitGridX, pitGridY) Then _
107:       pitGridX = -1
108:  End Sub
109:
110: Sub GetNextGridXY(pitGridX As Integer, pitGridY As Integer)
111:   pitGridX = pitGridX + 1
112:   If pitGridX = NUMPITSPERPLAYER Then
113:     pitGridX = 0
114:     If pitGridY = 0 Then
115:       pitGridY = 1
116:     Else
117:       pitGridY = 0
118:     End If
119:   End If
120: End Sub
121:
122: Sub GameOver()
123:   MsgBox "Game Over"
124:   InitGame
125: End Sub
126:
127: Sub DrawScoreBoxes()
128:   Form1.FillStyle = vbSolid
129:   Form1.Line (20, 400)-(108, 440), vbWhite, BF
130:   Form1.CurrentX = 34
131:   Form1.CurrentY = 408
132:   Form1.Print "HUMAN"
133:   Form1.CurrentX = 34
134:   Form1.CurrentY = 424
135:   Form1.Print Scores(HUMAN)
136:   Form1.Line (532, 400)-(620, 440), vbWhite, BF
137:   Form1.CurrentX = 548
138:   Form1.CurrentY = 408
139:   Form1.Print "COMPUTER"
140:   Form1.CurrentX = 548
141:   Form1.CurrentY = 424
142:   Form1.Print Scores(COMPUTER)
143: End Sub
144:
```

10

LISTING 10.3   continued

```
145: Sub Delay(amount As Single)
146:    Dim StartTime As Single
147:    Dim CurrentTime As Single
148:    StartTime = Timer
149:    Do
150:       CurrentTime = Timer
151:       DoEvents
152:    Loop While CurrentTime < StartTime + amount
153: End Sub
```

3. Add the following computer-player subroutines to the code window. You can either type the code or copy it from the Crystals4.txt file, which you can find in the Chap10\Code directory of this book's CD-ROM.

LISTING 10.4   The Code for the Computer Opponent

```
 1:   '=================================================
 2:   ' Computer-player subroutines and Functions.
 3:   '=================================================
 4:   Function CalcMoves() As Integer
 5:      Dim CompScores(7) As Integer
 6:      Dim comboScores(7) As Integer
 7:      Dim indexes(7) As Integer
 8:      Dim BestComboScore As Integer
 9:      Dim bestCompScore As Integer
10:      Dim count As Integer
11:      GetAllScores CompScores, comboScores
12:      BestComboScore = FindBestComboScore(comboScores)
13:      BuildBestComboIndexTable BestComboScore, _
14:         comboScores, indexes, count
15:      bestCompScore = FindBestCompScore(CompScores, _
16:         indexes, count)
17:      CalcMoves = SelectMove(bestCompScore, CompScores, _
18:         indexes, count)
19: End Function
20:
21: Function SelectMove(bestCompScore As Integer, _
22:    CompScores() As Integer, indexes() As Integer, _
23:    count As Integer) As Integer
24:    Dim index As Integer
25:    Dim r As Integer
26:    index = -1
27:    Do
28:       r = Int(Rnd * (count + 1))
29:       index = indexes(r)
30:       If Int(Rnd * 3) > 0 And _
```

LISTING 10.4   continued

```
31:          CompScores(index) <> bestCompScore Then _
32:       index = -1
33:     DoEvents
34:   Loop While index = -1
35:   SelectMove = index
36: End Function
37:
38: Function FindBestCompScore(CompScores() As Integer, _
39:     indexes() As Integer, count As Integer) As Integer
40:   Dim bestScore  As Integer
41:   Dim x As Integer
42:   bestScore = -100
43:   For x = 0 To count
44:     If CompScores(indexes(x)) > bestScore Then _
45:         bestScore = CompScores(indexes(x))
46:   Next x
47:   FindBestCompScore = bestScore
48: End Function
49:
50: Sub BuildBestComboIndexTable(BestComboScore As Integer, _
51:     comboScores() As Integer, indexes() As Integer, _
52:     count As Integer)
53:   Dim x As Integer
54:   count = -1
55:   For x = 0 To NUMPITSPERPLAYER - 1
56:     If comboScores(x) = BestComboScore Then
57:       count = count + 1
58:       indexes(count) = x
59:     End If
60:   Next x
61: End Sub
62:
63: Sub GetAllScores(CompScores() As Integer, _
64:     comboScores() As Integer)
65:   Dim tempBoard(NUMPITSPERPLAYER - 1, 1) As Integer
66:   Dim tempScores(1) As Integer
67:   Dim numCrystals As Integer
68:   Dim humanScore As Integer
69:   Dim pitGridX As Integer
70:   Dim pitGridY As Integer
71:   Dim x As Integer
72:   For x = 0 To NUMPITSPERPLAYER - 1
73:     CompScores(x) = -1
74:     comboScores(x) = -1
75:   Next x
76:   For x = 0 To NUMPITSPERPLAYER - 1
77:     CopyBoard tempBoard, Board
78:     If tempBoard(x, 1) <> 0 Then
```

10

LISTING **10.4** continued

```
79:        tempScores(HUMAN) = 0
80:        tempScores(COMPUTER) = 0
81:        pitGridY = COMPUTER
82:        pitGridX = x
83:        numCrystals = tempBoard(pitGridX, pitGridY)
84:        tempBoard(pitGridX, pitGridY) = 0
85:        While numCrystals
86:          GetNextGridXY pitGridX, pitGridY
87:          TestPutCrystalInPit pitGridX, pitGridY, _
88:              numCrystals, tempBoard, tempScores, COMPUTER
89:        Wend
90:        CompScores(x) = tempScores(COMPUTER) - _
91:            tempScores(HUMAN)
92:        humanScore = RunHumanTurn(tempBoard)
93:        comboScores(x) = CompScores(x) - humanScore
94:      End If
95:    Next x
96: End Sub
97:
98: Sub CopyBoard(dst() As Integer, src() As Integer)
99:    Dim x As Integer
100:    Dim y As Integer
101:    For x = 0 To NUMPITSPERPLAYER - 1
102:      For y = 0 To 1
103:        dst(x, y) = src(x, y)
104:      Next y
105:    Next x
106:  End Sub
107:
108:  Function FindBestComboScore(comboScores() _
109:      As Integer) As Integer
110:    Dim bestScore As Integer
111:    Dim x As Integer
112:    bestScore = -100
113:    For x = 0 To NUMPITSPERPLAYER - 1
114:      If comboScores(x) > bestScore And _
115:          comboScores(x) <> -1 Then _
116:        bestScore = comboScores(x)
117:    Next x
118:    FindBestComboScore = bestScore
119: End Function
120:
121: Function RunHumanTurn(tempBoard() As Integer) As Integer
122:    Dim bestScore As Integer
123:    Dim numCrystals As Integer
124:    Dim score As Integer
125:    Dim pitGridX As Integer
126:    Dim pitGridY As Integer
```

LISTING 10.4   continued

```
127:    Dim tempBoard2(NUMPITSPERPLAYER - 1, 1) As Integer
128:    Dim tempScores(1) As Integer
129:    Dim x As Integer
130:    bestScore = -100
131:    For x = 0 To NUMPITSPERPLAYER - 1
132:      CopyBoard tempBoard2, tempBoard
133:      If tempBoard2(x, 0) <> 0 Then
134:        tempScores(HUMAN) = 0
135:        tempScores(COMPUTER) = 0
136:        pitGridY = HUMAN
137:        pitGridX = x
138:        numCrystals = tempBoard2(pitGridX, pitGridY)
139:        tempBoard2(pitGridX, pitGridY) = 0
140:        While numCrystals
141:          GetNextGridXY pitGridX, pitGridY
142:          TestPutCrystalInPit pitGridX, pitGridY, _
143:              numCrystals, tempBoard2, tempScores, HUMAN
144:        Wend
145:        score = tempScores(HUMAN) - tempScores(COMPUTER)
146:        If score > bestScore Then bestScore = score
147:      End If
148:    Next x
149:    RunHumanTurn = bestScore
150: End Function
151:
152: Sub TestPutCrystalInPit(pitGridX As Integer, _
153:      pitGridY As Integer, numCrystals As Integer, _
154:      tempBoard() As Integer, tempScores() As Integer, _
155:      Player As Integer)
156:    Dim otherPlayer As Integer
157:    otherPlayer = 0
158:    If Player = 0 Then otherPlayer = 1
159:    numCrystals = numCrystals - 1
160:    tempBoard(pitGridX, pitGridY) = _
161:        tempBoard(pitGridX, pitGridY) + 1
162:    If tempBoard(pitGridX, pitGridY) = 3 Then
163:      If numCrystals = 0 Or pitGridY = 1 Then
164:        tempScores(Player) = tempScores(Player) + 3
165:      Else
166:        tempScores(otherPlayer) = tempScores(otherPlayer) + 3
167:      End If
168:      tempBoard(pitGridX, pitGridY) = 0
169:    End If
170:    If tempBoard(pitGridX, pitGridY) > 1 And _
171:        numCrystals = 0 Then
172:      numCrystals = tempBoard(pitGridX, pitGridY)
173:      tempBoard(pitGridX, pitGridY) = 0
174:    End If
175: End Sub
```

10

ANALYSIS These are the functions and subroutines that enable the computer to play a reasonably intelligent game against a human opponent. You'll examine these procedures in detail later in this chapter.

4. Add the following game functions to the code window. You can either type the code or copy it from the Crystals5.txt file, which you can find in the Chap10\Code directory of this book's CD-ROM.

LISTING 10.5   The Game's Functions

```
 1:  '===================================================
 2:  ' Game Functions.
 3:  '===================================================
 4:  Function PickUpCrystals(pitGridX As Integer, _
 5:      pitGridY As Integer) As Integer
 6:    Dim numCrystals As Integer
 7:    Dim pitPixelX As Integer
 8:    Dim pitPixelY As Integer
 9:    numCrystals = Board(pitGridX, pitGridY)
10:    Board(pitGridX, pitGridY) = 0
11:    pitPixelX = pitGridX * CELLWIDTH + OFFSETX
12:    pitPixelY = pitGridY * CELLHEIGHT + ROW1OFFSETY
13:    Form1.PaintPicture imgPit, pitPixelX, pitPixelY
14:    PickUpCrystals = numCrystals
15:  End Function
16:
17:  Function CalcScore(pitGridX As Integer, _
18:      pitGridY As Integer, numCrystals As Integer) _
19:      As Boolean
20:    Dim Winner As Integer
21:    Dim pitPixelX As Integer
22:    Dim pitPixelY As Integer
23:    Dim otherPlayer As Integer
24:    otherPlayer = 0
25:    If Player = 0 Then otherPlayer = 1
26:    If Board(pitGridX, pitGridY) = 3 Then
27:      Delay 0.5
28:      CrystalCount = CrystalCount - 3
29:      If numCrystals = 0 Or pitGridY = Player Then
30:        Scores(Player) = Scores(Player) + 3
31:        Winner = Player
32:      Else
33:        Scores(otherPlayer) = Scores(otherPlayer) + 3
34:        Winner = otherPlayer
35:      End If
36:      pitPixelX = pitGridX * CELLWIDTH + OFFSETX
37:      pitPixelY = pitGridY * CELLHEIGHT + ROW1OFFSETY
38:      Form1.PaintPicture imgPit, pitPixelX,  pitPixelY
39:      StoreCrystals Winner
```

LISTING 10.5   continued

```
40:        Board(pitGridX, pitGridY) = 0
41:        DrawScoreBoxes
42:    End If
43:    CalcScore = False
44:    If CrystalCount < 5 Then
45:        GameOver
46:        CalcScore = True
47:    End If
48: End Function
49:
50: Function ClickIsOnValidPit(mx As Single, my As Single, _
51:        pitGridX As Integer, pitGridY As Integer) As Boolean
52:    ClickIsOnValidPit = False
53:    If mx > MINX And mx < MAXX And my > MINY And my < MAXY And _
54:        mx < OFFSETX + pitGridX * CELLWIDTH + 42 And _
55:        my < ROW1OFFSETY + pitGridY * CELLHEIGHT + 42 And _
56:        Board(pitGridX, HUMAN) > 0 Then _
57:        ClickIsOnValidPit = True
58: End Function
59:
60: Function HaveMove(Player As Integer) As Boolean
61:    Dim x As Integer
62:    HaveMove = False
63:    For x = 0 To NUMPITSPERPLAYER - 1
64:        If Board(x, Player) > 0 Then HaveMove = True
65:    Next x
66: End Function
```

5. Add the following variable declarations and enumerations to the top of the code window. You can either type the code or copy it from the Crystals6.txt file, which you can find in the Chap10\Code directory of this book's CD-ROM.

LISTING 10.6   The Game's Declarations

```
1: '==================================================
2: ' Battle Bricks for Visual Basic 6
3: '    by Clayton Walnum
4: ' Copyright 2000 by Macmillan Computer Publishing
5: '==================================================
6: Option Explicit
7:
8: '==================================================
9: ' Constants.
10: '==================================================
11: Const CELLWIDTH = 56
12: Const CELLHEIGHT = 64
```

LISTING 10.6   continued

```
13: Const OFFSETX = 104
14: Const NUMPITSPERPLAYER = 8
15: Const ROW1OFFSETY = 196
16: Const ROW2OFFSETY = 260
17: Const MINX = 102
18: Const MAXX = 532
19: Const MINY = 198
20: Const MAXY = 240
21:
22: Enum PlayerEnum
23:    HUMAN
24:    COMPUTER
25: End Enum
26:
27: '=================================================
28: ' General Game Variables.
29: '=================================================
30: Dim Board(NUMPITSPERPLAYER - 1, 1) As Integer
31: Dim Scores(1) As Integer
32: Dim Player As Integer
33: Dim CrystalCount As Integer
34: Dim NumCrystalsInPit As Integer
35: Dim NumCrystalsInGame As Integer
36: Dim CrystalXY(49) As Integer
```

6. Copy the Crystals.dat file from this book's CD-ROM to your project's directory.
    This file contains the data that the computer loads into the CrystalXY() array.

7. Save your work.

You've now completed the Crystals program.

Understanding Crystals

Now that you've played the game and built your own version, it's time to examine the
code, starting with the game's constants and variables.

The Crystals Variables and Constants

Crystals relies on a set of global variables and constants that the game declares near the
top of the program. Table 10.1 lists the general global variables and their descriptions,
and Table 10.2 lists the constants.

TABLE 10.1 The Crystals General Game Variables

Variable	Type	Description
Board()	Integer	An array that holds the contents of each pit on the board
CrystalCount	Integer	The number of crystals remaining in the game
CrystalXY()	Integer	An array that holds the positions for placing crystals in the pits
NumCrystalsInPit	Integer	The starting number of crystals in each pit
Player	Integer	The current player
Scores()	Integer	The array that holds the human and computer game scores

TABLE 10.2 The Crystals Constants

Constant	Description
CELLHEIGHT	The height of a cell on the playing board
CELLWIDTH	The width of a cell on the playing board
MAXX	The maximum X value that's a valid mouse click in the grid
MAXY	The maximum Y value that's a valid mouse click in the grid
MINX	The minimum X value that's is a valid mouse click in the grid
MINY	The minimum Y value that's a valid mouse click in the grid
OFFSETX	The X coordinate of the left edge of the playing board
NUMPITSPERPLAYER	The number of pits in each player's row of the playing board
ROW1OFFSETY	The Y coordinate of the top edge of a pit in the first row
ROW2OFFSETY	The Y coordinate of the top edge of a pit in the second row
SCOREOFFSETY	The Y coordinate of the row and column scores
TOTALSCOREX	The X coordinate of the total score for the current game
TOTALSCOREY	The Y coordinate of the total score for the current game

The Crystals program also defines one enumeration, PlayerEnum, which defines constants for the human and computer opponent.

Programming Crystals

Crystals is a fairly easy game to program. All you need to do is keep track of the number of crystals in each pit and move them around as required by the game rules. You could probably write a very simple version of this program for two human players, without fancy graphics and a computer opponent, in a couple of pages of code.

This version of Crystals includes those fancy graphics, as well as a computer opponent. Still, there's not much new here, and the code is heavily commented. The program's computer opponent needs to be explored in depth, though.

Creating a Computer Opponent

Believe it or not, the computer opponent in Crystals knows absolutely nothing about strategy. It only knows how to count. That is, its strategy for winning a game is to run through all of its possible moves and see which move produces the highest score. It also checks all the possible moves that the human player can make for each move that the computer makes. Finally, the computer opponent picks the move that gives it the most points while giving the human player the poorest opportunity to score points.

This programming strategy works well for a game like Crystals, which has only eight possible moves per player per turn. When a player's turn comes around, he can choose only one of eight pits and then sow its crystals in each successive pit until they're gone, according to the rules of the game. After the player chooses the pit, he can do nothing to change the outcome of his turn.

Although the Crystals computer opponent looks forward only two turns (which actually requires analyzing 72 turns, which is eight computer turns, each with eight possible human responses), you can create game programs that look forward any number of turns, depending on how much time you want the computer to "think" and how much memory you have available.

Note

In a game like chess—whose board contains 16 possible moves for each player, each with 16 possible responses to each move (for a total of 256 responses)—it takes considerably more time and memory to process the board. To look forward two moves requires analyzing 272 possible moves and responses. To look forward three moves requires analyzing 4,368 moves and responses. And looking forward just four turns results in over 69,000 possible moves! (You calculate the total number of moves as follows: $16^1 + 16^2 + 16^3 + 16^4$.)

Programming the Computer's Strategy

The computer's turn begins in the subroutine ComputerPlay.

LISTING 10.7   The ComputerPlay Subroutine

```
 1:  Sub ComputerPlay()
 2:     Dim pitGridX As Integer
 3:     Dim pitGridY As Integer
 4:     Dim numCrystals As Integer
 5:     If HaveMove(COMPUTER) Then
 6:        PlayerMessage "Computer's turn."
 7:        pitGridY = COMPUTER
 8:        pitGridX = CalcMoves
 9:        numCrystals = PickUpCrystals(pitGridX, pitGridY)
10:        DistributeCrystals numCrystals, pitGridX, pitGridY
11:     Else
12:        PlayerMessage ("Computer has no move.")
13:     End If
14:     Player = HUMAN
15:     PlayerMessage "Human's turn."
16:  End Sub
```

ANALYSIS   This subroutine contains little more than calls to other subroutines that actually do the work. ComputerPlay first calls HaveMove (Line 5) to determine whether the computer opponent has a legal move it can make. If the computer does have a move, the program calls the subroutine PlayerMessage (Line 6) to display a message box on the screen. The message box just tells the human player that the computer opponent is about to take its turn. ComputerPlay then sets the computer's pit row (pitGridY) to the computer's row (Line 7) and calls the function CalcMoves (Line 8), which returns the pit number that will yield the best results for the computer's turn.

ANALYSIS   After finding the computer's move, the program calls the function PickUpCrystals (Line 9), which removes the crystals from the pit on the screen and returns the number of crystals picked up in the variable numCrystals. The DistributeCrystals subroutine (Line 10) then performs the computer's turn, sowing the crystals around the playing board. Finally, ComputerPlay sets the player to HUMAN (Line 14), shows the player message (Line 15), and ends.

The function CalcMoves is one of several functions that provide the computer with its smarts.

LISTING 10.8   The CalcMoves Function

```
 1:  Function CalcMoves() As Integer
 2:    Dim CompScores(7) As Integer
 3:    Dim comboScores(7) As Integer
 4:    Dim indexes(7) As Integer
 5:    Dim BestComboScore As Integer
 6:    Dim bestCompScore As Integer
 7:    Dim count As Integer
 8:    GetAllScores CompScores, comboScores
 9:    BestComboScore = FindBestComboScore(comboScores)
10:    BuildBestComboIndexTable BestComboScore, _
11:        comboScores, indexes, count
12:    bestCompScore = FindBestCompScore(CompScores, _
13:        indexes, count)
14:    CalcMoves = SelectMove(bestCompScore, CompScores, _
15:        indexes, count)
16: End Function
```

ANALYSIS   At the top of the function's body, you can see that the program uses three scoring arrays to keep track of the results of each move's analysis (Lines 2 to 4). A little later in this chapter, you'll see what the indexes() array does. The CompScores() array holds the net point value for each of the computer's eight possible moves. The program calculates this net value by subtracting any scores that the move generates for the human player from any scores that the move generates for the computer opponent.

For example, suppose that the computer opponent is analyzing the move starting at pit 2 (which is actually the third pit because the pit numbers start at 0). If, after sowing crystals around the board, the human player gains six points (because two pits in the human's row were brought up to three crystals but were not captured by the computer opponent) and the computer opponent gains nine points, that move's net point value for the computer opponent would be 3. The program would then store the value 3 in CompScores(2).

The comboScores() array contains the net point value of a move after the computer analyzes the human player's possible responses. To calculate this net value, the program subtracts from the score stored in CompScores() the highest possible net score for the human player's next move.

If all this sounds confusing, take a look at the following algorithm, which summarizes how the computer calculates the values for the CompScores() and comboScores() arrays:

1. Set pitGridX to 0 and pitGridY to the player's row.
2. Sow the crystals in pit pitGridX around the board, keeping track of scores for both the human and computer opponents.

3. Subtract the human's score gain from the computer's score gain, and store this net point value in CompScores(pitGridX).

4. Check each of the human's eight possible responses for the move taken in step 2 and return the highest net point value that the human player can achieve.

5. Subtract from CompScores(pitGridX) the human net point value generated in step 4, and store the result in comboScores(pitGridX).

6. Increment pitGridX and go back to step 1 if it's less than 8. Otherwise, the algorithm ends.

The program implements the preceding algorithm in the subroutine GetAllScores, which CalcMoves calls (Line 8) to fill the CompScores() and comboScores() arrays with their score values. After filling the score arrays, the comboScores() array contains the final net scores (which I call *combination scores* because they combine both the computer's move and the human player's response) for each of the computer's eight possible moves. The program calls the function FindBestComboScore (Line 9) to find the highest-rated move in the comboScores() array. FindBestComboScore returns this value into the variable BestComboScore.

CalcMoves then calls BuildBestComboIndexTable (Line 10), which scans the comboScores() array, looking for all scores that equal BestComboScore. Remember, several moves may result in scores equal to BestComboScore. To create a more unpredictable computer opponent, the program eventually chooses randomly from the moves whose net scores equal BestComboScore. After calling BuildBestComboIndexTable, the indexes() array contains indexes into the comboScores() array. These indexes point to all values in the comboScores() array that equal BestComboScore.

Next, CalcMoves calls FindBestCompScore (Line 12), which scans the CompScores() array and returns the highest score that it finds. Why does the program need this value? After all, the comboScores() array already takes CompScores() into consideration, right? Yes, but the comboScores() array stores net score values that assume that the human player will respond with the best possible move. However, the human player won't necessarily choose the best possible move. So, the computer should pick not the move that yields the highest combination score, but rather the move that yields the best combination score *and* that also has the highest possible score in CompScores().

To understand this logic better, look at Figure 10.4. In this figure, the highest possible point value in the comboScores() array is 3. (A -1 indicates that no crystals are in the pit, so no move is possible.) However, the computer can choose from six different moves, all of which yield a net point value of 3. The six best scores in the comboScores() array are at array indexes 0, 2, 3, 4, 5, and 6. Now look at the CompScores() array. The scores in this array indicate the net gain for the computer opponent without considering the human player's response. If you look at the scores in CompScores() at indexes 0, 2, 3, 4, 5, and 6, you'll see that the highest net score for the computer's move is 9.

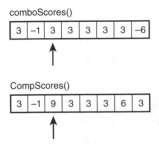

FIGURE 10.4

Using the score arrays.

The information you now have indicates that if the computer opponent chooses pit number 2 (counting from 0) and the human player responds with the best possible move, the computer will get three more points than the human player. CompScores(2) is 9, so this means that the player's best response can get six points because 9-6=3, which is the value in comboScores(2). However, if the human player fails to choose the best move, the computer opponent can net up to nine points (rather than just three) for the move starting at pit 2, depending on how many points the human player's response actually generates. Nine points is better than six or three, which are the net point values for other moves in the CompScores() array.

Getting back to the source code, CalcMoves now calls SelectMove, which returns the pit number that the computer opponent should choose for its current move.

Handling the Score Arrays

Of all the subroutines called in CalcMoves, GetAllScores and SelectMove are the only ones of real interest. The other functions just perform calculations for CalcMoves. The function GetAllScores provides the score arrays with their values:

LISTING 10.9   The GetAllScores Subroutine

```
1:  Sub GetAllScores(CompScores() As Integer, _
2:      comboScores() As Integer)
3:    Dim tempBoard(NUMPITSPERPLAYER - 1, 1) As Integer
4:    Dim tempScores(1) As Integer
5:    Dim numCrystals As Integer
6:    Dim humanScore As Integer
7:    Dim pitGridX As Integer
8:    Dim pitGridY As Integer
9:    Dim x As Integer
```

LISTING 10.9   continued

```
10:    For x = 0 To NUMPITSPERPLAYER - 1
11:       CompScores(x) = -1
12:       comboScores(x) = -1
13:    Next x
14:    For x = 0 To NUMPITSPERPLAYER - 1
15:       CopyBoard tempBoard, Board
16:       If tempBoard(x, 1) <> 0 Then
17:          tempScores(HUMAN) = 0
18:          tempScores(COMPUTER) = 0
19:          pitGridY = COMPUTER
20:          pitGridX = x
21:          numCrystals = tempBoard(pitGridX, pitGridY)
22:          tempBoard(pitGridX, pitGridY) = 0
23:          While numCrystals
24:             GetNextGridXY pitGridX, pitGridY
25:             TestPutCrystalInPit pitGridX, pitGridY, _
26:                   numCrystals, tempBoard, tempScores, COMPUTER
27:          Wend
28:          CompScores(x) = tempScores(COMPUTER) - _
29:                tempScores(HUMAN)
30:          humanScore = RunHumanTurn(tempBoard)
31:          comboScores(x) = CompScores(x) - humanScore
32:       End If
33:    Next x
34: End Sub
```

ANALYSIS   This subroutine uses two local arrays, tempBoard() and tempScores() (Lines 3 and 4), to keep track of its calculations. The array tempBoard() is a copy of the contents of the global Board() array, which contains the current status of the game board. Because the computer-player algorithm is only testing moves at this point, it can't change the contents of the global Board() array. Instead, it does all its work in the tempBoard() array.

GetAllScores first sets each element of the CompScores() and comboScores() arrays, which were passed into the function, to -1 (Lines 10 to 13). As mentioned previously, a -1 indicates that no move is possible at the pit. GetAllScores fills in only those array elements that actually have moves, so that the others are left with a -1.

Next, GetAllScores must loop through all eight of the computer opponent's possible moves (Line 14). It does this with a For loop. Within the loop, the program copies the Board() array into the tempBoard() array (Line 15). This ensures that each move starts with the current contents of the game board. Then, an If statement checks whether the current pit contains crystals (Line 16). If it doesn't, the entire contents of the For loop are skipped (except the If line, of course), leaving a -1 in the CompScores() and comboScores() arrays.

If the current pit contains crystals, the program initializes the tempScores() array to zeros (Lines 17 and 18) and sets the pit's grid coordinates (Lines 19 and 20). Then, in the temporary playing board stored in tempBoard(), the program distributes the crystals in the current pit (Lines 22 to 27). (The game screen displays none of this activity. The computer opponent isn't actually making a move, but simply weighing all its possible moves.) The subroutine GetNextGridXY calculates the next pit to receive a crystal (Line 24), and TestPutCrystalInPit places the crystal in the current pit in the temporary game board and calculates any points scored (Lines 25 and 26). (The program stores the scores in the tempScores() array.) TestPutCrystalInPit also adds crystals to the computer's "hand" (numCrystals) whenever appropriate. (By "hand," I mean the crystals that the computer picks up to sow around the board.)

After distributing all the crystals for a move, the program calculates the current move's net computer score by subtracting tempScores(HUMAN) from tempScores(COMPUTER) (Lines 28 and 29). It then calls RunHumanTurn to determine the point value of the human player's best response (Line 30). This value is stored in the variable humanScore. Finally, the program calculates the combination net score by subtracting humanScore from CompScores(x) and storing the result in comboScores(x) (Line 31).

The For loop continues until it has analyzed all eight moves and filled all the score arrays.

Selecting the Move

SelectMove is the function that finally determines exactly which move the computer opponent should pick:

LISTING 10.10   The SelectMove Function

```
 1:  Function SelectMove (bestCompScore As Integer, _
 2:     CompScores() As Integer, indexes() As Integer, _
 3:     count As Integer) As Integer
 4:     Dim index As Integer
 5:     Dim r As Integer
 6:     index = -1
 7:     Do
 8:        r = Int(Rnd * (count + 1))
 9:        index = indexes(r)
10:        If Int(Rnd * 3) > 0 And _
11:           CompScores(index) <> bestCompScore Then _
12:          index = -1
13:        DoEvents
```

LISTING 10.10 continued

```
14:    Loop While index = -1
15:    SelectMove = index
16: End Function
```

ANALYSIS This function chooses a random index from the indexes() array (Lines 8 and 9). As you've already learned, the indexes() array contains indexes into the comboScores() array. These indexes point to any scores in the array that equal BestComboScore. SelectMove checks whether the computer score at the chosen index in CompScores() is equal to bestCompScore (Lines 10 and 11) If it is, the function has found the computer's best move. If it isn't, the Int(Rnd * 3 > 0) in the If statement's conditional means that the chances are 1 in 3 that the computer opponent will choose the random move, even if it doesn't yield the highest value in CompScores(). This extra complication keeps the computer opponent from becoming too mechanical and predictable.

In any case, SelectMove returns the computer opponent's selected move. The move is then processed exactly as the human player's is. That is, you see the crystals being distributed around the game board just as you do when the human player uses the mouse to select a pit.

The speed of the computer-player algorithm is amazing. If the PlayerMessage subroutine didn't insert a two-second pause, the computer opponent's move would begin almost instantly after the human player's move.

Summary

Creating a computer opponent probably turned out to be an easier process than you expected. Of course, the computer opponent in Crystals has an advantage that the human player lacks: It can look forward at every possible set of two moves and find the best one. Imagine how long it would take you to think through 72 different moves. Without an additional playing board to keep track of things, you probably couldn't do it.

Q&A

Q Is it even possible to create a computer opponent than can beat an expert human player at a strategy game?

A Yep. Take chess, for example, which is considered to be the ultimate strategy game with no elements of luck. Chess programs have been created that can beat some of the best chess players in the world.

Q It seems to me that Crystals isn't all that hard to beat, once you get the hang of the game. Shouldn't it be tougher to beat a computer opponent?

A One reason you can beat Crystals with a little practice is that even a monkey can play the game and get a score. Just the process of sowing crystals around the board without any thought is bound to yield scoring moves. Still, a little strategy should improve your scores. Once you've developed that strategy, try to convert it to Visual Basic source code in order to make the computer opponent harder to beat.

Q What's the absolute easiest way to create a computer opponent for a game like Crystals?

A Well, because a monkey could beat this game, you could skip all the analyzing of moves and simply have the computer pick a random pit for each turn. The computer would then appear to be playing the game as a rank amateur.

Workshop

The workshop includes quiz questions to help gauge your grasp of the material. You'll find the answers to this quiz in Appendix A. Even if you feel that you totally understand the concepts presented here, you should work through the quiz anyway.

Quiz

1. What are two typical approaches for adding a computer opponent to a game?

2. Which approach for creating a computer opponent does Crystals use? Explain your answer.

3. What does the Crystals program use the `CompScores()` and `comboScores()` arrays for?

4. Briefly describe the algorithm that Crystals uses to determine the computer opponent's moves.

5. How does Crystals prevent the computer opponent from becoming too predictable?

DAY 11

Adding Sound to a Game

The real world is overflowing with sound. There's barely a moment of our lives when we're not barraged with hundreds of different sounds simultaneously. A computer game can't hope to compete with the real world in the aural department, but it doesn't have to. A few well-placed sound effects are all it takes to bring a game alive.

Today, you'll add a few sound effects to the Battle Bricks game you programmed on Day 7. Keep in mind that the sound effects included here are by no means the limit of what you can do. You should feel free to experiment and add as many other sound effects as you like. Specifically, today you'll learn the following:

- How to record and edit your own sound effects
- How to use the Microsoft Multimedia control
- How to use the Windows API to play sound effects
- How to use the DirectSound component of DirectX to play sound effects.

Recording Sound

If you've never recorded sound effects in Windows before, you're in for a treat. Not only is the job easy, but it's also fun. Most sound cards come with all the software you need to create sound effects for any game that can handle WAV files. Moreover, many of these sound-recording programs can also edit sounds in various ways, from clipping unwanted noise to adding echo or even reversing a sound effect.

Because I'm a musician, I have a bit of an upper hand thanks to my small home studio. If you have home-recording equipment, as well as an electronic instrument like a synthesizer, you can create all sorts of cool sound effects for your game. Add to that some sound manipulation software for your computer, and you're ready to become a sound-effects professional. Still, if you're just starting off, your computer probably has the basic programs you need already. If not, jump onto the Internet and look for freeware or shareware sound editors. Figure 11.1 shows WaveLab, the professional sound-editing software I have on my computer. It costs around $300.

FIGURE 11.1

The WaveLab sound application.

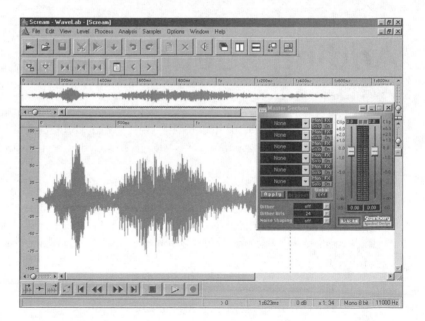

No matter what sound card you have and what software you'll be using to record and edit sound effects, the first step is to plug a microphone into the sound card. Then, any sounds the microphone picks up are transmitted to the sound card and the sound-editing program you're running.

Once you have the microphone plugged in, start up your sound-editing program and turn on the recording function. (You'll need to consult your program's documentation for specific instructions on recording sound.) Then, the sounds that the microphone picks up are converted to WAV format and saved to disk.

For example, suppose you want to record the words "Welcome, soldier, to Battle Bricks" to be used as a greeting when the player first runs the game. After plugging in your microphone and starting your sound program's record feature, just speak into the microphone (using a suitably impressive voice, of course). When you're done, turn off the record feature and save your spoken words to a WAV file. You can now play back those words with any program that can play WAV files.

Editing Sounds

Once you've recorded a sound effect, you'll almost always need to edit it somehow. Different sound programs have different editing features, but most of them let you delete various portions of the sound, as well as change the volume of the sound or add special effects such as reverb, echo, phasing, and so on.

One piece of editing you'll almost certainly have to do is to delete part of the beginning and the end of the sound, because you'll have a second or two of silence before the actual sound. Why? It takes a second or two to go from turning on the sound program's record function to actually creating the sound you want to record.

Figure 11.2 shows WaveLab ready to delete a silent area from the front of a sound effect. The user has marked the dark rectangular area with his mouse, in much the same way you'd highlight text in a word processor. Then, the user deletes the extraneous sound data by selecting the program's Delete function, as shown in Figure 11.3.

Another thing you might have to do is increase the volume of the sound effect. For some reason, they never seem to record loud enough. WaveLab has a Change Gain function that multiplies the amplitude of a sound wave by a percentage you select in the Gain Change dialog box (see Figure 11.4).

Your sound-editing program may have many other features as well, such as echo and reverse. You should also be able to cut and paste pieces of different sound effects together into one WAV file. Using this technique, you can come up with some pretty strange stuff! Figure 11.5 shows some of WaveLab's effects, open and ready to use.

11

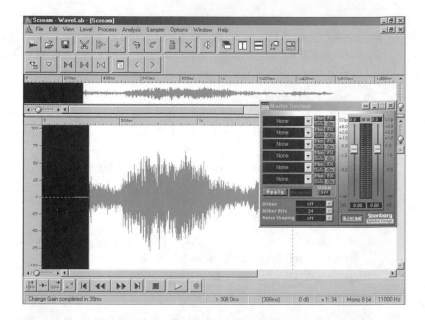

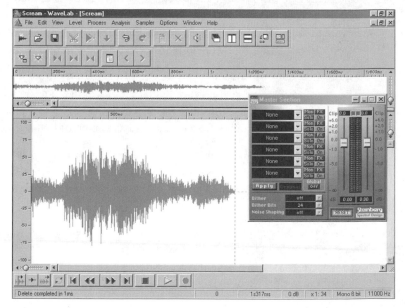

FIGURE 11.4

Scaling a sound effect's volume.

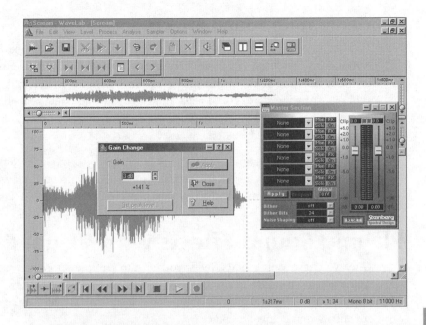

FIGURE 11.5

Most sound editors include special effects.

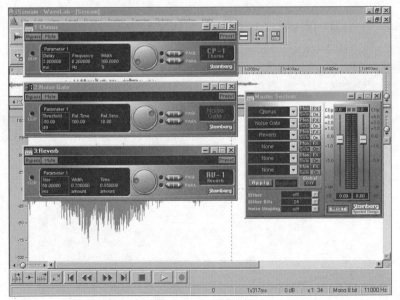

Generating Sound Effects

Just like most things in life, the sound effects you create for a game can be as simple or elaborate as you want. For most "homegrown" games, you can use items that you have laying around the house to generate sound effects. For commercial games that will be sold in a software store, you'll need a full-fledged studio and probably a sound engineer as well. Now you know why the major game companies are always complaining (or boasting) about their development costs!

I recorded the game sounds in this book in my home studio using objects laying around the house, along with a synthesizer. Later in this chapter, you'll play the new version of Battle Bricks and learn how the program plays back the sound effects.

Playing Sound Effects with Visual Basic

Once you have your sound effects, you need to set up your game program to play them. You can use Visual Basic's multimedia control, the Windows API, or the DirectSound component of DirectX. In this section, you'll examine all three methods of playing sounds in your computer games.

The Multimedia Control

The Microsoft Multimedia Control comes with all commercial versions of VB, except the Learning Edition. However, before you can use the control, you must add it to your project by selecting the Components command of the Project menu. This brings up the Components property sheet. On the Controls tab, select the Microsoft Multimedia Control 6.0, as shown in Figure 11.6. The Multimedia Control will then appear in your Visual Basic toolbox, along with the other controls that are loaded into your project.

FIGURE 11.6

Loading the
Multimedia Control.

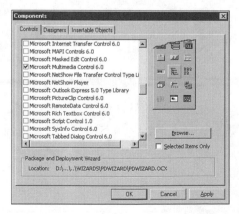

The Multimedia control encapsulates Windows' MCI (Media Control Interface), which is a library of functions for controlling multimedia devices. Although this powerful library enables you to control any multimedia device, we're only interested in the playback of WAV files.

To use the Multimedia Control to play back WAV files, you must add an instance of the control to your game's form, as shown in Figure 11.7. As you can see, the control features a full interface of buttons for controlling multimedia devices. The control can be manipulated programmatically, however. In that case, you'll almost certainly set the control's Visible property to False so the interface doesn't appear in the game's window.

FIGURE 11.7

Adding the Multimedia Control to a form.

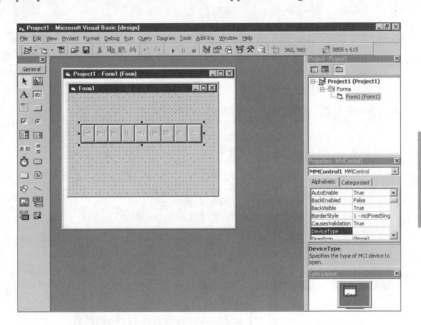

With the control added to your form, you can now set it up in your program. First, set the device type with the DeviceType property:

```
Form1.MMControl1.DeviceType = "WaveAudio"
```

Next, give the control the filename of the WAV file with the sound effect you want to play:

```
Form1.MMControl1.FileName = "sound.wav"
```

To load the WAV file, issue the "Open" command:

```
Form1.MMControl1.Command = "Open"
```

Finally, to play the sound, set the control's From property to 0 (which tells the control to play the sound from the start) and then issue the "Play" command:

```
Form1.MMControl1.From = 0
Form1.MMControl1.Command = "Play"
```

Whether you want to use the Multimedia Control depends on how sounds are incorporated into your game. For example, if you're writing an arcade game like Battle Bricks, the Multimedia Control probably won't work too well because of the brief pause before the sound is played. This latency may cause your program to bog down a bit. However, for many Visual Basic games (which don't tend to be arcade games anyway), the Multimedia Control may be the easiest way to go.

On this book's CD-ROM, you can find the MMControl example program, which plays a sound effect using the Microsoft Multimedia Control. The source code is very simple, as shown in Listing 11.1.

LISTING 11.1   The cmdPlay_Click Subroutine

```
1: Private Sub cmdPlay_Click()
2:   'ChDir "d:\tyvbgames\chap11\mmcontrol"
3:   Form1.MMControl1.DeviceType = "WaveAudio"
4:   Form1.MMControl1.FileName = "beamup.wav"
5:   Form1.MMControl1.Command = "Open"
6:   Form1.MMControl1.From = 0
7:   Form1.MMControl1.Command = "Play"
8: End Sub
```

 This procedure opens a wave (Lines 3 to 5) and plays it (using the multimedia control Lines 6 and 5).

Windows API Waveform Functions

Windows multimedia functions come in both high-level and low-level forms. The easiest way to play a sound using the Windows API from within your application is to call one of the high-level functions. These functions enable you to do everything from playing a WAV file to recording MIDI files. Unfortunately, it would take an entire book to cover all of the MCI's high-level functions. This section will show you how to use the multimedia high-level functions to control waveform audio, which is what you'll use most of the time. Windows supplies three high-level functions for playing waveform sounds: MessageBeep(), sndPlaySound(), and PlaySound().

Using the MessageBeep() Function

You can use the MessageBeep() function whenever you want to play a sound that's associated with one of Windows' alert levels. These sounds include the ubiquitous "ding" and other system sounds that inform you of various events. For example, if you click outside of a dialog box that's waiting for input, you hear a bell that reminds you to deal with the dialog box before you continue.

In a program, the various sounds associated with the Windows alert levels are defined by constants, including MB_ICONASTERISK, MB_ICONEXCLAMATION, MB_ICONHAND, MB_ICONQUESTION, and MB_OK.

When you use one of these constants in a call to MessageBeep(), the system plays the associated sound effect. Of course, before you can use MessageBeep() in a Visual Basic program, you must first declare the function and define the constants for the various alert levels, as shown here:

```
Public Declare Function MessageBeep Lib "user32" Alias _
    "MessageBeep" (ByVal wType As Long) As Long

Const MB_ICONHAND = &H10
Const MB_ICONQUESTION = &H20
Const MB_ICONEXCLAMATION = &H30
Const MB_ICONASTERISK = &H40
Const MB_ICONINFORMATION = MB_ICONASTERISK
Const MB_ICONSTOP = MB_ICONHAND
```

A typical call to MessageBeep in a Visual Basic program looks something like this:

```
Dim ErrorCode As Integer
ErrorCode = MessageBeep(MB_ICONASTERISK)
```

The function returns a 0 if it fails and a non-zero value if it succeeds.

Using the sndPlaySound() Function

Whereas the MessageBeep function limits you to only those sounds associated with system alert levels, the sndPlaySound function can play any waveform sound you like, including alert sounds. In a Visual Basic program, sndPlaySound is declared, as shown here:

```
Public Declare Function sndPlaySound Lib "winmm.dll" Alias _
    "sndPlaySoundA" (ByVal lpszSoundName As String, _
    ByVal uFlags As Long) As Long
```

The sndPlaySound function requires two parameters. The first is the name of the sound or WAV file that you want to play. The function first searches the system registry for the sound. These names aren't the names of waveform files, but rather names assigned to specific Windows events.

11

To play the SystemAsterisk sound, provide sndPlaySound() with the string SystemAsterisk as its first parameter. If sndPlaySound can't find the sound represented by the string, the function assumes that the sound string is the name of a waveform file. Then sndPlaySound searches for the file in the current directory, the main Windows directory, the Windows system directory, or directories included in the user's PATH environment variable. If the function can't find the file, it tries to play the SystemDefault sound. Finally, if it can't find this sound, it returns an error.

The second parameter for sndPlaySound is the sound-play option, which you'd set to SND_SYNC (&H0) for normal use.

A typical call to sndPlaySound() in a Visual Basic program looks something like this:

```
Dim ErrorCode As Integer
ErrorCode = sndPlaySound("sound.wav", &H0)
```

The function returns 0 if it fails and a non-zero number if it succeeds.

Using the PlaySound Function

The last high-level waveform function is PlaySound. It's a little more flexible than its cousin sndPlaySound, as you can see by its declaration in a Visual Basic program:

```
Public Declare Function PlaySound Lib "winmm.dll" Alias _
    "PlaySoundA" (ByVal lpszName As String, _
    ByVal hModule As Long, ByVal dwFlags As Long) As Long
```

Like sndPlaySound(), there are a number of flags you can use with PlaySound(), the most common of which are SND_ASYNC (&H1), SND_FILENAME (&H20000), and SND_LOOP (&H8). A typical call to PlaySound in a Visual Basic program looks something like this:

```
Dim ErrorCode As Integer
ErrorCode = PlaySound("sound.wav", 0, &H1 Or &H20000)
```

The arguments for the function are the sound's name (system name, resource name, or filename), the handle of the module that owns the resource (if the SND_RESOURCE flag is used), and the appropriate flags. The function returns 0 if it fails and a non-zero number if it succeeds.

In the Chap11\Playsounds directory of this book's CD-ROM, you'll find the PlaySounds program that demonstrates using the Windows API to play sounds. Listing 11.2 shows the complete source code.

LISTING 11.2   The PlaySounds Program

```
 1: Option Explicit
 2:
 3: Private Declare Function MessageBeep Lib "user32" _
 4:     (ByVal wType As Long) As Long
 5: Private Declare Function sndPlaySound Lib "winmm.dll" Alias _
 6:     "sndPlaySoundA" (ByVal lpszSoundName As String, _
 7:     ByVal uFlags As Long) As Long
 8: Private Declare Function PlaySound Lib "winmm.dll" Alias _
 9:     "PlaySoundA" (ByVal lpszName As String, _
10:     ByVal hModule As Long, ByVal dwFlags As Long) As Long
11:
12: Private Sub Form_Load()
13:   ChDir "d:\tyvbgames\chap11\playsounds"
14: End Sub
15:
16: Private Sub cmdMessageBeep_Click()
17:   Dim ErrorCode As Integer
18:   ErrorCode = MessageBeep(&H40)
19:   If ErrorCode = 0 Then _
20:     MsgBox "MessageBeep error.", vbExclamation, "Error"
21: End Sub
22:
23: Private Sub cmdSndPlaySound_Click()
24:   Dim ErrorCode As Integer
25:   ErrorCode = sndPlaySound("beamup.wav", &H0)
26:   If ErrorCode = 0 Then _
27:     MsgBox "sndPlaySound error.", vbExclamation, "Error"
28: End Sub
29:
30: Private Sub cmdPlaySound_Click()
31:   Dim ErrorCode As Integer
32:   ErrorCode = PlaySound("beamup.wav", 0, &H1 Or &H20000)
33:   If ErrorCode = 0 Then _
34:     MsgBox "PlaySound error.", vbExclamation, "Error"
35: End Sub
```

ANALYSIS   Lines 3 to 10 declare the Windows API functions called in the program. The
Form_Load subroutine (Lines 12 to 14) set the current directory so that the program can find its sound file. Lines 16 to 21 play a sound using the MessageBeep() function, and Lines 23 to 28 play a sound using the sndPlaySound() function. Finally, Lines 30 to 35 play a sound using the PlaySound() function.

When you run the program, you'll see the window shown in Figure 11.8. Each button shows the API function it calls. One thing to notice about the program is that it uses the sndPlaySound() function asynchronously (by specifying the flag &H0), which means that

11

control doesn't return to the program until the sound effect has finished playing. The PlaySound() function in this program, on the other hand, plays synchronously (by specifying the flag &H1), which mean control returns to the program immediately. For this reason, the PlaySound button immediately restarts the sound whenever it's clicked.

FIGURE 11.8

The PlaySounds program.

Using DirectSound

Probably the best way to play sound effects in your programs is with the DirectSound component of DirectX. In this section, you'll learn the basics of using DirectSound.

Adding DirectX to Your Project

Before you can use DirectX in your programs, you must add to your project a reference to the DirectX type library. To do this, select the Project menu's References command. The References dialog box appears. Place a check mark in the box next to the entry for DirectX 7 for Visual Basic Type Library, as shown in Figure 11.9. Click OK to close the dialog box, and you're set.

FIGURE 11.9

Adding DirectX to a VB project.

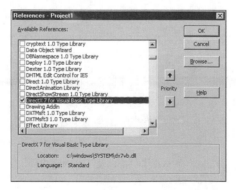

Declaring DirectSound Variables

After adding DirectX to your project, you can start adding DirectSound source code to your program. First, you need to declare the variables that'll hold references to the DirectX objects your program needs to access:

```
Dim DirectX7Obj As New DirectX7
Dim DirectSoundObj As DirectSound
Dim SoundBuffer As DirectSoundBuffer
```

Here, the first line defines a DirectX object using the New operator, the second line declares a DirectSound object, and the third line declares a buffer for the sound effect. You'll need to create a buffer like this for each sound effect in your program.

You can think of the DirectX object as the doorway into the DirectX library. Using the DirectX object (named DirectX7Obj in this example), your program can create other DirectX component objects, such as the DirectSound object that you'll create in the next section.

Creating a DirectSound Object

You need to create a DirectSound object in order to gain access to DirectSound's interface, which enables you to call DirectSound's methods. In Visual Basic, you create a DirectSound object like this:

```
Set DirectSoundObj = DirectX7Obj.DirectSoundCreate("")
```

Here, DirectSoundCreate's single argument is an empty string that tells DirectX that the DirectSound object will use the currently active driver.

Setting the Priority Level

Because the Windows environment allows multitasking, many applications may be running simultaneously. In order to keep things running smoothly, different aspects of the operating system are assigned priority levels. For this reason, DirectSound provides the SetCooperativeLevel method, which enables a program to request a priority level for the sound hardware. You typically call SetCooperativeLevel like this:

```
DirectSoundObj.SetCooperativeLevel Me.hWnd, DSSCL_PRIORITY
```

The program calls SetCooperativeLevel with two arguments: the handle of the window requesting a priority level and the flags representing the requested level. The DSSCL_PRIORITY flag gives the program exclusive use of the sound device.

11

Creating DirectSoundBuffer Objects

The next step is to create secondary DirectSoundBuffer objects for the sound effects in your program. First, declare two data types that hold the information that gets passed back and forth between DirectSound and your program:

```
Dim bufferDesc As DSBUFFERDESC
Dim waveFormat As WAVEFORMATEX
```

The DSBUFFERDESC structure holds information about DirectSoundBuffer objects. You transfer information to and from DirectSound by using structures such as DSBUFFERDESC. You fill in some of the information in the structure before you call certain DirectSound member functions, while DirectSound fills in other structure members to send information back to your program. You may or may not need any of this information.

To create a secondary buffer, the program loads a WAV file by way of the DirectSound object's CreateSoundBufferFromFile method:

```
SoundBuffer = DirectSoundObj.CreateSoundBufferFromFile _
    (FileName, bufferDesc, waveFormat)
```

CreateSoundBufferFromFile's three arguments are the path and filename of the WAV file, the DSBUFFERDESC data, and the WAVEFORMATEX data.

Playing the Sound

Finally, you're ready to get noisy with DirectSound. To play a sound, simply call the DirectSoundBuffer object's Play method:

```
SoundBuffer.Play 0
```

The Play method requires a single argument. A 0 indicates that the sound should play once, whereas a 1 indicates that the sound should be *looped*, or played again and again until it's explicitly stopped. Other important DirectSoundBuffer methods include Stop and SetCurrentPosition. The former stops a currently playing sound, and the latter sets a position within the sound at which to start playing:

```
SoundBuffer.Stop
SoundBuffer.SetCurrentPosition 0
```

Here, the argument of 0 for the SetCurrentPosition method tells DirectSound to set the sound back to the beginning.

The DirectSound Routines

You'll be thrilled to know that your humble author has put together a set of DirectSound routines that you can use in your programs without having to be a DirectSound expert. Those routines are shown in Listing 11.3.

LISTING 11.3   The DirectSound Routines

```
 1:  '****************************************************************
 2:  '* DirectSound Visual Basic Subroutines
 3:  '****************************************************************
 4:
 5:  'STEP 1
 6:  '****************************************************************
 7:  '* Place the following definitions at the top of your program.
 8:  '****************************************************************
 9:  Dim DirectX7Obj As New DirectX7
10:  Dim DirectSoundObj As DirectSound
11:
12:  ' STEP 2
13:  '****************************************************************
14:  '* Add the following line to the DirectSound definitions
15:  '* at the top of your program, changing the name "SoundBuffer"
16:  '* to the name of your sound effect. Add one of these lines for
17:  '* each sound effect in the program.
18:  '****************************************************************
19:  Dim SoundBuffer As DirectSoundBuffer
20:
21:  ' STEP 3
22:  '****************************************************************
23:  '* Call this subroutine, which initializes DirectSound, before
24:  '* calling any of the other DirectSound subroutines.
25:  '****************************************************************
26:  Sub InitDirectSound()
27:    On Local Error Resume Next
28:    Set DirectSoundObj = DirectX7Obj.DirectSoundCreate("")
29:    If Err.Number <> 0 Then
30:       MsgBox "DirectSound initialization failed."
31:       End
32:    End If
33:    DirectSoundObj.SetCooperativeLevel Me.hWnd,  DSSCL_PRIORITY
34:  End Sub
35:
36:  ' STEP 4
37:  '****************************************************************
38:  '* Call this function to initialize each sound effect buffer,
39:  '* passing as an argument the path to the sound effect's WAV
40:  '* file. This function returns the DirectSoundBuffer object for
41:  '* the sound effect.
42:  '****************************************************************
43:  Function CreateSound(FileName As String) As DirectSoundBuffer
44:    Dim bufferDesc As DSBUFFERDESC
45:    Dim waveFormat As WAVEFORMATEX
46:    bufferDesc.lFlags = DSBCAPS_STATIC
47:    Set CreateSound = _
48:        DirectSoundObj.CreateSoundBufferFromFile(FileName, _
```

11

LISTING **11.3**   continued

```
49:           bufferDesc, waveFormat)
50:   If Err.Number <> 0 Then
51:     MsgBox "unable to find sound file"
52:     End
53:   End If
54: End Function
55:
56: ' STEP 5
57: '****************************************************************
58: '* Call this subroutine to play a sound effect, passing
59: '* as arguments the sound effect's DirectSoundBuffer
60: '* object, as well as two Boolean values, the first of which
61: '* specifies whether the sound buffer should stop playing a
62: '* previous instance of the sound effect, and the second of
63: '* which specifies whether the sound should loop repeatedly.
64: '* If you choose to loop the sound effect, you must, when you
65: '* want to stop the looping, call the sound effect's Stop method
66: '* somewhere in your program.
67: '****************************************************************
68: Sub PlaySound(Sound As DirectSoundBuffer, _
69:     CloseFirst As Boolean, LoopSound As Boolean)
70:   If CloseFirst Then
71:     Sound.Stop
72:     Sound.SetCurrentPosition 0
73:   End If
74:   If LoopSound Then
75:     Sound.Play 1
76:   Else
77:     Sound.Play 0
78:   End If
79: End Sub
```

ANALYSIS   As you can see, the routines include complete instructions for use. You can find these routines under the name DirectSoundRoutines.txt in the Chap11\Code directory.

Adding Sound Effects to Battle Bricks

Now that you know everything (well, not *quite* everything) about creating and playing sound effects, you can beef up Battle Bricks with some cool sounds:

1. Add DirectX to your project by selecting the Project menu's References command and then checkmarking the DirectX 7 for Visual Basic Type Library item.

   You need to do this so that your program recognizes the various DirectSound symbols and methods.

2. Add the following DirectX declarations to the other variable declarations near the top of the program:

```
 1: '====================================================
 2: ' DirectSound variables.
 3: '====================================================
 4: Dim DirectX7Obj As New DirectX7
 5: Dim DirectSoundObj As DirectSound
 6: Dim BrickSoundBuffer As DirectSoundBuffer
 7: Dim BounceSoundBuffer As DirectSoundBuffer
 8: Dim BonusSoundBuffer As DirectSoundBuffer
 9: Dim MissSoundBuffer As DirectSoundBuffer
10: Dim FireSoundBuffer As DirectSoundBuffer
11: Dim ClappingSoundBuffer As DirectSoundBuffer
```

ANALYSIS   These lines declare the DirectSound objects that the program needs.

3. Add the following DirectSound routines to the end of the program's source code. You can find these routines in the DirectSoundRoutines.txt file in the Chap11\Code directory:

```
 1: '====================================================
 2: ' DirectSound Subroutines.
 3: '====================================================
 4: Sub InitDirectSound()
 5:   On Local Error Resume Next
 6:   Set DirectSoundObj = DirectX7Obj.DirectSoundCreate("")
 7:   If Err.Number <> 0 Then
 8:       MsgBox "DirectSound initialization failed."
 9:       End
10:   End If
11:   DirectSoundObj.SetCooperativeLevel Me.hWnd, DSSCL_PRIORITY
12: End Sub
13:
14: Function CreateSound(FileName As String) As DirectSoundBuffer
15:   Dim bufferDesc As DSBUFFERDESC
16:   Dim waveFormat As WAVEFORMATEX
17:   bufferDesc.lFlags = DSBCAPS_STATIC
18:   Set CreateSound = _
19:       DirectSoundObj.CreateSoundBufferFromFile(FileName, _
20:           bufferDesc, waveFormat)
21:   If Err.Number <> 0 Then
22:       MsgBox "unable to find sound file"
23:       End
24:   End If
25: End Function
26:
27: Sub PlaySound(Sound As DirectSoundBuffer, _
28:     CloseFirst As Boolean, LoopSound As Boolean)
```

11

```
29:    If CloseFirst Then
30:        Sound.Stop
31:        Sound.SetCurrentPosition 0
32:    End If
33:    If LoopSound Then
34:        Sound.Play 1
35:    Else
36:        Sound.Play 0
37:    End If
38: End Sub
```

ANALYSIS Lines 4 to 12 initialize the DirectSound libraries, and Lines 14 to 25 create a sound buffer from the given wave file. Finally, Lines 27 to 38 play the sound effect.

4. Add the following lines to the end of the Form_Load event handler:

```
InitDirectSound
CreateSounds
```

5. Add the following subroutine to the program. Note that you should change the explicit paths in the #Else section of the subroutine to your project's path.

```
1:  Sub CreateSounds()
2:    #If COMPILING Then
3:        Set BrickSoundBuffer = CreateSound("Brick.wav")
4:        Set BounceSoundBuffer = CreateSound("Bounce.wav")
5:        Set BonusSoundBuffer = CreateSound("Bonus.wav")
6:        Set MissSoundBuffer = CreateSound("Miss.wav")
7:        Set FireSoundBuffer = CreateSound("Fire.wav")
8:        Set ClappingSoundBuffer = CreateSound("Clapping.wav")
9:    #Else
10:       Set BrickSoundBuffer = CreateSound( _
11:           "d:\tyvbgames\chap11\battlebricks2\Brick.wav")
12:       Set BounceSoundBuffer = CreateSound( _
13:           "d:\tyvbgames\chap11\battlebricks2\Bounce.wav")
14:       Set BonusSoundBuffer = CreateSound( _
15:           "d:\tyvbgames\chap11\battlebricks2\Bonus.wav")
16:       Set MissSoundBuffer = CreateSound( _
17:           "d:\tyvbgames\chap11\battlebricks2\Miss.wav")
18:       Set FireSoundBuffer = CreateSound( _
19:           "d:\tyvbgames\chap11\battlebricks2\Fire.wav")
20:       Set ClappingSoundBuffer = CreateSound( _
21:           "d:\tyvbgames\chap11\battlebricks2\Clapping.wav")
22:    #End If
23: End Sub
```

ANALYSIS This subroutine simply loads the sound effects from disk. However, notice the use of compiler directives (Lines 2, 9, and 22) to control the paths from which the sounds are loaded. When you're running the program from within the Visual Basic

IDE, the second set of CreateSound calls provide an explicit pathname. When the COMPILING symbol is set to True, however, the first set of paths are used. This ensures that the executable can find the sound files in its own directory, no matter what that directory is named.

6. In the MoveBall subroutine, add the following line right before the KingSurrenders line that's already there:

```
PlaySound ClappingSoundBuffer, False, False
```

7. In the HandleBallActions subroutine, add the following line right before the StartNewBall line that's already there:

```
PlaySound MissSoundBuffer, False, False
```

8. In the CheckWalls subroutine, add the following line right before the second End If:

```
PlaySound BounceSoundBuffer, True, False
```

9. In the CheckWalls subroutine, add the following line right before the third End If:

```
PlaySound BounceSoundBuffer, True, False
```

10. In the CheckPaddle subroutine, add the following line right before the last End If:

```
PlaySound BounceSoundBuffer, True, False
```

11. In the DestroyBrick subroutine, add the following line right before the End If:

```
PlaySound BonusSoundBuffer, True, False
```

12. In the DestroyBrick subroutine, add the following line right after the End If:

```
PlaySound BrickSoundBuffer, True, False
```

13. In the WaitForReady subroutine, add the following line right before the End Sub:

```
FireSoundBuffer.Play 0
```

14. Add the following line to the top of the program, right after the Option Explicit line that's already there:

```
#Const COMPILING = False
```

When you set the COMPILING symbol to False, the program uses the full, explicit pathnames in the CreateSounds subroutine to locate the sound files. When you're ready to compile the program, change COMPILING to False. The program will compile only the lines containing the sound filenames with no explicit paths.

15. Copy to your project's directory all the WAV files from the Chap11\BattleBricks2 directory of this book's CD-ROM.

Now the Battle Bricks sound effects are complete, which makes the game much more interesting. Go ahead and play for a while!

11

Summary

Creating sound effects for Windows games is easier than you might expect. Just plug a microphone into your sound card and run a sound-recording program. Every sound that the microphone picks up is recorded by the sound program and stored on disk as a WAV (waveform) file. After recording the sound, you can edit it in various ways, including deleting parts of the sound, increasing the sound's volume, adding echo, and even reversing the sound. To play your sound effects, use the DirectSound routines provided in this chapter.

Q&A

Q Can I use commercial sound-effect recordings in my games?

A If you go to a large CD store, you'll probably find libraries of sound effects on CD. Whether you can use these sound effects in your games depends upon the licensing agreement that comes with the CD. In most cases, the lower-priced collections (around $15) are for personal use only. To get a sound-effect library that you can use legally in your games, you usually have to pay $50 or more.

Q How much do I have to spend to set up a simple studio for creating sound effects?

A You've already got the most important part of that studio: your computer. You can get fairly powerful sound-editing software for between $50 and $100, and you can get professional software for around $350. To get a decent synthesizer for creating sound effects, you'll probably have to spend at least $500, and more likely around $1,000. A decent microphone—such as a Shure SM-57, which is a great all-around mic—goes for around $90. But don't forget that household items, a microphone, a sound-editing program, and your sound card may be all you need to get started.

Q Is DirectSound really as simple to use as it's described to be in this chapter?

A Yes and no. If all you want to do is play sound effects from beginning to end, the simple routines I've provided should do the trick nicely. However, DirectSound provides a great deal of control over sound devices. If you're looking for that greater control and don't mind digging deeper into DirectSound, look it up in your Visual Basic online help.

Workshop

The workshop includes quiz questions to help gauge your grasp of the material. You'll find the answers to this quiz in Appendix A. Even if you feel that you totally understand the concepts presented here, you should work through the quiz anyway. The last section has a couple of exercises to help reinforce your learning.

Quiz

1. What's the minimum hardware and software you need for creating sound effects?
2. What are three ways of playing sound effects in your Visual Basic programs?
3. What would you use a sound editor for?
4. What does MCI stand for, and what is it?
5. Compare the `MessageBeep()` API function with the `PlaySound()` API function.
6. Which three DirectX objects does a program need in order to play a sound effect? Describe them.
7. What method do you call to play a sound effect with DirectSound? What method stops a sound from playing?

Exercises

1. Write a short program that plays a sound effect using DirectSound. (Don't use the DirectSound routines provided in this chapter. Also, don't forget to add the DirectX libraries to your project.)
2. Modify the Poker Squares program from Day 9 so that a sound effect plays when the player places a card in the grid, and also when the player clicks on a cell that already contains a card (an illegal-move sound).

11

DAY 12

Playing the Game: The Dragonlord RPG Project

If there's one thing that makes game players all fuzzy inside, it's the ability to create their own levels for a favorite game. For example, it's generally agreed that Doom's huge success, which led to many other similar games (including Quake), was due as much to the game's editability as it was to its playability. (Early on, game hackers figured out how to edit the game files and created their own editing tools before the official ones were released.) The funny thing about this discovery is that game programmers have long had the editors needed to create game levels for their games (a game editor is often one of the first programs created for a project); it just never occurred to anyone to release the editors for use by the general public.

Turns out, everyone thinks they've got what it takes to create great levels, and they love to do it. For the next few days, you'll work on a game called Dragonlord, which includes its own level editor. Today, you'll get an introduction to the game and have some fun hunting down skeletons and dragons in a mysterious dungeon. Tomorrow, you'll dig into the source code to see how the game works. Finally, the day after tomorrow, you'll build the level editor. Dragonlord will be your biggest project yet. Also, it will be good preparation for the last week of study, when you create the complete Moonlord strategy game.

What's an RPG?

If you're an avid computer game player, you probably already know what the letters *RPG* stand for: *role-playing game*. This type of game originated when a bunch of people got together and created characters that they used in a pencil-and-paper game of dungeon exploration. In the course of the game, the players told the game moderator (or *dungeon master*) what actions they wanted to take in the dungeon, and the moderator told them the results of those actions based on rolls of the dice. Before too long, the rules for such games become formalized. The most famous of these games is Dungeons and Dragons, or D&D as it's affectionately known among its adherents.

The rules for a role-playing game are so complex that it often takes several books to spell them out. Obviously, the dungeon master must do a lot of studying before he can run a game. When personal computers came along, role-playing games were created for them.

Unfortunately, creating a full-featured computer RPG these days takes dozens of people and several years. If this book tried to cover such a game, it would be the size of the Encyclopedia Britannica. Luckily, you can learn the basics of writing an RPG fairly easily. Then you can decide for yourself how far you want to go with it.

So, what makes an RPG different from other adventure games? The player takes on the role of another person, like a wizard, so a role-playing game must define one or more of these characters. In modern role-playing games, dozens of attributes define the way a character looks and acts in the game. These attributes typically include health (represented by hit points), strength, intelligence, race, occupation, class, religion, speed, skills, and so on. In addition to all these attributes are external modifiers, including the type of weapon the character has, the type of armor he's wearing, and the non-player characters (NPCs) with which the player must interact. The game must take all this data into account, throw in a bit of random chance, and determine the outcome of every event in the game.

In this book's RPG, Dragonlord, you'll get only a limited look at how to apply character attributes to the game rules in order to devise outcomes. Still, it's the same sort of programming that goes into today's mammoth RPGs, such as the Might and Magic series and the Ultima series.

Playing Dragonlord

Now that you know what an RPG is, let's have a little fun. Run Dragonlord, and you'll see the screen shown in Figure 12.1. Most of the screen consists of the dungeon map. At first, you can see only one room, which is where you're currently located. The other rooms on the map are marked by red squares. The current location of your game character is always a yellow square.

FIGURE 12.1

Dragonlord's main screen.

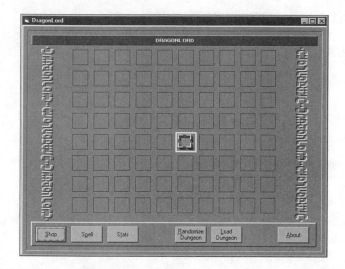

Below the dungeon map is Dragonlord's control bar, which displays the game's command buttons. You issue commands by clicking the buttons on the control bar. Table 12.1 lists the commands and what they do.

12

TABLE 12.1   Dragonlord's Commands

Command	Effect
Shop	Calls the shopkeeper
Spell	Casts a spell
Stats	Displays a statistics box for the game in progress
Randomize Dungeon	Randomizes the locations of the items in the currently loaded dungeon
Load Dungeon	Loads a dungeon file
About	Displays Dragonlord's About box

Shopping for Supplies

Before you explore the game any further, you need to get some supplies from the shop-keeper. To visit the shopkeeper, click the Shop button or press Alt+S. You'll see the YE OLDE SHOPPE dialog box (see Figure 12.2). Then choose the department where you want to shop by clicking the appropriate button or pressing the appropriate Alt+key combination (which is indicated by the underlined character on the button).

Figure 12.2

The YE OLDE SHOPPE dialog box.

The Health Department

When you click the Health button or press Alt+H, you'll see the HEALTH DEPART-MENT box (see Figure 12.3), which lists three items: Pie, Lodge, and Doctor. The box also lists the prices of the items. You can buy 5 meat pies for 10 gold pieces, a visit to the inn for 15 gold pieces, or a visit to the doctor for 15 gold pieces. When you click one of the buttons, the appropriate amount of money is deducted from your gold and you're thanked for your purchase. If you purchase a stay at the inn or a visit to the doctor, you'll also see the number of strength or hit points you've gained, as shown in Figure 12.4. To buy more of an item, you must click its button again.

Figure 12.3

The health depart-ment.

Figure 12.4

The game displays the number of hit points you've gained.

To maintain your strength in the dungeon, you need meat pies. Every time you move to a new room, you consume one-third of a pie, so they go pretty quickly. If you can handle the incredibly complex math, the 5 meat pies that you get for 10 gold pieces will last for only 15 moves. Of course, you can have more than 5 pies at a time, but you should do your best to conserve your gold.

 Caution   When your pies are gone, your strength diminishes twice as quickly.

When you need to restore some of your strength, visit the lodge. After a good night's sleep, you'll restore 21 to 35 strength points. However, you can never have more than 100 strength points, so it's probably unwise to visit the inn if you've got more than 70. When your strength drops to 0, you run in panic from the dungeon—and panicked adventurers always stumble upon an angry dragon. Aside from keeping you in the game, strength also affects how well you fight.

Hit points are a measure of the injuries you've sustained. When they're gone, so are you. If your hit points start getting low, you should visit the doctor. For a reasonable fee of 15 gold pieces, he'll patch you up, restoring 16 to 25 hit points. You can never have more than 50 hit points, so don't visit the doctor too often. As with strength, when your hit points reach 0, you run in panic from the dungeon and stumble upon a dragon. (Panicking adventurers don't pay much attention to where they're going.)

The Magic Department

When you click the Magic button or press Alt+M, you move to the magic department (see Figure 12.5), where you can buy spells, advice, and dragon brew. Spells are 10 gold pieces each, advice is 20 gold pieces per session, and the dragon brew is a whopping 80 gold pieces. You'll need to do some saving to accumulate such a large wad of cash!

12

FIGURE 12.5

The magic department.

Spells enable you to move instantly to any room on the map. This is an extremely useful power when you need to get somewhere fast. For example, you may stumble upon a teleport room that moves you far from where you want to be in the dungeon. A spell can get you right back on track. You can find spells lying around in the dungeon, so you shouldn't purchase any from the magic department until you're desperate.

When you buy advice, the shopkeeper tells you the direction of the dragon's room in relation to your current location. Getting advice at the beginning of the game is a good way to avoid the dragon until you're ready to take him on. If you stumble upon the dragon before you have the dragon brew, you're dragon chow.

Dragon brew is the most important item in the game. Normally the dragon is completely invincible in battle, so you must tame him with this magical potion. When you have the brew and you find the dragon's room, you and the dragon become good buddies. Otherwise… well, let's just say that dragons are always hungry, thanks to their huge bellies and nasty dispositions.

The Weapon Department

The dragon's dungeon is full of undead skeletons that would like nothing better than to make you one of them. When you find a skeleton, you must fight to the death. Obviously, the better your weapon, the better your chance of surviving a battle. Buy a decent weapon as soon as possible by clicking the Weapon button or pressing Alt+W. This takes you to the shopkeeper's weapon department, shown in Figure 12.6.

FIGURE 12.6

The weapon department.

Generally, the better your weapon, the easier the game is to beat. The sword is the best weapon, but it's expensive. If you buy the sword at the beginning of the game, you'll have no gold left to buy meat pies or advice.

When choosing a weapon, you can employ several strategies. You can spend all your gold on the sword and then hope you don't stumble upon the dragon before you can afford either advice or dragon brew. Or you might want to get advice from the very start and make do with a knife, which is almost as good as a sword. A club is only slightly more effective than no weapon at all, but it leaves you with a lot of gold to spend.

Keep in mind that weapons are expensive. You probably won't be able to afford another one at any time during the game, so choose wisely at the start. (By the way, if you don't buy a weapon, you fight with your fists.)

Moving Through the Dungeon

Each room in the dungeon has one or more doors. To move to another room, you must move in the direction of an exit. If you want to move north, for example, the north wall of your current room must have a door. If there is a door, simply click the room to which you want to move. The new room appears on the map, and you see whatever is in that room, if anything. Keep in mind that each move consumes 1 strength point and one-third of a pie.

Discovering Objects in the Dungeon

As you move from room to room, you'll stumble upon various objects, including gold, spells, serums, teleporters, skeletons, the thief, and, of course, the dragon. When you move to a room that has such an object, the DISCOVERY box appears. This box tells you what you've found and performs any action related to that object. After you discover an item in a room, you automatically pick it up, so it won't be in the room if you return there later in the game. The exceptions are skeletons and gold pieces, which can appear randomly in any room.

Gold Pieces

You use gold pieces (see Figure 12.7) to buy items from the shopkeeper. When you enter an empty room, you may stumble upon a small cache of gold. Also, whenever you defeat a skeleton, you get to keep his gold. Dragon brew is expensive, so you must spend your gold wisely. You'll not have much to spare.

12

FIGURE 12.7

Discovering gold pieces.

Spells

The spells that you find in the dungeon (see Figure 12.8) are exactly like those you buy from the shopkeeper. They enable you to move instantly to any room. To use a spell, click the control bar's Spell button or press Alt+P. A dialog box appears, telling you to click the room (or room square, if the room isn't on the map yet) where you want to move. When you click the room, you move there instantly.

FIGURE 12.8

Discovering spells.

Serums

Serums (see Figure 12.9) restore a portion of your strength. You cannot buy these magical potions from the shopkeeper. The only way that you can obtain them is to find them in the dungeon. You drink a serum automatically after a battle in which your strength drops below 20 points. Of course, if you have no serum, the only way to restore your strength is to visit the shopkeeper and purchase a stay at the inn.

FIGURE 12.9

Discovering serum.

Teleporters

A few of the rooms in the dungeon contain teleporter fields (see Figure 12.10) that instantly transfer you to another room. Often, this surprise move is helpful, taking you to a new area to explore. However, just as often, the teleporter plops you down near the dragon. In that case, your best bet is to use a spell to get back to where you were. If you don't have a spell or don't want to use one, you should take the most direct route to safety. If you stumble into the dragon's room without the dragon brew, the dragon will have a tasty meal.

FIGURE 12.10

FIGURE 12.10

A teleporter.

The Thief

One room in the dungeon hides the thief (see Figure 12.11). After you run into this pesky fellow, you'll find that 25 percent of your gold pieces are missing. The thief is an annoyance if you're carrying a lot of gold, but otherwise he does no harm. After the thief robs you once, he never appears again. With any luck, you'll manage to avoid him completely. (Yeah, right. Fat chance of that!)

FIGURE 12.11

The thief.

Skeletons

The dragon's dungeon is positively packed with skeletons (see Figure 12.12). These are nasty creatures that have nothing better to do than to make exploring miserable for innocent adventurers like yourself.

FIGURE 12.12

A skeleton.

12

When you discover a skeleton, you must battle him to the death (yours or his). To start the battle, click OK to exit the skeleton's DISCOVERY box. The battle box then appears, as shown in Figure 12.13.

FIGURE 12.13

The battle box.

The green die on the left represents your attack, and the green die on the right represents the skeleton's. For each attack, the fighter with the highest attack score delivers a blow to his opponent. Below the dice is your modifier score. This modifier is added to your roll to come up with your final attack score. For example, if you roll a 6 and have an attack modifier of 2, your total attack is 8. Then, if the skeleton rolls an 8 or less, you win. (In the case of a tie, you win.)

Each hit, against either you or the skeleton, scores between 1 and 5 points of damage. This damage is subtracted from the loser's hit points. Because a skeleton starts with 5 hit points, you can kill him with 1 to 5 hits. Each time you attack, you consume 1 strength point. If you're out of meat pies, you consume your strength twice as fast.

After you defeat a skeleton, you get his cache of gold. The amount of gold varies from skeleton to skeleton. If you fail to defeat the skeleton, the game ends because either your strength or hit points will have dropped to 0.

The Dragon

Like most objects in the dungeon, the dragon (see Figure 12.14) stays in the same room throughout the entire game. He doesn't come looking for you and really couldn't care less that you're reducing his skeleton army to heaps of moldy bones. However, the dragon doesn't like visitors, and if you stumble into his room, you'd better have the dragon brew to tame him. Otherwise, it's munch, munch, munch. If you do have the dragon brew when you discover His Scaly Majesty, you tame the dragon and win the game.

Randomizing a Dungeon

When you run Dragonlord, it always loads the default dungeon file, Dungeon.drg. This file (and every other Dragonlord dungeon file) defines the locations of all objects in the dungeon, so every time you load it, all the items are put back in the same rooms they were in before. Obviously, knowing where things are—especially the dragon—can make adventuring mucho boring. That's why the game gives you the Randomize Dungeon button. Click this button at the beginning of a game and Dragonlord shuffles the dungeon's contents. This way, you can play the same dungeon layout repeatedly.

Note

You can randomize the dungeon only at the beginning of a game. Once a game starts, the Randomize Dungeon button becomes disabled until the game ends.

Loading a Dungeon

To start a new game, you must load a dungeon file, which defines the layout of the rooms in the dungeon, as well as the items located in those rooms. To load a dungeon, click the Load Dungeon button, or press Alt+L, and choose the dungeon from the Open Dungeon File dialog box that appears. Figure 12.15 shows this dialog box as it appears in Windows Me. If you have an earlier version of Windows, the dialog box will look a bit different but will function similarly.

Note

At this point, your Dragonlord game features only a single dungeon file, Dungeon.drg. On Day 14, you'll create a dungeon editor that enables you to create your own dungeon files.

12

FIGURE **12.15**

The Open Dungeon File dialog box.

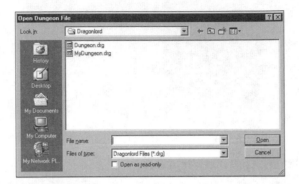

Building Dragonlord

So far you've had an easy lesson, spending most of your time playing the Dragonlord RGP. Unfortunately, learning how to *play* games is only a small part of learning how to *program* games. It's time to get back to the serious work!

In the following section, you'll build the program's user interface. In tomorrow's lesson, you'll add the source code that gets the game running. Crack your knuckles and stock up on gummy bears, because this will be your biggest project yet!

Creating Dragonlord's Main Form

The first step is to create the game's main form:

1. Start a new Standard EXE Visual Basic project.

2. Set the form's properties to the values listed here:

    AutoRedraw = True

    Caption = "Dragonlord"

    Height = 7590

    ScaleMode = Pixel

    Width = 9720

    This form will be the game's main screen.

3. Set the form's Picture property to the Dragonlord.gif image that you can find in the Images\Dragonlord directory of this book's CD-ROM.

4. Add an Image control to the project, giving it the name imgRoom and assigning the Room0.bmp file to the Picture property. (As with all of Dragonlord's image files, you can find Room0.bmp in the Images\Dragonlord directory of this book's CD-ROM.)

5. Select the new Image control by clicking it, and then press Ctrl+C to copy the control to the Clipboard. Press Ctrl+V to paste a new instance of the control into your form. When VB asks if you want to create a control array, answer Yes. Assign the Room1.bmp image file to this control's Picture property.

6. Add 13 more Image controls to the control array. Assign the remaining room images (Room2.bmp through Room14.bmp) to these controls. That is, the image control imgRoom(2) should get the Room2.bmp image, imgRoom(3) should get the Room3.bmp image file, and so on. The final control array will appear on your form as shown in Figure 12.16.

   Each of the different rooms in the dungeon has an image associated with it. The imgRoom control array contains these images.

FIGURE 12.16

The imgRoom control array.

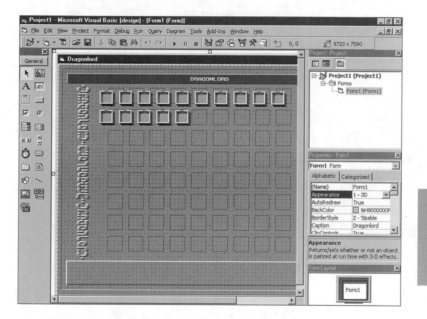

7. Create another Image control array called imgHall that contains two controls, and assign the Hall0.bmp and Hall1.bmp image files to the controls' Picture properties.

   This image array holds the two images that represent the hallways that lead from one room to another. When the player moves from one room to another, the connecting hallways appear on the screen.

12

8. Create another Image control array called `imgDice` that contains nine controls, and assign the Dice0.bmp through Dice8.bmp image files to the controls' `Picture` properties.

   The outcome of a battle is determined by a roll of the dice. However, Dragonlord's dice are special. Each die can represent a value from 1 to 9, rather than just 1 to 6.

9. Create another Image control array called `imgSkeleton` that contains four controls, and assign the Skeleton0.bmp through Skeleton3.bmp image files to the controls' `Picture` properties.

   When battling a skeleton, the player is treated with a couple of simple animation sequences. The `imgSkeleton` image array holds the images for these sequences.

10. Add seven more Image controls (not as a control array) to the form, and give them the following property settings:

   Image Control #1

   `Name` = imgGold

   `Picture` = Gold.bmp

   Image Control #2

   `Name` = imgThief

   `Picture` = Thief.bmp

   Image Control #3

   `Name` = imgSerum

   `Picture` = Serum.bmp

   Image Control #4

   `Name` = imgSpell

   `Picture` = Spell.bmp

   Image Control #5

   `Name` = imgTeleport

   `Picture` = Teleport.bmp

   Image Control #6

   `Name` = imgDragon0

   `Picture` = Dragon0.bmp

Image Control #7

Name = imgDragon1

Picture = Dragon1.bmp

These images will be used in the Discovery dialog box to illustrate what the player has found in a room.

11. Add a CommonDialog control to the form, keeping the object's default name. If the control isn't in your VB toolbox, you'll need to load it using the Project menu's Components command, as shown in Figure 12.17.

The program uses this control to enable the player to load different dungeon layouts.

FIGURE 12.17

Adding the CommonDialog control to a project.

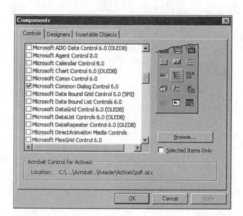

12. Add a Shape control to the form, giving it the following property settings:

Name = shpRoomMarker

BorderColor = Yellow

BorderWidth = 3

Height = 40

Shape = Rectangle

Width = 42

This shape control is the yellow rectangle that marks the player's current location in the dungeon.

12

13. Add six CommandButton controls to the form, giving them the following property settings:

CommandButton #1

`Name` = cmdShop

`Caption` = &Shop

`Height` = 34

`Left` = 30

`Top` = 418

`Width` = 65

CommandButton #2

`Name` = cmdSpell

`Caption` = S&pell

`Height` = 34

`Left` = 105

`Top` = 418

`Width` = 65

CommandButton #3

`Name` = cmdStats

`Caption` = S&tats

`Height` = 34

`Left` = 180

`Top` = 418

`Width` = 65

CommandButton #4

`Name` = cmdRandomize

`Caption` = &Randomize Dungeon

`Height` = 34

`Left` = 322

`Top` = 418

`Width` = 65

CommandButton #5

`Name` = cmdLoad

`Caption` = &Load Dungeon

`Height` = 34

`Left` = 398

`Top` = 418

`Width` = 65

CommandButton #6

`Name` = cmdAbout

`Caption` = &About

`Height` = 34

`Left` = 540

`Top` = 418

`Width` = 65

12

These buttons trigger the game's main commands.

14. Save your work, naming the form Dragonlord.frm and the project file Dragonlord.vbp.

You've now completed the game's main form, which should look something like Figure 12.18. However, you still need to add dialog boxes to the game's user interface, which you'll do in the following section.

FIGURE **12.18**

The completed form.

Adding Dialog Boxes to the User Interface

Dragonlord incorporates a number of dialog boxes into its user interface. These dialog boxes enable the user to shop for adventuring supplies, as well as display status information and battles. Perform the following steps to add the dialog boxes to the game:

1. Add a form to the project, giving the form the following property settings and controls:

   Name = frmBattle

   AutoRedraw = True

   BorderStyle = Fixed Dialog

   Caption = "Dragonlord"

   Font = MS Sans Serif, Bold, 10-point

   ForeColor = White

   Height = 4590

   Picture = Battle.gif

   ScaleMode = Pixel

   Width = 3105

CommandButton Control

Name = cmdOK

Caption = "&OK"

Height = 35

Left = 67

Top = 229

Width = 67

Figure 12.19 shows the completed dialog box, which appears when the player is battling a skeleton.

FIGURE 12.19

The completed frmBattle form.

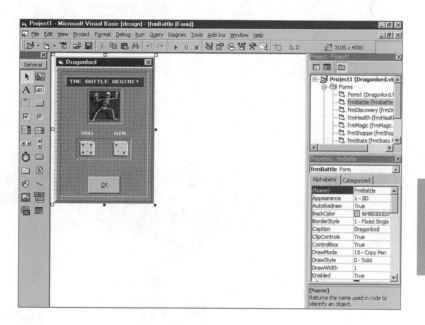

12

2. Add another form to the project, giving it the following property settings and controls:

    Name = frmDiscovery

    AutoRedraw = True

    BorderStyle = Fixed Dialog

    Caption = "Dragonlord"

Font = MS Sans Serif, Bold, 10-point

ForeColor = White

Height = 3705

Picture = Discovery.gif

ScaleMode = Pixel

Width = 3105

CommandButton Control

Name = cmdOK

Caption = "&OK"

Height = 36

Left = 66

Top = 168

Width = 67

Figure 12.20 shows the completed dialog box, which appears whenever the player discovers an object in a room.

FIGURE 12.20

The completed frmDiscovery form.

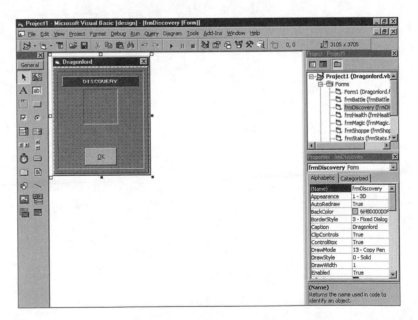

3. Add another form to the project, giving it the following property settings and controls:

Name = frmHealth

AutoRedraw = True

BorderStyle = Fixed Dialog

Caption = "Dragonlord"

ForeColor = White

Height = 3700

Picture = Health.gif

ScaleMode = Pixel

Width = 3880

CommandButton Control #1

Name = cmdPie

Caption = "&Pie"

Height = 34

Left = 23

Top = 169

Width = 65

CommandButton Control #2

Name = cmdLodge

Caption = "&Lodge"

Height = 34

Left = 93

Top = 169

Width = 65

12

CommandButton Control #3

Name = cmdDoctor

Caption = "&Doctor"

Height = 34

Left = 163

Top = 169

Width = 65

Figure 12.21 shows the completed form, which enables the player to purchase health-related items.

FIGURE **12.21**

The completed frmHealth form.

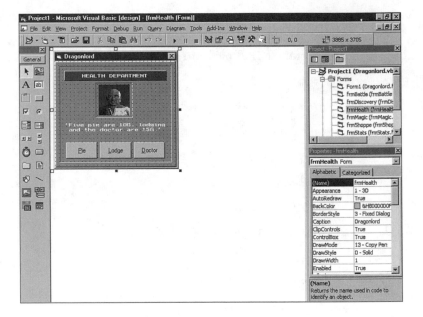

4. Add another form to the project, giving it the following property settings and controls:

Name = frmMagic

AutoRedraw = True

BorderStyle = Fixed Dialog

Caption = "Dragonlord"

```
ForeColor = White
```

```
Height = 3700
```

```
Picture = Magic.gif
```

```
ScaleMode = Pixel
```

```
Width = 3870
```

CommandButton Control #1

```
Name = cmdSpell
```

```
Caption = "&Spell"
```

```
Height = 34
```

```
Left = 23
```

```
Top = 169
```

```
Width = 65
```

CommandButton Control #2

```
Name = cmdAdvice
```

```
Caption = "&Advice"
```

```
Height = 34
```

```
Left = 93
```

```
Top = 169
```

```
Width = 65
```

CommandButton Control #3

```
Name = cmdBrew
```

```
Caption = "&Brew"
```

```
Height = 34
```

```
Left = 163
```

```
Top = 169
```

```
Width = 65
```

12

Figure 12.22 shows the completed form, which enables the player to purchase magic items.

FIGURE 12.22

*The completed
frmMagic form.*

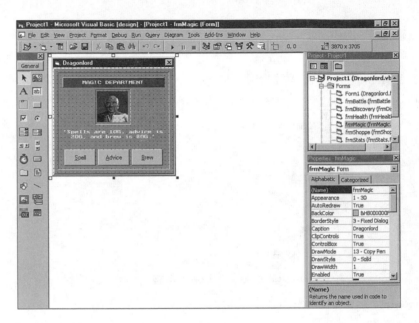

5. Add another form to the project, giving it the following property settings and controls:

Name = frmShoppe

AutoRedraw = True

BorderStyle = Fixed Dialog

Caption = "Dragonlord"

ForeColor = White

Height = 3700

Picture = Shoppe.gif

ScaleMode = Pixel

Width = 3880

CommandButton Control #1

Name = cmdHealth

Caption = "&Health"

Height = 34

Left = 23

Top = 169

Width = 65

CommandButton Control #2

Name = cmdMagic

Caption = "&Magic"

Height = 34

Left = 93

Top = 169

Width = 65

CommandButton Control #3

Name = cmdWeapon

Caption = "&Weapon"

Height = 34

Left = 163

Top = 169

Width = 65

Figure 12.23 shows the completed form, which enables the player to select the type of store he wants to shop in.

6. Add another form to the project, giving it the following property settings and controls:

Name = frmStats

AutoRedraw = True

BorderStyle = Fixed Dialog

12

Caption = "Dragonlord"

Font = MS Sans Serif, Bold, 10-point

ForeColor = White

Height = 3900

Picture = Stats.gif

ScaleMode = Pixel

Width = 3105

CommandButton Control

Name = cmdOK

Caption = "&OK"

Height = 26

Left = 28

Top = 185

Width = 145

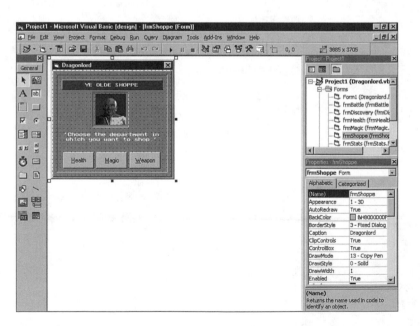

FIGURE 12.23

*The completed
frmShoppe form.*

Figure 12.24 shows the completed form, which displays the player's current attributes and statistics.

FIGURE **12.24**

The completed frmStats form.

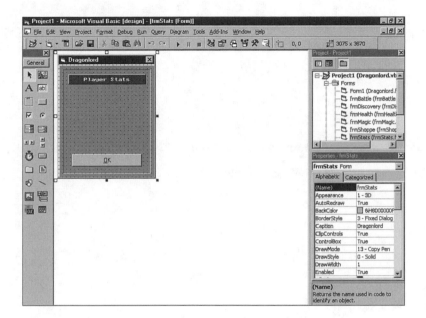

7. Add another form to the project, giving it the following property settings and controls:

  Name = frmWeapons

  AutoRedraw = True

  BorderStyle = Fixed Dialog

  Caption = "Dragonlord"

  ForeColor = White

  Height = 3700

  Picture = Weapons.gif

  ScaleMode = Pixel

  Width = 3890

12

CommandButton Control #1

Name = cmdClub

Caption = "&Club"

Height = 34

Left = 23

Top = 169

Width = 65

CommandButton Control #2

Name = cmdKnife

Caption = "&Knife"

Height = 34

Left = 93

Top = 169

Width = 65

CommandButton Control #3

Name = cmdSword

Caption = "&Sword"

Height = 34

Left = 163

Top = 169

Width = 65

Figure 12.25 shows the completed form, which enables the player to purchase weapons.

8. Save your work, giving the forms the default filenames supplied by Visual Basic.

You've now added a set of dialog boxes to your Dragonlord project. The next step is to start adding program code, which you'll do in tomorrow's lesson.

FIGURE 12.25

*The completed
frmWeapons form.*

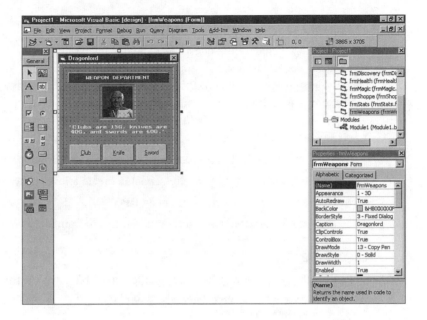

Summary

Computer role-playing games are among the most popular and complex games on the market. In today's lesson, you learned about RPG games in general and became familiar with this book's simple RPG game, Dragonlord.

Q&A

Q Why does it take so long for game companies to program computer RPG games?

A First of all, a modern computer RPG has a storyline that's large enough to fill a novel. How long would it take *you* to write a novel? Second, modern RPGs usually feature large worlds that include cities, dungeons, castles, deserts, oceans, lakes, forests, mountains, and more. Creating a world of this size and detail takes a lot of time.

Q Why would anyone want to take so much time to create a game?

A Creating a world and populating it with people and cities is a lot of fun (as well as a lot of work). It gives you the chance to act as a kind of god, dictating what your world will look like and what types of creates will live there. You also get to think up cool puzzles and watch while people try to solve them. And did I mention that RPG programmers get paid big bucks?

12

Workshop

The workshop includes quiz questions to help gauge your grasp of the material. You'll find the answers to this quiz in Appendix A. Even if you feel that you totally understand the concepts presented here, you should work through the quiz anyway. The last section is an exercise to help reinforce your learning.

Quiz

1. What makes an RPG different from other types of adventure games?
2. Give two reasons why you might want to create a level editor for a game.
3. How do you define a character in an RPG?
4. How are a character's attributes used in the program?

Exercise

1. Play the Dragonlord game until you're comfortable with it from a player's point of view. You'll need this experience in tomorrow's lesson, when you dig into the game's source code.

DAY 13

Programming a Simple RPG

Today you'll continue to develop Dragonlord, a full-fledged dungeon adventure game in which you must locate and tame a dragon hidden within a dungeon maze. To develop the Dragonlord program, you'll use many of the techniques that you've learned so far. Not only will you deal with various images, but you'll also play interesting sounds and learn how to manage a dungeon map. Specifically, today you'll do the following:

- Add object-handler code to the game
- Add initialization routines to the game
- Add general subroutines and functions to the game
- Add a module for global data types and routines
- Add source code to each of the dialog boxes
- Explore how Dragonlord works

Adding the Object Handlers

Now you need to associate code with the form that is the base object of the game's user interface, as well as with the various controls you've placed on the form:

1. Double-click the Form1 form to bring up the code window.

2. Add the following form handlers to the code window. You can either type in the source code or copy it from the Dragonlord01.txt file, which you can find in the Chap13\Code directory of this book's CD-ROM:

```
1:  '==================================================
2:  ' Main Form Handlers.
3:  '==================================================
4:  Private Sub Form_Load()
5:    FileName = "Dungeon.drg"
6:    InitSound
7:    InitObjects
8:    InitGame
9:  End Sub
10:
11: Private Sub Form_MouseDown(Button As Integer, _
12:     Shift As Integer, X As Single, Y As Single)
13:    If Randomizing Or Battling Then Exit Sub
14:    If Stats.CastingSpell = True Then
15:      SpellMove X, Y
16:    Else
17:      MovePlayer X, Y
18:    End If
19: End Sub
20:
21: Private Sub Form_Resize()
22:    On Error Resume Next
23:    If Form1.Width < 9690 Then Form1.Width = 9690
24:    If Form1.Height < 7560 Then Form1.Height = 7560
25:    On Error GoTo 0
26: End Sub
```

ANALYSIS The Form_Load event procedure (Lines 4 to 9) initializes the game when the form loads, and the Form_MouseDown event procedure handles mouse clicks on the playing board. The Form_Resize event procedure prevents the player from making the window too small to contain the playing board.

3. Add the following button handlers to the code window, directly after the code you added in the previous step. You can either type in the source code or copy it from the Dragonlord02.txt file, which you can find in the Chap13\Code directory of this book's CD-ROM:

```
1:  '==================================================
2:  ' Button Handlers.
3:  '==================================================
4:  Private Sub cmdAbout_Click()
5:    MsgBox "Dragonlord" & vbCrLf & "By Clayton Walnum" & _
6:        vbCrLf & vbCrLf & "Copyright 2000" & _
7:        vbCrLf & "by Macmillan Computer Publishing    ", _
8:        vbInformation, "About Dragonlord"
9:  End Sub
10:
11: Private Sub cmdRandomize_Click()
12:    Dim Room As Integer
13:    Dim SwapRoom As Integer
14:    Dim temp As Integer
15:    Dim RoomX As Integer
16:    Dim RoomY As Integer
17:    ToggleButtons False
18:    cmdRandomize.Enabled = False
19:    Randomizing = True
20:    For Room = 0 To NUMBEROFROOMS - 1
21:      If Map(Room) <> NOROOMDEFINED Then
22:        Do
23:          SwapRoom = Int(Rnd * NUMBEROFROOMS)
24:        Loop While Map(SwapRoom) = NOROOMDEFINED
25:        If Room <> STARTINGROOM And _
26:            SwapRoom <> STARTINGROOM Then
27:          GetPixelXY Room, RoomX, RoomY
28:          DrawCircle RoomX + 16, RoomY + 16, vbWhite
29:          Delay 0.001
30:          DrawCircle RoomX + 16, RoomY + 16, RGB(168, 168, 168)
31:          GetPixelXY SwapRoom, RoomX, RoomY
32:          DrawCircle RoomX + 16, RoomY + 16, vbWhite
33:          Delay 0.001
34:          DrawCircle RoomX + 16, RoomY + 16, RGB(168, 168, 168)
35:          temp = Items(Room)
36:          Items(Room) = Items(SwapRoom)
37:          Items(SwapRoom) = temp
38:        End If
39:      End If
40:    Next Room
41:    DragonRoom = GetDragonRoom
42:    ToggleButtons True
43:    cmdRandomize.Enabled = True
44:    Randomizing = False
45: End Sub
46:
47: Private Sub cmdSpell_Click()
48:    If Stats.Spells > 0 Then
49:      MsgBox "Click on the room to" & vbCrLf & _
50:          "which you want to move."
51:      Stats.CastingSpell = True
```

13

```
52:        Stats.Spells = Stats.Spells - 1
53:      Else
54:        MsgBox "You have no spells."
55:      End If
56:      cmdRandomize.Enabled = False
57: End Sub
58:
59: Public Sub cmdStats_Click()
60:      cmdRandomize.Enabled = False
61:      Load frmStats
62:      PrintStat 50, 50, "Hit Points: " & Stats.HitPoints
63:      PrintStat 50, 65, "Strength: " & Stats.Strength
64:      PrintStat 50, 80, "Pie: " & Stats.Pie
65:      PrintStat 50, 95, "Gold: " & Stats.Gold
66:      PrintStat 50, 110, "Spells: " & Stats.Spells
67:      PrintStat 50, 125, "Serums: " & Stats.Serums
68:      PrintStat 50, 140, "Brew: " & -Int(Stats.Brew)
69:      PrintStat 50, 155, "Weapon: " & Stats.Weapon
70:      frmStats.Show vbModal, Me
71: End Sub
72:
73: Private Sub cmdShop_Click()
74:      frmShoppe.Show , Me
75:      cmdRandomize.Enabled = False
76: End Sub
77:
78: Private Sub cmdLoad_Click()
79:      CommonDialog1.flags = cdlOFNFileMustExist
80:      CommonDialog1.CancelError = True
81:      CommonDialog1.FileName = ""
82:      CommonDialog1.InitDir = CurDir
83:      CommonDialog1.DefaultExt = "drg"
84:      CommonDialog1.Filter = _
85:          "Dragonlord Files (*.drg)|*.drg|All Files (*.*)|(*.*)"
86:      CommonDialog1.FilterIndex = 1
87:      CommonDialog1.DialogTitle = "Open Dungeon File"
88:      On Error GoTo DialogError
89:      CommonDialog1.ShowOpen
90:      FileName = CommonDialog1.FileName
91:      InitGame
92:      Exit Sub
93: DialogError:
94:      MsgBox "No file loaded.", vbInformation, "Open"
95: End Sub
```

ANALYSIS The cmdAbout_Click event procedure (Lines 4 to 9) displays the About dialog box when the player clicks the About button. The cmdRandomize_Click event procedure (Lines 11 to 45) randomizes the contents of the dungeon when the player clicks the Randomize Dungeon button. The cmdSpell_Click (Lines 47 to 57), `cmdStats_Click` (Lines 59 to 71), and `cmdShop_Click` (Lines 73 to 76) event procedures handle casting spells, viewing statistics, and shopping, respectively. Finally, the `cmdLoad_Click` event procedure (Lines 78 to 95) loads a dungeon file when the player clicks the Load Dungeon button.

Adding General Game Source Code

Now add the general game subroutines, functions, constants, and variables:

1. Add the following initialization subroutines to the code window, directly after the code you added in the previous section. You can either type in the code or copy it from the Dragonlord03.txt file, which you can find in the Chap13\Code directory of this book's CD-ROM:

```
 1:  '===================================================
 2:  ' Initialization Routines.
 3:  '===================================================
 4:  Sub InitObjects()
 5:    Dim i As Integer
 6:    Form1.Height = 7560
 7:    Form1.Width = 9690
 8:    Form1.Left = 200
 9:    Form1.Top = 200
10:    For i = 0 To 14
11:      imgRoom(i).Visible = False
12:      If i < 2 Then imgHall(i).Visible = False
13:      If i < 9 Then imgDice(i).Visible = False
14:      If i < 4 Then imgSkeleton(i).Visible = False
15:    Next i
16:    imgThief.Visible = False
17:    imgGold.Visible = False
18:    imgTeleport.Visible = False
19:    imgSpell.Visible = False
20:    imgSerum.Visible = False
21:    imgDragon0.Visible = False
22:    imgDragon1.Visible = False
23: End Sub
24:
25: Sub InitGame()
26:    Dim temp As Integer
27:    Dim PixelX As Integer
28:    Dim PixelY As Integer
29:    'ChDir "d:\TYVBGames\Chap13\DragonLord\"
30:    Open FileName For Binary As #1
31:    Get #1, , Map
32:    Get #1, , Items
33:    Close #1
34:    Randomize
35:    ResetStats
```

13

```
36:    Battling = False
37:    DragonRoom = GetDragonRoom
38:    Form1.PaintPicture Form1.Picture, 0, 0
39:    PixelX = (Stats.Room Mod NUMBEROFCOLS) * _
40:        CELLWIDTH + OFFSETX
41:    PixelY = (Stats.Room \ NUMBEROFCOLS) * _
42:        CELLHEIGHT + OFFSETY
43:    Form1.PaintPicture imgRoom(Map(Stats.Room) - 1), _
44:        PixelX, PixelY
45:    DrawRoomMarker
46:    cmdRandomize.Enabled = True
47: End Sub
```

ANALYSIS The InitObjects subroutine (Lines 4 to 23) initializes the Visual Basic objects in the game, setting form properties and making the various image objects invisible to the player. The InitGame subroutine (Lines 25 to 47) initializes the game's variables, including loading the default dungeon map.

2. Add the following general subroutines to the code window, directly after the code you added in the previous step. You can either type in the code or copy it from the Dragonlord04.txt file, which you can find in the Chap13\Code directory of this book's CD-ROM:

```
'=================================================
' General Game Subroutines.
'=================================================
Sub DrawCircle(X As Integer, Y As Integer, Color As Long)
  Form1.FillStyle = vbSolid
  Form1.FillColor = Color
  Form1.Circle (X, Y), 4, Color
End Sub

Sub MoveToRoom(newRoom As Integer, Direction As Integer)
  Dim stillAlive As Boolean
  stillAlive = UpdateStats
  If stillAlive Then
    PlaySound WalkSound, True, False
    DrawRoomMarker
    Stats.Room = newRoom
    DrawRoom
    DrawHallway Direction
    DrawRoomMarker
    ShowItem newRoom
  End If
End Sub

Sub CheckForRandomItem(Room As Integer)
  Dim randomItem As Integer
  If Items(Room) = I_EMPTY Then
    randomItem = Int(Rnd * 10)
```

```
      If randomItem = 8 Or randomItem = 9 Then
        Items(Room) = I_GOLD
      ElseIf randomItem > 4 And randomItem < 8 Then
        Items(Room) = I_SKELETON
      End If
   End If
End Sub

Sub DrinkSerum()
   Dim newStrength As Integer
   Stats.Serums = Stats.Serums - 1
   newStrength = Int(Rnd * 15) + 15
   MsgBox "You drink a serum." & vbCrLf & "+" & _
      newStrength & " strength points."
   SetStrength newStrength
End Sub

Sub ShowNoExit()
   MsgBox "You can't enter that" & vbCrLf & _
      "room from where you are."
End Sub

Sub DrawRoom()
   Dim Color As Long
   Dim RoomPixelX As Integer
   Dim RoomPixelY As Integer
   GetPixelXY Stats.Room, RoomPixelX, RoomPixelY
   Color = Point(RoomPixelX, RoomPixelY)
   If Color <> vbWhite Then _
     Form1.PaintPicture imgRoom(Map(Stats.Room) - 1), _
     RoomPixelX, RoomPixelY
End Sub

Sub DrawHallway(Direction As Integer)
   Dim RoomPixelX As Integer
   Dim RoomPixelY As Integer
   Dim HallPixelX As Integer
   Dim HallPixelY As Integer
   GetPixelXY Stats.Room, RoomPixelX, RoomPixelY
   GetHallPixelXY RoomPixelX, RoomPixelY, _
      HallPixelX, HallPixelY, Direction
   If Direction = NORTH Or Direction = SOUTH Then
     Form1.PaintPicture imgHall(0), HallPixelX, HallPixelY
   Else
     Form1.PaintPicture imgHall(1), HallPixelX, HallPixelY
   End If
End Sub

Sub GetHallPixelXY(RoomPixelX As Integer, _
     RoomPixelY As Integer, HallPixelX As Integer, _
     HallPixelY As Integer, Direction As Integer)
```

13

```
      Select Case Direction
        Case NORTH
          HallPixelX = RoomPixelX
          HallPixelY = RoomPixelY + 25
        Case EAST
          HallPixelX = RoomPixelX - 19
          HallPixelY = RoomPixelY
        Case SOUTH
          HallPixelX = RoomPixelX
          HallPixelY = RoomPixelY - 19
        Case WEST
          HallPixelX = RoomPixelX + 25
          HallPixelY = RoomPixelY
      End Select
End Sub

Sub DrawRoomMarker()
    Dim PixelX As Integer
    Dim PixelY As Integer
    GetPixelXY Stats.Room, PixelX, PixelY
    shpRoomMarker.Move PixelX - 4, PixelY - 4
End Sub

Sub GetPixelXY(Room As Integer, PixelX As Integer, _
      PixelY As Integer)
    PixelX = (Room Mod NUMBEROFCOLS) * CELLWIDTH + OFFSETX
    PixelY = (Room \ NUMBEROFCOLS) * CELLHEIGHT + OFFSETY
End Sub

Sub SpellMove(X As Single, Y As Single)
    Dim newRoom As Integer
    If X > OFFSETX And X < MAXX And _
        Y > OFFSETY And Y < MAXY Then
      Stats.CastingSpell = False
      PlaySound SpellSound, False, False
      newRoom = CalcRoomNumber(X, Y)
      DrawRoomMarker
      Stats.Room = newRoom
      DrawRoom
      DrawRoomMarker
      ShowItem newRoom
    End If
End Sub

Sub MovePlayer(X As Single, Y As Single)
    Dim Direction As Integer
    Dim Color As Long
    Dim newRoom As Integer

    If X > OFFSETX And X < MAXX And _
        Y > OFFSETY And Y < MAXY Then
```

```
      newRoom = CalcRoomNumber(X, Y)
      CalcMoveDirection newRoom, Color, Direction
    Else
      Exit Sub
    End If

    If (Color = vbWhite) Then
      ShowNoExit
    Else
      cmdRandomize.Enabled = False
      MoveToRoom newRoom, Direction
    End If
End Sub

Sub PrintStat(X As Integer, Y As Integer, Stat As String)
    frmStats.CurrentX = X
    frmStats.CurrentY = Y
    frmStats.Print Stat
End Sub

Sub CalcMoveDirection(newRoom As Integer, _
      Color As Long, Direction As Integer)
    Dim PixelX As Integer
    Dim PixelY As Integer
    GetPixelXY Stats.Room, PixelX, PixelY
    If newRoom = Stats.Room - 10 Then
      Color = Point(PixelX + 12, PixelY + 1)
      Direction = NORTH
    ElseIf newRoom = Stats.Room + 1 Then
      Color = Point(PixelX + 26, PixelY + 12)
      Direction = EAST
    ElseIf newRoom = Stats.Room + 10 Then
      Color = Point(PixelX + 12, PixelY + 25)
      Direction = SOUTH
    ElseIf newRoom = Stats.Room - 1 Then
      Color = Point(PixelX + 1, PixelY + 12)
      Direction = WEST
    Else
      Color = vbWhite
    End If
End Sub

Sub ShowItem(Room As Integer)
    Dim amount As Integer
    Dim loss As Integer
    Dim item As Integer
    CheckForRandomItem Room
    item = Items(Room)
    Items(Room) = I_EMPTY
    Select Case item
      Case I_GOLD
```

13

```
      amount = Int(Rnd * 3) + 2
      Stats.Gold = Stats.Gold + amount
      ShowDiscovery imgGold, amount & " GOLD PIECES", False
    Case I_SPELL
      Stats.Spells = Stats.Spells + 1
      ShowDiscovery imgSpell, "        A SPELL", False
    Case I_SERUM
      Stats.Serums = Stats.Serums + 1
      ShowDiscovery imgSerum, "      A SERUM", False
    Case I_THIEF
      loss = Stats.Gold / 4
      Stats.Gold = Stats.Gold - loss
      ShowDiscovery imgThief, "    THE THIEF!", False
    Case I_TELEPORT
      ShowDiscovery imgTeleport, "A TELEPORTER", False
      Teleport
    Case I_SKELETON
      Battling = True
      ToggleButtons False
      ShowDiscovery imgSkeleton(0), "  A SKELETON!", False
      FightSkeleton
    Case I_DRAGON
      FoundDragon
  End Select
End Sub

Sub ToggleButtons(Setting As Boolean)
  cmdShop.Enabled = Setting
  cmdSpell.Enabled = Setting
  cmdStats.Enabled = Setting
  cmdLoad.Enabled = Setting
  cmdAbout.Enabled = Setting
End Sub

Sub ShowDiscovery(img As Image, Msg As String, Sound As Boolean)
  If Sound Then _
      PlaySound DiscoverySound, True, False
  Load frmDiscovery
  frmDiscovery.Cls
  frmDiscovery.Left = Form1.Left + 1500
  frmDiscovery.Top = Form1.Top + 1500
  frmDiscovery.PaintPicture img.Picture, 68, 50
  frmDiscovery.CurrentX = 44
  frmDiscovery.CurrentY = 135
  frmDiscovery.Print Msg
  frmDiscovery.Show , Me
  Delay 2#
  Unload frmDiscovery
End Sub

Sub Delay(amount As Single)
  Dim StartTime As Single
```

```
      Dim CurrentTime As Single
      StartTime = Timer
      Do
         CurrentTime = Timer
         DoEvents
      Loop While CurrentTime < StartTime + amount
   End Sub

   Sub FoundDragon()
      Dim text1 As String
      Dim text2 As String
      Dim pic As Picture
      If Stats.Brew Then
      PlaySound DragonSound2, True, False
         text1 = "     and tamed him"
         text2 = "    with dragon brew."
         Set pic = imgDragon0.Picture
      Else
         PlaySound DragonSound, True, False
         text1 = "    and he's not happy!"
         text2 = "(Munch, munch, munch)"
         Set pic = imgDragon1.Picture
      End If
      frmDiscovery.cmdOK.Visible = False
      frmDiscovery.Left = Form1.Left + 1500
      frmDiscovery.Top = Form1.Top + 1500
      frmDiscovery.PaintPicture pic, 68, 50
      frmDiscovery.CurrentX = 22
      frmDiscovery.CurrentY = 135
      frmDiscovery.Print "You found the dragon,"
      frmDiscovery.CurrentX = 20
      frmDiscovery.CurrentY = 155
      frmDiscovery.Print text1
      frmDiscovery.CurrentX = 20
      frmDiscovery.CurrentY = 175
      frmDiscovery.Print text2
      frmDiscovery.Show , Me
      Form1.PaintPicture Form1.Picture, 0, 0
      InitGame
   End Sub

   Sub Dead()
      PlaySound DragonSound, False, False
      frmDiscovery.cmdOK.Visible = False
      frmDiscovery.Left = Form1.Left + 1500
      frmDiscovery.Top = Form1.Top + 1500
      frmDiscovery.PaintPicture imgDragon1.Picture, 68, 50
      frmDiscovery.CurrentX = 26
      frmDiscovery.CurrentY = 135
      frmDiscovery.Print "You run for your life,"
      frmDiscovery.CurrentX = 24
```

13

```
      frmDiscovery.CurrentY = 155
      frmDiscovery.Print "and stumble right into"
      frmDiscovery.CurrentX = 24
      frmDiscovery.CurrentY = 175
      frmDiscovery.Print "the dragon's jaws."
      frmDiscovery.Show vbModal, Me
      Form1.PaintPicture Form1.Picture, 0, 0
      InitGame
   End Sub

   Sub FightSkeleton()
      Dim Modifier As Integer
      Dim playerAlive As Boolean
      Dim amount As Integer
      Modifier = Stats.Weapon - 4 + Stats.Strength / 20
      playerAlive = DoBattle(Modifier)
      If playerAlive Then
         Delay 2#
         Unload frmBattle
         If Stats.Strength < 20 And Stats.Serums > 0 Then _
            DrinkSerum
         amount = Int(Rnd * 5) + 5
         ShowDiscovery imgGold, amount & " GOLD PIECES.", True
         Stats.Gold = Stats.Gold + amount
      Else
         Unload frmBattle
         Dead
      End If
   End Sub

   Sub Teleport()
      Dim newRoom As Integer
      PlaySound TeleportSound, False, False
      DrawRoomMarker
      Do
         newRoom = Int(Rnd * NUMBEROFROOMS)
      Loop While Map(newRoom) = NOROOMDEFINED Or _
         newRoom = Stats.Room
      Stats.Room = newRoom
      DrawRoom
      DrawRoomMarker
      ShowItem newRoom
   End Sub
```

3. Add the following game functions to the code window, directly after the code you
   added in the previous step. You can either type in the code or copy it from the
   Dragonlord05.txt file, which you can find in the Chap13\Code directory of this
   book's CD-ROM:

```
 1: '=================================================
 2: ' Game Functions.
 3: '=================================================
 4: Function UpdateStats() As Boolean
 5:   SetStrength -1 - 1 * (Stats.Pie < 1)
 6:   If Stats.Strength < 1 Then
 7:     Dead
 8:     UpdateStats = False
 9:     Exit Function
10:   End If
11:   Stats.PieMoveCount = Stats.PieMoveCount + 1
12:   If Stats.PieMoveCount = 3 Then
13:     SetPie -1
14:     Stats.PieMoveCount = 0
15:   End If
16:   UpdateStats = True
17: End Function
18:
19: Function CalcRoomNumber(PixelX As Single, _
20:     PixelY As Single) As Integer
21:   Dim mapx As Integer
22:   Dim mapy As Integer
23:   mapx = (PixelX - OFFSETX) \ CELLWIDTH
24:   mapy = (PixelY - OFFSETY) \ CELLHEIGHT
25:   CalcRoomNumber = mapy * NUMBEROFCOLS + mapx
26: End Function
27:
28: Function DoBattle(Modifier As Integer) As Boolean
29:   Dim damage As Integer
30:   Dim playerRoll As Integer
31:   Dim skeletonRoll As Integer
32:   Dim monsterHitPoints As Integer
33:   Dim alive As Boolean
34:   Dim X As Integer
35:   frmBattle.Left = Form1.Left + 1500
36:   frmBattle.Top = Form1.Top + 1000
37:   frmBattle.cmdOK.Enabled = False
38:   frmBattle.Show , Me
39:   frmBattle.CurrentX = 58
40:   frmBattle.CurrentY = 200
41:   frmBattle.Print "Modifier = " & Modifier
42:   monsterHitPoints = 5
43:   Battling = True
44:   alive = True
45:   Do
46:     playerRoll = RollDice(48, 155)
47:     Delay (0.5)
48:     skeletonRoll = RollDice(117, 155)
49:     damage = Int(Rnd * 5 + 1)
50:     SetStrength -1 - 1 * Abs(Stats.Pie < 1)
51:     If playerRoll + Modifier >= skeletonRoll Then
```

13

```
52:        PlaySound SkeletonHitSound, False, False
53:        frmBattle.PaintPicture imgSkeleton(2), 68, 50
54:        Delay 1#
55:        monsterHitPoints = monsterHitPoints - damage
56:        If monsterHitPoints < 1 Then Battling = False
57:      Else
58:        PlaySound PlayerHitSound, False, False
59:        frmBattle.PaintPicture imgSkeleton(1), 68, 50
60:        SetHitPoints -damage
61:        Delay 1#
62:        If Stats.Strength <= 0 Or Stats.HitPoints <= 0 Then
63:          Battling = False
64:          alive = False
65:        End If
66:      End If
67:      If Battling Then _
68:          frmBattle.PaintPicture imgSkeleton(0), 68, 50
69:    Loop While Battling
70:
71:    frmBattle.cmdOK.Enabled = True
72:    frmBattle.PaintPicture imgSkeleton(3), 68, 50
73:    cmdShop.Enabled = True
74:    cmdSpell.Enabled = True
75:    cmdStats.Enabled = True
76:    cmdLoad.Enabled = True
77:    cmdAbout.Enabled = True
78:    DoBattle = alive
79: End Function
80:
81: Function RollDice(X As Integer, Y As Integer)
82:    Dim num As Integer
83:    Dim roll As Integer
84:    For roll = 1 To 10
85:      PlaySound DiceSound, True, False
86:      num = Int(Rnd * 9)
87:      frmBattle.PaintPicture imgDice(num), X, Y
88:      Delay (0.1)
89:    Next roll
90:    RollDice = num
91: End Function
92:
93: Function GetDragonRoom()
94:    Dim X As Integer
95:    For X = 0 To 79
96:      If Items(X) = I_DRAGON Then GetDragonRoom = X
97:    Next X
98: End Function
```

ANALYSIS You'll explore these functions in detail later in this chapter. In general terms, the UpdateStats function (Lines 4 to 17) keeps the player's statistics up to date, the

CalcRoomNumber function (Lines 19 to 26) returns the room number located at the given coordinates, the DoBattle function (Lines 28 to 79) manages a battle between the player and a skeleton, the RollDice function (81 to 91) handles the rolling of dice during a battle, and the GetDragonRoom function (Lines 93 to 98) returns the number of the room in which the dragon is located.

4. Add the following variable declarations and enumerations to the top of the code window. You can either type in the code or copy it from the Dragonlord06.txt file, which you can find in the Chap13\Code directory of this book's CD-ROM:

```
 1:  '=================================================
 2:  ' Dragonlord for Visual Basic 6
 3:  '    by Clayton Walnum
 4:  ' Copyright 2000 by Macmillan Computer Publishing
 5:  '=================================================
 6:  Option Explicit
 7:
 8:  '=================================================
 9:  ' Constants.
10:  '=================================================
11:  Const NUMBEROFROOMS = 80
12:  Const CELLWIDTH = 44
13:  Const CELLHEIGHT = 44
14:  Const OFFSETX = 106
15:  Const OFFSETY = 50
16:  Const NUMBEROFCOLS = 10
17:  Const MAXX = 540
18:  Const MAXY = 398
19:  Const STARTINGROOM = 45
20:  Const NOROOMDEFINED = 0
21:
22:  Enum ItemEnum
23:    I_EMPTY
24:    I_SERUM
25:    I_SPELL
26:    I_GOLD
27:    I_SKELETON
28:    I_THIEF
29:    I_TELEPORT
30:    I_DRAGON
31:  End Enum
32:
33:  Enum DirectionEnum
34:    NORTH
35:    EAST
36:    SOUTH
37:    WEST
38:  End Enum
39:
```

13

```
40: '=================================================
41: ' General Game Variables.
42: '=================================================
43: Dim Randomizing As Boolean
44: Dim Items(NUMBEROFROOMS - 1) As Integer
45: Dim Map(NUMBEROFROOMS - 1) As Integer
46: Dim FileName As String
47:
48: '=================================================
49: ' Public Variables.
50: '=================================================
51: Public Battling As Boolean
52: Public DragonRoom As Integer
```

ANALYSIS Lines 11 to 20 define the game's constants, and Lines 22 to 38 define constants in enumerations. Lines 40 to 52 declare the game's general variables.

5. Save your work.

You've *almost* completed the Dragonlord program. (Whew!) All you need to do now is add one module of code and the DirectSound routines that play the game's sound effects.

Adding a Module for Data Types and Subroutines

Dragonlord uses a Visual Basic module for defining data types, subroutines, and functions that manage the player's game statistics. This module also contains the DirectSound stuff. To add this module, select the Project menu's Add Module command to display the Add Module dialog box (see Figure 13.1).

FIGURE 13.1

Adding a code module.

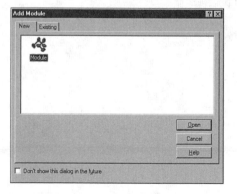

Then type the following source code into the new module's code window, or copy the source code from the Dragonlord07.txt file:

```
 1:  Option Explicit
 2:
 3:  Enum WeaponEnum
 4:     FIST
 5:     CLUB
 6:     KNIFE
 7:     SWORD
 8:  End Enum
 9:
10:  Type StatsType
11:     HitPoints As Integer
12:     Strength As Integer
13:     Pie As Integer
14:     Gold As Integer
15:     Spells As Integer
16:     Serums As Integer
17:     Brew As Boolean
18:     Room As Integer
19:     Weapon As Integer
20:     PieMoveCount As Integer
21:     CastingSpell As Boolean
22:  End Type
23:
24:  Public Stats As StatsType
25:
26:  '================================================
27:  ' DirectSound Variables.
28:  '================================================
29:  Dim DirectX7Obj As New DirectX7
30:  Dim DirectSoundObj As DirectSound
31:  Public DiceSound As DirectSoundBuffer
32:  Public TeleportSound As DirectSoundBuffer
33:  Public SkeletonHitSound As DirectSoundBuffer
34:  Public PlayerHitSound As DirectSoundBuffer
35:  Public WalkSound As DirectSoundBuffer
36:  Public SkeletonDieSound As DirectSoundBuffer
37:  Public DragonSound As DirectSoundBuffer
38:  Public DragonSound2 As DirectSoundBuffer
39:  Public SpellSound As DirectSoundBuffer
40:  Public DiscoverySound As DirectSoundBuffer
41:  Public ShopSound As DirectSoundBuffer
42:  Public CheckStatsSound As DirectSoundBuffer
43:
44:  Function CheckPurse(Cost As Integer)  As Boolean
45:     If Stats.Gold < Cost Then
46:        MsgBox "Your purse is too meager."
47:        CheckPurse = False
48:     Else
49:        CheckPurse = True
50:     End If
```

13

```
51: End Function
52:
53: Sub ResetStats()
54:    Stats.HitPoints = 50
55:    Stats.Strength = 100
56:    Stats.Pie = 1
57:    Stats.Gold = 60
58:    Stats.Spells = 0
59:    Stats.Serums = 0
60:    Stats.Brew = False
61:    Stats.Room = 45
62:    Stats.Weapon = FIST
63:    Stats.PieMoveCount = 0
64:    Stats.CastingSpell = False
65: End Sub
66:
67: Sub SetHitPoints(num As Integer)
68:    Stats.HitPoints = Stats.HitPoints + num
69:    If Stats.HitPoints > 50 Then Stats.HitPoints = 50
70:    If Stats.HitPoints < 15 Then
71:       PlaySound CheckStatsSound, False, False
72:       Form1.cmdStats_Click
73:    End If
74: End Sub
75:
76: Sub SetStrength(num As Integer)
77:    Stats.Strength = Stats.Strength + num
78:    If Stats.Strength > 100 Then Stats.Strength = 100
79:    If Stats.Strength < 15 Then
80:       PlaySound CheckStatsSound, False, False
81:       Form1.cmdStats_Click
82:    End If
83: End Sub
84:
85: Sub SetPie(num As Integer)
86:    Stats.Pie = Stats.Pie + num
87:    If Stats.Pie <= 0 Then Stats.Pie = 0
88:    If Stats.Pie < 2 Then
89:       PlaySound CheckStatsSound, False,  False
90:       Form1.cmdStats_Click
91:    End If
92: End Sub
93:
94: '==================================================
95: ' DirectSound Routines.
96: '==================================================
97: Sub InitSound()
98:    InitDirectSound
99:    'ChDir "d:\TYVBGames\Chap13\DragonLord\"
100:    Set WalkSound = CreateSound("Walk.wav")
101:    Set DiceSound = CreateSound("Dice.wav")
```

```
102:    Set TeleportSound = CreateSound("Teleport.wav")
103:    Set SkeletonDieSound = CreateSound("SkeletonHit.wav")
104:    Set DragonSound = CreateSound("Dragon.wav")
105:    Set DragonSound2 = CreateSound("Dragon2.wav")
106:    Set SkeletonHitSound = CreateSound("SkeletonHit.wav")
107:    Set PlayerHitSound = CreateSound("PlayerHit.wav")
108:    Set SpellSound = CreateSound("Spell.wav")
109:    Set DiscoverySound = CreateSound("Discovery.wav")
110:   Set ShopSound = CreateSound("Shop.wav")
111:   Set CheckStatsSound = CreateSound("CheckStats.wav")
112: End Sub
113:
114: Sub InitDirectSound()
115:   On Local Error Resume Next
116:   Set DirectSoundObj = DirectX7Obj.DirectSoundCreate("")
117:   If Err.Number <> 0 Then
118:      MsgBox "DirectSound initialization failed."
119:      End
120:   End If
121:   DirectSoundObj.SetCooperativeLevel Form1.hWnd, DSSCL_PRIORITY
122: End Sub
123:
124: Function CreateSound(FileName As String) As DirectSoundBuffer
125:   Dim bufferDesc As DSBUFFERDESC
126:   Dim waveFormat As WAVEFORMATEX
127:   bufferDesc.lFlags = DSBCAPS_STATIC
128:   Set CreateSound = _
129:      DirectSoundObj.CreateSoundBufferFromFile(FileName, _
130:          bufferDesc, waveFormat)
131:   If Err.Number <> 0 Then
132:     MsgBox "unable to find sound file"
133:     End
134:   End If
135: End Function
136:
137: Sub PlaySound(Sound As DirectSoundBuffer, _
138:    CloseFirst As Boolean, LoopSound As Boolean)
139:   If CloseFirst Then
140:     Sound.Stop
141:     Sound.SetCurrentPosition 0
142:   End If
143:   If LoopSound Then
144:     Sound.Play 1
145:   Else
146:     Sound.Play 0
147:   End If
148: End Sub
```

ANALYSIS Lines 3 to 8 define constants for the different weapon types, and Lines 10 to 24 define a data type for the player's game statistics. Lines 29 to 42 declare the

13

variables needed by the DirectSound routines, Lines 44 to 92 define functions for managing player statistics, and Lines 94 to 148 are the game's DirectSound routines.

Adding Dialog Box Source Code

All of the Dragonlord dialog boxes require a small amount of source code to implement their buttons and to control when and how they can be dismissed. For example, the dialog box that appears when the player battles a skeleton cannot be dismissed until the battle is over. Perform the following steps to add source code to the game's dialog boxes:

1. Bring up the source code window for the `frmBattle` dialog box. Type the following code into the code window, or copy it from the Dragonlord08.txt file (see Figure 13.2):

```
1: Private Sub cmdOK_Click()
2:   Unload Me
3: End Sub
4:
5: Private Sub Form_QueryUnload(Cancel As Integer,
6:     UnloadMode As Integer)
7:   If form1.Battling Then Cancel = True
8: End Sub
```

ANALYSIS Lines 1 to 3 unload the form when the player clicks the OK button, and Lines 5 to 8 prevent the player from closing the Battle dialog box when a battle is in progress.

FIGURE 13.2

Adding source code to the dialog box.

2. Bring up the source code window for the `frmDiscovery` dialog box. Type the following code into the code window:

```
Private Sub cmdOK_Click()
  Unload Me
End Sub
```

3. Bring up the source code window for the frmHealth dialog box. Type the following code into the code window, or copy it from the Dragonlord09.txt file:

```
1:  Option Explicit
2:
3:  Private Sub cmdDoctor_Click()
4:    Dim canAfford As Boolean
5:    Dim amount As Integer
6:    Unload Me
7:    canAfford = CheckPurse(15)
8:    If canAfford Then
9:      PlaySound ShopSound, False, False
10:     Stats.Gold = Stats.Gold - 15
11:     amount = Rnd(10) + 16
12:     SetHitPoints amount
13:     MsgBox "The doctor healed you." & vbCrLf & _
14:         vbCrLf & "+" & amount & " hit points."
15:   End If
16: End Sub
17:
18: Private Sub cmdLodge_Click()
19:   Dim canAfford As Boolean
20:   Dim amount As Integer
21:   Unload Me
22:   canAfford = CheckPurse(15)
23:   If canAfford Then
24:     PlaySound ShopSound, False, False
25:     Stats.Gold = Stats.Gold - 15
26:     amount = Rnd(15) + 21
27:     SetStrength amount
28:     MsgBox "You had a good night's sleep." & vbCrLf & _
29:         vbCrLf & "+" & amount & " strength points."
30:   End If
31: End Sub
32:
33: Private Sub cmdPie_Click()
34:   Dim canAfford As Boolean
35:   Unload Me
36:   canAfford = CheckPurse(10)
37:   If canAfford Then
38:     PlaySound ShopSound, False, False
39:     Stats.Gold = Stats.Gold - 10
40:     SetPie 5
41:   End If
42: End Sub
```

ANALYSIS   These subroutines handle the buttons on the Health dialog box. Specifically, Lines 3 to 16 enable the player to restore a portion of his hit points, and Lines 18 to 31 enable the player to recover strength points. Lines 33 to 42 enable the player to purchase pie.

13

4. Bring up the source code window for the frmMagic dialog box. Type the following
   code into the code window, or copy it from the Dragonlord10.txt file:

```
1:  Option Explicit
2:
3:  Private Sub cmdAdvice_Click()
4:     Dim canAfford As Boolean
5:     Dim Direction As String
6:     Unload Me
7:     canAfford = CheckPurse(20)
8:     If canAfford Then
9:       PlaySound ShopSound, False, False
10:      Stats.Gold = Stats.Gold - 20
11:      Direction = GetAdvice
12:      MsgBox "The dragon is " & Direction & _
13:          " of your current location."
14:    End If
15: End Sub
16:
17: Private Sub cmdBrew_Click()
18:    Dim canAfford As Boolean
19:    Unload Me
20:    canAfford = CheckPurse(80)
21:    If canAfford Then
22:      PlaySound ShopSound, False, False
23:      Stats.Gold = Stats.Gold - 80
24:      Stats.Brew = True
25:      MsgBox "You now have the dragon brew!"
26:    End If
27: End Sub
28:
29: Private Sub cmdSpell_Click()
30:    Dim canAfford As Boolean
31:    Unload Me
32:    canAfford = CheckPurse(10)
33:    If canAfford Then
34:      PlaySound ShopSound, False, False
35:      Stats.Gold = Stats.Gold - 10
36:      Stats.Spells = Stats.Spells + 1
37:    End If
38: End Sub
39:
40: Function GetAdvice() As String
41:    Dim dragonX As Integer
42:    Dim dragonY As Integer
43:    Dim playerX As Integer
44:    Dim playerY As Integer
45:    dragonX = Form1.DragonRoom Mod 10
46:    dragonY = Form1.DragonRoom \ 10
47:    playerX = Stats.Room Mod 10
48:    playerY = Stats.Room \ 10
```

```
49:    If dragonX = playerX Then
50:      If dragonY < playerY Then
51:        GetAdvice = "North"
52:      Else
53:        GetAdvice = "South"
54:      End If
55:    ElseIf dragonY = playerY Then
56:      If dragonX < playerX Then
57:        GetAdvice = "West"
58:      Else
59:        GetAdvice = "East"
60:      End If
61:    ElseIf dragonX < playerX And dragonY < playerY Then
62:      If Int(Rnd(2)) Then
63:        GetAdvice = "North"
64:      Else
65:        GetAdvice = "West"
66:      End If
67:    ElseIf dragonX > playerX And dragonY < playerY Then
68:      If Int(Rnd(2)) Then
69:        GetAdvice = "North"
70:      Else
71:        GetAdvice = "East"
72:      End If
73:    ElseIf dragonX > playerX And dragonY > playerY Then
74:      If Int(Rnd(2)) Then
75:        GetAdvice = "South"
76:      Else
77:        GetAdvice = "East"
78:      End If
79:    ElseIf dragonX < playerX And dragonY > playerY Then
80:      If Int(Rnd(2)) Then
81:        GetAdvice = "South"
82:      Else
83:        GetAdvice = "West"
84:      End If
85:    End If
86: End Function
```

ANALYSIS　These subroutines handle the buttons on the Magic dialog box. Specifically, Lines 3 to 15 enable the player to purchase a clue as to the dragon's location, and Lines 17 to 27 enable the player to purchase the dragon brew. Lines 29 to 38 enable the player to purchase a spell. Finally, Lines 40 to 86 are a helper function that's called from cmdAdvice_Click.

13

5. Bring up the source code window for the frmShoppe dialog box. Type the following code into the code window, or copy it from the Dragonlord11.txt file:

```
 1:  Option Explicit
 2:
 3:  Private Sub cmdHealth_Click()
 4:     Load frmHealth
 5:     frmHealth.Show
 6:     Unload frmShoppe
 7:  End Sub
 8:
 9:  Private Sub cmdMagic_Click()
10:     Load frmMagic
11:     frmMagic.Show
12:     Unload frmShoppe
13:  End Sub
14:
15:  Private Sub cmdWeapon_Click()
16:     Load frmWeapons
17:     frmWeapons.Show
18:     Unload frmShoppe
19:  End Sub
20:
21:  Private Sub Form_Load()
22:     Me.Left = form1.Left + 1000
23:     Me.Top = form1.Top + 1000
24:  End Sub
```

ANALYSIS   These subroutines handle the buttons on the Shoppe dialog box. Specifically, Lines 3 to 7 transfer the player to the health shop, Lines 9 to 13 transfer the player to the magic shop, and Lines 15 to 19 transfer him to the weapon shop. Finally, Lines 22 to 24 position the Shoppe dialog box when it appears.

6. Bring up the source code window for the frmStats dialog box. Type the following code into the code window:

```
Private Sub cmdOK_Click()
   Unload Me
End Sub
```

7. Bring up the source code window for the frmWeapons dialog box. Type the following code into the code window, or copy it from the Dragonlord12.txt file:

```
 1:  Option Explicit
 2:
 3:  Private Sub cmdClub_Click()
 4:     Dim canAfford As Boolean
 5:     Unload Me
 6:     canAfford = CheckPurse(15)
 7:     If canAfford Then
 8:        PlaySound ShopSound, False, False
 9:        Stats.Gold = Stats.Gold - 15
10:        Stats.Weapon = CLUB
11:     End If
```

```
12: End Sub
13:
14: Private Sub cmdKnife_Click()
15:   Dim canAfford As Boolean
16:   Unload Me
17:   canAfford = CheckPurse(40)
18:   If canAfford Then
19:     PlaySound ShopSound, False, False
20:     Stats.Gold = Stats.Gold - 40
21:     Stats.Weapon = KNIFE
22:   End If
23: End Sub
24:
25: Private Sub cmdSword_Click()
26:   Dim canAfford As Boolean
27:   Unload Me
28:   canAfford = CheckPurse(60)
29:   If canAfford Then
30:     PlaySound ShopSound, False, False
31:     Stats.Gold = Stats.Gold - 60
32:     Stats.Weapon = SWORD
33:   End If
34: End Sub
```

ANALYSIS These subroutines handle the buttons on the Weapon dialog box. Specifically, Lines 3 to 12 enable the player to purchase a club, and Lines 14 to 23 enable the player to purchase a knife. Finally, Lines 25 to 34 enable the player to purchase a sword.

Last-Minute Details

At last, you're almost ready to compile your own version of Dragonlord. First, though, you need to add the DirectX type library to your project. To do this, select the Project menu's References command and checkmark DirectX 7 for Visual Basic Type Library in the dialog box that appears (see Figure 13.3).

One last thing: You need to copy the default dungeon file, Dungeon.drg, into your game's directory so the game can load the file. You can find this file in the Chap13/Dragonlord directory of this book's CD-ROM. Failure to put this file where it belongs will cause the game to crash. You also need to copy all the WAV files from the Chap13/Dragonlord directory to your own Dragonlord directory. After this, you can compile the complete project.

13

Note Note that the program will run correctly only if you start it with the Dragonlord.exe file. If you want to run the program from within the Visual Basic programming environment, you need to add absolute paths to all the files the game needs to load.

FIGURE 13.3

Adding DirectX to a project.

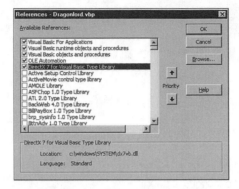

Understanding Dragonlord

Now that you've played the game and built your own version of it, it's time to examine the code, starting with the game's constants and variables. Because the program is so large, however, we won't look at every line of code. Most of it you can understand on your own. However, we *will* examine the parts of the program that handle the game's RPG elements.

Dragonlord's Variables and Constants

Dragonlord relies on a set of variables and constants that the game declares near the top of the program. Some variables are also declared in the Module1 program module. Table 13.1 lists the variables and their descriptions, and Table 13.2 lists the constants.

TABLE 13.1   Dragonlord's General Game Variables

Variable	Type	Description
Battling	Boolean	A flag that indicates that the game is in the battle mode
CheckStatsSound	DirectSoundBuffer	The buffer that holds the sound effect that warns the player when a statistic is getting dangerously low
DiceSound	DirectSoundBuffer	The buffer that holds the dice sound effect
DirectSoundObj	DirectSound	The program's DirectSound object
DirectX7Obj	DirectX7	The program's DirectX object
DiscoverySound	DirectSoundBuffer	The buffer that holds the sound effect that's played when the player discovers gold after defeating a skeleton

TABLE 13.1 continued

Variable	Type	Description
DragonRoom	Integer	The room containing the dragon
DragonSound	DirectSoundBuffer	The buffer that holds the sound effect for when the player finds the dragon and loses the game
DragonSound2	DirectSoundBuffer	The buffer that holds the sound effect for when the player finds the dragon and wins the game
FileName	String	The filename of the currently loaded dungeon
Items()	Integer	An array that holds the contents of each room in the dungeon
Map()	Integer	An array that holds the room types for each of the rooms in the dungeon
PlayerHitSound	DirectSoundBuffer	The buffer that holds the sound effect for when a skeleton hits the player
Randomizing	Boolean	A flag that indicates that the program is currently randomizing the dungeon
ShopSound	DirectSoundBuffer	The buffer for the item-purchase sound effect
SkeletonDieSound	DirectSoundBuffer	The buffer that holds the sound effect for when the player defeats a skeleton
SkeletonHitSound	DirectSoundBuffer	The buffer that holds the sound effect for when a skeleton gets hit by the player's weapon
SpellSound	DirectSoundBuffer	The buffer that holds the spell sound effect
Stats	StatsType	The player's game statistics
TeleportSound	DirectSoundBuffer	The buffer that holds the teleport sound effect
WalkSound	DirectSoundBuffer	The buffer for the sound effect of the player moving to a new room

13

TABLE 13.2 Dragonlord's Constants

Constant	Description
CELLHEIGHT	The height of a cell in the playing board
CELLWIDTH	The width of a cell in the playing board
MAXX	The maximum X value that is a valid mouse click in the grid
MAXY	The maximum Y value that is a valid mouse click in the grid
NOROOMDEFINED	The value that indicates that there's no room in the referenced map location
NUMBEROFCOLS	The number of rooms in a row of the dungeon map
NUMBEROFROOMS	The number of rooms in the dungeon
OFFSETX	The X coordinate of the left edge of the playing board
OFFSETY	The Y coordinate of the top edge of the playing board
STARTINGROOM	The room where the player starts

The Dragonlord program also defines one enumeration and a data type:

```
1: Enum WeaponEnum
2:    FIST
3:    CLUB
4:    KNIFE
5:    SWORD
6: End Enum
7:
8: Type StatsType
9:    HitPoints As Integer
10:    Strength As Integer
11:    Pie As Integer
12:    Gold As Integer
13:    Spells As Integer
14:    Serums As Integer
15:    Brew As Boolean
16:    Room As Integer
17:    Weapon As Integer
18:    PieMoveCount As Integer
19:    CastingSpell As Boolean
20: End Type
```

ANALYSIS The WeaponEnum enumeration (Lines 1 to 6) defines constants for the weapons that the player can purchase, and the StatsType data type (Lines 8 to 20) declares a data set for the player's statistics.

Dungeon Maps

Now let's look at how the game handles its dungeon map. Near the beginning of the program, you see the following array definition:

```
Dim Map(NUMBEROFROOMS - 1) As Integer
```

This is the dungeon map as it's stored in memory. Each number in the map represents a room. Because there are 15 possible combinations of exits from a room, there are 15 types of rooms, numbered from 0 to 14. For example, in the upper-left corner of the default map, there is a room type 7. This room has exits on the east and south walls. The next room in the default map is type 13, which has exits on the east, south, and west walls.

To create a different dungeon layout, you need only put different numbers in the map() array. Of course, all the numbers must be between 0 and 14 (inclusive), and you must ensure that the exits line up properly with the other rooms—that is, a north exit from a room should always lead to a south entrance in the other room.

The program loads the room-type numbers into the map() array from the Dungeon.drg file at the beginning of a game. As you learned yesterday, the player can load other dungeon files by clicking the Load Dungeon button. To make it easy to generate these dungeon files, Dragonlord comes with a visual dungeon editor, which you'll create in tomorrow's lesson.

Initializing the Game

Like any program, Dragonlord must assign starting values to certain variables before the user can start playing the game. Dragonlord must store items at random locations in the dungeon (if the player chooses to randomize the dungeon, that is) and set the player's statistics to their starting values.

The InitGame subroutine handles the game initialization. In this subroutine, the program first loads the default dungeon file:

```
Open FileName For Binary As #1
Get #1, , Map
Get #1, , Items
Close #1
```

InitGame then sets the player's starting statistics by calling the ResetStats subroutine, which is located in the Module1 program module:

```
1:  Sub ResetStats()
2:    Stats.HitPoints = 50
3:    Stats.Strength = 100
```

13

```
 4:     Stats.Pie = 1
 5:     Stats.Gold = 60
 6:     Stats.Spells = 0
 7:     Stats.Serums = 0
 8:     Stats.Brew = False
 9:     Stats.Room = 45
10:     Stats.Weapon = FIST
11:     Stats.PieMoveCount = 0
12:     Stats.CastingSpell = False
13: End Sub
```

ANALYSIS Here you can see the starting values for the many statistics that make up the player's character. If you wanted to give the player additional statistics to further define the character, you would add a variable for each new statistic to the `Stats` data type and then give each statistic a starting value in the `ResetStats` subroutine. How you handle the statistic in the game depends on how you want to use it, of course. For example, you might add an intelligence statistic that controls how well the player can cast spells. `InitGame` finishes the game initialization like this:

```
 1:     Randomize
 2:     Battling = False
 3:     DragonRoom = GetDragonRoom
 4:     Form1.PaintPicture Form1.Picture, 0, 0
 5:     PixelX = (Stats.Room Mod NUMBEROFCOLS) * _
 6:         CELLWIDTH + OFFSETX
 7:     PixelY = (Stats.Room \ NUMBEROFCOLS) * _
 8:         CELLHEIGHT + OFFSETY
 9:     Form1.PaintPicture imgRoom(Map(Stats.Room) - 1), _
10:         PixelX, PixelY
11:     DrawRoomMarker
12:     cmdRandomize.Enabled = True
```

ANALYSIS Here, `InitGame` randomizes the random number generator (Line 1), sets flags and variables to their starting values (Lines 2 and 3), and draws the first room (Lines 4 to 11).

Handling Character Stats

Throughout the game, the program must manipulate the character statistics when the player issues commands. For example, moving from room to room or fighting a skeleton requires energy. The more energy a player uses, the weaker he becomes. So, when the player does anything physical, the strength statistic goes down. Some statistics, such as those for hit points, require extra handling when they change, so the program provides member functions for manipulating those values. For example, to change the value of the player's `HitPoints` statistic, the program calls `SetHitPoints`:

```
1: Sub SetHitPoints(num As Integer)
2:    Stats.HitPoints = Stats.HitPoints + num
3:    If Stats.HitPoints > 50 Then Stats.HitPoints = 50
4:    If Stats.HitPoints < 15 Then
5:       PlaySound CheckStatsSound, False, False
6:       Form1.cmdStats_Click
7:    End If
8: End Sub
```

ANALYSIS Not only does this subroutine modify HitPoints by the amount in num (Line 2), but it also ensures that HitPoints doesn't exceed 50 (Line 3). In addition, when HitPoints drops below 15, this subroutine sounds an alarm (the CheckStatsSound sound effect) and displays the statistics window (Lines 4 to 7).

Two other data members—Strength and Pie—are changed by the subroutines SetStrength and SetPie, which are both similar to SetHitPoints.

Moving the Player

When the player clicks a room, the program must take the mouse coordinates of the click and calculate where the player wants to move. Then the program must move the player to the new room.

The movement begins in the MovePlayer subroutine, which first checks that the player has clicked within the screen limits of the dungeon map:

```
If X > OFFSETX And X < MAXX And _
    Y > OFFSETY And Y < MAXY Then
```

If the player clicks outside of the map, the program ignores the input. However, if the mouse coordinates check out okay, the program must calculate the number of the room where the player wants to move. It does this by calling CalcRoomNumber:

```
1: Function CalcRoomNumber(PixelX As Single, _
2:       PixelY As Single) As Integer
3:    Dim mapx As Integer
4:    Dim mapy As Integer
5:    mapx = (PixelX - OFFSETX) \ CELLWIDTH
6:    mapy = (PixelY - OFFSETY) \ CELLHEIGHT
7:    CalcRoomNumber = mapy * NUMBEROFCOLS + mapx
8: End Function
```

13

ANALYSIS This function takes the X,Y coordinates of the mouse click as parameters. It then takes these coordinates and calculates the row and column of the map where the player wants to move (Lines 5 and 6). Finally, it uses the row and column to get the room number (Line 7). In the calculations for mapx, the OFFSETX value is the number of pixels from the left edge of the screen to the left edge of the first map column, and

CELLWIDTH is the width of each column. In the calculations for mapy, OFFSETY is the distance from the top of the screen to the top of the map grid, and CELLHEIGHT is the height of each map row.

After MovePlayer calls CalcRoomNumber, the program has the room where the player wants to move. However, the program doesn't yet know whether the player should be allowed to move to that room. For the room to be a valid destination, it must connect directly to the room where the player is located. To check whether the move is valid, MovePlayer first calls CalcMoveDirection:

```
1:  Sub CalcMoveDirection(newRoom As Integer, _
2:      Color As Long, Direction As Integer)
3:    Dim PixelX As Integer
4:    Dim PixelY As Integer
5:    GetPixelXY Stats.Room, PixelX, PixelY
6:    If newRoom = Stats.Room - 10 Then
7:      Color = Point(PixelX + 12, PixelY + 1)
8:      Direction = NORTH
9:    ElseIf newRoom = Stats.Room + 1 Then
10:     Color = Point(PixelX + 26, PixelY + 12)
11:     Direction = EAST
12:   ElseIf newRoom = Stats.Room + 10 Then
13:     Color = Point(PixelX + 12, PixelY + 25)
14:     Direction = SOUTH
15:   ElseIf newRoom = Stats.Room - 1 Then
16:     Color = Point(PixelX + 1, PixelY + 12)
17:     Direction = WEST
18:   Else
19:     Color = vbWhite
20:   End If
21: End Sub
```

ANALYSIS This subroutine takes the following as parameters: the number of the destination room, a reference to the long integer that will hold a color value, and a reference to the integer that will hold a direction value.

The function calls GetPixelXY to retrieve the screen coordinates of the current room:

```
Sub GetPixelXY(Room As Integer, PixelX As Integer, _
    PixelY As Integer)
  PixelX = (Room Mod NUMBEROFCOLS) * CELLWIDTH + OFFSETX
  PixelY = (Room \ NUMBEROFCOLS) * CELLHEIGHT + OFFSETY
End Sub
```

CalcMoveDirection then uses a compound If statement that compares the destination room number (newRoom) to the current room number (stats.room). The subroutine uses this comparison to determine the direction in which the player is trying to move. For example, if the destination room is 15 and the current room is 25, the player is trying to move north because the room number to the north is always 10 less than the room number of the current location.

When the program determines the direction, it sets the variable Direction to one of the directions enumerated in DirectionEnum (NORTH, EAST, SOUTH, or WEST), and then it calls Point to retrieve the color of the pixel in the current room's exit area. For example, if the player is trying to move north, the program sets Direction to NORTH and gets the color of a pixel in the current room's northern exit area. The function returns both the direction and color values to MovePlayer for further processing.

MovePlayer examines the color value returned by CalcMoveDirection to check whether it is the color of the top of a wall (white):

```
If (Color = vbWhite) Then
  ShowNoExit
Else
  cmdRandomize.Enabled = False
  MoveToRoom newRoom, Direction
End If
```

This is a handy way to check for exits without having to store extra values in a program. In a way, you're using the screen as a storage area not only for graphics, but also for program data.

If the player is trying to move in an illegal direction, the program calls ShowNoExit to tell the player of his mistake. Otherwise, the program calls MoveToRoom, which handles the actual move. (The program also disables the Randomize Dungeon button, which prevents the player from randomizing the dungeon after he's made his first move.) This subroutine first calls UpdateStats to decrement the player's strength and pie counts:

```
stillAlive = UpdateStats
```

UpdateStats returns a Boolean value that indicates whether the player is still alive (that is, whether his strength is greater than 0). If he is, MoveToRoom calls DrawRoomMarker to move the current room marker (the yellow square) to the destination room:

```
DrawRoomMarker
```

The MoveToRoom subroutine then sets the player's room statistic to the new room, calls DrawRoom to display the new room, and calls DrawHallway to display the connecting hallway:

```
Stats.Room = newRoom
DrawRoom
DrawHallway Direction
```

13

Finally, MoveToRoom calls ShowItem to show the player what, if anything, he has found in the room:

```
ShowItem newRoom
```

The subroutine DrawRoom displays the new room:

```
1:  Sub DrawRoom()
2:    Dim Color As Long
3:    Dim RoomPixelX As Integer
4:    Dim RoomPixelY As Integer
5:    GetPixelXY Stats.Room, RoomPixelX, RoomPixelY
6:    Color = Point(RoomPixelX, RoomPixelY)
7:    If Color <> vbWhite Then _
8:      Form1.PaintPicture imgRoom(Map(Stats.Room) - 1), _
9:        RoomPixelX, RoomPixelY
10: End Sub
```

ANALYSIS DrawRoom first calls GetPixelXY (Line 5) to retrieve the screen coordinates at which the new room will be drawn. It then samples the color value (Line 6) at those coordinates to see whether the room has already been drawn. (The player may have been to the room before.) If the color value of the sampled pixel isn't white, the room has not yet been drawn (Lines 7 to 9).

After the program draws the room, it must draw the connecting hallway. The subroutine DrawHallway handles this task:

```
1:  Sub DrawHallway(Direction As Integer)
2:    Dim RoomPixelX As Integer
3:    Dim RoomPixelY As Integer
4:    Dim HallPixelX As Integer
5:    Dim HallPixelY As Integer
6:    GetPixelXY Stats.Room, RoomPixelX, RoomPixelY
7:    GetHallPixelXY RoomPixelX, RoomPixelY, _
8:        HallPixelX, HallPixelY, Direction
9:    If Direction = NORTH Or Direction = SOUTH Then
10:     Form1.PaintPicture imgHall(0), HallPixelX, HallPixelY
11:   Else
12:     Form1.PaintPicture imgHall(1), HallPixelX, HallPixelY
13:   End If
14: End Sub
```

ANALYSIS This subroutine calls GetPixelXY (Line 6) to get the screen coordinates of the new room and then uses those coordinates in a call to GetHallPixelXY (Line 7), which calculates the screen coordinates of the connecting hallway. DrawHallway uses its single parameter Direction to determine whether to draw a vertical or horizontal hall segment (Lines 9 to 13).

The subroutine ShowItem displays whatever the player may have found in the new room:

```
1:   Sub ShowItem(Room As Integer)
2:     Dim amount As Integer
3:     Dim loss As Integer
4:     Dim item As Integer
5:     CheckForRandomItem Room
6:     item = Items(Room)
7:     Items(Room) = I_EMPTY
8:     Select Case item
9:       Case I_GOLD
10:        amount = Int(Rnd * 3) + 2
11:        Stats.Gold = Stats.Gold + amount
12:        ShowDiscovery imgGold, amount & " GOLD PIECES", False
13:      Case I_SPELL
14:        Stats.Spells = Stats.Spells + 1
15:        ShowDiscovery imgSpell, "       A SPELL", False
16:      Case I_SERUM
17:        Stats.Serums = Stats.Serums + 1
18:        ShowDiscovery imgSerum, "     A SERUM", False
19:      Case I_THIEF
20:        loss = Stats.Gold / 4
21:        Stats.Gold = Stats.Gold - loss
22:        ShowDiscovery imgThief, "   THE THIEF!", False
23:      Case I_TELEPORT
24:        ShowDiscovery imgTeleport, "A TELEPORTER", False
25:        Teleport
26:      Case I_SKELETON
27:        Battling = True
28:        ToggleButtons False
29:        ShowDiscovery imgSkeleton(0), "  A SKELETON!", False
30:        FightSkeleton
31:      Case I_DRAGON
32:        FoundDragon
33:    End Select
34: End Sub
```

ANALYSIS This subroutine first calls CheckForRandomItem (Line 5), which is responsible for placing skeletons and caches of gold in empty rooms. If the destination room is empty, there's a chance that one of these items may appear in the room. After determining whether any random items will appear, the program saves the contents of the room by setting item equal to Items(Room) (Line 6) and then sets Items(Room) to I_EMPTY (Line 7), which indicates that the room is now empty.

The Select Case statement (Lines 8 to 33) then routes the program to the code that's needed to handle the current item. In most cases, the program only displays a DISCOV-ERY box and adds the item to the player's statistics. However, the teleport, skeleton, and dragon items get special handling, so the Select Case statement calls the appropriate

13

function: `Teleport`, `FoundDragon`, or `FightSkeleton`. `Teleport` transfers the player to a randomly selected room, and `FoundDragon` ends the game.

Battling Skeletons

`FightSkeleton` handles the battle between the player and the skeleton. The subroutine first calculates the player's attack modifier, which is based on the player's weapon and strength:

```
Modifier = Stats.Weapon - 4 + Stats.Strength / 20
```

Next, `FightSkeleton` calls `DoBattle`, which handles the actual fight:

```
playerAlive = DoBattle(Modifier)
```

`DoBattle` first displays the battle dialog box:

```
frmBattle.Left = Form1.Left + 1500
frmBattle.Top = Form1.Top + 1000
frmBattle.cmdOK.Enabled = False
frmBattle.Show , Me
frmBattle.CurrentX = 58
frmBattle.CurrentY = 200
frmBattle.Print "Modifier = " & Modifier
```

Then, the program sets the skeleton's hit points (`monsterHitPoints`) to 5, sets the `Battling` flag to `True`, and sets the `alive` flag to `True`:

```
monsterHitPoints = 5
Battling = True
alive = True
```

The `Battling` flag prevents the player from doing anything in the program before the battle is over. For example, the `Form_MouseDown` event handler will not process mouse clicks as long as the `Battling` flag is `True`:

```
If Randomizing Or Battling Then Exit Sub
```

A `Do` loop then iterates until `Battling` becomes `False`:

```
Do
{
   .
   .
   .
}
Loop While Battling
```

Inside the Do loop, the program calls RollDice to display the rolling dice and get the opponent's attack scores:

```
playerRoll = RollDice(48, 155)
Delay (0.5)
skeletonRoll = RollDice(117, 155)
```

When the player or skeleton scores a hit, DoBattle calculates the amount of damage scored by the hit. The program also subtracts an appropriate amount of strength from the player:

```
damage = Int(Rnd * 5 + 1)
SetStrength -1 - 1 * Abs(Stats.Pie < 1)
```

Notice how the preceding calculation uses the Boolean value (Stats.Pie < 1). If (Stats.Pie < 1) is true, it evaluates to -1. If (Stats.Pie < 1) is false, it evaluates to 0. Because the absolute value of the result of the Boolean expression is multiplied by -1, when the player's pie is less than 1, he loses an additional strength point. By using Boolean expressions in this way, you can eliminate the need for If statements in some circumstances.

Getting back to DoBattle, if the player's roll beats the skeleton's roll, the program displays the image of the hit skeleton, generates the winning sound, and deducts damage hit points from monsterHitPoints:

```
If playerRoll + Modifier >= skeletonRoll Then
  PlaySound SkeletonHitSound, False, False
  frmBattle.PaintPicture imgSkeleton(2), 68, 50
  Delay 1#
  monsterHitPoints = monsterHitPoints - damage
  If monsterHitPoints < 1 Then Battling = False
```

If monsterHitPoints is less than 1, the skeleton has lost the battle and Battling is set to False. However, if the skeleton's roll beats the player's roll, the program executes the Else portion of the If statement:

```
1:     Else
2:         PlaySound PlayerHitSound, False, False
3:         frmBattle.PaintPicture imgSkeleton(1), 68, 50
4:         SetHitPoints -damage
5:         Delay 1#
6:         If Stats.Strength <= 0 Or Stats.HitPoints <= 0 Then
7:           Battling = False
8:           alive = False
9:         End If
10:    End If
```

13

ANALYSIS Here, the program displays the attacking skeleton image (Lines 3), deducts damage from the player's hit points (Line 4), and generates the losing sound (Line 2). If the player's strength or hit points falls below 1 (Line 6), the player is dead, so the program sets Battling to False and alive to False (Lines 7 and 8).

Finally, if the battle is not yet over, the program restores the skeleton's normal image:

```
If Battling Then _
    frmBattle.PaintPicture imgSkeleton(0), 68, 50
```

After the program restores the skeleton's image, the Do loop performs another iteration. This continues until Battling equals False, at which point the program displays the skeleton as a pile of bones, enables the game's command buttons, and returns the alive flag to FightSkeleton:

```
frmBattle.cmdOK.Enabled = True
frmBattle.PaintPicture imgSkeleton(3), 68, 50
cmdShop.Enabled = True
cmdSpell.Enabled = True
cmdStats.Enabled = True
cmdLoad.Enabled = True
cmdAbout.Enabled = True
DoBattle = alive
```

Back in FightSkeleton(), if the player is still alive, the program gets rid of the battling window after a two-second delay:

```
Delay 2#
Unload frmBattle
```

Then, if the player has less than 20 strength points and also has a bottle of serum, the program calls DrinkSerum, which increases the player's strength points:

```
If Stats.Strength < 20 And Stats.Serums > 0 Then _
    DrinkSerum
```

The program then calculates how many gold pieces the player will find and displays the result in a DISCOVERY box:

```
amount = Int(Rnd * 5) + 5
ShowDiscovery imgGold, amount & " GOLD PIECES.", True
Stats.Gold = Stats.Gold + amount
```

If the player is no longer alive when the program returns to FightSkeleton, the program removes the battle window and calls the Dead subroutine, which ends the game:

```
Unload frmBattle
Dead
```

Creating Sound Effects

I created all of Dragonlord's sound effects in my home studio, using a Roland JP8000 synthesizer (see Figure 13.4), an Echo Layla professional PC sound card, and a Shure SM-58 microphone. I edited all the sounds using Steinberg WaveLab.

FIGURE 13.4

The Roland JP8000 synthesizer.

The program plays all sound effects with the DirectSound routines you learned about on Day 11, "Adding Sound to a Game."

Summary

Although you've examined only a portion of Dragonlord's source code, you should now understand how the rest of the program works. Before moving on to Day 14, however, you might want to spend some time going over the Dragonlord source code just to be sure that you understand it. It's a big program with a lot going on!

Q&A

Q What would be a typical number of attributes for a character in a profession-al RPG?

A The number of attributes that a game uses depends upon how realistic the game play will be. Full-fledged RPGs use dozens (hundreds?) of attributes that cover everything from basic stuff like strength, charm, luck, and health to a whole host of skills, such as swimming, mapping, understanding languages, repairing weapons, riding horses, bargaining, stealing, fighting, sneaking, and much more. The sky's the limit!

Q Dragonlord is played in a simple 2D, top-down viewpoint. How are 3D RPGs different?

A The only real difference is the graphics used to portray the character's current loca-tions. 3D programs handle character attributes the same way every other type of RPG does. The viewpoints may be different, but the basics of the game are the same. The player issues commands, and the program determines whether the

13

player's character has the correct abilities or statistics to complete the action. The program then determines an outcome for the command based on the character's attributes.

Workshop

The workshop includes quiz questions to help gauge your grasp of the material. You'll find the answers to this quiz in Appendix A. Even if you feel that you totally understand the concepts presented here, you should work through the quiz anyway. The last section is an exercise to help reinforce your learning.

Quiz

1. How does Dragonlord use the Map() array?

2. What does the Items() array represent?

3. What data does the program use to keep track of the player's statistics?

4. In general terms, explain the 15 room types.

5. How does the program use the Point function to control the player's movement through the dungeon?

6. What happens in the program when the player discovers a cache of gold, a spell, or a serum?

7. How does the Dragonlord program handle the fact that creatures in a dungeon are often on the move?

8. How do the Weapon and Strength attributes affect a fight?

9. What attributes do the skeleton characters have?

10. How can you use a Boolean expression to replace some types of If statements?

Exercise

1. Add a spell skill (attribute) to Dragonlord. This statistic should range from a minimum of 1 to a maximum of 5. At the start of the game, the spell skill should be set to 1. Each time the player casts a spell, the spell skill should go up 1. Use the spell skill so that the higher the player's skill, the closer the player gets to his target room when he casts the spell. That is, a spell skill of 1 should give the player only a 20% chance of reaching the selected room, whereas a spell skill of 5 should give the player a 100% chance of reaching the selected room. You should add more spell items to the dungeon to counteract the fact that they are now harder to use. (Hint: You can call the Teleport subroutine to easily transfer the player to a random room.)

DAY **14**

Creating a Level Editor

As I've said before, nothing gets people excited about a game more than being able to create their own levels. In a game like Dragonlord, a level is just a set of rooms and the items inside those rooms. This simplicity makes Dragonlord a perfect demonstration vehicle for creating a level editor. Today, you'll do just that. Specifically, you'll learn how to do the following:

- Use the editor
- Build the editor
- Save and load Dragonlord dungeon files
- Use control arrays to simplify the programming of editor toolboxes

Using the Dragonlord DungeonEditor

Before you learn how to build DungeonEditor on your own, you might like a little experience creating dungeons. Luckily, there's a version of DungeonEditor ready to go in the Chap14\DungeonEditor directory of this book's CD-ROM. (Well, okay, so luck had nothing to do with it.) When you run the program, you see the window shown in Figure 14.1.

FIGURE 14.1

The DungeonEditor application.

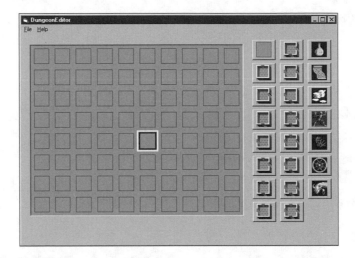

As you can see, the right side of the window has a set of buttons for the various types of rooms. To place a room in the dungeon, click on the corresponding button and then click the desired location on the dungeon grid. The selected room appears. You place items in the dungeon the same way, except you must place them in a location that already has a room.

To choose a new button in the toolbox, first click the activated button. This turns all the buttons back on again. Then you can select the new button you want to use.

To remove a room, click the first button in the toolbox, and then click the room. Both the room and any item it contains vanish from the map. Note that to remove an item, you must either replace the item with a different one or delete the room entirely.

The commands in the File and Help menus enable you to load and save files, start a new dungeon, exit the program, or view the program's About dialog box. Figure 14.2 shows what the default dungeon map looks like when it's loaded into the editor.

FIGURE 14.2

DungeonEditor displaying the default Dragonlord dungeon map.

Building the Dragonlord Dungeon Editor

Yesterday, you spent a lot of time building the Dragonlord game. Today, you'll build the game's dungeon editor. You'll be pleased to know that the editor is a small program that won't take too long to put together. In the following sections, you'll build the program one piece at a time.

Creating DungeonEditor's Main Form

The first step is to create the editor's main form:

1. Start a new Standard EXE Visual Basic project.

2. Set the form's properties to these values:

   AutoRedraw = True

   Caption = "DungeonEditor"

   Height = 6960

   ScaleMode = Pixel

   Width = 10005

3. Add a PictureBox control to the form, giving the control the following property settings:

   AutoRedraw = True

   AutoSize = True

   Font = MS Sans Serif, Bold, 8-point

   ForeColor = Blue

14

```
Left = 18
ScaleMode = Pixel
Top = 22
```

4. Set the PictureBox control's `Picture` property to the Grid.gif picture file, which you can find in the Images\DungeonEditor directory of this book's CD-ROM.

5. Add 16 CommandButton controls to the form, making them a control array named `cmdRoom`. Give the buttons the following property settings. You can find the buttons' picture files in the Images\DungeonEditor directory of this book's CD-ROM.

cmdRoom(0) Button

```
Caption = ""
Height = 42
Left = 483
Picture = Empty.bmp
Style = Graphical
Top = 13
Width = 49
```

cmdRoom(1) Button

```
Caption = ""
Height = 42
Left = 483
Picture = Room01.bmp
Style =Graphical
Top = 61
Width = 49
```

cmdRoom(2) Button

```
Caption = ""
Height = 42
Left = 483
Picture = Room02.bmp
Style = Graphical
Top = 109
Width = 49
```

cmdRoom(3) Button

```
Caption = ""
Height = 42
Left = 483
Picture = Room03.bmp
Style = Graphical
Top = 157
Width = 49
```

cmdRoom(4) Button

```
Caption = ""
Height = 42
Left = 483
Picture = Room04.bmp
Style = Graphical
Top = 205
Width = 49
```

cmdRoom(5) Button

```
Caption = ""
Height = 42
Left = 483
Picture = Room05.bmp
Style = Graphical
Top = 253
Width = 49
```

cmdRoom(6) Button

Caption = ""

Height = 42

Left = 483

Picture = Room06.bmp

Style = Graphical

Top = 301

Width = 49

cmdRoom(7) Button

Caption = ""

Height = 42

Left = 483

Picture = Room07.bmp

Style = Graphical

Top = 349

Width = 49

cmdRoom(8) Button

Caption = ""

Height = 42

Left = 541

Picture = Room08.bmp

Style = Graphical

Top = 13

Width = 49

cmdRoom(9) Button

Caption = ""

Height = 42

Left = 541

Picture = Room09.bmp

Style = Graphical

Top = 61

Width = 49

cmdRoom(10) Button

Caption = ""

Height = 42

Left = 541

Picture = Room10.bmp

Style = Graphical

Top = 109

Width = 49

cmdRoom(11) Button

Caption = ""

Height = 42

Left = 541

Picture = Room11.bmp

Style = Graphical

Top = 157

Width = 49

cmdRoom(12) Button

Caption = ""

Height = 42

Left = 541

Picture = Room12.bmp

Style = Graphical

Top = 205

Width = 49

cmdRoom(13) Button

Caption = ""

Height = 42

Left = 541

Picture = Room13.bmp

Style = Graphical

Top = 253

Width = 49

14

cmdRoom(14) Button

Caption = ""

Height = 42

Left = 541

Picture = Room14.bmp

Style = Graphical

Top = 301

Width = 49

cmdRoom(15) Button

Caption = ""

Height = 42

Left = 541

Picture = Room15.bmp

Style = Graphical

Top = 349

Width = 49

6. Add seven more CommandButton controls to the form, making them a control array named cmdItem. Give the buttons the following property settings. You can find the buttons' picture files in the Images\DungeonEditor directory of this book's CD-ROM. Figure 14.3 shows the finished controls.

cmdItem(0) Button

Caption = ""

Height = 42

Left = 599

Picture = Serum.bmp

Style = Graphical

Top = 13

Width = 49

cmdItem(1) Button

Caption = ""

Height = 42

Left = 599

Picture = Spell.bmp

Style = Graphical

Top = 61

Width = 49

cmdItem(2) Button

Caption = ""

Height = 42

Left = 599

```
Picture = Gold.bmp
Style = Graphical
Top = 109
Width = 49
```
cmdItem(3) Button
```
Caption = ""
Height = 42
Left = 599
Picture = Skeleton.bmp
Style = Graphical
Top = 157
Width = 49
```
cmdItem(4) Button
```
Caption = ""
Height = 42
Left = 599
Picture = Thief.bmp
Style = Graphical
Top = 205
Width = 49
```
cmdItem(5) Button
```
Caption = ""
Height = 42
Left = 599
Picture = Teleport.bmp
Style = Graphical
Top = 253
Width = 49
```
cmdItem(6) Button
```
Caption = ""
Height = 42
Left = 599
```

14

```
Picture = Dragon.bmp
Style = Graphical
Top = 301
Width = 49
```

FIGURE 14.3

The cmdRoom and cmdItem control arrays.

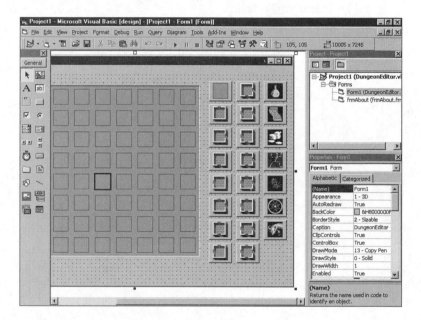

7. Add a CommonDialog control to the form, keeping the object's default name. If the control isn't in your VB toolbox, you'll need to load it using the Project menu's Components command, as shown in Figure 14.4.

FIGURE 14.4

Adding the CommonDialog control to the DungeonEditor project.

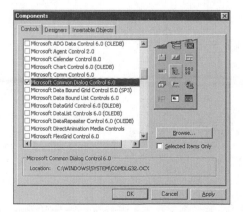

8. Add a Shape control to the form, giving it the following property settings:

BorderColor = Yellow

BorderWidth = 3

Height = 42

Left = 222

Shape = Rectangle

Top = 177

Width = 42

9. Save your work.

Your form should now look something like Figure 14.5.

FIGURE **14.5**

The completed form.

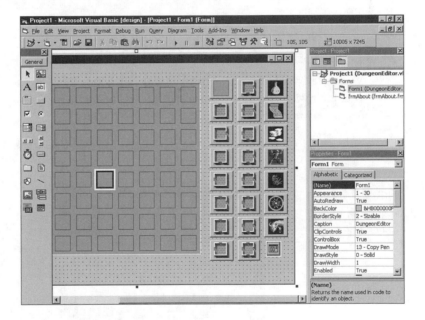

Next you'll take care of the program's menus.

Creating the Menus

14

Next step: the menus. Select the Menu Editor command from the Tools menu. When the editor appears, create the menus shown in Figure 14.6. Use the menu names mnuFile, mnuNew, mnuOpen, mnuSep (for the first menu separator in the File menu), mnuSave, mnuSaveAs, mnuSep2, mnuExit, mnuHelp, and mnuAbout.

FIGURE 14.6

*The menu editor,
displaying
DungeonEditor's
complete menus.*

You've now completed the game's menus. Next, you'll add the About dialog box to the project.

Adding the About Dialog Box

Visual Basic provides a readymade About dialog box that you can add to your projects if you don't want to create one from scratch. In the following steps, you'll include such a dialog box in the project and modify it for your own use.

1. Add a form to the project, selecting the About Dialog type, as shown in Figure 14.7.

FIGURE 14.7

*Adding an About
dialog box.*

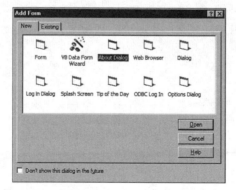

2. Set the picIcon PictureBox control in the dialog box to the Dragon.bmp file in the Images\DungeonEditor directory of this book's CD-ROM.

3. Change the dialog box's Caption property to the text "Copyright 2000 by Sams Publishing".

4. Delete the Warning label near the bottom of the dialog box.

Adding the Object Handlers

Now, you need to associate code with the form and its objects:

1. Double-click the Form1 form to bring up the code window.

2. Add the following form handlers to the code window. You can either type the source code or copy it from the DungeonEditor1.txt file, which you can find in the Chap14\Code directory of this book's CD-ROM.

LISTING 14.1   The Form Handlers

```
1:  '=================================================
2:  ' Main Form Handlers.
3:  '=================================================
4:  Private Sub Form_Load()
5:     InitVariables
6:  End Sub
7:
8:  Private Sub Form_Unload(Cancel As Integer)
9:     Dim Result As Integer
10:    Result = SaveIfNecessary()
11:    If Result <> vbCancel Then
12:       Unload frmAbout
13:    Else
14:       Cancel = True
15:    End If
16: End Sub
```

ANALYSIS   The Form_Load event procedure (Lines 4 to 6) initializes the editor's variables. This ensures that any changes are saved and that the frmAbout form is also unloaded.

3. Add the following button handlers to the code window. You can either type the source code or copy it from the DungeonEditor2.txt file, which you can find in the Chap14\Code directory of this book's CD-ROM.

LISTING 14.2   The Button Handlers

```
1:  '=================================================
2:  ' Button Handlers.
3:  '=================================================
4:  Private Sub cmdRoom_Click(Index As Integer)
5:     If RoomButton = NOBUTTONSELECTED Then
6:        RoomButton = Index
7:        DisableButtons
8:        cmdRoom(Index).Enabled = True
```

14

LISTING 14.2 continued

```
9:    ElseIf RoomButton = Index Then
10:      RestoreButtons
11:      RoomButton = NOBUTTONSELECTED
12:    End If
13: End Sub
14:
15: Private Sub cmdItem_Click(Index As Integer)
16:    If ItemButton = NOBUTTONSELECTED Then
17:      ItemButton = Index
18:      DisableButtons
19:      cmdItem(Index).Enabled = True
20:    Else
21:      RestoreButtons
22:      ItemButton = NOBUTTONSELECTED
23:    End If
24: End Sub
```

ANALYSIS These event procedures respond when the user clicks a room button or an item button, setting the variables that determine what type of object the player wants to place in the dungeon. The room number or item number is the index of the clicked button.

4. Add the following PictureBox handlers to the code window. You can either type the source code or copy it from the DungeonEditor3.txt file, which you can find in the Chap14\Code directory of this book's CD-ROM.

LISTING 14.3 The PictureBox Handlers

```
1:  '====================================================
2:  ' Picture Object Handlers.
3:  '====================================================
4:  Private Sub Picture1_Click()
5:    If RoomButton <> NOBUTTONSELECTED Then PlaceRoom
6:    If ItemButton <> NOBUTTONSELECTED Then PlaceItem
7:  End Sub
8:
9:  Private Sub Picture1_MouseMove(Button As Integer, _
10:     Shift As Integer, x As Single, y As Single)
11:    Dim Column As Integer
12:    Dim Row As Integer
13:    RoomX = x
14:    RoomY = y
15:    If RoomButton <> NOBUTTONSELECTED Or _
16:        ItemButton <> NOBUTTONSELECTED Then
17:      Column = X2Column(RoomX)
```

LISTING 14.3 continued

```
18:     Row = Y2Row(RoomY)
19:     Shape1.Move XOFFSET + Column * ROOMSIZE - 5, _
20:         YOFFSET + Row * ROOMSIZE - 5
21:   End If
22: End Sub
```

ANALYSIS The Picture1_Click event procedure (Lines 4 to 7) calls the subroutines that place a room or an item when the user clicks the dungeon grid. The Picture1_MouseMove event procedure (Lines 9 to 22) moves the yellow rectangle wherever the mouse pointer moves in the dungeon grid.

5. Add the following menu handlers to the code window. You can either type the source code or copy it from the DungeonEditor4.txt file, which you can find in the Chap14\Code directory of this book's CD-ROM.

LISTING 14.4 The Menu Handlers

```
1:  '================================================
2:  ' Menu Handlers.
3:  '================================================
4:  Private Sub mnuAbout_Click()
5:    frmAbout.Show
6:  End Sub
7:
8:  Private Sub mnuExit_Click()
9:    Dim Result As Integer
10:   Result = SaveIfNecessary()
11:   If Result <> vbCancel Then Unload Form1
12: End Sub
13:
14: Function SaveIfNecessary() As Integer
15:   Dim Answer As Integer
16:   Answer = vbYes
17:   If NeedToSave Then
18:     Answer = MsgBox("Do you want to save your changes?", _
19:         vbQuestion Or vbYesNoCancel)
20:     If Answer = vbYes Then mnuSaveAs_Click
21:   End If
22:   SaveIfNecessary = Answer
23: End Function
24:
25: Private Sub mnuNew_Click()
26:   Dim Result As Integer
27:   Result = SaveIfNecessary()
28:   If Result <> vbCancel Then
```

14

LISTING 14.4   continued

```
29:     InitVariables
30:     DrawScreen
31:   End If
32: End Sub
33:
34: Private Sub mnuOpen_Click()
35:   Dim Result As Integer
36:   On Error GoTo FileError
37:   Result = SaveIfNecessary()
38:   If Result <> vbCancel Then
39:     CommonDialog1.ShowOpen
40:     FileName = CommonDialog1.FileName
41:     Open FileName For Binary As #1
42:     Get #1, , Rooms
43:     Get #1, , Items
44:     Close #1
45:     NeedToSave = False
46:     DrawScreen
47:   End If
48:   Exit Sub
49: FileError:
50:     MsgBox "File not loaded.",  vbExclamation, "Save"
51: End Sub
52:
53: Private Sub mnuSave_Click()
54:   On Error GoTo FileError
55:   If FileName = "" Then
56:     mnuSaveAs_Click
57:   Else
58:     Open FileName For Binary As #1
59:     Put #1, , Rooms
60:     Put #1, , Items
61:     Close #1
62:     NeedToSave = False
63:   End If
64:   Exit Sub
65: FileError:
66:     MsgBox "File not saved.", vbExclamation, "Save"
67: End Sub
68:
69: Private Sub mnuSaveAs_Click()
70:   On Error GoTo FileError
71:   CommonDialog1.ShowSave
72:   FileName = CommonDialog1.FileName
73:   Open FileName For Binary As #1
74:   Put #1, , Rooms
75:   Put #1, , Items
76:   Close #1
```

LISTING 14.4 continued

```
77:    NeedToSave = False
78:    Exit Sub
79: FileError:
80:    MsgBox "File not saved.", vbExclamation, "Save As"
81: End Sub
```

ANALYSIS The mnuAbout_Click event procedure (Lines 4 to 6) displays the About dialog box when the user clicks the About menu command, and the mnuExit_Click event procedure closes the editor when the user clicks the Exit menu command. SaveIfNecessary (Lines 14 to 23) asks the user whether he wants to save his work, mnuNew_Click (Lines 25 to 32) starts a new dungeon file, mnuOpen_Click (Lines 34 to 51) opens an existing dungeon file, and mnuSave_Click (Lines 53 to 67) saves the current dungeon file. Finally, mnuSaveAs_Click (Lines 69 to 81) saves the dungeon layout under a new filename.

Adding General Source Code

Now, add the general subroutines, functions, constants, and variables by performing the following steps:

1. Add the following initialization subroutine to the code window. You can either type the code or copy it from the DungeonEditor5.txt file, which you can find in the Chap14\Code directory of this book's CD-ROM.

LISTING 14.5 The Initialization Routine

```
 1: '=================================================
 2: ' Initialization Routine.
 3: '=================================================
 4: Sub InitVariables()
 5:    Dim i As Integer
 6:    For i = 0 To ROOMCOUNT - 1
 7:      Rooms(i) = 0
 8:      Items(i) = 0
 9:    Next i
10:    RoomButton = NOBUTTONSELECTED
11:    ItemButton = NOBUTTONSELECTED
12:    NeedToSave = False
13:    FileName = ""
14: End Sub
```

ANALYSIS This subroutine initializes the program's variables.

14

2. Add the following general subroutines to the code window. You can either type the code or copy it from the DungeonEditor6.txt file, which you can find in the Chap14\Code directory of this book's CD-ROM.

LISTING 14.6 The General Subroutines

```
1:  '=====================================================
2:  ' General Subroutines.
3:  '=====================================================
4:  Sub DrawScreen()
5:     Dim Column As Integer
6:     Dim Row As Integer
7:     Dim Room As Integer
8:     For Column = 0 To COLUMNCOUNT - 1
9:       For Row = 0 To ROWCOUNT - 1
10:         Room = ColumnRow2Room(Column, Row)
11:         Picture1.PaintPicture _
12:           cmdRoom(Rooms(Room)).Picture, _
13:           XOFFSET + Column * ROOMSIZE, _
14:           YOFFSET + Row * ROOMSIZE
15:         If Items(Room) <> 0 Then
16:           Picture1.PaintPicture _
17:             cmdItem(Items(Room) - 1).Picture, _
18:             XOFFSET + Column * ROOMSIZE + 4, _
19:             YOFFSET + Row * ROOMSIZE + 4, 20, 20
20:         End If
21:       Next Row
22:     Next Column
23: End Sub
24:
25: Sub PlaceRoom()
26:    Dim Column As Integer
27:    Dim Row As Integer
28:    Dim Room As Integer
29:    Column = X2Column(RoomX)
30:    Row = Y2Row(RoomY)
31:    Room = ColumnRow2Room(Column, Row)
32:    Rooms(Room) = RoomButton
33:    If RoomButton = 0 Then Items(Room) = 0
34:    Picture1.PaintPicture _
35:      cmdRoom(RoomButton).Picture, _
36:      XOFFSET + Column * ROOMSIZE, _
37:      YOFFSET + Row * ROOMSIZE
38:    If Items(Room) <> 0 Then
39:      Picture1.PaintPicture _
40:        cmdItem(Items(Room)).Picture, _
41:        XOFFSET + Column * ROOMSIZE + 4, _
42:        YOFFSET + Row * ROOMSIZE + 4, 20, 20
43:    End If
```

LISTING 14.6 continued

```
44:    NeedToSave = True
45: End Sub
46:
47: Sub PlaceItem()
48:    Dim Column As Integer
49:    Dim Row As Integer
50:    Dim Room As Integer
51:    Column = X2Column(RoomX)
52:    Row = Y2Row(RoomY)
53:    Room = ColumnRow2Room(Column, Row)
54:    If Rooms(Room) = 0 Then
55:      MsgBox "You must place a room there first."
56:    Else
57:      Items(Room) = ItemButton + 1
58:      Picture1.PaintPicture _
59:        cmdRoom(Rooms(Room)).Picture, _
60:        XOFFSET + Column * ROOMSIZE, _
61:        YOFFSET + Row * ROOMSIZE
62:      Picture1.PaintPicture _
63:        cmdItem(ItemButton).Picture, _
64:        XOFFSET + Column * ROOMSIZE + 4, _
65:        YOFFSET + Row * ROOMSIZE + 4, 20, 20
66:      NeedToSave = True
67:    End If
68: End Sub
69:
70: Sub DisableButtons()
71:    Dim i As Integer
72:    For i = 0 To NUMROOMBUTTONS - 1
73:      cmdRoom(i).Enabled = False
74:      If i < 7 Then cmdItem(i).Enabled = False
75:    Next i
76: End Sub
77:
78: Sub RestoreButtons()
79:    Dim i As Integer
80:    For i = 0 To NUMROOMBUTTONS - 1
81:      cmdRoom(i).Enabled = True
82:      If i < 7 Then cmdItem(i).Enabled = True
83:    Next i
84: End Sub
```

ANALYSIS The DrawScreen subroutine (Lines 4 to 23) paints the dungeon grid with its rooms and items, PlaceRoom (Lines 25 to 45) paints a single room on the display, and PlaceItem (Lines 47 to 68) paints an item. The DisableButtons subroutine (Lines 70 to 77) disables all of the editor's buttons, and RestoreButtons (Lines 78 to 84) enables all the buttons.

14

3. Add the following functions to the code window. You can either type the code or copy it from the DungeonEditor7.txt file, which you can find in the Chap14\Code directory of this book's CD-ROM.

LISTING 14.7   The Program Functions

```
1:  '=================================================
2:  ' Program functions.
3:  '=================================================
4:  Function X2Column(x As Integer) As Integer
5:      X2Column = (x + 1 - XOFFSET) \ ROOMSIZE
6:  End Function
7:
8:  Function Y2Row(y As Integer) As Integer
9:      Y2Row = (y + 1 - YOFFSET) \ ROOMSIZE
10: End Function
11:
12: Function ColumnRow2Room(Column As Integer, _
13:      Row As Integer) As Integer
14:    ColumnRow2Room = Row * COLUMNCOUNT + Column
15: End Function
```

ANALYSIS   These functions convert X coordinates (Lines 4 to 6) to columns, Y coordinates (Lines 8 to 10) to rows, and grid columns and rows to room numbers (Lines 12 to 15).

4. Add the following variable declarations and enumerations to the top of the code window. You can either type the code or copy it from the DungeonEditor8.txt file, which you can find in the Chap14\Code directory of this book's CD-ROM.

LISTING 14.8   The Program Declarations

```
1:  '=================================================
2:  ' Dragonlord Dungeon Editor for Visual Basic 6
3:  '    by Clayton Walnum
4:  ' Copyright 2000 by Macmillan Computer Publishing
5:  '=================================================
6:  Option Explicit
7:
8:  '=================================================
9:  ' Constants.
10: '=================================================
11: Const XOFFSET = 7
12: Const YOFFSET = 6
13: Const ROOMSIZE = 44
14: Const COLUMNCOUNT = 10
15: Const ROWCOUNT = 8
```

LISTING 14.8   continued

```
16: Const ROOMCOUNT = 80
17: Const NOBUTTONSELECTED = -1
18: Const NUMROOMBUTTONS = 16
19:
20: '================================================
21: ' General Game Variables.
22: '================================================
23: Dim RoomButton As Integer
24: Dim ItemButton As Integer
25: Dim RoomX As Integer
26: Dim RoomY As Integer
27: Dim NeedToSave As Boolean
28: Dim FileName As String
29: Dim Rooms(ROOMCOUNT - 1) As Integer
30: Dim Items(ROOMCOUNT - 1) As Integer
```

5. Save your work.

You've now completed the Dragonlord DungeonEditor program. By now, you know what that means… Time to dig into the program's innards to see how it works.

Understanding DungeonEditor

Now that you've built your own version of DungeonEditor, it's time to examine the code, starting with the constants and variables. We won't look at every line of code in the program, however. Most of it you can understand on your own. Instead, we will examine the parts of the program that are most important.

DungeonEditor's Variables and Constants

DungeonEditor relies on a set of variables and constants that the game declares near the top of the program. Table 14.1 lists the variables and their descriptions, and Table 14.2 lists the constants.

TABLE 14.1   DungeonEditor's General Game Variables

Variable	Type	Description
FileName	String	The filename of the currently loaded dungeon
ItemButton	Integer	The index of the currently selected room button
Items()	Integer	An array that holds the items in each room of the dungeon
NeedToSave	Boolean	A flag that indicates whether or not the currently loaded dungeon needs to save its changes

14

TABLE 14.1   continued

Variable	Type	Description
RoomButton	Integer	The index of the currently selected room button
Rooms()	Integer	An array that holds the type of room in each dungeon location
RoomX	Integer	The X coordinate at which the user wants to place a room
RoomY	Integer	The Y coordinate at which the user wants to place a room

TABLE 14.2   DungeonEditor's Constants

Constant	Description
COLUMNCOUNT	The number of rooms in a row of the dungeon map
NOBUTTONSELECTED	A value indicating that the user hasn't selected a button in the toolbox
NUMROOMBUTTONS	The number of room buttons in the toolbox
ROOMCOUNT	The number of rooms in the dungeon
ROOMSIZE	The size of a room, in pixels
ROWCOUNT	The number of rooms in a column of the dungeon map
XOFFSET	The X coordinate at which the left edge of the dungeon map is located
YOFFSET	The Y coordinate at which the top edge of the dungeon map is located

The Toolbox

DungeonEditor is a simple program. All it has to do is write out to disk the integer values that represent the rooms and items in the dungeon. To make it easy for you to tell the program what those values are, DungeonEditor features a toolbox that contains a graphical button for each type of room and item that you can place in the dungeon.

DungeonEditor's toolbox is nothing more than two CommandButton control arrays. The first set of buttons represents the types of rooms you can use in the dungeon, and the second represents the types of items. Because these buttons are arranged in control arrays, it takes only one small event handler to handle all the buttons in an array. For example, when the user clicks a room button, VB calls the cmdRoom_Click event handler with the index of the clicked button:

LISTING 14.9 The cmdRoom_Click Event Procedure

```
1:  Private Sub cmdRoom_Click(Index As Integer)
2:    If RoomButton = NOBUTTONSELECTED Then
3:      RoomButton = Index
4:      DisableButtons
5:      cmdRoom(Index).Enabled = True
6:    ElseIf RoomButton = Index Then
7:      RestoreButtons
8:      RoomButton = NOBUTTONSELECTED
9:    End If
10: End Sub
```

ANALYSIS The subroutine simply sets the RoomButton variable to the index of the selected button (Line 3) and calls DisableButtons, which disables the remaining buttons in the toolbox (Line 4). If the user already had a button selected (Line 6), cmdRoom_Click reenables all buttons (Line 7) and sets RoomButton back to NOBUTTONSELECTED (Line 8). This leaves the toolbox ready for the user to select another button.

As you can see in the following source code, the cmdItem_Click event handler manages the item buttons in exactly the same way:

LISTING 14.10 The cmdItem_Click Event Procedure

```
1:  Private Sub cmdItem_Click(Index As Integer)
2:    If ItemButton = NOBUTTONSELECTED Then
3:      ItemButton = Index
4:      DisableButtons
5:      cmdItem(Index).Enabled = True
6:    Else
7:      RestoreButtons
8:      ItemButton = NOBUTTONSELECTED
9:    End If
10: End Sub
```

Placing a Room or Item into the Dungeon

If the user clicks the PictureBox control, the program assumes that he's trying to place a room or item at the clicked location. The Picture1_Click event handler routes the program to the correct subroutine depending upon the value of the RoomButton and ItemButton variables:

```
Private Sub Picture1_Click()
  If RoomButton <> NOBUTTONSELECTED Then PlaceRoom
  If ItemButton <> NOBUTTONSELECTED Then PlaceItem
End Sub
```

14

The `PlaceRoom` subroutine takes care of placing a room in the dungeon. First, `PlaceRoom` calls the `X2Column` and `Y2Row` functions to calculate the dungeon column and row in which the clicked room is located:

```
Column = X2Column(RoomX)
Row = Y2Row(RoomY)
```

Then, the program gets the room number from the `ColumnRow2Room` function:

```
Room = ColumnRow2Room(Column, Row)
```

The `RoomButton` variable, which is the index of the currently selected room button in the toolbox, contains the room type number for the selected location. (No, this isn't magic. I deliberately arranged the buttons in the toolbox this way.) The program sets the appropriate element of the `Rooms()` array to this value:

```
Rooms(Room) = RoomButton
```

If it happens that the user is deleting a room, the program also deletes any item that might be in the room:

```
If RoomButton = 0 Then Items(Room) = 0
```

At this point, the program has all the information it needs. After all, the only thing the program needs is the contents of the `Rooms()` and `Items()` arrays, which it has to write out to a file. However, because we humans cannot see into a computer's memory (at least, not yet), the program now must update the screen display to show these changes. It does this by painting the currently selected button's room image onto the dungeon grid:

```
Picture1.PaintPicture _
  cmdRoom(RoomButton).Picture, _
  XOFFSET + Column * ROOMSIZE, _
  YOFFSET + Row * ROOMSIZE
```

It's way cool that the buttons can act not only as graphical interface elements, but can also as storage places for images.

Next, if the user has just replaced one type of room with another, the program needs to redraw any item that was in the room:

```
If Items(Room) <> 0 Then
  Picture1.PaintPicture _
    cmdItem(Items(Room)).Picture, _
    XOFFSET + Column * ROOMSIZE + 4, _
    YOFFSET + Row * ROOMSIZE + 4, 20, 20
End If
```

Finally, because the user has changed the dungeon, the program sets the `NeedToSave` flag to `True`:

```
NeedToSave = True
```

The `PlaceItem` subroutine takes care of dropping items into dungeon rooms. It starts off by getting the room column, row, and number just as `PlaceRoom` did:

```
Column = X2Column(RoomX)
Row = Y2Row(RoomY)
Room = ColumnRow2Room(Column, Row)
```

Next, if the clicked location contains no room, the user isn't allowed to place an item there:

```
If Rooms(Room) = 0 Then
  MsgBox "You must place a room there first."
```

If a room exists at the selected location, the program places the item number in the `Items()` array:

```
Items(Room) = ItemButton + 1
```

In case the user is replacing an already existing item in the room, the program redraws the room:

```
Picture1.PaintPicture _
  cmdRoom(Rooms(Room)).Picture, _
  XOFFSET + Column * ROOMSIZE, _
  YOFFSET + Row * ROOMSIZE
```

Now the program can draw the item in the room:

```
Picture1.PaintPicture _
  cmdItem(ItemButton).Picture, _
  XOFFSET + Column * ROOMSIZE + 4, _
  YOFFSET + Row * ROOMSIZE + 4, 20, 20
```

As with any change to the dungeon, the `NeedToSave` flag must now be set to `True`:

```
NeedToSave = True
```

Saving and Loading Dungeon Data

Before DungeonEditor allows the user to exit the program, it calls the `SaveIfNecessary` function, which determines whether the disk file is up to date with the dungeon data. `SaveIfNecessary` checks the `NeedToSave` flag, and if the dungeon data is dirty (needs to

14

be saved), the program displays a message box asking the user if he wants to save the file:

```
If NeedToSave Then
    Answer = MsgBox("Do you want to save your changes?", _
        vbQuestion Or vbYesNoCancel)
```

If the user answers Yes, SaveIfNecessary calls mnuSaveAs_Click to save the file:

```
    If Answer = vbYes Then mnuSaveAs_Click
```

To save the file, the program simply shows a Save As dialog box so the user can choose a filename, opens the file, and writes out the contents of the Rooms() and Items() arrays:

```
CommonDialog1.ShowSave
FileName = CommonDialog1.FileName
Open FileName For Binary As #1
Put #1, , Rooms
Put #1, , Items
Close #1
```

Finally, the program sets the NeedToSave flag back to False because the contents of the disk file now match the data stored in the program:

```
NeedToSave = False
```

The program reads the file back into the program in almost exactly the same way, except that it's reading the data rather than writing it:

```
Open FileName For Binary As #1
Get #1, , Rooms
Get #1, , Items
Close #1
NeedToSave = False
```

And that's about all there is to the program. You should be able to understand the source code we haven't discussed here. Read through it to be sure that you understand how everything works. Then have fun making custom dungeons for Dragonlord. However, keep in mind that the default dungeon has been carefully balanced so that the game is neither too easy nor too hard. For example, if you place too many treasure items in your dungeon, the game may become too easy to beat. Also, be sure that the doors to your rooms match up properly. Just some stuff to think about.

Note

Balancing a game so that it's neither too easy nor too hard can be a tricky process. The only sure way is to play the game again and again. But keep in mind that you're already an expert at playing the game. This means that for a novice player, the game will be much more difficult. To account for this, it's a good idea to have some friends lined up who can test the game for you.

Summary

That finishes up our mini-project on creating simple RPGs. You can expand on what you've learned in the last few days to create just about any type of RPG, except those that require 3D graphics. You'll need to read a few more books before you can join the 3D gurus!

Now that your second week of study is complete, you're ready to jump into this book's major project—the Moonlord strategy game.

Q&A

Q Hey, building a dungeon editor was actually pretty easy. Should I start designing my own editor for Quake?

A Er... not really. Editors for 3D games are immensely more complex than Dragonlord's editor. Still, the basics are pretty much the same. The editor does little more than create the data that the game needs to load for each level. The rest is all visual icing on the cake for the user. Of course, with a game like Quake, we're talking a whole lot of icing!

Q When I create levels for my own games, can't I do away with all the fancy graphics in an editor? Can't I just plug values directly into the arrays and write the data out to a file?

A Sure. The idea is to create a file that the game program can read and interpret, nothing more and nothing less. However, think about what you'd have to do to design the level. At the minimum, you'd have to draw everything out on paper before translating the objects into numbers. Why not just let a computer program do the dirty work for you?

14

Q **DungeonEditor writes out its data in binary form. Instead, couldn't I have my editor create a text file that can be edited with a text editor, as well as with the dungeon editor?**

A Absolutely. The format of the data is completely up to you. You just have to be sure that both the editor and the game know how to read and interpret the same set of data. Of course, keep in mind that a text file is easy for game players to futz around with, which could yield corrupted data files.

Workshop

The workshop includes quiz questions to help gauge your grasp of the material. You'll find the answers to this quiz in Appendix A. Even if you feel that you totally understand the concepts presented here, you should work through the quiz anyway. The last section contains an exercise to help reinforce your learning.

Quiz

1. What's the only thing a level editor really needs to do?
2. How do DungeonEditor's buttons serve double duty in the program?
3. What's important about the order of the buttons in DungeonEditor's toolbox?
4. What's the advantage of grouping DungeonEditor's buttons into a control array?
5. Explain the purpose of the NeedToSave variable.
6. What are the values that the program stores in the Rooms() and Items() arrays?
7. What data does DungeonEditor need to write to disk in order to create a dungeon file that Dragonlord can load and interpret?

Exercises

1. Today's exercise will give you a chance to have a little fun. Use DungeonEditor to create several dungeons for Dragonlord. Try some different ideas, like creating a section of dungeon that can be reached only by casting a spell, or protecting the dragon by placing him at the end of a long, skeleton-infested corridor. You'll have to play your custom levels several times to make sure they aren't too easy or too hard.

WEEK 2

In Review

Before creating any class, you must consider the different ways to manipulate the data encapsulated in the class. After you've analyzed your game's needs, you can then write the class's functions. In Week 2, you created classes for a deck of cards.

Creating a complete card class is a nearly impossible task because you can never predict all the different ways that you may need to manipulate cards in your programs. However, you can write the functions that every card program needs—such as shuffling a deck and dealing hands—and then add more specific functions as you need them.

The Deck class you created features methods to shuffle the deck, deal cards, show a hand, erase cards, move cards, get card values, and restore a deck of cards to its state right after it was shuffled.

In Week 2, you also learned how to evaluate blackjack and poker hands. Evaluating a blackjack hand is easy, but writing the code to analyze a poker hand is another story. The Poker Squares program first checks the hand for a flush by determining whether all the cards in the hand are in the same suit. Then the program sorts the cards into an array and calls functions that check for the basic types of poker card combinations. These functions set flags that the program uses to determine the best possible hand.

There are a couple of ways to create a computer game opponent. You can program an opponent that "understands" the game's strategy and plays much like a human player. This solution is difficult to implement, however. Not only is it a programming challenge, but the game opponent will be only as good as you are at playing the game.

Another method of creating a computer opponent is to let the computer cheat by using its calculating power. This is the easiest approach to take. After you create a computer opponent in this "brute force" way, you can plug some of the holes in the way that the computer plays by adding strategy routines. Once you've created a competent opponent, adding your own strategies can only make it better.

When you built the Crystals game in Week 2, creating the computer opponent turned out to be relatively easy. Using the brute force method, the program simply looks forward at every possible set of two moves and finds the best one.

Most computer sound cards come with all the software you need to create sound effects for any game that can handle WAV files. Many of these sound-recording programs can also edit sounds in various ways, from clipping unwanted noise to adding echo, or even reversing a sound effect.

No matter what sound card you have and what software you'll be using to record and edit sound effects, the first step is to plug a microphone into the sound card. Then start up your sound-editing program and turn on the recording function.

Once you've recorded a sound effect, you'll almost always need to edit it somehow. Different sound programs have different editing features, but most of them let you delete various portions of the sound, as well as change its volume and add special effects such as reverb, echo, phasing, and so on.

Just like most things in life, the sound effects you create for a game can be as simple or as elaborate as you want. For most "homegrown" games, you can use items that you have lying around the house to generate sound effects. For commercial games, you'll need a full-fledged studio and probably a sound engineer as well.

Once you have your sound effects, you need to set up your game program to play them. There are several ways to do this, which include using Visual Basic's multimedia control, the Windows API, or the DirectSound component of DirectX.

Probably the best way to play sound effects in your programs is with DirectX. Before you can use it in your program, you must add a reference to the DirectX type library to your project. Then you can start adding DirectSound source code to your program. First, you need to declare the variables that'll hold references to the DirectX objects your program needs to access.

Because the Windows environment allows multitasking, many applications may be running simultaneously. In order to keep things running smoothly, different aspects of the operating system are assigned priority levels. For this reason, DirectSound provides the `SetCooperativeLevel` method, which enables a program to request a priority level for the sound hardware. The next step is to create secondary DirectSoundBuffer objects for the sound effects in your program. Finally, you can play the sound by calling the DirectSoundBuffer object's `Play` method.

A role-playing game must define one or more characters to represent the player in the game's world. In modern role-playing games, dozens of attributes define the way a character looks and acts in the game. These attributes typically include health, strength, intelligence, race, occupation, class, religion, speed, skills, and so on.

A player's abilities are a combination of all these attributes along with external modifiers, including the type of weapon the character has, the type of armor he's wearing, and the non-player characters with which he must interact. The game's rules take all this data into account, throw in a bit of random chance, and determine the outcome of an event in the game.

In Week 2, you created a simple RPG named Dragonlord, and you got a look at how to apply character attributes to the game rules in order devise outcomes. This game included a level editor for creating custom dungeon layouts.

WEEK 3

At a Glance

Week 3 is a seven-part, hands-on project in which you design and program Moonlord, a complex space strategy game. On Day 15, you'll learn how to play Moonlord, and then you'll get started on your own version of the project by creating the game's user interface. On Day 16, you'll add the source code needed to declare and initialize the game's many variables. Then, on Day 17, you'll program the first of the game's three screens. On Days 18 and 19, you'll program the game's two subscreens. Finally, on Days 20 and 21, you'll add animation and sound to the game.

Along the way, you'll revisit many topics that you've learned about in this book and use those skills as you complete this full-scale project. Specifically, you'll call upon the following skills to complete this final weeklong project:

- Drawing game screens
- Using Image controls to store game images
- Drawing text
- Writing game algorithms
- Displaying images
- Performing animation
- Playing sound effects
- Testing game programs

When you've completed this project successfully, you'll have polished up all the basic skills you need to write a sophisticated game program using Visual Basic. You'll then be ready to design and create your own original games.

At the end of Week 3, you will have programmed the following game:

- *Moonlord*—A commercial-quality space strategy game in which you explore outer space in an effort to destroy 50 alien ships before you run out of time and energy.

DAY 15

Game Play and the User Interface: The Moonlord Project

Here you are, already on your last week of studying VB game programming. Over the next seven days, you'll put all the knowledge you've attained into the building of your biggest, most sophisticated game yet: a full-featured space strategy game called Moonlord. Today you'll learn how to play the game, after which you'll start creating your own version of Moonlord by assembling the game's user interface. Specifically, today you'll learn about the following:

- The Moonlord story
- How to play Moonlord
- How to assemble the game's user interface
- How to incorporate predefined Visual Basic dialog boxes into a project

The Story

Like many games, Moonlord has a story that describes its setting and characters, as well as spelling out the mission you must complete to win the game. So, without further ado:

Moonlord Planetinsky was a bitter man.

Even though he had succeeded in almost single-handedly defeating last year's alien attack (the entire Titanian Territorial Guard had been stymied by the aliens' unusual strategies), and even though he returned home as a hero to the adulation of thousands, he found that deep inside, where it really counted, he was still as insecure as a newborn cub.

It was his name, you know.

The name Moonlord sounded so much like a title of office that people could rarely resist bowing when introduced. It was a matter of amusement for most, but Moonlord hated it.

His childhood had been no laughing matter, either. He had always been the kid with the cootiumphaloids (imaginary creatures about the size of a temphibootawep; if the other kids said you had them, you were an outcast). And now, as an adult, he still found that his unusual name was anything but an asset.

Why couldn't I have been given a normal name, *he often thought,* like Fredolotington Alnertopater or Eddyboperty Elnopilersop?

So he became tough—the toughest starfighter on the Saturnian moon of Titan. Nobody, nobody, dared cross him.

Now it seemed he had another job to do.

Moonlord stepped off the Sliderwalkatron and crossed to the headquarters of the Titanian Territorial Guard, clutching the telegramomessagecard in his left hand. It was from Leeryup Coddledoop, Commander-in-Chief of the TTG. He snickered to himself as he remembered the last time he had seen Leeryup, tucked into a hospital bed, every part of his body swollen like overfilled cameladesertliquibags.

"Guess he won't bow to me again!" Moonlord said out loud. A few people glanced in his direction, but none let his gaze linger. Moonlord was a hero, and they loved him—but they knew better than to draw attention to his peculiarities. He drew a deep lungful of smoke from his smokyngstickocancerlator and exhaled a swirling blue tornado.

When he stepped into Commander Coddledoop's office, the gray-haired man behind the desk stood up and saluted. Even though Moonlord was a civilian, he now received the

15

same respect as that awarded to an admiral of the fleet. To say the least, the TTG were inordinately impressed by Moonlord's handling of the last alien invasion.

Moonlord sat down without returning the salute and stared at the Commander, saying nothing.

The Commander sat slowly, fighting the urge to bow with all his soul. Heavens, but old habits died hard!

"Uh... ahem," he began eloquently. "...uh... To say the least, the TTG were inordinately impressed by your handling of the last alien invasion."

Wow, *thought Moonlord,* Deja vu. *But he said nothing; just sat, waiting.*

"We have a tiny problem," the Commander tried again, "One that requires your... er... delicate touch."

Moonlord's eyebrows climbed his forehead. "You wouldn't by any chance be referring to the new fleet the aliens have sent out, would you?"

"Well... it's a problem kind of... er... similar to that."

"Similar?"

"Um... very close to that, actually."

"How close?"

"Sort of... well... 'identical' would be the appropriate word, I guess."

Moonlord sighed. "Are you or are you not referring to the new alien threat?"

"I believe that would be an accurate paraphrase of my previous remarks."

"Have you ever considered politics?" Moonlord asked.

"Well..."

"Never mind. It was a rhetorical question."

Moonlord stood up and crossed to the Commander's newly installed compudigibinotometer-Pentium, the one that had recently replaced the long-loved compudigibinotometer-486, and called up the galactic map.

The aliens were everywhere.

"Let the good times roll," Moonlord muttered.

"Excuse me?" said the Commander, standing to get a better look at the screen.

"I'll take the job," Moonlord said, turning toward the Commander. "I'll show those alien scum that they can't mess with Titan."

The Commander positively glowed. "Thank you, thank you, thank you!" He was so delighted that he forgot to control his inner impulses. Before he knew it, he was bending at the waist, performing an elegant bow.

"Ohhhhh, nooooo…" he muttered.

It was the Commander's opinion that hospital food hadn't improved much since his last stay.

The Rules

When you run Moonlord and select the File menu's New Game command, you'll see the galactic map (see Figure 15.1) represented on your screen by an 18×8 grid. Each square in the grid is one sector of the galactic milieu, and hidden within these 144 sectors are the 50 alien craft you must locate and destroy. Since aliens always travel in pairs, only 25 sectors actually contain the enemy.

FIGURE 15.1

Moonlord at the start of a game.

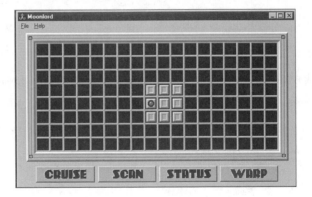

To make your job a little easier, there are two starbases where you can stock up on supplies and make repairs. There's one at each end of the galaxy, and just like the aliens, they're randomly placed at the beginning of each game, forcing you to explore.

To win the game, you must locate and destroy all 50 alien craft. You have only 100 Galactic Standard days to complete your mission. It'll take careful conservation of supplies and planned movement. If you like to leap into the fray without a strategy, you'll find failure a constant companion.

15

Although there's only one way to win the game, there are many ways to lose. (Can't make it *too* easy for you, now can we?) The first is to run out of time. You've got 100 days. No extensions. All begging will be ignored.

The second way to lose your hero status is to allow your energy to run out. Keep your eye on it; when it's gone, so are you. Remember to check the status of your weapons, too. If you're in the heat of battle and find that both your weapons systems are down, you'll have to resort to ramming the aliens (more on that later). That means heavy damage to your ship. Every time you ram an enemy, you're taking a one-in-ten chance of destroying your own ship.

Finally, using your ship's warp capabilities is a risky venture indeed. Each time you use them, you're taking a one-in-ten chance of destroying your engines and ending the game.

The Bridge

Below the galactic map, you'll find the bridge controls. This is where you gain access to the ship's main functions. There are four systems available here: cruise engines, scanners, a status display, and warp engines. (You access weapon systems from the scanner display.) To select a system, click its button.

Note that, at times, some systems will be damaged and thus unusable. You can tell at a glance which systems are down: their buttons in the bridge control bar will be disabled (see Figure 15.2). The only exceptions to this are the long-range scanners. They work automatically each time you move, so they have no system button. You can check them on the status display (see the "Status" section later in this chapter).

FIGURE 15.2

The control buttons for damaged systems are disabled.

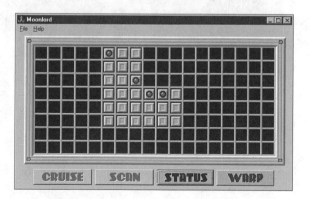

Cruise

To move your ship from one galactic sector to another, select the Cruise button. You are allowed to move in any of the eight compass directions, but you should note that diagonal moves are actually counted as two moves, and the required energy and time are deducted as if the move were completed with two non-diagonal moves. After clicking the Cruise button, select your destination sector by placing the mouse pointer over it and clicking. Each sector of movement uses ten units of energy and one day of time.

Note   If you click the Cruise button and then change your mind, you can click it a second time to shut off the Cruise system.

Status

Throughout the game, it's important to keep close tabs on your ship's condition and supplies. You can't afford to be stuck far from a starbase when your energy is almost depleted, and it helps to know which weapons are functional before you spring into battle. All this information is available in the status display (see Figure 15.3). To view the status display, select the Status system button on the bridge control bar.

FIGURE 15.3

Moonlord's status display.

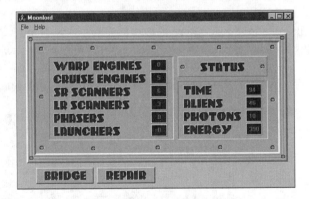

Your ship's six systems are displayed on the left, each followed by a number indicating how many days are needed to repair that system. A 0 means the system is fully functional.

On the right, you can find information on supplies, as well as the time remaining and the number of aliens remaining.

Click the Bridge button to return to the bridge display.

15

Damaged Systems

Damaged systems must be repaired before they can be used. Damage is measured by the number of days the crew requires to complete repairs. If you don't need the damaged system right away, you need do nothing. The crew will automatically get to work, applying their best efforts to the restoration of your ship. Remember: One sector of movement on the galactic map consumes one day. A system that requires three days to repair will be operative after a move of three sectors.

If you find you must make repairs immediately, you may do so by selecting the Repair button from the Status subsystem control bar. Each time you click the Repair button, a day goes by. That day's repairs are made and the status screen is updated.

System Repair Crews

If more than one system needs repair, the times are not added together. Each system has its own crew. For example, if your photon launchers require four days to repair and your short-range scanner needs two days, it'll take only four days to fix both systems. If you select only two days of repair time, the short-range scanner will be operational, but the launchers will require two additional days of repair before you can use them.

Don't forget that the time you spend waiting for repairs will be subtracted from the time available to your mission. Sometimes it's better to continue with a crippled ship than to waste a lot of time waiting for repairs to be completed.

Warp

If you find that you must move a long distance in a short amount of time, the warp engines may fill your need. Unfortunately, they're still experimental and their safety and reliability cannot be guaranteed. You have no control over where you'll end up, and each warp carries a one-in-ten chance of destroying your engines, leaving you helplessly afloat in the timeless void of space. In other words, the game could come to an abrupt end.

Each warp consumes one day and 30 units of energy. Due to its unreliability, you may have to jump several times before you get where you want (or at least in the general area).

Long-Range Scanners

You have two types of scanners on your ship: long-range and short-range. The long-range scanners fill in the galactic map as you move. They function automatically, so you need do nothing except repair them when they become damaged.

The long-range scanners examine the sectors adjacent to your position and mark the galactic map appropriately. An empty marker indicates empty sectors, a red light represents aliens, and a blue cross represents a starbase. A blue blinking light marks your current position. If your current sector contains aliens or a starbase, the blinking light alternates between green and red for aliens, or between blue and a blue cross for a starbase.

Short-Range Scanners

The Scan button on the bridge control bar activates the short-range scanners. When you select this system, the short-range scanner display pops up, as shown in Figure 15.4.

FIGURE 15.4

Moonlord's short-range scanner display.

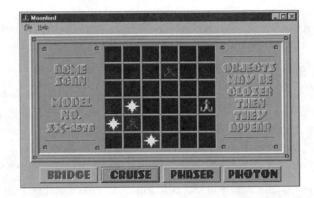

The short-range scan enables you to see your current sector in greater detail. Each sector of the galactic map is divided into 36 smaller sectors. Icons on the short-range scan screen represent all the suns, aliens, and starbases in the sector. Your own ship is marked, as well. The scanner control bar provides four system commands: Bridge, Cruise, Phaser, and Photon.

To return to the bridge, select the Bridge button.

Short-Range Cruise

Your movement in the short-range display is much the same as in the galactic map. Select the Cruise system from the scanner subsystem control bar, and then use the mouse to select your destination.

Unlike the galactic map, your movement here is somewhat restricted. You can't move through a sun, an alien, or a starbase. If anything is in your way, you must maneuver around it. Also, diagonal moves are not allowed because they're interpreted as two non-diagonal moves. Since the aliens attack each time you move, only single moves are allowed.

Movement on the short-range scanner display consumes no time, but it uses three energy points per sector.

Phasers

The phasers are the first and most powerful of your weapons systems. When activated, they release a burst of electromagnetic energy in every direction, damaging any alien craft on your scanners. Nothing can block their energy beams, not even a sun. The amount of damage done depends on the number of alien craft and their distance from your ship. Damage is cumulative. You may have to fire more than once to get the job done.

Select the Phaser button from the scanner subsystem control bar, and then enter the amount of power you want to apply to the phaser shot (see Figure 15.5). Each power point will be subtracted from your remaining energy, so allocate just enough to get the job done.

FIGURE 15.5

Allocating phaser power.

Photon Torpedoes

Photon torpedoes (destructive globes of energy) can be fired on any alien craft that is in alignment (horizontally, vertically, or diagonally) with your ship. Their range is sufficient to strike any ship on your scanners, and a strike is always fatal. Select the Photon button from the control bar, and then enter a photon vector (see Figure 15.6). A vector of 0 shoots a photon torpedo straight up, a vector of 1 shoots up and to the right, a vector of 3 shoots directly right, and so on.

FIGURE 15.6

Entering the photon torpedo vector.

Firing a photon torpedo consumes no energy, but nothing comes for free. In order to fire photon torpedoes, your launchers must be in working order and you must have torpedoes on hand. At the start of the game you're given ten torpedoes, and you have to dock with a starbase to get more. Obviously, you're going to have to use them judiciously.

Ramming

If you find yourself in the midst of battle with all your weapon systems down, you can still defeat the aliens by ramming them with your ship. Because your ship is much larger than the aliens' ships, this will always be fatal to the enemy. However, resorting to such desperate measures may cause excessive damage to your ship. There's a one-in-ten chance that the damage will be sufficient to cripple your ship permanently, thus ending the game.

Starbases

When you set out from Titan Base, your ship will be carrying all the supplies it can hold. It'll be necessary to stock up at certain points in the game. For this reason, there are two starbases, one at each end of the galactic milieu.

The starbases move from game to game, and they won't be marked on the galactic map until you locate them—one of your top mission priorities, obviously. After you locate a starbase (see Figure 15.7), you must go to the short-range scanners and dock with the base by moving your ship on top of it. All your supplies will be restocked and all systems will be repaired.

> **Note**
>
> A starbase looks just like your starship, except that it's purple rather than green and has a colored background.

FIGURE 15.7

A starbase in the short-range scanner screen.

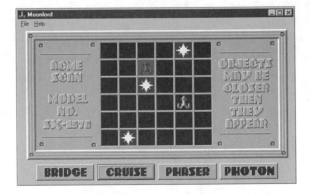

Building Moonlord's User Interface

The first step in building Moonlord's user interface is to create the editor's main form:

1. Start a new Standard EXE Visual Basic project.

2. Set the form's properties to the values listed here:

   AutoRedraw = True

   Caption = "Moonlord"

Height = 6645

ScaleMode = Pixel

Width = 8745

3. Set the form's `Icon` property to Moonlord.ico, which you can find in the Images\Moonlord directory of this book's CD-ROM.

   This icon will appear not only in the window's upper-left corner, but also in Windows Explorer and on the taskbar when the program's window has been minimized.

4. Add a PictureBox control to the form, giving it the following property settings:

   Name = picScreen

   AutoRedraw = True

   AutoSize = True

   BorderStyle = None

   Font = MS Sans Serif, Bold, 8-point

   ForeColor = Red (use the Palette tab)

   Left = 16

   ScaleMode = Pixel

   Top = 5

   This PictureBox control will hold the graphics for each of the game's three screens—the long-range, short-range, and status displays.

5. Set the PictureBox control's `Picture` property to the MainScreen.bmp picture file, which you can find in the Images\Moonlord directory of this book's CD-ROM.

   When the game begins, the screen image stored in the MainScreen.bmp file is what the player first sees.

6. Add four CommandButton controls to the form, giving them the following property settings. You can find the buttons' picture files in the Images\Moonlord directory of this book's CD-ROM.

   Button #1

   Caption = ""

   Height = 33

   Left = 36

   Picture = CrusBut.bmp

   Style = Graphical

   Top = 281

   Width = 121

Button #2

Caption = ""

Height = 33

Left = 164

Picture = ScanBut.bmp

Style = Graphical

Top = 281

Width = 121

Button #3

Caption = ""

Height = 33

Left = 292

Picture = StatBut.bmp

Style = Graphical

Top = 281

Width = 121

Button #4

Caption = ""

Height = 33

Left = 419

Picture = WarpBut.bmp

Style = Graphical

Top = 281

Width = 121

These four buttons make up the control panel for the game's three screens. The commands issued by the buttons depend upon the currently visible screen. On the main screen, for example, the four buttons issue the long-range cruise, short-range scan, status, and warp commands. On the short-range scan screen, however, these buttons issue the bridge, short-range cruise, phaser, and photon commands. Only two of the buttons appear on the status screen, issuing the bridge and repair commands.

7. Add 11 Image controls to the form, giving them the following property settings:

Image Control #1

Name = imgMarker

Left = 64

Picture = Marker.bmp

Top = 330

Image Control #2

Name = imgEmpty

Left = 94

Picture = Empty.bmp

Top = 330

Image Control #3

Name = imgOccupied

Left = 125

Picture = Occupied.bmp

Top = 330

Image Control #4

Name = imgCross

Left = 155

Picture = Cross.bmp

Top = 330

Image Control #5

Name = imgClear

Left = 186

Picture = Clear.bmp

Top = 330

Image Control #6

Name = imgAlien

Left = 230

Picture = AlienShp.bmp

Top = 330

15

Image Control #7
Name = imgSun

Left = 275

Picture = Sun.bmp

Top = 330

Image Control #8
Name = imgStarship

Left = 319

Picture = Starship.bmp

Top = 330

Image Control #9
Name = imgBase

Left = 364

Picture = Base.bmp

Top = 330

Image Control #10
Name = imgPhaser

Left = 408

Picture = Phaser.bmp

Top = 330

Image Control #11
Name = imgAlienShoot

Left = 453

Picture = AlienShoot.bmp

Top = 330

These are just some of the images required by the game. This set of image controls holds the pictures needed to display each sector of the long-range scan screen and the short-range scan screen, with the exception of the pictures used in the various animations.

15

8. Add the menus shown in Figure 15.8, naming them mnuFile, mnuNewGame, mnuHelp, and mnuAbout.

FIGURE 15.8

Moonlord's menus.

9. Save your work, naming the form Moonlord.frm and the project Moonlord.vbp.

Your form should now look something like Figure 15.9.

FIGURE 15.9

The completed form.

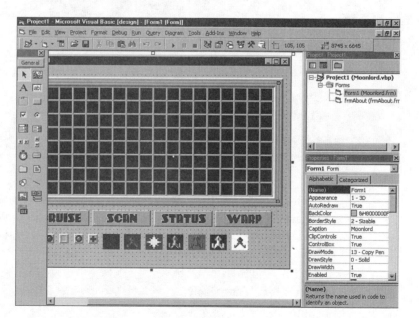

Adding the About Dialog Box

To complete this part of the Moonlord project, you must add the game's About dialog box:

1. Select the Project menu's Add Form command. When the Add Form dialog box appears (see Figure 15.10), double-click the About Dialog icon.

   As you can see in the Add Form dialog box, Visual Basic provides a number of prefab forms that you can add to your project and modify as needed.

FIGURE 15.10

The Add Form dialog box.

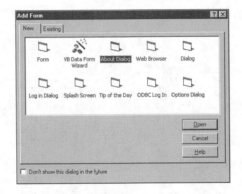

2. Give the lblTitle Label control the following property settings:

   Font = MS Sans Serif, Bold, 18-point

   Height = 331

   Left = 986

   Top = 165

   Width = 3648

   You don't need to set the label's Caption property because Visual Basic picks up the name of the application from the main form's name. You can change this type of automatically configured information from the Project Properties dialog box, as shown in Figure 15.11. To display this dialog box, select the Project menu's Properties command.

3. Give the form's lblDescription Label control the following property settings:

   Caption = "By Clayton Walnum"

   Height = 186

   Left = 986

   Top = 776

   Width = 3648

FIGURE 15.11

The Project Properties dialog box.

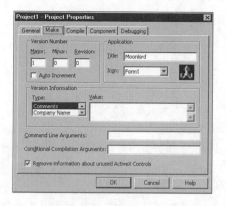

15

4. Add a Label control to the dialog box, giving it the following property settings:

   Caption = "Copyright 2000 by Macmillan Computer Publishing"

   Height = 196

   Left = 971

   Top = 993

   Width = 3620

5. On the cmdOK CommandButton control, change the following properties to the values shown:

   Height = 238

   Left = 718

   Top = 1366

   Width = 1183

6. On the cmdSysInfo CommandButton control, change the following properties to the values shown:

   Height = 238

   Left = 2662

   Top = 1366

   Width = 1183

7. Delete the "Warning" Label control from the dialog box.

8. Delete the two Shape controls (they look like lines) from the dialog box.

9. Give the About form the following property settings:

    Name = frmAbout

    Height = 2865

    Icon = Moonlord.ico

    Width = 4935

10. Set the `Picture` property of the `picIcon` object to the Moonlord.ico file.

11. Save the project, giving the About dialog box form the name frmAbout.frm.

At this point, your new About dialog box should look like Figure 15.12. Of course, you can make it look any way you like. The preceding steps only demonstrate how to use one of VB's predefined forms in your programs and how to edit it to fit your needs.

FIGURE 15.12

The new About dialog box.

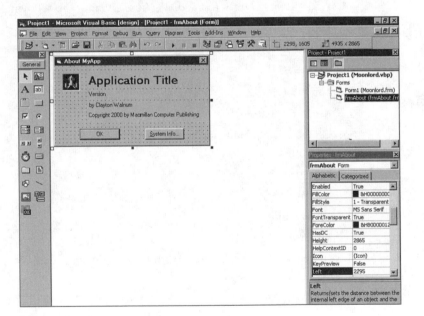

Summary

You've now completed Moonlord's user interface. You can run the program now, if you like, but it still needs a boatload of source code, graphical images, and sound effects before it will be complete. You'll start adding the source code in tomorrow's lesson.

Q&A

Q Come on, this game is impossible! I didn't even come close to winning.

A Like most strategy games, you have to learn to make the best of every move. Learning to travel the galactic milieu and to use your weapons in the most efficient manner possible is all part of becoming a Moonlord expert. (I'm the game's creator, and it even took me a while to get to the point where I could beat the game now and then.)

Q Where's the code that makes Visual Basic's predefined forms work (such as the About dialog box)?

A The predefined forms that come with Visual Basic are really no different than the forms you create yourself. If you double-click one of the forms (after adding it to your project, of course), you can see the source code that Microsoft's programmers provided for it. You can learn some cool stuff by examining this source code.

Q I finished building this part of the Moonlord project, but when I run it, all the images under the buttons show up. Did I do something wrong?

A Nope. Those images will disappear when you start adding source code to the program. Specifically, the program will change the height of the form so that the Image controls under the buttons are no longer visible. If the images really bug you, though, you can set all their `Visible` properties to `False`.

Workshop

The workshop includes quiz questions to help gauge your grasp of the material. You'll find the answers to this quiz in Appendix A. Even if you feel that you totally understand the concepts presented here, you should work through the quiz anyway. (Note that because today's lesson and the following Moonlord project lessons are extended exercises that draw upon previous chapters in the book, this chapter has no formal exercises after the quiz.)

Quiz

1. Explain how the picScreen PictureBox control in Moonlord's main form enables the form to act as the container for all three of Moonlord's game screens.

2. How do the four CommandButton controls help implement the different Moonlord game screens?

3. What is the purpose of all the Image controls you added to the main form?

4. Why does the About dialog box display the title "Application Title" at design time and the title "Moonlord" at runtime?

5. Where can you find the settings that Visual Basic uses for some of the strings in the About dialog box?

WEEK 3

DAY 16

Tracking Game Information: The Moonlord Project

Now that you've put together the game's main user interface, it's time to add the source code that makes the game work. The first part of that source code is the game's variables and constants, as well as the subroutines that initialize the variables.

Today you'll do the following:

- Define Moonlord's constants and variables
- Initialize the game's variables
- Study the game's variables
- Learn how the initialization routines work

Adding Enumerations, Constants, and Variables to Moonlord

In this section, you'll start adding source code to the Moonlord project you started in yesterday's lesson. First, you'll add enumeration, constant, and variable definitions to the program. Then you'll add the source code that initializes the game's variables to their starting values.

Adding the Declarations

1. Add the following enumerations to the main form's code window. You can type in the source code or copy it from the Moonlord1.txt file in the Chap16\Code directory:

```
 1:  '================================================
 2:  ' Moonlord for Visual Basic 6
 3:  '    by Clayton Walnum
 4:  ' Copyright 2000 by Macmillan Computer Publishing
 5:  '================================================
 6:  Option Explicit
 7:
 8:  '================================================
 9:  ' Enumerations.
10:  '================================================
11:  Public Enum GameModes
12:      MAINSCREEN
13:      SHORTSCANSCREEN
14:      STATSCREEN
15:      CRUISE
16:      SHORTCRUISE
17:      BATTLE
18:      WARP
19:      PHASER
20:      PHOTON
21:  End Enum
22:
23:  Public Enum Sectors
24:      CLEARSEC
25:      ALIENSSEC
26:      BASESEC
27:      SUNSEC
28:      STARSHIPSEC
29:  End Enum
30:
31:  Public Enum Stats
32:      TIMESTAT
33:      NUMOFALIENS
34:      PHOTONS
```

```
35:    ENERGY
36: End Enum
37:
38: Public Enum Systems
39:    WARPENGINES
40:    CRUISEENGINES
41:    SHORTRANGESCAN
42:    LONGRANGESCAN
43:    PHASERGUNS
44:    PHOTONLAUNCHER
45: End Enum
46:
47: Public Enum BlinkModes
48:    PLAYER
49:    OTHER
50: End Enum
51:
52: Public Enum GameResults
53:    GAMESTILLGOING
54:    GAMEWON
55:    GAMELOST
56: End Enum
```

16

ANALYSIS These enumerations define constants in groups of related values. For example, the Systems enumeration defines constants with values from 0 to 5 that will act as indexes into the array that holds information about the starship's systems.

2. Add the following constants to the main form's code window, beneath the declarations you added in Step 1. You can type in the source code or copy it from the Moonlord2.txt file in the Chap16\Code directory:

```
1:  '=================================================
2:  ' Constants.
3:  '=================================================
4:  Const OPERABLE = 0
5:  Const OFFSET = 25
6:  Const SHORTRANGEOFFSETX = 157
7:  Const SHORTRANGEOFFSETY = 26
8:  Const SECTORSIZE = 28
9:  Const SHORTRANGESECTORSIZEX = 39
10: Const SHORTRANGESECTORSIZEY = 36
11: Const SECTORCOUNT = 144
12: Const SHORTRANGESECTORCOUNT = 36
13: Const SHORTRANGECOLUMNCOUNT = 6
14: Const COLUMNCOUNT = 18
15: Const ROWCOUNT = 8
16: Const PLAYERSTARTSECTOR = 81
17: Const GRIDLOWX = 24
18: Const GRIDHIGHX = 521
19: Const GRIDLOWY = 23
```

```
20: Const GRIDHIGHY = 240
21: Const SHORTRANGEGRIDHIGHY = 235
22: Const SHORTRANGEGRIDLOWX = 157
23: Const SHORTRANGEGRIDHIGHX = 385
24: Const SHORTRANGEGRIDLOWY = 25
25: Const MAXALIENS = 50
26: Const MAXTIME = 100
27: Const MAXENERGY = 600
28: Const MAXPHOTONS = 10
29: Const PHOTONSPEED = 4
30: Const SUNYELLOW = 65535
31: Const ALIENBLUE = 8388608
```

ANALYSIS As you'll see later today, these constants define symbols for values that the program uses often. Defining a set of symbols like this and using them in your programming makes the source code easier to read and understand.

3. Add the following variables to the main form's code window, beneath the declarations you added in Step 2. You can type in the source code or copy it from the Moonlord3.txt file in the Chap16\Code directory:

```
 1: '================================================
 2: ' Global Variables.
 3: '================================================
 4: Dim GameMode As GameModes
 5: Dim BlinkMode As BlinkModes
 6: Dim Board(SECTORCOUNT - 1) As Integer
 7: Dim Drawn(SECTORCOUNT - 1) As Boolean
 8: Dim ShortRangeContents(SECTORCOUNT - 1, _
 9:      SHORTRANGESECTORCOUNT - 1)
10: Dim SystemStats(5) As Integer
11: Dim GameStats(3) As Integer
12: Dim AlienDamage(1) As Integer
13: Dim AlienPosition(1) As Integer
14: Dim GameOver As Integer
15: Dim PlayerSector As Integer
16: Dim ShortRangePlayerSector As Integer
17: Dim OldShortRangePlayerSector As Integer
18: Dim NumAliensDestroyed As Integer
19: Dim VectorsX1(8) As Integer
20: Dim VectorsY1(8) As Integer
21: Dim SystemNames(5) As String
```

ANALYSIS These variables represent all the data needed by the game as a whole. Later today, you'll see specifically how the program uses these values.

Adding the Initialization Code

1. Add the following form and menu handlers to the code window beneath the declarations you added in the previous section. You can type in the source code or copy it from the Moonlord4.txt file in the Chap16\Code directory:

```
1:  '====================================================
2:  ' Form Handlers.
3:  '====================================================
4:  Private Sub Form_Load()
5:     Form1.Height = 5505
6:     Form1.Width = 8745
7:     InitProgramVariables
8:  End Sub
9:
10: '====================================================
11: ' Menu Handlers.
12: '====================================================
13: Private Sub mnuNewGame_Click()
14:    InitGame
15:    Command1.Enabled = True
16:    Command2.Enabled = True
17:    Command3.Enabled = True
18:    Command4.Enabled = True
19: End Sub
```

ANALYSIS When the program starts, the Form_Load event handler sets the form's size and calls the InitProgramVariables subroutine, which initializes program variables.

2. Add the following initialization subroutines to the code window. You can type in the source code or copy it from the Moonlord5.txt file in the Chap16\Code directory:

```
1:  '====================================================
2:  ' Game Initialization.
3:  '====================================================
4:  Sub InitGame()
5:     Randomize
6:     InitGameVariables
7:     InitBoard
8:  InitShortRangeContents
9:  End Sub
10:
11: Sub InitProgramVariables()
12:    VectorsX1(0) = 0
13:    VectorsX1(1) = 1
14:    VectorsX1(2) = 1
15:    VectorsX1(3) = 1
16:    VectorsX1(4) = 0
17:    VectorsX1(5) = -1
18:    VectorsX1(6) = -1
```

```
19:     VectorsX1(7) = -1
20:     VectorsY1(0) = -1
21:     VectorsY1(1) = -1
22:     VectorsY1(2) = 0
23:     VectorsY1(3) = 1
24:     VectorsY1(4) = 1
25:     VectorsY1(5) = 1
26:     VectorsY1(6) = 0
27:     VectorsY1(7) = -1
28:     SystemNames(0) = "Warp Engines"
29:     SystemNames(1) = "Cruise Engines"
30:     SystemNames(2) = "Short Range Scan"
31:     SystemNames(3) = "Long Range Scan"
32:     SystemNames(4) = "Phasers"
33:     SystemNames(5) = "Photon Launcher"
34: End Sub
35:
36: Sub InitGameVariables()
37:     Dim i As Integer
38:     GameMode = MAINSCREEN
39:     GameOver = GAMESTILLGOING
40:     PlayerSector = PLAYERSTARTSECTOR
41:     BlinkMode = PLAYER
42:     NumAliensDestroyed = 0
43:     For i = 0 To 5
44:        SystemStats(i) = OPERABLE
45:     Next
46:     GameStats(TIMESTAT) = MAXTIME
47:     GameStats(NUMOFALIENS) = MAXALIENS
48:     GameStats(ENERGY) = MAXENERGY
49:     GameStats(PHOTONS) = MAXPHOTONS
50: End Sub
```

ANALYSIS InitGame is a top-level initialization subroutine that calls the other subroutines that actually perform the game initialization. The InitProgramVariables subroutine initializes variables whose values don't change in the game, and the InitGameVariables subroutine initializes variables that must be reinitialized each time a new game starts.

3. Add the following secondary initialization subroutines to the code window. You can type in the source code or copy it from the Moonlord6.txt file in the Chap16\Code directory:

```
1:  Sub InitBoard()
2:     ClearGameBoard
3:     PlaceAliens
4:     PlaceStarBases
5:  End Sub
6:
7:  Sub PlaceStarBases()
```

```
 8:    Dim column As Integer
 9:    Dim row As Integer
10:    Dim sector As Integer
11:    While Board(sector) <> BASESEC
12:      column = Int(4 * Rnd)
13:      row = Int(ROWCOUNT * Rnd)
14:      sector = row * COLUMNCOUNT + column
15:      If Board(sector) = CLEARSEC Then Board(sector) = BASESEC
16:    Wend
17:    sector = 14
18:    While Board(sector) <> BASESEC
19:      column = Int((4 * Rnd) + COLUMNCOUNT - 4)
20:      row = Int(ROWCOUNT * Rnd)
21:      sector = row * COLUMNCOUNT + column
22:      If Board(sector) = CLEARSEC Then Board(sector) = BASESEC
23:    Wend
24: End Sub
25:
26: Sub PlaceAliens()
27:    Dim placed As Boolean
28:    Dim i As Integer
29:    Dim column As Integer
30:    Dim row As Integer
31:    Dim sector As Integer
32:    For i = 0 To (MAXALIENS / 2) - 1
33:      placed = False
34:      While (Not placed)
35:        column = Int(COLUMNCOUNT * Rnd)
36:        row = Int(ROWCOUNT * Rnd)
37:        sector = row * COLUMNCOUNT + column
38:        If Board(sector) = CLEARSEC And _
39:            sector <> PLAYERSTARTSECTOR Then
40:          Board(sector) = ALIENSSEC
41:    placed = True
42:        End If
43:      Wend
44:    Next
45: End Sub
46:
47: Sub ClearGameBoard()
48:    Dim i As Integer
49:    For i = 0 To SECTORCOUNT - 1
50:      Board(i) = CLEARSEC
51:      Drawn(i) = False
52:    Next
53: End Sub
54:
55: Sub InitShortRangeContents()
56:    ClearShortRangeSectors
57:    PlaceShortScanSuns
58:    PlaceShortScanAliens
```

```
59:    PlaceShortScanBases
60:    PlaceShortScanStarships
61: End Sub
62:
63: Sub ClearShortRangeSectors()
64:    Dim sector As Integer
65:    Dim ShortRangeSector As Integer
66:    For sector = 0 To SECTORCOUNT - 1
67:      For ShortRangeSector = 0 To SHORTRANGESECTORCOUNT - 1
68:        ShortRangeContents(sector, ShortRangeSector) = CLEARSEC
69:      Next ShortRangeSector
70:    Next sector
71: End Sub
72:
73: Sub PlaceShortScanSuns()
74:    Dim sector As Integer
75:    Dim GotThreeSuns As Boolean
76:    Dim ClearSector As Integer
77:    For sector = 0 To SECTORCOUNT - 1
78:      ClearSector = Int(SHORTRANGESECTORCOUNT * Rnd)
79:      ShortRangeContents(sector, ClearSector) = SUNSEC
80:      ClearSector = GetClearShortRangeSector(sector)
81:      ShortRangeContents(sector, ClearSector) = SUNSEC
82:      GotThreeSuns = Int(2 * Rnd)
83:      If GotThreeSuns Then
84:        ClearSector = GetClearShortRangeSector(sector)
85:        ShortRangeContents(sector,  ClearSector) = SUNSEC
86:      End If
87:    Next
88: End Sub
89:
90: Sub PlaceShortScanAliens()
91:    Dim sector As Integer
92:    Dim ClearSector As Integer
93:    For sector = 0 To SECTORCOUNT - 1
94:      If Board(sector) = ALIENSSEC Then
95:        ClearSector = GetClearShortRangeSector(sector)
96:        ShortRangeContents(sector, ClearSector) = ALIENSSEC
97:        ClearSector = GetClearShortRangeSector(sector)
98:        ShortRangeContents(sector, ClearSector) = ALIENSSEC
99:      End If
100:   Next
101:End Sub
102:
103:Sub PlaceShortScanBases()
104:   Dim sector As Integer
105:   Dim ClearSector As Integer
106:   For sector = 0 To SECTORCOUNT - 1
107:     If Board(sector) = BASESEC Then
108:       ClearSector = GetClearShortRangeSector(sector)
109:       ShortRangeContents(sector, ClearSector) = BASESEC
```

```
110:    End If
111:  Next
112:End Sub
113:
114:Sub PlaceShortScanStarships()
115:  Dim sector As Integer
116:  Dim ClearSector As Integer
117:  For sector = 0 To SECTORCOUNT - 1
118:    ClearSector = GetClearShortRangeSector(sector)
119:    ShortRangeContents(sector, ClearSector) = STARSHIPSEC
120:  Next
121:End Sub
```

ANALYSIS These initialization subroutines get the game board ready for play by filling the game universe with aliens, suns, and bases.

4. Add the following function to the bottom of the code window. You can type in the source code or copy it from the Moonlord7.txt file in the Chap16\Code directory:

```
1:  '================================================
2:  ' Game Functions.
3:  '================================================
4:  Function GetClearShortRangeSector(sector As Integer) As Integer
5:    Dim GotClearSector As Boolean
6:    Dim ShortRangeSector As Integer
7:    GotClearSector = False
8:    While Not GotClearSector
9:      ShortRangeSector = Int(SHORTRANGESECTORCOUNT * Rnd)
10:     If ShortRangeContents(sector, ShortRangeSector) = CLEARSEC _
11:       Then GotClearSector = True
12:    Wend
13:    GetClearShortRangeSector = ShortRangeSector
14: End Function
```

Understanding Moonlord's Initialization

As you've seen, Moonlord features a large set of constants and variables. Because of the size and complexity of this variable set, it takes a lot of source code to initialize a game. In this section, you'll examine the initialization part of the Moonlord project in detail so that you understand what all the variables and constants do.

Moonlord's Variables and Constants

Moonlord relies on a set of global variables and constants that the program declares near the top of the source code. Table 16.1 describes Moonlord's constants, Table 16.2 describes the constants defined as enumerations, and Table 16.3 describes the game's global variables.

TABLE 16.1   Moonlord's Constants

Constant	Description
ALIENBLUE	The background color of an alien sector in the short-range scanner screen
COLUMNCOUNT	The number of columns in the long-range scanner screen
GRIDHIGHX	The highest valid X coordinate for mouse clicks on the long-range scanner screen
GRIDHIGHY	The highest valid Y coordinate for mouse clicks on the long-range scanner screen
GRIDLOWX	The lowest valid X coordinate for mouse clicks on the long-range scanner screen
GRIDLOWY	The lowest valid Y coordinate for mouse clicks on the long-range scanner screen
MAXALIENS	The maximum number of aliens in the game's universe
MAXENERGY	The maximum amount of energy the player can have
MAXPHOTONS	The maximum number of photons the player can have
MAXSUNS	The maximum number of suns in the game's universe
MAXTIME	The maximum amount of time the player has to complete the game
OFFSET	The distance from the left and top edges of the PictureBox control to the left and top edges of the long-range scanner grid
OPERABLE	A value that indicates that a ship system is operational
PHOTONSPEED	The speed at which the photon animation runs
PLAYERSTARTSECTOR	The long-range scanner sector at which the player begins the game
ROWCOUNT	The number of rows in the long-range scanner screen
SECTORCOUNT	The number of sectors in the long-range scanner screen
SECTORSIZE	The width and height in pixels of a sector in the long-range scanner screen
SHORTRANGECOLUMNCOUNT	The number of columns in the short-range scanner screen
SHORTRANGEGRIDHIGHX	The highest valid X coordinate for mouse clicks on the short-range scanner screen
SHORTRANGEGRIDHIGHY	The highest valid Y coordinate for mouse clicks on the short-range scanner screen
SHORTRANGEGRIDLOWX	The lowest valid X coordinate for mouse clicks on the short-range scanner screen
SHORTRANGEGRIDLOWY	The lowest valid Y coordinate for mouse clicks on the short-range scanner screen

TABLE 16.1   continued

Constant	Description
SHORTRANGEOFFSETX	The distance in pixels from the left edge of the PictureBox control to the left edge of the short-range scanner grid
SHORTRANGEOFFSETY	The distance in pixels from the top edge of the PictureBox control to the top edge of the short-range scanner grid
SHORTRANGESECTORCOUNT	The number of sectors in the short-range scanner screen
SHORTRANGESECTORSIZEX	The horizontal size in pixels of a sector in the short-range scanner screen
SHORTRANGESECTORSIZEY	The vertical size in pixels of a sector in the short-range scanner screen
SUNYELLOW	The color of a sun in the short-range scanner screen

TABLE 16.2   Moonlord's Enumerations

Constant	Defining Enumeration	Description
ALIENSSEC	Sectors	A value that indicates that there are aliens in the short-range scanner sector
BASESEC	Sectors	A value that indicates that there is a base in the short-range scanner sector
BATTLE	GameModes	A value that indicates that the player is currently in battle with aliens
CLEARSEC	Sectors	A value that indicates that there is nothing in the short-range scanner sector
CRUISE	GameModes	A value that indicates that the player is currently selecting a sector to which to cruise in the long-range scanner display
CRUISEENGINES	Systems	The index into the SystemStats() array for the cruise engines
ENERGY	Stats	The index into the GameStats() array for the player's remaining energy
GAMELOST	GameResults	A value that indicates that the game is over and the player has lost
GAMESTILLGOING	GameResults	A value that indicates that the player has not yet won or lost

TABLE 16.2   continued

Constant	Defining Enumeration	Description
GAMEWON	GameResults	A value that indicates that the game is over and the player has won
LONGRANGESCAN	Systems	The index into the SystemStats() array for the long-range scanners
MAINSCREEN	GameModes	A value that indicates that the player is currently in none of the other game modes
NUMOFALIENS	Stats	The index into the GameStats() array for the remaining number of aliens
OTHER	BlinkModes	A value that indicates that the sector graphic that shows the contents of the sector is the next graphic to draw in the blinking animation
PHASER	GameModes	A value that indicates that the player is currently using his phaser weapon system
PHASERGUNS	Systems	The index into the SystemStats() array for the phasers
PHOTON	GameModes	A value that indicates that the player is currently using his photon weapon system
PHOTONLAUNCHER	Systems	The index into the SystemStats() array for the photon launchers
PHOTONS	Stats	The index into the GameStats() array for the player's remaining photons
PLAYER	BlinkModes	A value that indicates that the next sector graphic to draw in the blinking animation is the player's marker
SHORTCRUISE	GameModes	A value that indicates that the player is currently selecting a sector to which to cruise in the short-range scanner display
SHORTRANGESCAN	Systems	The index into the SystemStats() array for the short-range scanners
SHORTSCANSCREEN	GameModes	A value that indicates that the player is currently viewing the short-range scanner screen
STARSHIPSEC	Sectors	A value that indicates that the player's starship is in the short-range scanner sector
STATSCREEN	GameModes	A value that indicates that the player is currently viewing the status scanner screen

TABLE 16.2 continued

Constant	Defining Enumeration	Description
SUNSEC	Sectors	A value that indicates that there is a sun in the short-range scanner sector
TIMESTAT	Stats	The index into the GameStats() array for the player's remaining time
WARP	GameModes	A value that indicates that the player is currently warping
WARPENGINES	Systems	The index into the SystemStats() array for the warp engines

TABLE 16.3 Moonlord's Global Variables

Variable	Type	Description
AlienDamage()	Integer	An array that contains the remaining damage for each of the two aliens in the short-range scanner screen
AlienPosition()	Integer	An array that contains the position of each of the two aliens in the short-range scanner screen
BlinkMode	BlinkModes	The current blink mode (the blink mode controls which long-range scanner sector image is displayed in the blinking sector)
Board()	Integer	An array that contains the contents of each sector in the long-range scanner screen
Drawn()	Boolean	An array that indicates which sectors in the long-range scanner screen have been drawn
GameMode	GameModes	Keeps track of the current game mode
GameOver	Integer	A value that indicates whether the game is running, the game is over and the player has won, or the game is over and the player has lost
GameStats()	Integer	An array that holds the status for the game values, such as the time remaining and the number of aliens still to find
NumAliensDestroyed	Integer	The number of aliens destroyed in the current short-range scanner sector

TABLE 16.3   continued

Variable	Type	Description
OldShortRangePlayerSector	Integer	The short-range scanner sector that the player occupied before moving
PlayerSector	Integer	The long-range scanner sector in which the player is currently located
ShortRangeContents()	Integer	The locations of all the suns, bases, aliens, and starships in the short-range grids
ShortRangePlayerSector	Integer	The short-range scanner sector in which the player is currently located
SystemNames()	String	An array containing the names of all ship systems
SystemStats()	Integer	An array that holds the current status of each ship system
VectorsX1()	Integer	A table of horizontal vectors used when calculating the movement of a photon
VectorsY1()	Integer	A table of vertical vectors used when calculating the movement of a photon

Initializing the Program Variables

I'm using the term *program variables* here to mean variables that the program must initialize only once, when the program first starts up. That is, if the player starts a new game without rerunning the program, the values of the program variables don't change. In Moonlord, these variables are three arrays. The first two, named VectorsX1() and VectorsY1(), are initialized as shown in Listing 16.1.

LISTING 16.1   Initializing the Vector Arrays

```
 1:    VectorsX1(0) = 0
 2:    VectorsX1(1) = 1
 3:    VectorsX1(2) = 1
 4:    VectorsX1(3) = 1
 5:    VectorsX1(4) = 0
 6:    VectorsX1(5) = -1
 7:    VectorsX1(6) = -1
 8:    VectorsX1(7) = -1
 9:    VectorsY1(0) = -1
10:    VectorsY1(1) = -1
11:    VectorsY1(2) = 0
12:    VectorsY1(3) = 1
```

LISTING 16.1   continued

```
13:    VectorsY1(4) = 1
14:    VectorsY1(5) = 1
15:    VectorsY1(6) = 0
16:    VectorsY1(7) = -1
```

ANALYSIS   The VectorsX1() and VectorsY1() arrays hold the vectors needed to animate a
photon. The numbers in VectorsX1() represent the required horizontal movement for each of eight directions, and VectorsY1() holds the same types of values for
vertical movement. For example, if the photon is supposed to travel directly upwards (the
player has chosen vector 0), the program gets the value 0 from VectorsX1(0) and the
value -1 from VectorsY1(0). By moving the photon 0 units horizontally and -1 units vertically, you make the photon move straight up the screen.

Another variable that must be initialized is the SystemNames() array, which holds the
names for each of the starship's systems. Listing 16.2 shows how the program initializes
this array.

LISTING 16.2   Initializing the SystemNames() Array

```
1:    SystemNames(0) = "Warp Engines"
2:    SystemNames(1) = "Cruise Engines"
3:    SystemNames(2) = "Short Range Scan"
4:    SystemNames(3) = "Long Range Scan"
5:    SystemNames(4) = "Phasers"
6:    SystemNames(5) = "Photon Launcher"
```

Initializing the Game Variables

I use the term *game variables* to mean variables that must be initialized at the beginning
of each new game. The program initializes one set of these variables in the
InitGameVariables subroutine, which first sets a couple of mode values:

```
GameMode = MAINSCREEN
GameOver = GAMESTILLGOING
```

The GameMode variable tracks what the player is currently doing. For example, if the
player is viewing the short-range scanner screen, GameMode is equal to SHORTSCANSCREEN.
The program uses the current mode to set buttons and to prevent the user from doing
things he shouldn't. If the player is in the CRUISE mode, for example, it means that he
has pressed the Cruise button on the long-range scanner screen and is about to select a
sector to which to move. You don't want the player to be able to click the Status button at

this time, so the CRUISE mode tells the program to disable that button. The various game modes are defined in the GameModes enumeration.

The GameOver mode variable can be one of three values: GAMESTILLGOING, GAMEONE, or GAMELOST. These modes are pretty self-explanatory and are defined in the GameResults enumeration.

Next, InitGameVariables initializes PlayerSector, BlinkMode, and NumAliensDestroyed:

```
PlayerSector = PLAYERSTARTSECTOR
BlinkMode = PLAYER
NumAliensDestroyed = 0
```

The PlayerSector variable holds the player's current location on the long-range scanner screen, BlinkMode helps control the blinking sector animation (as you'll see in an upcoming lesson), and NumAliensDestroyed tracks how many of the aliens in the current short-range scanner sector have been defeated. You'll see all these variables in action as you add more and more source code to the program.

InitGameVariables then sets all the starship systems to their undamaged condition:

```
For i = 0 To 5
  SystemStats(i) = OPERABLE
Next
```

If one of the elements of the SystemStats() array is set to something other than OPERABLE, that system can no longer be used.

Finally, InitGameVariables takes care of the GameStats() array:

```
GameStats(TIMESTAT) = MAXTIME
GameStats(NUMOFALIENS) = MAXALIENS
GameStats(ENERGY) = MAXENERGY
GameStats(PHOTONS) = MAXPHOTONS
```

You can tell which values this array holds by the names of the constants used as indexes into the array. As for how the game uses these values? If the player runs out of time or energy, the game is over. If he runs out of photons, the photon launcher will no longer work. Finally, if the player runs out of aliens, he's won the game.

Initializing the Game Board

The biggest task in setting up a game of Moonlord is initializing the game's universe with its contents. The first step, which happens in the ClearGameBoard subroutine, is to empty the game's universe and mark each sector as being undrawn (not yet displayed on the screen):

```
For i = 0 To SECTORCOUNT - 1
  Board(i) = CLEARSEC
  Drawn(i) = False
Next
```

Next, the program must place 25 pairs of aliens, as shown in Listing 16.3.

LISTING 16.3   Placing the Aliens

```
 1:    For i = 0 To (MAXALIENS / 2) - 1
 2:      placed = False
 3:      While (Not placed)
 4:        column = Int(COLUMNCOUNT * Rnd)
 5:        row = Int(ROWCOUNT * Rnd)
 6:        sector = row * COLUMNCOUNT + column
 7:        If Board(sector) = CLEARSEC And _
 8:            sector <> PLAYERSTARTSECTOR Then
 9:          Board(sector) = ALIENSSEC
10:          placed = True
11:        End If
12:      Wend
13:    Next
```

ANALYSIS   Each time through the For loop, the program places one pair of aliens. Inside the loop, the program calculates a random row and column. If the sector at that row and column is currently empty, the program places the aliens there.

The program must also place two starbases, one at each end of the game board. The PlaceStarBases subroutine handles this task. The subroutine places the first starbase as shown in Listing 16.4. PlaceStarBases places the second starbase similarly.

LISTING 16.4   Placing a Starbase

```
 1:    While Board(sector) <> BASESEC
 2:      column = Int(4 * Rnd)
 3:      row = Int(ROWCOUNT * Rnd)
 4:      sector = row * COLUMNCOUNT + column
 5:      If Board(sector) = CLEARSEC Then Board(sector) = BASESEC
 6:    Wend
```

ANALYSIS   To place a starbase, the program gets a random column and row in the first four columns of the board. If that sector is currently empty, the starbase is placed.

Otherwise, the While loop tries again to place the starbase. A similar While loop places the second starbase, but somewhere in the last four columns rather than in the first four.

Initializing the Short-Range Scanner Contents

Once the long-range scanner grid has been initialized, the contents of the game universe must be positioned within the short-range scanner grids. There is one short-range scanner grid for each sector in the long-range scanner grid, so there's a lot of work to be done. The InitShortRangeContents subroutine, shown in Listing 16.5, calls the various lower-level subroutines that perform each initialization task.

LISTING 16.5   The InitShortRangeContents Subroutine

```
1: Sub InitShortRangeContents()
2:    ClearShortRangeSectors
3:    PlaceShortScanSuns
4:    PlaceShortScanAliens
5:    PlaceShortScanBases
6:    PlaceShortScanStarships
7: End Sub
```

The first step is to call ClearShortRangeSectors, which sets all 25 short-range scanner sectors in each of the 144 long-range scanner sectors (that's a total of 3,600 short-range scanner sectors!) to their starting values, as shown here:

```
For sector = 0 To SECTORCOUNT - 1
  For ShortRangeSector = 0 To SHORTRANGESECTORCOUNT - 1
    ShortRangeContents(sector, ShortRangeSector) = CLEARSEC
  Next ShortRangeSector
Next sector
```

Now each sector must have two or three suns placed in the short-range grid. The PlaceShortScanSuns subroutine handles this task with a For loop, as shown in Listing 16.6.

LISTING 16.6   Placing Suns

```
1:    For sector = 0 To SECTORCOUNT - 1
2:      ClearSector = Int(SHORTRANGESECTORCOUNT * Rnd)
3:      ShortRangeContents(sector, ClearSector) = SUNSEC
4:      ClearSector = GetClearShortRangeSector(sector)
5:      ShortRangeContents(sector, ClearSector) = SUNSEC
6:      GotThreeSuns = Int(2 * Rnd)
7:      If GotThreeSuns Then
8:        ClearSector = GetClearShortRangeSector(sector)
```

LISTING 16.6   continued

```
 9:        ShortRangeContents(sector, ClearSector) = SUNSEC
10:     End If
11:  Next
```

ANALYSIS   Lines 2 and 3 place the first sun randomly in the short-range grid. Then, Line 4 calls GetClearShortRangeSector, which returns an empty random short-range scanner sector, after which Line 5 places the second sun in the selected sector. Line 6 determines whether this sector should have a third sun. If so, Lines 7 through 10 place the sun.

The program calls PlaceShortScanAliens to place the aliens in the short-range grids for each long-range scanner sector. Listing 16.7 shows the source code that actually places the aliens.

LISTING 16.7   Placing Aliens

```
1:  For sector = 0 To SECTORCOUNT - 1
2:    If Board(sector) = ALIENSSEC Then
3:      ClearSector = GetClearShortRangeSector(sector)
4:      ShortRangeContents(sector, ClearSector) = ALIENSSEC
5:      ClearSector = GetClearShortRangeSector(sector)
6:      ShortRangeContents(sector, ClearSector) = ALIENSSEC
7:    End If
8:  Next
```

ANALYSIS   The For loop starting in Line 1 iterates through each of the long-range scanner sectors. If the current sector contains aliens (Line 2), Lines 3 through 6 place the aliens randomly in the short-range grid, using the same method used to place the suns.

The program positions the two bases in the short-range grids in much the same way it placed the suns and aliens, as shown in Listing 16.8.

LISTING 16.8   Placing the Starbases

```
1:  For sector = 0 To SECTORCOUNT - 1
2:    If Board(sector) = BASESEC Then
3:      ClearSector = GetClearShortRangeSector(sector)
4:      ShortRangeContents(sector, ClearSector) = BASESEC
5:    End If
6:  Next
```

16

Finally, the program uses the same method yet again to initialize where the player's ship will appear in each short-range scanner sector:

```
For sector = 0 To SECTORCOUNT - 1
  ClearSector = GetClearShortRangeSector(sector)
  ShortRangeContents(sector, ClearSector) = STARSHIPSEC
Next
```

At this point, the game is fully initialized and ready to go.

Summary

Moonlord has a lot of variables that must be declared and initialized before the game can begin. Initializing these variables requires more than setting a few simple values. Arrays that represent the contents of the game's universe must be filled, using techniques that can be a little tricky.

With the game initialized, it's time to let the game play begin. You'll program the game's main screen tomorrow.

Workshop

The workshop includes quiz questions to help gauge your grasp of the material. You'll find the answers to this quiz in Appendix A. Even if you feel that you totally understand the concepts presented here, you should work through the quiz anyway.

Quiz

1. What's the difference between program variables and game variables?
2. What do the values in the `VectorsX1()` and `VectorsY1()` arrays mean?
3. Explain how the program will use the `GameMode` variable and the `GameModes` enumeration.
4. What do the values stored in the `SystemStats()` array represent?
5. What do the values stored in the `GameStats()` array represent?
6. What do the `Board()` and `Drawn()` arrays represent?
7. In general, explain how the program positions objects in the short-range grids.
8. What's the difference between how the starbases are placed in the long-range grid and how aliens are placed?

Exercise

1. Compile your new version of Moonlord and ensure that it runs correctly. When you run the program, the program variables should initialize without error. Then, when you select the File menu's New Game command, the game variables should initialize without generating errors. Of course, at this point the game isn't playable. You still have a lot of source code to add.

16

DAY 17

Programming the Main Screen: The Moonlord Project

With Moonlord's user interface put together and the game's variables declared and initialized, it's time to start adding the source code that makes the game work. Today you'll get the main screen up and running so that you can cruise or warp to any sector in the game's universe. You'll also make your long-range scanner operational.

Specifically, today you'll learn the following:

- How to program the main game screen
- How the buttons issue their commands
- How the game implements the game commands
- How the game displays graphics on the main screen

Adding Graphics for the Main Screen

The first step in getting the game's main screen up and running is to add some graphical images needed by the buttons and the screen. These images are stored in separate forms. Perform the following steps to add the forms and graphics to the program:

1. Add a new form to the project and name it frmMainScreen.

2. Set the new form's Picture property to the MainScrn.bmp bitmap file that you can find in the Images\Moonlord directory of this book's CD-ROM. Figure 17.1 shows what the form should look like.

   The program will use the picture contained in this form to update the screen whenever the player moves from the short-range scanner or status screens back to the main screen (the long-range scanner screen).

FIGURE 17.1

The complete frmMainScreen form.

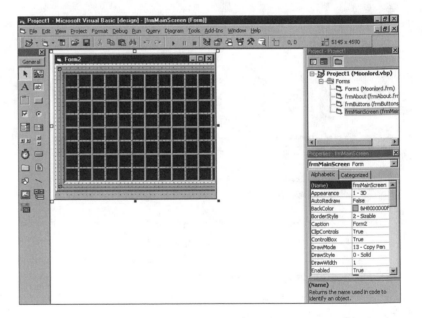

3. Add another form to the project and name it frmButtons.

4. Add eight Image controls to the frmButtons form, giving them the following property settings. When the form is complete, it should look like Figure 17.2.

   As the player moves from one game screen to another, the program must update the pictures displayed in the buttons. The program will get the graphics it needs to update the buttons from this form.

FIGURE 17.2

The complete frmButtons form.

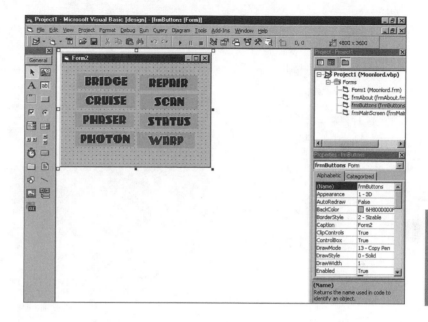

Image Control #1

Name = imgBridgeBut

Height = 480

Left = 450

Picture = BridgeBut.bmp

Top = 345

Width = 1860

Image Control #2

Name = imgCruiseBut

Height = 480

Left = 450

Picture = CrusBut.bmp

Top = 940

Width = 1860

Image Control #3

Name = imgPhaserBut

Height = 480

Left = 450

Picture = PhaserBut.bmp

Top = 1535

Width = 1860

Image Control #4

Name = imgPhotonBut

Height = 480

Left = 450

Picture = PhotonBut.bmp

Top = 2130

Width = 1860

Image Control #5

Name = imgRepairBut

Height = 480

Left = 2445

Picture = RepairBut.bmp

Top = 345

Width = 1860

Image Control #6

Name = imgScanBut

Height = 480

Left = 2445

Picture = ScanBut.bmp

Top = 940

Width = 1860

Image Control #7

Name = imgStatusBut

Height = 480

Left = 2445

Picture = StatBut.bmp

Top = 1535

Width = 1860

Image Control #8

Name = imgWarpBut

Height = 480

Left = 2445

Picture = WarpBut.bmp

Top = 2130

Width = 1860

5. Save your work, using the default names (frmButtons.frm and frmMainScreen.frm) for the new form files.

Updating Object Handlers

Now that you're making the main game screen functional, you need to update some object handlers and add a few new ones:

1. Replace the code in the mnuNewGame_Click event procedure with the following lines:

```
InitGame
picScreen.Picture = frmMainScreen.Picture
SetButtons
DrawSector PlayerSector
DoLongScan
```

2. Add the following Form_Unload procedure to the program, right after the Form_Load procedure:

```
Private Sub Form_Unload(Cancel As Integer)
  Unload frmButtons
  Unload frmMainScreen
End Sub
```

These lines remove the `frmButtons` and `frmMainScreen` forms from memory when the player exits the program.

3. Add the following line to the end of the Form_Load event procedure:

   ```
   DisableAllButtons
   ```

   The call to `DisableAllButtons` (a subroutine you'll add to the program later today) turns off all the game's command buttons. To turn the buttons on, the player must start a new game.

4. Add the following source code to the code window after the `PlaceShortScanStarships` subroutine. You can type in this source code, or you can paste it from the Moonlord1.txt file in the Chap17\Code directory of this book's CD-ROM:

```
 1:  '================================================
 2:  ' CommandButton Handlers.
 3:  '================================================
 4:  Private Sub Command1_Click()
 5:     If GameMode = MAINSCREEN Then
 6:        GameMode = CRUISE
 7:        SetButtons
 8:        Form1.MousePointer = 2
 9:     ElseIf GameMode = CRUISE Then
10:        GameMode = MAINSCREEN
11:        SetButtons
12:        Form1.MousePointer = 0
13:     End If
14: End Sub
15:
16: Private Sub Command2_Click()
17:     If GameMode = MAINSCREEN Then
18:        GameMode = SHORTSCANSCREEN
19:        SetButtons
20:        DoShortScan
21:     End If
22: End Sub
23:
24: Private Sub Command3_Click()
25:     If GameMode = MAINSCREEN Then
26:        DoStatus
27:     End If
28: End Sub
29:
30: Private Sub Command4_Click()
31:     If GameMode = MAINSCREEN Then
32:        GameMode = WARP
33:        SetButtons
34:        DoWarp
35:        If GameOver = GAMESTILLGOING Then
```

```
36:         GameMode = MAINSCREEN
37:         SetButtons
38:      End If
39:   End If
40: End Sub
```

ANALYSIS These are the four subroutines that respond to the player's command button clicks. As you can see by the If statements, what a command button does depends on the game's current mode. Later today, you'll examine these event procedures in greater detail.

5. Add the following button helper subroutines to the program right after the code you added in Step 4. You can type in this source code, or you can paste it from the Moonlord2.txt file in the Chap17\Code directory of this book's CD-ROM:

```
 1: '===================================================
 2: ' Button Helper Subroutines.
 3: '===================================================
 4: Sub SetButtons()
 5:    If GameOver = GAMESTILLGOING Then
 6:      Select Case GameMode
 7:        Case MAINSCREEN
 8:          SetMainButtons
 9:        Case CRUISE
10:          SetCruiseButtons
11:        Case WARP
12:          SetWarpButtons
13:      End Select
14:   End If
15: End Sub
16:
17: Sub SetMainButtons()
18:   Command1.Picture = frmButtons.imgCruiseBut.Picture
19:   Command2.Picture = frmButtons.imgScanBut.Picture
20:   Command3.Picture = frmButtons.imgStatusBut.Picture
21:   Command4.Picture = frmButtons.imgWarpBut.Picture
22:   Command3.Visible = True
23:   Command4.Visible = True
24:   Command1.Enabled = (SystemStats(CRUISEENGINES) = OPERABLE)
25:   Command2.Enabled = (SystemStats(SHORTRANGESCAN) = OPERABLE)
26:   Command3.Enabled = True
27:   Command4.Enabled = (SystemStats(WARPENGINES) = OPERABLE)
28: End Sub
29:
30: Sub SetCruiseButtons()
31:   DisableAllButtons
32:   Command1.Enabled = True
33: End Sub
34:
35: Sub SetWarpButtons()
```

17

```
36:    DisableAllButtons
37: End Sub
38:
39: Sub DisableAllButtons()
40:    Command1.Enabled = False
41:    Command2.Enabled = False
42:    Command3.Enabled = False
43:    Command4.Enabled = False
44: End Sub
```

ANALYSIS Depending on the current game mode, these subroutines enable and disable buttons, as well as update the buttons' graphics. You'll add more of these helper subroutines when you add the source code for the short-range scanner and status screens.

6. Add the following source code to the main form's code window, right after the `Command4_Click` event procedure. You can type in this source code, or you can paste it from the Moonlord3.txt file in the Chap17\Code directory of this book's CD-ROM:

```
1:  '===================================================
2:  ' Misc. Object Handlers.
3:  '===================================================
4:  Private Sub picScreen_MouseDown(Button As Integer, _
5:       Shift As Integer, x As Single, y As Single)
6:    If GameMode = CRUISE Then
7:      Command1.Enabled = False
8:      DoLongCruise x, y
9:      SetButtons
10:   End If
11: End Sub
```

ANALYSIS Whenever the player is in the game's cruise mode, he needs to select a destination sector. In this case, the `picScreen_MouseDown` event procedure gets the mouse click and passes the click's coordinates to the appropriate subroutine.

7. Add the following menu handler to the Menu Handlers section of the program:

```
Private Sub mnuAbout_Click()
  frmAbout.Show
End Sub
```

This subroutine does nothing more than display the About dialog box when the player clicks the About menu command.

8. Add the following general subroutines to the program. Place the code after the Menu Handlers section. You can type in this source code, or you can paste it from the Moonlord4.txt file in the Chap17\Code directory of this book's CD-ROM:

```
1:  '===================================================
2:  ' General Game Subroutines.
```

```
 3:  '=================================================
 4:  Sub DrawSector(sector As Integer)
 5:    Dim x As Integer, y As Integer
 6:    Dim pic As Picture
 7:    x = Sector2X(sector)
 8:    y = Sector2Y(sector)
 9:    If sector = PlayerSector Then
10:      Set pic = imgMarker.Picture
11:    ElseIf Board(sector) = CLEARSEC Then
12:      Set pic = imgEmpty.Picture
13:    ElseIf Board(sector) = BASESEC Then
14:      Set pic = imgCross.Picture
15:    ElseIf Board(sector) = ALIENSSEC Then
16:      Set pic = imgOccupied.Picture
17:    End If
18:    picScreen.PaintPicture pic, _
19:        OFFSET + x * SECTORSIZE, OFFSET + y * SECTORSIZE
20:    Drawn(sector) = True
21:  End Sub
22:
23:  Sub DoLongScan()
24:    Dim PlayerColumn As Integer, PlayerRow As Integer
25:    Dim ColumnLow As Integer, ColumnHigh As Integer
26:    Dim RowLow As Integer, RowHigh As Integer
27:    Dim column As Integer, row As Integer
28:    Dim sector As Integer
29:    If SystemStats(LONGRANGESCAN) <> OPERABLE Then Exit Sub
30:    PlayerColumn = Sector2Column(PlayerSector)
31:    PlayerRow = Sector2Row(PlayerSector)
32:    If PlayerColumn = 0 Then
33:      ColumnLow = 0
34:    Else
35:      ColumnLow = PlayerColumn - 1
36:    End If
37:    If PlayerColumn = COLUMNCOUNT - 1 Then
38:      ColumnHigh = PlayerColumn
39:    Else
40:      ColumnHigh = PlayerColumn + 1
41:    End If
42:    If PlayerRow = 0 Then
43:      RowLow = 0
44:    Else
45:      RowLow = PlayerRow - 1
46:    End If
47:    If PlayerRow = ROWCOUNT - 1 Then
48:      RowHigh = PlayerRow
49:    Else
50:      RowHigh = PlayerRow + 1
51:    End If
52:    For row = RowLow To RowHigh
53:      For column = ColumnLow To ColumnHigh
```

17

```
54:        sector = ColumnRow2Sector(column, row)
55:        If PlayerSector <> sector Then
56:          If Drawn(sector) = False Then
57:  DrawSector sector
58:            Delay 0.2
59:          End If
60:        End If
61:     Next column
62:   Next row
63: End Sub
64:
65: Sub Delay(amount As Single)
66:   Dim StartTime As Single
67:   Dim CurrentTime As Single
68:   StartTime = Timer
69:   Do
70:     CurrentTime = Timer
71:     DoEvents
72:   Loop While CurrentTime < StartTime + amount
73: End Sub
74:
75: Sub CalculateStats(StatType As Integer, amount As Integer)
76:   GameStats(StatType) = GameStats(StatType) + amount
77:   If GameStats(StatType) < 0 Then GameStats(StatType) = 0
78: End Sub
79:
80: Sub UpdateSystemRepairs(days As Integer)
81:   Dim i As Integer
82:   For i = 0 To 5
83:     SystemStats(i) = SystemStats(i) - days
84:     If SystemStats(i) < 0 Then _
85:         SystemStats(i) = OPERABLE
86:   Next
87: End Sub
88:
89: Sub CheckGame()
90:   If GameStats(NUMOFALIENS) = 0 Then
91:     EndGame (GAMEWON)
92:     GameOver = GAMEWON
93:   ElseIf (GameStats(TIMESTAT) = 0 Or _
94:       GameStats(ENERGY) = 0) Then
95:     EndGame (GAMELOST)
96:     GameOver = GAMELOST
97:   End If
98: End Sub
99:
100: Sub EndGame(GameStatus As Integer)
101:   If GameStatus = GAMEWON Then
102:     MsgBox "You win."
103:   ElseIf GameStatus = GAMELOST Then
104:     MsgBox "You Lose"
```

```
105:    End If
106:    DisableAllButtons
107: End Sub
```

ANALYSIS There's a lot of code here, and you'll examine it in more detail later today. For now, just know that this part of the program does a lot of the work for the subroutines that call upon these subroutines.

9. Add the following command handlers to the program, after the subroutines you added in Step 8. You can type in this source code, or you can paste it from the Moonlord5.txt file in the Chap17\Code directory of this book's CD-ROM:

```
1:  '=====================================================
2:  ' Command Subroutines.
3:  '=====================================================
4:  Sub DoStatus()
5:     MsgBox "Status"
6:     GameMode = MAINSCREEN
7:     SetButtons
8:  End Sub
9:
10: Sub DoShortScan()
11:    MsgBox "Short Scan"
12:    GameMode = MAINSCREEN
13:    SetButtons
14: End Sub
15:
16: Sub DoWarp()
17:    Dim OldPlayerSector As Integer
18:    OldPlayerSector = PlayerSector
19:    PlayerSector = Int(SECTORCOUNT * Rnd)
20:    DrawSector PlayerSector
21:    DrawSector OldPlayerSector
22:    CalculateStats TIMESTAT, -1
23:    CalculateStats ENERGY, -30
24:    UpdateSystemRepairs 1
25:    DoLongScan
26:    If Int(10 * Rnd) = 0 Then
27:       DisableAllButtons
28:       MsgBox "You Lose."
29:       GameOver = GAMELOST
30:    Else
31:       CheckGame
32:    End If
33:
34: End Sub
35:
36: Sub DoLongCruise(MouseX As Single, MouseY As Single)
37:    Dim NewPlayerColumn As Integer, NewPlayerRow As Integer
38:    Dim PlayerColumn As Integer, PlayerRow As Integer
39:    Dim ColumnDelta As Integer, RowDelta As Integer
```

17

```
40:    Dim OldPlayerSector As Integer
41:    Form1.MousePointer = 0
42:    If MouseX > GRIDLOWX And MouseX < GRIDHIGHX And _
43:        MouseY > GRIDLOWY And MouseY < GRIDHIGHY Then
44:      NewPlayerColumn = X2Column(MouseX)
45:      NewPlayerRow = Y2Row(MouseY)
46:      PlayerColumn = Sector2Column(PlayerSector)
47:      PlayerRow = Sector2Row(PlayerSector)
48:      ColumnDelta = Abs(PlayerColumn - NewPlayerColumn)
49:      RowDelta = Abs(PlayerRow - NewPlayerRow)
50:      OldPlayerSector = PlayerSector
51:      PlayerSector = ColumnRow2Sector(NewPlayerColumn, _
52:        NewPlayerRow)
53:      DrawSector PlayerSector
54:      DrawSector OldPlayerSector
55:      GameMode = MAINSCREEN
56:      CalculateStats TIMESTAT, -(ColumnDelta + RowDelta)
57:      CalculateStats ENERGY, -(ColumnDelta + RowDelta) * 10
58:      UpdateSystemRepairs ColumnDelta + RowDelta
59:      DoLongScan
60:      CheckGame
61:    End If
62: End Sub
```

ANALYSIS   These subroutines, which you'll examine in more detail a little later, perform the commands that the player selects when he clicks a command button.

   10. Add the following functions to the program, after the subroutines you added in Step 9. You can type in this source code, or you can paste it from the Moonlord6.txt file in the Chap17\Code directory of this book's CD-ROM:

```
1:  Function Sector2X(sector As Integer) As Integer
2:    Sector2X = sector - (sector \ COLUMNCOUNT) * COLUMNCOUNT
3:  End Function
4:
5:  Function Sector2Y(sector As Integer) As Integer
6:    Sector2Y = sector \ COLUMNCOUNT
7:  End Function
8:
9:  Function Sector2Column(sector As Integer) As Integer
10:   Sector2Column = sector Mod COLUMNCOUNT
11: End Function
12:
13: Function Sector2Row(sector As Integer) As Integer
14:   Sector2Row = sector \ COLUMNCOUNT
15: End Function
16:
17: Function X2Column(x As Single) As Integer
18:    X2Column = (x + 1 - OFFSET) \ SECTORSIZE
19: End Function
20:
```

```
21: Function Y2Row(y As Single) As Integer
22:    Y2Row = (y + 1 - OFFSET) \ SECTORSIZE
23: End Function
24:
25: Function ColumnRow2Sector(column As Integer, _
26:       row As Integer) As Integer
27:   ColumnRow2Sector = row * COLUMNCOUNT + column
28: End Function
```

ANALYSIS These functions perform the calculations needed to convert between screen coordinates, columns, rows, and sectors on the main screen display.

11. Save your work.

Understanding the Source Code

In the sections that follow, you'll closely examine the source code that you added to this portion of the Moonlord project.

The Button Handlers

As you already know, when the user clicks a CommandButton control, Visual Basic calls the control's Click event procedure. Moonlord has four command buttons, so it has four different Click event procedures for buttons. However, what these buttons actually do when they're clicked depends on the game's current mode. For example, in the Command1_Click event procedure (as it stands today; you'll add more code to it in later lessons), the program first checks whether the game is in the MAINSCREEN mode:

```
If GameMode = MAINSCREEN Then
  GameMode = CRUISE
  SetButtons
  Form1.MousePointer = 2
```

The MAINSCREEN game mode indicates that the player is viewing the game's main screen (the long-range scanner screen) and has no other commands pending. In this mode, the Command1 button is enabled and triggers the cruise command. So, when the player clicks the button in this mode, the program does the following:

- Changes the game mode to CRUISE.
- Calls the SetButtons subroutine to set the buttons as appropriate for the CRUISE mode (all buttons disabled except the Cruise button).
- Changes the mouse pointer to a cross for selecting the destination sector.

17

When the player clicks Command1, the game may already be in CRUISE mode. This eventuality is also accounted for in Command1_Click:

```
ElseIf GameMode = CRUISE Then
  GameMode = MAINSCREEN
  SetButtons
  Form1.MousePointer = 0
```

The CRUISE game mode indicates that the player has clicked the Cruise button but hasn't yet selected a destination sector. If the player clicks the Cruise button again in this mode, the program does the following:

- Changes the game mode back to MAINSCREEN.
- Calls the SetButtons subroutine to set the buttons as appropriate for the MAIN-SCREEN mode (all buttons enabled—unless a system associated with a button is damaged—and labeled with the Cruise, Scan, Status, and Warp commands).
- Changes the mouse pointer from a cross back to an arrow.

These actions cancel the player's original Cruise command, enabling him to select a different command.

The Command2_Click button, which triggers the Scan command in MAINSCREEN mode, works similarly:

```
If GameMode = MAINSCREEN Then
  GameMode = SHORTSCANSCREEN
  SetButtons
  DoShortScan
End If
```

Here, if the game is in the MAINSCREEN mode, the program does this:

- Changes the game mode to SHORTSCANSCREEN, which indicates that the player is now viewing the short-range scanner screen.
- Calls the SetButtons subroutine to set the buttons as appropriate for the SHORTSCANSCREEN mode (all buttons enabled—unless a system associated with a button is damaged—and labeled with the Bridge, Cruise, Phaser, and Photon commands).
- Calls DoShortScan to display the short-range scanner screen.

The Command3 button, which in the MAINSCREEN mode triggers the Status command, handles a mouse click like this:

```
Private Sub Command3_Click()
  If GameMode = MAINSCREEN Then
    DoStatus
  End If
End Sub
```

Right now, the Status command doesn't do a heck of a lot. In upcoming lessons, you'll add more source code to that part of the program. However, the Command4 button, which triggers the Warp command in the MAINSCREEN mode, is now fully implemented. In Command4_Click, the program first checks the game mode:

```
If GameMode = MAINSCREEN Then
```

If the player is clicking the button from the main screen (MAINSCREEN mode), the program sets the game to the WARP mode:

```
GameMode = WARP
```

Then the program sets the buttons for the WARP mode (all buttons disabled):

```
SetButtons
```

Next, the program performs the warp:

```
DoWarp
```

Now, because warping may bring on the end of the game (those dang experimental warp engines just aren't dependable!), the program must check that the GameOver variable has not been set to something other than GAMESTILLGOING. If the game's still afoot, the program sets the mode to MAINSCREEN and resets the buttons:

```
If GameOver = GAMESTILLGOING Then
  GameMode = MAINSCREEN
  SetButtons
End If
```

The Button Helper Subroutines

As you saw in the previous section, the SetButtons subroutine sets the state of the four command buttons depending upon the current game mode. As you were building this part of the program, you may have also noticed that the SetButtons subroutine (see Listing 17.1) doesn't do a heck of a lot on its own. It just calls other helper subroutines that get the job done.

LISTING 17.1   The SetButtons Subroutine

```
1:  Sub SetButtons()
2:    If GameOver = GAMESTILLGOING Then
3:      Select Case GameMode
4:        Case MAINSCREEN
5:          SetMainButtons
6:        Case CRUISE
7:          SetCruiseButtons
8:        Case WARP
```

LISTING 17.1   continued

```
 9:            SetWarpButtons
10:      End Select
11:   End If
12: End Sub
```

ANALYSIS   SetButtons first checks the GameOver flag to be sure that the game is still in action (that is, the player hasn't yet won or lost). Then SetButtons uses a Select Case statement to call the appropriate subroutine for the current game mode.

For an example of a button helper function, let's explore SetMainButtons. This subroutine is called whenever the buttons need to be set for the main screen. First, SetMainButtons transfers the correct images to the buttons:

```
Command1.Picture = frmButtons.imgCruiseBut.Picture
Command2.Picture = frmButtons.imgScanBut.Picture
Command3.Picture = frmButtons.imgStatusBut.Picture
Command4.Picture = frmButtons.imgWarpBut.Picture
```

Then, SetMainButtons ensures that the Command3 and Command4 buttons are visible because they may have been turned off on the Status screen, which uses only two of the buttons:

```
Command3.Visible = True
Command4.Visible = True
```

Now that the buttons have the correct images for the MAINSCREEN game mode and all the buttons are visible, the program must determine whether some buttons must be disabled due to damaged systems. Because each button's Enabled property is set to True or False, the program can use a Boolean expression to both check the associated system and set each button's state with the result. For example, this is the line that enables or disables the Command1 button:

```
Command1.Enabled = (SystemStats(CRUISEENGINES) = OPERABLE)
```

On the right side of the equals sign is a Boolean expression that returns True if the cruise engines are okay and False if they're not. The result of this Boolean expression is assigned to the button's Enabled property, which sets the button's state properly.

The program handles the other buttons' Enabled properties the same way, except for Command3, the Status command, which is always available:

```
Command2.Enabled = (SystemStats(SHORTRANGESCAN) = OPERABLE)
Command3.Enabled = True
Command4.Enabled = (SystemStats(WARPENGINES) = OPERABLE)
```

The other button helper functions work much the same way.

Getting Mouse Clicks

When the player clicks the Cruise button and thus sets the game to the CRUISE mode, the program must enable the player to click on the long-range scanner grid with the mouse. Because Windows is an event-driven system, the game can't sit around and wait for a mouse click; it has to go on about its business until the player clicks. One of the reasons Moonlord uses all these game modes is so it knows what to do with a mouse click when it gets one. The program retrieves and routes the mouse events in the picScreen_MouseDown subroutine. Why MouseDown instead of the usual Click? Because the MouseDown event procedure passes the coordinates of the mouse click to the program; Click doesn't.

In the current version of picScreen_MouseDown (you'll be adding more code to this procedure in upcoming lessons), the program first checks whether the game mode is CRUISE. If it is, the program disables the command button (until the cruise is finished), calls the subroutine that performs the cruise, and then resets the buttons:

```
If GameMode = CRUISE Then
  Command1.Enabled = False
  DoLongCruise x, y
  SetButtons
End If
```

The Command Subroutines

When the player clicks a button, he expects something to happen—specifically, the command indicated in the button's caption! You've already seen how the button controls route the commands based on the game's mode. Now it's time to look at the lower-level subroutines that actually perform the selected command.

You haven't yet done the programming for the Status screen, so the DoStatus subroutine only displays a message box and returns the game to the MAINSCREEN mode:

```
Sub DoStatus()
  MsgBox "Status"
  GameMode = MAINSCREEN
  SetButtons
End Sub
```

At this time, the same is true of the DoShortScan subroutine:

```
Sub DoShortScan()
  MsgBox "Short Scan"
  GameMode = MAINSCREEN
  SetButtons
End Sub
```

17

The DoLongCruise and DoWarp subroutines are fully implemented in this early version of Moonlord, however, because the program performs the Cruise and Warp commands on the main screen. Let's examine DoLongCruise first.

The DoLongCruise subroutine first sets the mouse pointer back to an arrow:

```
Form1.MousePointer = 0
```

Then the subroutine checks the coordinates of the mouse click to see whether the click falls within the boundaries of the long-range scanner grid:

```
If MouseX > GRIDLOWX And MouseX < GRIDHIGHX And _
    MouseY > GRIDLOWY And MouseY < GRIDHIGHY Then
```

If the mouse coordinates are okay, the subroutine converts the coordinates to the selected column and row:

```
NewPlayerColumn = X2Column(MouseX)
NewPlayerRow = Y2Row(MouseY)
```

The program also needs the current column and row:

```
PlayerColumn = Sector2Column(PlayerSector)
PlayerRow = Sector2Row(PlayerSector)
```

Using the new and current positions, the subroutine calculates the horizontal and vertical distance between the two locations:

```
ColumnDelta = Abs(PlayerColumn - NewPlayerColumn)
RowDelta = Abs(PlayerRow - NewPlayerRow)
```

Next, the program saves the current player sector, calculates the new player sector, and draws both sectors on the screen:

```
OldPlayerSector = PlayerSector
PlayerSector = ColumnRow2Sector(NewPlayerColumn, _
    NewPlayerRow)
DrawSector PlayerSector
DrawSector OldPlayerSector
```

With the cruise complete, the subroutine sets the game mode back to MAINSCREEN:

```
GameMode = MAINSCREEN
```

Because the cruise has eaten up some of the player's time and energy, the subroutine calls the CalculateStats and UpdateSystemRepairs subroutines to adjust these stats:

```
CalculateStats TIMESTAT, -(ColumnDelta + RowDelta)
CalculateStats ENERGY, -(ColumnDelta + RowDelta) * 10
UpdateSystemRepairs ColumnDelta + RowDelta
```

Finally, the game performs a long scan around the player's new location and checks whether the game should end (the player may be out of time or energy):

```
DoLongScan
CheckGame
```

The DoWarp subroutine works similarly to DoLongCruise, except that the program calculates a random destination sector:

```
PlayerSector = Int(SECTORCOUNT * Rnd)
DrawSector PlayerSector
DrawSector OldPlayerSector
```

Just as with a cruise, after a warp, the player's system stats must be updated and a long scan must be performed:

```
CalculateStats TIMESTAT, -1
CalculateStats ENERGY, -30
UpdateSystemRepairs 1
DoLongScan
```

Unlike a cruise, a warp carries with it a 1-in-10 chance of wrecking the ship and ending the game:

```
If Int(10 * Rnd) = 0 Then
   DisableAllButtons
   MsgBox "You Lose."
   GameOver = GAMELOST
```

If the ship survives the warp, it still has to survive the normal game check, which ensures that the player hasn't run out of time or energy:

```
Else
   CheckGame
End If
```

General Subroutines

Now you should have a good idea of how the main-screen portion of the game works, but there are still quite a few lower-level subroutines that you haven't examined yet. Guess what you're going to do now?

The DrawSector Subroutine

The first subroutine we'll examine is DrawSector, which receives the sector to draw as its single parameter. DrawSector first gets the X and Y coordinate at which to draw the sector:

```
x = Sector2X(sector)
y = Sector2Y(sector)
```

17

The subroutine then determines which image must be drawn in the sector, as shown in Listing 17.2.

LISTING 17.2   Determining the Correct Sector Image

```
1:   If sector = PlayerSector Then
2:     Set pic = imgMarker.Picture
3:   ElseIf Board(sector) = CLEARSEC Then
4:     Set pic = imgEmpty.Picture
5:   ElseIf Board(sector) = BASESEC Then
6:     Set pic = imgCross.Picture
7:   ElseIf Board(sector) = ALIENSSEC Then
8:     Set pic = imgOccupied.Picture
9:   End If
```

When the subroutine has determined the correct image, the only thing left to do is to draw the sector and mark it as drawn in the `Drawn()` array:

```
picScreen.PaintPicture pic, _
    OFFSET + x * SECTORSIZE,  OFFSET + y * SECTORSIZE
Drawn(sector) = True
```

The `DoLongScan` Subroutine

Every time the player moves on the long-range scanner screen, the program automatically performs a long-range scan (assuming that the long-range scanner is operational). The subroutine that performs this scan is the appropriately named `DoLongScan`. This subroutine first checks whether the long-range scanner is operational:

```
If SystemStats(LONGRANGESCAN) <> OPERABLE Then Exit Sub
```

If the scanner is working, the subroutine calculates the player's current column and row in the long-range scanner grid:

```
PlayerColumn = Sector2Column(PlayerSector)
PlayerRow = Sector2Row(PlayerSector)
```

Then `DoLongScan` must determine the minimum and maximum columns and rows to scan. These won't always be the eight adjacent sectors because the player's ship may be on the edge of the grid. `DoLongScan` sets the minimums and maximums, as shown in Listing 17.3.

LISTING 17.3   Determining the Minimum and Maximum Columns and Rows

```
1:   If PlayerColumn = 0 Then
2:     ColumnLow = 0
3:   Else
```

LISTING 17.3 continued

```
 4:        ColumnLow = PlayerColumn - 1
 5:    End If
 6:    If PlayerColumn = COLUMNCOUNT - 1 Then
 7:        ColumnHigh = PlayerColumn
 8:    Else
 9:        ColumnHigh = PlayerColumn + 1
10:    End If
11:    If PlayerRow = 0 Then
12:        RowLow = 0
13:    Else
14:        RowLow = PlayerRow - 1
15:    End If
16:    If PlayerRow = ROWCOUNT - 1 Then
17:        RowHigh = PlayerRow
18:    Else
19:        RowHigh = PlayerRow + 1
20:    End If
```

After determining the sectors to draw, DoLongScan does the drawing in nested For loops:

```
For row = RowLow To RowHigh
  For column = ColumnLow To ColumnHigh
```

Inside the loop, the subroutine converts the column and row to the sector:

```
    sector = ColumnRow2Sector(column, row)
```

The program then uses an If statement to skip drawing the player's current sector:

```
    If PlayerSector <> sector Then
```

Another If statement ensures that the sector is drawn only if it hasn't been drawn already:

```
    If Drawn(sector) = False Then
```

Finally, the subroutine draws the sector followed by a slight delay:

```
      DrawSector sector
      Delay 0.2
```

The CalculateStats Subroutine

The CalculateStats subroutine adds or subtracts values to or from game values, such as the amount of energy remaining:

```
Sub CalculateStats(StatType As Integer, amount As Integer)
  GameStats(StatType) = GameStats(StatType) + amount
  If GameStats(StatType) < 0 Then GameStats(StatType) = 0
End Sub
```

Notice the amount parameter. This value can be positive or negative, which determines whether the value is added to the game stat or subtracted from it. (When you add a negative number to something, it's the same as subtracting.)

The UpdateSystemRepairs Subroutine

Whenever the player cruises to a new location in the long-range scanner screen, time goes by. During this time, the ship's repair crews have been working diligently to repair any damaged systems. So each time the player moves, the program calls the UpdateSystemRepairs subroutine, which is shown in Listing 17.4.

LISTING 17.4   The UpdateSystemRepairs Subroutine

```
1: Sub UpdateSystemRepairs(days As Integer)
2:   Dim i As Integer
3:   For i = 0 To 5
4:     SystemStats(i) = SystemStats(i) - days
5:     If SystemStats(i) < 0 Then _
6:         SystemStats(i) = OPERABLE
7:   Next
8: End Sub
```

ANALYSIS   Line 3 starts a For loop that iterates through the SystemStats() array, and Line 4 subtracts the number of days that have passed from the number of days needed to repair the system currently indexed in SystemStats(). Lines 5 and 6 set the system back to operational if repairs are complete.

The CheckGame Subroutine

Because each move consumes energy and time, any move can bring about the end of the game. So after each move, the program calls the CheckGame subroutine, shown in Listing 17.5.

LISTING 17.5   The CheckGame Subroutine

```
 1:  Sub CheckGame()
 2:    If GameStats(NUMOFALIENS) = 0 Then
 3:      EndGame (GAMEWON)
 4:      GameOver = GAMEWON
 5:    ElseIf (GameStats(TIMESTAT) = 0 Or _
 6:        GameStats(ENERGY) = 0) Then
 7:      EndGame (GAMELOST)
 8:      GameOver = GAMELOST
 9:    End If
10:  End Sub
```

ANALYSIS Line 2 checks whether the player has exterminated all the aliens. If so, Lines 3 and 4 end the game with the player winning. Lines 5 and 6 check whether the player has run out of time or energy. If he has, Lines 7 and 8 end the game with the player losing.

The Functions

There's really not much to say about the functions that you've added to Moonlord in this lesson. They simply perform conversions between X and Y coordinates (pixel coordinates), columns and rows (sector coordinates in the grid), and sector numbers.

Summary

Now you're getting somewhere! Moonlord is actually doing something fun, which is good because games are *supposed* to be fun. (That's a fact that some game developers have yet to figure out, eh?) You've now got your cruise engines up and running, and you can even warp around the universe. The Scan and Status buttons don't do much yet, but you'll fix the Scan button in the next lesson when you program the Scan screen.

17

DAY 18

Programming the Short Range Scanner Screen: The Moonlord Project

Your Moonlord program is really starting to shape up, now that you have the main screen working. Still, you're quite a way from completing the game, so today you'll add the program code needed to make the short-range scanner screen work.

Specifically, today you'll do the following:

- Program the command buttons for the short-range scanner screen's game modes
- Implement the new commands represented by the short-range scanner buttons
- Add a new set of general subroutines
- Add functions for managing the short-range scanner screen

Adding Code to the Button Handlers

Moonlord's four command buttons do different things depending upon the current game mode. When the player switches to the short-range scanner screen, for example, the command buttons change to trigger the Bridge, Cruise, Phaser, and Photon commands. In this section, you'll add the source code needed to handle the buttons in the new game modes associated with the short-range scanner screen:

1. Add the following lines to `Command1_Click` after the `Form1.MousePointer = 0` line:

```
ElseIf GameMode = SHORTSCANSCREEN Then
    picScreen.Picture = frmMainScreen.Picture
    GameMode = MAINSCREEN
    SetButtons
    ShowBoard
```

   If the player clicks the `Command1` button when the game is in the `SHORTSCANSCREEN` mode, he is issuing the Bridge command, which returns the game to the main screen. These lines set up the main screen and put the game into the `MAINSCREEN` game mode.

2. Add the following lines to `Command2_Click` after the `DoShortScan` line. If you don't want to type this in, you can copy it from the Moonlord01.txt file in the Chap18\Code directory:

```
1:      If SectorHasAliens Then SetUpAliens
2:   ElseIf GameMode = SHORTCRUISE Then
3:      GameMode = SHORTSCANSCREEN
4:      SetButtons
5:      Form1.MousePointer = 0
6:   ElseIf GameMode = SHORTSCANSCREEN Then
7:      GameMode = SHORTCRUISE
8:      SetButtons
9:      Form1.MousePointer = 2
```

ANALYSIS These lines take care of the second command button when the player is viewing the short-range scanner screen. If the player previously selected the cruise command but has changed his mind (Line 2), Lines 3 to 5 return the game to the `SHORTSCANSCREEN` mode. On the other hand, if the player is already in the `SHORTSCANSCREEN` mode (Line 6), clicking the `Command2` button issues the cruise command, and Lines 7 to 9 set up the player to move his ship to a new short-range sector.

3. Add the following lines to `Command3_Click` after the `DoStatus` line. If you don't want to type this in, you can copy it from the Moonlord02.txt file in the Chap18\Code directory:

```
1:  ElseIf GameMode = SHORTSCANSCREEN Then
2:    GameMode = PHASER
3:    SetButtons
4:    ShootPhaser
5:    GameMode = SHORTSCANSCREEN
6:    SetButtons
```

ANALYSIS If the player clicks the Command3 button when the game is in SHORTSCANSCREEN mode (Line 1), he is firing the phaser. Lines 2 and 3 set up the game for the PHASER game mode, and Line 4 calls the subroutine that fires the phaser. Lines 5 and 6 return the game to SHORTSCANSCREEN after the phaser has fired.

4. Add the following lines to Command4_Click after the first End If line. If you don't want to type this in, you can copy it from the Moonlord03.txt file in the Chap18\Code directory:

```
1:  ElseIf GameMode = SHORTSCANSCREEN Then
2:    GameMode = PHOTON
3:    SetButtons
4:    ShootPhoton
5:    GameMode = SHORTSCANSCREEN
6:    SetButtons
```

ANALYSIS If the player clicks the Command4 button when the game is in SHORTSCANSCREEN mode (Line 1), he is firing a photon torpedo. Lines 2 and 3 set the game up for the PHOTON game mode, and Line 4 calls the subroutine that fires the photon torpedo. Lines 5 and 6 return the game to SHORTSCANMODE after the photon torpedo has been fired.

5. Add the following lines to SetButtons after the SetMainButtons line:

```
Case SHORTSCANSCREEN
  SetScanButtons
```

6. Add the following lines to SetButtons after the SetWarpButtons line. If you don't want to type this in, you can copy it from the Moonlord04.txt file in the Chap18\Code directory:

```
1:    Case SHORTCRUISE
2:      SetShortCruiseButtons
3:    Case PHASER
4:      SetPhaserButtons
5:    Case PHOTON
6:      SetPhotonButtons
```

ANALYSIS These lines call the appropriate button-setting subroutine for the game modes associated with the short-range scanner screen.

18

7. Add the following subroutines to the program, right after the `SetWarpButtons` subroutine. If you don't want to type this in, you can copy it from the Moonlord05.txt file in the Chap18\Code directory:

```
 1:  Sub SetScanButtons()
 2:    Command1.Picture = frmButtons.imgBridgeBut.Picture
 3:    Command2.Picture = frmButtons.imgCruiseBut.Picture
 4:    Command3.Picture = frmButtons.imgPhaserBut.Picture
 5:    Command4.Picture = frmButtons.imgPhotonBut.Picture
 6:    Command1.Enabled = Not SectorHasAliens
 7:    Command2.Enabled = True
 8:    Command3.Enabled = (SystemStats(PHASERGUNS) = OPERABLE)
 9:    Command4.Enabled = (SystemStats(PHOTONLAUNCHER) = _
10:       OPERABLE And GameStats(PHOTONS) > 0)
11: End Sub
12:
13: Sub SetShortCruiseButtons()
14:    DisableAllButtons
15:    Command2.Enabled = True
16: End Sub
17:
18: Sub SetPhaserButtons()
19:    DisableAllButtons
20: End Sub
21:
22: Sub SetPhotonButtons()
23:    DisableAllButtons
24: End Sub
```

ANALYSIS   These subroutines do nothing more than set the four command buttons properly for the current game mode. For example, if the game is the SHORTSCANSCREEN mode, the `SetScanButtons` subroutine is called. There, Lines 2 to 5 change the buttons' graphical captions. Line 6 disables the Bridge button if there are any aliens still on the screen, Line 7 enables the Cruise button, Line 8 enables the Phaser button only if the phasers are operational, and Lines 9 and 10 enable the Photon button only if the photon torpedo launcher is operational.

Command Subroutines

When the player clicks a button, more has to happen than just the game changing modes. (Talk about stating the obvious!) The game must also process the command and perform the task that the player has assigned it. In this section, you'll add the source code needed to perform the commands available on the short-range scanner screen:

1. Replace all the lines in the `DoShortScan` subroutine with the following lines. If you don't want to type this in, you can copy it from the Moonlord06.txt file in the Chap18\Code directory:

```
1:   Dim column As Integer, row As Integer
2:   Dim pic As Picture
3:   Dim ShortRangeSector As Integer
4:   GameMode = SHORTSCANSCREEN
5:   picScreen.Picture = frmScanScreen.Picture
6:   SetButtons
7:   For ShortRangeSector = 0 To SHORTRANGESECTORCOUNT - 1
8:     If ShortRangeContents(PlayerSector, _
9:        ShortRangeSector) = ALIENSSEC Then
10:      Set pic = imgAlien.Picture
11:    ElseIf ShortRangeContents(PlayerSector, _
12:        ShortRangeSector) = SUNSEC Then
13:      Set pic = imgSun.Picture
14:    ElseIf ShortRangeContents(PlayerSector, _
15:        ShortRangeSector) = BASESEC Then
16:      Set pic = imgBase.Picture
17:    ElseIf ShortRangeContents(PlayerSector, _
18:        ShortRangeSector) = STARSHIPSEC Then
19:      Set pic = imgStarship.Picture
20:      ShortRangePlayerSector = ShortRangeSector
21:    Else
22:      Set pic = imgClear.Picture
23:    End If
24:    column = ShortRangeSector2Column(ShortRangeSector)
25:    row = ShortRangeSector2Row(ShortRangeSector)
26:    picScreen.PaintPicture pic, _
27:      SHORTRANGEOFFSETX + column * SHORTRANGESECTORSIZEX, _
28:      SHORTRANGEOFFSETY + row * SHORTRANGESECTORSIZEY
29:   Next ShortRangeSector
```

ANALYSIS   The DoShortScan subroutine has a lot of work to do, starting on Line 5, where it changes the picture in the picScreen PictureBox control to the short-range scanner screen, and on Line 6, where the buttons are set up for the SHORTSCANSCREEN game mode. Line 7 starts a For loop that iterates once for each sector in the short-range scanner display. In the loop, Lines 3 to 23 determine the correct image to display in the sector. Lines 24 and 25 calculate the column and row at which to draw the image, and Lines 26 to 28 paint the image in the sector.

2. Add the following DoShortCruise subroutine to the program, right after the DoStatus subroutine. If you don't want to type this in, you can copy it from the Moonlord07.txt file in the Chap18\Code directory:

```
1:   Sub DoShortCruise(MouseX As Single, MouseY As Single)
2:   Dim newPlayerColumn As Integer, NewPlayerRow As Integer
3:   Dim cruiseOK As Boolean
4:   Dim aliensPresent As Boolean
5:   Dim clickIsValid As Boolean
6:   Dim sectorContents As Integer
7:   Dim targetSector
```

```
 8:    Form1.MousePointer = 0
 9:    clickIsValid = CheckShortRangeClick(MouseX, MouseY)
10:    If clickIsValid Then
11:      newPlayerColumn = X2ShortRangeColumn(MouseX)
12:      NewPlayerRow = Y2ShortRangeRow(MouseY)
13:      cruiseOK = CheckShortCruise(newPlayerColumn, NewPlayerRow)
14:      If cruiseOK Then
15:        targetSector = _
16:            ColumnRow2ShortRangeSector(newPlayerColumn, _
17:            NewPlayerRow)
18:        sectorContents = ShortRangeContents(PlayerSector, _
19:            targetSector)
20:        OldShortRangePlayerSector = ShortRangePlayerSector
21:        ShortRangePlayerSector = targetSector
22:        If sectorContents = BASESEC Then
23:          DockWithBase
24:        ElseIf sectorContents = ALIENSSEC Then
25:          DoRam (OldShortRangePlayerSector)
26:        Else
27:          ShortRangeContents(PlayerSector, _
28:              OldShortRangePlayerSector) = CLEARSEC
29:          ShortRangeContents(PlayerSector, _
30:              ShortRangePlayerSector) = STARSHIPSEC
31:          DoShortScan
32:          Delay 1#
33:          aliensPresent = SectorHasAliens
34:          If aliensPresent Then AliensAttack
35:          GameMode = SHORTSCANSCREEN
36:        End If
37:      Else
38:        MsgBox ("Can't cruise to that location.")
39:        GameMode = SHORTSCANSCREEN
40:      End If
41:    End If
42: End Sub
```

ANALYSIS The DoShortCruise subroutine is another one with a lot of work to do. Because of its size, you'll examine it in detail later in this chapter. Generally, though, this subroutine enables the player to move on the short-range scanner screen, and enables any aliens that may be in the sector to attack. This subroutine also calls the subroutines necessary to dock with a base or ram an alien ship.

3. Add the following DoRam subroutine to the program, right after the lines you added in Step 2. If you don't want to type this in, you can copy it from the Moonlord08.txt file in the Chap18\Code directory:

```
1:  Sub DoRam(OldPlayerSector As Integer)
2:    Dim NumberOfSystemsDamaged As Integer
3:    Dim i As Integer
4:    Dim column As Integer
```

```
 5:    Dim row As Integer
 6:    column = ShortRangeSector2Column(OldShortRangePlayerSector)
 7:    row = ShortRangeSector2Row(OldShortRangePlayerSector)
 8:    picScreen.PaintPicture imgClear.Picture, _
 9:       SHORTRANGEOFFSETX + column * SHORTRANGESECTORSIZEX, _
10:       SHORTRANGEOFFSETY + row * SHORTRANGESECTORSIZEY
11:    If (Int(10 * Rnd) = 0) Then
12:      GameOver = GAMELOST
13:      EndGame (GameOver)
14:    Else
15:      NumberOfSystemsDamaged = Int(4 * Rnd) + 1
16:      For i = 0 To NumberOfSystemsDamaged - 1
17:        DoSystemDamage
18:      Next i
19:      CalculateStats NUMOFALIENS, -1
20:      ShortRangeContents(PlayerSector, _
21:         ShortRangePlayerSector) = STARSHIPSEC
22:      ShortRangeContents(PlayerSector, _
23:         OldPlayerSector) = CLEARSEC
24:
25:      NumAliensDestroyed = NumAliensDestroyed + 1
26:      If NumAliensDestroyed = 2 Then
27:        Command1.Enabled = True
28:        NumAliensDestroyed = 0
29:        Board(PlayerSector) = CLEARSEC
30:      End If
31:      DoShortScan
32:      SetScanButtons
33:      CheckGame
34:    End If
35: End Sub
```

ANALYSIS Because of its size, you'll examine the DoRam subroutine in detail later in this chapter. Generally, this subroutine handles the ramming of an alien ship, including destroying the ship and damaging the starship's systems due to the crash.

4. Add the following ShootPhoton subroutine to the program, right after the lines you added in Step 3. If you don't want to type this in, you can copy it from the Moonlord09.txt file in the Chap18\Code directory:

```
 1:  Sub ShootPhoton()
 2:    Dim Vector As Integer
 3:    If SystemStats(PHOTONLAUNCHER) = OPERABLE And _
 4:       GameStats(PHOTONS) > 0 Then
 5:      Vector = GetVector
 6:      If Vector <> -1 Then
 7:        GameStats(PHOTONS) = GameStats(PHOTONS) - 1
 8:        TrackPhoton Vector
 9:        AliensAttack
10:      End If
11:    End If
12: End Sub
```

ANALYSIS As its name suggests, the ShootPhoton subroutine handles the shooting of a photon torpedo. First, Lines 3 and 4 check that the photon torpedo system is operational and that the player has photon torpedoes to shoot. If so, the call to GetVector (Line 5) gets the photon torpedo-aiming vector from the player. Line 6 ensures that the given vector is valid, and Line 7 removes a photon torpedo from the player's supplies. The call to TrackPhoton (Line 8) actually fires the photon torpedo, and Line 9 gives the aliens their turn to attack after the shot.

5. Add the following ShootPhaser subroutine to the program, right after the lines you added in Step 4. If you don't want to type this in, you can copy it from the Moonlord10.txt file in the Chap18\Code directory:

```
1:  Sub ShootPhaser()
2:    Dim power As Integer
3:    Dim alien As Integer
4:    Dim damage As Integer
5:    On Local Error GoTo InputError:
6:    power = InputBox("Enter amount of power:", _
7:       "Phaser Power", 50)
8:    Command3.Enabled = False
9:    If power > 0 Then
10:     CalculateStats ENERGY, -power
11:     For alien = 0 To 1
12:       If AlienDamage(alien) > 0 Then
13:          damage = CalculateDamage(power, alien)
14:          AlienDamage(alien) = AlienDamage(alien) - damage
15:          If AlienDamage(alien) < 1 Then _
16:             DestroyAlien (alien)
17:       End If
18:     Next alien
19:     AliensAttack
20:     CheckGame
21:    End If
22:    If GameOver = GAMESTILLGOING Then Command3.Enabled = True
23:    Exit Sub
24: InputError:
25: End Sub
```

ANALYSIS The ShootPhaser subroutine handles the firing of the phaser. First, Line 5 asks the player for the amount of power to apply to the phaser shot, after which Line 7 disables the Phaser button. If the amount of power to use is greater than 0 (Line 8), Line 9 subtracts the power from the player's ship, and Lines 10 to 15 deduct damage from any alien ships in the grid. Line 17 gives the aliens their turn to attack, and Line 18 checks for the end of the game. Finally, Line 20 turns the Phaser button back on.

General Subroutines

So far in this chapter, you've added a lot of source code to Moonlord. Many of the subroutines you've added call other subroutines that help them complete their tasks. In this section, you'll add those general, lower-lever subroutines:

1. Add the following `SetUpAliens` subroutine to the program, right after the `UpdateSystemRepairs` subroutine. If you don't want to type this in, you can copy it from the Moonlord11.txt file in the Chap18\Code directory:

```
1:  Sub SetUpAliens()
2:    Dim i As Integer
3:    Dim alien As Integer
4:    For i = 0 To SHORTRANGESECTORCOUNT - 1
5:      If ShortRangeContents(PlayerSector, i) = ALIENSSEC Then
6:        Command1.Enabled = False
7:        NumAliensDestroyed = 0
8:        AlienPosition(alien) = i
9:        AlienDamage(alien) = 5
10:       alien = alien + 1
11:     End If
12:   Next i
13: End Sub
```

ANALYSIS   If a sector contains aliens, they must be set up in preparation for battle. The `SetUpAliens` subroutine takes care of this task. Line 4 starts a `For` loop that iterates through all the sectors in the short-range scanner grid. If a short-range sector contains an alien (Line 5), Line 6 turns off the Bridge button, and Lines 7 to 10 initialize values needed by the rest of the program: the number of aliens that have been destroyed, the position of each alien on the grid, and the hit points for each alien ship.

2. Add the following `ShowBoard` subroutine to the program, right after the subroutine you added in the previous step. If you don't want to type this in, you can copy it from the Moonlord12.txt file in the Chap18\Code directory:

```
1:  Sub ShowBoard()
2:    Dim column As Integer, row As Integer
3:    Dim sector As Integer
4:    Dim pic As Picture
5:    For column = 0 To COLUMNCOUNT - 1
6:      For row = 0 To ROWCOUNT - 1
7:        sector = ColumnRow2Sector(column, row)
8:        If Drawn(sector) Then DrawSector sector

9:      Next row
10:   Next column
11: End Sub
```

18

ANALYSIS The `ShowBoard` subroutine steps through each sector in the long-range scanner grid, drawing the contents of each sector that was previously drawn. (The program doesn't draw sectors that the player has not yet explored.) As you can see, the `Drawn()` array keeps track of which sectors need to be drawn by `ShowBoard`.

3. Add the following `DockWithBase` subroutine to the program, right after the subroutine you added in the previous step. If you don't want to type this in, you can copy it from the Moonlord13.txt file in the Chap18\Code directory:

```
1:  Sub DockWithBase()
2:    Dim i As Integer
3:    Dim column As Integer, row As Integer
4:    For i = 0 To 5
5:      SystemStats(i) = OPERABLE
6:    Next i
7:    GameStats(ENERGY) = 600
8:    GameStats(PHOTONS) = 10
9:    GameMode = SHORTSCANSCREEN
10:   MsgBox "Docking complete."
11: End Sub
```

ANALYSIS The `DockWithBase` subroutine repairs all systems (Lines 4 to 6) and refills the player's energy and photon torpedoes (Lines 7 and 8). Then, Line 9 sets the game back to `SHORTSCANSCREEN` mode, and Line 10 informs the player that the docking was successful.

4. Add the following `AliensAttack` subroutine to the program, right after the subroutine you added in the previous step. If you don't want to type this in, you can copy it from the Moonlord14.txt file in the Chap18\Code directory:

```
1:  Sub AliensAttack()
2:    Dim i As Integer
3:    Dim r As Integer
4:    DisableAllButtons
5:    If Board(PlayerSector) = ALIENSSEC Then
6:      For i = 0 To 1
7:        If AlienDamage(i) > 0 Then
8:          r = Int(Rnd * 5)
9:          If r = 0 Then DoSystemDamage
10:       End If
11:     Next i
12:   End If
13: End Sub
```

ANALYSIS The `AliensAttack` subroutine takes care of alien attacks on the player. Because not every sector contains aliens, Line 5 first checks that the current sector does have aliens. If it does, the `For` loop in Lines 6 to 11 iterates twice, once for each alien.

Line 7 checks whether the current alien is able to attack. If so, Line 8 gets a random number from 0 to 5. If this number turns out to be 0, the alien's attack hits and does damage to the player's ship (Line 9).

5. Add the following `DoSystemDamage` subroutine to the program, right after the subroutine you added in the previous step. If you don't want to type this in, you can copy it from the Moonlord15.txt file in the Chap18\Code directory:

```
1:  Sub DoSystemDamage()
2:      Dim SystemDamaged As Integer
3:      Dim DamageAmount As Integer
4:      SystemDamaged = Int(6 * Rnd)
5:      DamageAmount = Int(6 * Rnd) + 1
6:      MsgBox "System: " & SystemNames(SystemDamaged) & vbCrLf & _
7:          "Damage: " & DamageAmount, vbExclamation, _
8:          "Damage Alert"
9:      SystemStats(SystemDamaged) = _
10:         SystemStats(SystemDamaged) + DamageAmount
11:     If SystemStats(SystemDamaged) > 9 Then _
12:         SystemStats(SystemDamaged) = 9
13:     SetScanButtons
14: End Sub
```

ANALYSIS   `DoSystemDamage` is the subroutine that determines which system an alien attack has damaged and how bad the damage is. Line 4 calculates which system to damage, and Line 5 calculates the amount. Lines 6 to 8 display a damage report to the player, and Lines 9 to 12 apply the damage to the ship's systems. Finally, Line 13 resets the short-range scanner display's buttons because a button that represents a damaged system must be disabled.

6. Add the following `TrackPhoton` subroutine to the program, right after the subroutine you added in the previous step. If you don't want to type this in, you can copy it from the Moonlord16.txt file in the Chap18\Code directory:

```
1:  Sub TrackPhoton(Vector As Integer)
2:      Dim x As Single
3:      Dim y As Single
4:      Dim xoff1 As Integer
5:      Dim yoff1 As Integer
6:      Dim hit As Boolean
7:      Dim outOfBounds As Boolean
8:      Dim color As Long
9:      Dim alienCol As Integer
10:     Dim alienRow As Integer
11:     Dim alienSector As Integer
12:     xoff1 = VectorsX1(Vector) * PHOTONSPEED
13:     yoff1 = VectorsY1(Vector) * PHOTONSPEED
14:     x = ShortRangeSector2X(ShortRangePlayerSector) + 15
15:     y = ShortRangeSector2Y(ShortRangePlayerSector) + 14
```

18

```
16:    Do
17:       color = picScreen.Point(x, y)
18:       picScreen.PSet (x, y), vbWhite
19:       Delay 0.05
20:       If color = SUNYELLOW Then hit = True
21:       If color = ALIENBLUE Then
22:         alienCol = X2ShortRangeColumn(x)
23:         alienRow = Y2ShortRangeRow(y)
24:         alienSector = ColumnRow2ShortRangeSector(alienCol, alienRow)
25:         If AlienPosition(0) = alienSector Then
26:           AlienDamage(0) = 0
27:           DestroyAlien (0)
28:         Else
29:           DestroyAlien (1)
30:           AlienDamage(1) = 0
31:         End If
32:         hit = True
33:       End If
34:       x = x + xoff1
35:       y = y + yoff1
36:       If x < SHORTRANGEGRIDLOWX Or x > SHORTRANGEGRIDHIGHX Or _
37:          y < SHORTRANGEGRIDLOWY Or y > SHORTRANGEGRIDHIGHY Then _
38:           outOfBounds = True
39:    Loop While hit <> True And outOfBounds <> True
40: End Sub
```

ANALYSIS Because of its size, you'll examine the `TrackPhoton` subroutine in detail later in this chapter. Generally, this subroutine draws the photon torpedo tracking line on the screen and determines when the torpedo hits something or goes off the grid.

7. Add the following `DestroyAlien` subroutine to the program, right after the subroutine you added in the previous step. If you don't want to type this in, you can copy it from the Moonlord17.txt file in the Chap18\Code directory:

```
1:    Sub DestroyAlien(alien As Integer)
2:       GameStats(NUMOFALIENS) = GameStats(NUMOFALIENS) - 1
3:       ShortRangeContents(PlayerSector, _
4:         AlienPosition(alien)) = CLEARSEC
5:       DoShortScan
6:       NumAliensDestroyed = NumAliensDestroyed + 1
7:       If NumAliensDestroyed = 2 Then
8:         Board(PlayerSector) = CLEARSEC
9:         Command1.Enabled = True
10:      End If
11: End Sub
```

ANALYSIS The `DestroyAlien` subroutine removes an alien from the sector when the player has destroyed the alien. Line 2 subtracts an alien from the game's total alien count, and Lines 3 and 4 clear the contents of the short-range sector that the alien used to occupy. Line 5 updates the short-range scanner display, and Line 6 increments the number of aliens that have been destroyed in the current sector. If that value is 2 (Line 7), the player has completely cleared the long-range sector of aliens. In that case, Line 8 clears the contents of the sector, and Line 9 enables the Bridge button so that the player can get back to the main display screen (the long-range scanner screen).

Game Functions

Just as some of the subroutines in the game rely on other lower-level subroutines to get work done, so do those same subroutines rely on various functions. In this section, you'll add the functions required by this chapter's version of Moonlord:

1. Add the following SectorHasAliens function to the end of the program function section. If you don't want to type this in, you can copy it from the Moonlord18.txt file in the Chap18\Code directory:

```
1:  Function SectorHasAliens() As Boolean
2:    Dim sector As Integer
3:    Dim FoundAliens As Boolean
4:    FoundAliens = False
5:    For sector = 0 To SHORTRANGESECTORCOUNT - 1
6:      If ShortRangeContents(PlayerSector, sector) = ALIENSSEC _
7:        Then FoundAliens = True
8:    Next
9:    SectorHasAliens = FoundAliens
10: End Function
```

ANALYSIS When the program needs to know whether a short-range sector contains an alien ship, it can call the SectorHasAliens function. In this function, Line 4 initializes the FoundAliens flag to False. The function will return the value of this flag. Lines 5 to 8 are a For loop that iterates through each of the short-range sectors. If any of these sectors contains an alien ship (Line 6), Line 7 sets the FoundAliens flag to True. Line 9 returns the value of the flag to the calling subroutine.

2. Add the following GetVector function to the end of the program function section. If you don't want to type this in, you can copy it from the Moonlord19.txt file in the Chap18\Code directory:

```
1:  Function GetVector() As Integer
2:    Dim result As Integer
3:    On Local Error GoTo InputError
4:    Do
5:      result = InputBox("Enter Photon Vector (0-7):")
6:    Loop While result < 0 Or result > 7
7:    GetVector = result
8:    Exit Function
9:  InputError:
10:   GetVector = -1
11: End Function
```

ANALYSIS The GetVector function displays an input box (Line 5) in which the player can
enter the vector for a photon torpedo shot. Thanks to the Do loop, the input box
keeps appearing until the player enters a valid value or clicks the Cancel button. The
Cancel button causes an error, which sends program execution to Line 10, which returns
an error value to the calling subroutine. Line 7 returns the vector value if no error occurs.

3. Add the following CheckShortRangeClick function to the end of the program
   function section. If you don't want to type this in, you can copy it from the
   Moonlord20.txt file in the Chap18\Code directory:

```
1:  Function CheckShortRangeClick(x As Single, _
2:      y As Single) As Boolean
3:  If x > SHORTRANGEGRIDLOWX And _
4:      x < SHORTRANGEGRIDHIGHX And _
5:      y > SHORTRANGEGRIDLOWY And _
6:      y < SHORTRANGEGRIDHIGHY Then
7:      CheckShortRangeClick = True
8:  Else
9:      CheckShortRangeClick = False
10: End If
11: End Function
```

ANALYSIS The CheckShortRangeClick function returns True if the mouse coordinates
passed as the x and y parameters are within the boundaries of the short-range
grid. Otherwise, the function returns False.

4. Add the following CheckShortCruise function to the end of the program function
   section. If you don't want to type this in, you can copy it from the Moonlord21.txt
   file in the Chap18\Code directory:

```
1:  Function CheckShortCruise(NewPlayerColumn, _
2:      NewPlayerRow) As Boolean
3:  Dim PlayerColumn As Integer, PlayerRow As Integer
4:  Dim CruiseOK As Boolean
5:  Dim DeltaX As Integer, DeltaY As Integer
6:  Dim OffsetX As Integer, OffsetY As Integer
7:  Dim column As Integer, row As Integer
8:  Dim sector As Integer, SectorContents As Integer
9:  Dim response As Integer
10: PlayerColumn = _
11:     ShortRangeSector2Column(ShortRangePlayerSector)
12: PlayerRow = _
13:     ShortRangeSector2Row(ShortRangePlayerSector)
14: CruiseOK = True
15: DeltaX = Abs(PlayerColumn - NewPlayerColumn)
16: DeltaY = Abs(PlayerRow - NewPlayerRow)
17: If DeltaX = 0 And DeltaY > 0 Then
18:     OffsetX = 0
19:     If NewPlayerRow < PlayerRow Then
```

```
20:       OffsetY = -1
21:     Else
22:       OffsetY = 1
23:     End If
24:   ElseIf DeltaX > 0 And DeltaY = 0 Then
25:     OffsetY = 0
26:     If NewPlayerColumn < PlayerColumn Then
27:       OffsetX = -1
28:     Else
29:       OffsetX = 1
30:     End If
31:   Else
32:       CruiseOK = False
33:   End If
34:   If CruiseOK Then
35:     column = PlayerColumn + OffsetX
36:     row = PlayerRow + OffsetY
37:     sector = ColumnRow2ShortRangeSector(column, row)
38:     While column <> NewPlayerColumn Or row <> NewPlayerRow
39:       SectorContents = _
40:           ShortRangeContents(PlayerSector,  sector)
41:       If SectorContents = ALIENSSEC Or _
42:           SectorContents = BASESEC Or _
43:           SectorContents = SUNSEC Then CruiseOK = False
44:       column = column + OffsetX
45:       row = row + OffsetY
46:       sector = ColumnRow2ShortRangeSector(column, row)
47:     Wend
48:   End If
49:   SectorContents = _
50:       ShortRangeContents(PlayerSector, sector)
51:   If SectorContents = SUNSEC Then
52:     CruiseOK = False
53:   ElseIf SectorContents = ALIENSSEC Then
54:     response = _
55:         MsgBox("Are you sure you want to ram that ship?", _
56:         vbYesNo)
57:     If response = vbNo Then CruiseOK = False
58:   End If
59:   CheckShortCruise = CruiseOK
60: End Function
```

ANALYSIS Because of its size, you'll examine the CheckShortCruise function in detail later in this chapter. Generally, this function determines whether the player is able to cruise to the short-range sector he has selected.

5. Add the following CalculateDamage function to the end of the program function section. If you don't want to type this in, you can copy it from the Moonlord22.txt file in the Chap18\Code directory:

```
 1:   Function CalculateDamage(power As Integer, _
 2:       alien As Integer) As Integer
 3:     Dim div As Double
 4:     Dim ASquared As Double, BSquared As Double
 5:     Dim damage As Integer
 6:     Dim ShipColumn As Integer, ShipRow As Integer
 7:     Dim alienColumn As Integer, alienRow As Integer
 8:     Dim distance As Integer
 9:     ShipRow = ShortRangePlayerSector \ 6
10:     ShipColumn = ShortRangePlayerSector - ShipRow * 6
11:     alienRow = AlienPosition(alien) \ 6
12:     alienColumn = AlienPosition(alien) - alienRow * 6
13:     ASquared = (ShipRow - alienRow) * (ShipRow - alienRow)
14:     BSquared = (ShipColumn - alienColumn) * _
15:         (ShipColumn - alienColumn)
16:     distance = Int(Sqr(ASquared + BSquared))
17:     If NumAliensDestroyed = 1 Then
18:       div = 3#
19:     Else
20:       div = 6#
21:     End If
22:     damage = Int(power / div / distance + 0.5)
23:     CalculateDamage = damage
24: End Function
```

ANALYSIS The CalculateDamage function figures out how much damage a phaser shot does to an alien ship. The damage depends on how much power is applied to the phaser and how far the alien ship is from the player's ship. Lines 9 to 12 get the columns and rows where the two ships are located, and Lines 13 to 16 use a little trigonometry to calculate the distance between the phaser and the alien ship. Because the phaser does more damage to one ship than it does to two, Lines 17 to 21 select a divisor for modifying the damage based on the number of alien ships that are absorbing power from the phaser shot. Finally, Line 22 calculates the damage, and Line 23 returns the damage value to the calling subroutine.

6. Add the following functions to the end of the program function section. If you don't want to type this in, you can copy it from the Moonlord23.txt file in the Chap18\Code directory:

```
 1:   Function ShortRangeSector2Column(sector As Integer) As Integer
 2:     ShortRangeSector2Column = sector Mod SHORTRANGECOLUMNCOUNT
 3:   End Function
 4:
 5:   Function ShortRangeSector2Row(sector As Integer) As Integer
 6:     ShortRangeSector2Row = sector \ SHORTRANGECOLUMNCOUNT
 7:   End Function
 8:
 9:   Function X2ShortRangeColumn(x As Single) As Integer
```

```
10:      X2ShortRangeColumn = _
11:          (x + 1 - SHORTRANGEOFFSETX) \ SHORTRANGESECTORSIZEX
12: End Function
13:
14: Function Y2ShortRangeRow(y As Single) As Integer
15:      Y2ShortRangeRow = _
16:          (y + 1 - SHORTRANGEOFFSETY) \ SHORTRANGESECTORSIZEY
17: End Function
18:
19: Function ColumnRow2ShortRangeSector(column As Integer, _
20:          row As Integer) As Integer
21:    ColumnRow2ShortRangeSector = row * _
22:          SHORTRANGECOLUMNCOUNT + column
23: End Function
24:
25: Function ShortRangeSector2X(sector As Integer) As Integer
26:    Dim col As Integer
27:    col = sector Mod SHORTRANGECOLUMNCOUNT
28:    ShortRangeSector2X = col * SHORTRANGESECTORSIZEX + _
29:          SHORTRANGEOFFSETX
30: End Function
31:
32: Function ShortRangeSector2Y(sector As Integer) As Integer
33:    Dim row As Integer
34:    row = sector \ SHORTRANGECOLUMNCOUNT
35:    ShortRangeSector2Y = row * SHORTRANGESECTORSIZEY + _
36:          SHORTRANGEOFFSETY
37: End Function
```

ANALYSIS These subroutines simply convert between short-range sectors, short-range X and Y coordinates, and short-range columns and rows.

Odds and Ends

Only a couple of things left to do, and then this chapter's version of Moonlord will be complete. First, you need to add the lines shown in Listing 18.1 to the picScreen_MouseDown event procedure. Place the new lines right after the SetButtons line.

LISTING 18.1 Code for picScreen_MouseDown

```
1:    ElseIf (GameMode = SHORTCRUISE Or GameMode = BATTLE) _
2:      And GameOver = GAMESTILLGOING Then
3:    Command2.Enabled = False
4:    DoShortCruise x, y
5:    If GameOver = GAMESTILLGOING Then
6:      GameMode = SHORTSCANSCREEN
7:      SetButtons
8: End If
```

ANALYSIS These lines handle mouse clicks on the short-range scanner screen when the game is in SHORTCRUISE or BATTLE mode. Line 1 checks the game mode, and Line 2 checks that the game is still in progress. Line 3 disables the Cruise button, and Line 4 calls DoShortCruise, the subroutine that performs the cruise on the short-range scanner screen. Finally, if the game hasn't ended as a result of the cruise (Line 5), Lines 6 and 7 reset the game mode and buttons.

Next, you need to add the short-range scanner screen's image to the program. To do this, add a new form to the project, and then set the form's Name property to frmScanScreen and the Picture property to ScanScrn.bmp. You can find this bitmap in the Images\Moonlord directory of this book's CD-ROM.

Finally, because the program is going to be loading the new form, it also has to unload it. Add the following line to the Form_Unload event procedure of the main form (Form1):

```
Unload frmScanScreen
```

You can now run Moonlord (after saving your work, of course) and try out your newly functional short-range scanner screen.

Understanding the Source Code

Much of the source code you've added to the project in this chapter was described in the construction steps. However, there are a few large subroutines and functions that need more space to explain. In this section, you'll examine those subroutines and functions in detail.

The DoShortCruise Subroutine

The DoShortCruise subroutine enables the player to move his ship on the short-range scanner screen. This subroutine must first check whether the player's mouse click was within the short-range grid's boundaries:

```
clickIsValid = CheckShortRangeClick(MouseX, MouseY)
```

If the click is okay, the subroutine calculates the row and column to which the player wants to move in the grid:

```
newPlayerColumn = X2ShortRangeColumn(MouseX)
NewPlayerRow = Y2ShortRangeRow(MouseY)
```

The function CheckShortCruise checks whether the move the player has requested is legal:

```
cruiseOK = CheckShortCruise(newPlayerColumn, NewPlayerRow)
```

If the move is legal, the subroutine calculates the sector number to which the player wants to move and gets the contents (sun, alien, base, or starship) of that sector:

```
targetSector = _
    ColumnRow2ShortRangeSector(newPlayerColumn, _
    NewPlayerRow)
sectorContents = ShortRangeContents(PlayerSector, _
    targetSector)
```

Next, the program saves the player's old location in the grid and sets the new one:

```
OldShortRangePlayerSector = ShortRangePlayerSector
ShortRangePlayerSector = targetSector
```

If the target sector contains a starbase or an alien ship, the program must call the DockWithBase or DoRam subroutines:

```
If sectorContents = BASESEC Then
  DockWithBase
ElseIf sectorContents = ALIENSSEC Then
  DoRam (OldShortRangePlayerSector)
```

If the destination sector is empty, the program moves the player to the sector and updates the short-range scanner display:

```
ShortRangeContents(PlayerSector, _
    OldShortRangePlayerSector) = CLEARSEC
ShortRangeContents(PlayerSector, _
    ShortRangePlayerSector) = STARSHIPSEC
DoShortScan
```

If there are aliens in the sector, they now get their chance to attack:

```
aliensPresent = SectorHasAliens
If aliensPresent Then AliensAttack
```

Then the game mode is set back to SHORTSCANSCREEN:

```
GameMode = SHORTSCANSCREEN
```

Finally, if the sector where the player is trying to move isn't a valid sector, the program tells the player so:

```
38:     MsgBox ("Can't cruise to that location.")
39:     GameMode = SHORTSCANSCREEN
```

The DoRam Subroutine

The DoRam subroutine enables the player to ram an alien ship. In The subroutine, the program first calculates the player's column and row in the grid:

```
column = ShortRangeSector2Column(OldShortRangePlayerSector)
row = ShortRangeSector2Row(OldShortRangePlayerSector)
```

Then, the program erases the image of the player's ship from the grid:

```
picScreen.PaintPicture imgClear.Picture, _
    SHORTRANGEOFFSETX + column * SHORTRANGESECTORSIZEX, _
    SHORTRANGEOFFSETY + row * SHORTRANGESECTORSIZEY
```

Whenever the player chooses to ram an alien ship, there's a 1-in-10 chance that the player's ship will be destroyed:

```
If (Int(10 * Rnd) = 0) Then
  GameOver = GAMELOST
  EndGame (GameOver)
```

If the ship survives the collision, it still sustains damage. How much damage the ship receives depends on a roll of the virtual dice. The program gets the number of systems damaged like this:

```
NumberOfSystemsDamaged = Int(4 * Rnd) + 1
```

A For loop then applies the damage by calling the DoSystemDamage subroutine:

```
For i = 0 To NumberOfSystemsDamaged - 1
  DoSystemDamage
Next I
```

Because a collision always destroys the alien ship (unless the collision destroys the player's ship, of course, in which case the game is over), an alien must be removed from the game:

```
CalculateStats NUMOFALIENS, -1
```

The player's starship is moved to the sector that used to hold the alien ship:

```
ShortRangeContents(PlayerSector, _
    ShortRangePlayerSector) = STARSHIPSEC
ShortRangeContents(PlayerSector, _
    OldPlayerSector) = CLEARSEC
```

The program then increments the number of aliens that have been destroyed in the current sector. If both aliens have been destroyed, the program enables the Bridge button again and clears the sector of aliens:

```
NumAliensDestroyed = NumAliensDestroyed + 1
If NumAliensDestroyed = 2 Then
  Command1.Enabled = True
  NumAliensDestroyed = 0
  Board(PlayerSector) = CLEARSEC
End If
```

Finally, the program updates the short-range scanner display and the buttons, and then it checks whether the game is over:

```
DoShortScan
SetScanButtons
CheckGame
```

The TrackPhoton Subroutine

When the player fires a photon torpedo, the program must draw the torpedo on the screen and determine whether it hits anything or just goes off the grid. The TrackPhoton subroutine handles this task. First, TrackPhoton calculates the vectors for photon torpedo movement. The xoff1 and yoff1 vectors are values that the program adds to the photon torpedo's current position in order to calculate its next position:

```
xoff1 = VectorsX1(Vector) * PHOTONSPEED
yoff1 = VectorsY1(Vector) * PHOTONSPEED
```

Next, TrackPhoton calculates the starting pixel location for the photon:

```
x = ShortRangeSector2X(ShortRangePlayerSector) + 15
y = ShortRangeSector2Y(ShortRangePlayerSector) + 14
```

The program then starts a Do loop that continues until the photon torpedo either hits something or travels off the short-range scanner grid. Inside the loop, the program gets the color of the pixel where the photon torpedo is about to be drawn:

```
color = picScreen.Point(x, y)
```

Then the photon torpedo is drawn at the same location:

```
picScreen.PSet (x, y), vbWhite
Delay 0.05
```

The next step is to check the old color of the pixel where the photon torpedo is located to see whether the torpedo has hit something. If the torpedo hits a sun, the loop ends with no further processing required:

```
If color = SUNYELLOW Then hit = True
```

The program then checks whether the photon torpedo hit an alien ship:

```
If color = ALIENBLUE Then
```

If the photon torpedo has hit an alien, there's a bit of work to be done. First, the program calculates the alien ship's sector:

```
alienCol = X2ShortRangeColumn(x)
alienRow = Y2ShortRangeRow(y)
alienSector = ColumnRow2ShortRangeSector(alienCol, alienRow)
```

18

Then, if the calculated sector is where the first alien ship is located, the alien ship is destroyed:

```
If AlienPosition(0) = alienSector Then
  AlienDamage(0) = 0
  DestroyAlien (0)
```

Otherwise, it must be the second alien that was hit:

```
Else
  DestroyAlien (1)
  AlienDamage(1) = 0
End If
```

Setting the hit flag enables the Do loop to end:

```
hit = True
```

The program then moves the photon torpedo's position. If the photon torpedo has gone beyond the bounds of the grid, the outOfBounds flag is set to True:

```
x = x + xoff1
y = y + yoff1
If x < SHORTRANGEGRIDLOWX Or x > SHORTRANGEGRIDHIGHX Or _
    y < SHORTRANGEGRIDLOWY Or y > SHORTRANGEGRIDHIGHY Then _
  outOfBounds = True
```

Finally, the Do loop ends if either the hit or outOfBounds flags have been set to True:

```
Loop While hit <> True And outOfBounds <> True
```

The CheckShortCruise Function

The CheckShortCruise function is one of the most complicated procedures in the program. This function must analyze the contents of the short-range scanner grid and determine whether the player is able to move to the sector that he has selected. The chosen sector must be empty, and no other objects, such as a sun or alien ship, can block the path to the sector. In CheckShortCruise, the program first gets the player's column and row:

```
PlayerColumn = _
    ShortRangeSector2Column(ShortRangePlayerSector)
PlayerRow = _
    ShortRangeSector2Row(ShortRangePlayerSector)
```

Then the program initializes the CruiseOK flag, which is the value that will be returned from the function, to True:

```
CruiseOK = True
```

In order to trace the path that the player's ship would have to take to get to the selected sector, the program must calculate the vectors for the player's movement, as shown in Listing 18.2.

LISTING 18.2   Calculating the Vectors

```
1:    DeltaX = Abs(PlayerColumn - NewPlayerColumn)
2:    DeltaY = Abs(PlayerRow - NewPlayerRow)
3:    If DeltaX = 0 And DeltaY > 0 Then
4:       OffsetX = 0
5:       If NewPlayerRow < PlayerRow Then
6:          OffsetY = -1
7:       Else
8:          OffsetY = 1
9:       End If
10:   ElseIf DeltaX > 0 And DeltaY = 0 Then
11:      OffsetY = 0
12:      If NewPlayerColumn < PlayerColumn Then
13:         OffsetX = -1
14:      Else
15:         OffsetX = 1
16:      End If
17:   Else
18:         CruiseOK = False
19:   End If
```

This code calculates vectors only for vertical or horizontal movement because diagonal movement is not allowed. If the player is trying to move diagonally, CruiseOK will be False. If CruiseOK is still True, the program calculates the next sector in the path of the player's movement:

```
If CruiseOK Then
   column = PlayerColumn + OffsetX
   row = PlayerRow + OffsetY
   sector = ColumnRow2ShortRangeSector(column, row)
```

Then a While loop checks each sector in the path:

```
While column <> NewPlayerColumn Or row <> NewPlayerRow
```

Inside the loop, the program gets the contents of the sector currently being checked:

```
SectorContents = _
    ShortRangeContents(PlayerSector, sector)
```

18

If that sector contains an object, the path to the destination sector is blocked:

```
If SectorContents = ALIENSSEC Or _
    SectorContents = BASESEC Or _
    SectorContents = SUNSEC Then CruiseOK = False
```

The loop then calculates the next sector in the path to the destination sector and continues for another iteration:

```
column = column + OffsetX
row = row + OffsetY
sector = ColumnRow2ShortRangeSector(column, row)
Wend
```

After the loop, the program checks the contents of the destination short-range sector:

```
SectorContents = _
    ShortRangeContents(PlayerSector, sector)
```

If the destination sector contains a sun, the move is disallowed:

```
If SectorContents = SUNSEC Then
    CruiseOK = False
```

However, if the destination sector contains an alien ship, the player probably wants to ram the ship. Just to make sure, the program asks whether that's the player's intention:

```
ElseIf SectorContents = ALIENSSEC Then
    response = _
        MsgBox("Are you sure you want to ram that ship?", _
        vbYesNo)
    If response = vbNo Then CruiseOK = False
End If
```

Finally, the function passes the value stored in the CruiseOK flag back to the calling subroutine:

```
CheckShortCruise = CruiseOK
```

Summary

Moonlord now has two functional screens, the main screen and the scanner screen. You can actually play the game a bit at this point, but you have no way of repairing damaged starship systems. This can quickly bring your game to a screeching halt. In Day 19, you'll take care of this problem when you program the Status screen, the last of Moonlord's three displays.

Workshop

The workshop includes quiz questions to help gauge your grasp of the material. You'll find the answers to this quiz in Appendix A. Even if you feel that you totally understand the concepts presented here, you should work through the quiz anyway.

Quiz

1. What does the program need to do with the four command buttons when the player switches from the main screen to the scanner screen and vice versa?

2. Explain the SHORTRANGESCAN and SHORTCRUISE game modes.

3. In general, what does the DoShortScan subroutine do?

4. Which subroutine must be called after every command the player issues on the sort-range scanner screen when aliens are present? Why?

5. How does the program determine how many ship systems are damaged after the player rams an alien ship?

6. In general, what does the SetUpAliens subroutine do?

7. How does the ShowBoard subroutine, which redraws sectors on the main screen, know which sectors to draw?

8. Why does the TrackPhoton subroutine get the color of a pixel before drawing the photon torpedo on the pixel?

9. In general, what does the CheckShortCruise function do?

18

Exercise

1. Compile your new version of Moonlord and ensure that it runs correctly. When you run the program, you should be able to switch between the main and scanner screens. When you switch between the screens, the buttons' captions should change to the commands appropriate for each screen. Test the buttons and all commands on the short-range scanner screen, including cruising, shooting phasers and photon torpedoes, ramming alien ships, and docking with a starbase.

DAY **19**

Programming the Status Screen: The Moonlord Project

Today, you'll program the status screen—the last screen in the game. Because there's not much for the player to do on this screen except view statistics and repair systems, this lesson will be on the short side. Consider this a reward for all your hard work up to this point!

Today you'll do the following:

- Update the button source code for the status screen
- Add the subroutines and functions that implement the STATSCREEN game mode
- Create a form for holding the status screen image

Updating the Button Code

When the player switches between the main screen and the short-range scan screen, the four command buttons get new captions and trigger different commands. The same is true when the player switches to the status screen. In this section, you'll add the source code needed to handle the buttons in the STATSCREEN game mode:

1. Add the following code to the Command1_Click event procedure right after the ShowBoard line that's already there:

   ```
   ElseIf GameMode = STATSCREEN Then
     picScreen.Picture = frmMainScreen.Picture
     GameMode = MAINSCREEN
     SetButtons
     ShowBoard
   ```

   These lines enable the Command1 button to return the program to the main screen and the MAINSCREEN game mode.

2. Add the following code to the Command2_Click event procedure right after the Form1.MousePointer = 2 line that's already there:

   ```
   ElseIf GameMode = STATSCREEN Then
     DoRepair
   ```

   These lines enable the player to click the Command2 button to initiate repairs to ship systems.

3. Add the following code to the SetButtons subroutine right after the SetScanButtons line that's already there:

   ```
           Case STATSCREEN
             SetStatusButtons
   ```

4. Add the following SetStatusButtons subroutine shown in Listing 19.1 to the program right after the SetShortCruiseButtons subroutine that's already there:

   ```
   1:  Sub SetStatusButtons()
   2:    Dim NeedRepairs As Boolean
   3:    Command1.Picture = frmButtons.imgBridgeBut.Picture
   4:    Command2.Picture = frmButtons.imgRepairBut.Picture
   5:    Command3.Visible = False
   6:    Command4.Visible = False
   7:    Command1.Enabled = True
   8:    NeedRepairs = CheckSystems
   9:    Command2.Enabled = NeedRepairs
   10: End Sub
   ```

ANALYSIS Lines 3 and 4 copy the correct graphic captions to the first two buttons, and Lines 5 and 6 remove the second two buttons from the screen. Line 7 enables the Command1 button, and Lines 8 and 9 enable or disable the Command2 button, depending on whether there are any repairs to be made to the ship's systems.

Adding Subroutines

Now you need to add a few more subroutines to the game. These subroutines manage most of the work needed to implement the commands that the player can issue on the status screen:

1. Replace the currently existing DoStatus subroutine with this one:

```
1: Sub DoStatus()
2:   GameMode = STATSCREEN
3:   picScreen.Picture = frmStatusScreen.Picture
4:   SetButtons
5:   ShowStatusValues
6: End Sub
```

ANALYSIS   This subroutine sets up the game for the STATSCREEN mode by setting the mode (Line 2), copying the status screen image to the main form (Line 3), setting the buttons for the mode (Line 4), and displaying the status values on the screen (Line 5).

2. Add the following ShowStatusValues subroutine to the program, right after the subroutine you added in the previous step. You can either type in the code or copy it from the Moonlord1.txt file in the Chap19\Code directory on this book's CD-ROM:

```
1:  Sub ShowStatusValues()
2:    Dim i As Integer
3:    picScreen.FillColor = RGB(0, 0, 0)
4:    picScreen.FillStyle = 0
5:    For i = 0 To 5
6:      picScreen.Circle (277, 65 + i * 27), 8, RGB(0, 0, 0)
7:      picScreen.CurrentX = 270
8:      picScreen.CurrentY = 58 + i * 27
9:      picScreen.Print SystemStats(i)
10:   Next i
11:   For i = 0 To 3
12:     picScreen.Circle (468, 117 + i * 27), 8, RGB(0, 0, 0)
13:     picScreen.Circle (480, 117 + i * 27), 8, RGB(0, 0, 0)
14:     picScreen.CurrentX = 460
15:     picScreen.CurrentY = 111 + i * 27
16:     picScreen.Print GameStats(i)
17:   Next i
18: End Sub
```

19

ANALYSIS   The ShowStatusValues subroutine prints the values for each of the game's systems and game statistics. Lines 2 and 3 set the form's fill style and color in preparation for the calls to the Circle method that will erase the existing values on the screen. The loop in Lines 5 to 10 prints the status of the ship's systems, and Lines 11 to 17 print the game statistics.

3. Add the following `DoRepair` subroutine to the program, right after the subroutine you added in the previous step. You can either type in the code or copy it from the Moonlord2.txt file in the Chap19\Code directory on this book's CD-ROM:

```
1:  Sub DoRepair()
2:    Dim stat As Integer
3:    GameStats(TIMESTAT) = GameStats(TIMESTAT) - 1
4:    For stat = 0 To 5
5:      If SystemStats(stat) > 0 Then _
6:          SystemStats(stat) = SystemStats(stat) - 1
7:    Next stat
8:    ShowStatusValues
9:    SetButtons
10: End Sub
```

ANALYSIS   Each time the player clicks the Repair button on the status screen, the program calls the `DoRepair` subroutine to apply one day's worth of repairs to the ship's systems. Line 3 subtracts a day from the time remaining, and the loop in Lines 4 to 7 subtracts a day from the time needed to repair each of the ship's six systems. Finally, Lines 8 and 9 update the display and the buttons.

Adding a Function

For this part of the Moonlord project, you need to add only a single CheckSystems function. Add this function anywhere in the function section of the program:

```
1: Function CheckSystems() As Boolean
2:   Dim i As Integer
3:   Dim damaged As Boolean
4:   For i = 0 To 5
5:     If SystemStats(i) > 0 Then damaged = True
6:   Next i
7:   CheckSystems = damaged
8: End Function
```

ANALYSIS   This function returns `True` if any of the ship's systems are damaged. The loop in Lines 4 to 6 checks each of the six systems for a repair time of one day or longer.

Odds and Ends

Only a couple of small tasks left, and you'll have completed this chapter's version of Moonlord, leaving you with a fully playable game. First, you need to add another form to the project. Name the form `frmStatusScreen`, and set its `Picture` property to the StatScrn.bmp file in the Images\Moonlord directory on this book's CD-ROM.

Finally, add the following line to the Form1 Form_Unload subroutine:

```
Unload frmStatusScreen
```

That's it. Now you can save your work, run the program, and check out your new status screen!

Summary

At this point, your Moonlord game should be fully operational. You should be able to play the game from beginning to end, although it may not be too exciting. Because the game is missing animation and sound, it's a lot like pancakes without butter and syrup. In the final two days, you'll fix that problem by adding animation and sound to your game.

Workshop

The workshop includes quiz questions to help gauge your grasp of the material. You'll find the answers to this quiz in Appendix A. Even if you feel that you totally understand the concepts presented here, you should work through the quiz anyway.

Quiz

1. What does Moonlord need to do to set up the buttons on the status screen?
2. In general, what does the DoRepair subroutine do?
3. In general, what does the ShowStatusValues subroutine do?
4. When does the CheckSystems function return a value of True?

Exercise

1. Compile your new version of Moonlord and ensure that it runs correctly. When you run the program, you should be able to switch between the main, scan, and status screens. When you switch between the screens, the buttons' captions should change to the commands appropriate for that screen. Test the Bridge and Repair commands on the status screen.

19

DAY 20

Adding Animation: The Moonlord Project

If you think your version of Moonlord looks a little dull at the moment, that's all about to change. Today you'll spice up Moonlord by adding animation sequences, bringing the game up to a more professional level. By the time you're done, you'll have alien ships that vanish in a whirl of power, starships that rattle when they get hit, and much more.

Specifically, today you'll do the following:

- Add animation sequences to the main screen
- Add animation sequences to the short-range scanner screen
- Add two functions required by the new subroutines

Animation on the Main Screen

In this section, you'll add the controls and source code needed to animate Moonlord's main screen (the long-range scanner screen). This animation includes a blinking marker at the player's current location, as well as an arrival animation when the player moves to a new sector:

1. Add a Timer control to the `Form1` form.

   This timer will control the blinking marker animation.

2. Add the following lines to the end of the `mnuNewGame_Click` event procedure:
   ```
   Timer1.Interval = 250
   Timer1.Enabled = True
   ```

   These lines turn on the timer and set it so that it generates a timer event every 250 milliseconds (1/4 second).

3. Add the following line to the `DoLongCruise` subroutine, right after the `PlayerSector = ColumnRow2Sector(newPlayerColumn, NewPlayerRow)` line:
   ```
   Timer1.Interval = 0
   ```

   This line turns off the timer so that it doesn't interfere with the arrival animation that's generated by the Cruise command.

4. Add the following line to the `DoLongCruise` subroutine, right after the `DrawSector OldPlayerSector` line:
   ```
   Timer1.Interval = 250
   ```

   This line turns the timer back on after the player's cruise command is completed.

5. Add the following `Timer1_Timer` event procedure to the program, placing it after the `picScreen_MouseDown` event procedure:
   ```
   Private Sub Timer1_Timer()
     AnimateMarker
   End Sub
   ```

   The `Timer1_Timer` event procedure calls the `AnimateMarker` subroutine every time Windows sends the program a timer event, the frequency of which is determined by the timer control's `Interval` property.

6. Add the following `AnimateMarker` subroutine to the program, placing it at the end of the existing source code. You can either type in the subroutine or copy it from the Moonlord1.txt file in the Chap20\Moonlord\Code directory on this book's CD-ROM:
   ```
   1:  '=================================================
   2:  ' Animation subroutines.
   3:  '=================================================
   4:  Sub AnimateMarker()
   5:    Dim column, row As Integer
   6:    Dim pic As Picture
   7:    If GameMode = MAINSCREEN Or GameMode = CRUISE Then
   8:      column = Sector2Column(PlayerSector)
   ```

```
 9:        row = Sector2Row(PlayerSector)
10:        If Board(PlayerSector) = ALIENSSEC Then
11:          Set pic = imgOccupied.Picture
12:        ElseIf Board(PlayerSector) = BASESEC Then
13:          Set pic = imgCross.Picture
14:        Else
15:          Set pic = imgEmpty.Picture
16:        End If
17:        If BlinkMode = PLAYER Then
18:          picScreen.PaintPicture pic, _
19:            OFFSET + column * SECTORSIZE, _
20:            OFFSET + row * SECTORSIZE
21:          BlinkMode = OTHER
22:        Else
23:          picScreen.PaintPicture imgMarker.Picture, _
24:            OFFSET + column * SECTORSIZE, _
25:            OFFSET + row * SECTORSIZE
26:          BlinkMode = PLAYER
27:        End If
28:      End If
29: End Sub
```

ANALYSIS Line 7 checks to be sure the player is on the main screen. (You don't want to animate the marker when the player is on some other screen.) Lines 8 and 9 get the player's current column and row in the grid. If the player is in a sector that contains aliens (Line 10), Line 11 gets the appropriate image for an occupied sector. Lines 12 and 13 are similar, except they check for a starbase. If the sector is empty, Lines 14 and 15 get the empty-sector image. Lines 17 to 21 then display the image representing the sector contents if the BlinkMode is set to PLAYER; otherwise, Lines 22 to 27 display the player's marker image. Alternating between these two images makes the player's location marker blink.

7. Add the following line to the DoLongCruise subroutine, right after the line Timer1.Interval = 0 that's already there:

   ```
   AnimateArrival PlayerSector
   ```

   This line animates the player's arrival at the target sector of a cruise command.

8. Add the following AnimateArrival subroutine to the program, right after the AnimateMarker subroutine you added in Step 6. You can either type in the subroutine or copy it from the Moonlord2.txt file in the Chap20\Moonlord\Code directory on this book's CD-ROM:

   ```
   1: Sub AnimateArrival(sector As Integer)
   2:    Dim x As Integer
   3:    Dim y As Integer
   4:    Dim i As Integer
   5:    x = Sector2X(sector)
   ```

20

```
6:    y = Sector2Y(sector)
7:    For i = 0 To 7
8:      picScreen.PaintPicture frmFrames.Picture, _
9:        OFFSET + x * SECTORSIZE, OFFSET + y * SECTORSIZE, _
10:        20, 20, i * 21 + 1, 1, 20, 20
11:     Delay 0.1
12:   Next i
13: End Sub
```

ANALYSIS   Lines 5 and 6 get the X and Y pixel locations of the player's destination sector, and Lines 7 to 12 display the arrival animation one frame at a time. Line 11 controls the speed of the animation.

Animation in the Short-Range Scanner Screen

In this section, you'll add the objects and source code needed to animate Moonlord's short-range scanner screen. This animation includes alien attacks, phaser firing, docking with a base, and an alien attack damaging the player's starship:

1. Add a new form to the project, giving it the name frmFrames and setting its Picture property to the Frames.bmp file, which you can find in the Images\Moonlord directory of this book's CD-ROM. Figure 20.1 shows the completed form.

   This form holds the images needed to perform several of the short-range scanner screen's animations. Each of the image sets contains eight animation frames. To create the animation, the program displays the frames one at a time in rapid succession.

2. Add the following line to the end of Form1's Form_Unload event procedure:

   Unload frmFrames

   This line unloads the frmFrames form from memory when the player closes the program.

3. Add the following line to the ShootPhaser subroutine, right after the If Power > 0 Then line:

   AnimatePhaser

   This line performs the phaser animation when the player clicks the Phaser button and selects a power setting greater than 0.

FIGURE 20.1

The frmFrames *form.*

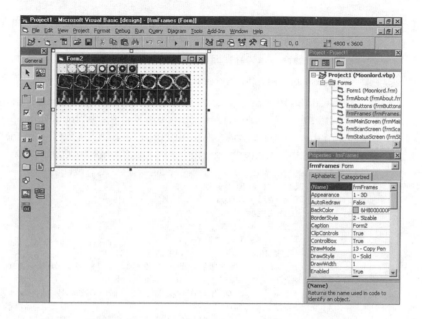

4. Add the following AnimatePhaser subroutine to the program, right after the AnimateArrival subroutine you placed there previously. You can either type in the subroutine or copy it from the Moonlord3.txt file in the Chap20\Moonlord\Code directory on this book's CD-ROM:

```
 1:  Sub AnimatePhaser()
 2:    Dim column, row As Integer
 3:    Dim i As Integer
 4:    column = ShortRangeSector2Column(ShortRangePlayerSector)
 5:    row = ShortRangeSector2Row(ShortRangePlayerSector)
 6:    For i = 0 To 9
 7:      picScreen.PaintPicture imgPhaser.Picture, _
 8:        SHORTRANGEOFFSETX + column * SHORTRANGESECTORSIZEX, _
 9:        SHORTRANGEOFFSETY + row * SHORTRANGESECTORSIZEY
10:      Delay 0.05
11:      picScreen.PaintPicture imgStarship.Picture, _
12:        SHORTRANGEOFFSETX + column * SHORTRANGESECTORSIZEX, _
13:        SHORTRANGEOFFSETY + row * SHORTRANGESECTORSIZEY
14:      Delay 0.05
15:    Next i
16:  End Sub
```

ANALYSIS The AnimatePhaser subroutine makes the player's ship blink. Lines 4 and 5 get the player's row and column in the grid. Then, in a For loop, Lines 6 to 15 alternate between showing a glowing starship image and the regular starship image.

20

5. Add the following line to the `DestroyAlien` subroutine, right after the
   `GameStats(NUMOFALIENS) = GameStats(NUMOFALIENS) - 1` line:

   ```
   AnimateAlienDestruction (alien)
   ```

   This line animates the destruction of an alien ship.

6. Add the following `AnimateAlienDestruction` subroutine to the program, right
   after the `AnimatePhaser` subroutine you placed there in Step 4. You can either type
   in the subroutine or copy it from the Moonlord4.txt file in the
   Chap20\Moonlord\Code directory on this book's CD-ROM:

   ```
   1:  Sub AnimateAlienDestruction(alien As Integer)
   2:    Dim alienRow As Integer
   3:    Dim alienColumn As Integer
   4:    Dim alienY As Integer
   5:    Dim alienX As Integer
   6:    Dim i As Integer
   7:    alienRow = AlienPosition(alien) \ 6
   8     alienColumn = AlienPosition(alien) - alienRow * 6
   9:    alienY = ShortRangeRow2Y(alienRow)
   10:   alienX = ShortRangeColumn2X(alienColumn)
   11:   For i = 0 To 7
   12:     picScreen.PaintPicture frmFrames.Picture, _
   13:         alienX + 1, alienY + 1, _
   14:         34, 31, i * 35 + 1, 22, 34, 31
   15:     Delay 0.1
   16:   Next i
   17: End Sub
   ```

ANALYSIS To animate the destruction of an alien ship, the program needs to display each of the eight animation frames, one after the other, in rapid succession. Lines 7 to 10 calculate the pixel coordinates at which the alien ship is located. The `For` loop in Lines 11 to 16 displays each of the animation sequence's eight frames. Notice how the program uses the loop variable `i` to calculate the location of the next image to display.

7. Add the following line to the `DockWithBase` subroutine, right after the `Dim column As Integer, row As Integer` line:

   ```
   AnimateDocking
   ```

   This line animates the starship docking procedure.

8. Add the following `AnimateDocking` subroutine to the program, right after the
   `AnimateAlienDestruction` subroutine you placed there in Step 6. You can either
   type in the subroutine or copy it from the Moonlord5.txt file in the
   Chap20\Moonlord\Code directory on this book's CD-ROM:

   ```
   1:  Sub AnimateDocking()
   2:    Dim column As Integer
   3:    Dim row As Integer
   ```

```
 4:    Dim i As Integer
 5:    column = ShortRangeSector2Column(OldShortRangePlayerSector)
 6:    row = ShortRangeSector2Row(OldShortRangePlayerSector)
 7:    picScreen.PaintPicture imgClear.Picture, _
 8:        SHORTRANGEOFFSETX + column * SHORTRANGESECTORSIZEX, _
 9:        SHORTRANGEOFFSETY + row * SHORTRANGESECTORSIZEY
10:    column = ShortRangeSector2Column(ShortRangePlayerSector)
11:    row = ShortRangeSector2Row(ShortRangePlayerSector)
12:    For i = 1 To 10
13:      picScreen.PaintPicture imgStarship.Picture, _
14:        SHORTRANGEOFFSETX + column * SHORTRANGESECTORSIZEX, _
15:        SHORTRANGEOFFSETY + row * SHORTRANGESECTORSIZEY
16:      Delay 0.25
17:      picScreen.PaintPicture imgBase.Picture, _
18:        SHORTRANGEOFFSETX + column * SHORTRANGESECTORSIZEX, _
19:        SHORTRANGEOFFSETY + row * SHORTRANGESECTORSIZEY
20:      Delay 0.25
21:    Next i
22:    ShortRangePlayerSector = OldShortRangePlayerSector
23:    column = ShortRangeSector2Column(ShortRangePlayerSector)
24:    row = ShortRangeSector2Row(ShortRangePlayerSector)
25:    ShortRangeContents(PlayerSector, _
26:        ShortRangePlayerSector) = STARSHIPSEC
27:    picScreen.PaintPicture imgStarship.Picture, _
28:        SHORTRANGEOFFSETX + column * SHORTRANGESECTORSIZEX, _
29:        SHORTRANGEOFFSETY + row * SHORTRANGESECTORSIZEY
30: End Sub
```

ANALYSIS   The docking animation is similar to the phaser animation (although a little trickier). Lines 5 to 9 erase the player's ship from its current sector, and Lines 10 and 11 get the column and row of the target sector (the one containing the starbase). Lines 12 to 21 blink the player's ship the same way the program did in the phaser animation. Finally, Lines 22 to 29 return the player's ship to its original sector.

9. Add the following line to the AliensAttack subroutine, right after the If AlienDamage(i) > 0 Then line:

    ```
    AnimateAlienShots i
    ```

    This line animates the alien ships when they fire on the player's starship.

10. Add the following AnimateAlienShots subroutine to the program, right after the AnimateDocking subroutine you placed there in Step 8. You can either type in the subroutine or copy it from the Moonlord6.txt file in the Chap20\Moonlord\Code directory on this book's CD-ROM:

    ```
    1:  Sub AnimateAlienShots(alien As Integer)
    2:    Dim alienRow As Integer
    3:    Dim alienColumn As Integer
    4:    Dim alienY As Integer
    ```

20

```
 5:    Dim alienX As Integer
 6:    Dim i As Integer
 7:    alienRow = AlienPosition(alien) \ 6
 8:    alienColumn = AlienPosition(alien) - alienRow * 6
 9:    alienY = ShortRangeRow2Y(alienRow)
10:    alienX = ShortRangeColumn2X(alienColumn)
11:    For i = 0 To 7
12:      picScreen.PaintPicture imgAlienShoot.Picture, _
13:          alienX, alienY
14:      Delay 0.05
15:      picScreen.PaintPicture imgAlien.Picture, _
16:          alienX, alienY
17:      Delay 0.05
18:    Next i
19: End Sub
```

ANALYSIS The firing alien is another blinking animation. Lines 7 to 10 get the alien ship's pixel coordinates, and the loop in lines 11 to 18 blinks the alien ship.

11. Add the following line to the `DoSystemDamage` subroutine, right after the `Dim DamageAmount As Integer` line:

    `AnimateDamage`

    This line animates the player's ship when an alien's shot damages it.

12. Add the following `AnimateDamage` subroutine to the program, right after the `AnimateAlienShots` subroutine you placed there in Step 10. You can either type in the subroutine or copy it from the Moonlord7.txt file in the Chap20\Moonlord\Code directory on this book's CD-ROM:

```
 1:  Sub AnimateDamage()
 2:    Dim column, row As Integer
 3:    Dim i As Integer
 4:    Dim playerX As Integer
 5:    Dim playerY As Integer
 6:    column = ShortRangeSector2Column(ShortRangePlayerSector)
 7:    row = ShortRangeSector2Row(ShortRangePlayerSector)
 8:    playerX = SHORTRANGEOFFSETX + column * SHORTRANGESECTORSIZEX
 9:    playerY = SHORTRANGEOFFSETY + row * SHORTRANGESECTORSIZEY
10:    For i = 0 To 7
11:      picScreen.PaintPicture frmFrames.Picture, _
12:          playerX + 1, playerY + 1, 34, 31, _
13:          i * 35 + 1, 54, 34, 31
14:      Delay 0.05
15:    Next i
16:    picScreen.PaintPicture imgStarship.Picture, _
17:        playerX, playerY
18:    Delay 1#
19:    Command3.Enabled = True
20: End Sub
```

ANALYSIS The `AnimateDamage` subroutine shakes the player's ship when an alien's shot has hit it. This subroutine works much like `AnimateAlienDestruction`, except that it uses a different set of animation frames. Specifically, Lines 6 to 9 calculate the pixel coordinates of the player's ship, and Lines 10 to 15 display the eight animation frames, one after the other. Finally, Line 16 restores the normal ship image to the sector.

Adding New Functions

In this section, you'll add two new functions required by a couple of the subroutines you just added to the program. You can either type in the functions (see Listing 20.1) or copy them from the Moonlord8.txt file in the Chap20\Moonlord\Code directory on this book's CD-ROM. Place the functions at the end of the program's Game Functions section.

LISTING 20.1 More Moonlord Functions

```
1: Function ShortRangeColumn2X(col As Integer) As Integer
2:     ShortRangeColumn2X = _
3:         col * SHORTRANGESECTORSIZEX + SHORTRANGEOFFSETX
4: End Function
5:
6: Function ShortRangeRow2Y(row As Integer) As Integer
7:     ShortRangeRow2Y = _
8:         row * SHORTRANGESECTORSIZEY + SHORTRANGEOFFSETY
9: End Function
```

ANALYSIS These functions simply convert between short-range scanner columns and rows and pixel screen coordinates.

Today's version of Moonlord is now complete. Make sure to save your work, giving the `frmFrames` form the default name of frmFrames.frm.

Summary

Moonlord is really shaping up, now that you've added some animation sequences to the mix. It's surprising how much of a difference these simple animations can make to the game. Playing Moonlord is a lot more fun now. And it'll be even more fun after you add the sound effects, which you'll do tomorrow.

20

Workshop

The workshop includes quiz questions to help gauge your grasp of the material. You'll find the answers to this quiz in Appendix A. Even if you feel that you totally understand the concepts presented here, you should work through the quiz anyway.

Quiz

1. What's the purpose of Moonlord's timer control?

2. Explain, in general, how the `AnimateMarker` subroutine works.

3. Several of Moonlord's animation sequences are made up of eight different images. Explain how the program uses those eight images to produce an animation.

4. How are the phaser, docking, and alien-shooting animations similar?

Exercise

1. Compile your new version of Moonlord and ensure that it runs correctly. When you run the program, try out all of the commands that are associated with animation sequences. These sequences are the blinking marker, long-range cruise, destroying an alien, shooting the phaser, an alien firing on your ship, getting hit by an alien shot, and docking with a starbase.

WEEK 3

DAY 21

Adding Sound: The Moonlord Project

The last step toward making Moonlord a professional-quality program is to add sound effects. Just as adding animation helped bring the program to life, sound effects raise the gaming experience to a whole new level. Remember that most of the sensory input that humans rely on comes from our eyes and ears. The more you stimulate these important senses, the better your game program will be.

Because you've already studied DirectSound, this will be one of the easiest chapters in the book. Consider this not only the last puzzle in the Moonlord project, but also your graduation party!

Today you will do the following:

- Add DirectSound support to Moonlord
- Associate sound effects with Moonlord's commands and animation sequences

Adding DirectSound Code

As you've already learned, one of the most powerful ways to add sound support to your program is through DirectSound. In this section, you'll add the code needed to get DirectSound and your sound effects up and running:

1. Add the following variable declarations to the program's existing variable declarations, right after the `Dim SystemNames(5) As String` line. If you don't want to type this in, you can copy the Moonlord1.txt file, which you can find in the Chap21\Moonlord\Code directory on this book's CD-ROM:

```
1:  '===================================================
2:  ' DirectSound Variables.
3:  '===================================================
4:  Dim DirectX7Obj As New DirectX7
5:  Dim DirectSoundObj As DirectSound
6:  Dim LongScanSound As DirectSoundBuffer
7:  Dim CruiseSound As DirectSoundBuffer
8:  Dim AlienDestructSound As DirectSoundBuffer
9:  Dim PhaserSound As DirectSoundBuffer
10: Dim ShortCruiseSound As DirectSoundBuffer
11: Dim AlienAttackSound As DirectSoundBuffer
12: Dim PlayerHitSound As DirectSoundBuffer
13: Dim PhotonSound As DirectSoundBuffer
14: Dim DockSound As DirectSoundBuffer
15: Dim ButtonSound As DirectSoundBuffer
```

ANALYSIS These variables represent the DirectSound objects and the DirectSound buffers for each of the sound effects.

2. Add the following `InitDirectSound` subroutine to the end of the program, right after the existing `AnimateDamage` subroutine. If you don't want to type this in, you can copy the Moonlord2.txt file, which you can find in the Chap21\Moonlord\Code directory on this book's CD-ROM:

```
1:  '===================================================
2:  ' DirectSound Routines.
3:  '===================================================
4:  Sub InitDirectSound()
5:     On Local Error Resume Next
6:     Set DirectSoundObj = _
7:        DirectX7Obj.DirectSoundCreate("")
8:     If Err.Number <> 0 Then
9:        MsgBox "DirectSound initialization failed."
10:       End
11:    End If
12:    DirectSoundObj.SetCooperativeLevel _
13:       Form1.hWnd, DSSCL_PRIORITY
14: End Sub
```

ANALYSIS Line 6 creates the program's DirectSound object, and Lines 8 to 11 handle any errors that arise. Lines 12 and 13 set the sharing level for the sound card.

3. Add the following `InitSound` subroutine to the end of the program, right after the subroutine you placed in the previous step. If you don't want to type this in, you can copy the Moonlord3.txt file, which you can find in the Chap21\Moonlord\Code directory on this book's CD-ROM:

```
1:  Sub InitSound()
2:      InitDirectSound
3:
4:      ' Comment out this line when compiling the program
5:      ChDir "d:\TYVBGames\Moonlord\"
6:
7:      Set LongScanSound = CreateSound("LongScan.wav")
8:      Set CruiseSound = CreateSound("FreezGun.wav")
9:      Set AlienDestructSound = CreateSound("Zing.wav")
10:     Set PhaserSound = CreateSound("Phaser.wav")
11:     Set ShortCruiseSound = CreateSound("ShortCruise.wav")
12:     Set AlienAttackSound = CreateSound("AlienAttack.wav")
13:     Set PlayerHitSound = CreateSound("PlayerHit.wav")
14:     Set PhotonSound = CreateSound("PlayerHit.wav")
15:     Set ButtonSound = CreateSound("Button.wav")
16:     Set DockSound = CreateSound("Dock.wav")
17: End Sub
```

ANALYSIS This subroutine first calls `InitDirectSound` (Line 2) to get DirectSound up and running. Line 5 enables Moonlord to run properly from the Visual Basic environment, but it should be removed when the program is compiled. Finally, Lines 7 to 16 load all of Moonlord's sound effects into their buffers.

4. Add the following `CreateSound` function to the end of the program, right after the subroutine you placed in the previous step. If you don't want to type this in, you can copy the Moonlord4.txt file, which you can find in the Chap21\Moonlord\Code directory on this book's CD-ROM:

```
1:  Function CreateSound(FileName As String) _
2:          As DirectSoundBuffer
3:      Dim bufferDesc As DSBUFFERDESC
4:      Dim waveFormat As WAVEFORMATEX
5:      bufferDesc.lFlags = DSBCAPS_STATIC
6:      Set CreateSound = _
7:          DirectSoundObj.CreateSoundBufferFromFile(FileName, _
8:              bufferDesc, waveFormat)
9:      If Err.Number <> 0 Then
10:         MsgBox "Unable to find sound file"
11:         End
12:     End If
13: End Function
```

21

ANALYSIS The `CreateSound` function loads a WAV file from disk and creates the sound effect's DirectSound buffer. Lines 3 to 5 set up the data needed to create a sound buffer. Then, Lines 6 to 8 load the sound effect identified by the filename passed to the function. Finally, Lines 9 to 12 handle an error caused by a missing sound file.

5. Add the following `PlaySound` subroutine to the end of the program, right after the function you placed in the previous step. If you don't want to type this in, you can copy the Moonlord5.txt file, which you can find in the Chap21\Moonlord\Code directory on this book's CD-ROM:

```
1:  Sub PlaySound(Sound As DirectSoundBuffer, _
2:      CloseFirst As Boolean, LoopSound As Boolean)
3:    If CloseFirst Then
4:      Sound.Stop
5:      Sound.SetCurrentPosition 0
6:    End If
7:    If LoopSound Then
8:      Sound.Play 1
9:    Else
10:     Sound.Play 0
11:   End If
12: End Sub
```

ANALYSIS The `PlaySound` subroutine plays the sound associated with the `DirectSoundBuffer` object passed to the function as its first parameter. If the `CloseFirst` parameter is `True`, Lines 3 to 6 turn off the sound before playing it again. Then, if the `LoopSound` parameter is `True`, Lines 7 and 8 play the sound with looping turned on. Otherwise, Lines 9 and 10 play the sound without looping.

6. Add DirectX libraries to the project. To do this, select the Project menu's References command and select DirectX 7 for Visual Basic Type Library from the list that appears.

7. Add the following line to the end of `Form1`'s `Form_Load` event procedure:

```
InitSound
```

8. Copy all the WAV files from this book's Chap15\Moonlord directory to the directory in which you've stored this version of the game.

Playing Sound Effects

Now you need to add the code that plays the sound effects at the appropriate times. This is just a matter of placing a number of calls to the `PlaySound` subroutine:

1. Add the following line to the beginning of the four button handlers, `Command1_Click`, `Command2_Click`, `Command3_Click`, and `Command4_Click`:

```
PlaySound ButtonSound, True, False
```

2. Add the following line to the `TrackPhoton` subroutine, right after the `Do` line that's already there:

```
PlaySound PhotonSound, True, False
```

3. Add the following line to `DoShortCruise`, right after the `If cruiseOK Then` line that's already there:

```
PlaySound ShortCruiseSound, False, False
```

4. Add the following line to `DoLongScan`, right after the `DrawSector sector` line that's already there:

```
PlaySound LongScanSound, False, False
```

5. Add the following line to the `AnimateArrival` subroutine, right after the `y = Sector2Y(sector)` Line that's already there:

```
PlaySound CruiseSound, False, False
```

6. Add the following line to the `AnimatePhaser` subroutine, right after the `row = ShortRangeSector2Row(ShortRangePlayerSector)` line that's already there:

```
PlaySound PhaserSound, False, False
```

7. Add the following line to `AnimateAlienDestruction` subroutine, right after the `Dim i As Integer` line that's already there:

```
PlaySound AlienDestructSound, False, False
```

8. Add the following line to the `AnimateDocking` subroutine, right after the `For i = 1 to 10` line that's already there:

```
PlaySound DockSound, True, False
```

9. Add the following line to the `AnimateAlienShots` subroutine, right after the `Dim i As Integer` line that's already there:

```
PlaySound AlienAttackSound, True, False
```

10. Add the following line to the `AnimateDamage` subroutine, right after the `playerY = SHORTRANGEOFFSETY + row * SHORTRANGESECTORSIZEY` line that's already there:

```
PlaySound PlayerHitSound, False, False
```

At long last, Moonlord is complete. Compile the program, slip on your starship pilot's cap, and go save the universe!

Summary

Your 21-day trek through the world of game programming is now at an end. Not only do you have a toybox full of games to play, but also the tools you need to create your own original games. Still, this book is just a sampling of the programming techniques used to

21

create computer games. If you want to continue this fascinating journey, be sure to check out Appendix E, "Game Programming Resources," for ideas on where to go next. Good luck, and may all your programs be bug-free!

Workshop

The workshop includes quiz questions to help gauge your grasp of the material. You'll find the answers to this quiz in Appendix A. Even if you feel that you totally understand the concepts presented here, you should work through the quiz anyway.

Quiz

1. By examining the DirectSound variables, can you tell how many sound effects the program uses?

2. What is the purpose of the line `ChDir "d:\TYVBGames\Moonlord\"` in the InitSound subroutine?

3. How does Moonlord synchronize its sound effects with its animations?

4. List the name of every variable you've declared in this book. If you answer this question correctly, you will become an honorary member of PWDKJWTSO (People Who Don't Know a Joke When They See One).

Exercise

1. Compile your new version of Moonlord and ensure that it runs correctly. When you run the program, try out all of the commands that are associated with sound effects, such as clicking the buttons, shooting weapons, and docking with starbases.

WEEK 3

In Review

Due to the nature of this week's lessons, there's really not much to review. Rather than learning new game-programming techniques, you spent Week 3 applying what you've learned to a full-scale strategy game. You created the game's user interface, programmed the game's three screens, and added animation and sound.

On Day 15, you created the game's interface, which involved not only adding the controls the player uses to manipulate the game, but also creating image controls that hold many of the game's bitmaps and a dialog box that presents the player with information about the game. With most of the interface stuff out of the way, on Day 16 you added the source code that defines and manipulates the data needed to play the game. This task included defining enumerations for sets of related constants, as well as writing the code that initializes the data in preparation for a new game. (Every game you write will need to define and initialize variables that track game data.)

On Day 17 you worked on the game's main screen. Completing Day 17's tasks included adding images for the graphical buttons and adding the source code that sets up, manipulates, and responds to the game's objects (such as the form and the buttons). You also wrote the source code that enables the player to play the portion of the game related to this main screen. Days 18 and 19 were similar to Day 17, except that you programmed the game's two subscreens. Not every game you write will have more than one screen, but the programming skills you practiced on these three days will help you design and implement game screens for your own projects.

Most games require some sort of animation, if for no other reason than to make them more visually exciting. On Day 20, you added several animation sequences to the game project, including the arrival of the player's starship in a new sector and the destruction of alien ships. Most games also require sound. On Day 21, you learned how to use DirectSound to add sound effects to any game.

APPENDIX **A**

Quiz Answers

Answers for Day 1

Quiz

1. Why does programming games make you a better all-around programmer?

   Because game programs often require you to get the most out of your computer's hardware. This will give you practice with solving problems you might encounter in many other programming projects. Along the way, you'll learn how to optimize your programs, which yields more efficient code.

2. Give at least four reasons why Visual Basic is a good language to use for game programming.

   Here are seven reasons: It's easy to use. Its controls enable quick creation of user interfaces. It enables fast program development. It's a powerful language. It features advanced graphical capabilities. It allows user-defined data types and classes. It can call Windows API functions directly.

3. Why isn't Visual Basic a good language for programming real-time 3D games such as *Quake*?

The number of calculations required, along with the need for very fast frame rates, make Visual Basic a poor choice for commercial-quality action and role-playing games.

4. What's a computer algorithm?

A set of steps for solving a programming problem.

5. How are artificial intelligence and computer algorithms related in game programming?

Computer algorithms determine how a computer player will play the game. Whether a computer player is easy or difficult to beat depends on how well the programmer has designed the algorithm.

Exercises

1. Imagine that you're going to write a computer version of checkers. How would you create the main game screen? What type of user interface might you use? What images would you need to design?

Everybody will come up with their own ideas on how best to design this game. For example, one programmer might want to create a screen that looks like a checkerboard viewed from an angle, while someone else might be happy with a simple straight-down view. In any case, the user interface will require a way to move the checkers, as well as commands for starting and ending games. You might have the user move a checker by clicking the source and destination squares, or you could get fancy and enable the player to drag the checker images around the board. You could use buttons for starting and ending games, but you'd also want these commands in the application's menu bar. As for images, you'll need to draw the checker board. You'll also need images of checkers, as well as a way to indicate when a checker has been kinged.

Answers for Day 2

Quiz

1. What are the five ways you can specify a color in a Visual Basic program?

By using standard color constants, Windows system color constants, the RGB function, the QBColor function, or hexadecimal values.

A

2. Why might you want to use system colors in your programs?

So the colors change appropriately whenever the user changes his Windows system color settings.

3. What are the three color elements of an RGB color value, and what are their minimum and maximum values?

The three color elements are red, green, and blue. Each element has a minimum value of 0 and a maximum value of 255.

4. What shapes can you draw with the `Line` method?

Lines and rectangles (including squares, of course).

5. What shapes can you draw with the `Circle` method?

Circles, ellipses, and arcs.

6. How does the `Step` keyword affect the coordinates given to the `Line` and `Circle` methods?

The coordinate associated with the `Step` keyword becomes relative to the settings of the `CurrentX` and `CurrentY` properties, rather than an absolute coordinate.

7. If you want to draw a shape filled with a predefined pattern, what property will you set for the object on whose surface you want to draw?

The `FillStyle` property determines how Visual Basic fills a shape.

8. What is the purpose of a drawing mode?

The drawing mode determines how Visual Basic combines source and destination colors when drawing.

9. Why are the `vbCopyPen` and `vbInvert` drawing modes especially useful?

The `vbCopyPen` mode replaces whatever is on the screen with what you're drawing. That way you get exactly what you ask for. The `vbInvert` mode, on the other hand, combines the source and destination colors in such a way that a second identical drawing operation erases what was drawn, returning the display to its original condition.

10. Which two Visual Basic controls can display shapes without your program having to draw them by using drawing methods?

The Line and Shape controls.

11. What Visual Basic object and control can act as drawing surfaces for the drawing methods?

The Form object and the PictureBox control.

12. Which two Visual Basic controls can display complex images such as bitmaps stored in a file?

The Image and PictureBox controls.

Exercises

1. Start a new Visual Basic project and draw a blue, two-pixel-wide line on the form from point 30,50 (measured in pixels) to point 100,75. (Hint: You can perform your drawing in the form's `Form_Load` method, but you must first set the form's `AutoRedraw` property to `True`.)

```
Private Sub Form_Load()
  Form1.AutoRedraw = True
  Form1.ScaleMode = vbPixels
  Form1.DrawWidth = 2
  Line (30, 50)-(100, 75), vbBlue
End Sub
```

2. In the same form, draw a yellow-filled rectangle with corners located at 20,30 and 75,60.

```
Private Sub Form_Load()
  Form1.AutoRedraw = True
  Form1.ScaleMode = vbPixels
  Form1.FillStyle = vbFSSolid
  Form1.Line (20, 30)-(75, 60), vbYellow, BF
End Sub
```

3. Add a PictureBox control to the form, and use the drawing methods to draw a scene in the PictureBox that includes a simple house on a green lawn and a sun in a blue sky. (Don't forget to set the PictureBox's `AutoRedraw` property to `True`.)

```
Private Sub Form_Load()
  Picture1.AutoRedraw = True
  Form1.ScaleMode = vbPixels
  Picture1.ScaleMode = vbPixels
  Picture1.FillStyle = vbFSSolid
  Picture1.Line (0, 0)-(Picture1.Width, _
    Picture1.Height / 2), vbBlue, BF
  Picture1.Line (0, Picture1.Height / 2)-(Picture1.Width, _
    Picture1.Height), vbGreen, BF
  Picture1.FillColor = vbYellow
  Picture1.Circle (50, 30), 15, vbYellow
  Picture1.Line (100, Picture1.Height / 2 - 30)-(180, _
    Picture1.Height / 2 + 30), vbWhite, BF
  Picture1.Line (130, Picture1.Height / 2)-(150, _
    Picture1.Height / 2 + 30), vbBlack, BF
End Sub
```

Answers for Day 3

A

Quiz

1. Which object property determines text color?

   The ForeColor property.

2. Which object property determines whether a line of text enables background graphics to show through?

   The FontTransparent property.

3. Which object property holds the attributes of the object's font?

   The Font property.

4. Name four font properties.

   The Font object supports eight properties: Bold, Charset, Italic, Name, Size, Strikethrough, Underline, and Weight.

5. How does the Weight property affect the appearance of text?

   The Weight property specifies the amount of "boldness" (thickness) applied to the text.

6. Which property enables a program to change the typeface of text?

   The Name property.

7. Can you set a single font to display several different attributes, such as bold, italic, and underline?

   Yes. A font can have all its attributes set simultaneously.

Exercises

1. Change the Nightshade text adventure so that all text appears as 10-point Arial.

   To do this, add the following lines to the beginning of the Form_Load subroutine:
   ```
   Form1.Font.Name = "Arial"
   Form1.Font.Size = 10
   ```

2. Add to the DoExamine subroutine the code needed to handle the command LOOK BED. The response to the command will be, "The bed has a blue comforter."

   To do this, add one of the following ElseIf clauses to the DoExamine subroutine:
   ```
   ElseIf Noun = "BED" And ItemLocations(BED) = -Room Then
      lblResult.Caption = "The bed has a blue comforter."
   ```
   or
   ```
   ElseIf Noun = "BED" And Room = 5 Then
      lblResult.Caption = "The bed has a blue comforter."
   ```

Answers for Day 4

Quiz

1. What's an algorithm?

   It's a series of steps that solve a problem.

2. Why do algorithms need to be efficient?

   So that computer programs can run as fast as possible.

3. How does the complexity of an algorithm relate to its efficiency?

   The more efficient an algorithm is, the more complex it tends to become.

4. How does a program store the location of a linked list in memory?

   A program uses a list-head pointer to store the location of the start of a list, and it usually uses a list-tail pointer to store the location of the end of the list.

5. What does the Life program use the LiveList and DieList linked lists for?

   The LiveList and DieList lists hold the cells that might come to life or might die in the next generation of the simulation.

6. In the Life program, what's the World array used for?

   The World array holds values that represent each cell in the grid, where 0 is a dead cell and 1 is a live cell.

7. How does the Neighbors array in the Life program help to speed the simulation's algorithm?

   The Neighbors array holds a running total of neighbor counts for all cells in the grid. By keeping this total and updating the neighbor counts only for those cells that have changed, the program doesn't need to do the complete count in each generation of the simulation.

8. Why must a program call the DoEvents method within a game loop?

   Because the operating system must be able to keep processing Windows messages. Otherwise, the system will come to a screeching halt.

Exercises

1. Come up with an algorithm that completely shuffles an array of 20 values, from 0 to 19. Write a short program that implements your algorithm and displays the shuffled values in the application's form.

   There are a number of ways that you might solve this problem. However, an efficient solution would be to move each element of the array only once. In the

A

following solution, the program iterates through the array, swapping each successive element with a randomly selected one. This algorithm requires only 20 swaps to shuffle the entire array fully:

```
Option Explicit

Dim values(19) As Integer

Private Sub Form_Load()
  Form1.AutoRedraw = True
  Form1.ScaleMode = vbPixels
  Form1.Height = 7000
  LoadArray
  ShuffleArray
  DisplayArray
End Sub

Sub LoadArray()
  Dim i As Integer
  For i = 0 To 19
    values(i) = i
  Next i
End Sub

Sub ShuffleArray()
  Dim i As Integer
  Dim r As Integer
  Dim temp As Integer
  Randomize
  For i = 0 To 19
    r = Int(Rnd * 20)
    temp = values(i)
    values(i) = values(r)
    values(r) = temp
  Next i
End Sub

Sub DisplayArray()
  Dim i As Integer
  For i = 0 To 19
    CurrentX = 40
    CurrentY = i * 20 + 20
    Print "values(" & i & ") = " & values(i)
  Next i
End Sub
```

2. Add constants to the program you wrote in Exercise 1 so that you can easily change the size of the array and the location where the program prints the array values.

```
Option Explicit

Const MAXELEMENTS = 20
Const XOFFSET = 40
Const YOFFSET = 20

Dim values(MAXELEMENTS - 1) As Integer

Private Sub Form_Load()
  Form1.AutoRedraw = True
  Form1.ScaleMode = vbPixels
  Form1.Height = 7000
  LoadArray
  ShuffleArray
  DisplayArray
End Sub

Sub LoadArray()
  Dim i As Integer
  For i = 0 To MAXELEMENTS - 1
    values(i) = i
  Next i
End Sub

Sub ShuffleArray()
  Dim i As Integer
  Dim r As Integer
  Dim temp As Integer
  Randomize
  For i = 0 To MAXELEMENTS - 1
    r = Int(Rnd * MAXELEMENTS)
    temp = values(i)
    values(i) = values(r)
    values(r) = temp
  Next i
End Sub

Sub DisplayArray()
  Dim i As Integer
  For i = 0 To MAXELEMENTS - 1
    CurrentX = XOFFSET
    CurrentY = i * 20 + YOFFSET
    Print "values(" & i & ") = " & values(i)
  Next i
End Sub
```

3. Modify the Life program so that it runs in a 30×18 grid, with cells that are 20 pixels high and 20 pixels wide. Change the size of the cell circles to a radius of 8. (Hint: Study the program's constants.)

At first this might seem like a tricky change to make, but thanks to the game's constants, it's actually very easy. Just change the following constants to the new values shown:

```
Const CELLWIDTH = 20
Const CELLHEIGHT = 20
Const MAXCOL = 30
Const MAXROW = 18
```

Answers for Day 5

Quiz

1. What is a significant difference between the Image and PictureBox controls?

   The PictureBox control is much like a form in that it can act as a container for other controls.

2. Which Image control property enables the control to scale pictures?

   The `Stretch` property.

3. What are two ways to move and resize an Image or PictureBox control?

   You can set the control's `Height`, `Width`, `Left`, and `Top` properties, or you can call the control's `Move` method.

4. When is it impossible to resize an Image control?

   When its `Stretch` property is set to `False`.

5. What are two techniques for loading a picture into a control?

   You can set the control's `Picture` property at design time, or you can set the property at runtime by calling the `LoadPicture` method.

6. Which of the two graphical controls can act as a drawing surface?

   The PictureBox control.

7. Is it possible to scale a picture in a PictureBox control?

   Yes, you can use the `PaintPicture` method to draw a picture at any size.

Exercise

1. Modify the Stretch3 program so that the PictureBox control displays the A.jpg picture file cut into two equal pieces when the user clicks the control. Hint: You'll need the `PaintPicture` method.

```
Option Explicit

Dim ImageWidth As Integer
Dim ImageHeight As Integer
Dim Split As Boolean

Private Sub Form_Load()
  Image1.Visible = False
  ImageWidth = Image1.Width
  ImageHeight = Image1.Height
  Picture1.Width = ImageWidth * 3
  Picture1.Height = ImageHeight * 3
  Split = False
  Picture1.PaintPicture Image1.Picture, 10, 10
End Sub

Private Sub Picture1_Click()
  Picture1.Cls
  If Split Then
    Picture1.PaintPicture Image1.Picture, 10, 10
  Else
    Picture1.PaintPicture Image1.Picture, _
        10, 10, ImageWidth / 2, ImageHeight, _
        0, 0, ImageWidth / 2, ImageHeight
    Picture1.PaintPicture Image1.Picture, _
        ImageWidth / 2 + 200, 10, _
        ImageWidth / 2, ImageHeight, _
        ImageWidth / 2, 0, _
        ImageWidth / 2, ImageHeight
  End If
  Split = Not Split
End Sub
```

Answers for Day 6

Quiz

1. What are the three steps needed to call a Windows API function from a Visual Basic program?

   Provide a function declaration, provide any required data type declarations, and call the function.

2. What's an easy way to get Windows API function, type, and constant declarations for your Visual Basic programs?

The easiest way is to load up the Apiload.exe application with the Win32api.txt file, and then copy declarations from Apiload.exe.

3. Name three bitmap attributes that you can find in a BITMAP structure.

The BITMAP structure provides the width of the bitmap in pixels, the height of the bitmap in pixels, the width of the bitmap in bytes, the number of color planes in the bitmap, the number of bits required to specify a pixel in the bitmap, and a pointer to the bitmap's image data.

4. Which two Windows API functions enable you to draw single lines?

The MoveToEx() and LineTo() functions do the trick.

5. Which Windows API function enables you to draw a set of lines?

The Polyline() function.

6. Name three Windows API functions that draw shapes.

Rectangle(), Ellipse(), and Polygon().

7. How can you get the handle of a bitmap associated with a Visual Basic object?

The handle is stored in the object's Image property.

8. What does DDB stand for?

Device-dependent bitmap.

9. What Windows API function retrieves information about a bitmap?

The GetObject() function.

10. What are the five most common pixel formats?

The five most common formats are 4-bit (16-color), 8-bit (256-color), 16-bit (High Color), 24-bit (True Color), and 32-bit (True Color).

11. Why must some bitmaps be padded with extra bytes?

Because each row of data in a bitmap must have an even number of bytes.

Exercises

1. Modify the 24-bit program so that it displays the color purple rather than red. (Hint: Purple is a combination of red and blue.)

All you have to do is change this line as shown:

```
BitmapBits(x) = 255 ' Blue color element
```

2. Write a short program that uses the Windows API to draw a circle that fits exactly inside a rectangle.

```
Option Explicit

Private Declare Function Rectangle Lib "gdi32" _
  (ByVal hdc As Long, ByVal X1 As Long, ByVal Y1 As Long, _
  ByVal X2 As Long, ByVal Y2 As Long) As Long

Private Declare Function Ellipse Lib "gdi32" _
  (ByVal hdc As Long, ByVal X1 As Long, ByVal Y1 As Long, _
  ByVal X2 As Long, ByVal Y2 As Long) As Long

Private Sub Form_Load()
  Picture1.ScaleMode = vbPixels
  Picture1.AutoRedraw = True
  Rectangle Picture1.hdc, 20, 20, 100, 100
  Ellipse Picture1.hdc, 21, 21, 99, 99
End Sub
```

3. Write a program that uses the Windows API to set the pixels of a PictureBox control's bitmap to display alternating lines of black and white. (Hint: Load the bitmap's data into a two-dimensional array.)

```
Option Explicit

Private Type BITMAP '14 bytes
  bmType As Long
  bmWidth As Long
  bmHeight As Long
  bmWidthBytes As Long
  bmPlanes As Integer
  bmBitsPixel As Integer
  bmBits As Long
End Type

Private Declare Function GetObject Lib "gdi32" _
    Alias "GetObjectA" (ByVal hObject As Long, _
    ByVal nCount As Long, lpObject As Any) As Long
Private Declare Function GetBitmapBits Lib "gdi32" _
    (ByVal hBitmap As Long, ByVal dwCount As Long, _
    lpBits As Any) As Long
Private Declare Function SetBitmapBits Lib "gdi32" _
    (ByVal hBitmap As Long, ByVal dwCount As Long, _
    lpBits As Any) As Long

Private Sub Form_Load()
  Picture1.AutoRedraw = True
End Sub

Private Sub Command1_Click()
  Dim BitmapSize As Long
  Dim BitmapBits() As Byte
```

A

```
Dim x As Long
Dim y As Integer
Dim bmp As BITMAP
Dim Color As Integer

GetObject Picture1.Image, Len(bmp), bmp
BitmapSize = bmp.bmWidthBytes * bmp.bmHeight
ReDim BitmapBits(1 To bmp.bmWidthBytes, 1 To bmp.bmHeight)
GetBitmapBits Picture1.Image, BitmapSize, BitmapBits(1, 1)
For y = 1 To bmp.bmHeight
  Color = 0
  If y Mod 2 Then Color = 255
  For x = 1 To bmp.bmWidthBytes
    BitmapBits(x, y) = Color
  Next x
Next y
SetBitmapBits Picture1.Image, BitmapSize, BitmapBits(1, 1)
End Sub
```

Answers for Day 7

Quiz

1. What's the purpose of a game loop in a real-time game?

   The game loop runs continuously, moving objects and performing calculations whether or not the program receives input from the user.

2. Explain how the BallX and BallY variables are used in Battle Bricks.

   The BallX and BallY variables hold the X and Y coordinates where the ball is currently located.

3. What is a vector, and how is it used to control ball movement in Battle Bricks?

   A vector is a line that indicates a direction. Battle Bricks controls the direction of the ball by adding the values contained in the BallVecX and BallVecY variables.

4. How does Battle Bricks finally manage to break out of its game loop?

   When the Done variable becomes True, the program breaks out of the loop.

5. What does the Bricks() array contain?

   It contains a value for each brick in the wall. A value of NOBRICK (which equals 0) in an element of the array indicates that that brick has been destroyed and is no longer in the game. A value of BRICK (which equals 1) indicates that the brick still appears on the screen.

6. How does the Battle Bricks program determine when to bounce the ball off of an object?

The program compares the coordinates of the ball with the coordinates of the different objects in the game. If the ball is about to overlap one of these objects—a wall, a brick, or the paddle—the program causes the ball to bounce away by reversing the one of the vectors, `BallVecX` or `BallVecY`.

7. What is the difference between candidate bricks and actual bricks?

A candidate brick is one of four brick locations that the ball may be overlapping. There may or may not be an actual brick (a brick that still appears on the screen) at one of these locations.

8. What does the program do to destroy a brick and remove it from the game?

To destroy a brick, the program erases it from the screen and then sets the associated element of the `Bricks()` array to `NOBRICK`.

Exercises

1. Modify Battle Bricks so that the paddle is 160 pixels wide.

All you have to do is change the following constants:

```
Const PADDLEWIDTH = 160
Const MAXPADDLEX = 340
```

2. Write a short program that bounces a ball around the display area of a form. Feel free to steal source code from the Battle Bricks game. Don't forget to use a game loop.

```
Option Explicit

Const BALLWIDTH = 30
Const BALLHEIGHT = 30
Const MAXBALLX = 610
Const MAXBALLY = 450

Dim BallX As Integer
Dim BallY As Integer
Dim BallVecX As Integer
Dim BallVecY As Integer
Dim Done As Boolean

Private Sub Form_Load()
  InitObjects
  InitGame
End Sub

Private Sub Form_KeyDown(KeyCode As Integer, _
    Shift As Integer)
```

```
    If KeyCode = vbKeyF2 Then GameLoop
End Sub

Private Sub Form_Unload(Cancel As Integer)
  Done = True
End Sub

Sub InitObjects()
  Form1.Height = 7575
  Form1.Width = 9675
  Form1.FillStyle = vbSolid
  Form1.BackColor = vbBlue
End Sub

Sub InitGame()
  BallX = 300
  BallY = 300
  BallVecX = 1
  BallVecY = -1
  Done = False
End Sub

Sub GameLoop()
  Do
    MoveBall
    DoEvents
  Loop While Not Done
End Sub

Sub MoveBall()
  Form1.DrawWidth = 1
  Form1.ForeColor = vbBlue
  Form1.FillColor = vbBlue
  Form1.FillStyle = vbSolid
  Form1.Circle (BallX + BALLWIDTH / 2, _
      BallY + BALLHEIGHT / 2), BALLHEIGHT / 2
  BallX = BallX + BallVecX
  BallY = BallY + BallVecY
  CheckWalls
  Form1.FillColor = vbRed
  Form1.ForeColor = vbBlack
  Form1.DrawWidth = 1
  Form1.Circle (BallX + BALLWIDTH / 2, _
      BallY + BALLHEIGHT / 2), BALLHEIGHT / 2
End Sub

Sub CheckWalls()
  If BallX < 1 Or BallX > MAXBALLX Then _
    BallVecX = -BallVecX
  If BallY < 1 Or BallY > MAXBALLY Then _
    BallVecY = -BallVecY
End Sub
```

Answers for Day 8

Quiz

1. Which real-world objects do the `clsCard` and `clsDeck` classes represent?

   The `clsCard` class represents a single card, and the `clsDeck` class represents a full deck of 52 cards.

2. How does the `clsDeck` class use the `clsCard` class?

   Each card in the deck is a `clsCard` object.

3. How can you calculate the suit of a card represented by a `clsCard` object?

   ```
   suit = value \ 13
   ```

4. How can you calculate the card's face value?

   ```
   faceValue = value mod 13
   ```

5. Which modules do you need to add to your programs to use the card classes?

   You need the clsCard.cls and clsDeck.cls class modules, of course. You also need the Cards.bas module, as well as the frmCards.frm form.

6. Which module defines the constants that are used with the card classes?

   Cards.bas

7. How do you get the cards represented by a `clsDeck` object into random order?

   Call the `clsDeck` object's `Shuffle` method.

8. How can you ensure that the frmCards.frm is removed from memory when the player quits your card game?

   Unload the form in your main form's `Form_Unload` event procedure.

Exercises

1. Write a short program that deals four, six-card hands. Overlap the cards in each hand by 10 pixels.

   ```
   Option Explicit

   Dim Deck As New clsDeck

   Private Sub Form_Load()
     CardForm.AutoRedraw = True
     CardForm.ScaleMode = vbPixels
   ```

A

```
    CardForm.BackColor = vbBlack
    Deck.Shuffle
    Deck.Deal 6, 0, 20, 20, -10, FaceUp
    Deck.Deal 6, 1, 20, 120, -10, FaceUp
    Deck.Deal 6, 2, 20, 220, -10, FaceUp
    Deck.Deal 6, 3, 20, 320, -10, FaceUp
End Sub

Private Sub Form_Unload(Cancel As Integer)
    Unload frmCards
End Sub
```

2. Write a short program that shuffles the deck and then deals 10 cards, one each time the user clicks the form. After the 10th card, reset the deck so that the same 10 cards are dealt again.

```
Option Explicit

Dim Deck As New clsDeck

Private Sub Form_Load()
    CardForm.AutoRedraw = True
    CardForm.ScaleMode = vbPixels
    CardForm.BackColor = vbBlack
    Deck.Shuffle
End Sub

Private Sub Form_Unload(Cancel As Integer)
    Unload frmCards
End Sub

Private Sub Form_Click()
    Dim NumCards As Integer
    Dim i As Integer
    NumCards = Deck.NumCardsInHand(0)
    If NumCards = 10 Then
        NumCards = 0
        Deck.Restore
        Cls
        For i = 1 To 10
            Deck.Discard 0, 0
        Next i
    End If
    Deck.Deal 1, 0, 20 + NumCards * 60, 20, 10, FaceUp
End Sub
```

Answers for Day 9

Quiz

1. What method of the `clsDeck` class makes it possible for Poker Squares to deal the same cards to two players?

   The `Restore` method restores the deck to its original state before any cards were dealt.

2. Explain how the `MINX`, `MAXX`, `MINY`, and `MAXY` constants are used in the Poker Squares program.

   These constants represent the minimum and maximum X and Y coordinates for valid mouse clicks in the card grid.

3. Why doesn't the Poker Squares program have `CheckForFullHouse` and `CheckForStraightFlush` functions?

   Because the program can use the `PairFlag` and `ThreeOfAKindFlag` flags to determine that the player has a full house. Likewise, the `StraightFlag` and `FlushFlag` flags can indicate a straight flush.

4. In the `GetBestHand` function, what does the program store in the `cards` array?

   The number of each type of card.

5. What does the global `Grid` array contain?

   The card values for the cards in the grid, with -1 meaning an empty cell.

6. Explain briefly how Poker Squares analyzes cards for scoring poker hands.

   The program checks each group (row and column) of five cards separately. First, it checks the current hand for a flush by checking whether all the cards in the hand are of the same suit. Then, the program sorts the cards into the `cards` array and calls functions like `CheckForStraight` and `CheckForThreeOfAKind` to check for the basic types of poker card combinations. These functions set flags that the program uses to determine the best possible hand.

7. Why does the `cards` array have 14 elements instead of only 13?

   The 14th element (`cards(13)`) enables the program to consider an ace as either a high card or a low card.

Exercises

1. Modify Poker Squares so that a pair of aces is worth 25 points.

   You first need to modify the `PokerHandsEnum` enumeration to include the `PairOfAces` hand:

```
Public Enum PokerHandsEnum
  NoHand
  Pair
  TwoPair
  ThreeOfAKind
  PairOfAces
  Straight
  Flush
  FullHouse
  FourOfAKind
  StraightFlush
End Enum
```

Then, you must modify the GetScore function to return 25 for a PairOfAces hand:

```
Function GetScore(BestHand As Integer) As Integer
  Select Case BestHand
    Case NoHand
      GetScore = 0
    Case Pair
      GetScore = 5
    Case TwoPair
      GetScore = 15
    Case ThreeOfAKind
      GetScore = 20
    Case PairOfAces
      GetScore = 25
    Case Straight
      GetScore = 30
    Case Flush
      GetScore = 35
    Case FullHouse
      GetScore = 45
    Case FourOfAKind
      GetScore = 60
    Case StraightFlush
      GetScore = 100
    End Select
End Function
```

Finally, you must modify the GetBestHand function to check for a hand that contains a pair, with that pair being aces:

```
Function GetBestHand(hand() As Integer) As Integer
  Dim FlushFlag As Boolean
  Dim StraightFlag As Boolean
  Dim PairFlag As Boolean
  Dim TwoPairFlag As Boolean
  Dim ThreeOfAKindFlag As Boolean
```

```
Dim FourOfAKindFlag As Boolean
Dim cards(13) As Integer

FlushFlag = CheckForFlush(hand)
SortCards cards, hand
StraightFlag = CheckForStraight(cards, hand)
PairFlag = CheckForPair(cards)
TwoPairFlag = CheckForTwoPair(cards)
ThreeOfAKindFlag = CheckForThreeOfAKind(cards)
FourOfAKindFlag = CheckForFourOfAKind(cards)

If (StraightFlag) And (FlushFlag) Then
  GetBestHand = StraightFlush
ElseIf FourOfAKindFlag Then
  GetBestHand = FourOfAKind
ElseIf (PairFlag) And (ThreeOfAKindFlag) Then
  GetBestHand = FullHouse
ElseIf FlushFlag Then
  GetBestHand = Flush
ElseIf (PairFlag) And (cards(0) = 2) Then
   GetBestHand = PairOfAces
ElseIf StraightFlag Then
  GetBestHand = Straight
ElseIf ThreeOfAKindFlag Then
  GetBestHand = ThreeOfAKind
ElseIf TwoPairFlag Then
  GetBestHand = TwoPair
ElseIf PairFlag Then
  GetBestHand = Pair
Else
  GetBestHand = NoHand
End If
End Function
```

Answers for Day 10

Quiz

1. What are two typical approaches for adding a computer opponent's to a game?

   One is to convert an expert player's strategy into computer algorithms. Another is to use a brute force method that takes advantage of the computer's calculating power to determine the outcome of its moves before making them.

2. Which approach for creating a computer opponent does Crystals use? Explain your answer.

   Crystals uses the brute force method. It calculates the outcomes of a set of moves and the human's responses to those moves before choosing the move that yields the highest score for the computer and the lowest score for the human player.

A

3. What does the Crystals program use the CompScores() and comboScores() arrays for?

   The CompScores() array holds the score the computer can get for each of its eight possible moves, and the comboScores() array holds the computer scores minus the scores for the human player's best response to the eight moves.

4. Briefly describe the algorithm that Crystals uses to determine the computer opponent's moves.

   First, the program fills the CompScores() and comboScores() arrays with their score values. The computer then finds the highest score in comboScores() that gets the highest score in CompScores(). This is the move the computer selects.

5. How does Crystals prevent the computer opponent from becoming too predictable?

   By inserting a random element into the SelectMove subroutine. This random element ensures that the computer opponent won't necessarily choose the same move in identical circumstances.

Answers for Day 11

Quiz

1. What's the minimum hardware and software you need for creating sound effects?

   You need a sound card, a microphone, and a sound editor.

2. What are three ways of playing sound effects in your Visual Basic programs?

   Using the Microsoft Multimedia Control, using Windows API MCI functions, or using DirectSound.

3. What would you use a sound editor for?

   A sound editor enables you to remove silences before and after recorded sound effects, as well as change the effect's volume and add special effects such as echo.

4. What does MCI stand for, and what is it?

   MCI stands for Media Control Interface, and it's a set of libraries for manipulating multimedia devices.

5. Compare the MessageBeep() API function with the PlaySound() API function.

   The MessageBeep() function only allows you to play system sound effects, whereas the PlaySound() function can play any WAV file.

6. Which three DirectX objects does a program need in order to play a sound effect? Describe them.

DirectX7, DirectSound, and DirectSoundBuffer objects. The DirectX7 object enables you to create component objects needed by your program (such as a DirectSound object). The DirectSound object provides access to the DirectSound libraries, enabling you to set priority levels and create sound buffers. The DirectSoundBuffer object represents a sound effect and provides the methods needed for manipulating the sound.

7. What method do you call to play a sound effect with DirectSound? What method stops a sound from playing?

   The Play method and the Stop method.

Exercises

1. Write a short program that plays a sound effect using DirectSound. (Don't use the DirectSound routines provided in this chapter. Also, don't forget to add the DirectX libraries to your project.)

```
Dim DirectX7Obj As New DirectX7
Dim DirectSoundObj As DirectSound
Dim BeamUpSound As DirectSoundBuffer

Private Sub Form_Load()
  Dim bufferDesc As DSBUFFERDESC
  Dim waveFormat As WAVEFORMATEX
  Set DirectSoundObj = DirectX7Obj.DirectSoundCreate("")
  DirectSoundObj.SetCooperativeLevel Me.hWnd, DSSCL_PRIORITY
  bufferDesc.lFlags = DSBCAPS_STATIC
  'ChDir "d:\tyvbgames\chap11\exercises\exercise1"
  Set BeamUpSound = _
      DirectSoundObj.CreateSoundBufferFromFile("beamup.wav", _
          bufferDesc, waveFormat)
End Sub

Private Sub cmdPlay_Click()
  BeamUpSound.Stop
  BeamUpSound.SetCurrentPosition 0
  BeamUpSound.Play 0
End Sub
```

2. Modify the Poker Squares program from Day 9 so that a sound effect plays when the player places a card in the grid and also when the player clicks on a cell that already contains a card (an illegal-move sound).

   You can find the answer to this exercise in the Chap11\Exercises\Exercise2 directory of this book's CD-ROM. All new source code added to the program is surrounded by the following comment lines:

```
'^^^^^^^^^^^^^^^^^^^^^^^^^^^^^^^^^^^^^^^^^^^^^^^^^^^

'^^^^^^^^^^^^^^^^^^^^^^^^^^^^^^^^^^^^^^^^^^^^^^^^^^^
```

Answers for Day 12

Quiz

1. What makes an RPG different from other types of adventure games?

   RPG games place the player in the role of a character with many attributes, which define the way the character can respond to game events.

2. Give two reasons why you might want to create a level editor for a game.

   The most obvious reason to program a level editor is to make it easy to create levels for your game. The bonus is that your game's players will probably create levels on their own. So when you're finished programming the game, you can include the editor as part of the package.

3. How do you define a character in a computer RPG?

   By defining a set of attributes—such as strength, speed, intelligence, and health.

4. How are a character's attributes used in the program?

   The character's attributes determine which actions the character can perform in the game, as well as the results of those actions. For example, a strong character wreaks more havoc in a battle than a weak character can.

Answers for Day 13

Quiz

1. How does Dragonlord use the Map() array?

   The Map() array contains numbers that specify the type of room (the available exits) that should appear in each location in the dungeon.

2. What does the Items() array represent?

   The Items() array contains numbers that specify the type of item (skeleton, gold, teleporter, etc.) hidden in each room.

3. What data does the program use to keep track of the player's statistics?

   The program defines a custom datatype, StatsType, that contains a variable for each statistic.

4. In general terms, explain the 15 room types.

   When a room can have up to four exits, one in each of the four primary directions (north, south, east, and west), there are 15 possible exit combinations. The room types 0 through 14 represent these 15 types of rooms.

5. How does the program use the `Point` function to control the player's movement through the dungeon?

The `Point` function returns the color of a specified pixel. By checking the color on the wall of a room, the program can determine whether that wall contains a door.

6. What happens in the program when the player discovers a cache of gold, a spell, or a serum?

The program adds the appropriate item to the player's inventory, which means adding it to the appropriate variable in the `Stats` data.

7. How does the Dragonlord program handle the fact that creatures in a dungeon are often on the move?

Every time the player moves into an empty room, there's a random chance that he'll encounter a skeleton.

8. How do the Weapon and Strength attributes affect a fight?

Both of these attributes affect the player's modifier, which is a value that's added to the player's dice roll. The better the player's weapon and the higher the player's strength, the higher this modifier will be, thus making the skeleton easier to defeat. Conversely, beating the skeleton is harder if these stats are low.

9. What attributes do the skeleton characters have?

Only one: hit points. Each skeleton starts with 5 hit points. When the player hits a skeleton, the program takes away some of its hit points. When the skeleton runs out of hit points, he's dead and the battle is over.

10. How can you use a Boolean expression to replace some types of `If` statements?

A Boolean expression has an actual numerical value. This value is 0 for `False` and -1 for `True`. You can use multiplication to take advantage of this value in order to add or subtract from statistics, just as Dragonlord does with the statement `SetStrength -1 - 1 * Abs(Stats.Pie < 1)`.

Exercises

1. Add a spell skill (attribute) to Dragonlord. This statistic should range from a minimum of 1 to a maximum of 5. At the start of the game, the spell skill should be set to 1. Each time the player casts a spell, the spell skill should go up 1. Use the spell skill in the program so that the higher the player's skill, the closer the player gets to his target room when he casts the spell. That is, a spell skill of 1 should give the player only a 20% chance of reaching the selected room, whereas a spell skill of 5 should give the player a 100% chance of reaching the selected room. You should add more spell items to the dungeon to counteract the fact that they are now harder

to use. (Hint: You can call the `Teleport` subroutine to transfer the player to a random room.)

You need to make changes to the source code shown below. Note that there is a special test dungeon named TestDungeon.drg on this book's CD-ROM that you can use to test your new version of Dragonlord. This test dungeon has spells in every room in order to make it easy to test the new `SpellMove` subroutine:

```
Type StatsType
  HitPoints As Integer
  Strength As Integer
  Pie As Integer
  Gold As Integer
  Spells As Integer
  Serums As Integer
  Brew As Boolean
  Room As Integer
  Weapon As Integer
  PieMoveCount As Integer
  CastingSpell As Boolean
  SpellSkill As Integer
End Type

Sub ResetStats()
  Stats.HitPoints = 50
  Stats.Strength = 100
  Stats.Pie = 1
  Stats.Gold = 60
  Stats.Spells = 0
  Stats.Serums = 0
  Stats.Brew = False
  Stats.Room = 45
  Stats.Weapon = FIST
  Stats.PieMoveCount = 0
  Stats.CastingSpell = False
  Stats.SpellSkill = 1
End Sub

Public Sub cmdStats_Click()
  cmdRandomize.Enabled = False
  Load frmStats
  PrintStat 50, 50, "Hit Points: " & Stats.HitPoints
  PrintStat 50, 65, "Strength: " & Stats.Strength
  PrintStat 50, 80, "Pie: " & Stats.Pie
  PrintStat 50, 95, "Gold: " & Stats.Gold
  PrintStat 50, 110, "Spells: " & Stats.Spells
  PrintStat 50, 125, "Serums: " & Stats.Serums
  PrintStat 50, 140, "Brew: " & -Int(Stats.Brew)
  PrintStat 50, 155, "Weapon: " & Stats.Weapon
  PrintStat 50, 170, "Spell Skill: " & Stats.SpellSkill
```

```
      frmStats.Show vbModal, Me
End Sub

Sub SpellMove(X As Single, Y As Single)
  Dim newRoom As Integer
  If X > OFFSETX And X < MAXX And _
      Y > OFFSETY And Y < MAXY Then
    Stats.CastingSpell = False
    PlaySound SpellSound, False, False
    Dim SpellFail
    SpellFail = Int(Rnd * 5) + 1
    If SpellFail > Stats.SpellSkill Then
      Teleport
    Else
      newRoom = CalcRoomNumber(X, Y)
      Stats.Room = newRoom
      DrawRoom
      DrawRoomMarker
      ShowItem newRoom
    End If
  End If
  If Stats.SpellSkill < 5 Then _
      Stats.SpellSkill = Stats.SpellSkill + 1
End Sub
```

Answers for Day 14

Quiz

1. What's the only thing a level editor really needs to do?

   Write to a disk file the data that the game needs to load a level.

2. How do DungeonEditor's buttons serve double duty in the program?

   Not only do they act as graphical buttons, but they also hold the images needed to paint the dungeon map display.

3. What's important about the order of the buttons in DungeonEditor's toolbox?

   The order reflects the numerical values for the rooms and items in the dungeon.

4. What's the advantage of grouping DungeonEditor's buttons into a control array?

   This technique enables the program to handle a set of buttons with a single event handler, rather than requiring a handler for every button.

A

5. Explain the purpose of the NeedToSave variable.

The NeedToSave variable is a Boolean value that indicates whether the user needs to save the current dungeon before exiting the program. By checking the value of this variable, the program knows when it needs to warn the user to save his work.

6. What are the values that the program stores in the Rooms() and Items() arrays?

The Rooms() array holds the room types for each room in the dungeon, and the Items() array holds the items that are located in each of the dungeon rooms.

7. What data does DungeonEditor need to write to disk in order to create a dungeon file that Dragonlord can load and interpret?

The editor only needs to write out the contents of the Rooms() and Items() arrays. These arrays hold all the data that defines a Dragonlord dungeon.

Answers for Day 15

Quiz

1. Explain how the picScreen PictureBox control in Moonlord's main form enables the form to act as the display for all three of Moonlord's game screens.

The PictureBox control will hold a different picture depending on the screen the player has switched to.

2. How do the four CommandButton controls help implement the different Moonlord game screens?

The buttons' captions and the commands they trigger will change when the currently displayed screen changes.

3. What is the purpose of all the Image controls you added to the main form?

These Image controls hold some of the pictures that the program needs to create the long-range and short-range scanner screens.

4. Why does the About dialog box display the title "Application Title" at design time and the title "Moonlord" at runtime?

At runtime, Visual Basic replaces the default title string with the application name you've supplied for the project.

5. Where can you find the settings that Visual Basic uses for some of the strings in the About dialog box?

These settings are on the Make page of the Project Properties dialog box. To display the dialog box, select the Project menu's Properties command.

Answers for Day 16

Quiz

1. What's the difference between program variables and game variables?

   Program variables are initialized only once when the program first starts. Game variables must be initialized for each new game.

2. What do the values in the VectorsX1() and VectorsY1() arrays mean?

   The values in these arrays determine the direction of a photon when it's fired.

3. Explain how the program will use the GameMode variable and the GameModes enumeration.

   The game modes determine how the screen's buttons are set up and what the player can and can't do at a given point in the game. The GameMode variable holds the currently active mode value, and the GameModes enumeration defines symbols for each of the game modes to which the GameMode variable can be set.

4. What do the values stored in the SystemStats() array represent?

   The current status (operational or damaged) of each of the ship's six systems.

5. What do the values stored in the GameStats() array represent?

   The time remaining, the number of aliens remaining, the number of photons remaining, and the energy remaining.

6. What do the Board() and Drawn() arrays represent?

   The Board() array holds the contents of the long-range grid, and the Drawn() array contains Boolean values that indicate which of the long-range scanner sectors have been drawn on the screen.

7. In general, explain how the program positions objects in the short-range grids.

   The program first generates a random column and row. Then it checks whether the sector at the generated column and row is empty. If it is, the program can place an object in that location. If the selected location is not empty, the program must choose another random column and row.

8. What's the difference between how the starbases are placed in the long-range grid and how aliens are placed?

   The starbases can be placed only in the first or last four columns of the long-range grid. Aliens can be placed anywhere, except where another object already exists.

Answers for Day 18

Quiz

1. What does the program need to do with the four command buttons when the player switches from the main screen to the scanner screen and vice versa?

    Change the captions on the buttons to the commands appropriate for the current screen.

2. Explain the SHORTRANGESCAN and SHORTCRUISE game modes.

    SHORTRANGESCAN is the default game mode when the player is viewing the short-range scanner screen. The SHORTCRUISE game mode is when the player has clicked the Cruise button on the short-range scanner screen but hasn't yet selected the sector where he wants to move.

3. In general, what does the DoShortScan subroutine do?

    DoShortScan iterates through each of the sectors in the short-range scanner grid, drawing the contents of each sector as it goes.

4. Which subroutine must be called after every command the player issues on the sort-range scanner screen when aliens are present? Why?

    The AliensAttack subroutine must be called because it's the subroutine that handles the aliens' turn.

5. How does the program determine how many ship systems are damaged after the player rams an alien ship?

    By getting a random number between 1 and 4 (inclusive).

6. In general, what does the SetUpAliens subroutine do?

    The SetUpAliens subroutine initializes variables that are used to track information about the aliens in a sector.

7. How does the ShowBoard subroutine, which redraws sectors on the main screen, know which sectors to draw?

    The Drawn() array contains a True value for each sector that must be drawn.

8. Why does the TrackPhoton subroutine get the color of a pixel before drawing the photon torpedo on the pixel?

    The pixel's color tells the program whether the photon torpedo has struck an alien ship or a sun.

9. In general, what does the CheckShortCruise function do?

The CheckShortCruise verifies that the player can move to the sector he has chosen. For example, the player isn't allowed to move past items such as suns and alien ships.

Answers for Day 19

Quiz

1. What does Moonlord need to do to set up the buttons on the status screen?

It must copy the correct bitmaps to the first two buttons and remove the second two buttons from the form (actually, it makes them invisible).

2. In general, what does the DoRepair subroutine do?

It subtracts a day from the time needed to repair each of the ship's damaged systems.

3. In general, what does the ShowStatusValues subroutine do?

This subroutine displays the current values of the ship system repair statuses and the game's statistics. It also updates the buttons, turning the Repair button on or off as appropriate.

4. When does the CheckSystems function return a value of True?

When one or more of the ship's systems are damaged.

Answers for Day 20

Quiz

1. What's the purpose of Moonlord's timer control?

The program uses the timer to time the blinking of the player's marker on the long-range scanner screen. The marker blinks every 1/4 second.

2. Explain, in general, how the AnimateMarker subroutine works.

Every 1/4 second, the Timer1_Timer event procedure calls the AnimateMarker subroutine. This subroutine displays an image in the player's current sector on the long-range scanner screen, alternating between the player's normal marker and one that represents the contents of the sector. The program uses the BlinkMode variable to keep track of which image to display each time AnimateMarker gets called.

3. Several of Moonlord's animation sequences are made up of eight different images. Explain how the program uses those eight images to produce an animation.

The program displays the images, one after the other, in rapid sequence.

4. How are the phaser, docking, and alien-shooting animations similar?

Each of these animation sequences uses only two images to create a blinking effect.

Answers for Day 21

Quiz

1. By examining the DirectSound variables, can you tell how many sound effects the program uses?

Yes, because each sound effect has its own DirectSoundBuffer object.

2. What is the purpose of the line `ChDir "d:\TYVBGames\Moonlord\"` in the `InitSound` subroutine?

This line ensures that Moonlord can find the sound-effect files when the program is being run from inside the Visual Basic programming environment. The compiled version of the program doesn't need this line because the executable knows to look inside its own directory for the files.

3. How does Moonlord synchronize its sound effects with its animations?

By triggering the sound effects at the same time the animation sequences start.

4. List the name of every variable you've declared in this book. If you answer this question correctly, you will become an honorary member of PWDKJWTSO (People Who Don't Know a Joke When They See One).

If you actually answered this one, you have way too much time on your hands!

APPENDIX B

Designing Computer Game Graphics

Probably the most important element of a computer game, aside from its playability, is its graphics. The better the graphics, the more the player will enjoy the game. In fact, graphics are so important that many mediocre games become popular solely because of their visual appeal.

Unfortunately, most programmers are about as artistically gifted as chimpanzees with cans of spray paint. To create a visually appealing game, many programmers hire artists. Many other gifted programmers—those who are capable of writing sensational games—simply give up on the idea of game programming when they discover their artistic limitations.

If this sounds familiar, here's good news: The graphics that are often used in computer games aren't particularly hard to draw. Learning to draw simple computer graphics is a lot like learning to make a cake from a mix. Much of computer graphic design is a matter of technique rather than skill. Of course, a few lessons in computer graphics won't make you an artist. If your game requires a lot of detailed graphics, such as people, monsters, and buildings, you'll probably still need to find an artist. But read on. You'll be amazed at how far you can get with just a few graphics lessons.

3D Made Simple

Games often boast of "realistic 3D graphics," but everything on your computer screen is flat and therefore two-dimensional. Although the images may *seem* to be three-dimensional, this is an illusion. What this book refers to as 3D graphics, then, are simply 2D images that give the illusion of depth (like photographs). Many of the graphics in the games in this book are *three-quarter view* or *pseudo-isometric view* graphics. In other words, the viewing angle for some objects is such that three sides are displayed: front, side, and top.

But before you get into three-quarter view graphics, it's time for a quick lesson in basic 3D computer drawing techniques. Some approaches to using graphics to create a sense of depth are very simple—so simple, in fact, that they require only a few lines. For example, one of the most common and useful 3D drawing techniques is based on the idea that all light comes from above. After all, sunlight never comes from below (unless you're in space), and even artificial light sources are usually placed at or above eye level. Therefore, people automatically associate brightly illuminated surfaces with the tops of objects and deeply shaded surfaces with the bottoms of objects.

Figure B.1 illustrates this principle. The drawing uses only three colors: white, gray, and black. Gray is the neutral background color, neither highlighted nor shadowed. On the background of the first image, the artist has drawn a reversed black "L," representing two sides of a rectangle. To create a 3D illusion for the rectangle in the middle of the figure, the artist completes the rectangle with white lines so that the rectangle seems to protrude from the background. To create the last rectangle in the figure, the artist makes a similar drawing, but uses white for the base "L" and black to complete the rectangle. This rectangle appears to be indented.

FIGURE B.1

A simple 3D drawing technique.

If you stack such elements (drawing one within the confines of another), you can create an illusion of multiple layers and varying depth. As Figure B.2 demonstrates, you can even use this technique to draw buttons that seem to be indented when they are selected.

Figure B.2

Stacking 3D objects.

Using light this way is a useful technique for several reasons. First, it's easy to do. Second, it takes advantage of human depth perception. Third, it's so simple that you can easily accomplish it through programming—just plotting a few lines on the screen— rather than having to draw the images in a paint application and then load the image into your program.

How to Make a 2D Square into a 3D Box

To create more detailed graphics, you must use a paint program. Images drawn with a paint program are called *bitmapped graphics* or just *bitmaps*. A bitmap can't be drawn with graphics function calls (at least, not very easily). Instead, you must transfer it to the screen as one complete image. This chapter teaches you some simple but effective bitmap-drawing techniques. (There's no point in trying to win the race before you know how to start the car!)

There are a lot of techniques for making flat computer graphics seem three-dimensional. The most sophisticated techniques require either a lot of artistic skill or some very specialized graphics tools (such as a 3D modeling and rendering package). These sophisticated methods are beyond the scope of this book. However, there are some techniques that even non-artists can use to create good-looking graphics with even the most rudimentary graphics editors or paint programs.

One basic trick for creating a 3D illusion is to add a simple shadow. This shadow is a dark silhouette, identical in shape to the primary object, placed so that it appears to be behind the object. You create the illusion of depth by offsetting the shadow away from the primary object. You can see this effect by drawing a solid white square on top of a solid black square, as shown in Figure B.3.

Figure B.3

Creating a shadow effect.

Many computer paint programs enable you to create this shadow effect simply by copying the object that you're drawing, coloring the copy darker than the original object so that the copy looks like a shadow, and then placing a copy of the original object over the new shadow object, as was done with the two squares in Figure B.3. The original object seems to be closer to you than its shadow.

You can get an even more realistic effect if you scale the shadow down slightly to simulate a perspective shift, as in Figure B.4. The farther away something is, the smaller it looks. Consequently, the smaller a shadow is in relation to the object casting it, the farther away the shadow appears.

FIGURE B.4

Adding greater depth to a shadow.

Although the preceding technique is a good way to create a 3D effect between an object and its background, it's not an good method for making the object itself look three-dimensional. However, you can use a variation of the shadow technique to draw three-dimensional objects. This variation is similar to the pencil-and-paper drawing technique, in which you change two overlapping squares into a cube by adding lines between the corners.

The images in Figure B.5 illustrate the principle. First, the artist draws two overlapping squares slightly diagonal to each other. Next, she draws lines connecting the equivalent corners on each square. This results in a wireframe cube, which gives the illusion of three dimensions but not of solidity. To make the cube look solid, the artist must select the square that she wants to be in front and then erase any lines that show through that front square and the top and facing squares. (The third cube in the figure shows the lines that the artist is going to remove in order to form a solid cube.) Presto! A solid cube.

FIGURE B.5

Creating a 3D cube.

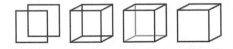

The less the squares overlap, the longer the object appears to be. (If the starting squares don't overlap at all, your drawing will look more like a railroad tie than a square cube.) This drawing technique isn't limited to squares. You can do the same thing with any shapes, from triangles to nonagons and more (see first image in Figure B.6). The technique works for virtually all geometric shapes, except circles and ellipsoids. They have no corners to connect, so the technique for making these objects look three-dimensional is a little different (see the second image in Figure B.6).

FIGURE B.6

Other three-dimension-al objects.

If you don't want your 3D object to look like it just came out of hyperspace, make sure to keep the two source objects properly aligned. In other words, don't rotate one object relative to the other, or you may end up with bizarre results like those shown in Figure B.7. The last time I saw a cube like that, my wife had to drive me home from the party!

B

FIGURE B.7

An improperly drawn 3D cube.

Now that you understand a few general principles, you can use them to create more sophisticated computer graphics, including the aforementioned three-quarter-view graphics. In the examples that follow, you'll continue to use the technique of creating a new three-dimensional object by connecting two copies of the same object. However, instead of using paper-and-pencil drawing techniques, you'll use the graphics power built into computer paint programs.

Offset Stamping for 3D Results

Dragonlord, one of the games in this book, requires a dungeon map made up of a matrix of individual rooms shown at three-quarter-view perspective. Creating such a room object is a good way to demonstrate a graphics technique known as *offset stamping*.

To use the offset stamping technique described here, you must have a graphics editor or paint program that enables you to clip a graphics element and stamp down copies without disturbing the original. Furthermore, you must be able to create transparent copies of objects. Such an object has a transparent background that doesn't erase the images beneath it.

To try offset stamping, first start your paint program and draw a square frame (*not* a filled square). Next, make a small opening in one of the sides to represent a door. Use your paint program's clipboard to copy the square, and then stamp a copy somewhere else on the screen. Pick a different color than you used for the first square and make the copy this new color. You use these two squares as source elements when you create a simulated 3D room, as shown in Figure B.8.

FIGURE B.8

Using offset stamping to create a room.

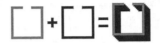

To use offset stamping to create the room, copy the square that you recolored, move to a blank area of the screen, and stamp a copy of the square there. Then stamp another copy over the first, just one pixel above and to the left of the first, as shown in Figure B.9. Do this several times, each time offsetting the stamp the same amount. Next, copy the first square that you drew and stamp it onto the stack that you just made, offsetting it as you did the other squares. When you're done, you should have a 3D room similar to the one shown in Figure B.8.

FIGURE B.9

The offset stamping technique.

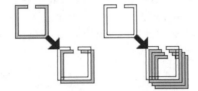

You can make your 3D objects look more realistic by adding more complex shading. One good method is to shade the faces of your starting shape with different colors and hues before you use the offset stamping technique. Figure B.10 shows an example of this shading. In this example, the source of the light on the object is above and to the right (as indicated by the sun symbol). You use the angle of the light source to determine how bright each object surface should be. To make the effect realistic, treat each face like a wall. If one side faces the light, make it brighter so that the other side is clearly in shadow.

FIGURE B.10

Shading an object before offset stamping.

After you finish the shading, use the offset stamping technique to create a room. First, stack several copies of the shaded object, offsetting each copy by one pixel both horizontally and vertically. Then fill the original shaded object with a single color and use that new object to "cap" the stack. If you start with the object shown in Figure B.10, you'll end up with objects like those shown in figure B.11. As you can see, altering the direction of the offset stamping changes the appearance of the objects.

FIGURE B.11

Shaded objects created by offset stamping.

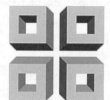

You can apply the offset stamping technique to virtually any shape. As Figure B.12 shows, you can even use offset stamping to create round objects (although they require more subtle shading).

FIGURE B.12

Shaded round objects created by offset stamping.

Special Tips and Tricks

Beyond 3D rooms and objects, you'll undoubtedly need many other graphical objects for your games. Some objects, such as bricks, are fairly simple to create. Others, such as teleport squares or glass spheres, require a bit more skill. To help you get started, the rest of this appendix is devoted to basic tips, techniques, and tricks for solving or avoiding difficult graphics problems.

Choosing Identifiable Objects

Sometimes the hardest task in drawing game graphics is to make an object look like the real-world object that it's *supposed* to look like. Resolution and color limitations often complicate your computer graphics drawing, but sometimes just figuring out how to symbolize an object can drive you to the medicine cabinet for aspirin.

For example, your game design might call for the hero to wear ultraviolet contact lenses that enable him to see certain other game objects. But contact lenses are little more than glass disks, which are difficult to render realistically. Would you recognize a graphic of contact lenses, no matter how well it was drawn?

In such circumstances, you should find a more easily identifiable object to replace the ambiguous object in your game. For example, you might use eyeglasses in your game instead of contact lenses. A player is unlikely to mistake a pair of eyeglasses for any other object.

Designing Icons

Creating icons for computer programs can be tougher than climbing a greased tree. Although a sword icon clearly represents fighting and a scissors icon obviously represents some kind of cutting function, how can you represent less visual functions, such as saving a game or displaying a high-score board?

Unfortunately, designing icons is a skill that can't be taught. It requires a lot of imagination and trial and error. Where icons are concerned, a picture is clearly *not* worth a thousand words!

Obviously, when you're designing icons, you should strive for simple, unambiguous images that easily identify their associated functions. If you can't come up with such images, you're far better off to use text labels instead. There are few things more annoying in computer interfaces than poorly designed icons.

Drawing Metal

Believe it or not, drawing metal surfaces is one of the easiest tasks in computer graphics, provided you have two or more shades of a specific color available. For flat metal surfaces, just draw diagonal highlights on the object. If you have more than two shades available, you can get more complex, alternating highlights by using darker reflections. Figure B.13 demonstrates this metal drawing technique. The more shades of a specific color you use, the more effective your result will be.

FIGURE B.13

Using highlights and reflections to draw metal surfaces.

You can use a similar technique to draw curved metal surfaces, but you must follow slightly different rules. First, highlights must appear near the edge closest to the light, and shadows must appear near the edges farthest from the light. Figure B.14 shows how you can make a cylinder appear metallic by changing hues and placing highlights appropriately. Notice that the harsh shadow along the dark left side of the cylinder softens to a lighter shade at the rim, which produces a more reflective look.

FIGURE B.14

Drawing a curved metal surface.

Because most metals are reflective, they display severe highlights and shadows. In other words, the more smoothly and evenly you blend shades into each other, the less metallic the surface appears. Adding specular highlights or "hot spots" (extremely bright points of reflected light, as shown in Figure B.14) helps make surfaces look more metallic.

Drawing Glass

Because glass is transparent, you don't draw it any more than you can draw air. What you *can* draw is the effect that glass has on objects that are seen through it. Often, the simplest way to create a glass object is to draw its general shape and then add highlights and shadows as you did when drawing metal. You then draw whatever shows through the glass, highlighting and shading it appropriately.

Figure B.15 shows how this works. You draw the bottle in light gray, with white highlights and dark gray shadows. Then you draw the liquid within the bottle by replacing the bottle's colors with different shades, but leaving a slim line of the original color at the perimeter of the bottle to show the thickness of the glass. The result looks transparent.

FIGURE B.15

Drawing a glass bottle.

Because glass is reflective, you can create glass surfaces by placing highlights on them, similar to those that you use to create metal surfaces. Highlights can either obscure objects seen through the glass or allow those objects to show through. If the object seen through the glass extends beyond the edges of the glass, you should degrade that part of the object by drawing it with slightly lighter colors. This is because glass isn't perfectly transparent and thus captures a tiny amount of light. This makes an image seen through glass look slightly dulled, as though it's lost some of its color. Also, glass sometimes bends light passing through it, resulting in some distortion of the image. To create this distortion, you can slightly enlarge the part of the object behind the glass as though it's being magnified.

Figure B.16 demonstrates the use of reflection, degradation, and distortion. It shows part of a metal rod as seen through a pane of glass.

FIGURE B.16

Using reflections, degradation, and distortion in drawing glass objects.

Drawing Luminous Objects

You can take advantage of several tricks when drawing luminous objects such as light bulbs or flaring stars. But if you're not careful, you may end up with a strange-looking object indeed. For example, if you draw a glow around a light bulb, almost anyone can tell that the light bulb is supposed to be glowing. However, if you place the same glow around an object shaped like a sheep, you get a lamb in need of shearing. Still, the glow effect is useful if used sparingly.

One of the best ways to create a luminous object is to draw the effect of the emitted light on the object's surroundings. For example, a glowing light-emitting diode (LED) is just a brightly colored blob. The only way you can show that the LED is lighted is by drawing the effects of its light on its surroundings. Likewise, when you draw a knight wielding a glowing sword, the sword should throw highlights on the knight while casting other parts of the figure into shadow. Figure B.17 shows these types of objects.

FIGURE B.17

Drawing glowing objects.

Fire, another type of glowing object, is difficult to draw because one of its distinguishing characteristics is its motion—the dance of the flame. Often, a static representation of flame looks like anything *but* fire. The colors that you use when drawing fire also can have a profound effect on the end result. The wrong hues may make your fire look more like a popsicle.

There are few good rules for drawing fire. Your best bet is to stick with the colors that people automatically associate with fire (reds and oranges), and place flames within recognizable contexts, such as camps, fireplaces, and torches.

Drawing Drop Shadows

A *drop shadow* is a shadow that you place under an item you've drawn. This is useful for a couple of reasons. First, if an object's drop shadow is immediately beneath and connected to the object, you can tell that the object is resting on the ground (or some other surface). Conversely, when an object's drop shadow is disconnected from and farther below the object, the object appears to be floating in the air.

There's not much to say about drop shadows. They're generally dark spots, often black, that appear around the base of an object or below an airborne one. The simplest drop shadows, such as those used in cartoons, are just spots. However, more elaborate drop shadows mimic the casting object's shape. Figure B.18 provides a couple of examples.

FIGURE B.18

Drawing drop shadows.

Smoothing Graphics

All display graphics on the PC are *raster* displays composed of thousands of illuminated dots on a vast grid. Therefore, the only perfectly smooth lines that you can draw are horizontal or vertical ones. Any line that deviates from perfect horizontal or vertical orientation is drawn across a series of rows and columns and appears to consist of staggered line fragments with obvious stairsteps. This stairstep effect is known as an *alias* (or colloquially as a "jaggie" because of its jagged look). The technique that you use to disguise this alias effect is called *antialiasing*.

Antialiasing blurs the edges of each stairstep by placing a pixel or pixels of an intermediate color or tone at the end of it. For example, to smooth the aliases between a blue or red area, place a purple pixel at each stairstep.

Figure B.19 demonstrates antialiasing on a black circle. The left circle of each pair is drawn black on white with no antialiasing. The right circle of each pair is antialiased, with two or more shades of gray used to blur the stairsteps. When the antialiasing is enlarged, as in the pair of circles on the right, it looks odd. However, when viewed at normal scale on a computer screen, as shown in the pair of circles on the left, antialiasing works wonderfully to reduce and even remove the stairstep effect.

FIGURE B.19

Antialiasing at work.

Many paint programs have a built-in feature for antialiasing part or all of a screen or graphic. Most of these antialiasing functions do a fairly good job, but like any automated procedure, sometimes you may not get the exact effect that you want. In such circumstances, you may have to retouch the antialiasing or even redo it from scratch.

Overusing antialiasing can result in fuzzy images. The fewer pixels that you use to draw an item, the more likely it is to become fuzzy when antialiased. Also, high-contrast images often look slightly muddy when antialiased.

Finally, if you antialias a graphic before placing it on its final background, you may get unexpected and unappealing results. Because the colors used in antialiasing are intermediate, placing a graphics element onto a different background color changes the antialiasing effect. You should make antialiasing the final step in preparing graphics. (Keep a copy of the original image, free of antialiasing, in case you have to make major changes or you just dislike the antialiasing effect.)

Summary

Although it takes many years of study and practice to become a competent computer artist, you can quickly learn several handy techniques for drawing effective—albeit simple—game graphics. These techniques include highlighting, shading, offset stamping, and antialiasing. You can combine all of these effects to create many types of pseudo-3D objects. These techniques even enable you to draw metal and glass surfaces.

APPENDIX C

Windows API Functions for Game Programmers

On Day 6, "Graphics Programming with the Windows API," you learned how to call Windows API functions. This appendix lists some of the API functions that you might find useful or interesting, along with their Visual Basic declarations. If you find something you like, look up the function in your online API reference to get all the details. Remember that some of these functions require that you also define special data types. If you've forgotten how to do this, refer back to Day 6.

AngleArc()

Draws an arc with a line segment connecting to it from the current drawing position:

```
Public Declare Function AngleArc Lib "gdi32" Alias "AngleArc" _
    (ByVal hdc As Long, ByVal x As Long, ByVal y As Long, _
    ByVal dwRadius As Long, ByVal eStartAngle As Double, _
    ByVal eSweepAngle As Double) As Long
```

Arc()

Draws an arc:

```
Public Declare Function Arc Lib "gdi32" Alias "Arc" _
    (ByVal hdc As Long, ByVal X1 As Long, ByVal Y1 As Long, _
    ByVal X2 As Long, ByVal Y2 As Long, ByVal X3 As Long, _
    ByVal Y3 As Long, ByVal X4 As Long, ByVal Y4 As Long) As Long
```

BitBlt()

Transfers a rectangular area of pixel color values from a source device context to a destination device context:

```
Public Declare Function BitBlt Lib "gdi32" Alias "BitBlt" _
    (ByVal hDestDC As Long, ByVal x As Long, ByVal y As Long, _
    ByVal nWidth As Long, ByVal nHeight As Long, _
    ByVal hSrcDC As Long, ByVal xSrc As Long, _
    ByVal ySrc As Long, ByVal dwRop As Long) As Long
```

Chord()

Draws a chord, which is the area formed when a line segment intersects an ellipse:

```
Public Declare Function Chord Lib "gdi32" Alias "Chord" _
    (ByVal hdc As Long, ByVal X1 As Long, ByVal Y1 As Long, _
    ByVal X2 As Long, ByVal Y2 As Long, ByVal X3 As Long, _
    ByVal Y3 As Long, ByVal X4 As Long, ByVal Y4 As Long) As Long
```

CreateBrushIndirect()

Creates a brush with the style, color, and pattern specified in a LOGBRUSH structure:

```
Public Declare Function CreateBrushIndirect Lib "gdi32" _
    Alias "CreateBrushIndirect" (lpLogBrush As LOGBRUSH) As Long
```

CreateDIBSection()

Creates a DIB (device-independent bitmap) that can be accessed directly in memory:

```
Public Declare Function CreateDIBSection Lib "gdi32" _
    Alias "CreateDIBSection" (ByVal hDC As Long, _
    pBitmapInfo As BITMAPINFO, ByVal un As Long, _
    ByVal lplpVoid As Long, ByVal handle As Long, _
    ByVal dw As Long) As Long
```

CreateHatchBrush()

Creates a brush with the given color and hatch pattern:

```
Public Declare Function CreateHatchBrush Lib "gdi32" _
    Alias "CreateHatchBrush" (ByVal nIndex As Long, _
    ByVal crColor As Long) As Long
```

CreatePatternBrush()

Creates a brush from the supplied bitmap image:

```
Public Declare Function CreatePatternBrush Lib "gdi32" _
    Alias "CreatePatternBrush" (ByVal hBitmap As Long) As Long
```

CreatePen()

Creates a pen of the given color, style, and thickness:

```
Public Declare Function CreatePen Lib "gdi32" Alias _
    "CreatePen" (ByVal nPenStyle As Long, _
    ByVal nWidth As Long, ByVal crColor As Long) As Long
```

CreateSolidBrush()

Creates a brush of the given solid color:

```
Public Declare Function CreateSolidBrush Lib "gdi32" _
    Alias "CreateSolidBrush" (ByVal crColor As Long) As Long
```

DeleteObject()

Deletes from memory a graphical object, such as a pen, bitmap, or brush:

```
Public Declare Function DeleteObject Lib "gdi32" _
    Alias "DeleteObject" (ByVal hObject As Long) As Long
```

Ellipse()

Draws an ellipse or circle:

```
Public Declare Function Ellipse Lib "gdi32" Alias "Ellipse" _
    (ByVal hdc As Long, ByVal X1 As Long, ByVal Y1 As Long, _
    ByVal X2 As Long, ByVal Y2 As Long) As Long
```

C

FloodFill()

Fills an area with the currently selected brush:

```
Public Declare Function FloodFill Lib "gdi32" Alias _
    "FloodFill" (ByVal hdc As Long, ByVal x As Long, _
    ByVal y As Long, ByVal crColor As Long) As Long
```

GetBitmapBits()

Retrieves the image data from the given bitmap:

```
Public Declare Function GetBitmapBits Lib "gdi32" _
    Alias "GetBitmapBits" (ByVal hBitmap As Long, _
    ByVal dwCount As Long, lpBits As Any) As Long
```

GetDC()

Gets the context for the window associated with the specified window handle:

```
Public Declare Function GetDC Lib "user32" Alias "GetDC" _
    (ByVal hwnd As Long) As Long
```

GetDIBColorTable()

Gets the RGB color values from a DIB:

```
Public Declare Function GetDIBColorTable Lib "gdi32" _
    Alias "GetDIBColorTable" (ByVal hDC As Long, _
    ByVal un1 As Long, ByVal un2 As Long, _
    pRGBQuad As RGBQUAD) As Long
```

GetDIBits()

Copies the image data from a bitmap into a buffer:

```
Public Declare Function GetDIBits Lib "gdi32" Alias _
    "GetDIBits" (ByVal aHDC As Long, ByVal hBitmap As Long, _
    ByVal nStartScan As Long, ByVal nNumScans As Long, _
    lpBits As Any, lpBI As BITMAPINFO, ByVal wUsage As Long) _
    As Long
```

GetObject()

Gets information about a graphical object, such as a bitmap, pen, or brush:

```
Public Declare Function GetObject Lib "gdi32" Alias _
    "GetObjectA" (ByVal hObject As Long, _
    ByVal nCount As Long, lpObject As Any) As Long
```

GetPixel()

Gets the RGB color value of the pixel at the given location:

```
Public Declare Function GetPixel Lib "gdi32" Alias _
    "GetPixel" (ByVal hdc As Long, ByVal x As Long, _
    ByVal y As Long) As Long
```

LineTo()

Draws a line from the current location to the given location:

```
Public Declare Function LineTo Lib "gdi32" Alias "LineTo" _
    (ByVal hdc As Long, ByVal x As Long, ByVal y As Long) As Long
```

MaskBlt()

Combines the pixels from a source and destination bitmap using a given mask and raster operation:

```
Public Declare Function MaskBlt Lib "gdi32" Alias "MaskBlt" _
    (ByVal hdcDest As Long, ByVal nXDest As Long, _
    ByVal nYDest As Long, ByVal nWidth As Long, _
    ByVal nHeight As Long, ByVal hdcSrc As Long, _
    ByVal nXSrc As Long, ByVal nYSrc As Long, _
    ByVal hbmMask As Long, ByVal xMask As Long, _
    ByVal yMask As Long, ByVal dwRop As Long) As Long
```

MessageBeep()

Plays one of the system-defined WAV sounds:

```
Public Declare Function MessageBeep Lib "user32" _
    Alias "MessageBeep" (ByVal wType As Long) As Long
```

C

PatBlt()

Fills the given rectangular area with the current brush, using the given raster operation:

```
Public Declare Function PatBlt Lib "gdi32" Alias "PatBlt" _
    (ByVal hdc As Long, ByVal x As Long, ByVal y As Long, _
    ByVal nWidth As Long, ByVal nHeight As Long, _
    ByVal dwRop As Long) As Long
```

Pie()

Draws a pie slice, such as you might use in a pie-type graph:

```
Public Declare Function Pie Lib "gdi32" Alias "Pie" _
    (ByVal hdc As Long, ByVal X1 As Long, ByVal Y1 As Long, _
    ByVal X2 As Long, ByVal Y2 As Long, ByVal X3 As Long, _
    ByVal Y3 As Long, ByVal X4 As Long, ByVal Y4 As Long) As Long
```

PolyBezier()

Draws a set of Bézier curves:

```
Public Declare Function PolyBezier Lib "gdi32" Alias _
    "PolyBezier" (ByVal hdc As Long, lppt As POINTAPI, _
    ByVal cPoints As Long) As Long
```

PolyDraw()

Draws a group of lines and Bézier curves:

```
Public Declare Function PolyDraw Lib "gdi32" Alias _
    "PolyDraw" (ByVal hdc As Long, lppt As POINTAPI, _
    lpbTypes As Byte, ByVal cCount As Long) As Long
```

Polygon()

Draws a polygonal shape:

```
Public Declare Function Polygon Lib "gdi32" Alias "Polygon" _
    (ByVal hdc As Long, lpPoint As POINTAPI, _
    ByVal nCount As Long) As Long
```

Polyline()

Draws a set of lines:

```
Public Declare Function Polyline Lib "gdi32" Alias _
    "Polyline" (ByVal hdc As Long, lpPoint As POINTAPI, _
    ByVal nCount As Long) As Long
```

PolyPolygon()

Draws a set of polygonal shapes:

```
Public Declare Function PolyPolygon Lib "gdi32" Alias _
    "PolyPolygon" (ByVal hdc As Long, lpPoint As POINTAPI, _
    lpPolyCounts As Long, ByVal nCount As Long) As Long
```

PolyPolyline()

Draws a set of polylines:

```
Public Declare Function PolyPolyline Lib "gdi32" Alias _
    "PolyPolyline" (ByVal hdc As Long, lppt As POINTAPI, _
    lpdwPolyPoints As Long, ByVal cCount As Long) As Long
```

Rectangle()

Draws a rectangle:

```
Public Declare Function Rectangle Lib "gdi32" Alias _
    "Rectangle" (ByVal hdc As Long, ByVal X1 As Long, _
    ByVal Y1 As Long, ByVal X2 As Long, ByVal Y2 As Long) _
    As Long
```

RoundRect()

Draws a rectangle with rounded corners:

```
Public Declare Function RoundRect Lib "gdi32" Alias _
    "RoundRect" (ByVal hdc As Long, ByVal X1 As Long, _
    ByVal Y1 As Long, ByVal X2 As Long, ByVal Y2 As Long, _
    ByVal X3 As Long, ByVal Y3 As Long) As Long
```

C

SelectObject()

Selects a graphical object—such as a bitmap, brush, or pen—into a device context:

```
Public Declare Function SelectObject Lib "gdi32" Alias _
    "SelectObject" (ByVal hdc As Long, ByVal hObject As Long) _
    As Long
```

SetBitmapBits()

Sets the image data in a bitmap:

```
Public Declare Function SetBitmapBits Lib "gdi32" Alias _
    "SetBitmapBits" (ByVal hBitmap As Long, _
    ByVal dwCount As Long, lpBits As Any) As Long
```

SetDIBColorTable()

Sets the colors in a DIB's color table:

```
Public Declare Function SetDIBColorTable Lib "gdi32" _
    Alias "SetDIBColorTable" (ByVal hDC As Long, _
    ByVal un1 As Long, ByVal un2 As Long, _
    pcRGBQuad As RGBQUAD) As Long
```

SetPixel()

Sets the RGB value of the pixel at the given coordinates:

```
Public Declare Function SetPixel Lib "gdi32" Alias _
    "SetPixel" (ByVal hdc As Long, ByVal x As Long, _
    ByVal y As Long, ByVal crColor As Long) As Long
```

SetROP2()

Sets the raster operation to be used in subsequent drawing operations:

```
Public Declare Function SetROP2 Lib "gdi32" Alias "SetROP2" _
    (ByVal hdc As Long, ByVal nDrawMode As Long) As Long
```

StretchBlt()

Copies a rectangular area of a bitmap to another rectangular area, stretching or shrinking the source data to fit the destination rectangle and using the given raster operation to determine how to combine the source and destination pixels:

```
Public Declare Function StretchBlt Lib "gdi32" Alias _
    "StretchBlt" (ByVal hdc As Long, ByVal x As Long, _
    ByVal y As Long, ByVal nWidth As Long, _
    ByVal nHeight As Long, ByVal hSrcDC As Long, _
    ByVal xSrc As Long, ByVal ySrc As Long, _
    ByVal nSrcWidth As Long, ByVal nSrcHeight As Long, _
    ByVal dwRop As Long) As Long
```

StretchDIBits()

Copies a rectangular area of a DIB to another rectangular area, stretching or shrinking the source data to fit the destination rectangle and using the given raster operation to determine how to combine the source and destination pixels:

```
Public Declare Function StretchDIBits Lib "gdi32" Alias _
    "StretchDIBits" (ByVal hdc As Long, ByVal x As Long, _
    ByVal y As Long, ByVal dx As Long, ByVal dy As Long, _
    ByVal SrcX As Long, ByVal SrcY As Long, _
    ByVal wSrcWidth As Long, ByVal wSrcHeight As Long, _
    lpBits As Any, lpBitsInfo As BITMAPINFO, _
    ByVal wUsage As Long, ByVal dwRop As Long) As Long
```

C

APPENDIX D

Getting Started with DirectX

There are several operating systems available for owners of PC-compatible computers, but Microsoft Windows has dominated the market. All the best applications are available for Windows, and just about every new computer comes with Windows already installed. When you consider the immense popularity of Windows, you might wonder why it took so long for Windows games to appear on the shelves.

If you've ever programmed games under Windows, you already know why all the best games used to run only under good old clunky DOS. Ironically, Windows, which is a graphical user interface that relies on tons of cute little icons and buttons, used to be slowest at handling graphics. And any operating system that can't handle graphics at blazing speeds can't handle games—at least not games that require transferring a lot of graphics between memory and the screen.

So why was DOS so much better at handling graphics? Because DOS lets you create your own custom graphics routines and access graphics directly in memory. Whereas Windows, in its attempt to provide a device-independent environment, required that all graphics handling go through its GDI (Graphics Device Interface), which is a library of handy but generally slow (compared to DOS) graphics functions for doing such things as drawing lines and transferring bitmaps to the screen.

Because of the GDI, games that required high-powered graphics engines were impossible to write for Windows... until DirectX came along, that is. This appendix shows you how to get started with DirectX in your game programs.

Why Game Programmers Need Fast Graphics

But before you start learning about DirectX, you need to understand why fast graphics are so important in games. The truth is that in most games, the slowest code is the code that moves graphics data around. One reason for this is that today's computers can handle very detailed images. These high-resolution images require huge amounts of memory.

Take, for example, a 256-color image with a resolution of 640×480. A 640×480 screen is made up of 307,200 individual dots of color, or *pixels*. Each of those pixels must be represented by eight bits in memory because it requires eight bits to allow for 256 different color combinations. (This is why 256-color pictures are often referred to as 8-bit images.) Therefore, storing a 640×480, 256-color image in memory requires 307,200 bytes. That's a third of a megabyte! In order to display that image on the screen, the program must transfer the image in RAM to the screen's memory.

Now, imagine that you're using this 256-color image as the background scene in a flight simulator game. Because the background scene is constantly changing, your program must repeatedly transfer new images to the screen. Thirty images a second wouldn't be unusual (it would be a fairly slow screen update, in fact). So now the program has to move 30×307,200 bytes—almost ten megabytes—of graphical data each second. Things are really starting to slow down now.

But there's still more. Suppose there are objects that move around on top of this constantly changing scene. These objects, called *sprites* in computer-gaming lingo, include the player's onscreen character and all the enemies the player is currently fighting. These sprites are graphical objects that must be transferred to the screen. So now, not only must the program transfer the background scene to the screen 30 times a second, but it must also transfer each sprite onto this image, one by one.

And this scenario ignores the problems you encounter when trying to animate sprites directly on the screen. Because simple animation produces an annoying flicker as sprites constantly appear and disappear, game programmers usually compose a complete scene in memory before transferring that scene to the screen. This can double the amount of graphical data that must be transferred because now the new background scene (or at least parts of it) must be transferred from one part of memory to another, the sprites are added, and then the whole thing is transferred to the screen. When you think about it, it's a miracle that computer games work at all!

Enter DirectX

DirectX is a set of COM objects for handling graphics, sound, input devices, and network play under Windows. COM, which stands for Component Object Model, is a specification for creating standalone Windows objects that can be called upon by any program in the system. COM objects provide an interface that applications use to call the member functions included in the object. For example, to use the DirectDraw component of DirectX, you create a DirectDraw object. Then you can call DirectDraw's member functions through the DirectDraw object.

If you've looked at DirectX's programmer's reference, you may have been shocked by the number of functions supplied by the library. The good news is that only a small subset of these functions is required for most game programs. For example, several DirectDraw functions give you the necessary tools to transfer bitmaps quickly between memory and the screen. In many cases, however, you may need to supply your own custom graphics functions for completing such tasks as loading bitmaps and sound files.

D

The Components of DirectX

DirectX actually comprises seven main components:

- **DirectDraw**—DirectDraw's specialty is graphics. It gives your program direct control over a computer's video hardware, enabling the program to quickly transfer graphics between memory and the screen. DirectDraw is designed to take advantage of any hardware capabilities that may be present on the user's video card. Moreover, DirectDraw can emulate most of these capabilities in software when they aren't available on the graphics card.

- **DirectSound**—DirectSound is to sound cards what DirectDraw is to video cards, providing an almost device-independent method for directly dealing with the user's sound devices. DirectSound allows you to more easily synchronize your sound effects with events on the screen because it responds much faster than other Windows sound functions, such as those included in the MCI (multimedia control interface). DirectSound can even handle 3D sound effects.

- **DirectInput**—Although most Windows games use the mouse as the control device, DirectInput provides the functionality your program needs to respond to a joystick. For this reason, you can now more easily create arcade-style games that use joysticks or control pads to control onscreen characters. Using DirectInput, your program can calibrate a joystick and read its position and buttons.

- **DirectPlay**—Today's most popular games enable players to compete head-to-head or cooperatively over a network. DirectPlay is the DirectX component that enables your programs to more easily include network-play support by generalizing the functionality needed by such support. As Microsoft so aptly puts it, "DirectPlay provides a transport-independent, protocol-independent, and online service-independent way for games developed for Windows to communicate with each other."

- **Direct3D**—Many of today's games are built around 3D graphics engines. The Direct3D component provides tools that help programmers create 3D-style games. You can use it to build games like Quake—assuming, of course, that you've got the advanced programming knowledge required to understand and use the Direct3D libraries.

- **DirectMusic**—The DirectX DirectSound component handles the playback of digital sound effects. Its cousin, DirectMusic, provides similar services for playing music in your games. DirectMusic takes message-based music (such as MIDI messages), converts it to WAV format, and then hands the music over to DirectSound for playing.

- **DirectSetup**—The DirectSetup component sets up DirectX on a player's system.

As you can see, DirectX includes just about everything you need except the game itself. Using DirectX, you can create full-featured, power-packed games that can compete with just about any game that used to run under DOS. In fact, creating games with DirectX is easier than creating games under DOS because DirectX's various components do so much of the work for you.

In spite of DirectX's richness of features, however, you need only a small subset of its functions to get started. By drawing upon a few functions supplied with DirectDraw and DirectSound, you can create just about any kind of game you like. This day will introduce you to DirectDraw, which is the most important DirectX component.

Installing the DirectX 7 SDK

Now that you have some idea of what DirectX is and why you should use it, it's time to install the DirectX developer's kit and sample applications on your system. On this book's CD-ROM, run the SETUP.EXE program in the dx7asdk/DXF folder and then follow the onscreen prompts.

When the installation is complete, you'll see that you now have a new program group named Microsoft DirectX 7 SDK on your start menu. The DirectX group contains many sample programs (including samples in Visual Basic) that demonstrate many of DirectX's talents, as well as utility programs for making programming with the SDK easier.

 Note   You don't need to install the full DirectX SDK in order to program DirectX programs with Visual Basic. You only need the DirectX runtime libraries. However, because the SDK includes tons of useful documentation, not to mention sample programs complete with source code, I recommend that you install the complete SDK.

Programming with DirectDraw

Now that you have some idea what DirectX does, it's time to use DirectDraw in an actual program. Not only will you get hands-on experience with DirectDraw, but you'll also be able to see it in action.

As you learn more about DirectDraw, keep in mind that its main purpose is to provide directly accessible drawing surfaces in memory and to allow you to transfer those drawing surfaces quickly to the screen. This process is important for game programmers because they frequently need to update the screen as often as 60 times a second.

Here's how to take advantage of DirectDraw in a Visual Basic program. You should keep the following programming steps in mind as you develop the DirectDraw application that follows:

1. Add a reference to the DirectX 7 For Visual Basic Type Library to your VB project.
2. Create a DirectX object in the program.
3. Create a DirectDraw object by calling the DirectX object's `DirectDrawCreate` method.
4. Call the DirectDraw object's `SetCooperativeLevel` method to set the cooperative level (normal or exclusive) between running applications.
5. Call the DirectDraw object's `CreateSurface` method to create a primary surface.
6. Call the DirectDraw object's `CreateSurface` method to create a back-buffer memory area for assembling images into a final display.
7. Call the DirectDraw object's `CreateSurfaceFromFile` method to load images into memory and to create surfaces for those images.
8. Set the clipping rectangle for the primary surface object.
9. Set the transparent color for surfaces holding non-rectangular sprites.
10. Assemble an image in the back buffer surface.
11. Call the back buffer `DirectDrawSurface` object's `Blt` method to copy the back buffer surface to the primary surface, which displays the image in the application's window.

This may seem like a lot of work, and no doubt much of it is still confusing to you. But fear not. All will be explained in the pages that follow. Once you get the hang of using DirectDraw, you'll discover that many of the steps in this list are little more than program overhead—something you do once when your program starts up.

Creating the DirectX Application

Perform the following steps to create your first DirectDraw program:

1. Create a new Standard EXE Visual Basic project.
2. Use the Project menu's References command to add a reference to the DirectX 7 for Visual Basic Type Library, as shown in Figure D.1.

*Adding a reference to
the DirectX type
library.*

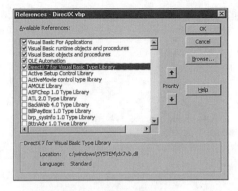

3. Set the form's `ScaleMode` property to Pixels.

4. Add a PictureBox control to the project's form.

5. Add two CommandButton controls to the form, giving them the following property settings:

   CommandButton #1

   Name = cmdStart

   Caption = "&Start"

   Height = 49

   Left = 424

   Top = 32

   Width = 49

   CommandButton #2

   Name = cmdStop

   Caption = "S&top"

   Height = 49

   Left = 424

   Top = 96

   Width = 49

D

6. Type the following source code into the project's code window, or copy it from the DirectX.txt file located in the AppendixD\Code directory of this book's CD-ROM:

```
Option Explicit

Const SPEEDX = 2
Const SPEEDY = 1
Const SPRITEHEIGHT = 64
Const SPRITEWIDTH = 64
Const BACKGROUNDHEIGHT = 400
Const BACKGROUNDWIDTH = 400


Dim DirectX7Obj As New DirectX7
Dim DirectDraw7Obj As DirectDraw7
Dim PrimarySurface As DirectDrawSurface7
Dim BackBufferSurface As DirectDrawSurface7
Dim BackgroundSurface As DirectDrawSurface7
Dim SpriteSurface As DirectDrawSurface7
Dim ClipperObj As DirectDrawClipper
Dim BackBufferRect As RECT
Dim PrimarySurfaceRect As RECT
Dim Running As Boolean
Dim SpriteX As Integer
Dim SpriteY As Integer
Dim SpriteOffsetX As Integer
Dim SpriteOffsetY As Integer

Private Sub Form_Load()
  InitObjects
  InitDirectDraw
  CreatePrimarySurface
  CreateBackBufferSurface
  CreateBackgroundSurface
  CreateSpriteSurface
  SetClipAndTransparency
  InitVariables
End Sub

Private Sub Form_Unload(Cancel As Integer)
  Set DirectDraw7Obj = Nothing
  Set DirectX7Obj = Nothing
  Running = False
End Sub

Private Sub cmdStart_Click()
  cmdStart.Enabled = False
  cmdStop.Enabled = True
  Running = True
```

```
    Animate
End Sub

Private Sub cmdStop_Click()
  cmdStart.Enabled = True
  cmdStop.Enabled = False
  Running = False
End Sub

Sub InitObjects()
  Form1.ScaleMode = vbPixels
  Picture1.ScaleMode = vbPixels
  Form1.AutoRedraw = True
  Picture1.AutoRedraw = True
  Form1.Width = 498 * Screen.TwipsPerPixelX
  Form1.Height = 440 * Screen.TwipsPerPixelY
  Picture1.BorderStyle = 0
  Picture1.Width = BACKGROUNDWIDTH
  Picture1.Height = BACKGROUNDHEIGHT
  Picture1.Left = 4
  Picture1.Top = 4
  cmdStop.Enabled = False
End Sub

Sub InitVariables()
  SpriteOffsetX = SPEEDX
  SpriteOffsetY = SPEEDY
End Sub

Sub SetClipAndTransparency()
  Set ClipperObj = DirectDraw7Obj.CreateClipper(0)
  ClipperObj.SetHWnd Picture1.hWnd
  PrimarySurface.SetClipper ClipperObj
  Dim key As DDCOLORKEY
  key.low = 0
  key.high = 0
  SpriteSurface.SetColorKey DDCKEY_SRCBLT, key
End Sub

Sub InitDirectDraw()
  Set DirectDraw7Obj = DirectX7Obj.DirectDrawCreate("")
  Call DirectDraw7Obj.SetCooperativeLevel _
      (Form1.hWnd, DDSCL_NORMAL)
End Sub

Sub CreatePrimarySurface()
  Dim ddsd As DDSURFACEDESC2
  ddsd.lFlags = DDSD_CAPS
  ddsd.ddsCaps.lCaps = DDSCAPS_PRIMARYSURFACE
```

D

```
      Set PrimarySurface = DirectDraw7Obj.CreateSurface(ddsd)
End Sub

Sub CreateBackBufferSurface()
   Dim ddsd As DDSURFACEDESC2
   ddsd.lFlags = DDSD_CAPS Or DDSD_HEIGHT Or DDSD_WIDTH
   ddsd.ddsCaps.lCaps = _
      DDSCAPS_OFFSCREENPLAIN Or DDSCAPS_SYSTEMMEMORY
   ddsd.lWidth = Picture1.Width
   ddsd.lHeight = Picture1.Height
   Set BackBufferSurface = _
      DirectDraw7Obj.CreateSurface(ddsd)
   BackBufferRect.Left = 0
   BackBufferRect.Right = Picture1.Width
   BackBufferRect.Top = 0
   BackBufferRect.Bottom = Picture1.Height
End Sub

Sub CreateBackgroundSurface()
   Dim ddsd As DDSURFACEDESC2
   ddsd.lFlags = DDSD_CAPS Or DDSD_WIDTH Or DDSD_HEIGHT
   ddsd.ddsCaps.lCaps = DDSCAPS_OFFSCREENPLAIN
   ddsd.lWidth = BACKGROUNDWIDTH
   ddsd.lHeight = BACKGROUNDHEIGHT
   Set BackgroundSurface = _
      DirectDraw7Obj.CreateSurfaceFromFile _
      ("d:\TYVBGames\Images\DirectX\Background.bmp", ddsd)
End Sub

Sub CreateSpriteSurface()
   Dim ddsd As DDSURFACEDESC2
   ddsd.lFlags = DDSD_CAPS Or DDSD_WIDTH Or DDSD_HEIGHT
   ddsd.ddsCaps.lCaps = DDSCAPS_OFFSCREENPLAIN
   ddsd.lWidth = SPRITEWIDTH
   ddsd.lHeight = SPRITEHEIGHT
   Set SpriteSurface = _
      DirectDraw7Obj.CreateSurfaceFromFile _
      ("d:\TYVBGames\Images\DirectX\Sprite.bmp", ddsd)
End Sub

Sub Animate()
   PaintBackground
   Do
      EraseSprite
      MoveSprite
      PaintSprite
      BltScreen
      DoEvents
```

```
  Loop While Running
End Sub

Sub MoveSprite()
  SpriteX = SpriteX + SpriteOffsetX * SPEEDX
  If SpriteX > BACKGROUNDWIDTH - SPRITEWIDTH Then
    SpriteX = BACKGROUNDWIDTH - SPRITEWIDTH
    SpriteOffsetX = -SpriteOffsetX
  ElseIf SpriteX < 0 Then
    SpriteX = 0
    SpriteOffsetX = -SpriteOffsetX
  End If
  SpriteY = SpriteY + SpriteOffsetY * SPEEDY
  If SpriteY > BACKGROUNDHEIGHT - SPRITEHEIGHT Then
    SpriteY = BACKGROUNDHEIGHT - SPRITEHEIGHT
    SpriteOffsetY = -SpriteOffsetY
  ElseIf SpriteY < 0 Then
    SpriteY = 0
    SpriteOffsetY = -SpriteOffsetY
  End If
End Sub

Sub EraseSprite()
  Dim ddResult As Long
  Dim SrcRect As RECT
  Dim DstRect As RECT
  SrcRect.Left = SpriteX
  SrcRect.Right = SpriteX + SPRITEWIDTH
  SrcRect.Top = SpriteY
  SrcRect.Bottom = SpriteY + SPRITEHEIGHT
  DstRect.Left = SpriteX
  DstRect.Right = SpriteX + SPRITEWIDTH
  DstRect.Top = SpriteY
  DstRect.Bottom = SpriteY + SPRITEHEIGHT
  ddResult = BackBufferSurface.Blt(DstRect, _
      BackgroundSurface, SrcRect, DDBLT_WAIT)
  If ddResult Then ShowError (ddResult)
End Sub

Sub PaintSprite()
  Dim ddResult As Long
  Dim SrcRect As RECT
  Dim DstRect As RECT
  SrcRect.Left = 0
  SrcRect.Right = SPRITEWIDTH
  SrcRect.Top = 0
  SrcRect.Bottom = SPRITEHEIGHT
  DstRect.Left = SpriteX
  DstRect.Right = SpriteX + SPRITEWIDTH
```

D

```
    DstRect.Top = SpriteY
    DstRect.Bottom = SpriteY + SPRITEHEIGHT
    ddResult = BackBufferSurface.Blt(DstRect, _
        SpriteSurface, SrcRect, DDBLT_KEYSRC Or DDBLT_WAIT)
    If ddResult Then ShowError (ddResult)
End Sub

Sub PaintBackground()
    Dim ddResult As Long
    Dim SrcRect As RECT
    Dim DstRect As RECT
    SrcRect.Left = 0
    SrcRect.Right = BACKGROUNDWIDTH
    SrcRect.Top = 0
    SrcRect.Bottom = BACKGROUNDHEIGHT
    DstRect.Left = 0
    DstRect.Right = BACKGROUNDWIDTH
    DstRect.Top = 0
    DstRect.Bottom = BACKGROUNDHEIGHT
    ddResult = BackBufferSurface.Blt(DstRect, _
        BackgroundSurface, SrcRect, DDBLT_WAIT)
    If ddResult Then ShowError (ddResult)
End Sub

Sub BltScreen()
    Dim ddResult As Long
    DirectX7Obj.GetWindowRect Picture1.hWnd, PrimarySurfaceRect
    ddResult = PrimarySurface.Blt(PrimarySurfaceRect, _
        BackBufferSurface, BackBufferRect, DDBLT_WAIT)
    If ddResult Then ShowError (ddResult)
End Sub

Sub ShowError(result As Long)
    Select Case (result)
    Case DDERR_GENERIC
        MsgBox "DDERR_GENERIC"
    Case DDERR_INVALIDOBJECT
        MsgBox "DDERR_INVALIDOBJECT"
    Case DDERR_INVALIDPARAMS
        MsgBox "DDERR_INVALIDPARAMS"
    Case DDERR_INVALIDRECT
        MsgBox "DDERR_INVALIDRECT"
    Case DDERR_NOALPHAHW
        MsgBox "DDERR_NOALPHAHW"
    Case DDERR_NOBLTHW
        MsgBox "DDERR_NOBLTHW"
    Case DDERR_NOCLIPLIST
        MsgBox "DDERR_NOCLIPLIST"
    Case DDERR_NODDROPSHW
        MsgBox "DDERR_NODDROPSHW"
    Case DDERR_NOMIRRORHW
```

```
      MsgBox "DDERR_NOMIRRORHW"
  Case DDERR_NORASTEROPHW
      MsgBox "DDERR_NORASTEROPHW"
  Case DDERR_NOROTATIONHW
      MsgBox "DDERR_NOROTATIONHW"
  Case DDERR_NOSTRETCHHW
      MsgBox "DDERR_NOSTRETCHHW"
  Case DDERR_NOZBUFFERHW
      MsgBox "DDERR_NOZBUFFERHW"
  Case DDERR_SURFACEBUSY
      MsgBox "DDERR_SURFACEBUSY"
  Case DDERR_SURFACELOST
      MsgBox "DDERR_SURFACELOST"
  Case DDERR_UNSUPPORTED
      MsgBox "DDERR_UNSUPPORTED"
  Case DDERR_WASSTILLDRAWING
      MsgBox "DDERR_WASSTILLDRAWING"
  End Select
End Sub
```

You've now completed the program. Run it, and then click the Start button. You'll see a window like the one shown in Figure D.2.

FIGURE D.2

The DirectX example program in action.

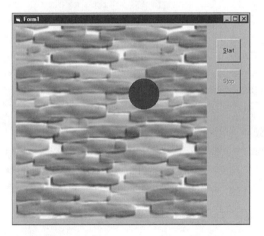

In the following sections, you'll examine the DirectX example program and learn how it works.

Initializing DirectDraw

Before a program can use DirectDraw, it must create a DirectDraw object and the DirectDrawSurface objects that will display the game's graphics. This requires a bit of work, as you'll see in the following sections.

Creating a DirectDraw Object

Creating a DirectDraw object is easy once you've added a reference to the DirectX type library to your project. First, create a DirectX object:

```
Dim DirectX7Obj As New DirectX7
```

Then call the DirectX object's `DirectDrawCreate` method:

```
Set DirectDraw7Obj = DirectX7Obj.DirectDrawCreate("")
```

You need to create a DirectDraw object in order to gain access to DirectDraw's interface, which enables you to call DirectDraw's member functions. `DirectDrawCreate` takes the video driver's GUID (globally unique identifier) as an argument. If you don't know anything about driver GUIDs, don't sweat it. Simply providing an empty string for this argument selects the currently active driver.

Requesting the Cooperative Level

Because the Windows environment allows multitasking, many applications may run simultaneously. This can mean hard times for a game program that's trying to retain control over the display hardware, including the screen resolution and the color palette. For this reason, DirectDraw provides the `SetCooperativeLevel` method. A DirectDraw application can share control of the screen resolution and the palette, or it can take exclusive control. You call `SetCooperativeLevel` like this:

```
DirectDraw7Obj.SetCooperativeLevel _
    Form1.hWnd, DDSCL_NORMAL
```

The `SetCooperativeLevel` method requires two arguments: the handle of the window and the flag representing the requested mode. In most cases, the flag should be `DDSCL_NORMAL`, which makes the application share the video resources just like any other Windows application. When you're writing a DirectX application that runs in the full-screen mode, you probably want to use the `DDSCL_EXCLUSIVE` mode.

Creating DirectDrawSurface Objects

The next step is to create the DirectDraw surfaces, which include the primary surface (the one that's displayed on the screen), the back buffer surface, and any surfaces needed for additional graphics, such as background images and sprites. Because this entails a bit of work, the code that accomplishes these tasks is tucked away in several subroutines, which are named after the surfaces they create. The first is `CreatePrimarySurface` (see Listing D.1).

LISTING D.1   The CreatePrimarySurface Subroutine

```
1: Sub CreatePrimarySurface()
2:   Dim ddsd As DDSURFACEDESC2
3:   ddsd.lFlags = DDSD_CAPS
4:   ddsd.ddsCaps.lCaps = DDSCAPS_PRIMARYSURFACE
5:   Set PrimarySurface = DirectDraw7Obj.CreateSurface(ddsd)
6: End Sub
```

ANALYSIS   This subroutine first declares a local variable named ddsd (Line 2), which is an instance of a DDSURFACEDESC2 data type. The DDSURFACEDESC2 data type is a structure that holds information about DirectDrawSurface objects. The DDSURFACEDESC2 data type looks like this:

```
Type DDSURFACEDESC2
    ddckCKDestBlt As DDCOLORKEY
    ddckCKDestOverlay As DDCOLORKEY
    ddckCKSrcBlt As DDCOLORKEY
    ddckCKSrcOverlay As DDCOLORKEY
    ddpfPixelFormat As DDPIXELFORMAT
    ddsCaps As DDSCAPS2
    lAlphaBitDepth As Long
    lBackBufferCount As Long
    lFlags As CONST_DDSURFACEDESCFLAGS
    lHeight As Long
    lLinearSize As Long
    lMipMapCount As Long
    lPitch As Long
    lRefreshRate As Long
    lTextureStage As Long
    lWidth As Long
    lZBufferBitDepth As Long
End Type
```

You communicate information to and from DirectDraw by using structures such as DDSURFACEDESC2. You fill in some of the information in the structure before calling certain DirectDraw member functions, while DirectDraw fills in other structure members to send information back to your program.

To create the primary surface, the CreatePrimarySurface subroutine first initializes the DDSURFACEDESC2 data, filling the lFlags member with flags that tell DirectDraw which structure members contain valid information (Line 3). In this case, the DDSD_CAPS flag indicates that DirectDraw should consider the values stored in the ddsCaps member to be valid. Setting the ddsCaps.lCaps member to DDSCAPS_PRIMARYSURFACE (Line 4) tells DirectDraw that the program wants to create the primary surface.

D

After initializing the DDSURFACEDESC2 data, the program calls the DirectDraw method CreateSurface to create the primary DirectDrawSurface object. The program declares this object near the top of the program:

```
Dim PrimarySurface As DirectDrawSurface7
```

CreateSurface's argument is the DDSURFACEDESC2 data.

To create the surface on which the program will assemble its display, the program calls the CreateBackBufferSurface subroutine (see Listing D.2).

LISTING D.2   The CreateBackBufferSurface Subroutine

```
 1: Sub CreateBackBufferSurface()
 2:   Dim ddsd As DDSURFACEDESC2
 3:   ddsd.lFlags = DDSD_CAPS Or DDSD_HEIGHT Or DDSD_WIDTH
 4:   ddsd.ddsCaps.lCaps = _
 5:     DDSCAPS_OFFSCREENPLAIN Or DDSCAPS_SYSTEMMEMORY
 6:   ddsd.lWidth = Picture1.Width
 7:   ddsd.lHeight = Picture1.Height
 8:   Set BackBufferSurface = _
 9:     DirectDraw7Obj.CreateSurface(ddsd)
10:   BackBufferRect.Left = 0
11:   BackBufferRect.Right = Picture1.Width
12:   BackBufferRect.Top = 0
13:   BackBufferRect.Bottom = Picture1.Height
14: End Sub
```

ANALYSIS   This subroutine is similar to CreatePrimarySurface, except that it provides more information to DirectDraw via the DDSURFACEDESC2 data. Specifically, this subroutine also specifies a width and height for the surface (Line 3) and specifies the DDSCAPS_OFFSCREEN flag (Lines 4 and 5), which means that the surface is an ordinary area of memory in which you're going to store and manipulate image data. The CreateBackBufferSurface function also initializes the BackBufferRect variable (Lines 10 to 13), which will be used in transferring data to and from the buffer.

Finally, the program requires two other offscreen surfaces, CreateBackgroundSurface and CreateSpriteSurface, one for the background image and one for the sprite (see Listing D.3).

LISTING D.3   The CreateBackgroundSurface and CreateSpriteSurface Subroutines

```
 1:  Sub CreateBackgroundSurface()
 2:    Dim ddsd As DDSURFACEDESC2
 3:    ddsd.lFlags = DDSD_CAPS Or DDSD_WIDTH Or DDSD_HEIGHT
 4:    ddsd.ddsCaps.lCaps = DDSCAPS_OFFSCREENPLAIN
 5:    ddsd.lWidth = BACKGROUNDWIDTH
 6:    ddsd.lHeight = BACKGROUNDHEIGHT
 7:    Set BackgroundSurface = _
 8:        DirectDraw7Obj.CreateSurfaceFromFile _
 9:        ("d:\TYVBGames\Images\DirectX\Background.bmp", ddsd)
10:  End Sub
11:
12:  Sub CreateSpriteSurface()
13:    Dim ddsd As DDSURFACEDESC2
14:    ddsd.lFlags = DDSD_CAPS Or DDSD_WIDTH Or DDSD_HEIGHT
15:    ddsd.ddsCaps.lCaps = DDSCAPS_OFFSCREENPLAIN
16:    ddsd.lWidth = SPRITEWIDTH
17:    ddsd.lHeight = SPRITEHEIGHT
18:    Set SpriteSurface = _
19:        DirectDraw7Obj.CreateSurfaceFromFile _
20:        ("d:\TYVBGames\Images\DirectX\Sprite.bmp", ddsd)
21:  End Sub
```

ANALYSIS   Notice that CreateBackgroundSurface and CreateSpriteSurface call the
CreateSurfaceFromFile (Lines 7 to 10 and Lines 18 to 20) DirectDraw method,
which enables you to easily create a surface from an image file.

Clipping and Transparency

The next step is to prepare the surfaces for animation by setting a clipping area and
defining a transparent color, which is a color that DirectDraw will not transfer when blitting the animation frames. The SetClipAndTransparency subroutine (see Listing D.4)
takes care of these tasks.

LISTING D.4   The SetClipAndTransparency Subroutine

```
1:  Sub SetClipAndTransparency()
2:    Set ClipperObj = DirectDraw7Obj.CreateClipper(0)
3:    ClipperObj.SetHWnd Picture1.hWnd
4:    PrimarySurface.SetClipper ClipperObj
5:    Dim key As DDCOLORKEY
6:    key.low = 0
7:    key.high = 0
8:    SpriteSurface.SetColorKey DDCKEY_SRCBLT, key
9:  End Sub
```

D

ANALYSIS The clipping area is the part of the screen to which all drawing operations must be confined. First, `SetClipAndTransparency` creates a clipper object by calling DirectDraw's `CreateClipper` method (Line 2), whose single argument is a 0. The program declares the clipper object itself near the top of the source code, like this:

```
Dim ClipperObj As DirectDrawClipper
```

To initialize the clipper object, the program passes the handle of the window to which drawing must be constrained to the clipper object via the object's `SetHWnd` method (Line 3). Finally, the program sets the clipping area by calling the primary surface's `SetClipper` method (Line 4), passing the newly created clipper object to the method.

Next, the subroutine sets the transparent color (Lines 5 to 8). Having a transparent color enables DirectDraw to copy the image of the bouncing ball without erasing areas on the background bitmap around the ball. For example, Figure D.3 shows what happens if you run the animation without defining a transparent color. The black area surrounding the ball image erases the background image. By defining a transparent color, you can tell DirectDraw not to transfer the black areas.

FIGURE D.3

The display without a transparent color defined.

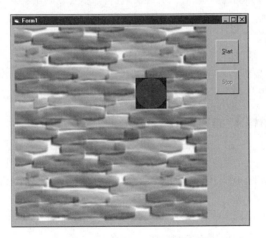

DirectDraw handles transparent colors through *color keys*, of which there are two types: source color keys and destination color keys. A *source color key* specifies a color (or colors) that DirectDraw will not copy when blitting (copying) an image. A *destination color key* specifies a color (or colors) that will be replaced when blitting an image.

The DirectX example program uses a source color key to prevent the background image from being wiped out when images of the ball are transferred to the surface. To do this, the program first declares an instance of the `DDCOLORKEY` data type:

```
Dim key As DDCOLORKEY
```

The Visual Basic version of DirectDraw declares the DDCOLORKEY structure, as shown here:

```
Type DDCOLORKEY
    high As Long
    low As Long
End Type
```

This data type holds only two values: the low index of the color space to define, and the high index of the color space to define. A *color space* is simply a range of colors. Because your program needs to define only one color key, the low and high values of the range are the same:

```
key.low = 0
key.high = 0
```

In the color palette, black is represented by the palette index 0.

After defining the DDCOLORKEY data, the program simply calls the sprite surface's SetColorKey method, like this:

```
SpriteSurface.SetColorKey DDCKEY_SRCBLT, key
```

SetColorKey's two arguments are a flag indicating the type of color key to create and the DDCOLORKEY data. The DDCKEY_SRCBLT value specifies that the color key is a sprite color that should not be transferred with the rest of the sprite image.

Performing the Animation

The first step in the animation process is painting the background image onto the back buffer, which the PaintBackground subroutine handles (see Listing D.5).

LISTING D.5   The PaintBackground Subroutine

```
 1:  Sub PaintBackground()
 2:    Dim ddResult As Long
 3:    Dim SrcRect As RECT
 4:    Dim DstRect As RECT
 5:    SrcRect.Left = 0
 6:    SrcRect.Right = BACKGROUNDWIDTH
 7:    SrcRect.Top = 0
 8:    SrcRect.Bottom = BACKGROUNDHEIGHT
 9:    DstRect.Left = 0
10:    DstRect.Right = BACKGROUNDWIDTH
11:    DstRect.Top = 0
12:    DstRect.Bottom = BACKGROUNDHEIGHT
13:    ddResult = BackBufferSurface.Blt(DstRect, _
14:        BackgroundSurface, SrcRect, DDBLT_WAIT)
15:    If ddResult Then ShowError (ddResult)
16: End Sub
```

ANALYSIS This subroutine first initializes two instances of the RECT data type (Lines 5 to 12). These instances, SrcRect and DstRect, represent the rectangular area of the background surface to be transferred to the back buffer and the rectangular area of the back buffer to which the source data should be copied. Because both the source and destination rectangles are the same size (the full size of the background image), both of these RECT instances are initialized the same.

A call to the back buffer surface's Blt method (Lines 13 and 14) transfers the background image to the back buffer. The Blt method's four arguments are the destination rectangle, the source surface, the source rectangle, and a flag specifying how the blit should be carried out. The DDBLT_WAIT flag specifies that Blt should not return until the blit is completed. (If DirectDraw is already busy with the surface, the copy will have to wait a while.)

With the background image in memory, the program can start animating the bouncing ball. The first step in the animation process is to erase the sprite from its current position. That's handled by the EraseSprite subroutine, which copies the portion of the background that was previously covered by the sprite (see Listing D.6).

LISTING D.6   The EraseSprite Subroutine

```
 1:  Sub EraseSprite()
 2:     Dim ddResult As Long
 3:     Dim SrcRect As RECT
 4:     Dim DstRect As RECT
 5:     SrcRect.Left = SpriteX
 6:     SrcRect.Right = SpriteX + SPRITEWIDTH
 7:     SrcRect.Top = SpriteY
 8:     SrcRect.Bottom = SpriteY + SPRITEHEIGHT
 9:     DstRect.Left = SpriteX
10:     DstRect.Right = SpriteX + SPRITEWIDTH
11:     DstRect.Top = SpriteY
12:     DstRect.Bottom = SpriteY + SPRITEHEIGHT
13:     ddResult = BackBufferSurface.Blt(DstRect, _
14:        BackgroundSurface, SrcRect, DDBLT_WAIT)
15:     If ddResult Then ShowError (ddResult)
16: End Sub
```

ANALYSIS Lines 5 to 8 set up the coordinates of the source rectangle, and Lines 9 to 12 set up the destination rectangle. Finally, Lines 13 and 14 restore the background surface by painting over the sprite image.

Then the program can paint the sprite in its new position, which was set by the MoveSprite subroutine. The PaintSprite subroutine paints the sprite on the back buffer (see Listing D.7).

LISTING D.7 The PaintSprite Subroutine

```
1:  Sub PaintSprite()
2:    Dim ddResult As Long
3:    Dim SrcRect As RECT
4:    Dim DstRect As RECT
5:    SrcRect.Left = 0
6:    SrcRect.Right = SPRITEWIDTH
7:    SrcRect.Top = 0
8:    SrcRect.Bottom = SPRITEHEIGHT
9:    DstRect.Left = SpriteX
10:   DstRect.Right = SpriteX + SPRITEWIDTH
11:   DstRect.Top = SpriteY
12:   DstRect.Bottom = SpriteY + SPRITEHEIGHT
13:   ddResult = BackBufferSurface.Blt(DstRect, _
14:       SpriteSurface, SrcRect, DDBLT_KEYSRC Or DDBLT_WAIT)
15:   If ddResult Then ShowError (ddResult)
16: End Sub
```

ANALYSIS Lines 5 to 8 set up the coordinates of the source rectangle, and Lines 9 to 12 set up the destination rectangle. Finally, Lines 13 and 14 copy the sprite image to its new location on the back-buffer surface.

Finally, the BltScreen subroutine copies the back buffer to the primary surface, which causes the image to appear in the window (see Listing D.8).

LISTING D.8 The PaintSprite Subroutine

```
1: Sub BltScreen()
2:   Dim ddResult As Long
3:   DirectX7Obj.GetWindowRect Picture1.hWnd, PrimarySurfaceRect
4:   ddResult = PrimarySurface.Blt(PrimarySurfaceRect, _
5:       BackBufferSurface, BackBufferRect, DDBLT_WAIT)
6:   If ddResult Then ShowError (ddResult)
7: End Sub
```

ANALYSIS Line 3 gets the size of the window's rectangle, and Lines 4 and 5 copy the newly updated back buffer to the screen.

As you can see in the `Animate` subroutine, this process of creating a frame of animation and copying it to the primary surface happens again and again in a loop (Lines 3 to 9) until the user stops it by clicking the Stop button or exiting the program (see Listing D.9).

LISTING D.9   The PaintSprite Subroutine

```
 1:  Sub Animate()
 2:     PaintBackground
 3:     Do
 4:        EraseSprite
 5:        MoveSprite
 6:        PaintSprite
 7:        BltScreen
 8:        DoEvents
 9:     Loop While Running
10:  End Sub
```

Summary

Programming a DirectX application with DirectDraw requires you to perform a number of steps. First, you call `DirectDrawCreate` to create a DirectDraw object. Then you can call the DirectDraw object's `SetCooperativeLevel` method to gain control over the display mode. Finally, the DirectDraw object's `CreateSurface` and `CreateSurfaceFromFile` methods enable you to create a primary surface and other surfaces you may need.

When you blit a bitmap from memory to the back buffer, often you need to specify a transparent color that won't be blitted with the rest of the image. To do this, you define a color key (which can contain one or more colors) and tell DirectDraw to use that color key when performing the blits. You also usually create a clipper object, which constrains all drawing to the application's window.

Finally, to perform your game's animation, you build the current image in a back buffer and then transfer the contents of the back buffer to the primary buffer. A surface's `Blt` method handles the task of moving image data from one surface to another.

APPENDIX E

Game Programming Resources

There's a lot of information about game programming out there. You could easily spend days, or even weeks, looking for information. In this appendix, I've done a little of the research for you, putting together a list of books and Web sites with additional tools and information about the exciting world of game programming.

Game Programming Books

There are quite a few game programming books out there, but most of them use C or C++ as the development language. For some reason, Visual Basic game programming books are almost nonexistent (which is why I wrote this one, of course). Still, if you want to advance as a game programmer, sooner or later you're going to have to learn C or C++. The following books are good choices for learning game programming with those languages:

Tricks of the Windows Game Programming Gurus: Fundamentals of 2D and 3D Game Programming
By Andre Lamothe
Macmillan Publishing Company
ISBN: 0672313618
Price: $49.99
1000 pages

Game Architecture and Design
By Andrew Rollings and Dave Morris
The Coriolis Group
ISBN: 1576104257
Price: $49.99
742 pages

Game Programming Gems
Edited by Mark Deloura
Charles River Media
ISBN: 1584500492
Price: $69.95
600 pages

Advanced 3D Game Programming With DirectX 7.0
By Adrian Perez and Dan Royer
Wordware Publishing
ISBN: 1556227213
Price: $59.95
500 pages

VB Game Programming Sites

Although there's a shortage of Visual Basic game programming books, there's no shortage of online resources. The following list includes some of the top Visual Basic sites, as well as some smaller (but still interesting) ones.

VB Game Programming Center

`http://www.vbexplorer.com/games.asp`

This site includes not only the usual tutorials (animation, sound, tiling, DirectX, game design, and so on), but also some cool free stuff, such as a free package of game art and a free sound library. Also featured are a tools library and game downloads.

Visual Basic Games, Code, and More

http://www.homestead.com/vbgames6/index.html

This site features tons of downloads, including games, source code, game art, and links. Of extra interest is the ongoing "Zelda" project, in which the site owner is designing and programming an RPG game in Visual Basic.

Lucky's VB Gaming Site

http://members.home.net/theluckyleper/

This is another site where the owner is building a sample RPG game. Also featured are tutorials on Windows API programming, playing WAV files, timing, blitting, game design, lighting effects, card games, and much more. Extras include a glossary of game terms, source code and library downloads, a message board, and a couple of online arcade game projects.

RaBit Zone Visual B Studio

http://www.interfold.com/rabit/main_index.htm

This site features news and tutorials. Also, a download section offers games, utilities, example code, tools, and a sample multimedia program written in Visual Basic.

Unlimited Realities

http://www.ur.co.nz/

This site features tons of tutorials, covering everything from sprites and bitmaps to advanced topics like image processing and 3D graphics.

Visual Basic Games

http://www.vbgames.co.uk/

This site's download area features over a dozen games written by the site's owner, an award-winning VB programmer. A majority of the games are written with DirectX, and all of them include full source code. The site also features a tutorials area and a links page.

Planet Source Code

http://www.planet-source-code.com/

This site boasts over 750,000 lines of Visual Basic source code, covering everything from data structures to COM and the Registry. A special games section offers 57,000 lines of sample code, including a game programming tutorial.

E

Voodoo VB

`http://www.redrival.com/voodoovb/`

This site features a message board, articles, tutorials, source code, and a long list of complete Visual Basic games you can download. The tutorials concentrate on DirectX Visual Basic programming, but also cover blitting, alpha blending, tiling, and frame counting, to mention a few.

vbX7: DirectX 7 and Game Programming for VB

`http://www.cason.addr.com/`

This site is dedicated to DirectX programming with Visual Basic. Featured are a discussion board, tutorials on virtually every aspect of VB DirectX programming, and a download center.

VB Game Planet

`http://vbgplanet.thenexus.bc.ca/`

Like many Visual Basic sites, VB Game Planet features tutorials, downloads, a message board, on-going projects (an RPG game), and a links page. The tutorials cover introductory game programming, blitting, animation, MIDI, algorithms, and RPG game design, including discussions of map editors, map scrolling, and game engines. Downloads include full games, as well as lots of demo source code.

Advanced Game Programming Sites

The sites listed in this section cover more advanced topics and usually concentrate on C or C++ programming rather than Visual Basic. Still, there's a lot of good general information available on these sites.

Pawn's Game Programming Pages

`http://www.aros.net/~npawn/`

Here you'll find programming tutorials on DirectSound, DirectDraw, loading WAV files, handling MIDI data, texture mapping, scrolling, collision detection, tile graphics, and more. There's a small download area that has, among other things, a C++ class for handling AVI files and a utility for converting sound files between formats. The site also has a page of links to other game resources.

Microsoft's DirectX Pages

http://www.microsoft.com/directx/

Here you can get up-to-date news about DirectX, and you can also download the home version of DirectX (only what's needed to run DirectX programs) or the full DirectX developer kit. You can also access Microsoft's new DirectX Developer Center, which brings together everything you can imagine about DirectX, including documentation, technical articles, downloads, newsgroups, events, books, and much more.

Game Programming Galaxy

http://www.geocities.com/SiliconValley/Vista/6774/

Includes articles on advanced topics like design, ray tracing, image filters, particle systems, sprites, and physics. Also features information on building tile-based worlds. Includes a small library of graphics and sound tools, as well as some libraries that should be useful to game programmers.

Visual Basic Game and Application Development

http://members.xoom.com/VBGAD/

Includes a FAQ section and a gallery of games, complete with source code. Features many tutorials on game programming and on programming in general, including playing sounds and displaying animated GIFs. Also includes a download section with source code, controls, and utilities.

Gamasutra

http://www.gamasutra.com/

This is a very nice, up-to-date site that features current news on the gaming industry, book excerpts, articles on the game-creation process, art galleries, and tutorials. Of great interest are the articles that describe how professional game developers created commercial games like *Age of Empires II*, *Vampire: The Masquerade*, and *Resident Evil 2*.

GameDev.Net

http://www.gamedev.net/gamedev.asp

Professional-level game development site that includes game development news, a reference section, and a game developer's community featuring chats, contests, and interviews. Lots of tutorials, covering everything from compilers to very advanced topics such as artificial intelligence, math and physics, and 3D graphics programming with OpenGL.

E

Game Dictionary

`http://www.gamedev.net/dict/`

Here you can find online definitions of over 500 game programming terms. The search engine enables you to find any term in the dictionary quickly, or you can search by category. Categories include Games, Hardware, People, 2D Graphics, 3D Graphics, Audio, Community, Network, OS, and others.

GameProgrammer.com

`http://gameprogrammer.com/`

This site features a bulletin board, a mailing list, want ads, and lots of tutorials on topics such as polygon rendering, texture mapping, and optimization.

Game Programming Resources and Links

`http://www.ziron.com/links/`

This site includes what is billed as "the world's largest game programming search engine." Also features a programming discussion board, an online programming bookstore, and library and utility downloads, as well as tutorials and source code for programming topics such as DirectX, Windows, multiplayer games, networks, 3D graphics, and much more.

INDEX

Symbols

Numbers

A

M

Read This Before Opening

Windows 95, Windows 98, Windows NT 4, and Windows 2000 Installation Instructions

1. Insert the CD-ROM into your CD-ROM drive.
2. From the Windows desktop, double-click on the "My Computer" icon.
3. Double-click on the icon representing your CD-ROM drive.
4. Double-click on the icon titled START.EXE to run the installation program.
5. Follow the onscreen instructions to finish the installation.

 Note

If Windows 95, Windows 98, Windows NT 4.0, or Windows 2000 is installed on your computer, and you have the AutoPlay feature enabled, the setup.exe program starts automatically whenever you insert the disc into your CD-ROM drive.